perspectives

Literacy

Academic Editor

C. Denise Johnson
University of Central Arkansas

coursewise
p u b l i s h i n g
inc.

Bellevue • Boulder • Dubuque • Madison • St. Paul

Our mission at **Coursewise** is to help students make connections—linking theory to practice and the classroom to the outside world. Learners are motivated to synthesize ideas when course materials are placed in a context they recognize. By providing gateways to contemporary and enduring issues, **Coursewise** publications will expand students' awareness of and context for the course subject.

For more information on **Coursewise,** visit us at our web site: http://www.coursewise.com

To order an examination copy, contact: Houghton Mifflin Sixth Floor Media: 800-565-6247 (voice); 800-565-6236 (fax).

Coursewise Publishing Editorial Staff

Thomas Doran, ceo/publisher: Environmental Science/Geography/Journalism/Marketing/Speech
Edgar Laube, publisher: Political Science/Psychology/Sociology
Linda Meehan Avenarius, publisher: **Courselinks**™
Sue Pulvermacher-Alt, publisher: Education/Health/Gender Studies
Victoria Putman, publisher: Anthropology/Philosophy/Religion
Tom Romaniak, publisher: Business/Criminal Justice/Economics
Kathleen Schmitt, publishing assistant

Coursewise Publishing Production Staff

Lori A. Blosch, permissions coordinator
Mary Monner, production coordinator
Victoria Putman, production manager

Note: Readings in this book appear exactly as they were published. Thus, inconsistencies in style and usage among the different readings are likely.

Cover photo: Copyright © 1997 T. Teshigawara/Panoramic Images, Chicago, IL. All Rights Reserved.

Interior design and cover design by Jeff Storm

Copyright © 1999 by Coursewise Publishing, Inc. All Rights Reserved.

Library of Congress Catalog Card Number: 99-90059

ISBN 0-395-97210-8

No part of this publication may be reproduced, stored in a retrieval system, or transmitted, in any form or by any means, electronic, mechanical, photocopying, recording, or otherwise, without the prior written permission of the publisher.

Printed in the United States of America by Coursewise Publishing, Inc.
7 North Pinckney Street, Suite 346, Madison, WI 53703

10 9 8 7 6 5 4 3 2 1

from the
Publisher

Sue Pulvermacher–Alt

Coursewise Publishing

I've lived a miracle. As a parent, I've witnessed the miracle of watching (if I can be so bold, even helping) my own two children become literate. My children are now able to recognize and know and attach meaning to letters, words, and symbols they encounter every day.

It really is a miraculous progression to experience. My son and daughter went through each stage at different ages. Nevertheless, they both have gone from discovering the ability to make sounds, to uttering one-syllable words, to recognizing symbols in the world around them (at least both of my kids knew the golden arches meant McDonalds by the age of 2). Each then matured from "reading" the book *Goodnight Moon* (amazingly sometimes without even turning the pages) to deliberately plodding word-by-word through *The Foot Book* to proudly finishing their first chapter books.

Now they're both in school, and their literacy skills must mature with them. It's not enough for them to be able to understand the written word on the page. They need to be literate about what they watch on television, what they listen to on the radio, what they read (or hear or see) at a web site. Increasingly, being literate means being a critical consumer of the words and symbols that come our way through a variety of mediums every day.

Good for you for expanding your understanding of literacy. Whether you're in a reading or language arts methods course, a children's literature course, a literacy issues course, or just reading this volume out of your own interest in the subject, you are taking a careful look at the phenomenon we call literacy. We hope you come away better equipped to facilitate the miracle of literacy for others.

The readings in this volume will help you better understand some of the important issues in literacy. In addition, the R.E.A.L. web sites you'll find listed throughout this *Perspectives: Literacy* volume and at the **Courselinks**™ site for Literacy have been chosen because they are particularly useful sites. Please don't take my word for it though. Read our annotations and decide if a site is worth visiting. Do the activities so you can get to know a site better. Search our **Courselinks** site by key topic and find the information you need to be a more literate student of literacy.

As publisher for this volume, I had the good fortune to work with Denise Johnson as the Academic Editor of *Perspectives: Literacy* and as the editor for the accompanying **Courselinks** site. Denise contacted me and asked how she could get involved. She liked our goal of publishing "connected learning" tools—connecting theory to practice and the classroom to the outside world. I liked her background—a blend of teaching experiences highlighted by a particular interest in the area of literacy and technology—and her enthusiasm. We agreed it made sense to work together to bring this literacy material to you. As a bonus, I've found someone who seems to enjoy the NFL as much as I do. (When the Packers next play the Cowboys, don't call. Denise and I will both be busy.)

We were helped by a top-notch Editorial Board. Readings and web sites were selected with our goal of "connected learning" in mind. Members of the Editorial Board offered critical feedback and posed interesting challenges. They know their content and are a web-savvy bunch. My thanks to Denise and the entire Editorial Board.

As you use our print and online resources and continue to build your understanding of literacy, I invite you to share your reactions to our materials. How'd we do in representing the subject of literacy? What worked and what didn't work in this *Perspectives: Literacy* volume and the accompanying **Courselinks** site? Are we helping you make the miracle of literacy happen for children you know?

Sue Pulvermacher-Alt, Publisher
suepa@coursewise.com

from the
Academic Editor

C. Denise Johnson
University of Central Arkansas

C. Denise Johnson is an assistant professor of reading education at the University of Central Arkansas. She received her Ed.D. in reading from the University of Memphis. She has taught as an elementary classroom teacher, a middle-school reading specialist, and a Reading Recovery teacher. She teaches graduate and undergraduate courses in literacy education, edits a column on literacy and technology in The Journal of Reading Education, *and conducts research on the integration of technology into preservice and inservice education courses and within elementary classrooms. Dr. Johnson has published articles on literacy and technology in a variety of journals and is active in several professional organizations. She enjoys traveling with her family and reading to her son, Derek.*

I will never forget my fifth-grade teacher, Miss Brightenstein. It is from her class that I hold my first memory of reading a book, *A Little Princess*, by Frances Hodgson Burnett. Oh, how I loved that book and Miss Brightenstein. Little did I know then what an impact her influence would have on me and my future decision to become a teacher. I believe that many of us hold a special place in our heart for a teacher who made a difference in our lives.

Teachers play a critical role in students' journey along the path to literacy. To be effective, teachers must be able to make insightful and thoughtful decisions about children and literacy instruction. This ability can be developed by observing children as they learn about print, by understanding the reading process, and by examining personal beliefs, assumptions, and theories of reading. One purpose of this volume is to provide readings that present a broad range of issues within the field of literacy and that can help teachers and prospective teachers become more knowledgeable about theory and practice in literacy.

The readings in this volume address seven topics of importance to literacy educators. The first section consists of readings about controversial issues under discussion among literacy educators. The sections that follow include readings on early reading and family literacy, reading comprehension, standards and integrated literacy instruction, assessment, diverse and at-risk learners, and technology. Critical reflection and thought about the issues discussed in the readings will lead you to define and refine your own beliefs about literacy instruction.

As we enter the new millennium, teachers will face the challenge of preparing an increasingly diverse student population for the workplace of tomorrow. Technology has already had a major impact on the form, context, and space for reading and writing. Teachers must make knowledgeable decisions about the best and most appropriate way to incorporate technology into literacy instruction to prepare children for the future. The Internet can be a powerful tool for professional development for teachers. The R.E.A.L. web sites listed at the end of each section in this volume, along with the **Courselinks**™ site for Literacy, provide additional information and resources for each topic. These informative web sites comprise the latest information on each topic and are usually updated periodically so they can serve as a resource over time.

Teachers significantly influence the lives of their students and the students' ability to read and write. Since reading and writing permeate every aspect of a child's life in and out of school, the decisions teachers make about literacy instruction are crucial. Teachers who are willing to examine theory, research, practice and their own beliefs about literacy can meet this challenge. By providing effective literacy learning opportunities that meet the needs of each student, teachers can really make a difference.

Editorial Board

We wish to thank the following instructors for their assistance. Their many suggestions not only contributed to the construction of this volume, but also to the ongoing development of our Literacy web site.

Allen Berger

Miami University

Dr. Allen Berger is the Heckert Professor of Reading and Writing at Miami University. He is the author of more than four hundred articles on reading and writing education that appear in major periodicals and publications. At Miami, he is the director of Teens for Literacy, a program he founded ten years ago to encourage inner-city students to improve literacy in their communities and to consider teaching as a profession. Dr. Berger has spoken at World Congresses on Reading in Buenos Aires, Singapore, Hamburg, and Manila, and at major conventions throughout Canada and the United States.

Regina G. Chatel

St. Joseph College

Dr. Regina G. Chatel is an assistant professor in the Department of Education at Saint Joseph College in West Hartford, Connecticut, where she teaches English language arts courses in a teacher preparation program. In addition to her work at Saint Joseph College, she has over twenty years of experience in public education as an English and social studies teacher (grades 7–12), a reading consultant (grades K–12), and a professional development specialist. Dr. Chatel received both her M.A. and her Ph.D. from the University of Connecticut. She is currently exploring research in assessment, urban education, and the use and impact of technology in education.

Sheila G. Cohen

State University of New York at Cortland

Dr. Sheila G. Cohen is an associate professor of education at the State University of New York at Cortland.

She teaches methods in reading and language arts, adult literacy tutoring, practicum in corrective reading, and the reading teacher and the reading program. Dr. Cohen received her Ed.D. in curriculum and instruction at the University of Kentucky.

Anita P. Davis

Converse College

Dr. Anita P. Davis is chair of the Department of Education and director of the Elementary Education and Teacher Education Program at Converse College in Spartanburg, South Carolina. She is the author of *Reading Instruction Essentials* (American Press, 1998, revised), and she has co-authored many publications, including *SAT I* (Research and Education Associates, 1997) and *The Best CLEP Review* (Research and Education Associates, 1997, revised). Dr. Davis received her Ed.D. in curriculum and instruction from Duke University.

Douglas Fisher

San Diego State University

Douglas Fisher is an assistant professor in the College of Education, Department of Teacher Education, at San Diego State University, where he teaches classes in English language development and literacy. His background includes adolescent literacy and instructional strategies for diverse student needs. He often presents at local, state, and national conferences, and has published a number of articles on reading/literacy, differentiated instruction, accommodations, and curriculum.

Amy Seely Flint

Indiana University, Bloomington

Dr. Amy Seely Flint is an assistant professor of language education at Indiana University, Bloomington, where she teaches methods of teaching elementary language arts and methods of teaching reading. Her research interests include the relationship between theoretical orientation and teaching effectiveness in elementary teachers, the social nature of literacy events in the classroom, and the roles of intertextuality and stance in the classroom. Dr. Flint received her Ph.D. in education, language, literacy, and culture from the University of California, Berkeley.

Jeannine Hirtle
Sam Houston State University

Kimberly Kimbell-Lopez
Louisiana Tech University

Dr. Kimberly Kimbell-Lopez is an assistant professor of education at Louisiana Tech University, where she currently teaches undergraduate and graduate classes in reading. Her areas of specialization include reading and language arts, and her research interests include studies of student talk in literature discussion groups and the integration of technology into reading and language arts. She is the author of *Connecting with Traditional Literature: Using Folktales, Fables and Legends to Strengthen Students' Reading and Writing* (in press), published by Allyn & Bacon. Dr. Kimbell-Lopez has presented at numerous local, state, and national conferences. She is a member of NRC, IRA, NCTE, AERA, and AACE. In 1997, Dr. Kimbell-Lopez was recognized as the outstanding doctoral student in curriculum and instruction at the University of Houston.

Sarah F. Mahurt
University of the Virgin Islands, St. Croix

Dr. Sarah F. Mahurt is an assistant professor of education at the University of the Virgin Islands, St. Croix, where she teaches reading and language arts courses at both the undergraduate and graduate level. Before entering academia, she taught for eight years as a remedial reading/language arts resource teacher for the Virgin Islands Department of Education. Dr. Mahurt is

president of the St. Croix Adult Literacy Alliance, and she has presented both nationally and internationally. She received her Ph.D. in literacy and language from Purdue University.

Dennis Mike
State University of New York at Geneseo

Margaret Morgan
Le Moyne College

Dr. Margaret Morgan is an assistant professor of education at Le Moyne College in Syracuse, New York, where she teaches graduate and undergraduate courses in literacy for persons preparing to become special education teachers. She previously taught for two years as an assistant professor at the Center for Teaching and Learning at the University of Southern Colorado in Pueblo, Colorado. Before entering higher education, Dr. Morgan worked as a reading specialist and teacher in the urban middle-school setting (grades 6–8). She is a certified speech-language pathologist, and she has worked in special education as both a teacher for the deaf and as a speech-language consultant to special education teachers. Dr. Morgan received her master's degree in communications disorders from Bowling Green State University, and her Ph.D. in 1993 in communications disorders and speech science from the University of Colorado in Boulder.

Carole S. Rhodes
Pace University

Dr. Carole S. Rhodes received her Ph.D. from New York University, where she specialized in literacy and teacher education. She is currently an associate professor at Pace University and has recently been awarded a FIPSE grant. Dr. Rhodes serves as a consultant to numerous school districts and works with teachers and administrators in literacy, middle and high school reform, and standards. She is an active member of IRA, NCTE, and NRC, and has chaired and served on several committees within these organizations.

Lynn Romeo
Monmouth University

Dr. Lynn Romeo is chair of the Department of Educational Leadership and Special Education, the program director for the MSEd programs, and a member of the graduate faculty at Monmouth University. Her expertise is in the area of literacy instruction, as well as the diagnosis and remediation of students and adults with learning difficulties. She has published in *Delta Kappa Gamma Bulletin, Reading Research and Instruction,* and *Reading Instruction Journal,* and she has presented at several state and national conferences. Dr. Romeo is also the advisor for the Council for Exceptional Children and the International Reading Association Student Interest Council at Monmouth.

Elizabeth Rudenga
Trinity Christian College

Elizabeth Rudenga is an associate professor and chair of the Education Department at Trinity Christian College in Palos Heights, Illinois, where she teaches courses in literacy and special education. Her research and areas of interest involve ways in which teachers can encourage, guide, and support students as they become literate, especially those students who do not immediately excel in the literacy process. She is also enthusiastic about the role that technology can play in the classroom and seeks to make future teachers aware of the many possibilities.

Barbara R. Schirmer
Kent State University

Dr. Barbara R. Schirmer is chair of the Department of Educational Foundations and Special Services at Kent State University. Her articles have appeared in such journals as *Teaching Exceptional Children* and *Reading Research and Instruction,* and she is the author of *Language and Literacy Development in Children Who Are Deaf*

(Allyn & Bacon, 1994). Dr. Schirmer received her M.Ed. in education of deaf and hard-of-hearing children and youth from the University of Pittsburgh and her Ed.D. in language minors: reading and special education from the University at Buffalo, State University of New York.

Kenneth J. Weiss
Nazareth College of Rochester

Dr. Kenneth J. Weiss is an assistant professor of education and the director of the Reading Education Program at Nazareth College of Rochester. He currently teaches courses in foundations of reading, reading in the content areas, and literature in the elementary and middle-school reading program. In addition to teaching, he also serves as a consultant for Literacy Consultants of Western New York and the Vocational Technical Reading Center Programs of the Connecticut State Department of Education. Dr. Weiss received his Ed.D. in reading at Rutgers University.

Nora L. White
University of Alaska, Fairbanks

Dr. Nora L. White is an assistant professor in the School of Education at the University of Alaska, Fairbanks, where she teaches undergraduate and graduate courses, such as foundations of literacy development, issues in literacy assessment, and cultural aspects of language and literacy. She is currently serving as a postdoctoral research fellow at the University of Western Sydney, Nepean, Australia. Her project, *Intersubjectivity: The Development of Home-School Literacy,* focuses on the similarities and differences between home and school literacy practices, the impact this has on students' school achievement, and how schools and families can work together to develop strong partnerships. Dr. White received her Ph.D. in language and literacy education from Ohio State University.

WiseGuide Introduction

Critical Thinking and Bumper Stickers

The bumper sticker said: Question Authority. This is a simple directive that goes straight to the heart of critical thinking. The issue is not whether the authority is right or wrong; it's the questioning process that's important. Questioning helps you develop awareness and a clearer sense of what you think. That's critical thinking.

Critical thinking is a new label for an old approach to learning—that of challenging all ideas, hypotheses, and assumptions. In the physical and life sciences, systematic questioning and testing methods (known as the scientific method) help verify information, and objectivity is the benchmark on which all knowledge is pursued. In the social sciences, however, where the goal is to study people and their behavior, things get fuzzy. It's one thing for the chemistry experiment to work out as predicted, or for the petri dish to yield a certain result. It's quite another matter, however, in the social sciences, where the subject is ourselves. Objectivity is harder to achieve.

Although you'll hear critical thinking defined in many different ways, it really boils down to analyzing the ideas and messages that you receive. What are you being asked to think or believe? Does it make sense, objectively? Using the same facts and considerations, could you reasonably come up with a different conclusion? And, why does this matter in the first place? As the bumper sticker urged, question authority. Authority can be a textbook, a politician, a boss, a big sister, or an ad on television. Whatever the message, learning to question it appropriately is a habit that will serve you well for a lifetime. And in the meantime, thinking critically will certainly help you be course wise.

Question Authority

Getting Connected

This reader is a tool for connected learning. This means that the readings and other learning aids explained here will help you to link classroom theory to real-world issues. They will help you to think critically and to make long-lasting learning connections. Feedback from both instructors and students has helped us to develop some suggestions on how you can wisely use this connected learning tool.

WiseGuide Pedagogy

A wise reader is better able to be a critical reader. Therefore, we want to help you get wise about the articles in this reader. Each section of *Perspectives* has three tools to help you: the WiseGuide Intro, the WiseGuide Wrap-Up, and the Putting It in *Perspectives* review form.

WiseGuide Intro

In the WiseGuide Intro, the Academic Editor introduces the section, gives you an overview of the topics covered, and explains why particular articles were selected and what's important about them.

Also in the WiseGuide Intro, you'll find several key points or learning objectives that highlight the most important things to remember from this section. These will help you to focus your study of section topics.

WiseGuide Intro

At the end of the WiseGuide Intro, you'll find questions designed to stimulate critical thinking. Wise students will keep these questions in mind as they read an article (we repeat the questions at the start of the articles as a reminder). When you finish each article, check your understanding. Can you answer the questions? If not, go back and reread the article. The Academic Editor has written sample responses for many of the questions, and you'll find these online at the **Courselinks**™ site for this course. More about **Courselinks** in a minute. . . .

WiseGuide Wrap-Up

Be course wise and develop a thorough understanding of the topics covered in this course. The WiseGuide Wrap-Up at the end of each section will help you do just that with concluding comments or summary points that repeat what's most important to understand from the section you just read.

In addition, we try to get you wired up by providing a list of select Internet resources—what we call R.E.A.L. web sites because they're **R**elevant, **E**xciting, **A**pproved, and **L**inked. The information at these web sites will enhance your understanding of a topic. (Remember to use your Passport and start at http://www.courselinks.com so that if any of these sites have changed, you'll have the latest link.)

Putting It in *Perspectives* Review Form

At the end of the book is the Putting It in *Perspectives* review form. Your instructor may ask you to complete this form as an assignment or for extra credit. If nothing else, consider doing it on your own to help you critically think about the reading.

Prompts at the end of each article encourage you to complete this review form. Feel free to copy the form and use it as needed.

The Courselinks™ Site

The **Courselinks** Passport is your ticket to a wonderful world of integrated web resources designed to help you with your course work. These resources are found at the **Courselinks** site for your course area. This is where the readings in this book and the key topics of your course are linked to an exciting array of online learning tools. Here you will find carefully selected readings, web links, quizzes, worksheets, and more, tailored to your course and approved as connected learning tools. The ever-changing, always interesting **Courselinks** site features a number of carefully integrated resources designed to help you be course wise. These include:

- **R.E.A.L. Sites** At the core of a **Courselinks** site is the list of R.E.A.L. sites. This is a select group of web sites for studying, not surfing. Like the readings in this book, these sites have been selected, reviewed, and approved by the Academic Editor and the Editorial Board. The R.E.A.L. sites are arranged by topic and are annotated with short descriptions and key words to make them easier for you to use for reference or research. With R.E.A.L. sites, you're studying approved resources within seconds—and not wasting precious time surfing unproven sites.

- **Editor's Choice** Here you'll find updates on news related to your course, with links to the actual online sources. This is also where we'll tell you about changes to the site and about online events.

- **Course Overview** This is a general description of the typical course in this area of study. While your instructor will provide specific course objectives, this overview helps you place the course in a generic context and offers you an additional reference point.

- **www.orksheet** Focus your trip to a R.E.A.L. site with the www.orksheet. Each of the 10 to 15 questions will prompt you to take in the best that site has to offer. Use this tool for self-study, or if required, email it to your instructor.

- **Course Quiz** The questions on this self-scoring quiz are related to articles in the reader, information at R.E.A.L. sites, and other course topics, and will help you pinpoint areas you need to study. Only you will know your score—it's an easy, risk-free way to keep pace!

- **Topic Key** The Topic Key is a listing of the main topics in your course, and it correlates with the Topic Key that appears in this reader. This handy reference tool also links directly to those R.E.A.L. sites that are especially appropriate to each topic, bringing you integrated online resources within seconds!

- **Web Savvy Student Site** If you're new to the Internet or want to brush up, stop by the Web Savvy Student site. This unique supplement is a complete **Courselinks** site unto itself. Here, you'll find basic information on using the Internet, creating a web page, communicating on the web, and more. Quizzes and Web Savvy Worksheets test your web knowledge, and the R.E.A.L. sites listed here will further enhance your understanding of the web.

- **Student Lounge** Drop by the Student Lounge to chat with other students taking the same course or to learn more about careers in your major. You'll find links to resources for scholarships, financial aid, internships, professional associations, and jobs. Take a look around the Student Lounge and give us your feedback. We're open to remodeling the Lounge per your suggestions.

Building Better Perspectives!

Please tell us what you think of this *Perspectives* volume so we can improve the next one. Here's how you can help:

1. Visit our **Coursewise** site at: http://www.coursewise.com

2. Click on *Perspectives*. Then select the Building Better *Perspectives* Form for your book.

3. Forms and instructions for submission are available online.

Tell us what you think—did the readings and online materials help you make some learning connections? Were some materials more helpful than others? Thanks in advance for helping us build better *Perspectives*.

Student Internships

If you enjoy evaluating these articles or would like to help us evaluate the **Courselinks** site for this course, check out the **Coursewise** Student Internship Program. For more information, visit:

http://www.coursewise.com/intern.html

Brief Contents

Contents

At **Coursewise,** we're publishing *connected learning tools.* That means that the book you are holding is only a part of this publication. You'll also want to harness the integrated resources that **Coursewise** has developed at the fun and highly useful **Courselinks**™ web site for *Perspectives: Literacy.* If you purchased this book new, use the Passport that was shrink-wrapped to this volume to obtain site access. If you purchased a used copy of this book, then you need to buy a stand-alone Passport. If your bookstore doesn't stock Passports to **Courselinks** sites, visit http://www.courselinks.com for ordering information.

section
1

Controversies and Commonalities: Issues in Literacy

section 2

Growing Readers: Early Reading and Family Literacy

section 3

"Teacher, What Does This Mean?": Understanding Text

section 4

The State of the Field: Standards and Integrated Literacy Instruction

section

5

Evaluating Readers and Writers: Comprehensive Assessment

section

6

When Children Struggle with the Reading Process: Literacy and Diversity and the At-Risk Learner

section 7

Technology as an Integral Part of Literacy Instruction

Topic Key

This Topic Key is an important tool for learning. It will help you integrate this reader into your course studies. Listed below, in alphabetical order, are important topics covered in this volume. Below each topic you'll find the reading numbers and titles, and also the R.E.A.L. web site addresses, relating to that topic. Note that the Topic Key might not include every topic your instructor chooses to emphasize. If you don't find the topic you're looking for in the Topic Key, check the index or the online topic key at the **Courselinks**™ site.

Assessment
18 Challenging Expectations: Why We Ought to Stand by the IRA/NCTE *Standards for the English Language Arts*
20 Motivating Readers: Better Ways to See and Support Student Reading Progress
22 Literacy Assessment Reform: Shifting Beliefs, Principled Possibilities, and Emerging Practices
23 New Writing Assessments: The Challenge of Changing Teachers' Beliefs About Students as Writers

National Assessment of Educational Progress
http://nces.ed.gov/nationsreportcard/

The National Center for Fair and Open Testing
http://www.fairtest.org

National Center for Research on Evaluation, Standards, and Student Testing (CRESST)
http://cresst96.cse.ucla.edu/index.htm

At-Risk Learners
24 There's More to Teaching At-Risk and Delayed Readers Than Good Reading Instruction
25 The 11 Deadly Sins of Remedial Reading Programs
26 Preventing Reading Failure: A Review of Five Effective Programs
28 Boosting Reading Success

Center for the Improvement of Early Reading Achievement
http://www.ciera.org/

Authenticity
15 Seeking Authenticity: What Is "Real" About Thematic Literacy Instruction?

Balanced Literacy
2 Where Are Teachers' Voices in the Phonics/Whole Language Debate? Results from a Survey of U.S. Elementary Classroom Teachers
7 Balanced Instruction: Insights and Considerations

Brain Processing
4 Why Andy Couldn't Read
5 Baby Talk

National Institute on Early Childhood Development and Education
http://www.ed.gov/offices/OERI/ECI/

Children's Literature
10 Talking about Books: Beyond Decodable Texts—Supportive and Workable Literature

Student Achievements: Sample Lesson Plans
http://users.neca.com/rchatel/Students.html#Lesson Plans

Comprehension
11 Mediation of Cognitive Competencies for Students in Need
12 Reading Comprehension: What Works
28 Boosting Reading Success

Cultural Literacy and Schema Theory
http://www.ils.nwu.edu/%7Ee_for_e/nodes/NODE-97-pg.html

ERIC Clearinghouse on Reading, English, and Communication
http://www.indiana.edu/~eric_rec/

Content Area Reading
24 There's More to Teaching At-Risk and Delayed Readers Than Good Reading Instruction
28 Boosting Reading Success

ERIC Clearinghouse on Reading, English, and Communication
http://www.indiana.edu/~eric_rec/

Critical Thinking
14 Critical Questions: Whose Questions?

Resources for The Center for Critical Thinking
http://www.sonoma.edu/cthink/K12/k12class/trc.nclk

ERIC Clearinghouse on Reading, English, and Communication
http://www.indiana.edu/~eric_rec/

Diversity
1 Literacy for All Students: Ten Steps Toward Making a Difference
6 Family Literacy: Examining Practice and Issues of Effectiveness
27 "Dat teacher be hollin at us"—What Is Ebonics?

Cultural Literacy and Schema Theory
http://www.ils.nwu.edu/%7Ee_for_e/nodes/NODE-97-pg.html

Equity
17 Innocent and Not-So-Innocent Contributions to Inequality: Choice, Power, and Insensitivity in a First-Grade Writing Workshop
18 Challenging Expectations: Why We Ought to Stand by the IRA/NCTE *Standards for the English Language Arts*
21 Can Grades Be Helpful *and* Fair?

Family Literacy Programs
6 Family Literacy: Examining Practice and Issues of Effectiveness

National Center for Family Literacy
http://www.famlit.org/

National Institute on Early Childhood Development and Education
http://www.ed.gov/offices/OERI/ECI/

section 1

Controversies and Commonalities: Issues in Literacy

Learning Objectives

- Define and describe the attributes of constructivism and holistic teaching.

- Summarize the debate over the role of phonics in beginning reading instruction, and analyze the effect it has had on teachers' instructional practices.

- Describe the conditions of natural language learning as they apply to literacy teaching.

- Describe the importance of parental involvement in identifying a child with a learning disability, and identify the challenges and solutions faced by parents of a child who has been identified as learning disabled.

WiseGuide Intro

Reading is an extremely complex process involving cognitive, affective, social, and linguistic elements. These elements, interacting dynamically, constitute the holistic act of reading. This concept is the foundation for various theories on how children use aspects of the reading process to become proficient readers, and these theories offer alternative ways to explain the reading process that have been neither proven nor disproven. Since literacy educators and researchers hold different theories, controversies have emerged about the best way to assist children in becoming proficient readers. These conflicting views have led to debates over what is known about reading instruction and the implications of that knowledge for classroom instruction. These controversies can be disconcerting to teachers who are concerned about providing the best instructional practices in reading.

Since there is no proven "best" approach to teaching reading, teachers base their instructional practices on their own beliefs, assumptions, and theories. Knowledgeable and masterful teachers are able to state distinctly and concisely what they believe about teaching and learning. The ability to express one's personal definition of *reading* can lead to understanding the reading process. Teachers who do not have a personal definition of *reading* or an understanding of the reading process are likely to assume the prevalent beliefs of others and the practices tacit in a given reading program or school. This can lead to teachers' teaching from tradition or unexamined beliefs, rather than from knowledge, experience, and critical evaluation.

In order to form a definition of *reading*, teachers must observe children to understand how they learn about print, they must clearly comprehend the cognitive, affective, social, and linguistic aspects of the reading process, and they must be knowledgeable about the various theories of reading and must understand that these theories drive instructional decisions in the classroom. One way to become informed about the issues being discussed about the various theories and practices is to read current articles.

The articles presented in Section 1 represent some of the issues currently being discussed among literacy educators. "Literacy for All Students: Ten Steps Toward Making a Difference" outlines a set of principles for becoming a holistic, constructivist teacher. "Where Are Teachers' Voices in the Phonics/Whole Language Debate? Results from a Survey of U.S. Elementary Classroom Teachers" presents the results of a nationwide survey of the instructional beliefs and practices of elementary public school teachers in the United States. "Toward an Educationally Relevant Theory of Literacy Learning: Twenty Years of Inquiry" provides insight into everyday natural learning and identifies conditions of learning as they apply to literacy instruction. "Why Andy Couldn't Read" highlights the educational challenges of parents, teachers, and children with language or learning disabilities.

Through examining these articles, teachers and prospective teachers can compare their beliefs with those presented in the articles and, in doing so, identify, refine, and critically reflect on their own beliefs. In this way, teachers can make their own informed decisions about literacy instruction.

? ? ? Questions ?

Reading 1. What is constructivism? What classroom practices reflect constructivism?

Reading 2. What was the controversy regarding reading instruction in the 1950s and 1960s? What is the debate about today?

Reading 3. What are the conditions for learning? What practices would reflect the conditions of learning if applied to literacy teaching in the classroom?

Reading 4. How can teachers inform parents about learning disabilities? What can parents do to assist their child if she or he is diagnosed with a learning disorder?

What is constructivism? What classroom practices reflect constructivism?

Literacy for All Students

Ten steps toward making a difference

In a fictitious letter to a new teacher taking a graduate-level course, Au explores questions often raised by young teachers and provides a set of principles for becoming a holistic, constructivist teacher.

Kathryn H. Au

Au, a former primary grade teacher, now works in the College of Education at the University of Hawaii. She is President of the National Reading Conference. She drafted the IRA resolution on cultural awareness. She can be contacted at the University of Hawaii, College of Education, 1776 University Ave., WA 2-223, Honolulu, HI 96822, USA.

Dear Maile,

In class yesterday afternoon, you described the challenges you face as a new teacher trying to conduct daily writers' and readers' workshops. You teach in a school with students of diverse cultural and linguistic backgrounds. Most are of Native Hawaiian ancestry, and the others are of many different ethnicities. Most speak a nonmainstream variety of English, Hawaii Creole English, as their first language, although a few speak other languages at home, such as Samoan, Ilokano, and Cantonese. Almost all are from low-income families.

Although your students are fourth graders, they do not appear to have had any previous experience with the process approach to writing or literature-based instruction. You have discovered that none of the other fourth-grade teachers are using these approaches, but you have heard that there is a fifth-grade teacher whose philosophy is similar to yours.

You want to continue with the writers' and readers' workshops, but you feel a great deal of uncertainty. Among the questions you raised were the following:

- Will the process approach to writing and literature-based instruction really prove effective with my students?

- Will it be possible to continue with these approaches on my own, even if my whole school is not moving in this direction?

- There is so much to do that I feel overwhelmed. What do I do first?

Your questions don't have simple answers; it's fortunate that we have the entire semester to address them. To focus our discussion, let me suggest 10 steps you might consider as you work to improve literacy instruction in your classroom.

1. Reflect Upon Your Own Philosophy of Literacy, Instruction, and Learning

Many teachers say, "Just tell me what to do!" They say they have no interest in philosophy. Yet I think it is vitally important to understand why we teach in one way or another. You may find it helpful to begin by organizing your thoughts about philosophy in three areas: literacy, instruction, and learning. Here are key ideas that have influenced my thinking.

Hansen (1992) writes of having students and teachers create literacy portfolios. The purpose of these portfolios is to answer the question, "Who am I as a reader and writer?" The portfolios contain artifacts along with brief, written reflections about why that artifact has been included.

Au, Kathryn Hu-Pei. (1997, November). Literacy for all students: Ten steps toward making a difference. *The Reading Teacher*, 51(3), 186–194.
Reprinted with permission of Kathryn H. Au and the International Reading Association. All rights reserved.

For example, one of the items in my literacy portfolio is a letter that I received from my grandmother. My favorite lines read:

Have to get ready now to go to the hospital to see the sick patients, long-term and daycare patients. We do this every Tuesday.

In my reflection I described how my grandmother wrote me this letter when she was 90 years old. I loved the idea that she was visiting the hospital to spread good cheer to people 20 or 30 years younger. Until I put my literacy portfolio together, I had not thought about the role of literacy in strengthening family ties.

One effect of creating a literacy portfolio is that we become aware of the power of literacy. Once we gain this awareness, we understand that part of our responsibility as teachers is to show students how literacy can be powerful in their lives. When students sense the power of literacy in their lives, they have ownership of literacy (Au, Scheu, & Kawakami, 1990). They value literacy and make it part of their everyday routines, at home as well as at school. I believe that ownership of literacy should be the overarching goal of the language arts curriculum (Au, Scheu, Kawakami, & Herman, 1990). We must teach students the skills and strategies they need to become proficient readers and writers. However, students who find literacy personally meaningful will have the motivation to learn and apply skills and strategies; other students may not.

My thinking about instruction has changed a great deal over the years. When I was a beginning teacher, I taught following a traditional basal reading program, which recommended teaching skills first. Students were supposed to develop an interest in reading and writing after they had learned the skills. We now know that interest does not develop automatically as a consequence of teaching students many skills (Shannon, 1989). When skills are overemphasized and meaningful activities neglected, students tend to find little value in reading and writing. They fail to develop ownership of literacy.

I now believe that instruction should begin with interest, with activities that students can find personally meaningful. Examples of such activities are reading and discussing a thought-provoking novel, such as *The Giver* by Lois Lowry (1993), or writing about events important in one's life. The samples you've brought to class show that your students are writing about a variety of topics: fishing at the boat harbor, visiting grandparents in Arizona, planting taro. Once students are engaged in meaningful literacy activities, they have reasons to learn the skills and strategies they need to complete the activities successfully.

Schools in low-income communities, like the one in which you teach, are the most susceptible to curricula that overemphasize skills (Allington, 1991). When scores on standardized tests are low, an increased emphasis on skills is often regarded as the logical solution. I fear this solution can be damaging to students' overall development as literacy learners. Even more than other students, struggling readers and writers need to be involved in meaningful literacy activities. These are the students who most need to experience ownership of literacy. Skill instruction can and should take place within the context of their engagement in meaningful activities.

The saying that children learn to read by reading and to write by writing applies as much to the struggling reader and writer as it does to other students. Skills and strategies are only as good as students' ability to apply them at the right time. Students have the best opportunity to gain experience with the application and orchestration of skills and strategies when they engage in the full processes of reading and writing. That is why authentic literacy activities—reading and writing that is real and meaningful—are central to a successful classroom literacy program, especially for students of diverse backgrounds.

of taking on too much at once. I've learned that it is best to focus on just one area at a time; for example, either the process approach to writing (Calkins, 1994; Graves 1994) or literature-based instruction (Roser & Martinez, 1995). Suppose you decide to focus on the process approach to writing. This means that you will concentrate your energies and attention on making changes to the writers' workshop. You will continue to conduct a readers' workshop and to teach reading as you are now doing, with only minor adjustments.

Teaching within the framework of a whole literacy curriculum—including the writers' workshop, the readers' workshop, and portfolio assessment—is extremely demanding for teachers (Au & Carroll, 1997). Teachers must relate to students in new ways, such as sharing their own literacy with students. It requires a great deal of thought, as well as trial and error in the classroom, to make the transformation. Teachers who try to do everything at once find that they are unable to gain a clear understanding of any particular aspect: writers' workshop, readers' workshop, or portfolio assessment (Au & Scheu, 1996).

You're wondering what to do first. Most of the teachers I know, who share a holistic, constructivist philosophy (Applebee, 1991; Raphael & Hiebert, 1996), judge the starting point to be the process approach to writing. In my experience, writing on self-selected topics—planning, drafting, revising, editing, and publishing—does more than anything else to build ownership of literacy for students of diverse backgrounds. I am a great believer in the power of literature to inspire and motivate students to become avid readers and lovers of literacy. But I have seen time and again, for students like those in your class, that ownership of literacy begins when they write and publish books about their own lives.

2. Choose a Focus for Change

You mentioned feeling overwhelmed because there are so many things you want to try. Sometimes, in our enthusiasm for new ideas, we run the risk

3. Make a Commitment to Full Implementation of Your Chosen Focus

You asked whether using a holistic, constructivist approach to literacy instruction would prove effective with your students. I'm convinced that this kind of approach can be highly effective in improving the literacy achievement and attitudes of students of diverse backgrounds. However, it will only be effective under conditions of full implementation (Au & Carroll, 1997). Full implementation means that all the key features of the innovation, such as the writers' workshop or portfolio assessment, are in place in your classroom. It is important to take change one step at a time and to move steadily toward full implementation.

One way of moving toward full implementation of your chosen focus is to work with a checklist. The checklist would contain all the features of classroom organization, teacher-led instruction, opportunities for student learning, and portfolio assessment that you believe to be important (Au & Carroll, 1997). The checklist can help you set goals for your own professional development. You begin by identifying the items you already have in place in your classroom. Then, perhaps once a month, you select the item or items that you would like to implement next.

You may want to look over several different checklists, such as those developed by Johnson and Wilder (1992) and Vogt (1991). If you are like most teachers, you will find yourself revising one of the checklists, drawing upon your own thinking and the ideas in other checklists. After all, unlike the authors of the original checklist, you know your own students and have a good sense of what will work effectively with them. In developing a checklist, you will also have started to plan your professional development as a teacher of literacy.

My colleagues and I (Au & Scheu, 1996) learned of the importance of full implementation while working with a checklist for the writer's workshop. We discovered that an implementation level of about 90% of checklist items is the point at which dramatic improvements in students' learning are seen. Below this level, although an increasing number of checklist items may be implemented, literacy achievement does not seem to improve. An implementation level of 90% proved to be what social scientists call a tipping

point, the point when the situation has finally changed enough so that positive results occur. To reach the tipping point, teachers had to have faith that they were on the right track and be patient and thorough in their work.

4. Establish Clear Goals for Students' Learning

Goals for student learning can help you know how to direct your teaching. Of course, you have already gained much of the information you need through observations of your students. You have a sense of their strengths as literacy learners and the areas in which they can benefit from instruction. Other information comes from outside the classroom, as you learn what other educators think about the goals for student learning at your grade level. In class we reviewed our state's language arts standards (Hawaii State Commission on Performance Standards, 1994), as well as the national standards for the English language arts proposed by the National Council of Teachers of English and the International Reading Association (1996). These documents are valuable resources, but they provide broad frameworks rather than ready-made solutions. Our state standards document describes goals across several grade levels (for example, kindergarten through Grade 3), while the national standards document lists goals appropriate from kindergarten through high school. Neither provides grade-level benchmarks—goals for student learning for each grade level—the form of standards most useful to the classroom teacher. For example, suppose that a broad goal at the state level is for students to understand and appreciate literature. A corresponding benchmark at the fourth-grade level would be that students write a response to literature, including story elements, the author's message, and connections to their own lives.

I've worked on the process of developing benchmarks at several schools, and in most cases it has not been difficult for teachers to reach consensus about the benchmarks appropriate for each grade. The diffi-

culty lies in moving from benchmarks as theoretical statements to benchmarks as actual goals that students will achieve. Schools like yours, in low-income communities, generally have a history of low student achievement. Given past experience, teachers may be skeptical about whether their students can actually reach the benchmarks (Au & Scheu, 1996). Teachers have told me, "I feel that these are the right benchmarks for my grade level, but I don't see how my students can achieve them."

Students of diverse backgrounds, like your students, can reach levels of performance consistent with state and national standards for achievement in the language arts (Au & Carroll, 1997; Au & Scheu, 1996). The teachers whose students achieved these results used practices that you may find helpful. They made benchmarks public and visible to students. They rewrote the benchmarks in language students could understand, and they posted charts with the benchmarks. They discussed the benchmarks so students knew what each one meant. They showed students examples, such as research reports completed by students the year before, of the kind of work that would be expected of them. They kept the benchmarks posted and frequently referred to them. Students knew the goals for literacy learning at their grade level; expectations were clear. With the cards on the table, so to speak, teachers and students can work collaboratively toward achievement of the benchmarks.

5. Share Your Own Literacy with Students

I mentioned earlier that the teacher's role is transformed in whole literacy classrooms. One of the characteristics of constructivist, holistic forms of teaching is that the teacher demonstrates to students that s/he engages in the same processes of literacy as they do. For example, if students are supposed to write in notebooks, the teacher shows how s/he writes entries in her/his notebook (Calkins, 1994). Teachers strive to be the kind of readers and writers they wish their students to be. As Graves (1990) suggests, teachers' discovery of their own literacy is the starting point for a successful writers' workshop.

It takes courage for teachers to share their own literacy with students. When we share our literacy with students we reveal ourselves as human beings with interests and feelings. Perhaps for this reason, teachers' sharing of their literacy makes a profound impression on students. Chris Tanioka, a fourth-grade teacher, wanted her students to understand how much she loved books.

One day she brought in a large bag of books and told the class she wanted to share some books she had on her nightstand and was currently reading. One by one she pulled out her books and told the class what they were about and why they were important to her. Some were "how to" books on flower arranging and swimming, one was a popular novel recommended to her by a colleague, and several were children's books. These she said she loved most of all. "I used to hide my books so no one would know I read children's books. But not anymore!" (Carroll, Wilson, & Au, 1996)

Nora Okamoto, a fifth-grade teacher, used her own writing as the basis for minilessons during the writers' workshop. In one minilesson, she focused on the benchmark *reconsiders and reorganizes writing*, showing students how she had changed a piece of writing from one genre to another.

Nora began by telling the students about a journal entry she had written about her father. She spoke about how hard it was to share her writing because the subject was a personal and emotional one. She talked about the feelings she had when her father experienced difficulties following the death of her mother. Nora explained how helpless she felt, not knowing what to do or say. She decided to write a piece about her father to express how much he meant to her. Then, reconsidering her writing, she saw how she could turn it into a poem, a less personal way to express her strong feelings. She showed the students how she circled thoughts and words from her journal entry and then began drafting. When Nora read the poem, the class was mesmerized. (Carroll et al., 1996)

Students in these classrooms did not have to be lectured about the power of literacy. Through their teachers' demonstrations, they saw it with their own eyes.

6. Make School Literacy Learning a Meaningful, Rewarding Experience for Students

You described how some students in your classroom have a negative attitude toward school and try to disrupt the class. They seem to be testing you to see how you will respond. You are working at winning them over, but you wonder if you will be successful. You worry that the time you are spending with this handful of students is taking time away from others, and you are concerned about negative effects on the whole class.

D'Amato (1988) points out that students of diverse backgrounds may not see the point of going to school. They may not have the understanding that doing well in school can improve their life opportunities, leading to college and a good job, because these connections have not been illustrated in their own families. D'Amato suggests that teachers must make school an interesting and rewarding daily experience, so that students will have a reason for coming to school and doing their best to learn.

In this view, literacy learning activities that students find meaningful are not a luxury but a necessity. Here are some ideas for making literacy meaningful for students.

- Before discussing a book, have students discuss their experiences related to the topic or theme of the book (Au, 1979). For example, before reading *The Giver* (Lowry, 1993), students might be asked what they would like to do when they grow up. Then they could be asked how they would feel if someone else were to make that decision for them.

- Teach students to write in notebooks about experiences important in their lives (Calkins, 1991). Demonstrate the process by reading entries from your own notebook.

- Interview students to learn about their tastes as readers. If students are indifferent to reading or do not yet have preferences, help them identify materials related to their interests. These materials may be surfing magazines or comic books, but that is a start. Make sure these materials are available to students during sustained silent reading.

- Invite older students, parents, and community members into the classroom to serve as literate role models. Have these individuals discuss the importance of literacy in their lives. For example, musicians who compose songs or raps can discuss the importance of writing. Students can gain the understanding that people in every occupation—*kumu hula*, lifeguards, farmers—use reading and writing to do their jobs well.

7. Involve Students in Portfolio Assessment

You are thinking of trying portfolio assessment. However, you have heard that it is a lot of work and wonder if it will be worth the trouble. Portfolio assessment is indeed worthwhile, because of what it can do to promote students' ownership of literacy. When portfolio assessment is successful, students take responsibility for their own literacy learning.

Once teachers have familiarized students with the grade-level benchmarks, they are ready to help students start portfolios. A list of benchmarks is attached to each student's portfolio. The teacher explains to students that they will be gathering evidence in their portfolios to show their progress in meeting the grade-level benchmarks. As each benchmark is reviewed, the teacher asks students if they can think of anything that might serve as evidence. For example, I observed a group of fifth graders who were asked to find evidence for the benchmark *plans writing*. Several students said they would use the topic lists and webs from their writing folders as evidence. One student asked if she could use as evidence a notebook entry that had been the basis for a published piece.

Teachers can help students understand portfolio assessment as a process that takes place across the year. When the portfolios are introduced, perhaps at the end of the first quarter, students may notice that they do not have evidence for all the benchmarks. For example, they may not have evidence for the benchmark *reads different genres of fiction and shows understanding of genre characteristics*, because they have only read realistic fiction. Students become aware of the need to work on this benchmark in the future. Teachers may ask students to write down the goals they will pursue during the next quarter. Students identify the benchmarks they will work on. They also identify personal goals that may not be represented by any benchmarks.

Valencia (1990) envisions the portfolio process as one in which students have the opportunity to reflect upon and evaluate their own learning. With portfolios, students take control of their own literacy learning, an important aspect of ownership. Through the use of benchmarks, students understand what others expect of them. By reflecting on their own progress as literacy learners, they understand what they should expect of themselves.

8. Keep Parents Involved in Students' Literacy Learning

You mentioned that you have already had some contact with parents. The mother of one of your students stopped by to talk with you. She had noticed her son's new enthusiasm for writing and was wondering if there was anything she could do to sustain this interest. A father wanted you to know that he was concerned about his daughter's spelling. He asked when his daughter would start having weekly spelling tests, and he was surprised when you explained that she would be learning correct spelling by editing her own writing.

One of our tasks in moving toward a holistic, constructivist approach to literacy instruction is to familiarize parents with the benefits of this approach. Most parents have not experienced readers' and writers' workshops and portfolio assessment in their own education. They may find it puzzling when they see drafts of students' writing with invented spelling, or they may wonder why teachers are not assigning phonics worksheets as homework.

Teachers can do much to address parents' questions and concerns. At evening meetings, some teachers have parents participate in a writers' or readers' workshop, to give them a sense of the learning experiences available to their children. Other teachers may explain these approaches to parents using slides of the classroom to illustrate different types of activities, such as peer conferences or literature circles. Some teachers communicate with parents through a monthly newsletter. Students participate in planning the newsletter and write most of the articles. Teachers may help parents learn new ways of helping their children with homework. For example, parents may feel uncomfortable eliciting children's ideas about a book. Through a monthly newsletter, teachers might share ideas for discussing books, such as suggestions for open-ended questions.

Some parents have schedules that allow them to work as volunteers in the classroom. During the readers' workshop, parents may bring a favorite book to read aloud to students, or they may listen to students read. Parents literate in a language other than English may be invited to the classroom to demonstrate that writing system, for example, Chinese calligraphy. Parents can confer with students about their writing and help students publish books by entering and printing texts on the computer.

Eleanor Baker, a university business writing instructor, spent a year as a volunteer in her son's first-grade class, assisting during the writers' workshop. On her first day, Baker (1994) found it difficult to work with young children in such a busy environment:

I felt overwhelmed because the children were so small with such tiny voices that could run a mile a minute. I felt that I couldn't focus on one child and make any sense of what he or she was saying because there was so much activity going on—children writing, children conferring with classmates or teacher, children brainstorming, and children drawing pictures. (Remember, I grew up at a time when neat rows of quiet students were the norm!) (p. 374)

Baker's words remind us of just how different classrooms today are from those parents usually recall. Gradually, as Baker interacted with the children and observed Martha Willenbrock, her son's teacher, she came to understand the benefits of the process approach to writing. Baker concludes:

The approach to writing that was used in this classroom does not turn all children into prolific writers; some children write much more than others. The approach does allow each child to write successfully, however, no matter what difficulties he or she encounters. (p. 377)

When teachers welcome parents as volunteers, parents have the chance to see the benefits of readers' and writers' workshops for themselves.

9. Network with Other Teachers

You have found the teachers at your grade level to be cordial and welcoming, but they do not appear interested in discussing instructional issues with you. You wonder if you should approach the fifth-grade teacher who seems to share your philosophy. That could be the first step toward forming your own teacher network. It would certainly be convenient to share ideas with the teachers at your grade level, but often teachers do not find themselves with such ready-made networks. Instead, they must create their own networks by doing just what you plan to do, actively seeking out others who share their philosophy. Being part of a teacher network is one of the best things you can do to further your own professional development.

I have heard many teachers use words like these to describe their experiences before joining a network:

I would go to a workshop and get all excited about this new approach. For the next few days, I would try it in my classroom. It wouldn't work. And I would think to myself, what am I doing wrong? I had so many questions, but there was no one to ask. So after a while, I would give up and go back to what I was doing before.

Most teachers have an interest in improving their teaching, but their past efforts have often been disappointing and frustrating. The typical one-day workshop provides inspiration and just enough knowledge to get started—but not enough to deal with the difficulties that arise in a particular classroom. Most teachers who hold a holistic, constructivist philosophy know that they must direct their own professional development. They have their own questions about literacy instruction, and they seek answers to these questions. They select carefully from the workshops offered by their school, their districts, and publishers. Most important, they belong to teacher networks so they can discuss and reflect upon the changes they are making in their classrooms.

Once you have identified colleagues interested in joining a network, you will face other challenges. It takes time to learn to describe one's classroom practices to other teachers and to articulate one's concerns about instruction. It takes practice to consult with other teachers: to listen, restate another's concerns, ask questions, offer suggestions. It takes practice to facilitate a discussion, make sure that everyone is heard, and keep the conversation focused on the key issues. Yet the rewards far outweigh the difficulties. Sometimes you will pose a question that spurs suggestions from the group. However, even when your colleagues cannot offer specific ideas, they will provide you with the encouragement to continue wrestling with the issues.

Finding the time to participate in a network may be the greatest challenge of all. Most teachers do not have time for network meetings during the school day. Sometimes they meet at lunch or after school. I belong to a teacher network that meets once a month over dinner. There are teachers who form carpools so they can network on the drive to and from school. Where there's a will, there's a way.

10. Allow Time for Change to Take Place

You have just begun your second year of teaching, and you are concerned about improving your literacy program, not to mention your teaching of math and other subjects. You know that this year is going more smoothly than last year, but you wish

your teaching would improve more quickly. You mentioned being surprised by how patient you could be with your students but noted that you have trouble being patient with yourself. You wonder how long it will take before you have the process approach to writing, literature-based instruction, and portfolio assessment all in place in your classroom.

I cannot say exactly, but it could well be several years before you feel comfortable with all these elements in your classroom language arts program. I see growth in your thinking since the beginning of our class, and I feel you are making more progress than you realize. If you have a holistic, constructivist philosophy, you will find that your vision of your classroom and your goals for professional development are constantly evolving. You have embarked on a journey that will continue for at least as long as you are a teacher.

I want to close by addressing a question that you have been too polite to raise in class. That is the question of what impact constructivist, holistic literacy instruction can really have on students' lives. Many of your students face difficult circumstances at home. Some are homeless. Some come to school hungry. Some have a parent in prison or addicted to drugs. Sometimes it seems as if there is little a teacher can do in the classroom that could possibly help students overcome these conditions. Yet literacy may help some students understand and come to terms with the challenges in their lives.

In one classroom, students engaged in dialogue journals with their teacher. A girl wrote about an incident that seemed to the teacher to involve sexual abuse. The teacher, the school counselor, and the student met to discuss the situation. Soon after, the student's parents took legal action to make sure the offender, a male relative, would not harm the girl again.

The student decided to write a book about these experiences, and she was determined to share the book with her classmates. When the teacher asked whether she really wanted to do this, the girl stood firm in her decision. She said that she hoped other students would learn from her experiences; if they were

being abused, they could do something about it.

This is a particularly dramatic example, but I know of many other instances in which students used literacy to address difficulties in their lives: witnessing the arrest of an older brother, moving in with relatives when a father lost his job, learning that a beloved grandmother had died. Accounts written by adolescents testify to the lasting impression of experiences in classrooms with holistic, constructivist teaching (e.g., Crockett & Weidhaas, 1992).

I can't say for a fact that your students will be convinced of the power of literacy, or that literacy will improve their lives. But it just might.

Sincerely yours,

Kathy Au

Author's Notes

The questions and responses in this letter are based on discussions with a graduate class in which about half the students were beginning teachers in low-income schools. The concerns attributed to Maile, a fictitious character, were the ones expressed by these teachers.

References

Allington, R.L. (1991). Children who find learning to read difficult: School responses to diversity. In E.H. Hiebert (Ed.), *Literacy for a diverse society: Perspectives, practices, and policies* (pp. 237–252). New York: Teachers College Press.

Applebee, A.N. (1991). Environments for language teaching and learning: Contemporary issues and future directions. In J. Flood, J.M. Jensen, D. Lapp, & J.R. Squire (Eds.), *Handbook of research on teaching the English language arts* (pp. 549–556). New York: Macmillan.

Au, K.H. (1979). Using the experience-text-relationship method with minority children. *The Reading Teacher, 32,* 677–679.

Au, K.H., & Carroll, J.H. (1997). Improving literacy achievement through a constructivist approach: The KEEP Demonstration Classroom Project. *Elementary School Journal, 97,* 203–221.

Au, K.H., & Scheu, J.A. (1996). Journey toward holistic instruction. *The Reading Teacher, 49,* 468–477.

Au, K.H., Scheu, J.A., & Kawakami, A.J. (1990). Assessment of students' ownership of literacy. *The Reading Teacher, 44,* 154–156.

Au, K.H., Scheu, J.A., Kawakami, A.J., & Herman, P.A. (1990). Assessment and accountability in a whole literacy curriculum. *The Reading Teacher, 43,* 574–578.

Baker, E.C. (1994). Writing and reading in a first-grade writers' workshop: A parent's perspective. *The Reading Teacher, 47,* 372–377.

Calkins, L.M. (1991). *Living between the lines.* Portsmouth, NH: Heinemann.

Calkins, L.M. (1994). *The art of teaching writing* (2nd ed.). Portsmouth, NH: Heinemann.

Carroll, J.H., Wilson, R.A., & Au, K.H. (1996). Explicit instruction in the context of the readers' and writers' workshops. In E. McIntyre & M. Pressley (Eds.), *Skills and strategies in whole language* (pp. 39–63). Norwood, MA: Christopher-Gordon.

Crockett, T., & Weidhaas, S. (1992). Scribbling down the pictures. In S. Benedict & L. Carlisle (Eds.), *Beyond words: Picture books for older readers and writers* (pp. 59–67). Portsmouth, NH: Heinemann.

D'Amato, J. (1988). "Acting": Hawaiian children's resistance to teachers. *Elementary School Journal, 88,* 529–544.

Graves, D. (1990). *Discover your own literacy.* Portsmouth, NH: Heinemann.

Graves, D. (1994). *A fresh look at writing.* Portsmouth, NH: Heinemann.

Hansen, J. (1992). Literacy portfolios: Helping students know themselves. *Educational Leadership, 49*(8), 66–68.

Hawaii State Commission on Performance Standards. (1994, June). *Final report.* Honolulu, HI: Author.

Johnson, J.S., & Wilder, S.L. (1992). Changing reading and writing programs through staff development. *The Reading Teacher, 45,* 626–631.

Lowry, L. (1993). *The giver.* Boston: Houghton Mifflin.

National Council of Teachers of English and International Reading Association. (1996). *Standards for the English language arts.* Urbana, IL and Newark, DE: Authors.

Raphael, T.E., & Hiebert, E.H. (1996). *Creating an integrated approach to literacy instruction.* Fort Worth, TX: Harcourt Brace.

Roser, N.L., & Martinez, M.G. (Eds.). (1995). *Book talk and beyond: Children and teachers respond to literature.* Newark, DE: International Reading Association.

Shannon, P. (1989). *Broken promises: Reading instruction in twentieth century America.* New York: Bergin & Garvey.

Valencia, S. (1990). A portfolio approach to classroom reading assessment: The whys, whats, and hows. *The Reading Teacher, 43,* 338–340.

Vogt, M. (1991). An observation guide for supervisors and administrators: Moving toward integrated reading/language arts instruction. *The Reading Teacher, 45,* 206–211.

 Article Review Form at end of book.

What was the controversy regarding reading instruction in the 1950s and 1960s? What is the debate about today?

Where Are Teachers' Voices in the Phonics/ Whole Language Debate?

Results from a survey of U.S. elementary classroom teachers

Elementary teachers opt for balance in their reading instruction programs. This article reports on a nationwide survey of the instructional beliefs and practices of elementary public school teachers in the United States.

James F. Baumann

James V. Hoffman

Jennifer Moon

Ann M. Duffy-Hester

Baumann and Hoffman teach courses in reading, language, and literacy at the University of Georgia and the University of Texas at Austin, respectively. Moon and Duffy-Hester are doctoral students in reading education at the University of Georgia. Baumann can be contacted at 309 Aderhold Hall, University of Georgia, Athens, GA 30602, USA.

A war is on between supporters of phonics and those who believe in the whole-language method of learning to read; caught in the middle—the nation's schoolchildren.

Time, October 27, 1997, p. 78

To assert that The Great Debate about the role of phonics in beginning reading instruction is alive and well today is an understatement. The 1950s (Flesch, 1955) and 1960s (Chall, 1967) controversy about whether reading instruction ought to involve a phonics or a look-say approach has evolved into the contemporary phonics versus whole language debate. Although pitting a method of teaching children to pronounce and spell words through instruction in symbol-sound relationships (phonics) against a comprehensive, holistic philosophy of language learning and teaching (whole language) may seem absurd to many within the literacy education community, the reality is that the debate lives on in professional and popular venues (Lehmann, 1997; Monoghan, 1997).

In this article, we address the current phonics versus whole language debate by presenting empirical evidence describing elementary teachers' beliefs, priorities, and reported practices involving phonics instruction and whole language practices. Our findings indicate that

Baumann, James F., Hoffman, James V., Moon, Jennifer, and Duffy-Hester, Ann M. (1998, May). Where are teachers' voices in the phonics/whole language debate? Results from a survey of U.S. elementary classroom teachers. *The Reading Teacher*, 51(8), 636–650. Reprinted with permission of James F. Baumann and the International Reading Association. All rights reserved.

teachers generally do not assume a polar, either-or approach to phonics and whole language, but instead provide children a balanced, eclectic program involving both reading skill instruction and immersion in enriched literacy experiences. Our data challenge the very crux of The Great Debate, which we consider neither great nor a debate. Rather, we view the controversy as an unfortunate straw man that diverts our attention, energy, and resources from the real challenges and concerns elementary teachers face when providing children appropriate, thoughtful, and effective reading and language arts instruction.

The Great Debate Past and Present

The phonics versus whole language debate has deep historical roots, going back at least to the early 20th century when William S. Gray and others argued for greater balance in elementary reading programs, which, at that time, involved heavy emphasis on intensive phonics instruction. This resulted in disagreements about whether phonics should be taught at all, and if so, how, how much, and when. Paul McKee, a significant figure in reading education during this period, described the "controversy" over phonics by commenting that "the writer knows of no problem [phonics instruction] around which more disputes have centered" (McKee, 1934, p. 191, cited in Cunningham, 1994, p. 915).

In *Learning to Read: The Great Debate*, Jeanne Chall (1967) popularized "The Great Debate" label when reviewing research that shed light on the disagreement about whether phonics should be taught to children or whether they should be taught to read words as wholes (i.e., whole-word, sight-word, or look-say approach). Chall concluded that direct, systematic instruction in phonics was necessary for children to develop word identification skill and reading fluency in an efficient manner.

Contemporary with Chall's work were the comprehensive U.S. Office of Education comparisons of beginning reading programs, the First Grade Studies (Bond & Dykstra, 1967; Stauffer, 1967). The results of the First Grade Studies suggested that systematic phonics instruction was related to success in decoding and fluency, but there was also considerable variation in achievement across and within classrooms, leading critics (e.g., Lohnes & Gray, 1972; Sipay, 1968) to argue that the debate was far from resolved.

With the rise of whole language in the 1980s, the debate nomenclature shifted from a phonics versus look-say conflict to a phonics versus whole language debate, an issue that has been addressed in numerous professional books (e.g., Adams, 1990; Goodman, 1986, 1993; Smith, 1994). The topic has likewise been discussed in articles in literacy education journals (e.g., Adams et al., 1991; Goodman, 1992; Spiegel, 1992; Stanovich, 1993–1994), in general education periodicals (e.g., Adams & Bruck, 1995), at professional conferences (e.g., Botel, Goodman, & Pearson, 1997), and in the popular press (e.g., Duff, 1996; "State Embraces Phonics," 1996).

The point of view, tenor, balance, and accuracy of such reports vary dramatically, but the topic is always controversial. The International Reading Association's position statement, *The Role of Phonics in Reading Instruction* (International Reading Association, 1997), acknowledged how the phonics versus whole language issue has achieved a visible, volatile status among educators, parents, politicians, journalists, and the general populace:

Today, the role of phonics in reading and writing has become as much a political issue as it has an educational one. Teachers and schools have become the focus of unprecedented public scrutiny as the controversy over phonics is played out in the media, state legislatures, school districts, and the home.

Fueling the public debate is the common perception that U.S. students' reading achievement has de-

clined because of whole language, literature-based instruction, or other holistic approaches. For example, Berliner (1997) commented on how a conservative educational watchdog group reported that "whole language has caused serious declines in reading achievement" (p. 407), with the alternative method of instruction typically being systematic, direct instruction in phonics (e.g., Sweet, 1995).

Along with the rhetoric, significant changes in educational policy and practices have been proposed or enacted. For example, on the basis of declining reading achievement test scores (Williams, Reese, Campbell, Mazzeo, & Phillips, 1995), the California Department of Education (1995) Reading Task Force declared in *Every Child a Reader* that "there is a crisis in California . . . a majority of California's children cannot read at basic levels" (p. 1). Blaming lower test scores on the *English-Language Arts Framework for California Public Schools, K–12*, which was implemented in the mid 1980s (California Department of Education, 1987) and put forward a holistic, literature-based perspective, "the Task Force concluded that many language arts programs have shifted too far away from direct skills instruction" (p. 2). As an alternative, the Task Force recommended a "balanced and comprehensive approach to reading" that includes "an organized, explicit skills program that includes phonemic awareness (sounds in words), phonics, and decoding skills to address the needs of the emergent reader" (p. 2).

But change has not been restricted to California. Other states have also recommended or enacted significant alterations in reading and language arts curricula and instruction on the assumption that teachers have adopted holistic practices to the point where they no longer teach phonics. *Newsweek* reported: "Alarmed by low reading scores, state after state is trying to return to phonics" (Hancock & Wingert, 1996, p. 75). Steps taken include legislative bills or department of education policies in a dozen or more states that mandate that phonics be part of the elementary curriculum or that specific phonics programs or materials

> We wonder how practicing physicians and lawyers or professors in medical and law schools would react if elected officials began to specify how they should practice or teach law or medicine.

be adopted and used (Monoghan, 1997). Some states have responded by legislating specific requirements for the teacher education curriculum. For example, a bill passed in Ohio requires preservice elementary teachers to take and pass a course in phonics instruction. It is a curious situation indeed when legislators in state houses define curriculum and instructional practices for professional educators working in elementary classrooms or university teacher education courses. We wonder how practicing physicians and lawyers or professors in medical and law schools would react if elected officials began to specify how they should practice or teach law and medicine.

It is important to note that the debate assumes that children are reading less well today than in years past, a conclusion not well supported, however, by large-scale assessment data. For example, National Assessment of Educational Progress results indicate that reading achievement levels of U.S. 9-, 13-, and 17-year-old students in 1994 did not differ significantly from 1971 cohorts (Campbell, Reese, O'Sullivan, & Dossey, 1996), challenging the let's-return-to-the-good-old-days argument.

International comparisons also fail to support the contention that the U.S. is behind the world in literacy, the International Association for the Evaluation of Educational Achievement (IEA) Reading Literacy Study (Binkley & Williams, 1996) being the prime example. The IEA Reading Literacy Study assessed the ability of fourth and ninth graders in many countries to comprehend narrative and expository prose and to obtain information from documents. U.S. fourth-grade students' performance exceeded all but 2 countries. U.S. fourth graders ranked behind only Finland, were tied with Sweden, and exceeded 24 other countries including France, Italy, New Zealand, Canada (British Columbia), and West Germany. Similarly, the performance of U.S. ninth graders was second only to Finland, exceeded 14 other countries, and was comparable with 15 other nations that included Sweden, France, New Zealand, and East and West Germany.

This does not mean that U.S. literacy educators ought to be smug about students' reading achievement. For example, 1994 NAEP results (Williams et al., 1995) indicated that scores for 12th-grade students and for some states or regions declined since the 1992 assessment, and NAEP data have yet to show consistent, long-term growth in the reading achievement of U.S. students. Nevertheless, large-scale, longitudinal achievement data do not support the assertion that there has been a steady decline in reading achievement across years or decades, or that the U.S. ranks low relative to achievement of children and adolescents in other developed countries (see Berliner & Biddle, 1995, and Kibby, 1995, for a detailed discussion).

In summary, the current phonics versus whole language debate, fueled by the belief that children are reading less well than in years past, assumes that as school systems and teachers adopted holistic and literature-based practices in reading and language arts instruction in the 1980s and early 1990s, they simultaneously abandoned phonics and decoding instruction. But is this so? What are teachers' instructional beliefs and actions with regard to whole language and phonics? Have they ceased teaching phonics in lieu of adopting holistic principles and practices?

It is the purpose of this article to address these questions. We do so by examining selected results from a large, U.S. survey of elementary classroom teachers. These data provide insight into teachers' beliefs and practices regarding phonics instruction and holistic teaching practices. Our results, which represent elementary teachers as disciplined eclectics with regard to phonics instruction and whole language practices, dispel yet one more myth embroiled in the contemporary version of The Great Debate.

A Survey of Elementary Teachers

The information we present in this article is from a larger study (Baumann, Duffy-Hester, Moon, & Hoffman, 1997) through which we sought to obtain a late 1990s perspective on public school elementary teachers' and administrators' beliefs

about reading instruction and their current classroom practices and administrative policies. Our inquiry was a modified replication of the classic study of reading instruction, *The First R: The Harvard Report on Reading in the Elementary Schools* by Mary C. Austin and Coleman Morrison (1963). In *The First R*, the researchers used mail surveys from a large, national sample of district-level administrators and elementary principals (responses from 1,023 districts) to assess reading instructional practices in U.S. elementary public schools. The surveys were supplemented by visits to 51 school districts, within which the researchers observed reading lessons and interviewed administrators and teachers.

Like Austin and Morrison (1963), we asked administrators and teachers about elementary reading and language arts instruction through mail surveys (Baumann et al., 1997). We queried educators about the same topics explored in *The First R*, although our surveys reflected contemporary nomenclature and changes in the field. For example, *The First R* questions about reading readiness were recast within an emergent literacy perspective, and we asked educators about new topics such as literature-based instruction, whole language, and alternative assessments. The results we report here are taken only from the elementary Teacher Survey. Due to budget limitations, we were unable to make site visits, so our results are restricted to teachers' self-reports of their beliefs and practices.

During the spring of 1996, we distributed surveys to 3,199 prekindergarten through Grade 5 public school teachers. These teachers were selected randomly from a national listing of 907,774 teachers, which was purchased from a commercial educational marketing and research firm that maintained that their sample included virtually the entire universe of preK–Grade 5 public school classroom teachers in the U.S.

The Survey Research Center (SRC) at the University of Georgia provided consultation service during survey construction and data analyses. The SRC was also responsible for disseminating and collecting all surveys and for coding and scoring objective items. A pilot version of the

Teacher Survey was field tested with public school elementary teachers and administrators and with university researchers, who were asked to evaluate the instrument for breadth of coverage, item bias, clarity, and format. The survey was revised in response to concerns expressed by these reviewers.

The final Teacher Survey consisted of 53 closed items (multiple choice and short fill-in blanks) and 2 open items (that included 4 questions, each followed by 3 to 4 write-on blanks). Because our research was designed to parallel *The First R* study, it included a full range of items that queried teachers about elementary reading instruction issues and practices. Items probed areas such as teachers' background and professional development; school, student, teacher, and district demographics; philosophy and program goals; instructional time, materials, and libraries; organization and assessment of the reading and language arts program; beginning reading instruction; programs for struggling and gifted readers; administrative leadership; and the changes teachers enacted and the challenges they faced in teaching reading.

We received 1,207 usable surveys (this value excludes surveys returned by the Postal Service, completed incorrectly or incompletely, or received after our data analysis cutoff date). This resulted in a conservatively calculated response rate of 37.7%, an acceptable value for a large mail survey (Weisberg, Krosnick, & Bowen, 1989). Our sampling margin of error for the survey was +/– 2.8%, a parameter that allowed for reliable generalizations from our probability sample to the population (Warwick & Lininger, 1975). The distribution of returned surveys paralleled the universe of the total population surveyed in terms of grade level, school type, and geographic region. The distribution by grade level of teacher respondents was prekindergarten 2%, kindergarten 15%, first grade 19%, second grade 18%, third grade 16%, fourth grade 17%, and fifth grade 13%.

Because the Teacher Survey was a modified replication of *The First R*, we constructed it to provide a comprehensive examination of issues and practices affecting elementary classroom teachers. Therefore, it was not written expressly to explore the phonics versus whole language issue, and we believe that the survey did not induce a Great Debate mind-set for those completing it. However, a number of items addressed the topics of phonics and whole language, and it is results from these items we report. Because of the replication nature of our study, we present mostly aggregate data (i.e., preK–Grade 5), although, when appropriate, we examine responses provided by teachers of beginning readers (i.e., K–Grade 2).

Teachers' Beliefs, Priorities, and Reported Practices vis-à-vis the Great Debate

The major finding from our survey related to the phonics versus whole language debate is that a majority of teachers embrace a balanced, eclectic approach to elementary reading instruction, blending phonics and holistic principles and practices in compatible ways. We present the data supporting this generalization by first providing an overall descriptive profile of U.S. public school elementary teachers and their students. We then present teachers' philosophies; the time they allocated to various aspects of their literacy instructional program; how teachers provide students instruction in phonics and other word identification skills; and how teachers provide students holistic, process, or immersion literacy experiences. Figure 1 presents a selective summary of these findings.

Overall profile of elementary teachers and students. The typical prekindergarten to Grade 5 teacher in a U.S. public elementary school is white (89%), female (93%), and experienced (an average of 16 years as an elementary teacher). Half have earned master's degrees or higher. Schools within our sample were situated within a mix of urban (23%), suburban (38%), and rural (38%) communities, with an average elementary school enrollment of about 550 students.

The majority of elementary teachers taught in a self-contained classroom setting (85%) with an average class size of 25 children (22 regular education and 3 special education students). Regarding the racial or ethnic identity of students, the average class composition was 68% white, 14% African American, 12% Latino/a, and 6% other racial or ethnic groups. Teachers reported that most children lived in middle- (46%) or low-income (45%) households, with relatively few (8%) living in upper-income households.

The elementary teachers estimated that a little over half (55%) of their students were average readers (i.e., reading within one grade level, plus or minus, of their grade placement), with the remainder split between above (20%) and below average (24%). Eighty-nine percent of the students spoke English as their first language, 8% spoke Spanish, and the remainder spoke other languages.

When asked to rate the quality of reading instruction provided elementary students, teachers gave high marks to their classroom reading programs and to their schools as a whole. Specifically, they were asked to assess how successful they were in developing skillful and strategic readers, critical and thoughtful readers, independent readers, and knowledgeable readers. Using an A to F grading scale, teachers consistently rated their schools in the B– to B range on these criteria and slightly higher (B to B+) for their own classroom reading programs.

Teachers' philosophical stances. Two items probed teachers' philosophical orientations toward reading and language arts instruction. The first item stated: "The following statements represent various perspectives, philosophies, or beliefs toward the teaching and learning of reading. Circle numbers in front of ALL of the following items that apply to you personally." Responses to this item revealed that, overall, teachers embraced a balanced or eclectic philosophy. Specifically, 89% of the teachers selected "I believe in a balanced approach to reading instruction which combines skills development with literature and language-rich activities." Three

Major Finding:

A majority of teachers embraced a balanced, eclectic approach to elementary reading instruction, blending phonics and holistic principles and practices.

Philosophically, a significant majority of teachers believed . . .

- In a balanced approach—combining skills with literature and language-rich activities (89%).
- In an eclectic approach—drawing from multiple perspectives and materials (76%).
- That phonics should be taught directly so readers become skillful and fluent (63%).
- That students need to be immersed in literature and literacy to achieve fluency (71%).

Teachers dedicated time for both skill instruction and holistic, immersion activities.

- Teachers, on average, spent 2 hours and 23 minutes each day on reading and literacy.
- 55 of these minutes were dedicated to teacher-directed skill or strategy instruction lessons.
- Teachers dedicated moderate or more time to instruction in reading strategies, vocabulary, phonics/decoding, comprehension, critical reading, content reading, and spelling.
- Teachers also dedicated moderate or more time to holistic, immersion practices such as reading aloud, students reading orally or silently, literature response, and process writing.

Teachers taught phonics, decoding, and word identification skills.

- Overall, 88% of teachers held the goal of developing readers who were skillful and strategic in word identification, fluency, and comprehension.

- When asked which reading skills were essential or important, the vast majority of K–2 teachers responded with instruction in phonics (99%), contextual analysis (99%), structural analysis (93%), sight words (96%), and meaning vocabulary (99%).
- K–2 teachers were most likely to employ systematic instruction in synthetic phonics (66%) or analytic phonics (40%), with fewer teaching phonics on an as-needed basis (19%).
- K–2 teachers embraced an emergent literacy perspective (70%) and rarely used conventional phonics workbooks.
- K–2 teachers complemented their explicit phonics instruction with phonics instruction through word families/phonograms (66%), in the context of children's literature (62%), and through spelling and writing activities (73%).

Teachers also employed holistic, process, and immersion instructional practice.

- Overall, 94% of teachers held the goal of developing readers who were independent and motivated to choose, appreciate, and enjoy literature.
- Teachers used children's literature: Most first-grade teachers reported moderate, predominant, or exclusive use of big books (84%) and picture trade books (81%); similarly, 72% of fourth-/fifth-grade teachers reported moderate or greater use of chapter trade books.
- PreK–2 teachers regularly read aloud (97%), accepted invented spellings (85%), and engaged children in oral language (83%), journal writing (78%), and reading response (69%) activities.
- Grades 3–5 teachers regularly taught comprehension (89%) and vocabulary (80%), provided literature response activities (79%), and used trade books instructionally (67%).

---

fourths (76%) of the teachers also selected "I have an 'eclectic' attitude toward reading instruction, which means that I would draw from multiple perspectives and sets of materials when teaching reading."

These balanced or eclectic positions are supported by preK–Grade 5 teachers' self-descriptions of the importance of teaching phonics (63% also selected "I believe that phonics needs to be taught directly to beginning readers in order for students to become fluent, skillful readers") and the importance of providing students a literature-rich environment (71% selected, "I believe students need to

be immersed in literature and literacy experiences in order to become fluent readers"). Therefore, teachers did not see holistic practices and phonics as a dichotomy, but instead viewed instruction in reading skills and strategies as something they ought to do along with and in the context of more holistic practices. In fact, from among the various philosophy and perspective statements, teachers tended *not* to identify with extreme positions. Only 22% chose the statement "I would describe myself as a 'traditionalist' when it comes to reading methods and materials," and only 34% selected "I would describe myself as a whole language teacher."

The balanced, eclectic reading instruction perspective was also supported by teachers' responses to the second philosophy item, which read: "The following statements represent various goals or objectives teachers might have for a reading instructional program. Circle numbers in front of ALL of the following statements that apply to you personally." Eighty-eight percent of the teachers selected "It is my goal to develop readers who are skillful and strategic in word identification, fluency, and reading comprehension," while 94% simultaneously selected "It is my goal to develop readers who are independent and motivated to choose, appreciate, and enjoy literature." Thus, a majority of teachers expressed the belief that children must acquire both the skill and motivation to read.

Time dedicated to and the nature of elementary reading instruction. Teachers dedicated time both to skill instruction and to reading and language arts practice and application activities. Teachers set aside an average of 55 minutes daily for teacher-directed reading skill or strategy instruction, which was defined as "reading 'groups,' skill or strategy lessons, teacher-guided reading of selections, etc." They also provided a daily average of 42 additional minutes for applying, practicing, and extending reading instruction, which was characterized as "reading aloud to children, students' independent reading or DEAR [Drop Everything and Read] periods, student-led response groups, cooperative reading activities, etc." Teachers provided another 46 minutes daily for language arts instruction and practice, which was described as "writing workshop, response journals, spelling, oral language activities, etc." This means that, on average, teachers spent 2 hours and 23 minutes on reading and language arts instruction and activities each school day.

Time spent on reading instruction (i.e., the 55 daily minutes) varied as a function of grade level, with teachers of beginning readers dedicating more time for instruction than upper elementary teachers. For example, whereas only 11% of the fourth- and fifth-grade teachers reported daily reading instruction periods in excess of one hour, 37% of first-grade and 27% of second- and third-grade teachers had reading instruction periods of over an hour in length. Therefore, the younger the child, the greater the time dedicated to "reading 'groups,' skill or strategy lessons, teacher-guided reading of selections, etc."

The notion of balance between instruction and practice/immersion is supported by how teachers partitioned their time for literacy activities. We asked teachers how much instructional time they devoted to various dimensions of the reading and language arts program on a scale of *Considerable* (4), *Moderate* (3), *Little* (2), and *None* (1). On average, teachers reported dedicating a *Moderate* amount of time for reading strategies instruction (i.e., an average scale score of 3.0), with at least a *Moderate* amount of time for teaching specific reading and language arts skills such as reading vocabulary (3.2), phonics/decoding (2.9), comprehension (3.6), critical reading (3.0), reading in the content areas (3.1), and spelling lists, activities, or games (2.8). But teachers also reported dedicating *Moderate* or greater time for more holistic, immersion, or process activities such as time practicing reading (students reading independently, 3.1; oral reading, 3.1; silent reading, 3.0), reading aloud to students (3.4), time spent engaged in literature response (3.1), and time spent on process writing (3.0).

Again, there was grade-level variation. For example, 58% of first-grade teachers reported dedicating *Considerable* time to phonics instruction, whereas this was true for only 3% of fourth- and fifth-grade teachers. But teachers of beginning readers also provided their students lots of exposure to literature and a positive reading model, with 98% of first-grade teachers reporting dedicating *Considerable* or *Moderate* amounts of time to reading aloud to their students.

Different skill/immersion balances were apparent for upper elementary teachers. For example, 91% of fourth- and fifth-grade teachers reported dedicating *Considerable* or *Moderate* amounts of time to instruction in reading in the content areas (as opposed to 69% for first-grade teachers), but they balanced this by providing students lots of time for independent reading (86% *Considerable* or *Moderate*), reading aloud to students (86% *Considerable* or *Moderate*), and literature response activities (81% *Considerable* or *Moderate*).

Balance or eclecticism was also apparent through teachers' decision making regarding instructional materials. Specifically, most teachers struck a balance between using basal reading programs and children's trade books in their reading programs. In a forced-choice item asking teachers about their use of basals and children's trade books, very few teachers across all grade levels indicated that they relied on basals exclusively (2%), with not a single first-grade teacher selecting this option. At the other extreme, a small proportion of teachers (16%) reported exclusive use of trade books in their classroom reading programs. The remaining, significant majority (83%) reported using basals supplemented by trade books (56%) or trade books supplemented by basals (27%).

Instruction in phonics, decoding, and word identification skills. Teachers valued and taught phonics, decoding, and word identification skills and strategies. As noted, 88% of teachers indicated that it was their goal to develop readers who were skillful and strategic. Consistent with this expressed value, teachers reported that they dedicated *Moderate* amounts of time to reading strategies instruction (3.0) and phonics and decoding (2.9). The emphasis on phonics and decoding was even more pronounced at the early grade levels. For example, 90% of first-grade teachers indicated that they dedicated *Considerable* (58%) or *Moderate* (32%) amounts of time to phonics and decoding instruction.

Teachers responsible for instructing beginning readers (i.e., teachers in kindergarten through Grade 2) were asked about their phonics, decoding, and word identification programs. In response to the question, "What is your opinion about the importance of teaching young children the following word reading strategies?", teachers were asked to respond to a 3-point scale (*Essential* = 3, *Important* = 2, *Not Important* = 1). For the item querying K–2 teachers' opinions about the importance of "teaching phonic analysis skills/strategies (decoding)," they expressed an overall rating between *Essential* and *Important* (2.6). Stated differently, 99% of the K–2 teachers indicated that phonics instruction was *Essential* (67%) or *Important* (32%), with only 0.6% indicating that phonics instruction was *Not Important*.

K–2 teachers expressed similar views toward the importance of teaching other word identification skills. Ninety-nine percent indicated that instruction in contextual analysis was *Essential* or *Important*, and 93% indicated that instruction in structural analysis was *Essential* or *Important*. Consistent with the balance theme, teachers also expressed the importance of instruction in sight words (96% *Essential* or *Important*) and meaning vocabulary (99% *Essential* or *Important*). Thus, teachers of young children believe in the importance of multiple strategies for reading and pronouncing unfamiliar words.

K–2 teachers who indicated that phonic analysis was *Essential* or *Important* were then asked how they taught phonics to their students. They were presented with various ways for providing phonics instruction and were asked to select all that described their teaching practices. Two thirds (66%) of the K–2 teachers indicated that they taught decoding through synthetic phonics, which was defined as "systematic instruction in which students are taught letter/sound correspondences first and then are taught how to decode words." Teachers were less likely (40%) to indicate they employed analytic phonics, which was defined as "systematic instruction in which students are taught some sight words first and then are taught phonics generalizations from these words." Only 19% indicated that phonics instruction was provided on an as-needed basis (i.e., "not systematic instruction; rather, students are taught phonic analysis skills as the need arises"). Thus, the majority of K–2 teachers indicated that they teach phonics systematically.

However, if teachers' use of systematic instruction in synthetic phonics conjures up the image of traditional phonics skill lessons employing recitation and use of workbooks or worksheets, that is far from the manner in which teachers taught phonics. First, when asked whether a reading readiness perspective or an emergent literacy perspective best represented their personal philosophy about beginning reading programs for young children, 70% of the K–2 teachers selected the emergent literacy perspective, which was defined as follows:

I believe in an emergent literacy perspective; that is, all children can benefit from early, meaningful reading and writing experiences (e.g., invented spelling, environmental print, being read to). Therefore, it is a teacher's job to provide students appropriate activities that will enable them to understand the functions and forms of literacy and to grow into conventional forms of reading and writing.

Thus, the majority of K–2 teachers held a contemporary perspective toward beginning reading instruction—one that incorporates activities that go well beyond traditional phonics lessons.

Second, even though two thirds of the K–2 teachers indicated that they employed synthetic phonics, they also embraced other approaches for teaching phonics. Specifically, approximately two thirds of the teachers likewise indicated that they provided phonics instruction through word families and phonograms (66%), taught phonics in the context of children's literature (62%), and taught phonics through spelling and writing activities (73%). Further, teachers eschewed conventional phonics instructional materials. Seventy percent of all teachers selected the *Never* (48%) or *Infrequently* (22%) option when asked about their use of phonics workbooks in their classrooms. Therefore, even though phonics instruction was pervasive and systematic, it was embedded within an emergent literacy perspective; it was provided through the medium of children's literature; and phonics usually was taught in the context of stories, writing, spelling, and word families, not through fill-in-the-blank workbook or worksheet exercises.

Holistic, process, and immersion instructional practices. Even though teachers clearly valued and implemented explicit instruction in phonics and other word identification and comprehension strategies, they likewise valued and simultaneously implemented literature and literacy immersion activities—practices that are typically viewed as whole language or process-oriented reading and language arts instruction. As noted, 71% of the sample indicated

that students should be immersed in literature and literacy experiences, and 94% concurred that it was their goal to develop independent, motivated readers who appreciate and enjoy literature. Consistent with these expressed values were teachers' reports that they relegated *Moderate* or greater amounts of time [according to a 4-point scale: *Considerable* (4), *Moderate* (3), *Little* (2), and *None* (1)] for reading aloud to students (3.4), for students to engage in independent, self-selected reading (3.1), for oral or written responses to literature (3.1), and for process writing (3.0).

Teacher's responses to other items also affirmed their desire and efforts to provide students an enriched literature environment. For example, when asked about the use of instructional materials, teachers indicated that they used children's and young adult literature as the primary instructional medium. Overall, elementary teachers indicated *Moderate* or greater use [according to a 5-point scale: *Exclusively* (5), *Predominantly* (4), *Moderately* (3), *Infrequently* (2), *Never* (1)] of fiction trade books (3.4) and nonfiction trade books (3.0) in their classrooms. When examining literature use by grade level and book type, however, the prevalence of an elementary literature-based environment was even more apparent. For instance, 84% of first-grade teachers reported *Moderate* (40%), *Predominant* (33%), or *Exclusive* (11%) use of big books in their classrooms, and 81% of first-grade teachers reported *Moderate* (43%), *Predominant* (32%), or *Exclusive* (6%) use of picture trade books for reading instruction. Similarly, 72% of upper elementary (fourth- and fifth-grade) teachers reported *Moderate* (37%), *Predominant* (31%), or *Exclusive* (4%) use of chapter trade books for reading instruction.

Other evidence of holistic or process-oriented practices emerged when teachers were asked about the reading and language arts materials, techniques, or activities they employed in their classrooms. Prekindergarten through Grade 2 teachers were provided one set of options, and third- through fifth-grade teachers were provided another. Each group was then asked, "Which of the following materials, techniques, or activities are likely to be found in your classroom regularly (define 'regularly' as three or more times per week)?"

Materials, techniques, or activities identified by two thirds or more of the preK–Grade 2 teachers as being employed regularly (in descending order) were reading aloud to children (97%), the acceptance of invented spelling (85%), oral language activities (83%), trade books used instructionally (80%), phonics and word identification lessons (79%), journal writing (78%), reading response activities (69%), and big books used instructionally (67%). Clearly, prekindergarten through Grade 2 teachers reported regularly engaging children in a variety of holistic or process-oriented activities.

> . . . balance, eclecticism, and common sense are the characteristics of reading . . . instructional practices employed by the vast majority of elementary teachers.

Materials, techniques, or activities identified by two thirds or more of the Grade 3–5 teachers are being employed regularly (in descending order) were comprehension strategy instruction (89%), vocabulary lessons/activities (80%), literature response activities (79%), instruction in literary elements (73%), instruction in comprehension monitoring (71%), and using trade books instructionally (67%). These teachers focused students on meaning by using, understanding, and responding to literature.

Limitations

Survey research, like any form of empirical inquiry, has limitations. One is that self-report data provide just a single means to evaluate attitudes and practices. Unlike *The First R* (Austin & Morrison, 1963), on which our study was based, we did not include a field component. Thus, we cannot claim that our results are supported by actual observations of teachers or by information gathered from face-to-face interviews. However, results from other recent surveys involving elementary teachers' beliefs and practices about reading instruction (Baumann & Heubach, 1996; Hoffman et al., 1995)

have corroborated results from observational studies (Barr & Sadow, 1989; Sosniak & Stodolsky, 1993), so there is some indication that field studies and mail surveys provide comparable information. Nevertheless, future field study research examining teachers' instructional practices would be highly illuminating on the phonics versus whole language debate, as well as on much broader issues in literacy education.

Second, we have primarily described common themes and patterns in the data, using measures such as aggregate percents and means (averages). While these are informative, we also acknowledge the variance that exists within any sample, and that measures of central tendency do not reveal the diversity. For example, although the average class size was 25 students, classes ranged from the low teens to over 40 students, and 8% of the teachers reported classes in excess of 30 children, excluding mainstreamed special education children. Although U.S. public school classrooms are integrated on average, some suburban or rural schools included classes of all-white students, whereas some inner-city schools had classrooms entirely of African American students. And some teachers' patterns of responses across items revealed them to be uniformly skills based, whereas others were consistently whole language. Therefore, it is important to consider both commonality and variation when painting a picture of elementary reading instruction.

A third limitation of survey research is the risk of response biases, such as courtesy, ingratiation, deception, or social desirability (Warwick & Lininger, 1975). The latter, social desirability bias, which is a tendency "to answer questions in a way that conforms to dominant belief patterns among groups to which the respondent feels some identification or allegiance" (Dillman, 1978, p. 62), raises the possibility that teachers responded to questions or issues in a manner that reflected their perception of educational norms rather than their own beliefs. However, research

has documented that mail surveys are much less prone to social desirability bias than are face-to-face or telephone surveys (e.g., Hochstim, 1967; Wiseman, 1972). After comparing research on different types of survey methods, Dillman concluded that "face-to-face interviews have the highest probability for producing socially desirable answers, the telephone survey next, and the mail survey least" (p. 63). Thus, we believe that the confidentiality afforded participants in our large, anonymous mail survey minimized social desirability bias in our study.

An Eclectic Philosophy

Given the limitations of our methods and study, what might we conclude from the data? For us, the findings lead to a clear and overpowering conclusion: The majority of U.S. public school elementary teachers do *not* assume polar or extreme positions when it comes to reading and language arts pedagogy. They neither teach phonics to the exclusion of providing children enriched literacy instruction nor immerse students in holistic literacy experiences devoid of reading skill instruction. Instead, we found that teachers design reading and language arts programs that provide children with a multifaceted, balanced instructional diet that includes an artful blend of direct instruction in phonics and other reading and writing strategies along with a rich assortment of literature, oral language, and written language experiences and activities.

If we were to create a composite, archetypal primary-grade teacher from our survey data, we would characterize this teacher as follows:

The U.S. public school primary-grade elementary teacher believes that the goal of reading instruction is to develop readers who are skillful, strategic, motivated, independent, knowledgeable, and appreciative of literature. This teacher embraces a literature-based perspective, combining trade book reading with the reading of basal anthology selections. This teacher dedicates at least 2.5 hours per day to a mixture of reading and language arts activities. These daily activities include reading aloud to children; providing time for children to engage in self-selected, independent reading;

creating opportunities for discussion and oral expression; engaging children in oral and written response-to-literature activities; scheduling journal writing and process writing periods; and directly teaching phonics skills, other word identification skills, and comprehension strategies. Phonics instruction is explicit, but it occurs in the context of literature, so that students can learn and practice pronouncing words presented in stories. This teacher also teaches words by sight and provides complementary instruction in structural and contextual analysis. In short, this teacher holds and practices a philosophy of disciplined eclecticism toward reading and language arts teaching and learning.

A profile of the prototypical intermediate-grade teacher would be very similar in philosophy and practice, with a decreased emphasis on word identification and an accentuation on vocabulary, comprehension, and content reading. In short, the typical elementary reading and language arts curriculum gleaned from our survey was very similar to the balanced instructional programs teachers and researchers have described recently in the professional literature (e.g., Baltas & Shafer, 1996; Johns & Elish-Piper, 1997; McIntyre & Pressley, 1996).

Teachers adopted aspects of whole language and literature-based perspectives in the 1980s and 1990s because such changes made sense and enhanced their instruction. Clearly, principles of whole language are reflected in the survey data and the preceding profile. It is inaccurate, however, to assert that teachers abandoned phonics and other skill instruction in the process of employing more holistic practices, for teachers know that children need to be taught how to read words and comprehend text in systematic, explicit ways.

When reporting on the 1997 International Reading Association Annual Convention, the *New York Times* (Steinberg, 1997) characterized the ongoing phonics versus whole language issue as "the increasingly politicized debate over reading instruction" (p. 34D), describing "fiery exchanges" between whole language advocates and phonics supporters. However, the *Times* also acknowledged that "what was perhaps most striking, in interviews with dozens of teachers this week, was how little relevance the pitched political debate

had to what they do in the classroom. Most teachers said they employed an eclectic approach that incorporated elements of both phonics and whole language" (p. 34D). This was expressed by a respondent to our survey who wrote: "I have become eclectic. I believe that student needs vary and therefore different approaches need to be taken. I use whatever works: sight words, phonics, whole language, chants, poems, reading groups, etc."

This teacher's voice is not alone. Indeed, our data document that balance, eclecticism, and common sense are the characteristics of reading and language arts instructional practices employed by the vast majority of elementary teachers. Teachers search for, select, and implement diverse, practical techniques that enable them to reach and teach their students, as Berliner (1997) noted when analyzing the phonics versus whole language debate:

Teachers are not often extremists on these issues [phonics vs. whole language]. Teachers tend to be pragmatists—using anything that seems to work—which is a reasonable strategy when confronted with children displaying a remarkable range of individual differences affecting how they learn. (p. 407)

Moving Beyond the Debate

We would fall short when interpreting our survey data by simply arguing that the reported generalizations about phonics and whole language are inaccurate. Teachers and schools are not static, and our findings reveal energy, change, and challenge in elementary reading instruction.

Near the end of our survey, we asked teachers if they had made any major changes or innovations in their reading instructional programs over the past few years. Sixty-nine percent stated that they had. Those indicating changes were then asked to respond to the open-ended question, "What was the nature of the change or innovation?" Analysis of the narrative responses to this question (interrater agreement of 85% across all open-ended items) revealed 23 separate categories of change and innovation. Teachers often reported changes that

involved a philosophy or programmatic shift (e.g., movement to trade books, whole language, balanced instruction, integrated instruction). Other changes involved the adoption of specialized programs to assist struggling readers, implementing new grouping or organizational patterns, the use of new materials, trying new writing initiatives, and employing new forms of alternative assessments. Three fourths of the teachers reported positive effects of the changes. They often attributed the success to their own initiative and ingenuity: "I initiated these changes based on current research about how kids learn to read." "I chose to take the training and change my approach." "Who? Myself. I'm constantly looking for new teaching techniques/activities."

In a final, open survey item, we asked, "As you work toward improving the quality of reading instruction in your classroom, what are the greatest challenges you face?" Teachers again responded with great diversity (31 separate categories), although there was a persistent theme of facing the challenge of accommodating children who found learning to read difficult (31% of all responses). Figure 2 presents some of the most prominent categories that emerged from this analysis, accompanied by selected teacher comments.

We find it interesting that the challenges teachers note rarely involve phonics and whole language. We believe this is because teachers have long since resolved The Great Debate, instead embracing and implementing a balanced, eclectic philosophy for teaching reading and language arts. While pundits, politicians, and the broader populace may deliberate whether teachers have ceased teaching phonics in lieu of whole language, teachers themselves focus on real-life classroom issues, such as how to accommodate the incredible range of students' needs and reading levels, how to deal with the frustration of not enough time to teach or insufficient quality materials to do it well, and how to accommodate large classes of diverse learners seated before them.

As so often happens when education issues become political, teachers are rarely consulted. For example,

Figure 2 | Prominent Categories and Selected Responses by Elementary Teachers Asked to Identify Their Greatest Challenges in Improving the Quality of Classroom Reading Instruction

- **Range of reading levels:** "Providing for the wide range of abilities." "Meeting such a diverse range in abilities, interest, and desire." "The level of reading the children have when they reach my room. Most are below grade level." "My range this year is first-grade level to 10th-grade level."

- **Lack of time:** "Too much time spent on unimportant or noncritical issues at school—not enough quality time to teach." "Finding enough time to devote to reading instruction." "Time interruptions and other curriculum demands." "In my classroom, first grade, time is one of my greatest challenges. With so many curriculum goals to cover, it can be difficult to get everything in." "*Time* to plan with colleagues and set up reading programs."

- **Not enough money or materials:** "I need more materials." "Money $ $ $ $ $." "Lack of materials—sharing one set of basals and trade books with five other teachers." "Money! My school system can't/won't fund literature-based classrooms, so I spend my own money (when I can afford it)." "Budget for materials." "I cannot continue to support the school by providing books and supplies. Our budget offers me no relief."

- **Teaching struggling readers:** "When children enter the third grade as nonreaders or emergent readers, it is virtually impossible

to bring them up to grade level in a year's time." "Struggling readers!" "The slow reader is always the challenge to me." "The students who are coming from second grade from other school systems who still cannot sound out words." "Meeting the needs of poor readers who struggle with skills and comprehension."

- **Parent support and involvement:** "Getting the parents to reinforce what I teach in the classroom." "Informing parents about our reading instruction and gaining their support." "Educating parents." "Instruction carrying over into the home."

- **Class size:** "Sheer numbers! I have 32 students for reading." "There are too many children in a class. This year I have 36." "The number of students in my class. I want to give them more of my time for individual instruction. Next year I am told I will have inclusion students in addition to 39 first-grade students."

- **Diverse students:** "Accommodating the needs of all different kinds of kids." "Accommodating linguistically diverse children." "I have many children with learning problems—the majority are LD and DH." "The children come with so many needs—emotional, physical, etc.—that academics is almost last on the list of things they need. I am nurse, parent, psychiatrist, etc., to more and more children each year."

---

the *Time* feature "How Johnny Should Read" (Collins, 1997), referenced at the beginning of this article, presented the opinions of whole language experts Kenneth Goodman and Frank Smith and phonics experts Marilyn Jager Adams and Jeanne Chall, with teachers represented only through anecdotes or brief glimpses into their classrooms. Missing was the voice of the other experts: the hundreds of thousands of teachers who provide children reading instruction daily. In the preparation of their feature, *Time* had solicited from us our survey data, and we provided a prepublication version of this article. None of our survey data appeared in the *Time* feature. *Time* argued that children are "caught in the middle" of the debate; we argue that teachers are left out of it.

Authors' Note

The study reported here was supported by the National Reading Research Center of the University of Georgia and the University of Maryland under the Educational Research and Development Centers Program (PR/Award No. 117A20007) as administered by the Office of Educational Research and Improvement, U.S. Department of Education. The findings and opinions expressed here do not necessarily reflect the position or policies of the National Reading Research Center, the Office of Educational Research and Improvement, or the U.S. Department of Education.

We thank the reviewers of our pilot instrument for their insightful comments and Jack Martin and Kathy Shinholser of the University of Georgia Survey Research Center for their expertise. We also thank the 1,207 classroom teachers who so generously contributed their time by responding to our survey with care and candor.

References

Adams, M.J. (1990). *Beginning to read: Thinking and learning about print.* Cambridge, MA: MIT Press.

Adams, M.J., Allington, R.L., Chaney, J.H., Goodman, Y.M., Kapinus, B.A., McGee, L.M., Richgels, D.J., Schwartz, S.J., Shannon, P., Smitten, B., & Williams, J.P. (1991). Beginning to read: A critique by literacy professionals and a response by Marilyn Jager Adams. *The Reading Teacher, 44,* 370–395.

Adams, M.J., & Bruck, M. (1995). Resolving the "great debate." *American Educator, 19*(2), 7, 10–20.

Austin, M.C., & Morrison, C. (1963). *The first R: The Harvard report on reading in elementary schools.* New York: Macmillan.

Baltas, J., & Shafer, S. (Eds.). (1996). *Balanced reading: Grades K–2.* New York: Scholastic.

Barr, R., & Sadow, M.W. (1989). Influence of basal programs on fourth-grade reading instruction. *Reading Research Quarterly, 24,* 44–71.

Baumann, J.F., Duffy-Hester, A., Moon, J., & Hoffman, J.V. (1998). *Describing the chimera: Philosophy and practices in U.S. elementary reading instruction.* Manuscript submitted for publication.

Baumann, J.F., & Heubach, K.M. (1996). Do basal readers deskill teachers? A national survey of educators' use and opinions of basals. *The Elementary School Journal, 96,* 511–526.

Berliner, D.C. (1997). Educational psychology meets the Christian Right: Differing views of children, schooling, teaching, and learning. *Teachers College Record, 98,* 381–416.

Berliner, D.C., & Biddle, B.J. (1995). *The manufactured crisis.* Reading, MA: Addison-Wesley.

Binkley, M., & Williams, T. (1996). *Reading literacy in the United States: Findings from the IEA reading literacy study.* Washington, DC: Office of Educational Research and Improvement, U.S. Department of Education.

Bond, G.L., & Dykstra, R. (1967). The cooperative research program in first-grade reading instruction. *Reading Research Quarterly, 2,* 5–142.

Botel, M., Goodman, K.S., & Pearson, P.D. (1997, May). Enduring issues: The continuing phonics controversy. Paper presented at Reading Hall of Fame cosponsored meeting at the annual convention of the International Reading Association, Atlanta, GA.

California Department of Education. (1987). *English-language arts framework for California public schools, K–12*. Sacramento, CA: Author.

California Department of Education. (1995). *Every child a reader* (Report of the California Reading Task Force). Sacramento, CA: Author.

Campbell, J.R., Reese, C.M., O'Sullivan, C., & Dossey, J.A. (1996, October). *Report in brief: NAEP trends in academic progress*. Washington, DC: Office of Educational Research and Improvement, U.S. Department of Education.

Chall, J. (1967). *Learning to read: The great debate*. New York: McGraw-Hill.

Collins, J. (1997, October 27). How Johnny should read. *Time, 150*(17), pp. 78–81.

Cunningham, P.M. (1994). Phonics and the phonics debate in reading. In A.C. Purves (Ed.), *Encyclopedia of English studies and language arts* (Vol. II, pp. 915–918). New York: Scholastic.

Dillman, D.A. (1978). *Mail and telephone surveys: The total design method*. New York: Wiley.

Duff, C. (1996, October 30). ABCeething: How whole language became a hot potato in and out of academia. *Wall Street Journal*, p. A1.

Flesch, R. (1955). *Why Johnny can't read—and what you can do about it*. New York: Harper & Brothers.

Goodman, K.S. (1986). *What's whole in whole language?* Portsmouth, NH: Heinemann.

Goodman, K.S. (1992). I didn't found whole language. *The Reading Teacher, 46,* 188–199.

Goodman, K.S. (1993). *Phonics phacts*. Portsmouth, NH: Heinemann.

Hancock, L., & Wingert, P. (1996, May 13). If you can read this . . . you learned phonics. Or so its supporters say. *Newsweek*, p. 75.

Hochstim, J.R. (1967). A critical comparison of three strategies of collecting data from households. *Journal of the American Statistical Association, 62,* 976–989.

Hoffman, J.V., McCarthey, S.J., Bayles, D., Price, D., Elliot, B., Dressman, M., & Abbott, J. (1995). *Reading instruction in first-grade classrooms: Do basals control teachers?* (Reading Research Rep. No. 43). Athens, GA: University of Georgia, National Reading Research Center.

International Reading Association. (1997, January). *The role of phonics in reading instruction: A position statement of the International Reading Association* [Brochure]. Newark, DE: Author.

Johns, J.L., & Elish-Piper, L. (1997). *Balanced reading instruction: Teachers' visions and voices*. Dubuque, IA: Kendall/Hunt.

Kibby, M.W. (1995). *Student literacy: Myths and realities* (Fastback No. 381). Bloomington, IN: Phi Delta Kappa.

Lehmann, N. (1997, November). The reading wars. *The Atlantic Monthly*, pp. 128–134.

Lohnes, P.R., & Gray, M.M. (1972). Intelligence and the cooperative reading studies. *Reading Research Quarterly, 7,* 466–476.

McIntyre, E., & Pressley, M. (Eds.). (1996). *Balanced instruction: Strategies and skills in whole language*. Norwood, MA: Christopher-Gordon.

McKee, P.G. (1934). *Reading and literature in the elementary schools*. Boston: Houghton Mifflin.

Monoghan, E.J. (1997, May). *Public opinion, professionalism and ideology: A historical look at controversies on phonics instruction*. Plenary address at Reading Research '97, International Reading Association, Atlanta, GA.

Sipay, E.R. (1968). Interpreting the USOE cooperative reading studies. *The Reading Teacher, 22,* 10–16.

Smith, C.B. (Ed.). (1994). *Whole language: The debate*. Bloomington, IN: ERIC Clearinghouse on Reading, English, and Communications.

Sosniak, L.A., & Stodolsky, S.S. (1993). Teachers and textbooks: Materials use in four fourth-grade classrooms. *The Elementary School Journal, 93,* 249–275.

Spiegel, D.L. (1992). Blending whole language and systematic direct instruction. *The Reading Teacher, 46,* 38–44.

Stanovich, K. (1993–1994). Romance and reality. *The Reading Teacher, 47,* 280–291.

State embraces phonics in approving new texts. (1996, December 13). *Los Angeles Times*, pp. A1, A29.

Stauffer, R.G. (1967). *The first grade studies: Findings of individual investigations*. Newark, DE: International Reading Association.

Steinberg, J. (1997, May 11). Teaching children to read: Politics colors a conference. *New York Times*, pp. D34, D61.

Sweet, R.W. (1995). Dr. Spock revisited. *Right to Read Report, 2*(8), 7.

Warwick, D.P., & Lininger, C.A. (1975). *The sample survey: Theory and practice*. New York: McGraw-Hill.

Weisberg, H.F., Krosnick, J.A., & Bowen, B.D. (1989). *An introduction to survey research and data analysis* (2nd ed.). Glenview, IL: Scott Foresman.

Williams, P.L., Reese, C.M., Campbell, J.R., Mazzeo, J., & Phillips, G.W. (1995). *NAEP 1994 Reading: A first look: Findings from the National Assessment of Educational Progress* (rev. ed.). Washington, DC: Office of Educational Research and Improvement, U.S. Department of Education.

Wiseman, F. (1972). Methodological bias in public opinion surveys. *Public Opinion Quarterly, 36,* 105–108.

 Article Review Form at end of book.

What are the conditions for learning? What practices would reflect the conditions of learning if applied to literacy teaching in the classroom?

Toward an Educationally Relevant Theory of Literacy Learning

Twenty years of inquiry

Cambourne reviews and expands upon his well-known conditions of learning, particularly as they apply to the teaching of literacy.

Brian Cambourne

A classroom teacher himself, Cambourne was awarded a Fulbright Fellowship and a postdoctoral Fellowship at Harvard University in the mid 1970s. He has been a visiting fellow at the Language Center of the University of Arizona and at the Center for the Study of Reading at the University of Illinois. Presently, he is Head of the Centre for Studies in Literacy at Wollongong University, where he has been working since 1982. He can be contacted there at Northfields Road, Wollongong, NSW Australia 2522.

Since the early 1970s I've been conducting research in natural settings. I've collected data from classrooms, homes, backyards, and supermarkets. The general focus of this research has been children learning

literacy. Essentially I have been motivated by the need to find an educationally relevant theory of learning.

This motivation is not recent. It first emerged when I was a young teacher, and I made an observation that both surprised and confused me. It was this: Many of the children I taught found school learning extremely difficult (especially reading and writing). However, within this group there was a significant number who seemed capable of successful learning in the world outside of school. I was continually surprised and confused by students who didn't seem able to learn the simplest concepts associated with reading, writing, spelling, or math, who nevertheless showed evidence of being able to learn and apply much more complex knowledge and skill in the everyday world.

The popular wisdom of the time added to my confusion. The prevailing explanation of why these children failed to learn in school was couched in terms like *deficit* or *deficiency*. In summary form this explanation was:

- Otherwise "normal" students who fail to learn in school are deficient in some way;

- This deficiency comprised either a tangible neurological impairment, a less tangible disabling learning condition (which was typically given an esoteric "scientific" label), a cultural deficiency, or all of the above.

This popular wisdom conflicted with what I observed day after day in my classroom. I knew from my conversations and interactions with

Cambourne, Brian. (1995, November). Toward an educationally relevant theory of literacy learning: Twenty years of inquiry. *The Reading Teacher,* 49(3), 189–190. Reprinted with permission of Brian Cambourne and the International Reading Association. All rights reserved.

these children that they did not display such deficits when it came to understanding and mastering the skills, tactics, and knowledge of complex sports like cricket, or sight reading music, or running a successful after-school lawn-mowing business, or reading and understanding the racing guide, or calculating odds and probabilities associated with card games, or speaking and translating across two or three languages. Although these contradictions caused me some intellectual unrest, I was too young and inexperienced to know how to resolve them.

Twenty years later when I was conducting research into language acquisition I again confronted the same issue. At the time I wrote this in my personal journal:

Learning how to talk, that is, learning how to control the oral language of the culture into which one has been born, is a stunning intellectual achievement of incredible complexity. It involves fine degrees of perceptual discrimination. It depends upon abstract levels of transfer and generalization being continually made. It demands that incredible amounts be stored in memory for instant retrieval. It necessitates high degrees of automaticity of very complex processes. Despite this complexity, as a learning enterprise, it is almost universally successful, extremely rapid, usually effortless, painless, and furthermore, it's extremely durable.

This was the same issue that had confused me as a young teacher, namely: How could a brain which could master such complex learning in the world outside school be considered deficient with respect to the kinds of learning that were supposed to occur inside school?

This time, however, I was neither young nor inexperienced. I'd learned at least three things in the intervening years. First, I'd learned that the discontinuities that existed between everyday learning and school learning could be better explained as the result of the pedagogies that were employed in each setting.

Second, I'd learned that all pedagogies are ultimately driven by a theory of learning. Accordingly, I tried to identify the theory of learning that drove the pedagogy I had used as young teacher. I discovered I had relied on a learning theory that could be summarised thus:

- Learning is essentially a process of habit formation.

- Complex habits are best formed (i.e., learned) if they are broken down into sequences of smaller, less complex, simpler habits and presented to learners in graded sequences of increasing complexity.

> I was continually surprised and confused by students who didn't seem able to learn the simplest concepts associated with reading . . . who nevertheless showed evidence of being able to learn and apply much more complex knowledge and skill in the everyday world.

- Habits are best formed by associating a desired response with the appropriate stimulus.

- Strong association leads to strong habits.

- Associative strength is a function of frequency of pairing an appropriate stimulus (S) with an appropriate response (R), (i.e., practice makes perfect).

- Inappropriate responses (i.e., approximations) are incipient bad habits and must be extinguished before they firm up and become fixed.

- Learners are too immature or underdeveloped to make decisions about their learning, so the process must be directed and controlled by the teacher.

This theory of learning resulted in a predictable pattern of teaching practice. Those "habits" that need to be "formed" were initially identified. These were then divided into subsets or hierarchies of smaller collections of subhabits. These, in turn, were then organised into "optimal" sequences or progressions, the mastery of any one being contingent upon the mastery of others earlier in the sequence. Repetitive drill and practice was the core teaching procedure employed. It was a theory which accorded special status to errors. Teachers (like me) who implemented this theory not only seemed to spend a lot of time and energy trying to develop automaticity, we spent almost as much en-

> . . . learning one's native language was probably the most universal exemplar of highly successful complex learning . . . outside of formal educational institutions.

ergy trying to extinguish errors from our students' repertoires.

I stated above that I'd learned three things in the intervening years. The third was this: I learned that the theory of learning that had underpinned my teaching still had strong currency among teachers, teacher educators, policy makers, curriculum designers, parents, and the general public. Although more than 20 years had passed since I had relied on this theory to drive my pedagogy, this theory (or one of its close relatives) still underpinned much of what went on in the name of education. I realized that the intellectual unrest I'd experienced some 20 years previously had suddenly resurfaced. This time, however, I felt more capable of resolving it.

A Closer Look at Everyday Natural Learning

I began by asking myself the following questions: What is an exemplar of highly successful complex learning? What made it successful? I decided that learning one's native language was probably the most universal exemplar of highly successful complex learning that occurred in the world outside of formal educational institutions. I therefore decided to learn more about this phenomenon.

I learned that there was a consensus that learning to talk is successful because human evolution had produced a nervous system that is specifically designed for the purpose. Initially I interpreted this to mean that it was merely a matter of neurological or genetic programming. However, I found other evidence that suggested there was more to it. For example, I discovered that there are humans born with intact and functioning nervous systems who sometimes do not learn to talk, or have great difficulty. Prelingually deaf children are an obvious example (Sacks, 1990). I also found case studies of so-called "feral" children (i.e., cut off from human contact) who did not successfully learn language:

As recently as 1970, a child called *Genie* in the scientific reports was discovered who had been confined to a small room under conditions of physical restraint, and who had received only minimal human contact from the age of eighteen months until almost fourteen years. She knew no language and was not able to talk, although she subsequently learned some language. (Fromkin & Rodman, 1978, p. 22)

The existence of such cases suggested that the acquisition of the oral mode of language might also be contingent upon the availability of environmental factors and/or conditions. I was reinforced in this thinking by the important conceptual connections between learning, language learning, and the teaching of reading which Don Holdaway (1979) Frank Smith (1981), and Ken Goodman and his colleagues (Gollasch, 1982) were making.

I believed that if such conditions could be identified, they might provide insights into promoting literacy learning in schools. Accordingly, I began some research to identify the conditions that supported oral language acquisition. I spent 3 years of my life bugging a group of toddlers as they interacted with parents, neighbors, friends, and acquaintances in homes, playgrounds, supermarkets, and other settings. One outcome of this research was the identification of a set of conditions that always seem to be present when language is learned.

The Conditions of Learning

Dictionary definitions of the term *conditions* carry a range of potential meanings including "particular modes of being," "existing cases or states," "circumstances indispensable to some results," "prerequisites on which something else is contingent," and "essential parts" (Macquarie University, 1981). The meaning I have attributed to *conditions* is an aggregate of all of these possibilities. I

want to convey the notion that the conditions I identified in this research are particular states of being (doing, behaving, creating), as well as being a set of indispensable circumstances that co-occur and are synergistic in the sense that they both affect and are affected by each other. Together they enable language to be learned. Each of the conditions I identified is briefly discussed below. (These conditions are discussed more fully in an earlier book [Cambourne, 1988].)

Immersion. This condition refers to the state of being saturated by, enveloped in, flooded by, steeped in, or constantly bathed in that which is to be learned. From the moment of birth, young language learners are immersed in the medium they are expected to learn. It is therefore a necessary condition for learning to talk, one that is denied prelingually deaf children and "feral" children.

Demonstration. This condition refers to the ability to observe (see, hear, witness, experience, feel, study, explore) actions and artifacts. All learning begins with a demonstration of some action or artifact (Smith, 1981). Father asking at the breakfast table, "Will you pass the butter, please?" and the subsequent passing of it is not only a demonstration of what that particular sequence of sound means but also a demonstration of what language can be used for, how it functions, how it can be tied to action, what kind of language is appropriate for the setting we call "breakfast," and so on. Young learners receive thousands of these demonstrations. They are the raw data that must be used to tease out how language is structured. The concept of demonstrations can be generalized to all learning. Potential horse riders need demonstrations of how a horse is ridden before they can begin learning to ride. The same applies to tying shoelaces, riding bikes, and singing, as well as to reading, writing, spelling.

Engagement. Immersion and demonstration are necessary conditions for learning to occur, but they are not sufficient. Potential learners must first engage with the demonstrations that immersion provides (Smith, 1981). Engagement incorporates a range of different behaviors. It has overtones of attention; learning is

unlikely if learners do not attend to demonstrations in which they are immersed. However, attention is unlikely if there is no perceived need or purpose for learning in the first place. Engagement also depends on active participation by the learner, which in turn involves some risk taking; learners can participate actively only if they are prepared to "have a go." Children learn to talk because they engage with the demonstrations of talking and language use that are constantly occurring around them.

Expectations. Expectations are essentially messages that significant others communicate to learners. They are also subtle and powerful coercers of behavior. Young learner-talkers receive very clear messages that not only are they expected to learn to talk, but also that they are capable of doing it. They are not given any expectation that it is "too difficult" or that they might fail. Quite the opposite. Try asking the parents of very young children whether they expect their offspring to learn to talk. Pay attention to the kind of response that you get.

Responsibility. When learning to talk, learner-talkers are permitted to make some decisions (i.e., take responsibility) about what they'll engage with and what they'll ignore. Nature does not provide language demonstrations that are specially arranged in terms of simple to complex. No one decides beforehand which particular language convention or set of conventions children will attend to and subsequently internalize. Learners are left some choice about what they'll engage with next. Learners are able to exercise this choice because of the consistency of the language demonstrations occurring in the everyday ebb and flow of human discourse. Such demonstrations (a) are always in a context that supports the meanings being transacted; (b) always serve a relevant purpose; (c) are usually wholes of language; and (d) are rarely (if ever) arranged according to some predetermined sequence.

The significant others in young learners' environments communicate very strong expectations that the learning task will ultimately be completed successfully, while simultaneously providing deep immersion with meaningful demonstrations. But the learners themselves decide the nature of the engagement that will occur.

Approximations. When learning to talk, learner-talkers are not expected to wait until they have language fully under control before they're allowed to use it. Rather they are expected to "have a go" (i.e., to attempt to emulate what is being demonstrated). Their childish attempts are enthusiastically, warmly, and joyously received. Baby talk is treated as a legitimate, relevant, meaningful, and useful contribution to the context. There is no anxiety about these unconventional forms becoming permanent fixtures in the learner's repertoire. Those who support the learner's language development expect these immature forms to drop out and be replaced by conventional forms. And they do.

Employment. This condition refers to the opportunities for use and practice that are provided by children's caregivers. Young learner-talkers need both time and opportunity to employ their immature, developing language skills. They seem to need two kinds of opportunity, namely those that require social interaction with other language users, and those that are done alone.

Parents and other caregivers continually provide opportunities of the first kind by engaging young learners in all kinds of linguistic give-and-take, subtly setting up situations in which they are forced to use their underdeveloped language for real and authentic purposes. Ruth Weir's (1962) classic study of the presleep monologues of very young children is an example of the second kind of opportunity. Her work suggests that young learner-talkers need time away from others to practice and employ (perhaps reflect upon) what they've been learning.

As a consequence of both kinds of employment, children seem to gain increasing control of the conventional forms of language toward which they're working. It's as if in order to learn language they must first use it.

Response. This condition refers to the feedback or information that learner-talkers receive from the world as a consequence of using their developing language knowledge and skills. Typically, these responses are given by the significant others in the learners' lives. When the learner-talker says, as he points to a glass on the table "Dat glass," the response from the parent if it's true (i.e., it is a glass) typically goes something like this: "Yes, that's a glass."

Exchanges like these serve the purpose of sharing information about the language and the degree of control that the learner has over it at any one time. The parent is supplying the missing bits of the child's approximation. The child is supplying the parent with an example of what he/she is currently capable of doing. It's as if the parent intuitively understands the importance of responsibility, and says to herself/himself: "I've no way of deciding which aspect of this learner's approximation is in need of adjustment just now. Therefore I'll demonstrate the conventional version of what I think was intended and leave the responsibility for deciding what is salient in this demonstration to the learner."

Applying the Conditions of Learning to Literacy Teaching

The identification of these conditions created a host of questions including: Could these conditions be applied to literacy learning? What happens when they are translated into classroom practice? Could they form the basis of an educationally relevant theory of literacy education?

To address these and related questions, I sought the help of teachers. Ten years ago, we employed a "teacher-as-coresearcher" methodology (Barton, 1992; Cambourne & Turbill, 1991) to explore the ramifications of these conditions for literacy learning and classroom practice. In what follows I will briefly describe some of what's emerged from this coresearching project.

Could these conditions be applied to literacy learning? We spent some time jointly exploring this question. We decided that the conditions that supported and enabled oral language learning could be transferred to literacy learning. The flow chart in Figure 1 summarizes the consensus we achieved.

Our joint exploration suggested that "engagement" was the key. It didn't matter how much immersion in text and language we provided; it didn't matter how riveting, compelling, exciting, or motivating our demonstrations were; if students didn't engage with language, no learning could occur. We were forced to look closely at the factors that affected the degree to which learners would engage (or not engage) with the demonstrations of literacy that were provided. As a consequence we formulated the following "Principles of Engagement":

- Learners are more likely to engage deeply with demonstrations if they believe that they are capable of ultimately learning or doing whatever is being demonstrated.

- Learners are more likely to engage deeply with demonstrations if they believe that learning whatever is being demonstrated has some potential value, purpose, and use for them.

- Learners are more likely to engage with demonstrations if they're free from anxiety.

- Learners are more likely to engage with demonstrations given by someone they like, respect, admire, trust, and would like to emulate.

We discovered that when these principles are consciously applied, teachers begin to employ a pro-learning, pro-reading, pro-writing discourse, which in turn sets in motion certain processes and personal relationships that are conducive to learning literacy. We also learned that if teachers consciously tried to maximize the degree to which they implemented expectations, responsibility, employment, approximations, and response, the probability of increasing the depth of learner engagement with the demonstrations they gave was dramatically increased.

What happened when these conditions were translated into classroom practice? As we began to explore the implementation of these conditions in classrooms, it became obvious that certain processes were necessary accompaniments of the literacy learning contexts that were created. So far we have identified transformation, discussion/reflection, application, and evaluation. It's hard to separate these processes from

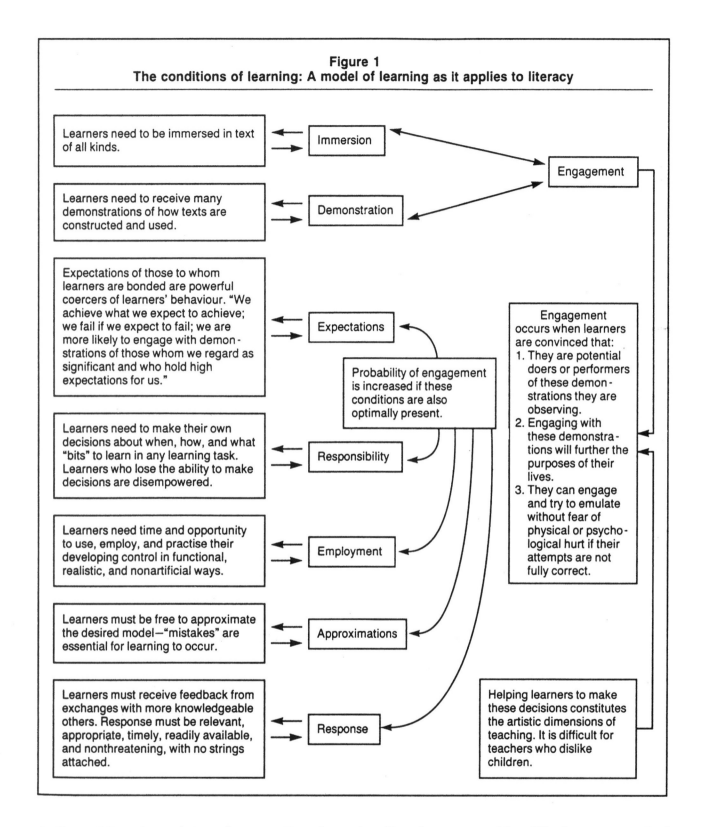

Figure 1
The conditions of learning: A model of learning as it applies to literacy

Learners need to be immersed in text of all kinds. → Immersion

Learners need to receive many demonstrations of how texts are constructed and used. → Demonstration

→ Engagement

Expectations of those to whom learners are bonded are powerful coercers of learners' behaviour. "We achieve what we expect to achieve; we fail if we expect to fail; we are more likely to engage with demonstrations of those whom we regard as significant and who hold high expectations for us." → Expectations

Probability of engagement is increased if these conditions are also optimally present.

Learners need to make their own decisions about when, how, and what "bits" to learn in any learning task. Learners who lose the ability to make decisions are disempowered. → Responsibility

Learners need time and opportunity to use, employ, and practise their developing control in functional, realistic, and nonartificial ways. → Employment

Learners must be free to approximate the desired model—"mistakes" are essential for learning to occur. → Approximations

Learners must receive feedback from exchanges with more knowledgeable others. Response must be relevant, appropriate, timely, readily available, and nonthreatening, with no strings attached. → Response

Engagement occurs when learners are convinced that:
1. They are potential doers or performers of these demonstrations they are observing.
2. Engaging with these demonstrations will further the purposes of their lives.
3. They can engage and try to emulate without fear of physical or psychological hurt if their attempts are not fully correct.

Helping learners to make these decisions constitutes the artistic dimensions of teaching. It is difficult for teachers who dislike children.

each other and from the conditions of learning. They co-occur and mutually shape each other. The seams between them are difficult to find. Despite this I will attempt to describe what we've learned so far.

Transformation. Transformation is the process that enables learners to "own" or be responsible for their learning. The process of making something one's own involves learners transforming the meanings

and/or skills that someone else has demonstrated into a set of meanings and/or skills that are uniquely theirs.

In the domain of language, this is highly similar to creating personal paraphrases. Expressing some concept or knowledge in one's own words while closely approximating the core meanings involved seems to co-occur with the decision to take control of (i.e., assume ownership of, take responsibility for) the concepts and knowledge involved. Our data suggest that learning that is not accompanied by transformation is shallow and transitory.

Discussion/reflection are language processes that are fundamental to human learning. Both have a similar purpose in learning, namely, to explore, transact, and clarify meaning. However, they differ with respect to audience. Reflection is really a discussion with oneself.

My classroom data show that the process of transformation is enormously enhanced through discussion with others. Such discussion allows the exchange and interchange of interpretations, constructed meanings, and understandings. Furthermore, these data support the claim that learning that has a mandatory social dimension to it is usually successful. Just as toddlers can learn to control the oral language of the culture into which they're born only by socially interacting with others, older learners also need a myriad of opportunities to interact with others in order to clarify, extend, refocus, and modify their own learning.

However, discussion with oneself (i.e., reflection) not only creates opportunities for clarification, extension, and refocusing, it also leads young learners to make explicit their unconscious language and literacy "know how." My data show a strong relationship between effective literacy learning and the development of conscious awareness of how language and learning works (i.e., metatextual awareness). Just as the prespeech monologues that Weir noticed seemed to be a necessary component of language learning, so "monologue with oneself" (which is a form of reflection) seems to enhance transformation. I feel confident in asserting that learning, thinking, knowing, and understanding are significantly enhanced when one is provided with opportunities for "talking one's way to meaning," both with others and with oneself.

Application is inherent in the condition of "employment." My data

suggest a multi-layered relationship among application, discussion/reflection, and transformation. When two or more persons collaborate in addressing or trying to resolve a problem, they are forced to interact with at least each other. This collaboration always requires discussion. Transformation occurs as a consequence of the discussion that typically accompanies jointly constructing, understanding new knowledge or mastering new skills. Often this new knowledge is reflected upon, and the new learning is further transformed.

Thus, teachers should create discussion opportunities for learners to apply their underdeveloped or naive knowledge and skills. These discussions often prompt other discussions. All this will maximise the probability that what learners hear and see others do, think, and say as they address the same problem will cause varying degrees of intellectual unrest which, in turn, will lead to a continuing cycle of transformation-reflection-discussion-reflection-transformation.

A continuous threat that runs through any teaching/learning process is *evaluation*. It is embedded in the condition of "response" described above. Learners are constantly evaluating their own performance as they engage, discuss/reflect, transform and apply what is to be learned. It doesn't matter whether learners are engaged in learning to iron, play tennis, write an economics essay, tie shoe laces, or acquire the oral language of the culture; they are continually asking of themselves "How am I doing?"

Those who adopt the teacher's role in any teaching/learning situation are also constantly engaged in evaluating. They are continually responding, giving the learners with whom they interact information that answers the "how-am-I-doing" question. This help or feedback typically comes in the form of some kind of response from whomever happens to be in the teacher role. It can come through discussion with other learners involved in similar kinds of learning, but only if there is a strong sense of collaboration and collegiality within the group. Figure 2 is a summary of this model of learning applied to a classroom setting.

Toward an Educationally Relevant Theory of Literacy Education

An educationally relevant theory of literacy education should have the following characteristics:

- Internal consistency: It should be able to explain both successful and unsuccessful literacy learning;

- Ecological validity: It should be applicable to both in-school and out-of-school contexts;

- Theory-into-practice congruence: It should be the basis for the design of instructional structures, processes, and activities;

- Pragmatic coherency: It should not make sense only to teachers and students, it should be "doable";

- Transferability: The principles inherent in the theory should be extendible to contexts other than literacy learning;

- High success rate: It should work in the sense that a significant number of learners acquire literacy as a consequence of applying the theory.

Since I first described this theory (Butler & Turbill, 1984) many thousands of teachers in hundreds of schools and school districts in Australia, New Zealand, the U.S., and Canada have adopted, adapted, and applied the principles to their own contexts. This theory has also been extended by creative educators to the teaching of mathematics (Semple & Stead, 1991; Stoessiger & Edmunds, 1987), music (Wilson, 1991), and teacher learning (Turbill, 1993).

The evidence that is emerging from these endeavors shows that the theory meets, in varying degrees, all of these criteria. I am quietly hopeful that someday I might be able to drop the word *Toward* from the title.

References

Barton, B. (1992). *An evaluation of "teacher-as-coresearcher" as a methodology for staff development.* Unpublished master's thesis, University of Wollongong, NSW, Australia.

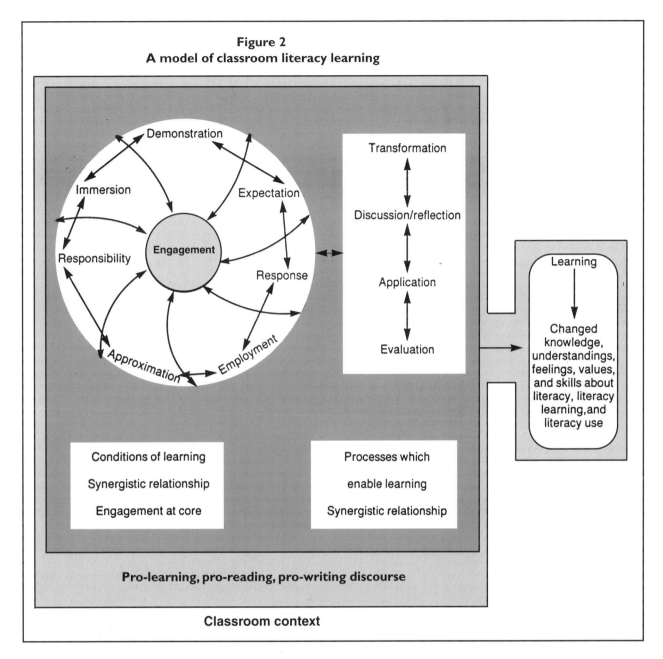

Figure 2
A model of classroom literacy learning

Demonstration

Immersion

Expectation

Engagement

Responsibility

Response

Approximation

Employment

Transformation

Discussion/reflection

Application

Evaluation

Learning

Changed knowledge, understandings, feelings, values, and skills about literacy, literacy learning, and literacy use

Conditions of learning

Synergistic relationship

Engagement at core

Processes which

enable learning

Synergistic relationship

Pro-learning, pro-reading, pro-writing discourse

Classroom context

Butler, A., & Turbill, J. (1984). *Toward a reading-writing classroom*. Sydney, NSW: Primary English Teaching Association.

Cambourne, B. L. (1988). *The whole story: Natural learning and the acquisition of literacy*. Auckland, New Zealand: Ashton-Scholastic.

Cambourne, B. L., & Turbill, J. (1991). *Teacher-as-coresearcher: How an approach to research became a methodology for staff development*. In J. Turbill, A. Butler, & B. Cambourne, *Frameworks: A whole language staff development program* (pp. 3–8). New York: Wayne-Fingerlakes BOCES.

Fromkin, V., & Rodman, R. (1978). *An introduction to language* (2nd ed.). New York: Holt.

Gollasch, F. (Ed.). (1982). *Language and literacy: The selected writings of Kenneth S. Goodman, volumes 1 & 2*. Boston: Routledge & Kegan-Paul.

Holdaway, D. (1979). *The foundations of literacy*. Sydney: Ashton-Scholastic.

Macquarie University. (1981). *The Macquarie dictionary*. Sydney: Macquarie Library Publishing.

Sacks, O. (1990). *Seeing voices*. New York: Harper Perennial.

Semple, C., & Stead, A. (1991, May). *Extending natural learning principles to mathematics in grade 5*. Paper presented at the meeting of the International Reading Association, Las Vegas, NV.

Smith, F. (1981). *Writing and the writer*. London: Heinemann.

Stoessiger, R., & Edmunds, J. A. (1987). *A process approach to mathematics*. Hobart, Tasmania, Australia: Tasmanian Department of Education, Curriculum Branch.

Turbill, J. B. (1993). *From a personal theory to a grounded theory of staff development*. Unpublished doctoral thesis, University of Wollongong, NSW, Australia.

Weir, R. (1962). *Language in the crib*. The Hague: Mouton and Co.

Wilson, L. (1991, May). *Extending natural learning principles to music reading and writing in primary school*. Paper presented at the meeting of the International Reading Association, Las Vegas, NV.

 Article Review Form at end of book.

How can teachers inform parents about learning disabilities? What can parents do to assist their child if he or she is diagnosed with a learning disorder?

Why Andy Couldn't Read

Millions of kids have been labeled learning disabled. Critics smell a scam here, but researchers say they've begun to unlock the puzzle of bright kids who can't learn.

Pat Wingert and Barbara Kantrowitz

Andrew Mertz was a very unhappy little boy in 1995. Third grade was a disaster, the culmination of a crisis that had been building since he entered kindergarten in suburban Maryland. He couldn't learn to read, and he hated school. "He would throw temper tantrums in the morning because he didn't want to go," recalls his mother, Suzanne. The year before, with much prodding from Suzanne, the school had authorized diagnostic tests for Andrew. The results revealed a host of brain processing problems that explained why he kept mixing up letters and sounds. Andrew's problem now had a label—he was officially classified as learning disabled—and he was legally entitled to help. But school officials, claiming bureaucratic delays, didn't provide any extra services.

In desperation, Suzanne, a trained reading specialist, pulled Andrew out of school and taught him at home for 10 months. It was an awesome task. To Andrew, lowercase p, q, b and d all looked like sticks with circles attached. Suzanne taught through touch and sound. She spent hours helping him make letters out of Play-Doh, shaving cream, sand and rice while exaggerating the sounds that went with them. The next year the district agreed to place him in a high-quality program for "gifted" children with learning disabilities. Teachers there continued many of the same practices. Now, at 10, Andrew is still struggling, but at least he can finally read.

Just about every teacher knows students like Andrew Mertz, bright kids who can't learn—no matter how hard they try. They are a painful puzzle to their parents and the subject of an intense educational controversy. In the last few years, researchers have made great strides in identifying and treating learning problems. But the explosion in knowledge has also led to what some say is an epidemic of diagnoses. According to 1996 figures, 2.6 million kids (4.36 percent of the nation's students) were in publicly funded learning-disabilities programs. In 1977, about 800,000 (1.8 percent of the student body) had been diagnosed. And this may only be the beginning. In an astonishing estimate, some researchers now say that as many as 20 percent of schoolchildren may have a neurological deficit, ranging from mild to severe, that makes it hard for them to read and write.

That's a lot of kids—and trying to help them is expensive. Largely as a result of lobbying by parents, federal law now mandates a "free and appropriate education" for the learning disabled; districts even have to pay tuition at private schools if they can't provide appropriate services.

Reading was especially hard for me becauxe the teachers did not teach me what I needed to know about reading. by: Andrew Mertz

From *Newsweek*, October 27, 1997. © 1997 Newsweek, Inc. All rights reserved. Reprinted by permission.

The parents of a child with a learning disability may be bombarded with Greek-rooted words that may confuse rather than clarify. Disabilities don't fit into neat categories; they are more likely to be a cocktail of disability types and associated problems.

Types of learning disabilities

Dyslexia Unusual difficulty sounding out letters and confusing words that sound similar. The most common form of disability.

Treatment: The latest techniques help students distinguish the different sounds that make up language and teach through touch (e.g., writing letters in sand). Word processors with spell-checking and speech-recognition software can help.

Dysgraphia Difficulty expressing thoughts on paper and with the act of writing itself. Characterized by problems gripping a pencil and unreadable penmanship.

Treatment: Students learn to describe thoughts orally as a precursor to writing. Paper with raised lines helps keep the hand aligned, and special pencil grips can ease hand strain. Children can benefit from learning the six or seven pencil strokes that combine to form roman letters.

Dyscalculia Incomprehension of simple mathematical functions. Often a child won't perceive shapes and will confuse arithmetic symbols.

Treatment: Having available in the classroom objects that a child can manipulate in order to add or subtract physically rather than on paper. Older students can perform calculations more easily by counting along a number line.

Associated problems

Dyspraxia (apraxia) Difficulty performing complex movements, including muscle motions needed for talking.

Treatment: For speech, facial exercises such as chewing gum or sucking and blowing through a straw. For other problems, kids can learn movement control through routine tasks like baking cookies.

Auditory discrimination Trouble distinguishing similar sounds ("pig" and "big") or confusing the sequence of heard or spoken sounds ("ephelant").

Treatment: Speech therapists and computer programs often use strategies like repetition and exaggerating the pronunciation of each letter so that

children will be better able to distinguish the sounds.

Attention deficit disorder Extreme hyperactivity and distractibility. Many children with learning disabilities suffer from ADD as well.

Treatment: Mild stimulants like Ritalin, but some kids respond poorly to medication. Behavior-modification techniques, such as motivating students to stay seated during a story reading, have been shown to help.

Dysnomia The inability to recall the names or words for common objects.

Treatment: Direct instruction by a speech or language therapist, who engages the child in word games and assigns large amounts of verbal practice.

Visual perception The inability to differentiate between foreground and background, as well as similar-looking numbers, letters, shapes, objects and symbols. Problems may include habitually skipping over lines of text.

Treatment: Direct, one-on-one instruction pointing out the child's mistakes and the visual cues they have overlooked.

Newsweek—"Learning Disabilities" by Janet Lerner. © 1997 Newsweek, Inc. All rights reserved. Reprinted by permission.

Teachers and clinicians have devised a wide range of techniques—from having kids write letters in sandboxes to using tape recorders, computers and other special equipment—to combat specific disabilities. The price tag: $8.12 billion last year, according to the Center for Special Education Finance.

This revolution has bred a new wave of critics who sneer at the learning-disabilities "epidemic." Some say many students labeled learning disabled are just lazy and looking for an easy way out. Other critics blame bad teaching for kids' reading problems and claim that school officials are inflating the number of disabled kids in order to wrest more money from the government. Still others contend that overly pushy parents—stereotypical hyperambitious Yuppie strivers—are behind the

dramatic increase in the numbers of learning-disabled students. These parents, the critics say, need a scientific excuse to explain why Jason or Jennifer isn't Harvard med-school material. The skeptics include prominent educators, like Boston University president Jon Westling, who was sued by students after he clamped down on accommodations for learning-disabled students.

But to parents whose children are struggling in school, the "epidemic" is real and heartbreaking. Learning disorders are often hard to accept because they afflict kids who appear perfectly healthy. It's easy to grasp the problems encountered by a child with a physical incapacity, such as blindness or paralysis. Yale University pediatrician and neuroscientist Sally Shaywitz, who studies the complex of reading problems

called dyslexia, says a learning problem is a "hidden disability." In fact, learning-disabled kids often display talent in other areas—perhaps art or science—while failing in one or more of the three R's.

Tammy Hollingsworth of suburban Dallas was optimistic when Joey, the oldest of her four children, entered kindergarten 15 years ago. Teachers had told her the boy was a genius. "His IQ was over 150 and he had a photographic memory," she recalls. But as he grew older and schoolwork became harder, he ran into serious problems. "Any assignment that required a transfer from the brain to paper, forget it. He couldn't do it." Over the years, teachers told Hollingsworth that Joey was just lazy and a discipline problem. He was 15 years old before he was tested for learning disabilities. Although the

Delays in normal development may be an early warning that your child has a learning disability—or a sign of a late bloomer. Here, a thumbnail guide to some common symptoms and the process of getting help:

1 Identification

The signs of learning disability vary with age. A parent or teacher of a child who consistently lags behind his or her peers and exhibits several of the following signs may consider an evaluation:

Preschool

- Starts talking later than other kids
- Has pronunciation problems
- Has slow vocabulary growth, is often unable to find the right word
- Has trouble learning numbers, the alphabet, days of the week

- Has difficulty rhyming words
- Is extremely restless and distractible
- Has trouble interacting with peers
- Displays a poor ability to follow directions or routines
- Avoids puzzles, drawing and cutting

Kindergarten through fourth grade

- Has a slow recall of facts
- Makes consistent reading and spelling errors, including letter reversals (b/d), inversions (m/w), transpositions (felt/left) and substitutions (house/home)

- Is slow to learn the connection between letters and sounds
- Transposes number sequences and confuses arithmetic signs (+,-,x,/,=)
- Is slow to learn new skills, relies heavily on memorization
- Is impulsive and lacks basic planning skills
- Has difficulty following directions or routines
- Has an unstable pencil grip
- Has trouble learning about time

2 Assessment

The parent or teacher takes the child to a school counselor or a pediatrician:

Physiological problems—like poor eyesight and hearing, as well as certain muscular diseases—can make normal children seem learning disabled. Psychological contributors, such as home life and emotional stability, should also be considered.

3 Testing

A referral is made to have the child evaluated by specialists:

Parents have the right to have their child evaluated after the age of 3, and public schools are obligated to arrange it. A psychologist, a social worker, a teacher, and a physician evaluate the student. Reading-comprehension, memory and spatial-relation tests help form a diagnosis.

4 Classification

The child is determined to be "learning disabled":

Some states require a discrepancy between a student's IQ and academic performance. Others need proof of dysfunction in things like perception and memory. Within 30 days of classification, children who qualify receive an individualized learning schedule.

5 Options/alternatives

By law, the child is entitled to an appropriate education:

A child's instruction must be continually monitored by his or her parents. If they are unsatisfied, they can lobby to change the curriculum or demand a transfer to another school—even a private one, paid at public expense.

Newsweek—Bill Youryoulias from National Center for Learning Disabilities. © 1997 Newsweek, Inc. All rights reserved. Reprinted by permission.

results showed he had real problems expressing his thoughts in writing (a disorder technically known as dysgraphia), it was too late to save his school career. Years of frustration and failure had taken their toll, and he dropped out at 17. Joey eventually earned a high-school-equivalency diploma; he is now enrolled in a local police academy.

If Joey were entering kindergarten today, he might have a better chance. The term "learning disabilities" is relatively new. It was introduced in 1963, when parents and educators from around the country organized the nonprofit group now known as the Learning Disabilities Association. Until then, children with learning problems were generally classified as "perceptually handi-capped," "brain injured" or "neuro-logically impaired." Many were turned away from public schools as uneducable, and if they couldn't afford private-school tuition, they just stayed home; some were even labeled mentally retarded. One advantage of combining the old diagnoses under a single new term was that it enabled educators to distinguish between children with below-average IQs (who were then put into classes for the mentally retarded) and kids of average or above-average intelligence who had trouble learning in specific areas but otherwise functioned normally.

More than three decades later, there is still no universal agreement about how to classify the constellation of problems that fall under this umbrella diagnosis. Medical doctors tend to accentuate differences in genetics, as well as brain organization and function. Psychologists focus on dysfunctions in areas like perception, processing, memory and attention. Teachers zero in on the specific areas of academic difficulty.

But researchers are getting closer to some concrete answers. The most tantalizing clues are coming from brain research that is still in the early stages, which is very promising. Using state-of-the-art functional magnetic resonance imaging (fMRI)—machines that take pictures of the brain in action—scientists are investigating disruptions in specific neurosystems. And they're learning even more from examining children and adults with brain injuries, says

One School's Solution

The Lab School of Washington, a private school, uses the arts—especially drama, music, painting and filmmaking—to teach a variety of academic and social skills. The goal is to encourage kids by building on their strengths.

Martha Bridge Denckla, a neuropsychologist with the Kennedy Krieger Institute in Baltimore. "Some of these traumatic brain cases simulate the exact picture we see all the time in learning-disabled cases where we don't know the cause," Denckla says. "These experiences make me very confident that what is causing LD affects the brain." But there's a long way to go. It was only four years ago that Shaywitz's team took one of the first fMRI pictures of a brain caught in the act of reading.

This is the most critical area of research because the most common learning disabilities relate to language—reading, writing and spelling. Some children have trouble comprehending words or letters in sequence. Others read words but don't understand the content. Still others are dyslexics, children and adults who have trouble naming letters and sounding out words, despite the fact that they often have large vocabularies and reason well.

Because dyslexia seems to run in families, scientists think that it is often inherited. For years, researchers, suspected it was caused by vision problems, and a stereotype developed that dyslexics commonly reverse letters (reading d's as b's, for example). Today, researchers like Yale's Shaywitz say dyslexics are no more likely to reverse letters than anyone else. Instead, Shaywitz and other researchers theorize that dyslexia is linked to a glitch in the brain's wiring that interferes with the ability to translate a written word into units of sound, or phonemes. Scientists have found that dyslexics often cannot recognize and break down spoken words into their phonetic segments or slice off one phoneme from a word—for example, they cannot figure out that "bat" without the b is "at." Technically, this problem is known as a "phonological awareness" deficit.

Researchers have identified four distinct steps in learning to read; breakdowns anywhere in this process can explain severe reading problems. G. Reid Lyon, acting chief of the child-development and behavior branch of the National Institutes of Child and Human Development, says that reading for all children begins with phonological awareness. Combinations of just 44 phonemes produce every English word. "Children who will be good readers," Lyon says, "just have a knack for understanding that words are made up of different sounds before they learn anything about the alphabet." The next step is linking these sounds with specific letters. This can be confusing because most letters—in English and many other languages—can have more than one sound. The reading-instruction methods known as linguistics (sound to letters) and phonics (letters to sound) focus on this part of the process by having kids sound out words. The third step, Lyon says, is for a child to become a fast reader—to make the association between symbol and sound virtually automatic so that the child can move on to the final step, concentrating on the meaning of the words. (Researchers around the country are testing ways to put these findings into reading programs for all kids, not just learning-disabled children.)

Some children also have spoken-language problems, which are often ignored because parents are told kids will "grow out of it." Kids with this disorder might mispronounce words because they're not processing sounds correctly. For example, they might call animals "aminals." They may also confuse specific sounds (thumb could become "fum") well after their peers are speaking clearly. School is a frustrating experience because they can't demonstrate what they know. They may, for example, recognize colors but not be able to name them. And their school troubles don't stop there. Studies indicate that preschoolers with oral-language problems often have difficulty later learning to read and write.

Another group of learning disorders revolves around difficulties in learning to compute or reason mathematically. In severe cases, these problems are called dyscalculia. Sometimes math difficulties appear without any other learning problems. At other times, these are the same children who have difficulty learning to speak and read. Janet Lerner, professor of education at Northeastern Illinois University and the author of the classic textbook for teachers of learning-disabled children, says some kids with math disabilities may suffer from "visual motor" problems that may make it difficult for them to count objects without physically touching them. They also have trouble adding one group of objects to another without counting them out, one by one. Others may have "visual perception" problems that, for example, render them unable to see a triangle as anything but three unrelated lines. They find it very arduous to copy letters and numbers and align numbers properly for computation.

Complicating the picture is the fact that many learning-disabled children also have a variety of motor, social, memory, organizational and attention problems that affect their schoolwork, such as attention deficit disorder (ADD). Researchers estimate that up to 30 percent of children with learning disabilities may have ADD, which makes it even harder for them to focus. Children humiliated by their inability to overcome their learning problems also tend to develop behavioral and emotional disorders. Kids with learning problems are twice as likely to drop out of school; a disturbingly high number end up with criminal records.

Even after they learn to read, write and add, many learning-disabled people don't find these basic skills easy. That's why educators believe early intervention is critical. "If we do not identify children early, by the end of second grade, the majority of them will have difficulty reading for the rest of their lives," says Lyon. "What we're finding is that there are sensitive periods when children can learn to read more easily, just like there are windows when children learn foreign language easier."

In many clinics and hospitals around the country, such as Evanston Northwestern Healthcare's Evanston Hospital north of Chicago, babies and toddlers who had a traumatic birth are regularly checked for signs of developmental delays—significant lags in reaching the milestones of smiling, sitting, walking and talking.

"We know problems at birth, including prematurity, increase the chances of developing learning problems later in childhood," says Joanne Bregman, director of Evanston's child development clinic. "All the research says that the first three years of life are critical. The sooner a problem is identified, the sooner it can be treated and the better the outcome is likely to be." Early intervention usually consists of speech, occupational or physical therapy. Every state has outreach programs that funnel children exhibiting significant delays in development into specialized public preschools.

A few nursery schools formally screen all children for early signs of learning problems. In Washington, D.C., Lynn A. Balzer-Martin, a pediatric occupational therapist, begins her multipart screening with a thorough questionnaire to parents and teachers about a child's health history, behavior and activities. Then she observes the child's movements, taking note of balance, positioning and coordination. Brain research has shown that the way a child moves or follows instruction can be an indicator of how well he processes information.

Someday, intervention may begin even earlier. Geneticists are working on procedures to identify inherited learning disorders. John DeFries, director of the Institute of Behavioral Genetics at the University of Colorado, says that researchers now believe that although as many as 20 genes may be involved in the reading process, just two or three "may account for most of the variation in reading difficulty that we see." If scientists can identify these genes, they could someday screen kids to determine which are at risk, and start working with them before they start to flounder.

At the moment, early intervention and diagnosis is the exception rather than the rule. Most children with learning disabilities don't get help until they're well along in school—usually between the ages of 9 and 14. That's because, under the law, funding follows failure. Children who are officially labeled learning disabled are eligible for special aid. But to win that, all 50 states and the federal government require proof of school problems.

Of course, that doesn't mean every child who is having trouble in school is learning disabled. Most states require a discrepancy between a child's actual achievement levels and his intellectual potential, usually determined by some type of IQ test. And that's another reason learning disabilities have become so controversial. Many critics of IQ tests believe they are culturally biased and underestimate the intellectual potential of poor and minority children. "Black kids have to be more severely disabled to be called LD," says Esther Minskoff of James Madison University. "White kids are picked up earlier."

Public and private schools around the country have developed programs for learning-disabled kids; the quality varies widely. At the Lab School of Washington, a private school with 285 students in kindergarten through 12th grade, founder and director Sally Smith uses the arts—especially music, dance, painting, drama and filmmaking—to teach academic skills. She has also created clubs based on different time periods to help develop social skills as well as provide a lively history curriculum. Kids start out as cavemen and move through Egypt, the Middle Ages and the Renaissance up to modern times. "It's very experiential, very hands-on," Smith says. "We want to build on their strengths." (One of the authors of this article, Washington correspondent Pat Wingert, sends a child to the Lab School.)

Public-school programs generally have fewer resources, but teachers still try to emphasize individual attention. At Eagle Rock Elementary School in suburban Los Angeles, Joyce Jerome and two aides preside over a class of 14 learning-disabled students in grades four to six. This year's theme is the ocean, and Jerome has decorated a wall with fishing nets, colorful seashells and pictures of whales and other sea life.

One recent morning, five students—all of whom read well below their grade level—were gathered around a half-moon desk trying to read the word "enormous." Finally, one child blurted out "eee nor moose" and smiled. He won a "ticket," which can be redeemed for prizes like colored pencils and carnival-type toys in the classroom "store."

Another student, an 11-year-old girl, gets the word "nothing." She is told to break it into syllables and does so after some obvious stress. Finally, she says two words: "no thing." Jerome prompts her. "What is like no thing? What sounds like no thing?" The girl rubs her forehead with her palm. "I don't know," she says, exasperated. "Why are these words so complicated?"

Some critics of the idea of learning disabilities claim that better instruction could eliminate the problem altogether. In the last few years, much of the controversy over these problems has become entwined with the often ferocious dispute over two alternate methods of teaching reading: phonics and "whole language," which is based on children's grasping the meaning of a word from its context in a story. While a pure whole-language approach works well for some kids, others—especially those with learning disabilities—struggle to read without help in phonics.

A few researchers have even suggested that whole language is the main reason for the huge increase in the number of kids diagnosed as disabled—fueling the idea that learning disabilities is a phony diagnosis, perhaps contrived to compensate for what are really teaching disabilities. In her new book, *Why Our Children Can't Read*, Diane McGuinness, a Florida psychologist, maintains that all children need direct instruction in decoding words and that the proportion of children labeled learning disabled would drop if whole-language programs were replaced with those that emphasize phonological awareness and linguistics.

Learning disabilities are hard to understand, and so is the law that attempts to help struggling kids. If a family can't work through the bureaucratic maze, a child can languish. Such was the case with Jennie Harvey. At 15, she's finally learning to read at the Cove School in suburban Chicago. Because she had severe speech problems, Jennie was enrolled in special-ed classes at the age of 3. Although she was promoted annually, by the seventh grade she still wasn't reading at a first-grade level.

Her parents accepted Jennie's teachers' assessment that they were doing all they could. But three years ago they hired Rose Pech, a retired special-education teacher turned tutor, who diagnosed a series of problems that required much more specialized instruction than Jennie had been receiving. With Pech's help, Jennie was admitted to Cove, a private school for severely learning-disabled children (the state pays the $16,000 annual tuition because the district cannot provide the same services).

Jennie's story is an extreme example of lost potential; because she's learning to read so late, her teachers doubt that she can ever really catch up.

Scientists want to spare other children a similar fate. And parents like Suzanne Mertz are learning how to make the system work for their kids. When her husband was recently transferred to Pennsylvania, she went school-shopping for Andrew before deciding which town to live in. She finally settled on Great Valley, which has an excellent learning-disabilities program. Her advice to other parents? "You can advocate for your child better than anyone," she says. "You know them best." Raising a child with learning disabilities will always be a long, hard road—but now, at least, there's reason to hope.

 Article Review Form at end of book.

WiseGuide Wrap-Up

- Teachers must reflect on their own beliefs about literacy learning in order to make informed decisions about literacy instruction.

- Students who are involved in personally meaningful literacy tasks will have the motivation to learn and apply skills and strategies.

- Most teachers use a balanced, eclectic approach to elementary reading instruction, blending phonics and holistic principles and practices in compatible ways.

- A set of conditions for natural learning can be implemented in the classroom to enhance language learning.

- Parents can play a vital role in early detection and intervention of learning disabilities in their children.

R.E.A.L. Sites

This list provides a print preview of typical **Coursewise** R.E.A.L. sites. There are over 100 such sites at the **Courselinks**™ site. The danger in printing URLs is that web sites can change overnight. As we went to press, these sites were functional using the URLs provided. If you come across one that isn't, please let us know via email to: webmaster@coursewise.com. Use your Passport to access the most current list of R.E.A.L. sites at the **Courselinks**™ site.

Site name: Reading Online—from ABC to Ready to Read: Perspectives on Reading in New Zealand

URL: http://www.readingonline.org/international/abc/index.html

Why is it R.E.A.L.? It provides a brief survey of the history of reading in New Zealand to show how whole language methods emerged. Until the 1960s, New Zealand's experiences with whole language were similar to those of North America. Phonics began to be increasingly downplayed as a gradual change in teaching methods occurred. The abstract states that "what happened in New Zealand has now happened on a wider scale in other countries as well, including Australia, Canada, England, and the United States, so the recent New Zealand experience will be useful for those who are currently being asked to teach whole language, and would like to know whether it has stood the test of time."

Key topics: history of literacy

Try this: Nicholson contrasts the two differing paradigms that appear to be at the forefront of the current debate concerning reading instruction. Delineate key elements for each of these paradigms, identify key people associated with each, and then discuss your thoughts about the two paradigms.

Site name: Time

URL: http://cgi.pathfinder.com/time/

Why is it R.E.A.L.? Time.com is the site that hosts articles from the newsmagazine *Time*. Over the past few years, *Time* has printed several articles on the state of education in the United States. One article in particular, "How Johnny Should Read," highlights the debate between supporters of phonics versus those who believe in the whole language method of learning to read.

Key topics: phonics, phonemic awareness, whole language

Try this: Find and read the article "How Johnny Should Read." In the conclusion of this article, the author states that "the fashionable word in the reading controversy right now is 'balance.' It would be tragic if the shift to phonics went to extremes and if the genuine contributions of whole language were abandoned, so this embrace of moderation is welcome." What does the author mean by this statement? Compare and contrast the following two excerpts from this article:

- In Adams' scheme, a reader does not have to learn all these combinations; once phonemic awareness is established and some sound-letter correspondences are learned, the brain begins to recognize new patterns on its own.

- From this work, he (Goodman) concluded that readers rely on context to guess an upcoming word rather than using the word's spelling. If this ability to guess were improved, and poring over individual letters discouraged, said Goodman, then reading would be more fluent.

section 2

Growing Readers:
Early Reading
and Family Literacy

There is nothing more exciting than watching a young child discover the joy of reading. This discovery occurs long before the child attends kindergarten or even preschool. Many parents begin reading aloud to their children when they are infants or toddlers. Indeed, children go to school with a wealth of knowledge about the forms and functions of printed language before formal instruction ever occurs. Parents play a major role in developing and providing an ongoing support of reading growth in their children.

Children go to school with a variety of cultural, ethnic, and socioeconomic backgrounds. Schools and teachers must be prepared to meet the individual needs of these children, as well as providing an environment that promotes language and literacy growth. Teachers must be intimately knowledgeable about the literacy development of young children, such as oral, reading, and written language development.

A key concern for teachers is helping beginning readers learn word-identification skills. A great deal of attention has been paid to the acquisition of such skills over the past three decades. Research in linguistics, psychology, and sociology has changed our understanding of the reading process. Various perspectives on how this research translates into classroom practice have led to several theories on how young readers acquire word-identification skills. Perhaps the most vigorous discussion revolves around the teaching of phonics. Some educators believe that phonics instruction should be a primary focus of beginning reading instruction. Others believe that reading can be taught successfully by teaching whole words and that phonics can be learned through analogy.

It is obvious that excellent instruction for beginning readers in the primary grades requires optimal school and family environments, as well as teachers who are well prepared and highly knowledgeable. The articles in Section 2 address issues concerning beginning reading instruction and family literacy. "Baby Talk" reports on the current research findings on the linguistic acquisition of children. "Family Literacy: Examining Practice and Issues of Effectiveness" highlights two family literacy programs and discusses the factors that are critical to their success. "Balanced Instruction: Insights and Considerations" examines the various definitions of *balanced literacy* and states implications for classroom practice. "Ready to Read" provides instructional practices and classroom examples of ways to combine phonics with comprehension for effective reading instruction. "Everything You Wanted to Know About Phonics (But Were Afraid to Ask)" discusses seven principles for effective phonics instruction and outlines the instructional practices of traditional as well as contemporary phonics instruction. "Talking About Books: Beyond Decodable Texts—Supportive

Learning Objectives

- Summarize major research findings on the acquisition of language and analyze the effect these findings have had on theories of language learning.

- Describe the key factors critical to the effectiveness of family literacy programs.

- Discuss the various definitions of *balanced literacy* and resulting classroom instructional practices.

- Identify effective principles of phonics instruction and understand how these principles are reflected in contemporary phonics instruction.

- Describe the difference between controlled vocabulary texts and quality children's literature in terms of their support for readers.

and Workable Literature" argues that high-quality children's literature is a better choice for reading instruction than is decodable text written specifically to give children practice in reading words to which they have been exposed in prior instruction.

? ? ? Questions ?

Reading 5. What are the major findings regarding the acquisition of language in children reported in this article? What might you question about the theories of language acquisition proposed in this article?

Reading 6. How do the two literacy projects reviewed in the article vary? How can family literacy programs ensure that they are working to meet the four key factors of effectiveness?

Reading 7. Discuss the definition of *balanced reading* and indicate several recommendations for practice based on each viewpoint. How do the discussions about balanced reading fit into the larger issues associated with reading instruction?

Reading 8. How can children in the same class but reading at different levels participate in the same activities described by Routman? How does your personal definition of *reading* compare with Routman's belief that phonics and meaning must be taught together?

Reading 9. Discuss the seven principles of effective phonics instruction described in this article. Compare and contrast traditional phonics approaches to contemporary phonics approaches in light of the qualities of effective phonics instruction.

Reading 10. Watson argues that quality children's literature is a better choice for reading instruction than is decodable text written specifically to give children practice in reading words to which they have been exposed in prior instruction. Locate some of the books discussed in this article and analyze them in terms of their support for readers, including patterns of words, syntax, concepts, and illustrations. List your findings.

What are the major findings regarding the acquisition of language in children reported in this article? What might you question about the theories of language acquisition proposed in this article?

Baby Talk

Learning language, researchers are finding, is an astonishing act of brain computation—and it's performed by people too young to tie their shoes.

Shannon Brownlee

Inside a small, dark booth, 18-month-old Karly Horn sits on her mother Terry's lap. Karly's brown curls bounce each time she turns her head to listen to a woman's recorded voice coming from one side of the booth or the other. "At the bakery, workers will be baking bread," says the voice. Karly turns her head left and listens, her face intent. "On Tuesday morning, the people have going to work," says the voice. Karly turns her head away even before the statement is finished. The lights come on as graduate student Ruth Tincoff opens the door to the booth. She gives the child's curls a pat and says, "Nice work."

Karly and her mother are taking part in an experiment at Johns Hopkins University in Baltimore, run by psycholinguist Peter Jusczyk, who has spent 25 years probing the linguistic skills of children who have not yet begun to talk. Like most toddlers her age, Karly can utter a few dozen words at most and can string together the occasional two-word sentence, like "More juice" and "Up, Mommy." Yet as Jusczyk and his colleagues have found, she can already recognize that a sentence like "the people have going to work" is ungrammatical. By 18 months of age, most toddlers have somehow learned the rule requiring that any verb ending in -ing must be preceded by the verb to be. "If you had asked me 10 years ago if kids this young could do this," says Jusczyk, "I would have said that's crazy."

Linguists these days are reconsidering a lot of ideas they once considered crazy. Recent findings like Jusczyk's are reshaping the prevailing model of how children acquire language. The dominant theory, put forth by Noam Chomsky, has been that children cannot possibly learn the full rules and structure of languages strictly by imitating what they hear. Instead, nature gives children a head start, wiring them from birth with the ability to acquire their parents' native tongue by fitting what they hear into a pre-existing template for the basic structure shared by all languages. (Similarly, kittens are thought to be hard-wired to learn how to hunt.) Language, writes Massachusetts Institute of Technology linguist Steven Pinker, "is a distinct piece of the biological makeup of our brains." Chomsky, a prominent linguist at MIT, hypothesized in the 1950s that children are endowed from birth with "universal grammar," the fundamental rules that are common to all languages, and the ability to apply these rules to the raw material of the speech they hear—without awareness of their underlying logic.

The average preschooler can't tell time, but he has already accumulated a vocabulary of thousands of words—plus (as Pinker writes in his book, *The Language Instinct*), "a tacit knowledge of grammar more sophisticated than the thickest style manual." Within a few months of birth, children have already begun memorizing words without knowing their meaning. The question that has ab-sorbed—and sometimes divided—linguists is whether children need a special language faculty to do this or instead can infer the abstract rules of grammar from the sentences they hear, using the same mental skills that allow them to recognize faces or master arithmetic.

The debate over how much of language is already vested in a child at birth is far from settled, but new linguistic research already is transforming traditional views of how the human brain works and how language evolved. "This debate has completely changed the way we view the brain," says Elissa Newport, a psycholinguist at the University of Rochester in New York. Far from being an orderly, computerlike machine that methodically calculates step by step, the brain is now seen as working more like a beehive, its swarm of interconnected neurons sending signals back and forth at lightning speed. An infant's brain, it turns out, is capable of taking in enormous amounts of information and finding the regular patterns contained within it. Geneticists and linguists recently have begun to challenge the common-sense assumption that intelligence and language are inextricably linked, through research on a rare genetic disorder called Williams syndrome, which can seriously impair cognition while leaving language nearly intact (box, page 39). Increasingly sophisticated technologies such as magnetic resonance imaging are allowing researchers to watch the brain in action, revealing that language literally

Copyright, June 15, 1998, *U.S. News & World Report*.

sculpts and reorganizes the connections within it as a child grows.

The path leading to language begins even before birth, when a developing fetus is bathed in the muffled sound of its mother's voice in the womb. Newborn babies prefer their mothers' voices over those of their fathers or other women, and researchers recently have found that when very young babies hear a recording of their mothers' native language, they will suck more vigorously on a pacifier than when they hear a recording of another tongue.

At first, infants respond only to the prosody—the cadence, rhythm, and pitch—of their mothers' speech, not the words. But soon enough they home in on the actual sounds that are typical of their parents' language. Every language uses a different assortment of sounds, called phonemes, which combine to make syllables. (In English, for example, the consonant sound "b" and the vowel sound "a" are both phonemes, which combine for the syllable *ba*, as in *banana*.) To an adult, simply perceiving, much less pronouncing, the phonemes of a foreign language can seem impossible. In English, the p of *pat* is "aspirated," or produced with a puff of air; the p of *spot* or *tap* is unaspirated. In English, the two p's are considered the same; therefore, it is hard for English speakers to recognize that in many other languages the two p's are two different phonemes. Japanese speakers have trouble distinguishing between the "l" and "r" sounds of English, since in Japanese they don't count as separate sounds.

Polyglot Tots

Infants can perceive the entire range of phonemes, according to Janet Werker and Richard Tees, psychologists at the University of British Columbia in Canada. Werker and Tees found that the brains of 4-month-old babies respond to every phoneme uttered in languages as diverse as Hindi and Nthlakampx, a Northwest American Indian language containing numerous consonant com-

binations that can sound to a nonnative speaker like a drop of water hitting an empty bucket. By the time babies are 10 months to a year old, however, they have begun to focus on the distinctions among phonemes of their native language and to ignore the differences among foreign sounds. Children don't lose the ability to distinguish the sounds of a foreign language; they simply don't pay attention to them. This allows them to learn more quickly the syllables and words of their native tongue.

An infant's next step is learning to fish out individual words from the nonstop stream of sound that makes up ordinary speech. Finding the boundaries between words is a daunting task, because people don't pause . . . between . . . words . . . when . . . they speak. Yet children begin to note word boundaries by the time they are 8 months old, even though they have no concept of what most words mean. Last year, Jusczyk and his colleagues reported results of an experiment in which they let 8-month-old babies listen at home to recorded stories filled with unusual words, like *hornbill* and *python*. Two weeks later, the researchers tested the babies with two lists of words, one composed of words they had already heard in the stories, the other of new unusual words that weren't in the stories. The infants listened, on average, to the familiar list for a second longer than to the list of novel words.

The cadence of language is a baby's first clue to word boundaries. In most English words, the first syllable is accented. This is especially noticeable in words known in poetry as trochees—two-syllable words stressed on the first syllable—which parents repeat to young children (BA-by, DOG-gie, MOM-my). At 6 months, American babies pay equal amounts of attention to words with different stress patterns, like gi-RAFFE, or TI-ger. By 9 months, however, they have heard enough of the typical first-syllable-stress pattern of English to prefer listening to trochees, a predilection that will show up later, when they start uttering their first

words and mispronouncing giraffe as *raff* and banana as *nana*. At 30 months, children can easily repeat the phrase "TOM-my KISS-ed the MON-key," because it preserves the typical English pattern, but they will leave out the *the* when asked to repeat "Tommy patted the monkey." Researchers are now testing whether French babies prefer words with a second-syllable stress—words like be-RET or ma-MAN.

Decoding Patterns

Most adults could not imagine making speedy progress toward memorizing words in a foreign language just by listening to somebody talk on the telephone. That is basically what 8-month-old babies can do, according to a provocative study published in 1996 by the University of Rochester's Newport and her colleagues, Jenny Saffran and Richard Aslin. They reported that babies can remember words by listening for patterns of syllables that occur together with statistical regularity.

The researchers created a miniature artificial language, which consisted of a handful of three-syllable nonsense words constructed from 11 different syllables. The babies heard a computer-generated voice repeating these words in random order in a monotone for two minutes. What they heard went something like "bidakupadotigolabubidaku." *Bidaku*, in this case, is a word. With no cadence or pauses, the only way the babies could learn individual words was by remembering how often certain syllables were uttered together. When the researchers tested the babies a few minutes later, they found that the infants recognized pairs of syllables that had occurred together consistently on the recording, such as *bida*. They did not recognize a pair like *kupa*, which was a rarer combination that crossed the boundaries of two words. In the past, psychologists never imagined that young infants had the mental capacity to make these sorts of inferences. "We were pretty surprised we could get this result with babies, and with only brief exposure," says Newport. "Real language, of course, is much more complicated, but the exposure is vast."

Little polyglots. An infant's brain can perceive every possible sound in every language. By 10 months, babies have learned to screen out foreign sounds and to focus on the sounds of their native language.

Kristen Aerts is only 9 years old, but she can work a room like a seasoned pol. She marches into the lab of cognitive neuroscientist Ursula Bellugi, at the Salk Institute for Biological Studies in La Jolla, Calif., and greets her with a cheery, "Good morning Dr. Bellugi. How are you today?" The youngster smiles at a visitor and says, "My name is Kristen. What's yours?" She looks people in the eye when she speaks and asks questions—social skills that many adults never seem to master, much less a third grader. Yet for all her poise, Kristen has an IQ of about 79. She cannot write her address; she has trouble tying her shoes, drawing a simple picture of a bicycle, and subtracting 2 from 4; and she may never be able to live independently.

Kristen has Williams syndrome, a rare genetic disorder that affects both body and brain, giving those who have it a strange and incongruous jumble of deficits and strengths. They have diminished cognitive capacities and heart problems, and age prematurely, yet they show outgoing personalities and a flair for language. "What makes Williams syndrome so fascinating," says Bellugi, "is it shows that the domains of cognition and language are quite separate."

Genetic Gap Williams syndrome, which was first described in 1961, results when a group of genes on one copy of chromosome 7 is deleted during embryonic development. Most people with Williams resemble each other more than they do their families, with wide-set hazel eyes, upturned noses, and wide mouths. They also share a peculiar set of mental impairments. Most stumble over the simplest spatial tasks, such as putting together a puzzle, and many cannot read or write beyond the level of a first grader.

In spite of these deficits, Bellugi has found that children with the disorder are not merely competent at language but extraordinary. Ask normal kids to name as many animals as possible in 60 seconds, and a string of barnyard and pet-store examples will tumble out. Ask children with Williams, and you'll get a menagerie of rare creatures, such as ibex, newt, yak, and weasel. People with Williams have the gift of gab, telling elaborate stories with unabashed verve and incorporating audience teasers such as, "Gadzooks!" and "Lo and behold!"

This unlikely suite of skills and inadequacies initially led Bellugi to surmise that Williams might damage the right hemisphere of the brain, where spatial tasks are processed, while leaving language in the left hemisphere intact.

That has not turned out to be true. People with Williams excel at recognizing faces, a job that enlists the visual and spatial-processing skills of the right hemisphere. Using functional brain imaging, a technique that shows the brain in action, Bellugi has found that both hemispheres of the brains of people with Williams are shouldering the tasks of processing language.

Bellugi and other researchers are now trying to link the outward characteristics of people with Williams to the genes they are missing and to changes in brain tissue. They have begun concentrating on the neocerebellum, a part of the brain that is enlarged in people with Williams and that may hold clues to their engaging personalities and to the evolution of language. The neocerebellum is among the brain's newest parts, appearing in human ancestors about the same time as the enlargement of the frontal cortex, the place where researchers believe rational thoughts are formulated. The neocerebellum is significantly smaller in people with autism, who are generally antisocial and poor at language, the reverse of people with Williams. This part of the brain helps make semantic connections between words, such as *sit* and *chair*, suggesting that it was needed for language to evolve.

Learning words is one thing; learning the abstract rules of grammar is another. When Noam Chomsky first voiced his idea that language is hard-wired in the brain, he didn't have the benefit of the current revolution in cognitive science, which has begun to pry open the human mind with sophisticated psychological experiments and new computer models. Until recently, linguists could only parse languages and marvel at how quickly children master their abstract rules, which give every human being who can speak (or sign) the power to express an infinite number of ideas from a finite number of words.

There also are a finite number of ways that languages construct sentences. As Chomsky once put it, from a Martian's-eye view, everybody on Earth speaks a single tongue that has thousands of mutually unintelligible dialects. For instance, all people make sentences from noun phrases, like "The quick brown fox," and verb phrases, like "jumped over the fence." And virtually all of the world's 6,000 or so languages allow phrases to be moved around in a sentence to form questions, relative clauses, and passive constructions.

Statistical Wizards

Chomsky posited that children were born knowing these and a handful of other basic laws of language and that

they learn their parents' native tongue with the help of a "language acquisition device," preprogrammed circuits in the brain. Findings like Newport's are suggesting to some researchers that perhaps children can use statistical regularities to extract not only individual words from what they hear but also the rules for cobbling words together into sentences.

This idea is shared by computational linguists, who have designed computer models called artificial neural networks that are very simplified versions of the brain and that can "learn" some aspects of language. Artificial neural networks

Discriminating minds. Toddlers listen for bits of language like the, which signals that a noun will follow. Most 2-year-olds can understand "Find the dog," but they are stumped by "Find gub dog."

mimic the way that nerve cells, or neurons, inside a brain are hooked up. The result is a device that shares some basic properties with the brain and that can accomplish some linguistic feats that real children perform. For example, a neural network can make general categories out of a jumble of words coming in, just as a child learns that certain kinds of words refer to objects while others refer to actions. Nobody has to teach kids that words like *dog* and *telephone* are nouns, while *go* and *jump* are verbs; the way they use such words in sentences demonstrates that they know the difference. Neural networks also can learn some aspects of the meaning of words, and they can infer some rules of syntax, or word order. Therefore, a computer that was fed English sentences would be able to produce a phrase like "Johnny ate fish," rather than "Johnny fish ate," which is correct in Japanese. These computer models even make some of the same mistakes that real children do, says Mark Seidenberg, a computational linguist at the University of Southern California. A neural network designed by a student of Seidenberg's to learn to conjugate verbs sometimes issued sentences like "He jumped me the ball," which any parent will recognize as the kind of error that could have come from the mouths of babes.

But neural networks have yet to come close to the computation power of a toddler. Ninety percent of the sentences uttered by the average 3-year-old are grammatically correct. The mistakes they do make are rarely random but rather the result of following the rules of grammar with excessive zeal. There is no logical reasoning for being able to say, "I batted the ball" but not "I holded the rabbit," except that about 180 of the most commonly used English verbs are conjugated irregularly.

Yet for all of grammar's seeming illogic, toddlers' brains may be able to spot clues in the sentences they hear that help them learn grammatical rules, just as they use statistical regularities to find word boundaries. One such clue is the little bits of language called grammatical morphemes, which among other things tell a listener whether a word is being used as a noun or as a verb. *The*, for instance, signals that a noun

will soon follow, while the suffix *ion* also identifies a word as a noun, as in vibration. Psycholinguist LouAnn Gerken of the University of Arizona recently reported that toddlers know what grammatical morphemes signify before they actually use them. She tested this by asking 2-year-olds a series of questions in which the grammatical morphemes were replaced with other words. When asked to "Find the dog for me," for example, 85 percent of children in her study could point to the right animal in the picture. But when the question was "Find *was* dog for me," they pointed to the dog 55 percent of the time. "Find *gub* dog for me," and it dropped to 40 percent.

Fast Mapping

Children may be noticing grammatical morphemes when they are as young as 10 months and have just begun making connections between words and their definitions. Gerken recently found that infants' brain waves change when they are listening to stories in which grammatical morphemes are replaced with other words, suggesting they begin picking up grammar even before they know what sentences mean.

Such linguistic leaps come as a baby's brain is humming with activity. Within the first few months of life, a baby's neurons will forge 1,000 trillion connections, an increase of 20-fold from birth. Neurobiologists once assumed that the wiring in the baby's brain was set at birth. After that, the brain, like legs and noses, just grew bigger. That view has been demolished, says Anne Fernald, a psycholinguist at Stanford University, "now that we can eavesdrop on the brain." Images made using the brain-scanning technique positron emission tomography have revealed, for instance, that when a baby is 8 or 9 months old, the part of the brain that stores and indexes many kinds of memory becomes fully functional. This is precisely when babies appear to be able to attach meaning to words.

Masters of pattern. Researchers played strings of three-syllable nonsense words to 8-month-old babies for two minutes. The babies learned them by remembering how often syllables occurred together.

Other leaps in a child's linguistic prowess also coincide with remarkable changes in the brain. For instance, an adult listener can recognize *eleph* as *elephant* within about 400 milliseconds, an ability called "fast mapping" that demands that the brain process speech sounds with phenomenal speed. "To understand strings of words, you have to identify individual words rapidly," says Fernald. She and her colleagues have found that around 15 months of age, a child needs more than a second to recognize even a familiar word, like *baby*. At 18 months, the child can get the picture slightly before the word is ending. At 24 months, she knows the word in a mere 600 milliseconds, as soon as the syllable *bay* has been uttered.

Fast mapping takes off at the same moment as a dramatic reorganization of the child's brain, in which language-related operations, particularly grammar, shift from both sides of the brain into the left hemisphere. Most adult brains are lopsided when it comes to language, processing grammar almost entirely in the left temporal lobe, just over the left ear. Infants and toddlers, however, treat language in both hemispheres, according to Debra Mills, at the University of California–San Diego, and Helen Neville, at the University of Oregon. Mills and Neville stuck electrodes to toddlers' heads to find that processing of words that serve special grammatical functions, such as prepositions, conjunctions, and articles, begins to shift into the right side around the end of the third year.

From then on, the two hemispheres assume different job descriptions. The right temporal lobe continues to perform spatial tasks, such as following the trajectory of a baseball and predicting where it will land. It also pays attention to the emotional information contained in the cadence and pitch of speech. Both hemispheres know the meanings of many words, but the left temporal lobe holds the key to grammar.

This division is maintained even when the language is signed, not spoken. Ursula Bellugi and Edward Klima, a wife and husband team at the Salk Institute for Biological Studies in La Jolla, Calif., recently demonstrated this fact by studying deaf people who were lifelong signers of American Sign Language and who also had suffered a stroke in specific areas of the brain. The researchers found, predictably, that signers with damage to the right hemisphere had great difficulty with tasks involving spatial perception, such as copying a drawing of a geometric pattern. What was surprising was that right hemisphere damage did not hinder their fluency in ASL, which relies on movements of the hands and body in space. It was signers with damage to the left hemisphere who found they could no longer express themselves in ASL or understand it. Some had trouble producing the specific facial expressions that convey grammatical information in ASL. It is not just speech that's being processed in the left hemisphere, says MIT's Pinker, "or movements of the mouth, but abstract language."

Nobody knows why the left hemisphere got the job of processing language, but linguists are beginning to surmise that languages are constructed the way they are in part because the human brain is not infinitely capable of all kinds of computation. "We are starting to see how the universals among languages could arise out of constraints on how the brain computes and how children learn," says Johns Hopkins linguist Paul Smolensky. For instance, the vast majority of the world's languages favor syllables that end in a vowel, though English is an exception. (Think of a native Italian speaking English and adding vowels where there are none.) That's because it is easier for the auditory centers of the brain to perceive differences between consonants when they come before a vowel than when they come after. Human brains can easily recognize *pad, bad,* and *dad* as three different words; it is much harder to distinguish *tab, tap,* and *tad.* As languages around the world were evolv-

Strict grammarians. Most 3-year-olds rarely make grammatical errors. When they do, the mistakes they make usually are the result of following the rules of grammar with excessive zeal.

ing, they were pulled along paths that minimize ambiguity among sounds.

Birth of a Language

Linguists have never had the chance to study a spoken language as it is being constructed, but they have been given the opportunity to observe a new sign language in the making in Nicaragua. When the Sandinistas came to power in 1979, they established schools where deaf people came together for the first time. Many of the pupils had never met another deaf person, and their only means of communication at first was the expressive but largely unstructured pantomime each had invented at home with their hearing families. Soon the pupils began to pool their makeshift gestures into a system that is similar to spoken pidgin, the form of communication that springs up in places where people speaking mutually unintelligible tongues come together. The next generation of deaf Nicaraguan children, says Judy Kegl, a psycholinguist at Rutgers University, in Newark, N.J., has done it one better, transforming the pidgin sign into a full-blown language complete with regular grammar. The birth of Nicaraguan sign, many linguists believe, mirrors the evolution of all languages. Without conscious effort, deaf Nicaraguan children have created a sign that is now fluid and compact, and which contains standardized rules that allow them to express abstract ideas without circumlocutions. It can indicate past and future, denote whether an action was performed once or repeatedly, and show who did what to whom, allowing its users to joke, recite poetry, and tell their life stories.

Linguists have a long road ahead of them before they can say exactly how a child goes from babbling to banter, or what the very first languages might have been like, or how the brain transforms vague thoughts into concrete words that sometimes fly out of our mouths before we can stop them. But already, some practical conclusions are falling out of the

new research. For example, two recent studies show that the size of toddlers' vocabularies depends in large measure on how much their mothers talk to them. At 20 months, according to a study by Janellen Huttenlocher of the University of Chicago, the children of talkative mothers had 131 more words in their vocabularies than children whose mothers were more taciturn. By age 2, the gap had widened to 295 words.

In other words, children need input and they need it early, says Newport. Parking a toddler in front of the television won't improve vocabulary, probably because kids need real human interaction to attach meaning to words. Hearing more than one language in infancy makes it easier for a child to hear the distinctions between phonemes of more than one language later on.

Newport and other linguists have discovered in recent years that the window of opportunity for acquiring language begins to close around age 6, and the gap narrows with each additional candle on the birthday cake. Children who do not learn a language by puberty will never be fluent in any tongue. That means that profoundly deaf children should be exposed to sign language as early as possible, says Newport. If their parents are hearing, they should learn to sign. And schools might rethink the practice of waiting to teach a foreign language until kids are nearly grown and the window on native command of a second language is almost shut.

Linguists don't yet know how much of grammar children are able to absorb simply by listening. And they have only begun to parse the genes or accidents of brain wiring that might give rise, as Pinker puts it, to the poet, the raconteur, or an Alexander Haig, a Mrs. Malaprop. What is certain is that language is one of the great wonders of the natural world, and linguists are still being astonished by its complexity and its power to shape the brain. Human beings, says Kegl, "show an incredible enthusiasm for discourse." Maybe what is most innate about language is the passion to communicate.

Article Review Form at end of book.

How do the two literacy projects reviewed in the article vary? How can family literacy programs ensure that they are working to meet the four key factors of effectiveness?

Family Literacy

Examining practice and issues of effectiveness

Here is a study for the U.S. National Center on Adult Literacy that identified a variety of family literacy programs in Michigan. Programs were examined to show how they adapt their practice to their participants' special needs. Two sample cases are discussed.

Andrea DeBruin-Parecki
Scott G. Paris
Jennifer Siedenberg

DeBruin-Parecki is a doctoral candidate in the Combined Program in Education and Psychology at the University of Michigan (1406 School of Education Building, 610E University Avenue, Ann Arbor, MI 48109-1259, USA). Paris teaches and Siedenberg is a research assistant at the same university. The authors wish to thank Michelle Everett for her help with this article.

Poverty, illiteracy, poor education, and social risks are intercorrelated problems in the U.S. According to the National Adult Literacy Survey (Kirsch, Jungeblut, Jenkins, & Kolstad, 1993), the majority of adults who demonstrated literacy skills in the lowest levels of proficiency were living in poverty. Research has shown that children in these homes are less likely to enter school prepared to learn and are more likely to drop out before they complete high school (Edwards, 1995; Fine, 1991;

Heath, 1983). Higher levels of adult education have a positive impact on both the income level and the educational future of the children in a family. Education may be instrumental for improving the lives of impoverished people; however, it has not been a panacea for many who, rebuffed by past school failure, do not regard further education as a solution to their problems.

During the past decade, policy makers, educators, and business people at the national, state, and local levels have explored ways to make adult education programs more meaningful and useful to adults and their children. A common goal of these diverse endeavors has been to strengthen the skills that parents need to enhance a family's learning experiences and to improve their children's success in school (*Congressional Oversight Hearing*, 1992; Darling, 1988). The emphasis on family resources as a pathway to remedy low literacy skills and academic problems led to the creation of innovative family literacy programs that promote intergenerational learning activities.

Although widely endorsed by policy makers and educators, the field of family literacy is struggling to define its goals and practices. A single description of family literacy is not possible because each program must adapt its goals and services to the population it serves. Family literacy professionals seeking to design flexible, culturally responsive, and effective programs can turn to concepts derived from theories in adult literacy, emergent literacy, developmental psychology, multiculturalism, and social justice, as well as to the growing body of research being done in the field itself for assistance in planning. Direct collaboration with clients and community members helps to ensure the goals of the program match those of the populations served. Morrow, Paratore, and Tracey (1994), in an attempt to describe family literacy, stated:

Family Literacy encompasses the ways parents, children, and extended family members use literacy at home and in their community. Sometimes, Family Literacy occurs naturally during routines of daily living and helps adults and children get things done. . . . Family Literacy may be

DeBruin-Parecki, Andrea, Paris, Scott G., and Siedenberg, Jennifer. (1997, May). Family literacy: Examining practice and issues of effectiveness. *Journal of Adolescent & Adult Literacy*, 40(8), 596–605. Reprinted with permission of Andrea DeBruin-Parecki and the International Reading Association. All rights reserved.

initiated purposefully by a parent or may occur spontaneously as parents and children go about the business of their daily lives. Family Literacy activities may also reflect the ethnic, racial, or cultural heritage of the families involved.

This description reveals how family literacy programs are adapted to diverse family characteristics, but does not describe instructional components. Most family literacy programs include adult education, early childhood education, and parenting components, as well as some type of interactive literacy component for families (Darling, 1988; St. Pierre et al., 1995). How these components are envisioned and enacted depends on many issues and varies widely across programs.

Many researchers, administrators, teachers, and policy makers believe that an integrated approach to family literacy that balances mainstream educational skills, cultural sensitivity, bilingual education for nonnative speakers, collaborative learning and teaching, and family support is the key to establishing successful programs (Auerbach, 1989, 1995a, 1995b; Gadsden, 1992, 1994; Morrow, 1995; Weinstein-Shr, 1993, 1995). Programs that have become elaborate systems that offer more than just the teaching of reading and writing appear to be more successful than those with a strict literacy emphasis.

In addition to skills instruction, issues of access, child care, transportation, community and cultural orientation, and personal meaningfulness are considered in these programs. However, these programs often develop without a coherent vision that integrates program goals, instructional practices, assessment methods, staff training, and social support for participants. This makes it difficult to assess the effectiveness of existing programs and to assist new programs as they search for ways to implement family literacy.

Michigan Family Literacy Research

The purpose of this study was to examine the broad range of family literacy programs throughout Michigan, a state selected for the cultural diversity of the population, the wide variety of rural, urban, and suburban settings, and a long-term historical involvement with adult literacy instruction, which has taken place outside of traditional school settings. The goals of this project were to identify and describe existing family literacy programs throughout the state in order to: (a) distribute a comprehensive list of statewide services that could inform and assist participants, practitioners, and administrators in locating needed information; (b) document how goals, instructional practices, assessment methods, staff training, collaboration with surrounding community agencies, and social support for participants varied across different programs; and (c) identify critical factors of effective programs.

Approximately 700 literacy programs in Michigan were telephoned or mailed surveys to determine if they could be classified as family literacy programs. We found these programs by examining lists from organizations such as Even Start and Head Start and by contacting public libraries, school systems, Literacy Volunteers of America, churches, and community centers. Although family literacy programs can have many components, programs we focused on had to include an interactive literacy component between children and parents.

According to our criteria, 50 of the 700 contacted programs were categorized as family literacy programs and more detailed information on their structure, curricula, target population, and philosophy was obtained by telephone interviews. These data were organized according to program location (rural, urban, suburban), population characteristics (e.g., ethnicity, gender), size, use of specific models and funding sources, goals, instructional practices, assessment methods, staff training, collaboration with surrounding community agencies, and social support for participants.

From this information, a representative sample of 11 family literacy programs was chosen for in-depth study based on variation across these key characteristics. During planned visits to all of these 11 programs, administrators, participants, and teachers were interviewed, classes were observed, and survey information was collected. The combination of these data sources provided information for descriptive case studies that demonstrate both the commonalities and differences among programs. Examination of these 11 cases illustrated multiple interpretations of family literacy and revealed critical attributes of effective programs.

Case studies of two family literacy programs will be presented here to demonstrate how these attributes are implemented in very differing circumstances. The first program adapted a nationally recognized model, whereas the second one is a community-based program, which developed its own model.

Maple Tree Even Start

Maple Tree Even Start program is located in a suburb of Detroit where it primarily serves a population of Chaldean-speaking women and their children who have immigrated from Iraq. It was established in the spring of 1991 and emphasizes training in English as a Second Language (ESL) in order to meet the needs of the community. Currently, the program has day classes operating at three local elementary schools and offers an additional home visiting component. Those involved advocate improving the educational level of the whole family and support Even Start's general philosophy that "Parents are the child's first teacher" (McKee & Rhett, 1995).

Maple Tree Even Start employs one director, two half-time coordinators who are also half-time teachers, one full-time preschool teacher, one full-time adult education/parent teacher, three preschool aides and one full-time bilingual aide. All are women and all are Caucasian with the exception of the bilingual aide, who is of Middle Eastern descent. They range in age from early 30s to mid 40s. Each has her own area of expertise within the field of education as reflected in her educational degrees and experience.

This program has served as many as 186 parents and children per year. Participants are primarily young mothers with low levels of education who have not yet obtained their high school diplomas. The majority of these mothers do not use

English as a first language, and they lack the conventional literacy skills needed for daily activities. Most of the participants come from low-income families and receive some form of government assistance. To be eligible for enrollment as specified by national Even Start guidelines, participants must qualify for adult basic education services and must have a child under the age of 8.

Maple Tree Even Start classes are held 4 days a week for 2½ hours. Transportation is provided for those in need, as is child care for children too young to participate. Lunch is often served. The average parent class size ranges from 15 to 20 participants with a similar number in the children's classes. In addition to the center-based classes, staff also visit the families at home once or twice a month to provide additional support and literacy instruction for both adult and child. A certified teacher and a paraprofessional visit the home with materials and activities that promote skill development of the child, encourage parent/child interaction, and teach basic skills appropriate to the subject and level the adult is trying to improve.

The program's curriculum follows the Kenan Family Literacy Model, which was initiated in 1986 when the Kentucky Legislature funded the Parents and Child Education (PACE) program in six rural counties throughout the state. Because of the program's early success in raising families' literacy skills and self-esteem, the William R. Kenan, Jr. Charitable Trust funded a large grant to be used to expand the existing program. In 1989, in response to the national recognition given to the newly modified PACE model, now called the Kenan Family Literacy Model, the National Center for Family Literacy was established with funds from the Kenan Trust. This center was charged with continually improving this model and disseminating information about family literacy across the U.S., thus providing programs such as Maple Tree with a workable framework to follow (Brizius & Foster, 1993; Seaman, Popp, & Darling, 1991).

The Kenan model addresses the broad areas that are important within an integrative family literacy program. However, much of the time is

spent on separate activities for adults and children with interactive time representing only a small portion of the suggested plan. Programs such as Maple Tree are usually left on their own to design curricula within the four large components or to find ready-made instructional plans to borrow. This is not easy for many new programs to accomplish. The National Center for Family Literacy does attempt to provide training and support for programs, but even within this training there is little opportunity for program personnel to gain direct knowledge of curriculum or assessment design.

The Kenan Family Literacy Model is based on a curriculum that includes four key components: adult education, parenting support, early childhood education, and interactive parent-child activities. All of these components are present in the Maple Tree Even Start Program. Adult education classes in which parents spend 6 hours a week are geared toward passing the General Educational Development (GED) test, job employability skills, and/or ESL improvement. The instructional program promotes adult literacy through individualized educational plans established for each participant through testing, observation, and parent assessment forms. Practical and achievable goals are set and reset throughout the year to meet the adults' individual needs. Group instruction, one-on-one teaching, flashcards, independent study, and computerized instruction are among the variety of methods used during this time.

The Maple Tree program bases the parenting support component of the Kenan model on the Bowdoin Method Parenting Course (Bowdoin, 1993) which focuses on the skills parents need to help their children with school readiness. Parents participate for 4 hours a week in this component, which includes viewing videos, reading parenting skills books, and participating in educational activities that focus on both cognitive and affective skills in parenting. Other aspects of parent education at the Maple Tree program include a 6-week nutrition course, expert speakers discussing health and environmental issues, and a free "make-and-take" children's game workshop.

While the parents attend their adult classes, the children are in a supervised preschool room participating in readiness activities to help prepare them for school. The children are assessed by standardized tests when they enter the program and teachers use this information along with their observations and knowledge of age-appropriate skills to plan individual and small-group activities that extend what the children already know. Because the majority of the participants are nonnative speakers, the results of standardized tests are not always useful, but are required by funders. A whole-language/thematic approach is used in the preschool classroom where a creative, organized curriculum revolves around a central theme, with an emphasis on play and hands-on activities.

The final component of Maple Tree Even Start is the Parents and Children Together (PACT) interaction time where parents actively support and participate in the education of their children. For a total of 2½ hours a week, adults and children come into the preschool room to work together on a child-selected activity, such as painting or playing with manipulatives. PACT time may also involve group storytelling sessions that often focus on a theme being used in both the child and adult classrooms. Supportive ways of reading are modeled to the parent during this time and emphasis is placed on the importance of interactive reading, asking questions, and having children reread the stories. Parents and children are then given time to read together. In addition, family field trips are often taken to places such as the zoo or library.

Assessment for the Maple Tree Even Start program includes pre, post, and ongoing evaluation of participants' progress. During the time this study was initiated, the Comprehensive Adult Student Assessment System (CASAS, 1980–93), given to obtain the participants' reading levels, was required, as was the Botel Reading Inventory (BRI, 1961–70) and/or the Adult Basic Learning Examination, second edition (ABLE II, 1986–90), which was administered to adults to assess grade levels in reading, math, and specific living skills.

Adult students with limited English skills were also tested on the Basic English Skills Test (BEST, 1982–88) to determine a beginner, intermediate, or advanced level of study. Currently, due to changes in requirements, the BEST and Tests of Adult Basic Education (TABE, 1987–94) are being given. Informal assessments for adults include interviews and journal writing.

The children are evaluated with the Brigance Diagnostic Inventory of Early Development—Revised (IED–R, 1978–91) to ascertain the appropriate focus for educational activities. The children are also tested with the Preschool Inventory (PSI, 1965–91) for any major developmental delays and were formerly tested with the Peabody Picture Vocabulary Test—Revised (PPVT–R, 1959–84) to determine receptive vocabulary. In addition, portfolios are beginning to be used to document the educational and developmental progress of each child involved in the program.

Perhaps due to language issues, results of all of these tests have been poor for adults and children and have not shown significant changes. Anecdotal reports gathered from personal and telephone interviews, however, indicated that parents felt that they had benefited from participation, as had their children. The parents' fluency in English, their reading skills, and the amount of time they spent around literacy activities with their children greatly improved. This program has had much difficulty demonstrating its success through traditional means and seeks to find more authentic methods of assessment, which can more easily demonstrate the progress participants report.

Maple Tree's strongest collaborative effort in support of family education is with the Job Training Partnership Act (JTPA). Even Start adult participants attend JTPA's computer lab 2 days a week where they work on improving their skills in academic areas for their GED, along with learning computer and job skills. A bilingual aide works in both Even Start and JTPA to help foster communication between staff, participants, and their families. JTPA recognizes that participants are literate in their own cultures and uses these literacy abilities through computer programs

that accommodate the Arabic dialect. Participants use the program to create newsletters distributed in both English and Arabic to students, their families, and other community members. In addition, a family literacy component is incorporated into JTPA by using software that teaches adult participants vocabulary that corresponds to the vocabulary used in a children's book series. These books are available for the adults to take home and read with their children.

In a further attempt at enriching the program, Maple Tree Even Start has also reached out to the surrounding community in various cooperative efforts. They coordinate their recruitment advertising efforts with Head Start and collaborate on several parenting programs. Connections with local health agencies and hospitals permit them to bring in qualified speakers to discuss important medical and hygiene issues. A cooperative program with the public library allows parents to visit the library regularly and learn how to select books for their children. The program has further involved itself with many social agencies by making cross-references.

Maple Tree Even Start provides a comprehensive program that is informed in part by participants' cultural backgrounds. Program administrators and teachers feel that they still must continue to learn more about their clients' unique culture in order to address their needs sensitively. There is also a pressing demand for the creation of additional bilingual materials, more authentic means of assessment, and better communication between parents and teachers. In general, the staff would like to create more of their own curricula, to design more authentic evaluations, and to find ways in which to blend their individual areas of expertise to enrich the family component of the program.

Christian Outreach Center

The Christian Outreach Center has for many years been in the process of actively developing a family literacy program to prepare children for school success by promoting family involvement. The center is located in

an impoverished neighborhood that has a high incidence of crime, violence, and drug abuse. Low-income African Americans constitute over three fourths of the people in the community and there is a high predominance of single-parent, female-headed households. The students who attend the local elementary school across the street from the center have the lowest standardized test scores in the city.

The center was established in 1988 in a former church facility to provide one-on-one literacy tutoring for adults. Transportation and child care, as well as lunch or dinner, are always provided if desired. This adult literacy component was soon expanded to include an after-school program for children and teenagers where they could receive help with their schoolwork and learn new skills on the computers that were added to supplement both the adult and child literacy programs.

Food is always available after school, and children may be dropped off by school buses. In response to the community need for assistance in learning how to help their children get ready to attend school, the Christian Outreach Center also began a Reading Partners program. Here, preschool children and their mothers attend a storytelling session where effective reading strategies are modeled as the story is told.

Another unique effort to promote family literacy was established on the basketball court. Basketball Literacy targets fathers and their children by providing recreational activities on an indoor basketball court on Saturday mornings, as well as offering reading assistance and a wide selection of literacy activities and books for fathers to read to their children during their time off the court.

The popularity of this program has spawned a teenage version several evenings a week. Both girls and boys are able to remain in the center and play as long as they spend their time off court engaged in one of the many supervised literacy activities available to them, such as individual tutoring, operating computers, or watching educational videos. This innovative program provides a safe haven in a violent area and a chance for teenagers to have positive experiences with literacy activities.

Hundreds of adults, children, and families have been served here.

There are four paid members on the center staff associated with family literacy. There are three females—two Caucasian, one African American—and one African American male, ranging in age from early 30s to mid 40s. Their positions are as follows: Adult/Family Literacy Administrator (who oversees the entire program), Youth Coordinator (who is in charge of parent/child interaction centering around books, tapes, and videos, as well as the after-school and Basketball Literacy programs), Child Coordinator (who assists with child care issues, arranges story times, and devises thematically based hands-on activities and crafts for the preschool child/parent program), and Computer Coordinator (a Volunteer in Service to America worker who supervises activities in the lab and instructs participants in learning computer skills and in the use of specific math and language arts computer programs).

The staff has had to learn a great deal about literacy and families as the program evolved. Although they all have a minimum of a bachelor's degree, their educational backgrounds did not necessarily prepare them for their positions. However, even without a background in education, the Youth Coordinator, having been raised in a similar neighborhood, has excellent rapport with the teenagers and young adults.

The center recently received a matching grant. This allowed the board of directors, administrators, and teachers to expand the family literacy program and concentrate more on bringing parents and their children together in activities revolving around literacy and mathematics. The design of a new program that focused on interaction between preschool children and their parents was planned collaboratively and the curriculum was borrowed from a variety of sources. Along with the creation of this program, a mission statement was authored that reads: "The purpose of our focus on family literacy is to provide a flexible program for building reading and math skills through involving parents with children in the learning process." To

begin to accomplish this goal, 16 dyads of adults and children were scheduled to attend classes twice a week for 3-hour sessions over a 10-week period.

Because the staff had limited resources and were unfamiliar with particular early childhood curricula, they decided to base their family literacy instruction on age-appropriate math and literacy computer software that was already in their possession. They had originally found this software in an educational catalog.

The participants are divided into four groups, with one working on literacy activities on the computer, another with the print and tape versions, a third with a related hands-on activity, and the fourth working on separate computer math programs. There are multiple components within the literacy software that allow the staff to build literacy activities based on the included stories. Each week a story with a particular theme is used. The stories allow for individual input and are represented in three versions: computer, print, and tape. This weekly theme is extended into a hands-on activity. Parents help guide their children in all activities. In addition, parents receive educational handouts and take home activities centered on the theme of the week.

The computer curriculum begins to provide instruction in the skills children need to master before entering school. Additional noncomputer activities focus on skill building in the areas of drawing, writing, and cutting while familiarizing children with shapes, numbers, colors, and letters. Storytellers from the local library present culturally diverse books and songs and involve children and parents interactively in music, literature, and dance. Assessment is virtually nonexistent. Observations and volunteered work samples provide some idea of child and adult progress in this part of the program, but it is clearly not well organized. A collection of adults' and children's work is beginning to be placed in portfolios in an attempt to study progress. This collection of work is not systematic. The Christian Center is more interested in promoting literacy as an important and enjoyable activity than in judging

families and perhaps causing them unnecessary discomfort, resulting in their departure.

The computer is also used to assist adults and teenagers in improving their literacy skills through a variety of individual programs. In addition, one-on-one tutoring is available from volunteers who generally follow the curricula prescribed by the Literacy Volunteers of America. Assessment of adults is informal in most cases and serves only to assist the tutors and computer coordinator in determining where to begin instruction and how to proceed. Many of the program's adults have an aversion to school-like assessments due to low self-esteem and possibly to bad experiences in the public school system. When adults without high school degrees appear to be ready (as seen through observation and informal assessment), if they are willing they are referred to local agencies that sponsor GED classes.

The Christian Outreach Center makes a great effort to support members of the community in need of assistance. It obtains many referrals from a nearby drug rehabilitation program, from the court system, and from mailings to several social agencies. The center's affiliation with a large Christian church provides a large portion of its funding as well as many volunteer tutors for its one-on-one literacy instruction and after-school programs. It has also established many outside contacts and through these can refer participants for job training and GED skills classes. In addition, the center has a liaison with a prominent local children's hospital. The Center hopes that collaboration with this hospital will result in the design of an effective parenting component to supplement the existing family literacy activities.

Christian Outreach Center aims to assist families in improving their lives in ways that are congruent with their expressed needs and goals. The family literacy program is being implemented to build the bond between the child and the parent while improving adult literacy skills and preparing children for more successful academic and social experiences in the school environment. Center workers need more knowledge about emergent literacy, adult education methods, and systematic means of assessment. However, even with these needs, they are still able to serve the neighborhood by providing a safe and educational environment for community members, helping adults build basic skills, and assisting parents in preparing their young children for school.

Four Key Factors

The people involved in each of the two programs presented here consider their programs to be effective in their community. They pride themselves on high attendance. Maple Tree Even Start is concerned, however, because the same families attend regularly and it is often hard to reach others in the community. The Christian Outreach Program personnel, while hoping for stability, feel strongly that touching the lives of many if even briefly is most beneficial to families. Effectiveness of family literacy programs is very difficult to judge due to the different purposes they serve for their clients. Recognizing that not all programs need to possess the same traits to be successful in their surroundings, we identified four comprehensive factors that are linked with program effectiveness.

Our examination of six features (goals, instructional practices, assessment methods, staff training, collaboration with surrounding agencies, and social support for participants) within 11 representative programs revealed four critical and comprehensive factors that need to be considered when attempting to design effective Family Literacy programs.

Participation

The first factor revolves around participation. To achieve some form of success, programs need to enable increased access and participation by reducing physical barriers such as transportation and child care, by negotiating emotional barriers such as fear of school and low self-esteem, and by recognizing, incorporating, and respecting cultural and familial differences. Close connections to the community and a well integrated referral system are also of major impor-

tance. Families have to be able to survive and carry on day-to-day living before literacy can become important to them. Many families served are unable to stay in one place for a long period for many reasons; the chief among these is poverty. Every attempt should be made to serve families for as long as they are able to participate, and to try to help them find stability in their community so that they can continue in the program.

Curriculum

The second factor focuses on curriculum, which best serves clients when it is meaningful and useful in their lives. Program components should be balanced and include a significant amount of time spent on age-interactive literacy activities, which include good instruction and modeling. An emphasis on understanding family and child development and providing developmentally appropriate materials should occur. Curriculum is best when it increases self-efficacy through successful learning experiences, and builds bridges between parents, teachers, and children, as well as between home and school.

Prepackaged curricula that are not easily modified or curricula designed without theoretical backing are poor choices. Collaboratively designed, theoretically sound curricula that can clearly be modified for individual, cultural, and program differences and objectives are a better choice for promoting learning. To show progress of participants, programs need assessment that is matched to curriculum as opposed to that which is disconnected or irrelevant to participants' lives. Self-reflection is a key component of such assessment methods.

Staff and Administration

The third critical issue centers on staff and administration. An effective family literacy program is made up of a stable, collaborative staff with varied credentials in fields that may include adult education, early childhood education, elementary education, community education, social work, and educational administration. Expertise is also needed from

the community at large, as well as the participants. The key is collaboration. Staff are most successful in assisting participants when they are willing to collaborate with other staff, blend their expertise with that of others, and work directly with clients to help them to meet their own goals. Staff training is important and should consist of more than theory and introductions to assessment instruments and curricula. It should also include learning about the population being served, not only from text but also by communicating with participants and neighborhood leaders and agencies.

Fund-Raising

The fourth critical issue is funding. Programs always seem to be scrambling for funds (often unstable), which is a highly competitive pursuit. Most large funders require complex grant applications, and many smaller programs do not have the expertise to write them or the funds to hire someone to do it for them. This puts them at a distinct disadvantage. Funders also have specific criteria for renewed funding that revolve around evaluative outcomes. Programs often have great difficulty showing what to them is obvious progress. Unstable funding also affects staff who, unsure of when their job may end, become uninvested and constantly look for more stable employment. Programs with little capital are not able to provide the amalgam of services needed or to purchase appropriate materials and books. It is not encouraging to community members to have programs appear and disappear, making promises they are unable to keep.

In conclusion, the four factors discussed provide a broad overview of the critical issues that most influence the effectiveness of family literacy programs. The field of family literacy is changing rapidly. It needs theory, research, cultural and community participation, and knowledge to guide services and practices. A greater integration of emergent literacy and adult literacy is needed to make practices interactive and intergenerational. Curricula have to be carefully designed to be individualized and goal oriented, meaningful, and relevant to participants' lives.

Programs need authentic, process-oriented assessments that are outcome based and reflect progress accurately. Staff must collaborate and gain knowledge beyond academe, becoming invested in and enlightened about the populations they serve. Because family literacy programs influence more than conventional literacy skills, program staffers also have to consider a wide range of client needs in order to help clients reach their goals and improve their lives.

References

Auerbach, E.R. (1989). Toward a social-contextual approach to family literacy. *Harvard Educational Review*, 59, 165–187.

Auerbach, E. (1995a). Deconstructing the discourse of strengths in family literacy. *Journal of Reading Behavior*, 27, 643–661.

Auerbach, E.R. (1995b). Which way for family literacy: Intervention or empowerment? In L. M. Morrow (Ed.), *Family Literacy: Connections in schools and communities* (pp. 11–18). Newark, DE: International Reading Association.

Bowdoin, R. (1993). *Bowdoin method I manual.* Brentwood, TN: Webster's International.

Brizius, J.A., & Foster, S. A. (1993). *Generation to generation: Realizing the promise of family literacy.* Ypsilanti, MI: High Scope Press.

Congressional Oversight Hearing on the Even Start Program: Hearing before the Subcommittee on Elementary, Secondary, and Vocational Education of the Committee on Education, Labor, House of Representatives, 102d Cong., 2d sess. Serial no. 102–136. (1992).

Darling, S. (1988). *Family Literacy: Replacing the cycle of failure with the legacy of success: Evaluation report of the Kenan Trust Family Literacy Project.* Louisville, KY: Kenan Trust. (ERIC Document Reproduction Service No. ED 332 794)

Edwards, P.A. (1995). Connecting African-American parents and youth to the schools reading curriculum: Its meaning for school and community literacy. In V. L. Gadsden & D. A. Wagner (Eds.), *Literacy among African-American youth: Issues in learning, teaching, and schooling* (pp. 261–280). Cresskill, NJ: Hampton Press.

Fine, M. (1991). *Framing dropouts: Notes on the politics of an urban public high school.* Albany, NY: SUNY Press.

Gadsden, V.L. (1992). Giving meaning to literacy: Intergenerational beliefs about access. *Theory Into Practice*, 31, 328–336.

Gadsden, V.L. (1994). Understanding family literacy: Conceptual issues facing the field. *Teachers' College Record*, 96, 58–86.

Heath, S.B. (1983). *Ways with words: Language, life and work in communities and classrooms.* Cambridge, England: Cambridge University Press.

Kirsch, I.S., Jungeblut, A., Jenkins, L., & Kolstad, A. (1993). *Adult literacy in America: National Adult Literacy Survey.* Princeton, NJ: Educational Testing Service.

McKee, P.A., & Rhett, N. (1995). The Even Start family literacy program. In L. M. Morrow (Ed.), *Family literacy: Connections in schools and communities* (pp. 155–166). Newark, DE: International Reading Association.

Morrow, L.M. (1995). *Family literacy: Connections in schools and communities.* Newark, DE: International Reading Association.

Morrow, L.M., Paratore, J. R., & Tracey, D. H. (1994). *Family literacy: New perspectives, new opportunities.* Newark, DE: International Reading Association.

Seaman, D., Popp, R., & Darling, S. (1991). *Follow-up study of the impact of the Kenan Trust Model for Family Literacy* (Report No. PS 020180). Louisville, KY: National Center for Family Literacy. (ERIC Document Reproduction Service No. ED 340 479)

St. Pierre, R., Swartz, J., Gamse, B., Murray, S., Deck, D., & Nickel, P. (1995). *National evaluation of the Even Start Family Literacy Program Final Report.* Washington, DC: U.S. Department of Education. (ERIC Document Reproduction Service No. ED 386 328)

Weinstein-Shr, G. (1993). *Restoring the intergenerational cycle of family teaching: Family literacy in multilingual communities.* Washington, DC: Southport Institute for Policy Analysis. (ERIC Document Reproduction Service No. ED 373 604)

Weinstein-Shr, G. (1995). Learning from uprooted families. In G. Weinstein & E. Quintero (Eds.), *Immigrant learners and their families: Literacy to connect the generations* (pp. 113–133). McHenry, IL: Delta Systems.

 Article Review Form at end of book.

Discuss the definition of *balanced reading* and indicate several recommendations for practice based on each viewpoint. How do the discussions about balanced reading fit into the larger issues associated with reading instruction?

Balanced Instruction

Insights and considerations

Penny A. Freppon

University of Cincinnati, Ohio, USA

Karin L. Dahl

Ohio State University, Columbus, Ohio, USA

Balanced instruction, with its emphasis on elementary and beginning reading, has gained considerable media attention and is of interest to many teachers and literacy researchers. To describe balanced instruction and its classroom implications requires identifying the relevant scholarly works. For the most part, information on balanced instruction itself is not yet in research reports. Instead, specific versions of balanced instruction are described in books in which the authors cite various supportive bodies of research. . . .

In this article we present some of these conceptions of balanced instruction, provide information about the research and theory supporting each one, and describe some of the practical implications for classroom practice. We include recent books about balanced instruction and manuscripts that are in press as well as two state reports. . . .

To clarify and do justice to the breadth of information on balanced instruction and its implications for classroom practice, we include interview information. In addition to interviewing the authors of selected works, we also interviewed teacher educators and teachers. Prior to interviewing these people we interviewed practicing teachers in our classes, asking them the same questions in order to gain more insight into balanced instruction from teachers' perspectives. The interview discussions we present broaden the information base on balanced instruction, sharpen the focus on issues, and help connect this article to classroom practice.

In the preparation of this article we monitored the rising tide of messages flowing from the media and e-mail networks. We found a great deal of political proclaiming about balanced instruction. . . . We include some of what is political about balanced instruction in this article because it was not possible to exclude it and do justice to the topic. Classroom practice is always subjected to political pressures. At this time and in specific places, the wave of media interest about balanced instruction significantly impacts many teachers' and teacher educators' lives.

The California Reform: Defining Two Distinct Instructional Strands for Literacy

The discussion about balanced instruction seems to have gained wide attention with a perceived crisis in the state of California and the resulting reports: *Every Child a Reader* (California Department of Education, 1995) and *Teaching Reading: A Balanced Comprehensive Approach to Teaching Reading in Prekindergarten Through Grade Three* (California Department of Education, 1996). Much from these reports is included in Bill Honig's (1996) *Teaching Our Children to Read: The Role of Skills in a Comprehensive Reading Program.* . . .

Honig's (1996) book and these reports stressed that a balanced reading program provides separate, explicit skill instruction and language-rich literature instruction. Honig described daily instruction that provides 1 hour of directly teaching letter-sound correspondences, practicing previously taught material in texts with familiar word patterns, and working on words and spelling. An additional 1-hour period is to be set aside for instruction in

Adapted from Freppon, Penny A., and Dahl, Karin L. (1998, Apr/May/Jun). Balanced instruction: Insights and considerations. *Reading Research Quarterly*, 33(2), 240–251. Reprinted with permission of Penny Freppon and the International Reading Association. All rights reserved.

shared reading, reading children's literature, reader response interactions, and the teaching of writing.

The point of this balanced instruction reading program is to achieve the general goal of independent reading by mid-first grade through the two distinct strands of instruction. This program expresses the need for flexible instruction based on individual needs, separate systematic phonics, and appropriate early intervention. There is a focus on the primary grades, especially first grade; specific recommended levels of skill development by grade level, and a stated need for rich language teaching. . . .

All three volumes stated that (a) research has produced the framework for a comprehensive reading program that will succeed, and (b) reading comprehension and higher order thinking depend on early alphabetic and word knowledge acquisition. Good classroom practice requires knowing each child's skill attainment and assuring that children receive what is necessary to achieve recommended specific progress within the described specific time frame. For example, key benchmarks include (a) acquiring basic phonemic awareness at mid-K, (b) decoding simple *cvc* words at mid-first grade, followed by *ccvc* and long vowels; and (c) reading and understanding grade-appropriate material at the end of first grade. In an interview, Honig (personal communication, May 29, 1997) elaborated on his conception of balanced instruction:

Meaning (in reading) comes from both the concept behind the word and from stringing those words together. Word recognition is an automatic system in which readers scan virtually every word and each letter in words. Beginning students need to recognize 19 out of 20 words in most materials so they can think about what they are reading.

The key instructional question is how readers become automatic with a growing number of words. Since letters are stored in one part of the brain, the sounds in another, and the meaning of the word in a third [part of the brain], readers need to connect these parts when first reading a word. That is why the tool of sounding out words or decoding is so predictive of reading success. Sounding out by definition connects letters and sounds with meaning of the word in beginning readers.

Almost all children will be accelerated by explaining how the system works, and all children need to be evaluated to see if they actually know it or have just memorized words. Most children should have this tool by mid-first grade.

The implications for classroom practice from Honig included the following points:

- Phonics and word knowledge are prerequisites to successful reading.

- Each grade level has specific skill components that should be taught.

- Use decodable texts for teaching phonics; use other, predictable texts for motivating children, teaching the concept of a word, and teaching other concepts of print.

- Continually diagnose and work with children who are learning the same concepts and have whole-class and small-group activities.

Connecting Culture, Motivation, and Skills in Balanced Instruction

In their new book, *Balanced Literacy Instruction: A Teacher's Resource Book* (in press), Kathryn Au, Jacquelyn Carroll, and Judith Scheu followed principles of balanced instruction set down by Dorothy Strickland. These educators have consistently focused on minority children and demonstrated a strong concern for building home, community, and school connections for at-risk children. . . .

Skills and skill instruction in phonics, decoding, and vocabulary building are discussed extensively. For example, in early phonics instruction, children are taught to compare unknown words to known words and to work with onsets and rimes as much as possible. Instruction is shaped according to children's development in alphabetic learning through a whole-part-whole routine. Au et al. (in press) addressed the problems of struggling learners through a workshop approach. Each year teachers can expect to encounter some children in need of more support. Specific advice is provided on getting these children into conven-

tional reading as soon as possible. Au (personal communication, April 14, 1997) elaborated on some of these and other issues in the following interview excerpt:

Of course, there are many issues [in balanced instruction]. But given my interests, the key issues have to do with the successful literacy instruction of students of diverse backgrounds. I'm convinced that we cannot be successful with these students if they do not first see the reasons for becoming literate. First, they must fall in love with books and, as Lucy Calkins puts it, they must write from the heart. Then they can see the point of skill instruction.

I find it distressing to read in the popular press that phonics instruction is supposed to lay the foundation for reading. This prevalent but misguided notion ignores 20 years of research on emergent literacy that clearly demonstrates the priority of functions of literacy over forms (sounds, letters, mechanics) in young children's development.

It's a long story, but I am convinced after our last 5 years of research at KEEP (Au & Carroll, 1997) that word identification is simply not the main problem. The danger, as I see it, is that an overemphasis on word identification will result in students of diverse backgrounds being denied opportunities to acquire the full processes of reading and writing. They end up as poor readers and writers with a bunch of isolated skills, while other students become good readers and writers, able to read with appreciation and understanding and to write movingly and convincingly.

The Au et al. text on balanced instruction includes specific suggestions for practice. This practice holds that in becoming literate, students' ownership (the value children place on and feelings they have for reading and writing), reading comprehension, the writing process, and skills are critical. Some recommendations for practice include the following:

- Achieving a balance in literacy instruction involves a process of exploring pros and cons, with no expectations for a recipe that can be followed.

- Acknowledging the tensions between the set curriculum, and the students' needs or interests.

- Referring to the set curriculum but not feeling obligated to teach skills in exact order given.

- Establishing structures for teaching small groups, the whole class, and individual children.

- Emphasizing change and growth in reading and writing workshops and decreasing normed testing.

Contrasting Models and Discussions: Balanced Instruction Texts for Teachers

California teacher educator Gail Tompkins has written a 1997 textbook, *Literacy for the 21st Century: A Balanced Approach,* specifically for beginning teachers. . . .

Tompkins's preface expressed her concerns about literacy as a controversial topic that may lead researchers, parents, and teachers to tout and defend one instructional approach after another. She adopted the term *balance* as the best one to describe her theoretical stance on integrating the language arts with a focus on children's literature. Tompkins contended that alphabetic knowledge and phonics skills arise both as a prerequisite for, and a consequence of, learning to read. She made very specific recommendations for practice:

- High-utility phonics concepts (e.g., teach word patterns) rather than rule learning, and instruction that uses a whole-part-whole perspective.

- Teaching with minilessons; helping children use multiple cues for getting words; and implementing explicit instruction that uses word walls, word sorting, and rich literature discussions.

- A high level of teacher scaffolding with individual and small-group help as well as some whole-class instruction.

In her interview Tompkins talked openly about public education as she has experienced it. She did not shy away from the complexities of teaching, or from the current political situation that affects teachers in her state. . . . Also at issue is the burden that rapid change and new instructional programs impose on teachers. Tompkins (personal communication, July 19, 1997) elaborated in the summarized interview that follows:

Californians demanded a change when the 1994 National Assessment of Educational Programs reported that California's fourth graders read well below the national average (and tied with Louisiana at the bottom of the ranking). The result was the California Reading Initiative of 1996 in which the legislature allocated $1 billion to improve reading instruction. The mandate called for balanced instruction or the explicit teaching of skills in a literature-based program.

I think the recent economic turndown in our state contributed to the neglect of public schools. Class size is one problem. Many teachers have 32–36 students in cramped classrooms, and students often speak three different native languages in the same classroom. One real benefit of the Reading Initiative has been a reduction of class size to 20 students in the primary grades. However, class size must be reduced at all grade levels, and school libraries have had little money to purchase new books. . . .

Many beginning teachers are not well prepared to teach reading. . . . It is simply not possible to teach everything beginning teachers need to know about reading in a single course. Many universities and professors are revising programs and courses in light of the new mandate. Practicing primary-grade teachers are now receiving staff development in the California balanced instruction program. . . .

Our multicultural and multilingual student population presents many challenges. Teachers have learned new ways of teaching and working with these students' families. Even so, the job of teaching reading and writing is not easy. Other problems, social and political, are part of teaching. Teachers have had to calm the fears of some students that they and their families would be deported after the passage of Proposition 167, and I've been in inner-city schools where there are bars on the windows and drills for drive-by shootings.

Explicit Skills and Strategies in Whole Language

The common ground between whole language and explicit instruction in strategies and skills is the focus of Ellen McIntyre and Michael Pressley's book *Balanced Instruction:* *Strategies and Skills in Whole Language* (1996). With the purpose of blending perspectives, the authors, nevertheless, operated generally in the whole language philosophy. They anchored their views of instruction within whole language principles including (a) respect for children as learners, (b) belief in the functional uses of reading and writing, (c) belief that children must engage in the whole processes of reading and writing, and (d) regard for the significance of social and cultural dimensions of learning. McIntyre's central argument is that explicit, planned instruction in specific skills has often not been a part of whole language programs, despite publications that encouraged their inclusion (Camborne, 1988; Dudley-Marling, 1995; Dudley-Marling & Dippo, 1991; Freppon & Headings, 1996; Goodman, Brooks, Meredith, & Goodman, 1987; Newman & Church, 1990). Instead, instruction in comprehension strategies, phonemic awareness, word recognition, and spelling have been given short shrift in some whole language programs. . . .

In her interview, McIntyre (personal communication, May 15, 1997) explained that balanced instruction is a useful term for what good teaching is, viz., thoughtful, planned instruction based on children's background, interests, strengths, and needs. She continued:

The theoretical base for balanced instruction is cultural and psycholinguistic. Instruction must take into account the child's culture and understand the child's way of learning. People learn based on their existing understandings and cultural backgrounds in socially constructed settings, particularly through conversations. Whole language and explicit instruction come together in the instructional conversation.

Some practices that are specifically recommended in this volume include:

- Using an assessment-to-instruction model of teaching.

- Respecting children's backgrounds, language, interests, and abilities.

- Using information about the learners' culture, values, knowledge, and interests to plan instruction.

- Teaching strategies and skills explicitly using a whole-part-whole approach that returns the learner to meaningful whole text.

- Providing planned, systematic instruction on needed strategies.

Explicit Skills as Separate Practice and Literature Immersion

In his forthcoming book, *Effective Reading Instruction: The Case for Balanced Teaching,* Michael Pressley (in press) advocated separating explicit skills instruction with accompanying practice sessions. This text presented his version of balanced instruction that values explicit skills instruction as well as whole language-like literature immersion experiences. His point was that teachers should refer to skills lessons learned as memorable events as they coach the child's actual reading.

Throughout the book Pressley described key elements of this balanced instruction program and cited supportive research. This interpretation of balanced instruction includes systematic, explicit instruction and practice focused on decoding and comprehension. . . .

Pressley also emphasized specific strategy research such as the work on reciprocal teaching (Palincsar & Brown, 1984) and focused on metacognitive knowledge about using strategies (Meichenbaum & Asarnow, 1979).

This conception of balanced instruction drew heavily on research about scaffolding (Wood, Bruner, & Ross, 1976) and the need for delivery of instruction to be matched to the student's level of competence. . . . In this conception of balanced instruction these exemplary programs included high levels of motivation as the key element in balanced instruction. Pressley cited the work of Morrow (1992) showing that motivation comes from challenging and interesting literature experiences, and the studies by Guthrie (1996) and Turner (1995) about the value of learner choice and engagement.

Pressley (personal communication, July 2, 1997) described balanced instruction in his interview as a program with "more systematic instruc-

tion of skills than would be present in classroom versions of whole language with their emphasis on teaching only when there is a demonstrated need." Pressley argued for a separation of skill practices and actual reading and writing experiences. In classroom practice this meant the following:

- Explicit skill lessons that are memorable to learners.

- Practice opportunities for specific skills.

- Coaching from the teacher during reading or writing in ways that reference previous skill practice.

Balancing Instruction Within Whole Language

In Constance Weaver's new book *Reconsidering a Balanced Approach to Reading* (in press), a view of balanced instruction was presented along with extended documentation of supportive research and reprints of selected studies. Weaver described instruction that focuses on meaning. She maintained that meaning is the emphasis in beginning reading, strategy and skill instruction, and assessment. Weaver advocated teaching phonics in the context of reading and writing and keeping letter-sound cues in balance with other kinds of knowledge. She argued that phonemic awareness, letter-sound knowledge, and word knowledge develop in the process of becoming an independent reader. They are not an end unto themselves. Thus, "a balanced reading program focuses on using skills like phonemic awareness and phonics knowledge in the service of strategies for constructing meaning from text" (p. 12).

The research supporting these arguments (and the bulk of this book) included studies of proficient reading, phonemic awareness and phonics, and reading assessment. For example, to show the reader's orchestration of different kinds of information during reading, Weaver cited miscue research of Goodman (1973) and the synthesis of miscue research by Brown, Goodman, and Marek (1996). . . .

In basic processing research Weaver highlighted the work of

Moustafa (1995) that shows that readers read in chunks of letters rather than letter by letter. Weaver also discussed a study by Ayres (1993) showing that kindergartners who encounter an emphasis on meaning in reading before instruction on phonics were more able to take advantage of subsequent phonics instruction. With assessment, Weaver argued that some versions of balanced instruction may lead to increased assessment of arbitrary performance standards and an overemphasis on skills and remediation.

Weaver cited general agreement that (a) phonics knowledge can develop through repeated exposure to familiar texts, and (b) children should receive some explicit help with phonics. Direct instruction can be planned and well thought through, without necessarily becoming a formal set of instructional sequences. Finally, she asserted that there is consensus that children do not need phonics rules, phonics first, or phonics drill worksheets.

In her interview Weaver (personal communication, March 27, 1997) supported contextualized teaching, where "skills are taught as children are engaging in meaningful acts of reading and writing." She also raised the question of who gets to decide how children will be taught to read. She argued that informed professionals should play a critical role. Practical classroom practices drawn from Weaver's reconsiderations included:

- Helping children develop phonics knowledge through language play with familiar texts, (reading, rereading, rhymes, poems, songs, and playing with sound elements).

- Talking about letter-sound relationships when writing in front of children and helping them write word sounds they hear.

- Keeping the emphasis on meaning during reading and writing.

Discussion of Balanced Instruction: Interviews and Commentary

As noted earlier, we interviewed teachers and others about balanced instruction. Interviews were conducted because they provided both breadth about this topic with various perspectives and access to more information linked to practice. We talked individually with people, asking each of them the same questions, namely, What is balanced instruction? What issues does it raise? and What is its theory and/or research base?

We interviewed Betty Shockley-Bisplinghoff, an author, researcher, and primary-grade teacher at Barnett Shoals Elementary School in Georgia. She was selected because she is an exemplary teacher and a whole language educator. We included her interview because some of the press about balanced instruction condemns this philosophy, and because Shockley-Bisplinghoff's (personal communication, May 15, 1997) discussion mirrored that of other teachers with whom we talked.

I think that its aim was to balance phonics and holistic instruction. But the ways balanced instruction is getting implemented in schools I have seen are not balanced. Programs (commercial) are the name of the game. We may be trying to come up with a term that may pacify all of us—that will appeal to both camps.

My concern as a whole language teacher is that the term *balanced instruction* is reactionary. Whole language is a grassroots movement begun and sustained by classroom teachers. I wonder if this term *balanced* chips away at the philosophy base and thinking of teachers. From whole language comes the only time that I know of when teachers defined their own philosophy. Balanced instruction seems to say be eclectic. It may encourage teachers who don't have a well-defined philosophy to think they can just do lots of things or anything without hard thinking and identification of their philosophical base. Whole language teachers do many things to help children learn. And they know how to instruct, organize, plan, and teach. It is structured. Good practice is not a matter of activities, or a way that is activity-based because an activity approach takes the why and how out of instruction.

Whole language leads some teachers to formal inquiry, being a coresearcher with colleagues, and with children, and it means owning and defining teaching for ourselves. Good whole language teaching is and always has been balanced. If we keep using whole language and phonics as mutually exclusive things, we will get nowhere.

We also interviewed Shari Ettenberger, a first-grade teacher at Herman L. Brandt Elementary School in New York. As an author and researcher she was also selected because she was identified as an exemplary balanced instruction teacher (Wharton-McDonald, Pressley, & Mistretta, in press) and because her thinking echoed that of other teachers with whom we talked. Ettenberger (personal communication, May 28, 1997) made the following points in her interview:

Balanced instruction is a fine blend of a variety of teaching strategies and styles through scaffolding and personalized instruction that best meets the needs of students. It provides a positive, print-rich environment where students' interests and opinions are valued.

Teachers in this setting explicitly model and facilitate learning by providing meaningful hands-on experiences that motivate and engage learners. These teachers are accountable for recording students' progress by using a variety of tools (running records, anecdotal notes, rubrics, and portfolios). They have flexible groups according to children's needs, interests, and activities. Theme studies are used and integrated across the curriculum, and reading and writing focus on quality and use for a variety of purposes and audiences. Peer collaboration and lots of sharing are important.

I think there is an issue about the complexity of creating a substantial, consistent, and accountable program and the lack of the public's awareness about this method of instruction and assessment. There is also the issue of administrators, teachers, and communities unwilling to change and the requirements of organization, commitment, having proper resources, and having high expectations.

Teacher educators were also interviewed. Those contacted had an interest in balanced instruction, and their responses helped capture the breadth of perspectives, issues, and considerations for practice. . . .

Dick Allington, author, researcher, and former president of the National Reading Conference, began his interview by noting that understanding what balanced instruction means was a problem for him since so many kinds of research are being used as supporting evidence by so many different people with quite divergent notions. Allington's (personal communication, August 1, 1997) summarized interview follows:

My own view of balanced instruction comes from working with Gerry Duffy in the late 1970s on a project in which some teachers came to be identified as informed eclectics. More recently some researchers have done exemplary teachers' surveys and found that most exemplary teachers look a lot like Duffy's informed eclectics. These teachers teach kids, not materials.

A key issue in framing balanced instruction has to do with reading and writing in the curriculum. Is balanced instruction integrated language arts, or just about reading?

Another issue is critical, and that is who controls the decisions about what is balanced instruction and what isn't. Is it the state, the district, the teacher?

Often I'm not sure which [version of] balanced instruction people are talking about. . . . Defining balanced instruction seems to revolve around the question of the role of decoding instruction, what is to be taught, in what manner, and with what sorts of texts for children to read and the importance of these reading materials in initial reading acquisitions.

P. David Pearson, another former president of the National Reading Conference, invited us to frame his interview response by drawing on his writing (Pearson, 1996). Pearson's response (personal communication, June 11, 1997) follows:

I propose some core principles, the sources of which are myriad and many are happily and readily consistent with the whole language movement. The sources are also consistent with much of the work that has been pushed into the margins, too, in the ascendancy of whole language.

The first principle (for balanced instruction) is that teachers build code-based instruction on their deep knowledge of language and learning; they take advantage of the natural (though not identical) relationship between oral and written language and use it to help children learn from the language wellspring deep in their being. Once children discover the principle of representing their words with the letters they are learning, they are helped to embrace the alphabetic principle and acquire a concept for the whole system of representation.

Good practice grounded in deep knowledge of language and literacy will lead us to regard learning to read as an intellectual achievement rather than an acquisition of skills. I have never understood why there is so much furor over learning the letters and sounds of language. Granted we sometimes make a fetish of them, testing children until they are weary and remediating kindergartners who do not master early assessments. This sort of action is as irresponsible as is failing to provide opportunities for students to learn the letters and sounds of language.

I have seen enough competent, engaging instruction to conclude that both phonemic awareness and letter recognition can be acquired in engaging settings and activities and can be assessed in productive engaging tasks rather than decontextualized activities. We must never forget that phonics is a means to an end. To view it otherwise is to risk deceiving ourselves into believing we have actually accomplished something of value by having taught the system. The value is realized only when students use phonics to make and monitor meaning. We must get phonics off workbook pages and into real reading and writing.

Other key principles in my program for a balanced literacy curriculum include authenticity (of text and task), community (settings in which tasks are rendered authentic), integration (among language arts and with subject matter curriculum), optimism (high expectations for all), modeling (to help students see how literacy works), student control (making sure students make decisions about what they read and how they are doing), and connectedness (worrying about how all we teach connects with students' lives).

Thoughtful teachers help students develop a sense of control of their learning by holding high expectations for all their students and by providing within classroom learning communities the sort of authentic, integrated curriculum and real-life demonstrations of literacy that will help students understand the connectedness of school learning to lifelong learning.

Conclusions and Discussion

As noted at the beginning of this article, the information on balanced instruction is in flux. It varies across research bases and in the interpretations of research implications for practice. While much of balanced instruction appears to be focused on beginning reading, phonetic skills, holistic teaching, and the aggregation of best practices, it nevertheless acts as a lightning rod for larger issues. All of these issues, from techniques for developmentally appropriate skills teaching to control of classrooms, have implications for practice. We have tried to provide a reason-able representation of much that is being said on this topic thus far. Teachers and interested others can learn from considering the content presented here and in further reading of these and other works. In this final section we address some points on classroom practice, political implications, and ideas about teaching itself that we found important in balanced instruction.

Implications for Classroom Practice

There are explicit messages associated with balanced instruction. The principal one is that good practice is terribly complex and requires time to learn. Good practice requires much hard work and extensive knowledge of many areas in literacy, and it needs support. These areas include the research on phonetic and word learning, emergent literacy and beginning reading, the writing and reading process, reader response, varied texts and materials, the nature and practice of scaffolded instruction, and so-cial-cultural constructivist learning.

Although the California 1995 and 1996 state reports and subsequent media accounts drew considerable attention, literacy researchers and teachers have long been concerned about sound practice and research on important aspects such as phonics instruction and word level skills. Much of the work we have discussed here substantiates this point. Across philosophies and theoretical stances researchers and teachers have repeatedly emphasized the importance of phonics teaching and learning with holistic, literature-based, and language-based instruction. Constructivist teaching values the importance of phonetic learning and attends to its teaching; however, *how* this teaching is carried out is at issue. Several balanced instruction researchers repeatedly emphasized the importance of phonics teaching and learning within integrated language-based instruction; however, others argued for separating phonics teaching and learning. This is an essential difference found in the work that we reviewed for this article. This difference is important not only in implementing reading programs but also in the development of exemplary practice.

The journey toward exemplary teaching requires time and hard work. An emphasis focused only on implementing reading programs falls short of providing sufficient understanding for this journey. A recent study reported in *The Elementary School Journal* (Au & Carroll, 1997) provided insights about supporting teachers' work in schools *and* improving children's achievement. This study found that a dual model—one focused on teachers' knowledge and skills and one on empowerment and professional growth—promotes the kind of complex teaching called for in balanced instruction. This dual model demonstrated that teachers need developmental programs and support not only to learn more about skills instruction but also to become stronger professionals. Some conceptions of balanced instruction seemed to recommend a transmission model of teaching and of teacher learning and change. We believe that the dual model described by Au and Carroll will better achieve the goals of balanced instruction. We also believe this model is clearly evident in the whole language philosophy that is condemned by some balanced instruction enthusiasts.

Balanced instruction is helpful. For example, it helps us look again at what we now know about phonemic awareness, spelling, word learning, and scaffolded instruction (Wilde, 1988, 1992, 1996; Wood, Bruner, & Ross, 1976). Balanced instruction also invites revisiting the supportive research on these topics (e.g., Cunningham, 1990; Ehri, 1995; Gentry & Gillet, 1993; Henderson & Beers, 1980; Perfetti, Beck, Bell, & Hughes, 1987; Read, 1975; Treiman, 1993). However, some balanced instruction writings can also gloss over what we know about good teacher thinking and action. It can present a negative view of public education.

We begin this section by saying that balanced instruction has some clear messages for practice. Yet, there are also some mixed messages that essentially have to do with *how* teaching is conducted and who decides how teachers practice. A comprehensive discussion of these messages is beyond the scope of this article; however, we addressed one of these points earlier, and we conclude this article with a brief discussion of some others.

Implications of Some Larger Issues

Some versions of balanced instruction and associated issues smack of control of both schools and teachers' work (Berliner, 1997). These versions (usually in the popular press) serve as a quick fix or a rush to judgment about the complex problems experienced by teachers, children and their families, and communities. Some depend on an overly generalized negative view of public education. However, recent research by Berliner and Biddle (1995) challenged the notion of a uniform crisis in reading achievement across all of the U.S. and documents the success of particular groups. Mainstream children who are not living in poverty tend to do well in U.S. schools. These children's schools usually have a sound economic base and strong, supportive administrators.

The political alarm about widespread public school failure has been used by some to reformulate and mandate selected curriculum. It also glosses over the complexities of teaching and learning. It tends to marginalize and cover up the hard work of teaching and the need for good leadership and better funding of schools for children of poverty. Beginning teachers and teachers in complex situations need more time, support, and understanding than ever before. They need to be heard.

The role of research is another matter of concern in our considerations of balanced instruction. We believe, as do many others, that we know much more now about literacy learning and how good teachers practice. Clearly, research has made and is making significant and useful contributions. Still, it can never provide *the answer*. As we have pointed out, factors other than reading instruction, such as community, home, young children's unique personal characteristics, and school leadership are paramount in literacy learning. We need to build responses to these factors and count them into the culture of the classroom.

Early literacy instruction needs a wide research and professional-development base. Moreover, various voices in balanced instruction speak to the importance of teachers' autonomy and authority. Teachers' interpretations of relevant research that informs the reading program and their unique transactions with children in individual classrooms are pivotal (Lloyd & Anders, 1994; Samuels & Pearson, 1980). Teachers' interpretations change as they grow professionally and encounter more and more children with various needs and strengths.

As noted previously, there are differences by degree and in the ways that people think research into practice occurs in balanced instruction. These differences are grounded in alternative models of the nature of teaching itself and in accounts of what teachers actually do in reflection and action (Schon, 1983; Yinger, 1986, 1987). A transmission model (e.g., a fixed scope and sequence applied in the classroom) echoes the process-product movement of the past. Newer research, such as that on situated learning (Brown, Collins, & Duguid, 1989; Rogoff & Lave, 1984), and research projects conducted with teachers (Allen & Shockley, 1996; Allen, Shockley, & Baumann, 1995; Lloyd & Anders, 1994) suggest that teachers mediate the research they know according to many factors (e.g., continuous changes in their own learning, students' needs, daily classroom events).

Teachers grow as professionals and learn to improve practice in better ways through grappling intellectually with this mediation. Our interpretation of balanced instruction aligns with Roehler's (1990) emphasis on acceptance of complex classroom dilemmas and Duffy's (1990) emphasis on teachers relying on themselves to establish a theory-based philosophy, learn the research, and make informed instructional decisions.

References

Adams, M. (1990). *Beginning to read: Thinking and learning about print.* Cambridge, MA: Harvard University Press.

Allen, J., & Shockley, B. (1996). Composing a research dialogue: University and school research committees encountering a cultural shift. *Reading Research Quarterly, 31,* 220–228.

Allen, J., Shockley, B., & Baumann, J. (1995). Gathering 'round the kitchen table: Teacher inquiry in the NRRC School Research Consortium. *The Reading Teacher, 48,* 526–529.

Anderson, R.C., & Pearson, P.D. (1984). A schema-theoretical view of basic processes in reading. In P.D. Pearson (Ed.), *Handbook of reading research* (pp. 255–292). New York: Longman.

Au, K., & Carroll, J. (1997). Improving literacy achievement through a constructivist approach: The KEEP demonstration classroom project. *The Elementary School Journal, 97,* 203–221.

Au, K., Carroll, J., & Scheu, J. (in press). *Balanced literacy instruction: A teacher's resource book.* Norwood, MA: Christopher-Gordon.

Ayres, L.R. (1993). *The efficacy of three training conditions on phonological awareness of kindergarten children and the longitudinal effect of each on later reading acquisition.* Unpublished doctoral dissertation, Oakland University, Rochester, MI.

Ayres, L.R. (1996, Spring). *Balanced reading instruction.* Orlando, FL: University of Central Florida.

Berliner, D.C. (1997). Educational psychology meets the Christian right: Differing views of schooling, children, teaching, and learning. *Teachers College Record, 96,* 381–415.

Berliner, D.C., & Biddle, B. (1995). *The manufactured crisis.* Reading, MA: Addison-Wesley.

Brown, J., Goodman, K.S., & Marek, A.M. (1996). *Studies in miscue analysis: An annotated bibliography.* Newark, DE: International Reading Association.

Brown, S., Collins, A., & Duguid, P. (1989). Situated cognition and the culture of learning. *Educational Researcher, 18*(1) 32–42.

California Department of Education. (1987). *California English-language arts framework.* Sacramento, CA: Author.

California Department of Education. (1995). *Every child a reader.* Sacramento, CA: Author.

California Department of Education. (1996). *Teaching reading: A balanced comprehensive approach to teaching reading in prekindergarten through grade three.* Sacramento, CA: Author.

Calkins, L.M. (1994). *The art of teaching writing.* Portsmouth, NH: Heinemann.

Cambourne, B. (1988). *The whole story: Natural learning and the acquisition of literacy in the classroom.* Auckland, New Zealand: Scholastic.

Clay, M. (1985). *The early detection of reading difficulties* (3rd ed.). Portsmouth, NH: Heinemann.

Clay, M. (1991). *Becoming literate: The construction of inner control.* Portsmouth, NH: Heinemann.

Cunningham, A.E. (1990). Explicit versus implicit instruction in phonemic awareness. *Journal of Experimental Child Psychology, 50,* 429–444.

Cunningham, A.E., & Stanovich, K. E. (1993). Children's literacy environments and early word recognition skills. *Reading and*

Writing: An Interdisciplinary Journal, 5, 193–204.

Cunningham, P. (1995). *Phonics they use: Words for reading and writing* (2nd ed.). New York: HarperCollins.

Dahl, K.L., & Freppon, P.A. (1995). A comparison of inner-city children's interpretations of reading and writing instruction in the early grades in skills-based and whole language classrooms. *Reading Research Quarterly, 30,* 50–74.

Delpit, L.D. (1986). Skills and other dilemmas of a progressive black educator. *Harvard Educational Review, 58,* 208–287.

Dressel, J.H. (1990). The effects of listening and discussing different qualities of children's literature on narrative writing of fifth graders. *Research in the Teaching of English, 24,* 397–414.

Dudley-Marling, C. (1995). Whole language: It's a matter of principles. *Reading and Writing Quarterly, 11,* 109–117.

Dudley-Marling, C., & Dippo, D. (1991). The language of whole language. *Language Arts, 68,* 548–554.

Duffy, G. (1990). What counts in teacher education? Dilemmas in educating empowered teachers. In J. Zutell & S. McCormick (Eds.), *Learner factors/teacher factors: Issues in literacy research and instruction.* 40th yearbook of the National Reading Conference (pp. 1–18). Chicago: National Reading Conference.

Duffy, G., Roehler, L.R., & Hermann, B. (1988). Modeling mental processes helps peer readers become strategic readers. *The Reading Teacher, 41,* 762–757.

Eeds, M., & Wells, D. (1989). Grand conversations: An exploration of meaning construction in literature study groups. *Research in the Teaching of English, 23,* 4–29.

Ehri, L.C. (1995). Phases of development in reading words. *Journal of Research in Reading, 18,* 116–125.

Freppon, P.A., & Headings, L. (1996). Keeping it whole in whole language: A first grade teacher's phonics instruction in an urban classroom. In E. McIntyre & M. Pressley (Eds.), *Balanced instruction: Strategies and skills in whole language* (pp. 65–82). Norwood, MA: Christopher Gordon.

Gentry, J.R., & Gillet, J.W. (1993). *Teaching kids to spell.* Portsmouth, NH: Heinemann.

Goldenberg, C. (1994). Promoting early literacy development among Spanish speaking children: Lessons from two studies. In E. H. Hiebert & B. M. Taylor (Eds.), *Getting reading right from the start: Effective early literacy intervention* (pp. 171–199). Boston: Allyn & Bacon.

Goodman, K.S. (1973). *Theoretically based studies of patterns of miscues in oral reading performance.* Detroit, MI: Wayne State University. (ERIC Document Reproduction Service No. ED 079 708)

Goodman, K.S. (1976). Reading: A psycholinguistic guessing game. In H. Singer & R. Ruddell (Eds.), *Theoretical models and processes of reading*

(pp. 497–508). Newark, DE: International Reading Association.

Goodman, K.S. (1986). *What's whole in whole language?* Portsmouth, NH: Heinemann.

Goodman, K.S. (1992). Why whole language is today's agenda in education. *Language Arts, 69,* 354–363.

Goodman, K., Brooks, E., Meredith, R., & Goodman, Y. M. (1987). *Language and thinking in school: A whole language curriculum* (3rd ed.). New York: Richard C. Owen.

Goswami, U. (1988). Orthographic analogies and reading development. *Quarterly Journal of Experimental Psychology, 40,* 73–83.

Graves, D. (1983). *Writing: Teachers and children at work.* Exeter, NH: Heinemann.

Graves, D. (1994). *A fresh look at writing.* Portsmouth, NH: Heinemann.

Guthrie, J. T. (1996). Educational contexts for engagement in literacy. *The Reading Teacher, 49,* 432–445.

Henderson, E.H., & Beers, J. W. (1980). *Developmental and cognitive aspects of learning to spell.* Newark, DE: International Reading Association.

Holdaway, D. (1979). *The foundations of literacy.* Portsmouth, NH: Heinemann.

Honig, W. (1996). *Teaching our children to read: The role of skills in a comprehensive reading program.* Thousand Oaks, CA: Corwin Press.

Juel, C. (1994). *Learning to read and write in one elementary school.* New York: Springer-Verlag.

Lloyd, C., & Anders, P. (1994). Research-based practices as the content of staff development. In V. Richardson (Ed.), *Teacher change and the staff development process: A case in reading instruction* (pp. 68–89). New York: Teachers College Press.

Lyon, G.R. (1994). *Research in learning disabilities at the NICHD.* Bethesda, MD: NICHD Technical Document/Human Learning and Behavior Branch.

Lyon, G.R. (1995). Research initiative in learning disabilities: Contributions from scientists supported by the National Institute of Child Health and Human Development. *Journal of Child Neurology, 10,* 120–128.

McIntyre, E. (1996). Strategies and skills in whole language: An introduction to balanced teaching. In E. McIntyre & M. Pressley (Eds.), *Balanced instruction: Strategies and skills in whole language* (pp. 1–22). Norwood, MA: Christopher Gordon.

McIntyre, E., & Freppon, P.A. (1994). A comparison of children's development of alphabetic knowledge in a skills-based and a whole language classroom. *Research in the Teaching of English, 28,* 391–417.

McIntyre, E., & Pressley, M. (Eds.). (1996). *Balanced instruction: Strategies and skills in whole language.* Norwood, MA: Christopher-Gordon.

Meichenbaum, D., & Asarnow, J. (1979). Cognitive-behavioral modification and metacognitive development: Implications

for the classroom. In P. C. Kendall & S. D. Hollon (Eds.), *Cognitive-behavioral interventions* (pp. 11–35). New York: Academic Press.

Moats, L.C. (1994). The missing foundation in teacher education: Knowledge of the structure of spoken and written language. *Annals of Dyslexia, 44,* 157–168.

Moll, L.C. (1988). Some key issues in teaching Latino students. *Language Arts, 65,* 465–472.

Moll, L.C. (1990). *Vygotsky and education: Instructional implications and applications of sociohistorical psychology.* Cambridge, England: Cambridge University Press.

Moll, L.C. (1992). Literacy research in community and classrooms: A sociocultural approach. In R. Beach, J. L. Green, M. L. Kamil, & T. Shanahan (Eds.), *Multidisciplinary perspectives on literacy research* (pp. 211–244). Urbana, IL: National Conference on Research in English and the National Council of Teachers of English.

Morrow, L.M. (1992). The impact of a literature-based program on literacy achievement, use of literature, and attitudes of children from minority backgrounds. *Reading Research Quarterly, 27,* 250–275.

Moustafa, M. (1995). Children's productive phonological recoding. *Reading Research Quarterly, 30,* 464–476.

Newman, J., & Church, S. (1990). The myths of whole language. *The Reading Teacher, 44,* 20–26.

O'Brien, K.L. (1991). A look at one successful literature program. *The New Advocate, 4,* 113–123.

Palincsar, A.B., & Brown, A.L. (1984). Reciprocal teaching of comprehension-fostering and monitoring activities. *Cognition and Instruction, 1,* 117–175.

Paris, S.G., Lipson, M.Y., & Wixson, K. K. (1983). Becoming a strategic leader. *Contemporary Educational Psychology, 2,* 293–316.

Pearson, P.D. (1996). Reclaiming the center. In M. Graves, P. van den Broek, & B. Taylor (Eds.), *The first R: Every child's right to read* (pp. 259–274). New York: Teachers College Press.

Pearson, P.D., & Fielding, L. (1991). Comprehension instruction. In R. Barr, M. L. Kamil, P. B. Mosenthal, & P. D. Pearson (Eds.), *Handbook of reading research: Volume II* (pp. 815–860). White Plains, NY: Longman.

Perfetti, C.A., Beck, I., Bell, L.C., & Hughes, C. (1987). Phonemic knowledge and learning to read are reciprocal: A longitudinal study of first grade children. *Merrill-Palmer Quarterly, 33,* 283–319.

Pressley, M. (in press). *Effective reading instruction: The case for balanced teaching.* New York: Guilford Press.

Pressley, M., Rankin, J., & Yokoi, L. (1996). A survey of instructional practices of primary teachers nominated as effective in promoting literacy. *The Elementary School Journal, 96,* 363–384.

Purcell-Gates, V. (1995). *Other people's words: The cycle of low literacy.* Cambridge, MA: Harvard University Press.

Read, C. (1975). *Children's categorizations of speech sounds in English.* Urbana, IL: National Council of Teachers of English.

Roehler, L. (1990, May). *Embracing the complexities.* Paper presented at the University of Maryland Conference on Cognitive Research and Instructional Innovation, University of Maryland, College Park.

Rogoff, B., & Lave, J. (1984). *Everyday cognition: Its development in social contexts.* Cambridge, MA: Harvard University Press.

Rosenblatt, L. (1978). *The reader, the text, the poem: The transactional theory of the literary work.* Carbondale, IL: Southern Illinois University Press.

Samuels, S.J., & Pearson, P.D. (1980). Caution: Using research in applied settings. *Reading Research Quarterly, 15,* 1–5.

Schon, D.A. (1983). *The reflective practitioner.* New York: Basic Books.

Smith, F.S. (1992). Learning to read: The never-ending debate. *Phi Delta Kappen, 73,* 432–441.

Stanovich, K.E. (1986). Matthew effects in reading: Some consequences of individual differences in the acquisition of literacy. *Reading Research Quarterly, 21,* 360–407.

Stanovich, K.E., Cunningham, A.E., & Freeman, D. J. (1984). Relation between early reading acquisition and word decoding with and without context: A longitudinal study of first-grade children. *Journal of Educational Psychology, 76,* 668–677.

Tompkins, G. (1997). *Literacy for the 21st century: A balanced approach.* Englewood Cliffs, NJ: Prentice-Hall.

Torgesen, J.K. (1995). Instruction for reading disabled children: Questions about knowledge into practice. *Issues in Education: Contributions From Educational Psychology, 1,* 91–95.

Treiman, R. (1993). *Beginning to spell.* New York: Oxford University Press.

Turner, J. (1995). The influence of classroom contexts on young children's motivation for literacy. *Reading Research Quarterly, 30,* 410–441.

Weaver, C. (in press). *Reconsidering a balanced approach to reading.* Urbana, IL: National Council of Teachers of English.

Wharton-McDonald, R., Pressley, M., & Mistretta, J. (in press). Outstanding literacy instruction in first grade: Teacher practices and student achievement. *The Elementary School Journal.*

Wharton-McDonald, R., Pressley, M., Rankin, J., Mistretta, J., Tokio, L., &

Ettenberger, S. (1997). Effective primary-grades literacy instruction = balanced instruction. *The Reading Teacher, 50,* 518–521.

Wilde, S. (1988). Learning to spell and punctuate: A study of eight- and nine-year-old children. *Language and Education: An International Journal, 2,* 35–59.

Wilde, S. (1992). *You kan red this!* Portsmouth, NH: Heinemann.

Wilde, S. (1996). *What's a schwa sound anyway? A holistic guide to phonetics, phonics, and spelling.* Portsmouth, NH: Heinemann.

Wood, S.S., Bruner, J.S., & Ross, G. (1976). The role of tutoring in problem solving. *Journal of Child Psychology and Psychiatry, 17,* 89–100.

Yinger, R.J. (1986). Examining thought in action: A theoretical and methodological critique of research on interactive teaching. *Teaching and Teacher Education, 3,* 263–282.

Yinger, R.J. (1987). Learning the language of practice. *Curriculum Inquiry, 17,* 293–318.

 Article Review Form at end of book.

How can children in the same class but reading at different levels participate in the same activities described by Routman? How does your personal definition of *reading* compare with Routman's belief that phonics and meaning must be taught together?

Ready to Read

This reading classroom really works. Does yours measure up?

Regie Routman

How do kids learn to read? I've been teaching reading in the public schools for almost 30 years—as a classroom teacher, a reading specialist, a learning-disabilities teacher, and currently as a mentor for other teachers. And I've noticed some important things along the way. The most significant is that phonics (the association of letters with certain sounds) comes easily to most young children. But that may not be enough. The most recent reports from the National Assessment of Educational Progress indicate that 92 percent of students can read and understand words at a basic level by the age of 9. However, the majority cannot satisfactorily analyze and interpret what they read, even by the age of 17. Clearly, for children to understand concepts as well as sound out words, teaching must combine phonics with methods that enable them to grasp meaning.

Reading success really begins long before the first day of school. By age 1 or 2, in fact, children should be regularly read to by parents. The U.S. Commission on Reading examined more than 10,000 studies and issued a landmark report stating, "The single most important activity for . . . eventual success in reading is reading aloud to children." This rich background in language provides a foundation of interest and experience on which teachers can build. When it's missing, it's harder, but still possible, for kids to catch up.

What goes on in a first-grade classroom that's geared to reading success? Inside teacher Hallie Stewart's classroom at the Mercer School in Shaker Heights, Ohio, the excitement about reading and writing is palpable. The books the teacher has chosen are memorable stories by well-known children's authors and illustrators—books with rhythmic language, a repetitive structure, and a predictable story line. In fact, experts have found that young readers read more easily when the context is familiar, the text well written, and the plot interesting. By contrast, "controlled language" books, which focus on teaching a particular phonics sound rather than telling a good story, turn many kids off to reading and are actually more difficult for them to understand. With sentences like "Pam's cat Tab can wag, wag, wag," such books make no sense— they're written to teach phonics rather than to delight children.

Children in the Same Class Read at Different Levels

It's midyear in Ms. Stewart's class, and these 6- and 7-year-olds know the routine. In pairs or small groups, they're reading aloud, pointing to words, and discussing stories. Several children have taken the initiative to create a phonics chart of words that contain "at." Two students are listening to a story on cassette, while following along in their

books. Others are writing in their journals.

Reading and writing go on all day long in all subject areas— whether it's science, social studies, or math. And children don't simply use these new skills in teacher-directed assignments; they choose to read and write for their own purposes. For example, Nat, who's fascinated with reptiles, is poring over a book on snakes. Emma, who thinks that the lunchroom is too noisy, has just finished writing a letter of complaint to the principal.

Today Ms. Stewart is introducing the whole class to *Caps for Sale*, a beloved children's classic. Her 23 children are at different reading levels: A few are still learning the names and sounds of the letters of the alphabet, while "rereading" familiar stories they've memorized (an important early stage of reading); some are using phonics and other strategies to read simple picture books; others are up to easy chapter books; and several are fluent readers who can read just about anything. Later in the day, teaching will be individualized to each child's level. But for now, everyone gathers on the colorful rug in the "reading center," a large, comfortable space set off by low bookcases. This is the all-essential classroom library, which contains multiple copies of outstanding children's books, arranged by author, topic, and difficulty so children can choose their own books easily. Also on display are stories that the kids have written and illustrated them-

Regie Routman, *Parents,* October 1997. Copyright 1997 Gruner & Jahr USA Publishing. Reprinted from *Parents* magazine by permission.

selves, typed and bound by parent volunteers.

Ms. Stewart sits next to an easel that holds a "big book," an enlarged replica of the original storybook text and pictures. She doesn't just talk "at" the kids, but invites them to join in the process. "Today, we'll be reading a new book together," she begins. "Some of you may already know the story. Perhaps someone in your family has read it to you. Let's read the title together." Pointing to each word, she reads aloud, "Caps for Sale," and many students chime in.

"Look at the cover," she continues, "and see if you can predict what the story is about." The cover shows a man asleep in a tree with lots of caps piled up on the ground and monkeys peeking out from behind the tree. Tricia ventures, "I think it's about a man who has lots of hats." Sheila adds, "Some monkeys will play a trick on him." Douglas ventures, "The monkeys will run off with his hats." Such prediction gives kids a sense of purpose in reading and encourages them to think about the story and not just decode the words.

Predicting Events in a Story Piques Kids' Interest

"Let's see if you're right. Look under the title—there's a subtitle that says, 'A tale of a peddler, some monkeys, and their monkey business.' What's 'monkey business'? Has anyone ever heard that expression?" asks Stewart.

"Yeah," says Douglas. "My dad tells me and my brother, 'Cut out that monkey business' when we're fooling around at the dinner table."

Ms. Stewart then goes through the pictures in the story, asking the children to predict what might happen before she reads aloud. She also discusses new words (peddler, ordinary, wares) that appear in the story.

After this five- to ten-minute introduction, Ms. Stewart starts to read, pointing to each word and occasionally stopping to discuss the story as she goes along. Then she begins a second reading and invites her students to read with her. While the focus is always on enjoying and understanding the story, in subsequent readings she'll take the opportunity to teach skills she knows the children

will need to read independently. For instance, she may pause at a word she knows the children are familiar with and expect them to fill it in. She may call attention to the "ed" at the end of "looked," "checked," "walked," and "refreshed," or note special punctuation. All students follow the text with their eyes as she points to each word and reads aloud. Many join in with her, reading the parts they can.

Writing Stories Can Enhance the Joy of Reading

Then Ms. Stewart guides the class in rereading together several familiar "big books," as well as several poems, chants, or songs written in enlarged print on chart paper. Reading, and rereading, together help build fluency, confidence, comprehension, and, most of all, enjoyment. Later on, when Ms. Stewart meets with students in small groups and individually, she assesses exactly what students can read and what she needs to teach.

Writing goes hand in hand with reading in this first-grade class. For many young children, that "aha" moment—when the concept of reading really clicks in—takes place when they read back what they themselves have written. Ms. Stewart models the writing process for the whole class by thinking out loud and writing a true story about her dog. She begins, "Today, my dog woke me up with his barking," writing each word on large chart paper in front of the class. She slowly enunciates, drawing out the sounds of each word as she writes the letters, so that the children hear and see the sound-letter connections. Sometimes she asks the children to supply some of the letters and punctuation. "How do we spell 'ing'?" she asks, and some kids respond correctly. "What do I need to put at the end of my sentence? That's right. A period." Finishing a few sentences, she adds, "What do I need to do now?"

"Reread," comes the answer. "Yes, that's right. I need to reread to see if my story is just the way I want it and to check my spelling." After rereading the story a few times and

pointing to each word as she reads, Ms. Stewart goes back and underlines "today," "my" and "up" and tells the class, "These are words I expect you to be able to spell now. Look at my story if you need to know how to spell them."

Then, after brainstorming with the whole class, she calls on several students who have volunteered to talk about a significant experience from their lives. In the process, she elicits details and descriptive language that will reappear in the children's writing. This talk before the children plunge into journal-writing is essential. Hearing other children's stories jogs their memories and convinces them that they, too, have interesting stories to tell. Such talk also leads many children to write ongoing stories that often continue for days and weeks.

"Invented" Spelling Gradually Becomes Correct

As the children begin to write, Ms. Stewart uses the time for individual help. She stops to kneel by each student, encouraging them to use their best "invented" (phonics-based) spelling and helping them draw on their knowledge of letters, sounds, and words. She also encourages them to use the resources she's displayed around the room. "Would you read me what you've written?" she asks 6-year-old Nancy. Nancy reads her first sentence, which she's written as: "My grandpa is cuming ovr my hous today."

"Good for you," observes her teacher. "How did you know how to write grandpa and today?"

" 'Today' is on our calendar board," Nancy points out, and 'grandpa' is on our family-words chart."

"That's right. And 'today' is also in my story and on our word wall."

Sensing that Nancy is probably ready to learn how to spell "house," she adds, "I also like the way you wrote the word 'house.' You heard a lot of the sounds. There's a silent letter at the end of that word. What do you think it could be?"

When Nancy correctly answers, "e," Ms. Stewart says, "I'm

going to write house under your 'hous.' Next time you want to write the word, you can look here." Sure enough, in the following day's journal writing, Nancy checks back and spells "house" correctly. Each day after about a half hour of journal writing, Ms. Stewart meets with small groups (five to eight children who have been grouped together according to skills they need to work on) and guides them through a book, which has been carefully chosen to offer a bit of a challenge. Since they are grouped this way for only 20 minutes a day, kids do not feel stigmatized. The goal is to have students problem-solve the tough spots with minimal help. But Ms. Stewart also uses this time to listen to students read aloud and to make detailed notes. By observing her students individually and in groups, she notices what problem-solving strategies they are using—or not—and what she needs to teach next. For instance, Stephanie, who volunteers to read aloud from *Caps for Sale*, stops at the word "hungry." "Can you think of a strategy to figure that out?" Ms. Stewart asks.

Stephanie pauses for a few seconds. "It starts with the 'h' sound," she says. "I know 'un' like in 'fun' and 'lunch.' The peddler wants to eat lunch, so he must be 'hungry.' "

"You used what you know and checked with the story," Ms. Stewart tells her warmly. "Good for you!"

After everyone has read, Ms. Stewart reviews the strategies they've used today: rereading, putting in what makes sense and sounds right, sounding out, checking against what's going on in the picture and story, and using their previous knowledge of words. Near the end of group time, Ms. Stewart has the children pair up to finish reading

their stories and write down any words they can't figure out for tomorrow's class.

The focus all day—indeed, all year—is on meaning, as well as word recognition. Phonics and predicting go hand in hand in Ms. Stewart's class, leading to understanding and to the best outcome of all—a lifetime love of reading.

 Article Review Form at end of book.

What If Your Child Can't Read?

Don't panic if your child hasn't learned to read well by the end of first grade. (She should be reading something but may not yet be fluent.) **Kids learn at different rates,** and some don't catch on until second grade. However, if by the middle of second grade your child isn't reading fairly well, **you should request an evaluation by the school's child-study team.** Ask to be present when the evaluation results are discussed and be part of the school's plan to create a program for your child. While up to 20 percent of children may experience reading difficulties and need extra help, **approximately 5 to 7 percent are so reading-disabled** that they need intensive, systematic phonics teaching in order to learn.

—Regie Routman

Reprinted from *Parents* magazine by permission.

Reading Pointers

- **Read to your child every day.** Make reading, enjoying books, and talking about books a way of life. Hearing stories builds vocabulary, listening skills, and continued interest in reading.

- **Use the "five-finger test"** to help your child choose books to read on his own. Have him read aloud from one page in the new book. When he comes to a word he can't read or doesn't understand, he puts up one finger. If all five fingers go up, the book is too difficult to read independently. You may want to read it to him.

- **If your child cannot read a certain word,** use other strategies along with "sound it out," such as:

  "What makes sense there?"

  "Say the sound of the first letter, read to the end of the sentence, and then come back to it."

  "Look at the picture."

  "What you said didn't sound right—try that again."

- **Don't forget to praise your child for her efforts.**

—Regie Routman

Reprinted from *Parents* magazine by permission.

Discuss the seven principles of effective phonics instruction described in this article. Compare and contrast traditional phonics approaches to contemporary phonics approaches in light of the qualities of effective phonics instruction.

Everything You Wanted to Know About Phonics (But Were Afraid to Ask)

Steven A. Stahl

Ann M. Duffy-Hester

University of Georgia, Athens, USA

Katherine Anne Dougherty Stahl

Clark County Public Schools, Georgia, USA

It is difficult to talk about phonics. Regie Routman (1996) used to say that "Phonics is a lot like sex. Everyone is doing it behind closed doors, but no one is talking about it" (p. 91). This has changed. People are talking about it, mostly in confusion about how to do it (phonics, that is). This is true in the media (e.g., Collins, 1997; Levine, 1994) as well as among teachers we talk to. In California, a bellwether state in education, a new report from the California Task Force on Reading (California Department of Education, 1995) recommended that "every school and district must organize and implement a comprehensive and bal-anced reading program that is re-search-based and combines skill de-velopment with literature and language-rich activities," and as-serted that "the heart of a powerful reading program is the relationship between explicit, systematic skills in-struction and literature, language and comprehension. While skills alone are insufficient to develop good readers, no reader can become proficient without those foundational skills" (p. 3).

There is a consensus of belief that good reading instruction in-cludes some attention to decoding. Whole language advocates such as Church (1996) and Routman (1996) devoted chapters of their recent books to teaching phonics, and Goodman (1993) wrote a book de-voted entirely to phonics. These whole language advocates argued that whole language teachers should be teaching phonics and that decod-ing instruction had always been part of whole language teaching. To quote Routman again:

It would be irresponsible and inexcusable not to teach phonics. Yet the media are having a field day getting the word out that many of us ignore phonics in the teaching of reading. It just isn't so. Some of us may not be doing as good a job as we need to be doing, but I don't know a knowledgeable teacher who doesn't teach phonics. (1996, p. 91)

Results of a recent U.S. national sur-vey of elementary school teachers in-dicated that 99% of K–2 teachers consider phonics instruction to be es-sential (67%) or important (32%) (Baumann, Hoffman, Moon, & Duffy-Hester, 1998).

Beliefs and Phonics

A lot of people are talking about phonics but in different ways. How people talk about phonics depends on their belief systems about reading in general. Different people have dif-ferent beliefs about how reading should be defined (DeFord, 1985; Stahl, 1997), which might affect how they think about phonics instruction. Some people believe that if one can recognize all of the words in a text quickly and accurately, one will be able to understand and appreciate that text. Therefore, the primary task in teaching reading for people who

Adapted from Stahl, Steven A., Duffy-Hester, Ann M., and Stahl, Katherine Anne Dougherty. (1998, July/Aug/Sept). Everything you wanted to know about phonics (but were afraid to ask). *Reading Research Quarterly*, 33 (3), 338–355. Reprinted with permission of Steven A. Stahl and the International Reading Association. All rights reserved.

hold this belief is to teach students how to recognize words (e.g., Gough & Hillinger, 1980). Others believe that reading should begin with interpretations of whole texts, and that phonics should be used only to support the reader's need to get meaning from text (e.g., Goodman, 1993). It is not difficult to see how these different belief systems might lead to different forms of phonics instruction.

The whole language movement helped to change the way we talk about phonics. This movement exploded onto the educational scene, rapidly changing basic beliefs about education (Pearson, 1989) and basal reading programs (Hoffman et al., 1994), as well as views on reading and reading instruction, and focusing on uses of written language for communication and on individual responses to literature and exposition (e.g., Goodman, 1986). Whole language advocates generally include phonics (or graphophonemics) as one of the cuing systems used in identifying words. Their model of reading is partially based on Goodman (1976) who suggested that readers use three cuing systems—graphophonemic, syntactic, and semantic—to identify words as they encounter them in meaningful text.

Goodman based his model on his work with miscue analysis (e.g., Goodman & Goodman, 1977), or the analysis of oral reading miscues that readers make during reading. Whole language teachers have advocated teaching children about letter-sound correspondences, but *only as an aid to a child's ongoing process of getting meaning from a text or producing a text*, and *only as needed*. In some instructional programs based on the whole language philosophy, the teacher does not teach from a predetermined scope and sequence but instead gives children the information they need to understand texts.

Although the issue should never have been whole language versus phonics but instead issues of how best to teach children to decode, the polarizing rhetoric used by some on the whole language movement seems to have convinced people that whole language and phonics are opposed to each other (McKenna, Stahl, & Reinking, 1994; Moorman, Blanton, & McLaughlin, 1994). Many teachers adopting a whole language philoso-phy perceived that they should never teach words in isolation, should provide phonics instruction only when students demonstrate the need for this instruction, and should never use unauthentic literature, such as books chosen for spelling patterns, in instruction. Although these rules are often violated by knowledgeable whole language teachers (see McIntyre & Pressley, 1996; Mills, O'Keefe, & Stephens, 1992; Pressley, Rankin, & Yakoi, 1996), they were nonetheless somehow communicated to many others.

These (mis)perceptions of whole language teaching resulted in confusion for many whole language teachers. Further, when some teachers (or their administrators) perceived a need for phonics instruction, they added on a program unrelated to their regular, literature-based program. These *Frankenclasses* were stitched together, with neither part of the curriculum informing the other. Such a curriculum may be no more desirable than the omission of phonics instruction.

In this article, we will review basic principles underlying word learning and phonics instruction. These principles are applicable in many primary-grade classrooms. Next, we will discuss approaches to teaching phonics. Finally, we will draw some tentative conclusions on how an integrated language arts program that includes phonics instruction may look in first-grade classrooms.

Understanding Phonics Instruction

When evaluating phonics instruction, we can rely on a research base going back to the 1920s for some empirical principles, but we also need to rely on some common sense. Research tells us that an early and systemic emphasis on teaching children to decode words leads to better achievement than a later or more haphazard approach (Adams, 1990; Chall, 1989, 1996). Further, being able to decode words is necessary for children to become independent word learners and thus be able to develop as readers without teacher assistance (Share, 1995). This much seems clear. But such instruction can occur in a vari-ety of settings, including traditional classes and whole language classes (Church, 1994; Dahl & Freppon, 1995; Mills et al., 1992). What is important is that phonics instruction is done well. Research (and common sense) suggest the following principles of good phonics instruction.

Good Phonics Instruction Should Develop the Alphabetic Principle

The key to learning to decode words is the principle that letters can represent sounds. Many languages such as Chinese use logographs, or stylized pictures, to represent meanings. Others use symbols to represent whole syllables. English, like many other languages, uses letters to represent individual sounds in words. Although English is not entirely regular—that is, there is not always a one-to-one correspondence between letters and sounds—understanding that letters do have a relationship with the sounds in words is a hallmark of successful beginning readers (Adams, 1990). . . .

Good Phonics Instruction Should Develop Phonological Awareness

The key to the development of the alphabetic principle, word recognition, and invented spelling is phonological awareness. Phonological awareness is one of the most important concepts to arise out of the past 20 years of research in reading (Stanovich, 1991). Phoneme awareness is the awareness of sounds in *spoken* words. As words are spoken, most sounds cannot be said by themselves. For example, the spoken word /cat/ has one continuous sound and is not pronounced "kuh-a-tuh." Children ordinarily concentrate on the meaning and do not think of the sounds in the word. But, since letters represent sounds, a child must learn to think of words as having *both* meaning and sound in order to understand the alphabetic principle (Stahl & Murray, 1998). . . .

Good Phonics Instruction Should Provide a Thorough Grounding in the Letters

The other part of learning letter-sound relationships is learning the forms of letters. Efficient word recognition is dependent on children's thorough familiarity with letters. They should not have to think, for example, that the letter *t* is the one with the up and down line and the cross thingy. Instead, children should recognize *t* immediately. Adams (1990) suggested that children need to recognize the forms of the letters automatically, without conscious effort, to be able to recognize words fluently.

There is some uncertainty about whether knowing the names of letters is absolutely necessary. On one hand, children can learn to recognize words without knowing the names of letters, and some reading programs do not require that children learn the names of the letters (Adams, 1990). On the other hand, knowing the names of letters is one of the best predictors of success in reading (Chall, 1996). Knowing the names of letters also helps children talk about letters. All in all, it is preferable to teach the names of letters, although children can begin to learn to read without knowing *all* the names of the letters. Thus, children should be reading and listening to connected texts before they know, and as they are learning, the names of all of the letters of the alphabet. . . .

Good Phonics Instruction Should Not Teach Rules, Need Not Use Worksheets, Should Not Dominate Instruction, and Does Not Have to Be Boring

There are a number of misconceptions about phonics instruction. Although traditional phonics instruction did teach rules, used worksheets, and was, frankly, often boring, it does not have to be. . . .

What seems to work in phonics instruction is direct teacher instruction, not practice on worksheets. Two observational studies by Haynes and Jenkins (1986) and Leinhardt, Zigmond, and Cooley (1981) found that the amount of time students spent on worksheets did not relate to gains in reading achievement. This may be because completing worksheets takes students' time away from reading stories or content material, and because instructional aspects of worksheets are often poorly designed (Osborn, 1984). What appeared to be most relevant was time spent reading connected text (Leinhardt et al., 1981). . . .

Good Phonics Instruction Provides Sufficient Practice in Reading Words

There are three types of practice that might be provided in a phonics program—reading words in isolation, reading words in stories (i.e., expository and narrative texts), and writing words. The ultimate purpose of phonics instruction is for children to learn to read words. Many researchers (see Adams, 1990, for a review) conclude that people identify words by using spelling patterns. These patterns are learned through continued practice in reading words containing those patterns. In addition, all successful phonics programs provide a great deal of practice in reading words containing the letter-sound relationships that are taught. Therefore, the practice given in reading words is extremely important. . . .

Good Phonics Instruction Leads to Automatic Word Recognition

In order to read books, children need to be able to read words quickly and automatically. If a child stumbles over or has to decode slowly too many words, comprehension will suffer (Samuels, Schermer, & Reinking, 1992). Although we want children to have a strategy for decoding words they do not know, we also want children to recognize many words automatically and be able to read them in context. . . .

Good Phonics Instruction Is One Part of Reading Instruction

It is necessary to remember that phonics instruction is only one part of a total reading program. Reading instruction has many different goals. We want children to enjoy reading and be motivated to read. We want children to comprehend what they read. We want children to be able to recognize words quickly and automatically. We know that children do not enjoy reading if they cannot comprehend or if they have to struggle sounding out each and every word.

Therefore, we want children to have a good background in letter-sound correspondences and be able to apply this knowledge to recognizing words quickly and automatically. But at the same time, children will not enjoy reading if the only reading they do is sounding out words. Good reading instruction contains a balance of activities around these different goals. . . .

Specific Approaches to Phonics Instruction

The conditions under which these principles can be met occur in a variety of reading programs. Reviews of research in this area suggest that it is the emphasis on early and systematic phonics instruction that makes a program effective and that differences between approaches are relatively small (Chall, 1996; Dahl & Freppon, 1995). In this section, we will discuss and review phonics instruction, both traditional and contemporary, from a variety of instructional philosophies. What we call traditional approaches are approaches that were in vogue during the 1960s and 1970s but seem to be returning as teachers grapple with how to teach phonics. Contemporary phonics approaches are those that have been used frequently in the past decade.

Traditional Phonics Approaches

Research on traditional phonics approaches includes mammoth federally funded studies (Abt Associates, 1977; Bond & Dykstra, 1967; Dykstra, 1968), large-scale district evaluations (Kean, Summers, Raivetz, & Farber, 1979), and reviews of research such as that of Adams (1990) and Chall (1996). These reviews consistently find that early and systematic phonics instruction is more effective than later and less systematic instruction.

The differences in quality between phonics approaches are small. Generally, reviews have found a slight advantage for synthetic approaches over analytic approaches (e.g., Chall, 1996), but these differences may be due not to differences in method but instead to differences in coverage, practice, or other factors.

Analytic Phonics Approaches

Analytic approaches begin with a word that a child already knows and breaks this word down into its component parts. . . .

Linguistic approaches. Another variety of phonics instruction that might be called analytic is the so-called linguistic method. This method is based on the theories of linguist Leonard Bloomfield (Bloomfield & Barnhart, 1961) who reasoned that one cannot pronounce many of the sounds that consonants make in isolation (that is, the first sound of *cat* is not /kuh/ but the unpronounceable /k/). Because children cannot sound words out, they should learn words in patterns (such as *cat, rat,* and *fat*) and induce the pronunciations of unknown words from known patterns. . . .

Synthetic Phonics Approaches

The other major division of traditional phonics approaches are the synthetic phonics approaches. Such phonics approaches begin with teaching students individual letters or groups of letters and then showing students how to blend these letters together to form words. . . .

Orton-Gillingham approaches. Approaches based on Orton-Gillingham methods begin with direct teaching of individual letters paired with their sounds through a VAKT (i.e., visual, auditory, kinesthetic, and tactile) procedure that involves tracing the letter while saying its name and sound, blending letters together to read words and sentences, and finally reading short stories constructed to contain only taught sounds. . . .

Direct instruction approaches. The Direct Instruction approach of Englemann was first published under the name of Distar (Englemann & Bruner, 1969), later Reading Mastery. The Distar approach is a synthetic phonics approach, based on a behavioral analysis of decoding (Kameenui, Simmons, Chard, & Dickson, 1997). . . .

Contemporary Phonics Approaches

In this section, we discuss three contemporary phonics approaches:

(a) spelling-based principles; (b) analogy-based approaches, and (c) embedded phonics approaches. All of these approaches are usually described in the literature as components of larger reading instruction programs. For example, spelling-based approaches are implemented in programs such as the Multimethod, Multilevel Instruction Program (e.g., Cunningham & Hall, 1997), the Charlottesville Volunteer Tutorial or Book Buddies Project (e.g., Invernizzi, Juel, & Rosemary, 1996/1997; Johnston, Juel, & Invernizzi, 1995), and the Howard Street Tutoring Program (e.g., Morris, 1992). Analogy-based approaches are one aspect of the Benchmark Word Identification Program (e.g., Gaskins et al., 1996/1997), and embedded phonics approaches are utilized in programs such as Reading Recovery (Clay, 1993) or in whole language classrooms (e.g., Dahl & Freppon, 1995; Freppon & Headings, 1996). Thus, it is important to consider the instructional context in which these contemporary phonics approaches often occur.

Spelling-Based Approaches

Three contemporary approaches to phonics instruction, Word Study (e.g., Bear, Invernizzi, Templeton, & Johnston, 1996), Making Words (e.g., Cunningham & Cunningham, 1992; Cunningham & Hall, 1994), and Meta-Phonics (Calfee, 1998; Calfee & Henry, 1996), are based on spelling principles.

Word Study. In Word Study, students examine words and word patterns through strategies such as sorting, in which students categorize words and pictures according to their common orthographic features. Word Study instruction is based on students' developmental levels of orthographic knowledge and is an approach to teaching phonics, vocabulary, spelling, and word recognition. . . .

Making Words. In Making Words (e.g., Cunningham & Cunningham, 1992; Cunningham & Hall, 1994), students are given six to eight different letters on letter cards. Then, the teacher calls out words with two, three, four, and more letters that can be formed using the students' letters, with the teacher and

students first making the words and then sorting words based on their common spelling patterns or other orthographic features. . . .

Making Words is one component of the Working With Words block in the Multimethod, Multilevel Instruction Program (e.g., Cunningham & Hall, 1997). . . .

Meta-phonics. In this approach, reading and spelling are taught simultaneously through social interaction and group problem solving. Sounds are introduced through phonemic awareness instruction. This instruction stresses articulation as a key to learning sounds (Calfee, 1998; Calfee et al., 1973). . . .

Analogy-Based Approaches

In analogy-based approaches to phonics instruction, students learn how to decode words they do not know by using words or word parts they do know. . . .

Analogy-based approaches are currently used as one instructional component in the Benchmark Word Identification Program (e.g., Gaskins, Gaskins, & Gaskins, 1991, 1992). . . .

Embedded Phonics Approaches

In embedded phonics approaches, phonics instruction occurs in the context of authentic reading and writing experiences. The phonics instruction in Reading Recovery and in many whole language classrooms are examples of embedded approaches to phonics instruction. . . .

Phonics in Reading Recovery. . . . Lessons are based on Goodman's (1976) model, suggesting that readers use three cuing systems to recognize words in context. Clay (1993) called these systems visual, structural, and meaning cues. . . .

Research on Contemporary Approaches to Phonics

Although there are indications that the contemporary approaches discussed in this section were effective, there is a notable lack of controlled research to validate the effectiveness of these approaches. Part of the reason for the lack of research is the newness of these approaches. Another possible reason is the general trend of the field away from comparative research and toward descriptive research (McKenna et al., 1994). Although descriptive research can give us insights, without some sort of comparison it is difficult to tell whether these new approaches are more effective than traditional approaches. Such comparative research need not be a horse race in which different approaches are saddled up to see which one produces the highest scores on a standardized achievement test. Instead, such comparisons may include qualitative aspects, such as in Dahl and Freppon's (1995) study, and should be directed toward what each approach might be effective at rather than toward choosing the most effective.

Constructions of Knowledge About Words

The principles discussed in the beginning of this article all relate to a teacher guiding students' constructions of knowledge about words. From a constructivist perspective, learners are thought to be actively constructing knowledge through their interactions with the world. This, of course, includes interactions with teachers and reading materials. Ordinarily, researchers have used a constructivist perspective to talk about comprehension, especially in conjunction with schema theory (e.g., Anderson & Pearson, 1984). Researchers in decoding rely on other psychological models, such as connectionism (Adams, 1990) and behaviorist models (Carnine, Silbert, & Kameenui, 1990). Neither of these models explicitly views the learner as actively constructing information about words.

Our observations of children show them very actively trying to make sense of words, in both their writing and their reading. A child who makes two or three attempts at a word in a text before coming up with one that makes sense and accommodates the letter-sound relationships that he or she knows is actively constructing word knowledge, as is the child who stretches out the letters in the word *camel* and produces *caml*.

Viewing decoding through a constructivist lens may be a whole language perspective (e.g., Weaver, 1994), but one need not adopt teaching techniques commonly associated with the whole language philosophy if one takes this perspective. A constructivist perspective is consistent with any of the methods discussed in the second section of this paper. Constructivism is not synonymous with discovery learning, since children can be guided in their constructions more or less explicitly. What constructivism implies is that the child is an active learner.

What children construct is a network of information about letters. They know, for example, that *t* is more likely to be followed by *r* or *h* than by *q* or *p*, that *ck* never starts a word, that *q* is nearly always followed by *u* (with the exception of some Arabic and Chinese words) (see Adams, 1990; Venezky, 1970). Much of this information could be directly taught or learned from repeated experiences with print. Children do differ in their need for guidance. Some children will learn much of what they need to know about words from exposure (e.g., Durkin, 1966), but most children need some explicit support. This support might be provided in context, as in the embedded phonics instruction approaches, through analogy- or spelling-based approaches, or through more direct instruction. It could be that some children with reading problems require more direct instruction (Carnine et al., 1990).

The notion that children construct knowledge about words may explain why the differences among programs are small. As long as one provides early and systematic information about the code (Chall, 1996), it may not matter very much how one does it. If each of the programs discussed previously provides similar amounts of coverage with similar amounts of practice reading words in isolation and in context, they might all have similar effects. From a constructivist perspective, children learn by acting upon information; if the information is similar, the learning should be as well. The principles discussed in the first part of this article suggest the information that should be taught in a phonics program. If this information is made available to children, then it may not matter exactly how the instruction occurs.

An effective first-grade reading program, for example, might involve some systematic and direct instruction in decoding, with associated practice in decodable texts (Juel & Roper/Schneider, 1985). These may include some contrived texts, if they are artfully and interestingly done. They also might include authentic literature chosen for repetition of taught patterns (Trachtenburg, 1990). Children also need a variety of engaging but easy texts, both for interest and for practice in reading a variety of materials. Some of these texts might be predictable where the context supports word recognition, at least until the child develops more independent word recognition strategies (Clay, 1993; Fountas & Pinnell, 1996). Predictable texts by themselves, however, may limit children's word learning (Duffy, McKenna, Vancil, Stratton, & Stahl, 1996), unless the teacher draws specific attention to words in those texts (Johnston, 1995). Writing, using invented spelling, is useful for developing word knowledge (Clarke, 1989). As they invent spellings, children need to integrate their developing phoneme awareness with their knowledge of sound-symbol correspondences (Stahl & Murray, 1998).

Because first-grade children are focused on decoding in their text reading (Chall, 1996), children's comprehension growth might best be accommodated by the teacher reading aloud to the children. Studies have found that children can learn new vocabulary words from hearing stories (e.g., Elley, 1989). In addition, teachers can model more advanced comprehension strategies with stories they read out loud to children since these stories are likely to have richer contexts than stories a child can read independently. This is not to say that comprehension should be ignored during children's reading. Basic strategies such as recall (Koskinen et al., 1988) or story grammars (Beck & McKeown, 1981) can be profitably taught to children at this age. An extensive reading program would likely improve first graders' motivation toward reading, as would a daily period of choice reading (Morrow & Tracey, 1998).

Thus, an effective first-grade program might involve elements associated with whole language (teacher reading aloud, invented spelling, free reading, extensive use of literature) as well as more direct instructional approaches (direct sound-symbol instruction, limited use of decodable or contrived texts). How these elements might be managed might also depend on the needs of the children. Children who enter first grade with a low literacy background may need more direct instruction to develop concepts that other children may have learned through print-based home experiences with literacy. Children with print-based literacy backgrounds may benefit from more time to choose their reading, with teacher support to read more and more complex materials.

Effective reading instruction requires that a teacher recognize multiple goals for reading instruction, and that different means are required to reach these multiple goals. Juggling these goals will always be a challenge. We are not sure, however, that the alleged balance we are seeing in some classroom reading programs is based on a forward-looking examination of what is needed for effective reading instruction; rather, it may be based, at least in part, on false allegations popularized by the media and accepted by some legislators and administrators describing the limited success of past reading programs.

The balance in some of today's reading programs appears to be an attempt to lay phonics instruction on top of a literature-based curriculum. This is easy. Good reading instruction, however, is difficult. It involves all teachers asking themselves what skills their students have, what their goals are, and how reading instruction can be directed toward all of their goals.

References

ABT Associates. (1977). *Education as experimentation: A planned variation model. Volume IV-B, Effects of follow-through models.* Cambridge, MA: Author.

Adams, G.L., & Englemann, S. (1996). *Research on direct instruction: 25 years beyond DISTAR.* Seattle, WA: Educational Achievement Systems.

Adams, M. J. (1990). *Beginning to read: Thinking and learning about print.* Cambridge, MA: MIT Press.

Anderson, R.C., Hiebert, E.F., Scott, J.A., & Wilkinson, I.A.G. (1985). *Becoming a nation of readers.* Champaign, IL: National Academy of Education and Center for the Study of Reading.

Anderson, R.C., & Pearson, P.D. (1984). A schema-theoretic view of basic processes in reading. In P.D. Pearson (Ed.), *Handbook of reading research* (pp. 255–292). White Plains, NY: Longman.

Barnes, G.W. (1989). Word sorting: The cultivation of rules for spelling in English. *Reading Psychology, 10,* 293–307.

Baumann, J.F., Hoffman, J.V., Moon, J., & Duffy-Hester, A. M. (1998). Where are teachers' voices in the phonics/whole language debate? Results from a survey of U.S. elementary classroom teachers. *The Reading Teacher, 51,* 636–650.

Bear, D.R., & Barone, D. (1989). Using children's spellings to group for word study and directed reading in the primary classroom. *Reading Psychology, 10,* 275–292.

Bear, D.R., Invernizzi, M., Templeton, S., & Johnston, F. (1996). *Words their way: Word study for phonics, vocabulary, and spelling instruction.* Upper Saddle River, NJ: Merrill.

Beck, I.L., & McKeown, M.G. (1981). Developing questions that promote comprehension: The story map. *Language Arts, 58,* 913–918.

Bloodgood, J. (1991). A new approach to spelling in language arts programs. *Elementary School Journal, 92,* 203–211.

Bloomfield, L., & Barnhart, C.L. (1961). *Let's read: A linguistic approach.* Detroit, MI: Wayne State University Press.

Bond, G., & Dykstra, R. (1967). The cooperative research program in first grade reading. *Reading Research Quarterly, 2,* 5–142.

Bruck, M., & Treiman, R. (1992). Learning to pronounce words: The limitations of analogies. *Reading Research Quarterly, 27,* 374–388.

Byrne, B., & Fielding-Barnsley, R. (1991). Evaluation of a program to teach phonemic awareness in young children. *Journal of Educational Psychology, 83,* 451–455.

Calfee, R. (1998). Phonics and phonemes: Learning to decode in a literature-based program. In J. Metsala & L. Ehri (Eds.), *Word recognition in beginning literacy.* Mahwah, NJ: Erlbaum.

Calfee, R. & Henry, M. (1996). Strategy and skill in early reading acquisition. In J. Shimon (Ed.), *Literacy and education: Essays in memory of Dina Feitelson* (pp. 97–118). Cresskill, NJ: Hampton Press.

Calfee, R.C., Lindamood, P., & Lindamood, C. (1973). Acoustic-phonetic skills and reading: Kindergarten through twelfth grade. *Journal of Educational Psychology, 64,* 293–298.

California Department of Education. (1995). *Every child a reader: The report of the California Reading Task Force.* Sacramento: Author. (http://www.cde.ca.gov/ cilbranch/eltdiv/rdg_init.htm).

Carnine, D., Silbert, J., & Kameenui, E. (1990). *Direct instruction reading* (2nd ed.). Columbus, OH: Merrill.

Center, Y., Wheldall, K., Freeman, L., Outhred, L., & McNaught, M. (1995). An evaluation of Reading Recovery. *Reading Research Quarterly, 30,* 240–263.

Chall, J.S. (1989). Learning to read: The great debate twenty years later. A response to "Debunking the great phonics myth." *Phi Delta Kappan, 71,* 521–538.

Chall, J.S. (1996). *Learning to read: The great debate* (revised, with a new foreword). New York: McGraw-Hill.

Church, S.M. (1994). Is whole language really warm and fuzzy? *The Reading Teacher, 47,* 362–371.

Church, S.M. (1996). *The future of whole language: Reconstruction or self-destruction.* Portsmouth, NH: Heinemann.

Clarke, L.K. (1989). Encouraging invented spelling in first graders' writing: Effects on learning to spell and read. *Research in the Teaching of English, 22,* 281–309.

Clay, M.M. (1991). Introducing a new storybook to young readers. *The Reading Teacher, 45,* 264–273.

Clay, M.M. (1993). *Reading Recovery: A guidebook for teachers in training.* Portsmouth, NH: Heinemann.

Clymer, T. (1963). The utility of phonic generalizations in the primary grades. *The Reading Teacher, 16,* 252–258.

Clymer, T. (1996). The utility of phonic generalizations in the primary grades. *The Reading Teacher, 50,* 182–187.

Collins, J. (1997, October 27). How Johnny should read. *Time Magazine, 150*(17), 78–81.

Cunningham, P.M. (1975/1976). Investigating a synthesized theory of mediated word identification. *Reading Research Quarterly, 11,* 127–143.

Cunningham, P.M. (1978). Decoding polysyllabic words: An alternative strategy. *Journal of Reading, 21,* 608–614.

Cunningham, P.M. (1979). A compare/ contrast theory of mediated word identification. *The Reading Teacher, 32,* 774–778.

Cunningham, P.M. (1980). Applying a compare/contrast process to identifying polysyllabic words. *Journal of Reading Behavior, 12,* 213–223.

Cunningham, P.M. (1995). *Phonics they use* (2nd ed.). New York: HarperCollins.

Cunningham, P.M., & Cunningham, J.W. (1992). Making words: Enhancing the invented spelling-decoding connection. *The Reading Teacher, 46,* 106–115.

Cunningham, P.M., & Hall, D.P. (1994). *Making words.* Carthage, IL: Good Apple.

Cunningham, P.M., & Hall, D.P. (1997, May). *A framework for literacy in primary classrooms that work.* Paper presented at the 42nd annual convention of the International Reading Association, Atlanta, GA.

Dahl, K.L., & Freppon, P.A. (1995). A comparison of innercity children's interpretations of reading and writing instruction in the early grades in skills-based and whole language classrooms. *Reading Research Quarterly, 30,* 50–74.

DeFord, D.E. (1985). Validating the construct of theoretical orientation in reading instruction. *Reading Research Quarterly, 20,* 351–367.

Duffy, A.M., McKenna, M., Vancil, S., Stratton, B., & Stahl, S. A. (1996, December). *Tales of Ms. Wishy-Washy: The effects of predictable books on learning to recognize words.* Paper presented at the annual meeting of the National Reading Conference, Charleston, SC.

Durkin, D. (1966). *Children who read early.* New York: Teachers College Press.

Durkin, D. (1978/1979). What classroom observations reveal about reading comprehension instruction. *Reading Research Quarterly, 14,* 481–533.

Durkin, D. (1988). *A classroom observation study of reading instruction in kindergarten* (Tech. Rep. No. 422). Champaign, IL: Center for the Study of Reading, University of Illinois at Urbana-Champaign.

Dykstra, R. (1968). The effectiveness of code- and meaning-emphasis beginning reading programs. *The Reading Teacher, 22,* 17–23.

Ehri, L.C. (1992). Reconceptualizing the development of sight word reading and its relationship to recoding. In P. Gough, L. C. Ehri, & R. Treiman (Eds.), *Reading acquisition* (pp. 107–143). Mahwah, NJ: Erlbaum.

Ehri, L.C. (1995). Phases of development in learning to read words by sight. *Journal of Research in Reading, 18,* 116–125.

Ehri, L.C., & Robbins, C. (1992). Beginners need some decoding skill to read words by analogy. *Reading Research Quarterly, 27,* 12–26.

Eldredge, J.L. (1995). *Teaching decoding in holistic classrooms.* Englewood Cliffs, NJ: Merrill.

Eldredge, J.L., & Butterfield, D. (1986). Alternatives to traditional reading instruction. *The Reading Teacher, 48,* 32–37.

Elkonin, D.B. (1973) U.S.S.R. In J. Downing (Ed.), *Comparative reading* (pp. 551–579). New York: Macmillan.

Elley, W.B. (1989). Vocabulary acquisition from listening to stories. *Reading Research Quarterly, 24,* 174–187.

Englemann, S., & Bruner, E. (1969). *Distar reading program.* Chicago: SRA.

Fayne, H.R., & Bryant, N.D. (1981). Relative effects of various word synthesis strategies on the phonics achievement of learning disabled youngsters. *Journal of Educational Psychology, 73,* 616–623.

Feitelson, D., Kita, R., & Goldstein, Z. (1986). Effects of listening to series stories on first graders' comprehension and the use of language. *Research in the Teaching of English, 20,* 339–356.

Flack, M. (1931). *Angus and the cat.* Garden City, NY: Doubleday.

Fleisher, L.S., Jenkins, J.R., & Pany, D. (1979/1980). Effects on poor readers' comprehension of training in rapid decoding. *Reading Research Quarterly, 15,* 30–48.

Fountas, I.C., & Pinnell, G.S. (1996). *Guided reading: Good first teaching for all children.* Portsmouth, NH: Heinemann.

Freppon, P.A., & Dahl, K.L. (1991). Learning about phonics in a whole language classroom. *Language Arts, 68,* 190–197.

Freppon, P.A., & Headings, L. (1996). Keeping it whole in whole language: A first grade teacher's instruction in an urban whole language classroom. In E. McIntyre & M. Pressley (Eds.), *Balanced instruction: Strategies and skills in whole language* (pp. 65–82). Norwood, MA: Christopher-Gordon.

Gambrell, L.B., Wilson, R.M., & Gantt, W.N. (1981). Classroom observations of task-attending behaviors of good and poor readers. *Journal of Educational Research, 74,* 400–404.

Gaskins, I.W., Downer, M.A., Anderson, R.C., Cunningham, P.M., Gaskins, R.W., Schommer, M., & The Teachers of the Benchmark School. (1988). A metacognitive approach to phonics: Using what you know to decode what you don't know. *Remedial and Special Education, 9,* 36–41.

Gaskins, I.W., Ehri, L.C., Cress, C., O'Hara, C., & Donnelly, K. (1996/1997). Procedures for word learning: Making discoveries about words. *The Reading Teacher, 50,* 312–327.

Gaskins, R.W., Gaskins, J.C., & Gaskins, I. (1991). A decoding program for poor readers—and the rest of the class, too! *Language Arts, 68,* 213–225.

Gaskins, R.W., Gaskins, J.C., & Gaskins, I. (1992). Using what you know to figure out what you don't know: An analogy approach to decoding. *Reading and Writing Quarterly: Overcoming Learning Disabilities, 8,* 197–221.

Gill, J.T. (1992). Development of word knowledge as it relates to reading, spelling, and instruction. *Language Arts, 69,* 444–453.

Gillet, J.W., & Temple, C. (1990). *Understanding reading problems* (3rd ed.). Glenview, IL: Scott Foresman.

Gillingham, A. (1956). *Remedial training for children with specific disability in reading, spelling, and penmanship.* Cambridge, MA: Educators Publishing Service.

Goodman, K.S. (1976). Reading: A psycholinguistic guessing game. In H. Singer & R. B. Ruddell (Eds.), *Theoretical models and processes of reading* (2nd ed., pp. 497–508). Newark, DE: International Reading Association.

Goodman, K.S. (1986). *What's whole in whole language? A parent/teacher guide to children's learning.* Portsmouth, NH: Heinemann.

Goodman, K.S. (1993). *Phonics phacts.* Portsmouth, NH: Heinemann.

Goodman, K.S., & Goodman, Y.M. (1977). Learning about psycholinguistic processes by analyzing oral reading. *Harvard Educational Review, 47,* 317–333.

Goswami, U. (1993). Toward an interactive analogy model of reading development: Decoding vowel graphemes in beginning reading. *Journal of Experimental Child Psychology, 56,* 443–475.

Goswami, U. (1998). The role of analogies in the development of word recognition. In J. Metsala & L. Ehri (Eds.), *Word recognition in beginning literacy.* Mahwah, NJ: Erlbaum.

Gough,P.B., & Hillinger, M.L. (1980). Learning to read: An unnatural act. *Bulletin of the Orton Society, 30,* 179–196.

Hall, D.P., & Cunningham, P.M. (1996). Becoming literate in first and second grades: Six years of multimethod, multilevel instruction. In D.J. Leu, C.K. Kinzer, & K.A. Hinchman (Eds.), *Literacies for the 21st century.* 45th yearbook of the National Reading Conference (pp. 195–204). Chicago: National Reading Conference.

Harste, J.C., Burke, C.L., & Woodward, V.A. (1982). Children's language and world: Initial encounters with print. In J.A. Langer & M.T. Smith-Burke (Eds.), *Reader meets author/Bridging the gap* (pp. 105–131). Newark, DE: International Reading Association.

Haskell, D.W., Foorman, B.R., & Swank, P. A. (1992). Effects of three orthographic/phonological units on first grade reading. *Remedial and Special Education, 13,* 40–49.

Haynes, M.C., & Jenkins, J.R. (1986). Reading instruction in special education resource rooms. *American Educational Research Journal, 23,* 161–190.

Herman, P.A. (1985). The effect of repeated readings on reading rate, speech pauses, and word recognition accuracy. *Reading Research Quarterly, 20,* 553–565.

Hiebert, E.H. (1994). A small group literacy intervention with Chapter I students. In E.H. Hiebert & B. M. Taylor (Eds.), *Getting reading right from the start* (pp. 85–106). Boston: Allyn & Bacon.

Hoffman, J.V., McCarthey, S.J., Abbott, J., Christian, C., Corman, L., Curry, C., Dressman, M., Elliott, B., Matherne, D., & Stahle, D. (1994). So what's new in the new basals? A focus on first grade. *Journal of Reading Behavior, 26,* 47–73.

Hohn, W.E., & Ehri, L.C. (1983). Do alphabet letters help pre-readers acquire phonemic segmentation skill? *Journal of Educational Psychology, 75,* 752–762.

Invernizzi, M., Abouzeid, M., & Gill, T. (1994). Using students' invented spellings as a guide for spelling instruction that emphasizes word study. *Elementary School Journal, 95,* 155–167.

Invernizzi, M., Juel, C., & Rosemary, C.A. (1996/1997). A community volunteer tutorial that works. *The Reading Teacher, 50,* 304–311.

Iversen, S., & Tunmer W.E. (1993). Phonological processing skills and the Reading Recovery program. *Journal of Educational Psychology, 85,* 112–126.

Johnston, F.R. (1995, December). *Learning to read with predictable text: What kinds of words do beginning readers remember?* Paper presented at the annual meeting of the National Reading Conference, New Orleans, LA.

Johnston, F., Juel, C., & Invernizzi, M. (1995). *Guidelines for volunteer tutors of emergent and early readers.* Charlottesville, VA: University of Virginia McGuffey Reading Center.

Juel, C., & Roper/Schneider, D. (1985). The influence of basal readers on first grade reading. *Reading Research Quarterly, 20,* 134–152.

Kameenui, E.J., Simmons, D.C., Chard, D., & Dickson, S. (1997). Direct instruction reading. In S.A. Stahl & D.A. Hayes (Eds.), *Instructional models in reading* (pp. 59–84). Mahwah, NJ: Erlbaum.

Kean, M. H., Summers, A.A., Raivetz, M.J., & Farber, I.J. (1979). *What works in reading? Summary and results of a joint school district/Federal Reserve Bank empirical study in Philadelphia.* Philadelphia: Office of Research and Evaluation. (ERIC Document Reproduction Service ED 176 216).

Kline, C.L., & Kline, C.L. (1975). Follow-up study of 216 dyslexic children. *Bulletin of the Orton Society, 25,* 127–144.

Koskinen, P.S., Gambrell, L.B., Kapinus, B.A., & Heathington, B.S. (1988). Retelling: A strategy for enhancing students' reading comprehension. *The Reading Teacher, 41,* 892–896.

Leinhardt, G., Zigmond, N., & Cooley, W. (1981). Reading instruction and its effects. *American Educational Research Journal, 18,* 343–361.

Levine, A. (1994, December). Education: The great debate revisited. *Atlantic Monthly, 274*(6), 38–44.

Lovitt, T.C., & Demier, D.M. (1984). An evaluation of the Slingerland method with LD youngsters. *Journal of Learning Disabilities, 17,* 267–272.

Lovitt, T.C., & Hurlburt, M. (1974). Using behavior-analysis techniques to assess the relationship between phonics instruction and oral reading. *Journal of Special Education, 8,* 57–72.

McIntyre, E., & Pressley, M. (1996). *Balanced instruction: Strategies and skills in whole language.* Norwood, MA: Christopher-Gordon.

McKenna, M.C., Stahl, S.A., & Reinking, D. (1994). A critical commentary on research, politics, and whole language. *Journal of Reading Behavior, 26,* 211–233.

Meyer, L.A. (1983). Increased student achievement in reading: One district's strategies. *Research in Rural Education, 1,* 47–51.

Mills, H., O'Keefe, T., & Stephens, D. (1992). *Looking closely: Exploring the role of phonics in one whole language classroom.* Urbana, IL: National Council of Teachers of English.

Monroe, M. (1932). *Children who cannot read.* Chicago: University of Chicago Press.

Moorman, G.B., Blanton, W.E., & McLaughlin, T. (1994). The rhetoric of whole language. *Reading Research Quarterly, 29,* 308–329.

Morris, D. (1992). *Case studies in teaching beginning readers: The Howard Street tutoring manual.* Boone, NC: Fieldstream Publications.

Morris, D., Ervin, C., & Conrad, K. (1996). A case study of middle school reading disability. *The Reading Teacher, 49,* 368–377.

Morrow, L.M., & Tracey, D. (1998). Motivating contexts for young children's literacy development: Implications for word recognition development. In J. Metsala & L. Ehri (Eds.), *Word recognition in beginning literacy.* Mahwah, NJ: Erlbaum.

Murray, B.A. (1995). *Which better defines phoneme awareness: Segmentation skill or identity knowledge?* Unpublished doctoral dissertation, University of Georgia, Athens.

Murray, B.A., Stahl, S.A., & Ivey, M.G. (1996). Developing phoneme awareness through alphabet books. *Reading and Writing: An Interdisciplinary Journal, 8,* 307–322.

Ogden, S., Hindman, S., & Turner, S.D. (1989). Multisensory programs in the public schools: A brighter future for LD children. *Annals of Dyslexia, 39,* 247–267.

Osborn, J. (1984). The purposes, uses, and contents of workbooks and some guidelines for publishers. In R. C. Anderson, J. Osborn, & R.J. Tierney (Eds.), *Learning to read in American schools: Basal readers and content texts* (pp. 45–112). Hillsdale, NJ: Erlbaum.

Osborn, J., Stahl, S.A., & Stein, M. (1997). *Teachers' guidelines for evaluating commercial phonics packages.* Newark, DE: International Reading Association.

Pearson, P.D. (1989). Reading the whole language movement. *Elementary School Journal, 90,* 231–241.

Pressley, M., Rankin, J., & Yokoi, L. (1996). A survey of instructional practices of primary teachers nominated as effective in promoting literacy. *Elementary School Journal, 96,* 363–384.

Rasinski, T.V. (1991). Fluency for everyone: Incorporating fluency instruction in the classroom. *The Reading Teacher, 43,* 690–692.

Routman, R. (1996). *Literacy at the crossroads.* Portsmouth, NH: Heinemann.

Samuels, S.J., Schermer, N., & Reinking, D. (1992). Reading fluency: Techniques for making decoding automatic. In S. J. Samuels & A. E. Farstrup (Eds.), *What research says about reading instruction* (2nd ed., pp. 124–144). Newark, DE: International Reading Association.

Schlagal, R.C., & Schlagal, J.H. (1992). The integral character of spelling: Teaching strategies for multiple purposes. *Language Arts, 69,* 418–424.

Seuss, Dr. (1957). *The cat in the hat.* Boston: Houghton Mifflin.

Shanahan, T., & Barr, R. (1995). Reading Recovery: An independent evaluation of the effects of an early instructional intervention for at-risk learners. *Reading Research Quarterly, 30,* 958–996.

Share, D.L. (1995). Phonological recoding and self-teaching: Sine qua non of reading acquisition. *Cognition, 55,* 151–218.

Silberberg, N.E., Iversen, I.A., & Goins, J.T. (1973). Which remedial reading method works best? *Journal of Learning Disabilities, 6,* 547–556.

Spaulding, R., & Spaulding, W.T. (1962). *The writing road to reading.* New York: Morrow.

Stahl, K.A.D., Stahl, S.A., & McKenna, M. (1997). *The development of phonological awareness and orthographic processing in Reading Recovery.* Unpublished manuscript, University of Georgia, Athens.

Stahl, S.A. (1997). Models of reading instruction: An introduction. In S.A. Stahl & D.A. Hayes (Eds.), *Instructional models in reading* (pp. 1–29). Hillsdale, NJ: Erlbaum.

Stahl, S.A., Heubach, K., & Cramond, B. (1997). *Fluency oriented reading instruction* (Research Report). Athens, GA: National Reading Research Center.

Stahl, S.A., & Murray, B.A. (1994). Defining phonological awareness and its relationship to early reading. *Journal of Educational Psychology, 86,* 221–234.

Stahl, S.A., & Murray, B.A. (1998). Issues involved in defining phonological awareness and its relation to early reading. In J. Metsala & L.C. Ehri (Eds.), *Word recognition in beginning literacy* (pp. 65–87). Mahwah, NJ: Erlbaum.

Stahl, S.A., Osborn, J., & Pearson, P.D. (1994). *Six teachers in their classrooms: Looking closely at beginning reading* (Tech. Rep. No. 606). Champaign, IL: Center for the Study of Reading, University of Illinois at Urbana-Champaign.

Stahl, S.A., Suttles, C.W., & Pagnucco, J.R. (1996). The effects of traditional and process literacy instruction on first graders' reading and writing achievement and orientation toward reading. *Journal of Educational Research, 89,* 131–144.

Stanovich, K.E. (1991). The psychology of reading: Evolutionary and revolutionary developments. *Annual Review of Applied Linguistics, 12,* 3–30.

Sullivan, H.J., Okada, M., & Niedermeyer, F.C. (1971). Learning and transfer under two methods of word-attack instruction. *American Educational Research Journal, 8,* 227–240.

Tangel, D. M., & Blachman, B. A. (1992). Effects of phoneme awareness instruction on kindergarten children's invented spellings. *Journal of Reading Behavior, 24,* 233–262.

Taylor, B.M., Short, R., & Shearer, B. (1990, December). *Early intervention in reading: Prevention of reading failure by first grade classroom teachers.* Paper presented at the annual meeting of the National Reading Conference, Miami, FL.

Templeton, S. (1989). Tacit and explicit knowledge of derivational morphology: Foundations for a unified approach to spelling and vocabulary development in the intermediate grades and beyond. *Reading Psychology, 10,* 233–253.

Templeton, S. (1991). Teaching and learning the English spelling system:

Reconceptualizing method and purpose. *Elementary School Journal, 92,* 185–201.

Templeton, S. (1992). New trends in an historical perspective: Old story, new resolution—Sound and meaning in spelling. *Language Arts, 69,* 454–463.

Templeton, S., & Bear, D.R. (Eds.). (1992). *Development of orthographic knowledge and the foundations of literacy: A memorial Festschrift for Edmund H. Henderson.* Hillsdale, NJ: Erlbaum.

Trachtenburg, P. (1990). Using children's literature to enhance phonics instruction. *The Reading Teacher, 43,* 648–653.

Traub, N. (1977). *Recipe for reading* (2nd ed.). New York: Walker.

Turner, J.C. (1995). The influence of classroom contexts on young children's motivation for literacy. *Reading Research Quarterly, 30,* 410–441.

Venezky, R.L. (1970). *The structure of English orthography.* The Hague, The Netherlands: Mouton.

Vickery, K.S., Reynolds, V.A., & Cochran, S. W. (1987). Multisensory training approach for reading, spelling and handwriting: Orton-Gillingham based curriculum in a public school setting. *Annals of Dyslexia, 37,* 189–200.

Wasik, B.A., & Slavin, R.E. (1993). Preventing early reading failure with one-to-one tutoring: A review of five programs. *Reading Research Quarterly, 28,* 178–200.

Watson, D.J. (1989). Defining and describing whole language. *Elementary School Journal, 90,* 129–142.

Weaver, C. (1994). *Reading process and practice: From socio-psycholinguistic to whole language.* Portsmouth, NH: Heinemann.

White, T.G., & Cunningham, P.M. (1990, April). *Teaching disadvantaged students to decode and spell by analogy.* Paper presented at the annual meeting of the American Educational Research Association, Boston.

Yaden, D.B., Smolkin, L.B., & MacGillivray, L. (1993). A psychogenetic perspective on children's understanding about letter associations during alphabet book readings. *Journal of Reading Behavior, 25,* 43–68.

Zutell, J., & Rasinski, T. (1989). Reading and spelling connections in third and fifth grade students. *Reading Psychology, 10,* 137–155.

Article Review Form at end of book.

Watson argues that quality children's literature is a better choice for reading instruction than is decodable text written specifically to give children practice in reading words to which they have been exposed in prior instruction. Locate some of the books discussed in this article and analyze them in terms of their support for readers, including patterns of words, syntax, concepts, and illustrations. List your findings.

Talking About Books

Beyond decodable texts—supportive and workable literature

Dorothy Watson

Dorothy Watson, Guest Editor and author of this month's Talking About Books *column, challenges the concept of decodable texts with a review of contemporary children's books that support readers predictable features. The following people have contributed to this column: Ann Alof, Carol Gilles, Jenine Loesing, Cheryl Schofield, Beverly Vick, Virginia Walker, and their students, Patricia Jenkins, Sheryl McGruder, and Peter Hasselriis provided insights, references and encouragement.*

In September, Alvin was asked to choose a book to read from a pile of five books. He flipped through them, stopping along the way to look at the engaging illustrations that were in three of the books. Alvin made two piles and then surprisingly said, pointing to the stories with illustrations, "These look great but," pointing to the other pile, "I can *say* some of the words in these. I guess I'd better do these." I was dismayed to find that he had rejected three beautifully written and illustrated books to settle on two that resembled controlled-vocabulary basals. Alvin sounded out some of the words of his first selection. He also yawned, rubbed his eyes, and jabbed at the print with his finger. Wanting to take us both out of our torment, I asked, "Is this as boring for you as it is for me?" Alvin replied, "I don't know what it's about." The truth: The "book" wasn't about anything, but it was, in part, "decodable" text.

Throughout the year Alvin and I began each session with the same selection procedure. Mid-year, after many experiences in his classroom with a teacher who was knowledgeable about literature and the reading process, and after experiences in our sessions with a variety of texts that could never be described as "sequentially ordered," "controlled vocabulary," "leveled," or "decodable," Alvin began to make quick work of the selection procedure. The decodable texts were discarded with "boring," "too easy," "naw," and the all time put-down "yuckola." Alvin made it clear why he *rejected* books,

but I wanted him to think through and articulate why he *chose* certain books. When I asked him to help me understand his selection process, I fully expected him to talk about the beauty of the pictures and about stories that interested him. His explanation came thoughtfully, "I can *work* this story." Alvin explained that a *workable* book was one that he "liked enough to try hard."

Alvin's words intrigued Charlie Robb, a third grade teacher, who asked his colleagues in a graduate class in Miscue Analysis to think of a favorite book and then to consider the elements of the book that supported their reading. These experienced educators talked about what they brought to the book from their own lives and interests. They mentioned the grace and flow of language that invited them in and moved them along, and their feeling of accomplishment as they made their way through a challenging book. For these proficient adult readers, their favorite books were ones that they could, to use Alvin's term, work.

Dorothy Watson, "Talking About Books: Beyond Decodable Texts—Supportive and Workable Literature," *Language Arts,* December 1997, by the National Council of Teachers of English. Reprinted with permission.

To further understand Alvin's concept of working a story, we turn to Ken Goodman's model of reading (1965). Goodman's work sheds light on how readers work text, how they *sample* from the array of print and illustrations, how they *predict* what may come next and how they *draw inferences* from the intersections of their lives and the text. The model prompts teachers to observe readers as they reject or accept their predictions and inferences, as they resample from the text or from the content of their lives if their work doesn't result in meaning or if it doesn't "sound right." The model further points up the role of integration of new information with the reader's existing knowledge.

Predictable Books as Support for Readers

In *Phonics Phacts* (1993), Goodman says that active readers don't wait until they have all the information before making up their minds; readers anticipate where a text is going, what will come next, and what structures they will meet. He tells us, "A *prediction* is an anticipation of what will come in the text" (p. 113).

Goodman's model helps teachers understand that linguistic and cognitive risk-taking enables proficient readers to make predictions. Many less proficient readers, however, are afraid of taking risks and do so only if the syntax, semantics, and letter-sound relationships within the texts are very secure and dependable—that is, highly predictable. Teachers realize that text itself, if it is predictable enough, helps children learn to read. "Predictable books" became a basic part of reading for young children. Steve Bialostok (1992) categorized predictable language books in terms of patterns of words, syntax, concepts, and illustrations. The following are his categories with some typical examples.

1. Books in which there is a relationship between picture and text such as *Rosie's Walk* by Pat Hutchins and *Rain* by Robert Kalan.

2. Books in which the text remains almost identical on each page except for a substitution of a word or phrase, such as *Cat on a Mat* by Brian Wildsmith and *I Was Walking Down the Road* by Sarah Barchas.

3. Books with cumulative language, such as the new, exciting, and informative *Hungry Animals, A Seed Grows,* and *A New Butterfly* by Pamela Hickman and Heather Collins.

4. Response books in which the text is often in the form of questions and answers or conversation, such as *Whose Mouse Are You?* by Robert Kraus and *Chick and the Duckling* by Mirra Ginsburg.

5. Books with repeated portions, such as *It Didn't Frighten Me* by Janet Goss and Jerry Harste and *Sitting Down to Eat* by Bill Harley (illustrations by Kitty Harvill).

6. Rhythmic books, such as *Jamberry* by Bruce Degan and *Brown Bear, Brown Bear, What Do You See?* by Bill Martin, Jr.

7. Interlocking books in which one idea engages with another idea until an entire chain of text is formed, as in *When the Elephant Walks* by Keiko Kosza and *Fortunately* by Remy Charlip.

8. Poetry and books of songs in which rhyme, alliteration, repetition, and rhythm provide predictability, as in *How Sweet the Sound: African-American Songs for Children* by Wade and Cheryl Hudson and *Inch by Inch: The Garden Song* by David Mallet.

Many struggling readers gain both support for their reading and confidence in their own abilities through their use of predictable books (some of which find their way into enlarged books called big books). Such books continue to constitute a significant part of children's early reading material in many literature-filled classrooms. Critics often diminish the experience of shared reading using predictable texts with, "Those kids aren't reading. They've just memorized the story." Nevertheless, teachers and struggling readers are aware that human memory, aided by the linguistic and cognitive support found in predictable books, help them work the story.

Cheryl Schofield understands the role of memory in early reading and therefore spends a great deal of time reading and rereading predictable books to her kindergartners and first-graders, many of whom need highly supportive books to interest, motivate, and ease them into successful reading. Many of Cheryl's selections could be described as linguistically predictable, but they also support her blossoming readers in other ways. The following books are workable not only because of their predictability, but also because of their potential for successful inference making, text references (both forward and backward in the story), descriptions, and examples. Of *Cat Among the Cabbages* (1996) by Alison Bartlett, Cheryl comments,

When I read, 'The cat walks past a quiet red hen and a noisy red rooster. Cock-a-doodle-dooooooooooo!' everybody joined in. We liked the way describing words were printed to match their meaning. We liked the fold-out pages, especially the one of the kittens. One child loved the guessing part at the end of the book. This story lends itself to quick dramatization:

The cat wakes up and yawns. Then it takes a long stretch. . . . The cat crouches low to the ground and wriggles its tail. . . . It leaps! And a large yellow butterfly flutters high into the sky. . . . The cat struts past short pink piglets and scoots around a fat pink pig. (Unpaged)

Off-the-page references to life and known literature make books more workable for emerging readers. *Winnie-the-Pooh Tells Time* inspired by A. A. Milne (illustrations by Ernest Shepard, 1997) supports readers who are familiar with Pooh and Piglet in other Milne books or who are familiar with time-telling and counting experiences. Cheryl says her kids are not thrown by words like smackerel and Poohsticks, but enjoy talking about them.

Jenine Loesing chose *From Head to Toe* (1997) by Eric Carle to capture her first graders' interest. Familiarity with the love of Carle's stories encourages and gives the same confidence and support that only an old friend can provide. Jenine says,

"True to Eric Carle's style, the reader is engaged from page one. Animals introduce a movement, 'I am a cat and I arch my back. Can you do it?' followed by the answer, 'I can do it!' The supportive text allows even the very young child to read this book." Matthew commented, "The title matches the book. It starts at his head and ends at his toes." Forrest observed, "It's kind of like a Simon Says book." Carroline wanted to move around when she read it and Grant thought it was like exercising.

Jenine invited her students to make their own books: "I am (child's name). I can (action). Can you? Yes, I can!" Then each child drew an animal that fit the action.

Daisy as a Mommy (1996) by Lisa Kopper is a delightful book that will kindle lots of discussion about babies and puppies. Daisy and the pups captivate the kids and repetitive language helps the readers: "Mommy gives her baby the best breakfast. So does Daisy. . . . Mommy gives her baby a bath. So does Daisy." (Unpaged)

The text of children's lives as it intersects with Kopper's story will help readers work the story on their own after a few readings with their teacher, parent, or an older reading buddy.

Grace Hallworth's collection of Afro-Caribbean rhymes, games, and songs for children, *Down by the River* (illustrations by Caroline Binch, 1996), begins with a wake-up rhyme for baby:

Pinchy, pinchy, pinchy,
Fly, fly away.
Birdy, birdy, birdy,
Fly, fly, away. (Unpaged)

These rhymes and songs that have been passed down by generations originally came from diverse cultural backgrounds and have their roots in France, Africa, England, and America. The support of captivating rhythm, rhyme, action, and illustrations is evident. Children will enjoy working the pieces and extending the collection by adding games, songs, jokes, and rhymes from their own backgrounds. (One can't help but notice that "Pinchy, pinchy, pinchy" is more palatable than making "lip-poppers" in phonemic awareness exercises.)

Teachers will not give up on inviting even their most non-proficient readers into literature that is rich in language and thought. They know that rereading of these special books is necessary, so they make tapes for listening, they pair students for collaborative reading, they ask older readers to read with their students and, of course, they reread books to their classes. But teachers also know that needy readers must have texts that they can work with on their own after a limited number of read alouds. Many series specifically designed for non-proficient readers are now available. It takes searching, but with patience and a determination to ignore the levels assigned, some gems can be found in a few of these series. Several of the eight-page books in the Visions: African-American Experiences, Young Readers Series are examples of good workable texts. Favorites include: *Pockets, My Buddy, My Friend, Mama Goes to School, Skating Whiz, Family Names, Glasses,* and *Am I Ready Now?* by Claudette Mitchell, Gracie Porter, and Patricia Cousin (illustrations by James Threalkill and Michael McBride, 1996). In these books, readers gain support through illustrations, rhyme, repetition, and pace that includes a twist at the end. For example, *Pockets* reads: "The pocket on my pants (p. 2), holds my ants. (p. 3), The pocket on my shirt (p. 4), holds my dirt. (p. 5), The pocket on my coat (p. 6), holds my boat. (p. 7), The pocket on my vest is the best (p. 8)." (Check out the vest pocket surprise.)

My Best Sandwich by Susan Hartley and Shane Armstrong (illustrations by Peter Townsend, 1996), *Shadows* by Margaret Ballinger and Rachel Gosset (illustrations by Stephen Michael King, 1996), and *Snap Likes Gingersnaps* by Rachel Gosset (illustrations by Peter Townsend, 1996) in Scholastic's Reading Discovery series, provide multiple supports for young readers. Each of the seven-page books has a clever little yarn that will make children smile. Several books in the series published by MONDO Publishing, One Plaza Rd. in Greenvale, New York are worthy of children's time, appeal to their interests, and are supportive. They deserve an examination.

Text, Lives and Other Literature as Support for Inferencing and Predicting

Goodman's insights into predictability provide criteria for supportive text, but his model also points out other natural reading strategies that help learners create meaning. The concept of *inferencing* has not been explored as thoroughly as has the notion of *predicting*. With additional information from a model of reading that is not only theoretically sound but that supports practice, teachers are now searching for stories and materials that have rich potential for children to work the text by *making inferences* and then *confirming* or *rejecting* their inferences and predictions.

According to Goodman (1993), "Inferences are possible and necessary because no text is a complete representation of the meaning" (p. 113). Inferences are the information readers supply. Proficient readers go beyond the author's explicit information; they make use of implicit information. They do this by tapping into the vast store of knowledge gained from their lives which includes experiences with literature.

It probably won't surprise anyone that the first questions asked by the teachers who introduced these books to their students was, "How appropriate are the stories to the lives of my kids? Will they be interested?" These teachers know that children won't willingly read (and can't work) what they have no interest in and what they can't understand. This is in keeping with the two predictability criteria that Ken and Yetta Goodman suggested in "Consumer Beware! Selecting Materials for Whole Language Readers," (Goodman & Goodman, 1991):

1. Language that is natural for the text and the reader.

2. Conceptual information is known by the reader to a considerable extent though it often contains new information which interests the reader. (p. 119)

Additionally, the teachers mentioned all the criteria for material selection that the Goodmans wrote about in the same article:

1. Literary quality

2. Authentic social/cultural significance

3. Cohesion and coherence—the way in which the text hangs together.

4. Illustrations

5. Teaching possibilities

6. Psychological possibilities. (p. 119)

Based on their questions and the criteria above, teachers chose the following books to present to their students.

Because so many of her first graders were losing teeth, Jenine Loesing chose *The Seed Bunny*, by Jennifer Selby (1996). Sam, after many unsuccessful attempts to pull his big bunny front tooth, finally drifts off to sleep. Out comes Sam's tooth and the Seed Bunny rewards him with a package of carrot seeds complete with planting directions. Carrie comments, "This book is good for anyone who may be afraid about losing their teeth." Anju predicts that Sam will begin to work on his other big front tooth and that the same thing will happen again.

Jenine suggests that teachers might use this book as a read aloud each time a child loses a tooth. The text will soon become so familiar that individuals or partners will be able to read it on their own.

On a very warm day during the last few weeks of school, Ann Alofs read Cynthia Rylant's *Mr. Putter and Tabby Row the Boat* (illustrations by Arthur Howard, 1997) to her second and third graders. Ann writes,

The children listened intently as I read the story. After the second chapter, Josh pointed out that each chapter seemed to lead into the next. As I read similar sentences: 'They sweated on the front porch. They sweated in the kitchen. They sweated under the oak tree,' and lines repeated across text: "It was a hot walk. It was a sweaty walk. It was a slow walk" (Unpaged) the children chimed in. After reading the book, we had a great time talking about it.

Starr: "I like when the bird came down and tried to eat the grapes on Mrs. Teaberry's hat."

Logan: "And the hat goes with Mrs. Teaberry's name because it had berries on it!"

Cissy: "You can make good guesses because you can look at the pictures. You know the words better because they repeat things over and over."

Deasha: "They kept saying sweat, sweat, sweat."

Logan: "Whenever they are walking, it repeats, like it was a hot walk, and a sweaty walk."

Kiana: "It's good that Mr. Putter and Tabby is a series. I like to read books in a series."

When Ann read *Mr. Putter and Tabby Fly the Plane* by the same author and illustrator, she couldn't help but notice the enthusiasm with which Will and Zach talked about the book.

Will: "I read that book! It was about Mr. Putter and he loved planes. He saw this plane he'd never seen before. He bought it. He got everything . . ."

Zach: (interrupting and eager to take the book to his desk) "Can I read it?"

Will: (refusing to be stopped) ". . . ready to go but it still didn't work. But it did in the end."

Ann says the children noticed other books in the series listed on the book jacket and asked to get them in their room. Later Ann commented,

Mr. Putter and Tabby Row the Boat had been in our room a week. Many children picked it up to read, but two boys in particular chose the book over and over during 'choices' time. Both boys are second graders currently receiving Title One services for reading. One began reading the book and asked the other for help. The boys and I talked about the book. One commented, 'It was funny. It also repeated. I like books that repeat because that makes it easier to read.'

Another book that had strong appeal to Ann's kids was *The Summer of Stanley* by Natalie Kinsey-Warnock (illustrations by Donald Gates, 1997). According to Matthew the book has ". . . great pictures and an outstanding plot." He tells us that the book is about "people in World War II who have a goat that's driving them insane." Matt who read the book "by myself" pays it the ultimate compliment, "I'd buy it if I could." *The Summer of Stanley* supports young readers through its winning plot, its familiar characters (annoying big sister, irritating neighbor, and exasperated mom) and, a familiar story line about an unwanted animal becoming a hero.

Detective Donut and the Wild Goose Chase by Bruce Whatley (illustrations by Rosie Smith, 1997) was a favorite of Ann's kids. Matthew wrote in his review, "People who like mysteries will like this book!" The text and the illustrations complement each other and provide necessary support for the reader to grasp the

many subtle inferences that need to be made in order to construct meaning. As it turns out, Detective Donut (the print tells his story) is not as swift of thought and deduction as his alert and vigilant partner, Mouse (the illustrations tell his story). This is a book to talk about with a reading buddy or in a small group in which the children can search for the clues provided in both print and picture. What a dynamic duo: Detective Donut and Mouse, print and picture!

Beverly Vick's culturally, ethnically, and linguistically diverse class of second-graders chose many books because of their beautiful and interesting language, repetition, humor and familiarity with themes and strong characters. Beverly selected four class favorites. A charmer that is sure to capture any reader is *A Mouse Told His Mother* by Bethany Roberts (illustrations by Maryjane Begin, 1997). The reader is supported by the repetitious "A mouse told his mother, 'I . . . am going to the moon, . . . am off to catch a crocodile, . . . will dive for pirate treasure,' followed by, 'Take your toothbrush, . . . Don't forget to wash your feet, . . . You'd better bring a towel,' 'said his mother'" (Unpaged). The interlocking talk between mouse and mom, as well as the lovely complementary pictures, provide children with immediate support for their own reading.

Bunny Cakes (1997) by Rosemary Wells is a favorite of Beverly's kids. It wasn't the delightful story that first drew them in, but rather Ruby's grocery lists and Max's invented writing. Once into the book, Bev's multi-lingual class loved words like raspberry-fluff icing and Red-Hot Marshmallow Squirters. According to Bev, her little linguists are "Hooked on homophones, so a discussion on flour and flower was inevitable." There are lots of symbols, environmental print, and darling (the word fits!) pictures that lend support to listeners who will soon want to read the story on their own.

On Bev's recommendation, I roped my tough-to-please neighbor, Kevin, into joining me in reading Jez Alborough's *Watch Out! Big Bro's Coming!* (1997). He grinned all the way through it, laughed out loud at the ending and made me smile with, "I love that book!" I do too. Readers are supported by lines with sparkling word substitutions, " 'Look out!' croaked the frog. 'Big Bro's coming!' ", " 'Watch out!' squawked the parrot. 'Big Bro's coming!' " and the repetitious "He's rough, he's tough, and he's really big," along with the brilliant pictures. My friend, a fifth-grader, suggested that the book would be great to read to kindergarten bookpals; "You know, they'd sit still for this one!"

Children's interest in their own family histories and in the topic of adoption will draw them into Jamie Lee Curtis' *Tell Me Again About the Night I Was Born* (1996). Laura Carnell's whimsical but right-on illustrations complement a tender story. Kids and adults will find themselves and their family members in the pictures and will ask that this story be read again and again.

Dancing With the Wind by Stanton Orser (illustrations by James Bernardin, 1997) begins, "Did you know," he asks, "that long ago you could see the wind?" With that, father calms his daughter's fears by telling her about a beautiful woman who was the wind. This is a many-layered story of how the wind was freed from her captor through the abilities of seemingly natural enemies. The bear, the deer, the fox, the rabbit, the owl, the mouse, the porcupine, and even the tiny tick join their individual strengths and talents to save the wind, their woods and their lives. Readers will gain support through the strength of the plot, the beauty and clarity of the language and the illustrations.

Searching for supportive books for older readers, Carol Gilles found *Spider Boy* by Ralph Fletcher (1997). Carol says,

This chapter book about the new boy at school helps readers work the text through familiar characters they can relate to. Bobby isn't happy with his move to New Paltz. He keeps his wrist watch on Illinois time and waits for calls from his real friends. Rather than making new friends, Bobby lies to everyone in New Paltz and they believe him. He doesn't, however, have to lie about his love for spiders. Through Bobby's diary, Fletcher weaves factual information about spiders, 'People don't understand spiders. They think of them as blood thirsty vampires. The truth is spiders make the world a better place. They try to give us a bug-free environment. Spider experts estimate that the insects eaten by spiders in one year weigh more than fifty million people'

(p. 1). Another supportive feature is Fletcher's careful use of context to help readers understand unfamiliar words and concepts. For example, Bobby's sister comments about her boyfriend, 'Luke is . . . a *phenomenal* swimmer, one of the best in the state' (p. 77). Or later, when Bobby has a confrontation with Butch, 'Ever heard of an African king baboon spider? . . . I didn't think so. You know what the word *lethal* means? How about *fatal*? This is one of the deadliest spiders on earth' (p. 139). This book has a strong story line about loneliness and, of course, would appeal to spider enthusiasts.

Carol also chose Andrea Johnston's *Girls Speak Out: Finding Your True Self*, with an introduction by Gloria Steinem (1997). Carol says,

The author speaks in simple direct language, including poems and excerpts from short stories by popular authors, about the concerns of teenage girls. Issues include making choices, being a daughter, and finding their true selves. The writings are an outgrowth of a program initiated by the author and held at YWCAs that emphasizes that everyone matters. It was created using an advisory committee of 11- to 19-year-old young women who "talked, listened, laughed, read, sewed, ate, shopped, hiked, field-tested artifacts, and kept journals so they could give other girls what they themselves hoped to experience" (p. xii). The directness of the messages, familiar style, and quality of the excerpts makes this a workable text for teenaged girls. As fifth grader Nadia exclaimed, "This is a real book. I want to share it with my friends and family."

Curricular Support for Reading

Goodman provided a "theoretical model" of reading that is much more than theory; it is a foundation for curricular experiences and materials. His sociopsycholinguistic model reminds us that readers must be invited to bring to the text their thoughts, language and lives. Doing so, some children, even without curricular support, can successfully read a wide range of books in a variety of genres. Even so, all readers—even proficient ones but most particularly hesitant readers—can benefit from thematic studies that provide background information and connectedness through conceptually related materials and ideas. Classrooms that encourage discussions, questions and

student research offer curricular support that helps learners make sense of texts that might otherwise be too difficult for them.

Logan (Ann Alofs multi-age primary) sees that certain books lend themselves to thematic cycles and that readers will get support in their understanding from the information gained through theme studies. Logan writes of *Look to the North: A Wolf Pup Diary* by Jean Craighead George (illustrations by Lucia Washburn, 1997),

I think other kids would like this book. I think teachers should get it because it would be good for science—it has the life cycle of a wolf. The wolves start out one day old and at the end they start over and have more babies.

On each lyrical and informative page, George invites young readers to "look to the north" in order to watch the wolf pups from birth to seven months. Readers gain support from the author and illustrator's beautiful language and pictures that describe, define, and depict the lives of Boulder, Scree, and Talus. In turn, readers have a responsibility; they must work the text by bringing information to it and by finding connections in the details of the wolves' lives. A curricular theme with conceptually related materials will help readers with their work.

The poetic text and clear crisp pictures of *Shaker Hearts* by Ann Turner (illustrations by Wendell Minor, 1997) intrigued Virginia Walker's fifth graders. According to Ouai, the book is ". . . a story that is a poem," and Shi Shi spoke of it as "a story that sings like a song." Other class members described it as "a rhyme that goes over and over," "a book with elegant words," "simple but interesting with great pictures," and "a book that tells about another culture." Virginia's class is a community of scholars in which social and cultural issues are freely discussed. The study of multiethnic, cultural, and social groups infuse the dynamic and literature-filled inquiry curriculum. Such a setting supports children's thinking, reading, and writing.

Another poetic narrative is Carolyn Lesser's *Storm on the Desert* (illustrations by Ted Rand, 1997). Carol Gilles sees this beautiful picture story book as a resplendent example of the mutual support illustrations and text can offer. Carol writes,

This non-fiction rendition of a desert storm is an unrhymed poem coupled with brilliant illustrations, done in pencil, pastel, chalk, and watercolor. The combination of text and pictures extend meaning and allows readers to work the text. As we read,

> Sun burns the crackly earth.
> Flickers and elf owl
> Tuck into holes in saguaros (Unpaged)

we see a *saguaro* with an owl holed up in a small burrow and a bird (must be a flicker) pecking a larger burrow. "Reading" such illustrations, children construct meaning and deepen understanding. When the storm hits, the text and illustrations work together to make us see and hear it:

> Lightning flashes inside clouds.
> Distant thunder growls,
> Nears, rumbling between mountains,
> Bony fingers of lightening streak,
> Strike. (Unpaged)

The illustration portrays bony finger lightning angling out of the sky, with all the animals in dark chalky silhouette, fleeing the storm.

Rand uses color and broad brush strokes to show us how the desert is transformed after the rain, a striking contrast to the white and brown illustrations prior to rain and the murky brown during the rain. A harmonious merger of text and illustrations offers readers a chance to understand the life of a desert.

The Vision Seeker by James Whetung (illustrations by Paul Morin, 1996) while challenging, invites readers to bring their interest and knowledge of legends and culture to it and to construct their own meaning. Such background information can come from ideas and materials found within a theme cycle that includes discussions on human struggles and personal growth. The story is filled with symbolism and beauty as Spirit Bird travels back to Long Ago, and it begins, "My spirit name is Spirit Bird. My mother's clan is, of common knowledge, Otter. My father says his clan is Black Duck; others say it is Cormorant." (Unpaged). Britney (fifth grade) commented, "One thing that caught my eye was the Indian signs. I wonder what they all mean?" Sam explains, "This is a cool legend about warring clans and of a vision-seeking boy who saved them and brought peace."

A Reader in Every Child

We've focused here on the supportive nature of real literature that is written for children by authors who care about their craft and their talents. These books are offered to students by teachers who know that within all children there are readers hungry for the stories. Teachers also know that to read, children need help from the story itself. Help must come from captivating books that reach out to the reader. Clearly, our search leads us far beyond non-dimensional decodable text.

References

Alborough, Jez. (1997). *Watch out! big bro's coming!* Cambridge, MA: Candlewick Press. Unpaged. ISBN: 0-7636-0130-6.

Ballinger, Margaret, & Gosset, Rachel. (1996). *Shadows*. Illus. Stephen Michael King. New York: Scholastic. Unpaged. ISBN: 0-590-23793-4.

Barchas, Sarah. (1993). *I was walking down the road*. New York: Scholastic. Unpaged. ISBN: 0-590-7183-5.

Bartlett, Alison. (1996). *Cat among the cabbages*. New York: Dutton Children's Books. Unpaged. ISBN: 0-525-45755-0.

Bialostok, Steve. (1992). *Raising readers: Helping your child to literacy*. New York: Peguis. 161 pp.; ISBN: 1-895411-37-8.

Carle, Eric. (1997). *From head to toe*. New York: HarperCollins Publishers. Unpaged. ISBN: 0-06-023515-2.

Charlip, Remy. *Fortunately*. New York: Macmillan. Unpaged. ISBN: 0-590-07762-7.

Curtis, Jamie Lee. (1996). *Tell me again about the night I was born*. Illus. Laura Cornell. New York: Joanna Cotler Books. Unpaged. ISBN: 0-06-024528-X.

Degan, Bruce. (1983). *Jamberry*. New York: Harper and Row. Unpaged. ISBN: 0-06-443068-5.

Fletcher, Ralph. (1997). *Spider boy*. New York: Clarion Books. 182 pp.; ISBN: 0-395-77606-6.

George, Jean Craighead. (1997). *Look to the north: A wolf pup diary*. Illus. Lucia Washburn. New York: HarperCollins. Unpaged. ISBN: 0-06-023641-8.

Ginsburg, Mirra. (trans. from the Russian.). (1972). *The chick and the duckling* by V. Suteev. New York: Macmillan. Unpaged. ISBN: 0-24-102380-7.

Gollasch, Frederick (Ed.). (1982). *Language and literature: Selected writing of Kenneth Goodman* (Vol. 1). Boston, MA: Routledge & Kegan, Paul. 304 pp.; ISBN: 0-7100-0875-9.

Goodman, K.S. (1965). Cues and Miscues in Reading. *Elementary English Review, 42*(6), pp. 639–643.

Goodman, Kenneth. (1993). *Phonics Phacts*. Portsmouth, NH: Heinemann. 120 pp.; ISBN: 0-435-08810-6.

Goodman, K., & Goodman, Y. (1991). Consumer beware! Selecting materials for whole language readers. In K. Goodman, L. Bridges, & Y. Goodman (Eds.), *The whole language catalog*. (p. 119). New York: American School Publishers. 445 pp.; ISBN: 0-07-020102-1.

Goss, Janet, & Harste, Jerry. (1981). *It didn't frighten me*. School Book Fairs, Inc. Unpaged. ISBN: none listed.

Gosset, Rachel. (1996). *Snap likes gingersnaps*. Illus. Peter Townsend. New York: Scholastic. Unpaged. ISBN: 0-590-23785-3.

Hallworth, Grace. (Compiler). (1996). *Down by the river: Afro-Caribbean rhymes, games, and songs for children*. Illus. Caroline Binch. New York: Scholastic Inc. Unpaged. ISBN: 0-590-69320-4.

Harley, Bill. (1996). *Sitting down to eat*. Illus. Kitty Harvill. Little Rock: August House. Unpaged. ISBN: 0-87483-460-0.

Hartley, Susan, & Armstrong, Shane. (1996). *My best sandwich*. Illus. Peter Townsend. New York: Scholastic. Unpaged. ISBN: 0-590-23788-8.

Hickman, Pamela, & Collins, Heather. (1997). *Hungry Animals*. Toronto, Ontario: Kids Can Press Ltd. Unpaged. ISBN: 1-55074-204-3.

Hickman, Pamela, & Collins, Heather. (1997). *A New Butterfly*. Toronto, Ontario: Kids Can Press Ltd. Unpaged. ISBN: 1-55074-202-7.

Hickman, Pamela, & Collins, Heather. (1997). *A Seed Grows*. Toronto, Ontario: Kids Can Press Ltd. Unpaged. ISBN: 1-55074-200-0.

Hudson, Wade, & Cheryl. (1995). *How sweet the sound: African-American songs for children*. Illus. Floyd Cooper. New York: Scholastic. 48 pp.; ISBN: 0-590-48034-0.

Hutchins, Pat. (1968). *Rosie's walk*. New York: Macmillan. Unpaged. ISBN: 0-027458050-4.

Johnston, Andrea. (1997). *Girls speak out: Finding your true self*. New York: Scholastic. 209 pp.; ISBN: 0-590-89795-0.

Kalan, Robert. (1978). *Rain*. New York: Greenwillow. Unpaged. ISBN: 0-688-84139-2.

Kinsey-Warnock, Natalie. (1997). *The summer of Stanley*. Illus. Donald Gates. New York: Cobblehill Books/Dutton. Unpaged. ISBN: 0-525-65177-2.

Kopper, Lisa. (1996). *Daisy is a mommy*. New York: Dutton Children's Books. Unpaged. ISBN: 0-525-45722-4.

Kosza, Keiko. (1990). *When the elephant walks*. New York: Putnam. Unpaged. ISBN: 0-399-21755-X.

Kraus, Robert. (1970). *Whose mouse are you?* New York: Macmillan. Unpaged. ISBN: 0-027-51190-1.

Lesser, Carolyn. (1997). *Storm on the desert*. Illus. Ted Rand. San Diego: Harcourt Brace & Company. Unpaged. ISBN: 0-15-272198-3.

Mallett, David. (1995). *Inch by inch: The garden song.* Illus. Ora Eitan. New York: HarperCollins Publishers. Unpaged. ISBN: 0-06-024304-X.

Martin, Jr. Bill. (1967). *Brown bear, brown bear, what do you see?* New York: Holt, Rinehart and Winston. Unpaged. ISBN: 0-8050-0201-4.

Milne, A.A. (Inspired by). (1997). *Winnie-the-Pooh tells time.* Illus. Ernest H. Shepard. New York: Dutton Children's Books. Unpaged. ISBN: 0-525-45535-3.

Mitchell, Claudette, Porter, Gracie R., & Cousins, Patricia Tefft. (1996). *Am I ready now?* Illus. James R. Threalkill and Michael J. McBride. San Diego: Arborlake Publishing, Inc. Unpaged. ISBN: 1-57518-044-8.

Mitchell, Claudette, Porter, Gracie R., & Cousins, Patricia Tefft. (1996). *Family names.* Illus. James R. Threalkill and Michael J. McBride. San Diego: Arborlake Publishing, Inc. Unpaged. ISBN: 1-57518-048-0.

Mitchell, Claudette, Porter, Gracie R., & Cousins, Patricia Tefft. (1996). *Glasses.* Illus. James R. Threalkill and Michael J. McBride. San Diego: Arborlake Publishing, Inc. Unpaged. ISBN: 1-57518-049-9.

Mitchell, Claudette, Porter, Gracie R., & Cousins, Patricia Tefft. (1996). *Mama goes to school.* Illus. James R. Threalkill and Michael J. McBride. San Diego: Arborlake Publishing, Inc. Unpaged. ISBN: 1-57518-051-0.

Mitchell, Claudette, Porter, Gracie R., & Cousins, Patricia Tefft. (1996). *My buddy, my friend.* Illus. James R. Threalkill and Michael J. McBride. San Diego: Arborlake Publishing, Inc. Unpaged. ISBN: 1-57518-053-7.

Mitchell, Claudette, Porter, Gracie R., & Cousins, Patricia Tefft. (1996). *Pockets.* Illus. James R. Threalkill and Michael J. McBride. San Diego: Arborlake Publishing, Inc. Unpaged. ISBN: 1-57518-055-3.

Mitchell, Claudette, Porter, Gracie R., & Cousins, Patricia Tefft. (1996). *Skating whiz.* Illus. James R. Threalkill and Michael J. McBride. San Diego: Arborlake Publishing, Inc. Unpaged. ISBN: 1-57518-067-7.

Orser, Stanton. (1997). *Dancing with the wind.* Illus. James Bernardin. Flagstaff, AZ: Rising Moon. Unpaged. ISBN: 0-87358-639-5.

Roberts, Bethany. (1997). *A mouse told his mother.* Illus. Maryjane Begin. New York: Little, Brown and Company. Unpaged. ISBN: 0-316-74982-6.

Rylant, Cynthia. (1997). *Mr. Putter and Tabby fly the plane.* Illus. Arthur Howard. San Diego: Harcourt Brace & Company. Unpaged. ISBN: 0-15-256253-2.

Rylant, Cynthia. (1997). *Mr. Putter and Tabby row the boat.* Illus. Arthur Howard. San Diego: Harcourt Brace & Company. Unpaged. ISBN: 0-15-256257-5.

Selby, Jennifer. (1996). *The seed bunny.* San Diego: Harcourt Brace & Co. Unpaged. ISBN: 0-15-201397-0.

Turner, Ann. (1997). *Shaker hearts.* Illus. Wendell Minor. New York: Harper Collins Publishers. Unpaged. ISBN: 0-06-25369-X.

Wells, Rosemary. (1997). *Bunny cakes.* New York: Dial Books for Young Readers. Unpaged. ISBN: 0-8037-2143-9.

Whatley, Bruce. (1997). *Detective Donut and the wild goose chase.* Illus. Rosie Smith. New York: Harper Collins Publishers. Unpaged. ISBN: 0-06-026604-X.

Whetung, James. (1996). *The vision seeker.* Illus. Paul Morin. Toronto: Stoddart. Unpaged. ISBN: 0-7737-2966-6.

Wildsmith, Brian. (1982). *Cat on the mat.* Oxford: Oxford University Press. Unpaged. ISBN: 0-19-272123-2.

Dorothy Watson is Professor Emerita at the University of Missouri, where she taught for 20 years. Dorothy was the first president of the Whole Language Umbrella, has won numerous awards for her teaching and has made significant contributions to literacy education. Her books include: *Reading Miscue Inventory: Alternative Procedures* (with Y. Goodman and C. Burke), *Ideas and Insights: Language Arts in the Elementary School,* and most recently, *Making a Difference: Selected Writings of Dorothy Watson.*

All of the contributors are members of Mid-Missouri TAWL (Teachers Applying Whole Language).

Ann Alof and Cheryl Schofield teach in multi-age settings at Benton Elementary School in Columbia, Missouri.

Jenine Loesing teaches first grade and Sheryl McGruder teaches second grade at Fairview Elementary in Columbia, Missouri.

Virginia Walker teaches fifth grade at Robert E. Lee Elementary School in Columbia, Missouri.

Beverly Vick teaches second grade at Patrick Henry Elementary School in Alexandria, Virginia and is a resent Ph.D. graduate from the University of Missouri–Columbia.

Carol Gilles, Patricia Jenkins, and Peter Hasselrüs teach literacy classes in the Department of Curriculum and Instruction and also work with Continuing Professional Education at the University of Missouri–Columbia.

 Article Review Form at end of book.

WiseGuide Wrap-Up

- Recent research in the language acquisition of infants has found that language learning is an astonishing act of brain computation.

- Effective family literacy programs revolve around participation; provide a curriculum that best serves clients; use stable, collaborative, and certified staff and administration; and use effective fund-raising practices.

- The definition of *balanced literacy* differs according to people's perceptions of how research into practice transpires and is grounded in alternative models of teaching.

- Teachers' interpretations of relevant research will change as they interact with children to establish a theory-based philosophy that will inform instructional practices.

- Phonics instruction must be an integral part of all reading instruction but must be guided by common sense and effective teaching practices.

- The supportive features of quality children's literature are better texts for reading instruction than are controlled-vocabulary, decodable texts.

R.E.A.L. Sites

This list provides a print preview of typical **Coursewise** R.E.A.L. sites. There are over 100 such sites at the **Courselinks**™ site. The danger in printing URLs is that web sites can change overnight. As we went to press, these sites were functional using the URLs provided. If you come across one that isn't, please let us know via email to: webmaster@coursewise.com. Use your Passport to access the most current list of R.E.A.L. sites at the **Courselinks**™ site.

Site name: Center for the Improvement of Early Reading Achievement
URL: http://www.ciera.org/
Why is it R.E.A.L.? The purpose of this site is to improve reading achievement by generating and disseminating theoretical, empirical, and practical solutions to persistent problems in the learning and teaching of beginning reading.
Key topics: reading achievement, reading research
Try this: Summarize the ten research-based principles related to how the reading achievement of young children could be improved.

Site name: National Institute on Early Childhood Development and Education
URL: http://www.ed.gov/offices/OERI/ECI/
Why is it R.E.A.L.? This comprehensive site focuses on research and resources for families, educators, communities, and policy makers—in an effort to assist all children, regardless of societal, economic, family, linguistic, and/or disability conditions.
Key topics: early childhood development and learning, family and community support
Try this: Review the offerings of the web site; then select one online publication to read and review.

Site name: National Center for Family Literacy
URL: http://www.famlit.org/
Why is it R.E.A.L.? This resource promotes the advancement and support of family literacy services for families across the United States through programming, training, research, advocacy, and dissemination of information about family literacy.
Key topics: family literacy
Try this: Explore this site and list the resources available to parents to support family literacy.

section

3

Learning Objectives

- Define *mediated learning experiences* and explain why they are beneficial to students.

- Identify the components of a successful program of comprehension instruction.

- Explain, from a theoretical perspective, how and why different ways of talking about text can be important for learning to read literature.

- Define *critical literacy* and identify ways to involve students in analyzing text.

"Teacher, What Does This Mean?": Understanding Text

 **WiseGuide Intro**

The purpose of writing is to express a thought or an idea. The purpose of reading is to comprehend the author's message. Words and letters are taught, so that children will be able to construct meaning from written text. From their very first encounters with books, children should expect reading to make sense.

Over the past thirty years, research in the area of reading comprehension has led to new theoretical understandings about the complex process of constructing meaning from text. Schema theory has profoundly influenced our understanding of how people store information in memory and how previously learned information can lead to new knowledge. Schema are sets of related concepts that form a network of interrelated knowledge and experiences. The growth and development of the schema are influenced by experiences and educational opportunities.

Schema theory has provided a powerful explanation of the extremely complex act of comprehending text, with strong instructional implications. Teachers who understand schema theory realize the importance of the prior knowledge children bring to the classroom. Students with a substantial amount of knowledge about a subject are apt to recall more information from reading than are students who do not possess as much or any prior knowledge. Thus, activating and building on prior knowledge before reading is essential to optimal comprehension.

Since comprehension is invisible, students are not able to see the strategies teachers use to comprehend text, and teachers are unable to see where children may be having difficulty comprehending text. Therefore, it is important for teachers to make "visible" effective comprehension strategies. It is critical for teachers to understand the strategies children use to comprehend text and the ways in which teachers can facilitate reading comprehension.

The articles in Section 3 discuss the roles of prior knowledge, schema, and reading for meaning in literacy development. "Mediation of Cognitive Competencies for Students in Need" explains the theory of mediated learning experiences and its importance for children who are not prepared to deal with the cognitive challenges confronting them as they enter school. "Reading Comprehension: What Works" discusses effective classroom strategies that teachers can implement to improve reading comprehension. "Changing Talk About Text: New Roles for Teachers and Students" offers a theoretical discussion on how and why different ways of talking about text can be so important in learning to read literature. "Critical Questions: Whose Questions" provides insight into ways to promote critical literacy in the classroom, while cautioning that teachers must be able to accept students' questions, even when they do not appear to lead to the kinds of critical understanding that teachers hope to achieve.

Questions

Reading 11. Define the three characteristics of mediated learning experiences (MLE). The author states that, even though MLE theory is "naturally appealing," it is really more demanding than it is comforting; it makes our expectations grow and our accomplishments shrink. Explain what you think the author means by this statement.

Reading 12. Why do teachers encourage students to talk to one another about things they have read? Describe what the authors mean by peer and collaborative learning.

Reading 13. What is meant by "different ways of talking" about books?

Reading 14. What is meant by the term *critical questions?* Why do teachers want students to be able to ask critical questions?

Define the three characteristics of mediated learning experiences (MLE). The author states that, even though MLE theory is "naturally appealing," it is really more demanding than it is comforting; it makes our expectations grow and our accomplishments shrink. Explain what you think the author means by this statement.

Mediation of Cognitive Competencies for Students in Need

Children who have not received sufficient Mediated Learning Experiences are not prepared to deal with the cognitive challenges confronting them as they enter school and are thus unable to benefit from the wealth of classroom experiences offered, Mr. Ben-Hur points out.

Meir Ben-Hur

Meir Ben-Hur is a consultant for Sky-Light Training and Publishing, Inc., Arlington Heights, Ill. He has worked closely with Reuven Feuerstein and has presented his work in Brazil, Israel, France, Canada, Mexico, and the U.S. © 1998, Meir Ben-Hur.

Keith, an average fifth-grade student, has just completed an exciting hands-on science unit investigating "planet Earth." It lasted four months. Wanting to assess Keith's new understanding, his science teacher engages in a clinical interview with him.[1]

Teacher: Where is the sun after it sets?

Keith (pausing): I don't know . . .

Teacher (pointing to the student-made colorful globes with attached labels hanging from the classroom ceiling and to students' pictures and drawings on the walls):

Is there anything in our classroom exhibit that can help you think about this?

Keith (looking around): No . . . but I know it doesn't go into the ocean.

Teacher: How do you know that?

Keith: Because it would splash the water.

Teacher: Oh. So where does it really go?

Keith (pausing): Maybe to China?

Teacher (relieved): And where is it when it sets in China?

Keith (troubled): I don't know . . .

Sound familiar? Have you ever wondered why it is that some students experiences—even rich, exciting, hands-on types of active learning—do not result in real learning of new concepts? Have you wondered how it happens that some students (perhaps as many as half)

do not understand what they experience even in the most engaging classes?

Why Learning Needs to Be Mediated

The Piagetian constructivist school of developmental psychology, which views cognitive abilities as a product of the combination of the maturation of the central nervous system and earlier exposures, provides little help to our troubled teacher. She needs to find ways to facilitate the construction of concepts in mathematics, science, and other subjects for the half of her students who cannot build them on their own.

"Meaning" is not implicit in objects and events. Our concept of the world is, for the most part, not a product of our perception of the world. Rather, our perception is generally the product of our concept of

© 1998 Skylight Training and Publishing, Inc.

the world. What we learn from our direct exposure to objects and events (direct learning) is strictly determined by our preconceived notions of these objects and events and by our ability to relate them to our previous learning. Our concepts, in turn, may be modified by those experiences that are incompatible with them. However, such modifications are unlikely to happen without some form of intervention or mediation. Remember, it took humans millions of years to change their idea that the Earth is flat, and they did not change their thinking until the interventions of maps and exploration provided evidence incompatible with their beliefs.

While children learn much of what they know and can do incidentally, mediation is not incidental teaching.

Keith's learning about planet Earth could not depend entirely upon his own ideas of planet Earth even in a hands-on, exciting, active-learning science class. His perceptions of the objects and events in his science class were entirely different from those his teacher expected.

Lev Vygotsky, a world-renowned social psychologist, argued that the origin of our concepts of the world must be found in our early learning of such things as language, culture, and religion.[2] This learning cannot happen without the help, or mediation, of such people as parents, caretakers, and siblings.

Reuven Feuerstein terms this form of learning Mediated Learning Experience (MLE), as opposed to Direct Learning Experience (DLE). He argues that the "mediators" of our early learning interpose themselves between us and the world to help make our experiences meaningful. Furthermore, he argues that, in their deliberate attempts to change our concepts, mediators promote the development of our cognitive systems.

How MLE Promotes Cognitive Development

In an attempt to produce mental models, modalities, and dispositions for our later experiences, mediated learning experiences transform our cognitive systems and facilitate our cognitive development. To "show us the meaning," mediators confront us with and draw our attention to selected stimuli. They teach us how to look at the world selectively, how to "see meaning." They schedule the appearance and disappearance of stimuli, they bring together stimuli that are separated by time and/or space, and they focus our attention on certain transformations in stimuli that we otherwise would overlook. In the process, they teach us how to focus and how to register the temporal and spatial properties of objects and events and the changes that occur in them. They teach us how to compare the same experiences using different criteria and how to sort relevant data from irrelevant data. They help us learn how to label our experiences, and they teach us how to group them by categories. Through MLEs, we learn how to learn and how to think. MLEs prepare us for future learning.

Consider, for example, two groups of parents and children who visit a hands-on, exploratory science museum. In one group, a child skips eagerly from exhibit to exhibit, touching displays and occasionally pressing a button or listening to a recorded message. In the second group, the child and parents walk to each exhibit together. Then the parents direct the child's attention to specific features, they ask questions, they interpret displays, they search for causal relationships, and they eventually help the child formulate concepts about the exhibit. In the first group, there is no comparing of this new experience to what the child already knows, no new insights are gained, and no new learning takes place. In the second group, the parents provide an MLE, and the child learns and acquires meaning.

Children who have not received sufficient MLEs are not prepared to deal with the cognitive challenges confronting them as they enter school and are thus unable to benefit from the wealth of classroom experiences offered. Even when faced with hands-on, active-learning opportunities, they fail to find the meaning. They may enjoy creating the model planets, but they do not understand the related "whys." They fail to achieve academically, fall be-hind, and lose interest. These children often experience the world in a random, impulsive way and grasp it episodically. They cannot consider several sources of information simultaneously and do not compare their experiences. They do not form relationships between ideas or look for causes. They do not identify problems and are bored even in classes that teachers believe are challenging. They are children who do not feel a need to reason and draw inferences, children who have difficulties in making representations. Keith was one of these children, and, as such, he benefitted little from typical classroom experiences.

Why MLEs May Be Withheld

Children may not receive Mediated Learning Experiences as a result of certain biological, emotional, or social factors. Extensive research—such as studies on Down's syndrome or emotionally disturbed children—has been done on biological and emotional factors. Indeed, the literature is replete with evidence of their importance in the cognitive development of children. Some of the research shows that even the consequences of biological and emotional conditions can be ameliorated with effective MLEs.

Feuerstein specifically directs our attention to social factors. He points to the social condition of many culturally different children as a determinant of their academic failure. He has observed that it is this population of children—those likely to be deprived of the benefit of a stable cultural context—who do not receive MLEs as a matter of their parents' choice. Because they do not see their own culture as necessary, or even appropriate, for the future of their children, many minority parents withhold MLEs from their children and delegate the responsibility for their cognitive development to the social institutions of the government. Cultural discontinuity, which turns into MLE deprivation, is indeed a growing social problem, as reported in comparative studies with minority children. The population of minority students with learning problems, including the gifted underachievers, continues to grow.

Feuerstein's theory of MLE is tied to his belief that our cognitive abilities are modifiable, that we can change our abilities from the expected course of cognitive development. One of his fundamental premises is that the structure of the intellect can be transformed to enable one to learn better. Feuerstein argues that, regardless of age, irrespective of the cause, and despite a poor level of functioning, humans' cognitive abilities are malleable. This argument is well supported by research on the brain. If a child did not receive sufficient MLEs as part of his or her early childhood experiences, MLEs in the classroom can change the course of the child's early cognitive development.

MLE in the Classroom

Feuerstein's theory of MLE offers a refreshing outlook on education, and many teachers find his humanistic approach exciting. However, he warns against the misuse of his ideas. Good learning is not necessarily mediated, and, according to Feuerstein, mediation is not always good teaching.

A teacher must first decide whether a student needs mediated learning. If mediation is not needed, then it is useless and may even be harmful. Mediation, by definition, replaces independent work. If a student has formed an appropriate goal for his or her science observations (i.e., has formed a relevant hypothesis); can follow written directions; can record, compare, and sort data; can write a report; and can present findings, and if his or her learning requires only these processes, then mediation is not needed. If the student cannot perform any one, or more, of these functions, then mediation should be offered to ameliorate the specific deficiency. Furthermore, mediation should be withheld as soon as the student achieves mastery. Ultimately, all students should be able to benefit from all types of learning opportunities, including direct learning experiences—such as lectures, the Internet, and independent study—because they have learned how to learn.

If you decide to offer MLE, you may want to follow Feuerstein's guidelines for mediators. Feuerstein lists three characteristics that define MLE and distinguish it from other teacher/student interactions.[3] None of these is sufficient by itself; rather, each provides a necessary dimension for MLE. These characteristics are intentionality and reciprocity, transcendence, and meaning.

Intentionality and Reciprocity

While children learn much of what they know and can do incidentally, mediation is not incidental teaching. In MLE the teacher interposes himself or herself intentionally and systematically between the children and the content of their experiences. At the same time, both the teacher and the children reciprocate with shared intentions. It is easy to apply this principle when a student initiates MLE—that is, when a student feels a need for the teacher's guidance. In such cases, a teacher intentionally addresses the existing need that engages the student in learning and responds to a child's need for mediation. The more challenging case for mediators is when a child does not feel the need for mediation. How can the teacher's imposed intentions achieve a reciprocal response?

New learning experiences should always be built on past successful ones, with a manageable progression between the two.

Skillful mediators create *student-felt* needs by manipulating all the available classroom resources, including the content of instruction, the students' level of alertness, and the teacher's own behavior. The model of Feuerstein's Instrumental Enrichment (FIE) program helped me to understand this idea.

Let us first consider the choice of instructional content and material. The FIE program includes hundreds of problem-solving exercises—all using alternatives to the cultural content (ideas, values, beliefs, vocabulary, traditions, and so on) that is known to foster MLEs naturally in the childhood environment but that is often absent in the experiences of culturally deprived students. Teachers are always impressed by the students' excited responses to FIE tasks and by the power of the program to generate a felt need for mediation. FIE tasks challenge students appropriately both by their novelty (their unusual appearance and struc-

ture) and by their level of difficulty (not too easy, but progressively more difficult).

Teachers who have access to or are creative in developing and collecting alternative instructional content usually know how to use variations to engage students. Such teachers may find or develop a variety of content for the mediation of specific abilities. For example, a teacher may want to mediate the sorting of data. If a student is not interested in sorting with one kind of content, the teacher may offer an alternative that does engage the student.

We also need to consider how a teacher's actions help to create student-felt needs for mediation. As teachers, we often behave in the classroom in unusual ways in order to keep students alert. We raise our voices, use exaggerated body movements, and ask direct questions of students who seem to be drifting off. Other teaching strategies, however, enhance the reciprocity in mediation. They focus on student expectations and intrinsic motivation. FIE teachers trained in MLE use questions to create a student-felt need for mediation. Questions are carefully chosen to be as challenging and rewarding as the FIE tasks are. This model can be applied throughout the curriculum.

The choice of questions reflects the mediator's expectations of students. If the expectations are low, the questions are simple. If they are high, the questions are difficult. If the expectations are wrong, the instructional pace is too slow or too fast, or the questions are unchallenging, the mediation is likely to fail. Therefore, the choice of questions must be based on a fair assessment and analysis of the needs and abilities of the students. The analysis, assessment, and expectations of students must be dynamic, reflecting the changes sought by the MLE.

We often think about the choice of teacher questions in terms of levels, such as those represented by Bloom's taxonomy. When a teacher asks students "why" and "how" rather than "what," students need to generate ideas rather than reproduce and copy ideas. For example, a science teacher whose students completed a sorting procedure will ask the students to explain *how* they did the procedure rather than *what* the result of their work was.

New learning experiences should always be built on past successful ones, with a manageable progression between the two. When the challenge of the teacher's questions is manageable, students become intrinsically motivated to engage further in MLE. If the questions are too simple or too difficult, students disengage from the MLE.

The way we choose our questions is related to the time we allow students to think before they respond and to our reactions to their responses. Teachers are often impatient. The average pause or "wait time" after teachers ask a question in the classroom is two to three seconds. This impatience generally has three negative consequences. First, students may need more time to think a question through carefully. Premature student responses are likely to misguide teachers in forming subsequent questions. Second, short wait time reinforces students' impulsiveness. Third, when students don't respond during the short pause, teachers tend to become uncomfortable and replace the original question with another, lower-level question, thereby reducing the challenge to students, possibly below the optimal level. A mediator's (in this case a teacher's) patience, even an "exaggerated" pause, is critical to the learning experience.

The mediator's response to a student's answer must foster reciprocity in the interaction. Mediators may encourage and invite further elaboration and discussion or probe if initial responses are incomplete, unclear, or incorrect. At the same time, mediators should remain nonjudgmental in their comments. Examples of appropriate teacher responses are "Thank you for your answer," "Interesting answer," "Could you explain your thinking in a different way, so that all the students can understand?" and "Could you think of another answer?" Responses of this kind reflect the reciprocal nature of the interaction between mediator and learner, and they foster intrinsic motivation.

To summarize, teacher behaviors that foster reciprocity in an MLE include:

- choosing content that students like to think about;
- changing stance, facial and body expressions, and level and inflection of voice;
- asking "why" and "how" questions rather than "what" questions;
- allowing sufficient wait time for student responses;
- responding to student reflections in a nonjudgmental manner;
- encouraging students to offer alternative ideas;
- revealing interest in student learning;
- listening carefully to students;
- showing readiness to spend more time for the benefit of a student's learning; and
- taking special interest in struggling learners.

Transcendence

While it may be an appropriate teaching goal, content knowledge by itself is not the mediator's concern. Content serves only as a means to reach the goals of MLEs. An MLE seeks changes in the way students learn and think. Such changes must transcend the content and context of the MLE. A teacher may use the science class to mediate the process and utility of sorting data by different criteria. However, the teacher's mediation must be aimed at the cognitive behavior and not at the specific data to which the process is applied. In fact, content may be a restrictive factor in an MLE.

Abstract as it may be, content always defines specific contextual, functional, or even conceptual boundaries. In order to ensure the transfer of learning to other content areas and contexts, mediators should attempt to *eliminate* the boundaries that intrinsically tie the target cognitive behavior in the learning experience to its content; that is, they must decontextualize the learning of cognitive behavior. To do this, mediators need to vary the content while focusing on the *same* target behavior. For example, if the mediator is focusing on representational thinking, then the classroom model for the rotation of Earth around the sun would be just one instance in which the students discuss the spatial configuration and relationships involved. The mediator would engage the students with other contents that model the same cognitive function. Thus a science teacher might ask students to model eclipses of the sun and the moon and to explain these conditions as observed from Earth, the moon, and the sun. When the students realize that the view differs depending on the point of reference, the teacher would ask them to think of other cases in which the outcome depends on the point of view.

Typical examples of the transcendence principle can be found in mediated learning at home. As parents mediate the concept of organization, they choose different content areas and contexts. These may include the organization of toys, drawings, crayons, chairs, tools, the contents of a school bag, and so on.

The organization of these objects will vary with the criteria applied. First, the items might be ordered by size or color, then grouped by function, and, eventually, by age or according to the different relationships between them.

The transcendent goal in these MLEs is to develop the child's need and ability to organize different objects and events by different criteria for different purposes. If the mediated learning of organization is limited to certain objects, certain criteria, and specific purposes, then the transfer or application of this learning will be limited. Similarly, parents use different content and contexts to mediate reflective behavior, comparative behavior, the concepts of space and time, the search for causal relationships, logic, communication skills, and so on. When parents mediate, they foster lifelong learning abilities.

Mediated learning experiences must seek the development of learning and thinking abilities that will be useful with mostly unpredictable content.

If the goal of MLE is to foster independence and lifelong learning, then teachers, too, must focus on processes rather than content. Just think about the magnitude of change in the world since you were in grade school. If you are currently a teacher, then the amount of knowledge in the world has grown at least eightfold since you went to grade school; school curricula have been changed many times; work has changed radically; life has become vastly different. It is projected that in 20 years knowledge will double every 73 days! Can you imagine how our lives will differ in 20 years? Mediated learning experiences must seek the development of learning and thinking abilities that will be useful with mostly unpredictable content.

The key to teacher mediation is identifying appropriate transcendent goals. Current national and state standards for different academic fields call for the pursuit of such goals. For example, among the standards for science literacy established by the American Association for the Advancement of Science, the benchmarks for the use of patterns and relationships include measuring, estimating, seeing the shape of things, making graphs, comparing two groups of data, analyzing patterns, and so on.[4] These goals describe cognitive processes and dispositions rather than contents. While the content used to achieve these goals may vary, the transcendent MLE goals are quite specific. The cognitive processes described by these goals are likely to be applicable even in the unforeseeable future.

Transcendent goals turn MLEs into deliberate and systematic, rather than incidental, experiences. Such goals provide the mediator with a context for structuring learning experiences. However, as indicated above, despite the implicit order in the learning experiences, students still might not make connections between current and previous learning and might not anticipate future learning experiences without the help of a mediator.

Mediators employ several practices to ensure that students understand how their learning is connected to transcendent goals. First, mediators help students make a clear connection between a current learning experience and previous ones by asking them to review their past experiences, summarize a new experience, and compare both sets of experiences. Mediation of transcendent goals again takes the form of higher-level questions. Questions that elicit students' insights about "how" and "why" they perform the way they do help them to connect current and past experiences.

Second, mediators are always instrumental in bringing the learning outcomes to the level of the child's awareness. The typical questions "What was new today?" followed by "How did you change?" provide the vehicle for the production of this awareness of or insight into the learning outcomes.

Third, mediators help students relate current learning experiences to transcendent goals by asking questions that anticipate future uses, such as "What is it good for?" and "Where can it be used?" Student examples of such applications are meaningful because they illustrate the transcendence of the learning experience beyond the specific content. For example, if a child learns to organize his room and is asked to elaborate on the value of organization and to anticipate the future uses of this idea, the child might recognize that he needs to organize his school bag and that, when he is older, he will need to organize his tool box, and so on.

Teacher behaviors that model transcendence in an MLE include:

- selecting a variety of instructional content in accordance with transcendent cognitive developmental goals,

- asking "why" and "how" questions rather than informative "what" questions,

- making a clear connection between a current learning experience and previous ones,

- discussing learning outcomes, and

- relating learning experiences and transcendent goals.

Meaning

The basic tenet of the theory of MLE is that mediation endows the learning experience with meaning. Meaningful learning may be considered the successful product of emotional and cognitive excitement. An MLE provides the student with the emotional excitement of learning and with the feeling of competence. An MLE also successfully targets the "whys" and "what fors" of the learning. Thus the learning experience simultaneously becomes a meaningful emotional experience and a meaningful cognitive one. Mediators do not expect their students to readily "see" this meaning in the learning experience. They guide the students through their learning in the search for this meaning.

Much has been said about "making learning fun." I will not discuss this important idea here. Rather, it is my intention to elaborate the cognitive aspect of the mediation of meaning. In this article I am concerned with the common case of students who learn content and procedures and may have fun learning them but are still left without an understanding of why what they learned is important. Tricks, no less wonderful than magic, make such students absorb content and procedures whose meaning they don't understand. Unfortunately, in many cases, and certainly in the long term, even magic does not work and meaningless learning stops. Students may graduate or drop out of school without ever appreciating the utility of mathematics, the beauty of art and literature, the purpose and process of scientific experiments, the importance of physical education, or the value of a healthy diet. These are the kinds of meanings mediators guide students to find in their learning experiences.

Discovering how our theories apply to our observations—i.e., finding meaning—involves comparing experiences, grouping and regrouping them, considering when and where they occur, and examining relationships between them. Children are not the only ones who fail to do this. I remember an adult student in the FIE Program who suddenly realized that his failure in school had to do with the fact that he did not know how to learn. One day he appeared extremely excited and instructed me to "look at this textbook!" I took the book from him, looked at the cover, scanned its contents, and struggled to find some intelligent comment to match his excitement as he exclaimed, "Look, I highlighted the whole book!" Indeed, his yellow marks covered the entire contents of the book. He said that he never knew that learning is not memorizing. Only now did he understand that to find meaning he needed to reorganize the information he read to fit his theories—or to adapt his theories of "why" and "how" things are or happen. Indeed, many students process their experiences this way only when a mediator guides them to do so. Experienced and independent learners do so automatically. They do it because they learned why and how to do it at some point in the past.

The mediation of meaning is essentially teaching how to learn. First, mediation makes it understood that learning has a target. By asking questions, the mediator helps the student anticipate a learning goal: "What are we looking for?" and "Why is it important?" Then the mediator makes sure that the student compares and classifies the new information or connects it with what has been previously learned, asking such questions as "How is it the same as before?" "What is new here?" and "How is it different?" Then the mediator helps the student construct new meaning, asking such questions as "What did you learn today?" "How did you find out?" "Why is it important?" and "Where can you use what you learned?" Eventually, the mediator will bring the process of learning it-

self into the student's conscious awareness: "What did you learn about learning [e.g., experimenting, thinking, and so on]?" and "Where will you use it?"

Teaching behaviors associated with the mediation of meaning are:

- discussing learning goals with students;

- repeating concepts in their different applications;

- encouraging students to identify applications for what they learned;

- expecting students to transfer their learning across the curriculum;

- giving explicit value to a given experience;

- changing stance, facial and body expressions, and level and inflection of voice; and

- asking "why" and "how" questions, rather than "what" questions.

Throughout my career as an educator I have found that Feuerstein's theory of MLE, while "naturally appealing," is more a source of concern for educators than a source of relief. It is more demanding than it is comforting; it makes our expectations grow and our accomplishments shrink. Feuerstein's theory is hard to implement, for it requires the utmost in commitment, continuous learning,

and systematic work. At the same time, I have learned that there is no alternative to hard work for enabling children to learn.

The reward for that hard work is well deserved. Keith is now 18 and will graduate from high school this year. The dialogue with Keith less than a decade ago was an important milestone in his teacher's career. She has since become a mediator and has helped many other students in Brooklyn, New York, develop appropriate science concepts. Together, a student and his teacher found out where the sun is before it rises.

1. Madeleine Long and Meir Ben-Hur, "Informing Learning Through the Clinical Interview," *Arithmetic Teacher,* February 1991, pp. 44–47.
2. Lev Vygotsky, *Mind in Society* (Cambridge, Mass.: Harvard University Press, 1978).
3. Reuven Feuerstein, Rafi Feuerstein, and Yaron Schur, "Process as Content in Education of Exceptional Children," in Arthur L. Costa and Rosemarie M. Liebmann, eds., *Supporting the Spirit of Learning: When Process Is Content* (Thousand Oaks, Calif.: Corwin Press, 1997).
4. American Association for the Advancement of Science, *Project 2061: The Nature of Mathematics, Grades 3–5* (New York: Oxford University Press, 1993).

 Article Review Form at end of book.

Why do teachers encourage students to talk to one another about things they have read? Describe what the authors mean by peer and collaborative learning.

Reading Comprehension
What works

To set the stage for students to succeed at reading, teachers can supply ample time for text reading, direct strategy instruction, and opportunities for collaboration and discussion.

Linda G. Fielding and P. David Pearson

Linda G. Fielding is Assistant Professor of Curriculum and Instruction, The University of Iowa, N275 Lindquist Center, Iowa City, IA 52242. P. David Pearson is Professor and Dean, College of Education, University of Illinois at Urbana-Champaign, 38 Education Bldg., 1310 S. Sixth St., Champaign, IL 61820.

Perhaps the most sweeping changes in reading instruction in the last 15 years are in the area of comprehension. Once thought of as the natural result of decoding plus oral language, comprehension is now viewed as a much more complex process involving knowledge, experience, thinking, and teaching. It depends heavily on knowledge—both about the world at large and the worlds of language and print. Comprehension inherently involves inferential and evaluative thinking, not just literal reproduction of the author's words. Most important, it can be taught directly.

Two years ago we reviewed the most recent research about comprehension instruction (Pearson and Fielding 1991). Here, we revisit that research, supplementing it with current thinking about reading instruction, and transform the most consistent findings into practical guidelines for teachers.

We contend that a successful program of comprehension instruction should include four components:

- large amounts of time for actual text reading,

- teacher-directed instruction in comprehension strategies,

- opportunities for peer and collaborative learning, and

- occasions for students to talk to a teacher and one another about their responses to reading.

A program with these components will set the stage for students to be interested in and to succeed at reading—providing them the intrinsic motivation for continual learning.

Ample Time for Text Reading

One of the most surprising findings of classroom research of the 1970s and '80s was the small amount of time that children spent actually reading texts. Estimates ranged from 7 to 15 minutes per day from the primary to the intermediate grades (Anderson et al. 1985). Children typically spent more time working on reading skills via workbook-type assignments than putting these skills to work in reading connected texts. The skill time/reading time ratio was typically the highest for children of the lowest reading ability (Allington 1983b). Allocating ample time for actual text reading and ensuring that students are actually engaged in text reading during that time are among teachers' most important tasks in comprehension instruction.

Why is time for text reading important? The first benefit of time for reading is the sheer opportunity to orchestrate the skills and strategies that are important to proficient reading—including comprehension. As in sports and music, *practice makes perfect* in reading, too.

Second, reading results in *the acquisition of new knowledge*, which, in turn, fuels the comprehension process. Research of the late 1970s and early '80s consistently revealed a strong reciprocal relationship be-

Fielding, Linda G. and Pearson, P. David (1994). "Reading Comprehension: What Works," *Educational Leadership* 51, 5: 62–68. Reprinted with permission of the Association for Supervision and Curriculum Development. Copyright © 1994 by ASCD. All rights reserved.

tween prior knowledge and reading comprehension ability. The more one already knows, the more one comprehends; and the more one comprehends, the more one learns new knowledge to enable comprehension of an even greater and broader array of topics and texts.

The first part of this reciprocal relationship was the focus of much research of the last 15 years—developing methods for activating and adding to readers' knowledge base before reading to increase text understanding (Beck et al. 1982, Hansen and Pearson 1983). More recently, researchers have emphasized the second part of the relationship: the role that actual text reading plays in building knowledge. For example, increases in vocabulary and concept knowledge from reading silently (Nagy et al. 1987, Stallman 1991) and from being read to (Elley 1989) have been documented. Further, the positive statistical relationship between amount of time spent reading and reading comprehension (Anderson et al. 1988) may be largely attributable to the knowledge base that grows through text reading.

Recent research has debunked the misconception that only already-able readers can benefit from time spent in actual text reading, while less able readers should spend time on isolated skills instruction and workbook practice (Anderson et al. 1988, Leinhardt et al. 1981). A newer, more compelling argument is that the differing amounts of time teachers give students to read texts accounts for the widening gaps between more able and less able readers throughout the school grades (Allington 1983b, Stanovich 1986).

How much time should be devoted to actual text reading? At present research offers no answers, but we recommend that, of the time set aside for reading instruction, students should have more time to read than the combined total allocated for *learning* about reading and *talking or writing* about what has been read.

Getting the Most Out of Reading Time

The equivocal results of sustained silent reading programs throughout the years (Manning and Manning 1984) suggest, though, that simply allocating time is not enough. Teachers can increase the likelihood that more time for contextual reading will translate into improved comprehension skills in the following ways.

1. *Choice.* Teachers can give children opportunities and guidance in making text selections. Although we know of no research that directly links choice to reading comprehension growth, we speculate that choice is related to interest and motivation, both of which are related directly to learning (Anderson et al. 1987).

2. *Optimal difficulty.* Teachers can monitor students' and their own selections to ensure that all students spend most of their time reading books that are appropriate in difficulty—not so hard that a student's cognitive resources are occupied with just figuring out how to pronounce the words and not so easy that nothing new is likely to be learned.

3. *Multiple readings.* Teachers can honor and encourage rereading of texts, which research suggests leads to greater fluency and comprehension (Allington 1983a). Although most research about repeated reading of passages has focused on improvements in reading speed, accuracy, phrasing, and intonation, a growing number of studies have documented improved comprehension as well (Dowhower 1987).

Once thought of as the natural result of decoding plus oral language, comprehension is now viewed as a much more complex process involving knowledge, experience, thinking, and teaching.

4. *Negotiating meaning socially.* "Silent" reading time shouldn't be entirely silent. Teachers can (a) allow part of the time for reading in pairs, including pairs of different abilities and ages (Koskinen and Blum 1986, Labbo and Teale 1990); and (b) provide regular opportunities for readers to discuss their reading with the teacher and with one another. We view reading comprehension as a social as well as a cognitive process. Conversation not only raises the status of independent silent reading from a time filler to an important part of the reading program; it also gives students another opportunity to practice and build comprehension skills collaboratively, a topic to which we return below. Atwell (1987) and Hansen (1987) further argue that these conversations help to build the all-important community of readers that is the essence of literature-based programs.

Teacher-Directed Instruction

Research from the 1980s indicated that in traditional reading classrooms, time for comprehension instruction was as rare as time for actual text reading. After extensive observations in intermediate-grade classrooms, Durkin (1978–1979) concluded that teachers were spending very little time on actual comprehension instruction. Although they gave many workbook assignments and asked many questions about text content, Durkin judged that these exercises mostly tested students' understanding instead of teaching them how to comprehend.

In response to Durkin's findings, much research in the 1980s was devoted to discovering how to teach comprehension strategies directly. In the typical study of this type, readers were directly taught how to perform a strategy that skilled readers used during reading. Then, their abilities both in strategy use and text comprehension were compared either to their own performance before instruction or to the performance of similar readers who were not taught the strategy directly. *Explicit instruction*, the name given to one such widely researched model, involves four phases: teacher modeling and explanation of a strategy, guided practice during which teachers gradually give students more responsibility for task completion, independent practice accompanied by feedback, and application of the strategy in real reading situations (Pearson and Dole 1987).

In one of the biggest success stories of the time period, research showed repeatedly that comprehension can in fact be taught. Many strategies have been taught successfully:

- using background knowledge to make inferences (Hansen and Pearson 1983) or set purposes (Ogle 1986);

- getting the main idea (Baumann 1984);

- identifying the sources of information needed to answer a question (Raphael and Pearson 1985); and

- using the typical structure of stories (Fitzgerald and Spiegel 1983) or expository texts (Armbruster et al. 1987) to help students understand what they are reading.

One of the most exciting results of this body of research was that comprehension strategy instruction is especially effective for students who began the study as poor comprehenders—probably because they are less likely to invent effective strategies on their own. In some studies, less able readers who had been taught a comprehension strategy were indistinguishable from more able readers who had not been taught the strategy directly.

After more than a decade of research and criticism from both sides of the controversy about comprehension strategy instruction, we have a much clearer understanding of what quality instruction looks like and how to make it part of a larger comprehension instructional program.

Authenticity of strategies. First, the strategies students are taught should be as much as possible like the ones actual readers use when they comprehend successfully. To meet this criterion of authentic use, instruction should focus on the flexible application of the strategy rather than a rigid sequence of steps. It

should also externalize the thinking processes of skilled readers—not create artificial processes that apply only to contrived instructional or assessment situations.

Demonstration. Teachers should also demonstrate how to apply each strategy successfully—what it is, how it is carried out, and when and why it should be used (Duffy et al. 1988, Paris et al. 1991). Instead of just talking about a strategy, teachers need to illustrate the processes they use by thinking aloud, or modeling mental processes, while they read.

Guided practice. A phase in which teachers and students practice the strategy together is critical to strategy learning, especially for less-successful comprehenders. During this time teachers can give feedback about students' attempts and gradually give students more and more responsibility for performing the strategy and evaluating their own performance (Pearson and Dole 1987). This is also the time when students can hear about one another's reasoning processes—another activity especially important for less strategic readers.

Authenticity of texts. Finally, students must be taught, reminded, and given time to practice comprehension strategies while reading everyday texts—not just specially constructed materials or short workbook passages. We would like to see real texts used more and earlier in comprehension strategy instruction. Using real texts, we believe, will increase the likelihood that students will transfer the use of taught strategies to their independent reading—and that, after all, is the ultimate goal of instruction.

Opportunities for Peer and Collaborative Learning

We are becoming more and more aware of the social aspects of instruction and their influence on cognitive outcomes. In addition to equity and the sense of community fostered through peer and collaborative learning, students gain access to one another's thinking processes.

Perhaps the most widely researched peer learning model is *coop-*

erative learning. This approach has been examined in a variety of academic disciplines (Johnson and Johnson 1985, Slavin 1987)—with the focus in a few cases on literacy learning, including comprehension (Meloth 1991, Stevens et al. 1987). A synthesis of this research suggests that cooperative learning is most effective when students clearly understand the teacher's goals, when goals are group-oriented and the criterion of success is satisfactory learning by each group member, when students are expected and taught to explain things to one another instead of just providing answers, and when group activities supplement rather than supplant teacher-directed instruction. At its best, cooperative learning has positive social and cognitive benefits for students of all abilities.

Other models of peer teaching also have been investigated—for example, *reciprocal teaching.* In this model, students take turns leading dialogues that involve summarizing, asking an important question about what was read, predicting information, and attempting to clarify confusions. Reciprocal teaching is effective when students, not just teachers, teach their peers to engage in these dialogues (Palincsar et al. 1987).

Time to Talk About Reading

Some form of discussion or explication of a text has been a feature of reading classrooms for years, but traditional teacher-student discussions have been consistently criticized because they emphasize teacher control and learning a single interpretation. Critics have tended to advocate student-centered discussions that honor multiple interpretations. Cazden (1986) and many others noted a universal format of traditional teacher-student discussions, called the IRE format. The teacher *initiates* a question, a student *responds*, and the teacher *evaluates* the response before moving to another question.

Recently, various forms of teacher-student discussions have been geared toward achieving the following three goals.

1. Changing Teacher-Student Interaction Patterns

In the traditional recitation format, teachers choose the topics and, through feedback to students, control which student answers are viewed as correct and incorrect. One outcome of the recitation format is that teachers talk a lot! Typically, teachers talk as much as or more than all students combined, because their questions and feedback focus on transmitting the text interpretation they have in mind and because of the monitoring function that teachers naturally perform when they are in charge of a discussion.

Tharp and Gallimore (1989) use the terms *responsive teaching* and *instructional conversations* to contrast effective teacher-student dialogues with such recitations. In responsive teaching, teachers plan instruction by anticipating a range of student responses in addition to thinking about their own interpretations. They then use student input into discussions and student text interpretations to move the discussion to higher levels. Teachers might still nominate topics and opinions for group consideration, but student input drives the discussion forward.

Changing the pattern of classroom discussions to allow more student input and control is no easy task. Alvermann and Hayes (1989), for example, found that it was much easier for teachers to change the *level* of questions they asked (for example, move to more inferential, evaluative, and critical thinking questions) than it was for them to change the basic *structure* or pattern of interactions in classroom discussions. Teachers suggested two main reasons for the persistence of the recitation format in their classrooms: maintaining control and ensuring coverage of important information and canonical interpretations.

2. Accepting Personal Interpretations and Reactions

A broader definition of comprehension, one that includes the possibility of multiple interpretations and the importance of readers' responses to their reading, is behind many of the changes proposed for discussions in recent years. This respect for individual response and interpretation has been nurtured by the growth in popularity of the response to literature tradition (Beach and Hynds 1991). In particular, Rosenblatt's (1978) distinction between *efferent reading*—that from which a reader gets information or basic meaning—and *aesthetic reading*—the actual lived-through experience of reading and responding personally to a text—has allowed us to treat reading experiences differentially. Recently, the process of allowing students to build, express, and defend their own interpretations has become a *re*valued goal of text discussions.

Eeds and her colleagues use the term *grand conversations* to describe literature discussions in which the teacher's role is to be a coequal in the discussion, instead of the leader of a *gentle inquisition* (Eeds and Wells 1989, Peterson and Eeds 1990). In this role, the teacher can capitalize on teachable moments, help clarify confusions, keep track of students' ideas, and suggest ideas for consideration without insisting on a unitary interpretation of the text.

A typical concern about such discussions is that students might spend a lot of time talking about personal reactions but come away from the discussion not really "understanding" what they have read or not having taken the opportunity to discuss important text features. In analyses of such discussions of literary texts, however, Eeds and Wells (1989) and others (Raphael et al. 1992, Rogers 1991) have found that students engage in a variety of activities important to understanding:

- using the whole range of responses, from literal to critical and evaluative;

- clarifying the basic meaning of the text when there are confusions or disagreements; and

- using the opinions of others—including classmates, teacher, and published critics—to help clarify their thinking about a text.

In some of these studies, writing also has been an important avenue for students to understand text: (a) by documenting their independent thinking before group discussion and, (b) by synthesizing information and figuring out how their thinking has changed after discussion.

3. Embedding Strategy Instruction in Text Reading

Even in teacher-student discussions focused around a shared understanding of important text information, new ideas are emerging about how to build this shared understanding in a way that will teach students something about comprehension as well as text information. For example, in *situated cognition* (Brown et al. 1989), learning about comprehension strategies is embedded in discussions about texts. The cognitive activities students engage in are much like the ones that have been the focus of research about explicit instruction in comprehension strategies, such as summarizing and getting the main idea. The difference is that the focus is on learning authentic information in the texts—for example, discovering how photosynthesis works by reading a chapter about it—with comprehension strategy learning as a secondary outcome of repeated engagement in such discussions about many different texts. The belief is that students will internalize effective comprehension strategies through repeated situations in which they read and discuss whole texts with a teacher and peers.

A Call for Multiple Approaches

When we teach courses about reading instruction for preservice and in-service teachers, we sometimes hear the complaint that researchers seem to pit approaches against one another instead of exploring how a particular innovation might operate as part of a total program. This is a legitimate concern, because if innovations are viewed as dichotomous, children may end up with instruction that is deficient in some areas.

> Clearly, then, multiple approaches to comprehension improvement are in order.

Anything less than a well-rounded instructional program is a form of discrimination against children who have difficulty with reading. Delpit (1988), for example, asserts that children from nonmainstream backgrounds deserve to be taught directly what their mainstream teachers want them to do in order to read and comprehend texts. Slavin (1987) contends that an important outcome of cooperative learning is that it eliminates the segregation along racial and socioeconomic lines that often accompanies ability grouping. And Stanovich (1986) argues that if less able readers continually are denied opportunities to read actual texts, they will inevitably fall further and further behind—the rich will get richer and the poor will get poorer. Clearly, then, multiple approaches to comprehension improvement are in order. To use the recent language of the standards debate, a full portfolio of teacher strategies designed to promote a full portfolio of student strategies could be construed as essential in meeting opportunity-to-learn standards.

We see no reason why all four of the components described here—ample time for actual text reading, teacher-directed comprehension strategy instruction, opportunities for peer and collaborative learning, and time to talk about what has been read—should not complement one another in the same classroom. Nor do we see why the appropriateness of any component would depend on whether the primary reading material is children's literature or basal readers. We do believe, however, that if our ultimate goal is to develop independent, motivated comprehenders who choose to read, then a substantial part of children's reading instructional time each day must be devoted to self-selected materials that are within the students' reach. It is through such reading that children can experience the successful comprehension, learning, independence, and interest that will motivate future reading.

References

Allington, R.L. (1983a). "Fluency: The Neglected Reading Goal." *The Reading Teacher* 36: 556–561.

Allington, R.L. (1983b). "The Reading Instruction Provided Readers of Differing Reading Abilities." *Elementary School Journal* 83: 548–559.

Alvermann, D.E., and D.A. Hayes. (1989). "Classroom Discussion of Content Area Reading Assignments: An Intervention Study." *Reading Research Quarterly* 24: 305–335.

Anderson, R.C., E.H. Hiebert, J.A. Scott, and I.A.G. Wilkinson. (1985). *Becoming a Nation of Readers.* Washington, D. C.: National Institute of Education.

Anderson, R.C., L. Shirey, P.T. Wilson, and L.G. Fielding. (1987). "Interestingness of Children's Reading Material." In *Aptitude, Learning, and Instruction. Vol. 3: Conative and Affective Process Analyses,* edited by R. Snow and M. Farr. Hillsdale, N.J.: Erlbaum.

Anderson, R.C., P.T. Wilson, and L.G. Fielding. (1988). "Growth in Reading and How Children Spend Their Time Outside of School." *Reading Research Quarterly* 23: 285–303.

Armbruster, B.B., T.H. Anderson, and J. Ostertag. (1987). "Does Text Structure/Summarization Instruction Facilitate Learning From Expository Text?" *Reading Research Quarterly* 22: 331–346.

Atwell, N. (1987). *In the Middle.* Montclair, N.J.: Boynton/Cook.

Baumann, J. F. (1984). "Effectiveness of a Direct Instruction Paradigm for Teaching Main Idea Comprehension." *Reading Research Quarterly* 20: 93–108.

Beach, R., and S. Hynds. (1991). "Research on Response to Literature." In *Handbook of Reading Research: Vol. II,* edited by R. Barr, M. Kamil, P. Mosenthal, and P. D. Pearson. New York: Longman.

Beck, I.L., R.C. Omanson, and M.G. McKeown. (1982). "An Instructional Redesign of Reading Lessons: Effects on Comprehension." *Reading Research Quarterly* 17: 462–481.

Brown, J. S., A. Collins, and P. Duguid. (1989). "Situated Cognition and the Culture of Learning." *Educational Researcher* 18, 1: 32–42.

Cazden, C. (1986). "Classroom Discourse." In *Handbook of Research on Teaching,* 3rd ed., edited by M. C. Wittrock. New York: Macmillan.

Delpit, L. (1988). "The Silenced Dialogue: Power and Pedagogy in Educating Other People's Children." *Harvard Educational Review* 58, 3: 280–298.

Dowhower, S. L. (1987). "Effects of Repeated Reading on Second-Grade Transitional Readers' Fluency and Comprehension." *Reading Research Quarterly* 22: 389–406.

Duffy, G., L. Roehler, and B. Hermann. (1988). "Modeling Mental Processes Helps Poor Readers Become Strategic Readers." *The Reading Teacher* 41: 762–767.

Durkin, D. (1978–1979). "What Classroom Observations Reveal About Reading Comprehension Instruction." *Reading Research Quarterly* 15: 481–533.

Eeds, M., and D. Wells. (1989). "Grand Conversations: An Exploration of Meaning Construction in Literature Study Groups." *Research in the Teaching of English* 23: 4–29.

Elley, W. B. (1989). "Vocabulary Acquisition from Listening to Stories." *Reading Research Quarterly* 24: 174–187.

Fitzgerald, J., and D. L. Spiegel. (1983). "Enhancing Children's Reading Comprehension Through Instruction in Narrative Structure." *Journal of Reading Behavior* 15, 2: 1–17.

Hansen, J. (1987). *When Writers Read.* Portsmouth, N. H.: Heinemann.

Hansen, J., and P. D. Pearson. (1983). "An Instructional Study: Improving Inferential Comprehension of Good and Poor Fourth-Grade Readers." *Journal of Educational Psychology* 75: 821–829.

Johnson, D., and R. Johnson. (1985). "The Internal Dynamics of Cooperative Learning Groups." In *Learning to Cooperate, Cooperating to Learn,* edited by R. Slavin, S. Sharon, S. Kagan, R. Hertz Lazarowitz, C. Webb, and R. Schmuck. New York: Plenum Press.

Koskinen, P., and I. Blum. (1986). "Paired Repeated Reading: A Classroom Strategy for Developing Fluent Reading." *The Reading Teacher* 40: 70–75.

Labbo, L., and W. Teale. (1990). "Cross-Age Reading: A Strategy for Helping Poor Readers." *The Reading Teacher* 43: 362–369.

Leinhardt, G., N. Zigmond, and W. Cooley. (1981). "Reading Instruction and Its Effects." *American Educational Research Journal* 18: 343–361.

Manning, G. L., and M. Manning. (1984). "What Models of Recreational Reading Make a Difference?" *Reading World* 23: 375–380.

Meloth, M. (1991). "Enhancing Literacy Through Cooperative Learning." In *Literacy for a Diverse Society: Perspectives, Practices, and Policies,* edited by E. Hiebert. New York: Teachers College Press.

Nagy, W. E., R. C. Anderson, and P. A. Herman. (1987). "Learning Word Meanings from Context During Normal Reading." *American Educational Research Journal* 24: 237–270.

Ogle, D. (1986). "K-W-L: A Teaching Model That Develops Active Reading of Expository Text." *The Reading Teacher* 39: 564–570.

Palincsar, A. S., A. L. Brown, and S. M. Martin. (1987). "Peer Interaction in Reading Comprehension Instruction." *Educational Psychologist* 22: 231–253.

Paris, S. G., B. A. Wasik, and J. C. Turner. (1991). "The Development of Strategic Readers." In *Handbook of Reading Research: Vol. II*, edited by R. Barr, M. Kamil, P. Mosenthal, and P. D. Pearson. New York: Longman.

Pearson, P. D., and J. A. Dole. (1987). "Explicit Comprehension Instruction: A Review of Research and a New Conceptualization of Instruction." *Elementary School Journal* 88, 2: 151–165.

Pearson, P. D., and L. G. Fielding. (1991). "Comprehension Instruction." In *Handbook of Reading Research: Vol. II*, edited by R. Barr, M. Kamil, P. Mosenthal, and P. D. Pearson. New York: Longman.

Peterson, R., and M. Eeds. (1990). *Grand Conversations: Literature Groups in Action.* New York: Scholastic.

Raphael, T., S. McMahon, V. Goatley, J. Bentley, F. Boyd, L. Pardo, and D. Woodman. (1992). "Research Directions: Literature and Discussion in the Reading Program." *Language Arts* 69: 54–61.

Raphael, T. E., and P. D. Pearson. (1985). "Increasing Students' Awareness of Sources of Information for Answering Questions." *American Educational Research Journal* 22: 217–236.

Rogers, T. (1991). "Students as Literary Critics: The Interpretive Experiences, Beliefs, and Processes of Ninth-Grade Students." *Journal of Reading Behavior* 23: 391–423.

Rosenblatt, L. (1978). *The Reader, the Text, the Poem: The Transactional Theory of a Literary Work.* Carbondale, Ill.: Southern Illinois University Press.

Slavin, R. E. (1987). "Cooperative Learning and the Cooperative School." *Educational Leadership* 45, 3: 7–13.

Stallman, A. (1991). "Learning Vocabulary from Context: Effects of Focusing Attention on Individual Words During Reading." Doctoral diss., University of Illinois, Urbana-Champaign.

Stanovich, K. (1986). "Matthew Effects in Reading: Some Consequences of Individual Differences in the Acquisition of Literacy." *Reading Research Quarterly* 21: 360–407.

Stevens, R., N. Madden, R. Slavin, and A. Famish. (1987). "Cooperative Integrated Reading and Composition: Two Field Experiments." *Reading Research Quarterly* 22: 433–454.

Tharp, R. G., and R. Gallimore. (1989). *Rousing Minds to Life: Teaching, Learning and Schooling in Social Context.* New York: Cambridge University Press.

 Article Review Form at end of book.

What is meant by "different ways of talking" about books?

Changing Talk About Text

New roles for teachers and students

Many language arts educators champion discussion as a way of building and deepening reader response to literature. This article offers a theoretical perspective on how and why different ways of talking about text can be so important for learning to read literature.

James R. Gavelek and Taffy E. Raphael

James R. Gavelek is an associate professor in the departments of Teacher Education and Educational Psychology at Michigan State University. Taffy E. Raphael, a professor at Michigan State University, coordinates the Masters Program in Literacy Instruction.

Like many researchers and teachers today, we have shared the excitement over changing perspectives about literacy instruction. We have read chapters and articles that suggest the importance of *more* and *different kinds* of language interactions between teacher and students and among students as they talk about the texts that they read and those that they create (Roser & Martinez, 1995; Short & Pierce, 1990). Scholars (e.g., Eeds & Wells, 1989; Raphael & Goatley, 1994; Wells & Chang-Wells, 1992) have suggested changing the nature of teacher leadership in classroom literature and other content area discussions. For example, some scholars (Freedman, 1993; Villaume, Worden, Williams, Hopkins, & Rosenblatt,

1994) have suggested that teachers facilitate or participate in rather than dominate talk about text. Others argue for what Wiencek and O'Flahavan (1994) refer to as "decentralized structures" (p.488), in which teachers drastically reduce their role or remove themselves entirely from the students' discussions.

In the work within the Book Club Project (see McMahon, 1994; Raphael, Goatley, McMahon, & Woodman, 1995; Raphael & McMahon, 1994), we have had the opportunity to study teacher-student interactions during talk about text, as well as the interactions among children within their student-led discussions known as book clubs. We observed three important aspects of book clubs. First, like others (e.g., Gilles, 1994), we found that initial discussions among students were not as highly developed as the talk about text we had encountered in many chapters and articles. Second, we noted that teachers' talk within whole-class settings appeared to play a crucial role in students' developing the language of talk about text, whether the language was about

literary elements, authors' craft, response to literature, or understanding and clarification. Third, multiple opportunities for students to engage in talk about text appeared to be critical. Such talk occurs in the public settings of whole-class and small-group discussions, as well as in more private settings where students engage in internal dialogues as they write in their reading logs or respond to literature as they read alone.

The reading we have engaged in and the research observations and analysis we have done are the basis for this paper. In this paper, we examine the critical and formative role of teachers in orchestrating students' talk about text. We first explore the theoretical basis for talk about text that is appropriate and crucial to language arts education. Second, we detail a model of language use within the classroom and its implications about teachers' and students' roles within literature discussions, as well as the contexts in which these discussions occur. Third, we consider implications of the model for the instruction and assessment of language and literacy.

James R. Gavelek and Taffy E. Raphael, "Changing Talk About Text: New Roles for Teachers and Students," *Language Arts,* March 1996, by the National Council of Teachers of English. Reprinted with permission.

Social Constructionism and the Crucial Role of Language

Underlying much of the current work that explores language practices in classrooms, specifically conversation about text, is frustration with traditional models of instruction. Traditional models are characterized by teachers' dominating classroom talk, students' responding to questions provided at the end of stories or within teachers' manuals, and students' lacking opportunities to participate in meaningful discussions with both their teacher and their peers (Denyer & Florio-Ruane, 1995; Ulichny & Watson-Gegeo, 1989). Many educational researchers have dealt with this frustration by closely studying classroom language practices and experimenting with ways of reconceptualizing the teacher's role to encourage talk about text that is more meaningful and more educative than talk fostered by past practices (Eeds & Wells, 1989; Green & Dixson, 1993).

Emphases in the research literature on the importance of changing roles for teachers and increasing language opportunities for students reflect a fundamental shift in the theoretical perspective that guides our development of instructional practices. Halliday (1993) suggests that language should be at the center of any concept of learning. Many current researchers have adopted a *social constructionist* perspective, which encompasses both Vygotsky's (1978) sociohistorical theory and more recent contributions from sociolinguists and discursive psychologists (Bruner, 1990; Wertsch, 1985). Others have applied social constructionist ideas to language and literacy instruction (see Au & Kawakami, 1986; Bruffee, 1986; Gavelek, 1986; Langer, 1991; McMahon, 1992; Wells & Chang-Wells, 1992). Central to this perspective is the constitutive role of language in mediating the relationship between the *student as knower* and the *text as known*; both the construction of what comes to be understood as knowledge of a text and the development of student as knower of texts depend critically upon language practices. We first discuss the role of language in knowledge construction, the development of literate minds, and the interrelationship between the two processes. We then explore these concepts within the context of classroom literacy events that emphasize talk about text.

Language and the Construction of (Textual) Knowledge

Traditional theories of learning suggest that knowledge corresponds to or "pictures" the world as it "really" is. In other words, the world unambiguously presents itself to us. Using traditional theories, our goal as teachers is to *re*-present or transmit those rules (e.g., grammatical), conceptual categories (e.g., scientific), or facts (e.g., historical) that we assume to be true. In contrast, proponents of a social constructionist perspective suggest that knowledge is constructed collaboratively by individuals as they discuss and argue a particular perspective or interpretation. Proponents of this view question those who assume the "givenness" and unchanging nature of knowledge. Instead of viewing knowledge as immutable, those who adopt a social constructionist perspective suggest that what we accept as knowledge is based on conventions that we, as a community, have constructed and agreed on. For example, our sense of narrative structure is a reflection of our culture's way of presenting stories, but there is nothing inherently "real" about our narrative structures.

This perspective has the potential to shift our focus on talk about text away from seeking "facts" or "truths" toward constructing "interpretations" and offering "warranted justifications" for interpretations. From this perspective, the teacher's role would shift from asking questions to ensure that students arrive at the "right" meaning to creating prompts that encourage students' exploratory talk (Barnes, 1995). Teachers would encourage talk that elicits a range of possible interpretations among individuals reading and responding at any given time. Teachers would also encourage talking about previously read texts be-cause individuals construct different readings at different periods in life or within different contexts (Rosenblatt, 1938). Textual meaning is not "out there" to be acquired; it is something that is constructed by individuals through their interactions with each other and the world. In classrooms, these interactions take the form of discussions, and the teacher helps guide and participates in them. Underlying the processes of interpretations and justifications in discussions is language.

Language and the Development of Literate Minds

The second way in which language, from a social constructionist perspective, plays a central role in the development of literate minds is in mediating students' abilities to think, feel, and act. To appreciate the importance of language in this development of mind, it is helpful to turn to Vygotsky's sociohistorical theory. In his general law of cultural development, Vygotsky suggests that the acquisition and use of all higher psychological processes have their origins in individuals' interactions with others. That is, "any function appears on the social plane, and then on the psychological plane. First, it appears between people as an interpsychological category, and then within the child as an intrapsychological category" (Vygotsky, 1981, p. 163). Vygotsky's distinction between elementary and higher psychological functions is crucial to understanding the important role that he attached to language-mediated interactions.

On the one hand, humans are uniquely constituted as biological individuals to acquire and make use of the various oral and literate practices that constitute a language. It is the existence of these biologically based, elementary psychological processes (e.g., involuntary perception, memory) that is necessary but not sufficient for the emergence of mind (e.g., oral and literate language, human emotions). Our biological potential to think, feel, and act as humans can only be realized through our interactions with others. Each language's creation—and the meanings and processes that are a part of every one—is to be understood as a cultural achievement with a unique history.

Through our interactions with more knowledgeable others, we acquire the culturally variable and historically changing higher psychological functions that make possible the intelligence unique to humankind. The higher psychological processes that define us as cultural beings thus emerge from, but are not reducible to, the elementary psychological processes that characterize us as biological beings.

Language Practices in Talk About Text

Vygotsky's general law of cultural development carries profound implications for how we think about language arts education—specifically, teaching talk about text. Social constructionists place individuals such as the teacher, other adults, and more knowledgeable peers in the crucial role of mediating the learning of the individual. Several relatively recent descriptions illustrate the importance placed on language use in literacy learning (see Dyson, 1992; Graves & Hansen, 1983; Raphael et al., 1995).

Raphael and her colleagues (e.g., Goatley, Brock, & Raphael, 1995; McMahon, 1994; Raphael et al., 1995) offer many descriptions of students' participating in Book Club, a literacy learning program centered around talk about text. Within whole-class settings, Ms. Woodman (teaching fourth grade) and Mrs. Pardo (teaching fifth grade) shared their personal responses and framed discussions with students to encourage similar contributions. Students also participated in student-led response groups. They had the responsibility for identifying topics of interest, raising questions, and clarifying confusions for their peers. Their teachers observed them carefully during this time, using the students' language as a window into their thinking. In subsequent whole-class settings, the students' ideas formed the basis for whole-class discussions, which were orchestrated by the teacher to help students extend their small-group conversations. The teachers also created opportunities within the whole-class setting for "teachable moments" based on students' own questions and comments. Teachers' roles shifted among direct teaching to scaffolding, facilitating, and participating in the conversations (Raphael & Goatley, 1994).

Other researchers have focused specifically on the role of peers and the educative importance of their language use through discussion and play and the ultimate impact of this language on their ability to create and talk about text. Dyson (1992) describes her study of early elementary readers and writers and the role of drama and play in developing literacy abilities. She shows how students' language and discussion among peers re-emerges in their writing and their talk about that writing. Graves and Hansen (1983) describe the learning that occurs through student-teacher and student-student interactions during author's chair. Graves and Hansen also demonstrate that students did not simply share favorite texts they or others have written; rather, students had engaged in conversation that pushed each others' thinking in ways that helped their development as readers and writers.

The point of these studies is that the public language about text does not simply create an authentic audience or purpose for text production and comprehension, nor does it simply motivate students. Rather, these social settings are the very *means* by which students come to acquire and construct new knowledge, new meanings, and new interpretations of text through interactive use of language. Students need leadership from their teachers in making these situations educative and meaningful, as well as multiple opportunities in which to engage in discussions.

Jason, a student who had participated in Book Club in both fourth and fifth grades, helps to illustrate the idea of social origins of higher psychological processes through his experiences in Book Club. Jason was invited to the state reading association conference to speak to teachers about Book Club. In his talk, he stated:

One of my favorite things about Book Club is that we get a chance to talk to our peers. When we talk with our peers, we find out about other people's ideas, have a chance to say something really important, get to tell what the author should do better or different, ask questions about the book, and express our feelings and ideas.

Also, sometimes books were hard for me to understand. In Book Club, the other students or the teacher helped another to understand the story. . . . Talking is important because you can say what you feel you want to say, and you can listen to others. This helps you get other ideas or feelings. What I mean is you get to say what you want to say. This is important because kids have important things to say.

Jason experienced an environment that encouraged him to try new ways of using language, of talking about text. His comments suggest that he has internalized key concepts about language and literacy that form the basis of his argument for having opportunities to talk with his peers about books.

The transition from interpsychological to intrapsychological functioning, which is illustrated by Jason's remarks, has important implications for teaching. The transition suggests that whatever children are able to do as individuals originates in social interactions with more knowledgeable others (e.g., teachers, parents, older siblings, peers). *Public discourse* in which children participate provides a foundation for their later *inner speech.* Where does public discourse related to literacy occur? As Heath (1989) and others have documented, one important place is the home. However, there is little argument that most of children's talk about text occurs in school settings. Student interactions with teachers and with peers provide the basis for their eventual independent abilities.

Social psychologist and philosopher Rom Harré (1984; Harré,

> **Public language about text does not simply create an authentic audience or purpose for text production and comprehension, nor does it simply motivate students. Rather, these social settings are the very means by which students come to acquire and construct new knowledge, new meanings, and new interpretations of text through interactive use of language.**

Clarke, & De Carlo, 1985) created a model that helps clarify how learners such as Jason move from using new meanings or strategies publicly and in interaction with others to individually appropriating and transforming these concepts and strategies into newly invented ways of thinking. Harré's model, the *Vygotsky Space,* illustrates the relationship between the public discourse that occurs (between teachers and students, among students themselves) and individuals' subsequent ability to think, feel, and act. We describe the Vygotsky Space, extending Harré's model to language and literacy education.

Conceptualizing Student's Talk About Text: The Vygotsky Space

The Vygotsky Space highlights five features of a social constructionist perspective on learning. First, it represents the relationship between discourse among students and between teacher and students. Second, it speaks to the idea that many voices contribute to an individual's learning. Third, it delineates how conventional knowledge supports invention. Fourth, it suggests reasons why creating an environment that fosters risk taking is critical to the development of higher psychological processes. Finally, it helps to explain the idea that learning is not linear, nor does it develop in the space of a single event. Harré (1984; Harré et al., 1985) created the Vygotsky Space (see Figure 1) by overlaying two dimensions.

The first dimension is *public ↔ private,* characterizing the degree to which any cognitive activity is visible and thus available for observation. That is, cognitive activities, such as strategies used to interpret text, can be public and observable or they can be private and unobservable.

Public cognitive activity may occur in a whole-class instructional setting or smaller one-to-one settings, such as a teacher-student writing conference. An example of a whole-class setting is teachers' reading aloud to their students, frequently thinking aloud as they read. Teachers' use of "think-alouds" makes what would otherwise be invisible cognitive activity visible to students through the modeling of particular ways to think about or respond to text. For example, during a Book Club unit thematically organized around the study of the Civil War, Mrs. Pardo read Hunt's (1964) *Across Five Aprils* aloud to her students each day. She often paused to make comments such as, "I wonder what Bill is worrying about here, what the decision is that he keeps thinking about," then continued the reading without further discussion. Through language, she made visible a skilled reader's ability to keep a question in mind and read for further information. In another unit, when reading about the plane crash in the novel *Hatchet* (Paulsen, 1987), she paused to comment, "This is getting exciting—I'll bet having his hatchet attached to his belt is going to make a big difference in his survival!" She thought aloud to share both the feeling she had in response to the text and a point at which a prediction may make sense. In short, thinking aloud is one way of making thinking and feeling public in a large-group setting.

In contrast, when cognitive activity is private, the thinking can only be inferred—for example, by reading something a child has written (i.e., inferring, based on that public performance, what might have preceded it). Thus, private cognitive activity involves the individual's largely unobservable engagement with language, such as reading independently and engaging in personal response. We cannot know directly what processes the child has used.

Sometimes the public and the private seem to merge, as is the case when children are asked to record their responses in reading logs. The writing is observable, giving the response the status of a public act, but the thinking that led to the response—the intertextual or cross-situational connections the child has made—is unobservable. We infer the kinds of cognitive activities that the child might have utilized from the public record created by the reading log entry. In short, on the *public ↔ private* dimension, performances range from being observable to being unobservable.

The second dimension of the Vygotsky Space is *social ↔ individual.* This dimension reflects the degree to which students either use the knowledge learned from others or make what was learned their own. In the social world of classroom discourse, students are introduced to a vast number of concepts, meanings, and strategies. The goal of education is usually two-fold: Educators want students to possess the conventional knowledge of our culture and be able to use the knowledge in ways that help them construct meanings for themselves (Dewey, 1916). This second dimension of the Vygotsky Space represents the movement from what is taught and learned as part of the classroom's social setting to what eventually becomes an individual's personalized learning. This process of internalizing and personalizing what has been taught is characterized in terms of degrees instead of absolutes. That is, personalization is an ongoing process within which the learning is evolving and changing over time and with experiences.

For example, in Book Club students are introduced to ways of writing in their reading logs, which are used, in turn, as a basis for Book Club discussions. There is a social aspect to reading logs in that students use particular forms of response in the same way as they were taught. To the extent that students continue to use the forms without variation from the original examples of the teacher, they are performing on the social end of social ↔ individual dimension. The reading logs of such students often share similar features. For example, a character map that Jason created for Sadako, the main character in Coerr's (1977) novel *Sadako and the Thousand Paper Cranes,* was identical in format and in many of the features to his peers' reading log entries. However, when Jason made changes in the forms of response to tailor them to his own purposes and needs, he moved toward the individual end of the social ↔ individual dimension. For example, Jason invented a type of reading log response called "titles," which focused on an analysis of the titles authors use for chapters within their books, their decisions of whether to use titles or numbers, and the readers' creation of alternate possibilities for chapter titles (Pardo, in press). The social use of taught strategies provided a basis from which students invented their own types of response.

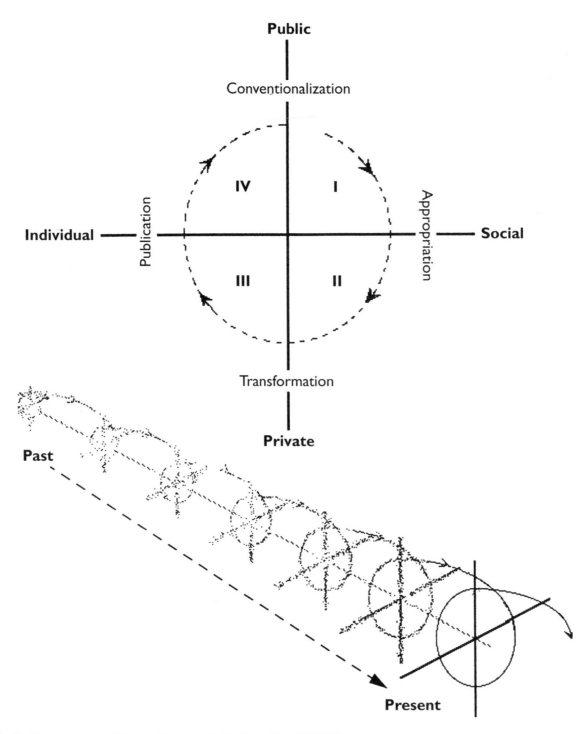

Figure 1. The Vygotsky Space (Adapted from model by Rom Harré [1984]).

When these two dimensions are combined as shown in Figure 1, they define the Vygotsky Space, which consists of four parts: (1) public/social, (2) private/social, (3) private/individual, and (4) public/individual. At any given time, learners' cognitive functioning may be characterized schematically as occurring within one of the quadrants. Quadrants I and IV (Q_I, Q_{IV}) consist of observable events that differ in terms of the location. Q_I reflects a collective, social setting, while Q_{IV} reflects the individual. Quadrants II and III (Q_{II}, Q_{III}) reflect unobservable cognitive activity through which learners progress as they make strategies their own. Following Vygotsky, Harré (1984; Harré et al., 1985) proposes that in the course of their development, individuals move recursively through these quadrants.

Harré identifies four processes that characterize developmental transitions between adjoining quadrants, transitions that shed light on the sequential and recursive movement through the quadrants. Movement between Q_I and Q_{II} describes the process of *appropriation.* Appropriation refers to learners' "uptake" of concepts and strategies that are introduced and used within the public/social setting of the first quadrant. The meanings and ways of knowing discussed in the public/social quadrant arise from various sources. Teachers may predict what students need based on past experiences. Teachers may decide to focus on instructional areas based on inferences about the private/individual cognitions of students. Students themselves may explicitly raise questions within the public/social quadrant, try out new meanings, and begin the process of appropriation of those ideas for their private use.

For example, Mrs. Pardo's modeling during a unit she taught with third-grade students illustrates language-based activity within the public/social quadrant (Pardo & Raphael, 1991). She taught ways for organizing the information that small groups of students had gathered about particular forms of communication (e.g., newspapers, radio). Mrs. Pardo had used the same sources as the students (i.e., informational texts, interviews, tradebooks) to gather information. She then modeled how to generate categories and organize all she had learned within relevant categories. This was a public event (a think-aloud) in a social setting (a whole-class session).

Students appropriated much of what was modeled. They used formats similar to the ones Mrs. Pardo had modeled, and they often identified similar categories. Although students' thinking was no longer easily visible, Mrs. Pardo was able to infer what students had been thinking by eavesdropping on their small-group discussions and analyzing the written work they created on their own. The students' individual thinking in this case was still strongly social in nature, with evidence of appropriation in sections of the chart that they produced. In both labels used and in items listed within categories, these sections mirrored ones Mrs. Pardo

had used, though they were not simply copied since the choices of categories changed according to the students' particular topics.

As students move from the private/social (Q_{II}) to the private/individual (Q_{III}), they engage in a process of *transformation.* Transformations frequently occur within the private dimension and, therefore, can only be inferred from students' individual work once it is made public. By examining students' publications, teachers can infer the process by which students transform meanings and strategies appropriated within the social domain, making those strategies their own.

Students showed evidence of transformation in classrooms over the 2 years of their participation in Book Club. For example, we can infer from Jason's presentation of analyses of titles as a new type of reading log entry that he had transformed taught entries in a way that he found interesting and meaningful. Jason's teachers, Ms. Woodman in fourth grade and Mrs. Pardo in fifth, modeled numerous log entries and the criteria for evaluating types of log entries. Further, they both modeled how new ways of responding in the logs could be invented. Such a climate invited students to consider knowledge as something that is actively constructed, and this invitation empowered students to make their thinking public.

Publication describes the process by which a person's meanings and strategies are made public so that others can respond. Publications can make visible appropriated meanings and strategies that have changed little in the ways the individual learner has used them. Alternatively, publications may show evidence of transformations of appropriated meanings and strategies. Jason illustrated the process of publication when he analyzed the titles of chapters the authors of various tradebooks had used, shared this new response category with peers, and taught them how he analyzed the titles. His thoughts were made public through oral discourse and written logs.

> By examining students' publications, teachers can infer the process by which students transform meanings and strategies appropriated within the social domain, making those strategies their own.

Finally, *conventionalization* describes the processes by which individuals' public manifestations of thinking (i.e., their actions and their ideas) are incorporated as part of the community of discourse in which they participate. For example, when Jason's title analysis was added to a chart that listed types of reading log response entries, other students in the class began to use the category. Conversation about response in his classroom included analysis of titles. Through conventionalization, Jason's appropriation, transformation, and publication of a concept related to response to literature became part of the conventional knowledge of his classroom, knowledge that was now available to his teacher and peers. Further, the process of inventing new reading log entries was also conventionalized as other students developed new forms of response. For example, Mei—one of Jason's classmates—introduced the category of "feelings," modifying a more general form of personal response.

We believe that Harré's (1984; Harré et al., 1985) model is rich in its capacity to help us conceptualize the relationship between the discourse that students are guided to participate in through social venues and the text-related thinking that they independently demonstrate over time. With Harré's model, we can see that language doesn't simply reflect thought; language makes possible what individuals think. That is, through classroom discourse students' knowledge is actually constructed. The model highlights the importance of the public/social aspects of discourse, for it is in public where both meanings and the processes by which those meanings are constructed are "out in the open" to be acquired and subsequently become the subject of discussion, clarification, and further development by students.

The model also highlights the importance of considering the power relationships that exist in school settings, for it is in the public/social quadrant that students' meanings are most fragile. It is here that teachers can either create an atmosphere in which taking intellectual risks is safe and encouraged, or one in which risk taking leaves students vulnerable to both adults' and peers' harsh criticisms. The teachers play a critical role in establishing the environment in which students learn to respect one another, to engage in conflict around ideas rather than personalities, and to encourage each other and support peers' learning. In short, language used within the public/social quadrant may be positive, but there are no guarantees that such an environment will naturally emerge without explicit attention to its development (Lensmire, 1994).

Further, the model provides a framework for teachers to help students develop facility with and ownership of a range of cognitive and metacognitive strategies. Instructional conversations can encourage movement among the quadrants. Alternative and flexible grouping patterns can provide students with a range of opportunities for talking and writing about text with the support of more knowledgeable others, both adults and peers. Creating opportunities for students to transform what they have learned and inventing ways of using their knowledge to support their own literacy activities can encourage lifelong habits of literate thinking. Students' individual learning arises from, but is not reducible to. these social interactions. In other words, students develop a "mind of their own." Students' individual learning is the result of public/social interactions with many different individuals. What better place than the classroom to create such opportunities? In the next section, we discuss implications of the Vygotsky Space for literacy instruction.

Implications of the Model for Literacy Instruction

Adopting Harré's (1984; Harré et al., 1985) model for teaching provides a lens for thinking about the kind of collaborative classroom environment teachers create for their students, the content of the curriculum they offer, the mutual negotiation of the content between teachers and students, and the ways students' progress is evaluated.

The Classroom Environment

The public-discourse (e.g., modeling and the uptake of others' ideas) in which teachers engage and also encourage in their students within Q_I sets the climate of the classroom. What is more, this climate strongly influences the willingness of students to go public in Q_{IV} with their own thinking and thus make their invented ideas open to further refinement. As Short (1990) notes in her description of communities of learners, "The kinds of social relationships and conversations that are encouraged will greatly impact the thinking processes of learners" (p. 34).

It is not surprising that students such as Jason and Mei felt comfortable sharing their text interpretations and inventing categories for response and sharing them with their peers. The public/social discourse in both classrooms had encouraged the students to see knowledge consisting of both conventional knowledge to be learned and concepts and ideas to be constructed. Over their 2 years of participating in Book Club, they both had developed a range of responses to draw upon. The students saw strategies as tools to be used and adapted, and learning as something to be shared. Their talk about text, often prompted by the thinking they had engaged in while writing in their logs, became richer and more varied as they learned a range of personal, creative, and critical responses to the texts they read and as they learned to invent new ways of responding.

The Curricular Content

The very ability to transform rests in students' mastering conventions that have been developed over time within the culture. These conventions make possible more inventive ways of using language if they are taught in a manner that helps students realize that convention and invention don't stand in opposition to each other. To transform or invent presupposes certain conventions. In Book Club, students talked about text in ways that spanned several response types: personal response, or reacting individually to issues and ideas; creative response, or "playing with" ideas (e.g., placing themselves in the character's situation or considering alternative events in one of the stories they'd read); and critical response, or evaluating authors' use of the craft or the success of various literary elements within the story. Their ability to engage in these conversations reflected not only an understanding of the language conventions and tools that comprise writing and reading but also their understanding of the inventive and interpretive aspects of reading and discussing texts. Thus, from the perspective of the Vygotsky Space, one aspect of the curriculum to be taught is the conventional knowledge of our culture, for it is this knowledge that provides a foundation for students' invention, their transformation of taught concepts and ideas.

The sense of convention *versus* invention in the language arts stems from lack of consensus about the role of skill instruction in a move toward an emphasis on process and on more holistic ways of teaching. We suggest that knowledge of skills, strategies, and conventions provides a much needed bases for engaging in more interpretive aspects of literacy. It is not an issue of *whether* conventional knowledge is appropriate to teach, but a question of *when, how,* and *under what circumstances.* The Vygotsky Space helps illustrate the relation between convention and invention and the role of the teacher in creating the climate for both to occur, as well as creating opportunities for students to learn. In this model, the public/social discourse of the classroom is the vehicle by which students come to understand the conventional knowledge of our culture and society. Through such discourse they can be encouraged to take what they have learned, examine it closely, experiment with their knowledge, and transform it in ways meaningful to them (as e e cummings did when he chose to reject uppercase letters). Through public/individual discourse, such transformations can be made public and,

> The Vygotsy Space helps underscore the fact that convention and invention do not oppose each other; rather, they represent two sides of the critical developmental part of learning.

thus, become part of the conventionalized knowledge of the classroom. In short, the Vygotsky Space helps underscore the fact that convention and invention do not oppose each other; rather, they represent two sides of the critical developmental part of learning.

Negotiating the Curriculum Content

Terms such as *teacher-centered* and *child-centered* imply a polarity that is neither as simple as the terms might convey, nor as oppositional, when it relates to the classroom curriculum. Certainly, we expect our educational system to have a vision. But we also expect that our students enter school with a rich background and set of interests, both of which can guide curricular decisions. Teachers use the public/social space of Q_I to make visible the educational system's goals; at the same time, they elicit from the students their own interests and questions for inquiry.

Mrs. Pardo recognizes the potential tension between the educational system's and children's goals and has worked with her students to negotiate the content of the literature that forms the basis of the reading program in her classroom. She draws on district curriculum content guidelines and from grade-level documents. She has lists of tradebook sets that are available to her grade from the district Language Arts Center. She also interviews her students, asking them to complete interest surveys and questionnaires about authors and books they have read and/or want to read. She merges the students' interests with the district guidelines in order to create interdisciplinary units (see Lipson, Wixson, Valencia, & Peters, 1993) that provide broad areas of study and choices within the parameters she has identified.

Evaluating Student Progress

Traditional means of assessment often limit the teacher's ability to make ongoing evaluations of students' progress. Measures such as end-of-unit tests or standardized achievement tests signal problems, but often they do so at a point in time when intervention is no longer possible. Further, single-point assess-

ments, such as end-of-story questions, may even be misleading (Dekker, 1991; Watson, 1990). The Vygotsky Space underscores the complexity of learning and the different entry points a teacher has to observe and make decisions about formal intervention or informal guidance. It also makes clear the fragility of the evaluative context in which much school learning occurs. How and, indeed, whether students make their thinking public on subsequent occasions is determined to a large extent by the ways in which their teachers provide critical feedback. In going public with their thinking (Q_{IV}), students provide teachers with opportunities to engage in on-site, formative assessments and to offer suggestions as to how students might improve upon and further develop their newly formulated ways of comprehending or composing texts.

For example, students in Ms. Woodman's room had elected to read and discuss Lowry's (1989) Newbery award-winning book *Number the Stars* in the spring of 1991, shortly after the award had been announced. A group of students had read one of the chapters in which the Danish king was tormented by German forces. In the small group, one student asked, "Why would Hitler want to take over Denmark?" Another student responded authoritatively that the Danish king had a lot of oil and wouldn't share it with his neighbors, so the Germans went in to get the oil. The student had applied his knowledge of the Persian Gulf War (which was in progress at this time) to his reading of Lowry's novel. Peer-led discussions helped to make visible students' confusions and their initial attempts to construct meaning. The public discourse in their small-group settings provided a window into the information they had drawn upon to try to make sense of the text and, at the same time, signaled the need to talk about some of the conventional historical knowledge.

Concluding Comments

Within the field of language arts education, we have focused considerable energy and debate on both oral and written language practices within schools. A number of scholars (e.g.,

Corson, 1984; Wells, 1990) have argued persuasively for the importance of oral language opportunities within classrooms, opportunities that support and encourage the development of literate thinking. Recent books have been devoted to the importance of talk among students in response to the books they have read (Roser & Martinez, 1995; Short & Pierce, 1990) and the writing they have, created (Calkins, 1986; Graves, 1983). Others (e.g., Barone, 1990; Dekker, 1991) have argued for written language exchanges between teachers and students and among students (Bromley, 1989) to make students' thinking and learning more visible. Language and language practices are crucial to students' intellectual, social, and emotional development. But it is not simply the language practices themselves that are inherently important. Rather, what matters greatly are the ways these different language opportunities connect among each other, the ways teachers mine these opportunities for their instructional potential, and the ways students come to understand that language is one of the most important tools of our culture. Using language in these ways suggests we reexamine the teacher's role within language arts instruction.

When changes in teachers' roles are suggested, it often seems as though we are faced with a series of either/or choices: teacher-controlled versus student controlled; convention versus invention; whole class versus small groups. The Vygotsky Space opens the possibility that educators are not faced with a series of forced choices; rather, different goals invite different ways of using language, different foci for instruction, and different instructional contexts. It helps us think about relationships among various classroom structures and related talk that promote students' literacy learning and lifelong valuing of language and literacy. As Phelps (1988) has noted, "We need a more complex, subtle, and variable model of the ways in which teachers and learners negotiate power, creativity, wisdom, purpose, consciousness, and action in their transactions" (p. 109). By identifying relations among public ↔ private and social ↔ individual language use, the Vygotsky Space provides a way of unpacking the relatively straightforward mandate to increase language opportunity and use in our schools. It is not simply the use of language, but language itself that helps teachers and learners achieve the multiple and varied goals of schooling.

References

Au, K.H., & Kawakami, A.J. (1986). The influence of the social organization of instruction on children's text comprehension ability: A Vygotskian perspective. In T.E. Raphael (Ed.), *The contexts of school-based literacy* (pp. 63–78). New York: Random House.

Barnes, D. (1995). Talking and learning in classrooms: An introduction. *Primary Voices K–6, 3*(l), 2–7.

Barone, D. (1990). The written responses of young children: Beyond comprehension to story understanding. *The New Advocate, 3,* 49–56.

Bromley, K.D. (1989). Buddy journals make the reading-writing connection. *The Reading Teacher, 43,* 122–129.

Bruffee, K.A. (1986). Social construction, language, and the authority of knowledge. *College English, 48,* 773–790.

Bruner, J. (1990). *Acts of meaning.* Cambridge, MA: Harvard University Press.

Calkins, LM. (1986). *The art of teaching writing.* Portsmouth, NH: Heinemann.

Coerr, E. (1977). *Sadako and the thousand paper cranes.* New York: Putnam.

Corson, D. (1984). The case for oral language in schooling. *The Elementary School Journal, 81,* 458–467.

Dekker, M.M. (1991). Books, reading and response: A teacher-researcher tells a story. *The New Advocate, 4,* 37–46.

Denyer, J., & Florio-Ruane, S. (1995). Mixed messages and missed opportunities: Moments of transformation in writing conferences and teacher education. *Teaching and Teacher Education, 15*(6), 539–551.

Dewey, J. (1916). *Democracy and education.* New York: The Free Press.

Dyson, A.H. (1992). *Social worlds of children learning to write.* New York: Teachers College Press.

Eeds. M., & Wells, D. (1989). Grand conversations: An explanation of meaning construction in literature study groups. *Research in the Teaching of English, 23*(l), 4–29.

Freedman, L. (1993). Teacher talk: The role of the teacher in literature discussion groups. In K. Pierce & C. Gilles (Eds.), *Cycles of meaning: Expanding the potential of talk in learning communities* (pp. 219–235). Portsmouth, NH: Heinemann.

Gavelek, J.R. (1986). The social context of literacy and schooling: A developmental perspective. In T. E. Raphael (Ed.), *The contexts of school-based literacy* (pp. 3–26). New York: Random House.

Gilles, C., with Dickson, J., McBride, C., & Vandover, M. (1994). Discussing our questions and questioning our discussions: Growing into literature study. *Language Arts, 71,* 499–508.

Goatley, V.J., Brock C., & Raphael, T.E. (1985). Diverse learners in regular education books clubs. *Reading Research Quarterly, 30,* 352–380.

Graves, D. (1983). *Writing: Teachers and children at work.* Exeter, NH: Heinemann.

Graves, D.H., & Hansen, (1983). The author's chair. *Language Arts, 60,* 176–183.

Green, J.L., & Dixson, C.N. (1993). Talking knowledge into being: Discoursive and social practices in classrooms. *Linguistics and Education: An International Research Journal, 5*(3,4), 231–239.

Halliday, M. A. K. (1993). Toward a language-based theory of learning. *Linguistics & Education, 5,* 93–116.

Harré, R. (1984). *Personal being: A theory for individual psychology.* Cambridge, MA: Harvard University Press.

Harré, R., Clarke, D., & DeCarlo, N. (1985). *Motives and mechanisms.* New York: Methuen.

Heath, S.B. (1989). Oral and literate traditions among black Americans living in poverty. *American Psychologist, 44,* 367–373.

Hunt, I. (1964). *Across Five Aprils.* New York: Berkeley.

Langer, J.A. (1991). Literacy and schooling: A sociocognitive perspective. In E. H. Hiebert (Ed.), *Literacy for a diverse society* (pp. 9–27). New York: Teachers College Press.

Lensmire, T. (1994). *When children write: Critical re-visions of the writing workshop.* New York: Teachers College Press.

Lipson, M.Y., Valencia, S.W., Wixson, K.K., & Peters. C.W. (1993). Integration and thematic teaching: Integration to improve teaching and learning. *Language Arts, 70,* 252–263.

Lowry, L. (1989). *Number the stars.* South Holland, IL: Yearling Books.

McMahon, S.I. (1994). Student-led Book Clubs: Transversing a river of interpretation. *The New Advocate, 7,* 109–125.

Pardo, L.S. (in press). Reflective teaching for continuing development of Book Club. In S.I. McMahon & T.E. Raphael (Eds.), *The Book Club Project: Exploring literature-based literacy instruction.* New York: Teachers College Press.

Pardo, L.S., & Raphael, T.E. (1991). Classroom organization for instruction in content areas. *The Reading Teacher, 44,* 556–565.

Paulsen, G. (1987). *Hatchet.* New York: Puffin Books.

Phelps, L.W. (1988). *Composition as a human science.* New York: Oxford University Press.

Raphael, T.E., & Goatley, V.J. (1994). The teacher as "more knowledgeable other": Changing roles for teaching in alternative reading instruction programs. In C.

Kinzer & D. Leu (Eds.), *Multidimensional aspects of literacy research, theory and practice* (pp. 527–536). Chicago: National Reading Conference.

Raphael, T.E., Goatley, V.J., McMahon, S.I., & Woodman, D. A. (1995). Promoting meaningful conversations in student book clubs. In N. Roser & M. Martinez (Eds.), *Book talk and beyond: Children and teachers respond to literature* (pp. 71–83). Newark, DE: International Reading Association.

Raphael, T.E., & McMahon, S.I. (1994). 'Book Club': An alternative framework for reading instruction. *The Reading Teacher, 48,* 102–116.

Rosenblatt, L.M. (1938). Literature as exploration. New York: Appleton-Century.

Roser, N.L., & Martinez, M.G. (Eds.). (1995). *Book talk and beyond: Children and teachers respond to literature.* Newark, DE: International Reading Association.

Short, K.G. (1990). Creating a community of learners. In K. G. Short & K. M. Pierce (Eds.), *Talking about books: Creating literate communities* (pp. 32–52). Portsmouth, NH: Heinemann.

Short, K.G., & Pierce, K.M. (1990). *Talking about books: Creating literate communities.* Portsmouth, NH: Heinemann.

Ulichny, P., & Watson-Gegeo, K. (1989). Interactions and authority: The dominant interpretive framework in writing conferences. *Discourse Processes, 12,* 309–328.

Villaume, S.K., Worden, T., Williams, S., Hopkins, L., & Rosenblatt, C. (1994). Five teachers in search of a discussion. *The Reading Teacher, 47,* 480–487.

Vygotsky, L.S. (1978). *Mind in society.* Cambridge, MA: Harvard University Press.

Vygotsky, L.S. (1981). The genesis of higher mental functions. In J.V. Wertsch (Ed.), *The concept of activity in psychology* (pp. 144–188). Armonk, NY: M.E. Sharpe.

Watson, D.J. (1990). Show me: Whole language evaluation of literature groups. In K.G. Short & K.M. Pierce (Eds.), *Talking about books: Creating literate communities* (pp. 157–174). Portsmouth, NH: Heinemann.

Wells, G. (1990). Talk about text: Where literacy is learned and taught. *Curriculum Inquiry, 20,* 369–404.

Wells, G., & Chang-Wells, G.L. (1992). *Constructing knowledge together.* Portsmouth, NH: Heinemann.

Wertsch, J.V. (1985). *Vygotsky and the social formation of mind.* Cambridge, MA: Harvard University Press.

Wiencek, J., & O'Flahavan, J.F. (1994). From teacher-led to peer discussions about literature: Suggestions for making the shift. *Language Arts, 71,* 488–498.

 Article Review Form at end of book.

What is meant by the term *critical questions?* Why do teachers want students to be able to ask critical questions?

Critical Questions

Whose questions?

In trying to teach children to become critical readers, we must help them to ask questions and accept that many of these questions will not appear on the surface to lead to the kinds of critical understandings we are seeking.

Anne Simpson

Simpson is currently head of the School of Language and Literacy Education at the University of Southern Australia. She may be contacted at Holbrooks Road, Underdale, South Australia 5045.

Which part do we question, Miss? The first part or the last part?

Miss, would it be a good question of why would he wear purple and that in the jungle?

How did the tribesmen get their hair cut and get their earrings?

These questions were among some posed by students in a year 7 Australian classroom, where a teacher was attempting to foster critical literacy. She was exploring a number of strategies for teaching children to challenge the texts they read and to identify how texts position readers to respond in particular ways (Wilson, 1995). Having spent some weeks modelling critical questions using texts describing Australian Aborigines, she selected Phantom comics and a Tarzan movie for the students to work on to pose their own questions. The questions the children asked intrigued me and prompted me to explore the issue of how we deal with children's agendas and the questions they raise around texts.

Critical Literacy

I will begin by briefly reviewing some claims that have been made for critical literacy, with the understanding that "ideals of critical literacy are at best provisional. They are the most favourable constructions possible at given times out of what we have available in the way of theory and practice" (Lankshear, 1994, p. 4). Indeed most proponents of critical literacy resist providing succinct definitions but rather focus upon what they believe it does or should aim to achieve, such as to "help readers resist certain kinds of assaults presented by written texts; to challenge, that is, particular ways of talking about persons, places, events and phenomena and ways of talking to the reader—of positioning her/him in particular ways" (Wallace, 1992, p. 61). Luke (as cited in Jongsma, 1991) believes "our aim is to get students to construct and to challenge texts, to see how texts provide selective versions of the world . . . with an eye towards transforming social, economic and cultural conditions" (p. 518). Others are even more ambitious in their vision.

Shannon (as cited in Jongsma, 1991) sees critical literacy as "a means for understanding one's own history and culture and their connection to current social structure . . .

and for fostering an activism toward equal participation for all the decisions that affect and control our lives" (p. 519). And Shor (as cited in Lankshear, 1994) describes critical literacy as "analytical habits of thinking, reading, writing, speaking or discussing which go beneath the surface impressions, traditional myths, mere opinions, and routine clichés; understanding the social contexts and consequences of any subject matter; discovering the deep meaning of any event, text, technique, process, object, statement, image, or situation; applying that meaning to your own context" (p. 22).

My own interpretation, for the purposes of this investigation at least, is much more modest and is shaped by my interest in children's reading and children's books and by my experiences in upper primary and lower secondary classrooms. In the middle class primary school in which I was working, I chose to focus upon the following critical understandings:

- characters are not real but are constructed by authors.

- stories are not reflections of reality but are selective versions of it, told from a particular view.

- in telling a story an author will leave gaps in the text that the reader must fill.

Simpson, Anne. (1996, October). Critical questions: Whose questions? *The Reading Teacher,* 50(2), 118–127. Reprinted with permission of Anne Simpson and the International Reading Association. All rights reserved.

- readers will fill these gaps differently.

- the author positions the reader to respond in particular ways through use of language, point of view, etc.

- it is possible to challenge and resist this preferred or dominant reading.

- authors write for particular audiences and assume that audiences have specific cultural knowledge and values.

- some values are privileged by the social and cultural context through which they are mediated.

My purpose in doing this work with children is to help them become more conscious of how texts work upon them and less susceptible to manipulation by what they read and view. In saying this, I believe we have to accept that often our work does not have the desired effect. For example, children may learn to identify stereotypes and media manipulation in texts, particularly in advertising, and yet still accept and enjoy these messages. In this sense, they learn to give us what we want and to say what we want to hear, while at the same time resist our purposes in identifying these messages. In other words, helping readers (and this includes ourselves) uncover the implicit cultural values in texts and highlighting how texts work, will not necessarily lead them to reject of the values or ideology of these texts or mar the pleasure they find in them (Christian-Smith, 1993).

Nor perhaps should that be our main objective. My primary intention in leading students toward the critical understandings outlined above is to open up issues for debate—to make them explicit and make it possible for readers to then decide whether or not to accept the values and positioning of the text. At the same time, I accept that teaching cannot be neutral and that teaching literacy—the texts we select to work with, the ways in which we work with them, and the contexts in which we use them—is a

> **In this sense, they learned to give us what we want and to say what we want to hear, while at the same time resisting our purposes in identifying these messages.**

political practice (Luke, 1988). Furthermore, as a teacher I have my own agendas and beliefs that will inevitably, through my position of power in the classroom, influence my students' responses to texts—privileging some responses above others.

Teaching Critical Literacy

There are a number of approaches to the teaching of critical text analysis. Some, which have been demonstrated by teachers such as Mellor, O'Neill, and Patterson (1992), Morgan (1992), and Gilbert (1994), include:

- setting questions (e.g., how else could the author have presented this information?);

- disrupting the text (e.g., changing words, rewriting sections);

- juxtaposing texts (e.g., comparing different accounts of the same event);

- supplying alternative endings (e.g., writing a different outcome);

- role playing, role reversal (e.g., uncovering what's been left out or what is inconsistent);

- making insertions and additions (e.g., adding new information or someone else's version);

- deleting (e.g., withholding or omitting information);

- introducing parody (e.g., highlighting social and cultural assumptions and values through play); and

- examining the social context (e.g., who wrote it, for whom, when, why?).

The strategies a teacher selects will depend upon the texts she or he is using, the program, the class, what other resources are available, and the teacher's own experience. It is possible to use more than one strategy at a time. My decision to focus upon questions was prompted by my interest in those raised about *The Phantom*

comics, and a sense that if children become used to asking critical questions, these questions can be asked of many kinds of texts and media and thus have a transferability that some of the other strategies lack. Questions can also, of course, be used to explore some of these other strategies.

Critical Questions

Using the ideas and kinds of questions that have been suggested by people like Mellor et al. (1992), Corcoran (1992), and Wallace (1992), I formulated questions based upon the understandings I wished to foster:

- Characters are not real but are constructed by authors. *How/why has the author . . . ? (i.e., Continually bring to the foreground the role of the author or illustrator in constructing the story or text. How could it have been written differently?)*

- Stories are not reflections of reality but are selective versions of it. *Whose voices aren't heard? Who is telling this story? Whose point of view is presented and whose isn't?*

- In telling a story, an author will leave gaps. *What's missing in this version? What's been left out?*

- Readers will respond to these gaps differently. *How does your reading of this compare with mine? Why is it different?*

- The author positions the reader to respond in particular ways through use of language, point of view, etc. *What does the author want you, the reader, to think and feel about particular characters or events? How does he or she achieve this?*

- It is possible to challenge and resist this preferred or dominant reading. *What is another way—an alternative way—of reading this text?*

- Authors write for particular audiences and assume that these audiences have specific cultural knowledge and share certain values. *What has the author assumed is the "natural" way things are or should be? What is he or she assuming is "best"? What kinds of people, contexts, and experiences are either ignored or devalued?*

Paula Willson is an experienced year 6/7 teacher whose classroom I have often observed. She and I have previously explored her reading circle program (Willson & Simpson, 1994), and it seemed to offer an ideal opportunity for working with questions. Reading circles comprise groups of five to seven children meeting once a week with her to discuss a section of a novel they have all read. The group members decide on the book they want to read and how much of it they will read each week. They use sticky notes to write ideas, questions, and comments that occur to them as they read, and attach these to the relevant pages of the book. These notes are of great value in the group discussions. The children are sometimes required to write a short response after each discussion and a longer one at the end of the book. At the beginning of each year Willson gives the children a page of general guidelines and questions to refer to when they write their notes and weekly responses. These guidelines include generic reader-response questions, such as Does this remind you of anything that has happened to you?; What do you think might happen next?; How do you feel about the characters?; What bits do you like or dislike?

Willson and I wanted to use new questions to help children gain some of the insights into texts and adopt some of the reading practices outlined at the beginning of this article. We were, however, uneasy about the form of the questions I had constructed, but we were not sure how to rework them so that they would be understandable, interesting, and relevant to these 11-, 12- and 13-year-olds. We were concerned that the questions were not meaningful to them, we were not likely to engage the children in the kind of critical exploration of texts we hoped for. However, like Commeyras (1994), we still believed that it was possible for us to work on these questions so that eventually they would lead to the outcomes sought.

My previous tangles with Tarzan and The Phantom indicated that there was more involved than just simplifying questions, and I want to signal a few of the questions we had as we planned our program:

- do all the questions we raise about texts need to be *critical*?

- will a focus on *critical* questions spoil readers' enjoyment?

- what about children's own questions? what do we do with them?

- before we can ask *critical* questions, do readers need experience and opportunities to read texts in other ways?

Reading Texts

Beginning with the last of these issues we found "four roles of the reader" (Freebody & Luke, 1990) useful in providing one model to conceptualise the ways in which we read. They suggest that good reading programs promote the following four roles:

1. code breaker (How do I crack this? What do the symbols or letters or combinations of letters signify?);

2. text participant (What does this mean?);

3. text user (What can I do with this information here and now? What is this text for? How can I talk about it? Could I produce such a text? How do others use it?); and

4. text analyst (What does this text do to me? How does it position me? What does it expect me to know/value?).

If we use this model, we can describe what Willson and I were trying to do as generating questions that would help children operate as *text analysts*. At the same time we knew that these children would, as readers, also be operating as code breakers, text participants, and text users. Freebody and Luke (1990) believe that it is possible to read in these four roles simultaneously and that to be a text analyst does not always imply that children have first to be skilled

We felt that if the questions were not meaningful to the children, we were not likely to engage them in the critical exploration of texts we hoped for.

readers of complex or sophisticated texts. For example, in a context of big book shared reading, teachers can introduce children to all four of these reading positions. It is also possible to work with very simple texts, as Jennifer O'Brien has demonstrated with Mother's Day catalogues (O'Brien, 1994) and as Barbara Comber and I have described with cereal boxes and packaging, having children decode, interpret, analyse, evaluate, and produce texts (Comber & Simpson, 1995).

For this investigation, we decided to work with picture books for the following reasons:

- these books usually generate immediate enthusiasm and interest. We felt there was less likelihood of children's enjoyment being compromised.

- students would be able to read the complete text relatively quickly and therefore review the whole book as well as specific features of it.

- visual texts put students on a more equal footing—some who might not be as confident with print could participate as fully as skilled readers.

- with illustrated texts, students seem more able to step back and talk about how the author/ illustrator has portrayed/ constructed a story or a product.

- because the text is relatively short, students often have time to read it more than once, as we teachers usually do with the novels we teach. This gives readers more opportunity for reflection.

We chose *The Wolf* (Barbalet, 1991); *Gorilla* (Browne, 1983), *Willy the Wimp* (Browne, 1984), *Piggybook* (Browne, 1987), *Window* (Baker, 1991), *Black & White* (Macaulay, 1990), and *The Eleventh Hour* (Base, 1988). We selected books we thought were sophisticated, thought provoking, and entertaining. We believed it would be more productive to work with these texts as opposed to seeking out material that was clearly stereotyped, biased, or otherwise flawed. We wanted to use books that *we* enjoyed and that offered aesthetic, intellectual, and emotional rewards to readers, rather than introduce books that were simplistic and easy to criticise for a lesson on critical literacy.

Although it is easier to work with popular texts (e.g., magazines and advertisements) and popular series (e.g., romances), our decision to use books that were sanctioned by the school and the classroom as "good literature" (texts that were highly regarded by teachers, librarians, and parents) was based on the desire to demonstrate that critical analysis is not a negative practice, but one that is appropriate for all texts. By using attractive texts that we valued and that were within the students' familiar literature circle structure, Willson and I hoped students would be more likely to adopt a critical perspective toward other texts they commonly encountered inside and outside school.

Our Questions

We thought that the kinds of critical questions we wanted to pose might be more easily understood and answerable if they were tailored to individual books, so we began by constructing sets of specific questions and activities for each of the books and gave these to the students to use when writing their responses. We wanted to offer questions about each book to help them focus upon the text as a cultural construction that used a number of linguistic and visual devices to position the reader to read and respond in particular ways. Our initial set of questions for *Gorilla* looked like this:

1. Do you think this book has any particular kind of message? What might it be?
2. Are there any bits that puzzle you? Why?
3. If you had written or illustrated this book, are there any pages you would have done differently or filled in or told more about? How? What haven't you been told that you would like to know?
4. Who's missing from this story? Give a reason why they might not be there.
5. Which picture tells you most about Hannah's situation? How does the illustrator achieve this?

6. How do you think Browne feels about gorillas? Which words or pictures lead you to think this?
7. If Browne had made the main character a boy, would the story work the same way, or would some things have to be changed? Explain.
8. Who is telling this story?
9. What do you think is the most important thing for people to talk about in relation to this book?
10. Can you retell this story from another point of view? Whose?

Clearly we were getting carried away here, and so we reduced the number of questions to four for each book. For *Piggybook* we settled on the following:

In your response to this book, we would like you to think and write about the following:

1. Where do you think the author might have got the ideas for this book?
2. If you lived in Africa, or China, or India, apart from the look of the people, would the idea of the story still work? That is to say, do you think families are like this in other countries?
3. What are the various ways the author has used our understanding and associations for the word *pig*?
4. Why has he chosen to turn the father and boys into pigs? Why not, for example, gorillas? Is this fair to pigs?

In retrospect, it was hardly surprising that the children's written responses to these questions were very short, monosyllabic where possible, and disappointing insofar as they did not appear to reflect any kind of consideration of the issues we were attempting to raise. Most students answered each question separately as if it were a test. For example: *Q1. I think he got his idea from a pig farm. Q2. No, because their lives are different. Q3. The author used the word* pig *for the animal and for saying they were pigs. Q4. If they were gorillas it wouldn't make sense.*

Some students elaborated a little more, and the opportunity we offered to create a text for *Window* or retell *Gorilla* from another point of view produced more satisfactory results. On the whole, however, it seemed to us that the kinds of questions we were asking were not striking a responsive chord with the children. Something was seriously amiss. It became painfully obvious that we were raising issues that were of no interest to the students and that

demanded too much in a written response. We believed we needed not only to change our strategy but also to provide a structure for ourselves and for the children to clarify, elaborate, and share ideas.

The Children's Questions

Our next step, after every group had the opportunity to read and discuss one or more books and write something in response to our questions, was to give pairs of students a book they had not previously discussed and to ask them to read it and then write approximately four questions to guide another group in their discussions and responses. We asked students to think of questions that focussed upon what the author or illustrator was trying to do in the book and upon what *they* thought would be important to talk about. Below are some questions we collected from pairs reading *The Wolf* and *Piggybook*.

Piggybook
Why does the mum do all the housework?
Why don't they know how to cook?
Why is the lady cut out of the photo?
Why do the kettle and the cup and the saucepan have holes in them?
Why doesn't the mum have a piggy face?
Why are they looking for food when they can go to the shop?
Why is there some word or drawing of a pig on every page?
Why won't they clean up the mess?
How enjoyable was the story?
How many pigs are there in the book?
Do the dad and the kids respect the mother?
How many questions can you think of?
What do the men learn?
What did they do to please the mum?
Do you understand why they have pig heads?
I really would like to know why they treat their mother like a slave.
Would the mother know how to fix a car?
How come the boys and the father are the only part of the family to have a pig face?
Why does the mum have to do everything at the start?
Why do they have to go to an important school if they are such pigs?
Why did the mum come back if they had got worse than they were?

The Wolf
Why doesn't the wolf want to come inside?
Why isn't the wolf afraid of humans?
What does the illustrator do to the pictures to make them correspond to the story?

What do you think the story is about?
How does the wolf feel about the humans?
What has the illustrator used for the illustrations?
What kind of emotions does the family have about the wolf around the house?
What message is behind the story?
What did the wolf look like?
What might the wolf be?
What do they think the wolf will do?
Where do they live?
Might it be a ghost wolf?
How do they know it's a wolf?
Why can't they go outside, because the wolf only comes at night?
Wolves can't open doors with their hands.
Maybe the wolf wants food.

After quickly reviewing the questions, we grouped them into four general categories:

- literal (or trivial)—*How many pigs are there in the book?*

- genuine (or authentic)—*Why don't they just clean up and wash the dishes?*

- rote (or stock, learned)—*What is the message behind the story?* and

- thoughtful (probing)—*What might the wolf be?*

There were not many questions (apart from ones we considered rote) that we could easily identify as being *critical* in the sense we have discussed—that is, standing back from the story as it was presented to question how and why it had been constructed the way it was. We were somewhat puzzled and disappointed by this, but our initial concerns evaporated when the children came together to talk about their questions. What soon became apparent was that the kind of question did not matter. The children's understandings were developed through the responses, not the questions. Nearly every child's questions provoked interested responses from the other children and stimulated discussion that reflected the kinds of insights we were trying to encourage.

Willson and I believe two factors were at work to produce this—the children themselves had constructed the questions, and they were able to explore these ideas together through the structure of Willson's literature circle program. In what follows, I will give examples from several of these exchanges, tease out what I think was occurring, and suggest some of the implications for teaching critical literacy through the use of questions.

Addressing the Questions

Having a structure in which children could present and discuss their questions about the texts proved to be vital to exploring and developing critical analysis of texts. Discussion in small groups provided an excellent context for pursuing multiple meanings and expanding levels of understandings. Willson's children (like many) dislike writing. Setting the agenda for their writing the way we did (with *critical* questions) meant they lost interest and commitment, and this was reflected in their writing. When the students were given the task of writing their own questions as the basis for oral work, however, they set about the task with enthusiasm. They clearly enjoyed the challenge of coming up with questions of their own, and the most exciting time was the group discussions when the children posed and explained their questions and other students responded.

We also found that having students ask questions in literature circles meant others in the group listened more closely and found it easier to respond than they had to statements that began "I liked it where . . ." or "It's funny when. . . ." By being encouraged to ask the questions, to direct the focus, and to set the agenda, the children were inevitably more interested in the outcomes and in the answers. As Ash (1992) found when she was looking for strategies to engage a group of at-risk junior high students in reading *Sounder* (Armstrong, 1989), what made the readers pay attention was "not a set of predetermined, teacher questions, but a student generated question" (p. 64). When readers came to the group with questions, students' commitment to the discussions was heightened, and this involvement led to them pursuing ideas and features of the text that at least some students might otherwise have missed. For example, the question "Why has Hannah's father got a banana in his back pocket?" (something several students had overlooked) led to a discussion of why the illustrator might have put it there and what it might signify.

As far as we could tell, there was no set of questions or kind of question that worked better than others. Consistent with what Commeyras (1994) concluded from her research, we came to see that "good discussion questions are the ones students want to discuss" (p. 519). As long as the questions were appropriate to the context, the texts, and the children's interests, they provoked useful discussion, and this provided a foundation for pursuing critical understandings. Although the questions in themselves may not often have led to the critical analysis we sought without teacher input, many of them at least offered us that possibility. As an illustration, the following exchange was initiated by the question "Why doesn't the wolf want to come inside?" Other students responded:

S1: He does, but they won't let him.
S2: No, he doesn't.
S3 We can't even see him.
S4: Maybe he isn't real.
S5: Yes, he is, because they hear him.
S6: He's trying to but it's all boarded up.
Teacher: Maybe the author is trying to keep us guessing.
(pause)
S1: I reckon he wants to get in!
(pause)
Teacher: How has the illustrator made you think that, Jimmy?
S2: You can tell by their faces.
Teacher: Why has the author chosen a wolf? What is it about wolves that is so scary? What other stories do you know that have wolves in them?

In this discussion Willson was trying to direct attention and make explicit those features of the text that lead readers to respond with fear of the wolf and to sympathise with the family. With her question about wolves, she was able to raise the issue of cultural assumptions about wolves and some of the implicit literary associations that readers (even very young readers) bring to bear in their responses to this text—why we expect wolves to be dangerous and how the author of this book plays upon and then disrupts this reading. We can't be sure what the children took away from this discussion, but we would hope that their awareness of some of the techniques producers of texts use to elicit particular responses had been heightened.

Children's Agendas

We were careful to value *all* the children's questions, though inevitably there were some that we thought more worthwhile than others. No doubt our responses revealed this. However, when the discussion seemed to us to be focussing upon irrelevant and trivial features of the text in response to questions like "How many gorillas are in the cage?" we found if we allowed time and space for these questions and let such topics take their own course, they would often lead to other issues, such as why the author might have included the picture and what was the point he might have been trying to make. Several children argued that Browne obviously felt sorry for gorillas and thought it was cruel to put them in cages. They explained that he made them look sad so we would feel sorry for them. This led to a consideration of zoos and the benefits and disadvantages for people and for animals and to the question of whose interests are served by zoos.

Even when the children served up questions that we felt we were just giving us what we wanted or what they could remember from the ones we had previously given them, we found, as did Roller and Beed (1994), that these rote or stock questions often served useful purposes, such as allowing less confident participants to enter the discussion with a safe question. Furthermore, stock questions such as "What is the message behind the story?" or "How is the author trying to make you feel?" could lead to discussions, which then offered us the opportunity of gently directing the talk to a critical focus. The rote question "Who's missing?" both in *Gorilla* and in *The Wolf* opened up discussion of alternative viewpoints and voices (e.g., other parents—real and imaginary—who would have different perspectives and stories to tell).

In another example, the question "What does the illustrator do to the pictures to make them correspond to the story?" seemed to me on first hearing to ask simply how well the illustrations reflected what the text said. However, the other group members were excited by the question and started talking about mood, colour, and technique and focussing upon particular pictures that conveyed the fear and nightmarish undertones of the story. From here we were able to consider some of the cultural assumptions and literacy associations we have about tunnels, long winding staircases, wells, and other similar visual images.

However, rather than always grasping the opportunities offered for critical question, we allowed the children to continue with *their* discussion, even if they weren't always discussing important issues—important to us, that is. If their talk was lively and around the text, it was apparent that there were valuable opportunities for them to gain experience, skills, and confidence in all four of the reader roles described earlier and for the teacher to support them in acquiring the language to talk critically about texts.

The Teacher's Role

If the teacher accepts the children's social experiences as significant and allows them to use their own ways of contextualising issues or readings, she or he can take advantage of their language and experiences in order to build upon their already established repertoire of literate thinking. (Roller & Beed, 1994, p. 513)

We found this was excellent advice. When we followed it we were more likely to discover what the children thought was significant and why, and thus create an opportunity to contribute a perspective that had some chance of being genuinely considered and accepted, rather than politely ignored. Slowly we learnt to keep quiet, let the other children answer, and to concentrate on what was behind any question. Where was it coming from? What was the child getting at? In a sense, we were reversing traditional roles and, instead of the students trying to guess what was in the teacher's head, we put ourselves in the position of trying to guess what was in the student's head.

As we continued along this path of allowing talk about text to arise from the children's own questions, we could see that Willson's role in literature circles would have to change. Rather than asking the questions, she would now be supporting students to clarify and articulate questions that mattered to them, so that they would become less dependent upon our models and frames. Another substantial part of her role would be to gradually familiarise students with a repertoire of language to talk critically about texts and a new perspective from which to do this. One way to do this might be to bring to the foreground the role of the author or illustrator in constructing the story and positioning the reader to respond in particular ways. For example, we tried to preface our comments and responses with phrases such as "Perhaps Barbalet was trying to . . .."; "How do you think Tanner expects readers to respond to . . .?"; "I think it's interesting the way Baker has . . .."; "Did you notice the colours and lines Macaulay has chosen to . . .?"; "I wonder why Base selected that word to . . .?"

We were sensitive to children's resistance to some of our interpretations and purposes and tried not to push our agendas upon them. For example, most children rejected outright any notion that Hannah might have dreamt about her night escapades with the gorilla or that the wolf did not exist, that it may just have been a symbol. We had to learn to accept inconsistencies and contradictions in the children's responses, while at the same time drawing attention to them and exploring their implications. It seemed as long as we didn't insist upon any closure of interpretation, the students remained enthusiastic and willing to take risks with their questions and responses.

Our experience did not lead us to conclude we had to resist explicit teaching. Clearly the modelling that had preceded the children's posing and discussing their own questions had been influential. Also, whilst not dismissing questions that did not appear interesting to us, we gave positive reinforcement to particular questions that we judged might lead to a consideration of issues related to our goals, such as "Why is the lady cut out of the photo?"; "Do the dad and the kids respect the mother?"; "Might it be a ghost wolf?" But although we were constantly alert to possibilities in the discussions to model critical questions, highlight features of the text we believed significant, and explore alternative meanings, at the same time we consciously restrained ourselves from pouncing on every opportunity. This was consistent with our concern to respect children's agendas and not to compromise their enjoyment of the books.

Summary

In many respects this investigation does not conclude so much with what the children learned about critical text analysis through questioning, as it does with what Willson and I learned about how to set the stage for such learning. In this instance, it was talk and the sharing of responses, together with the opportunity to ask the questions, which laid the basis for the children to deepen their awareness, appreciation, and critical insights into texts. The established structure of small reading discussion groups gave the children a safe and supportive forum for exploring their questions.

Questions are not the only way, or even the best way, to work toward the critical understandings we may seek. Not all texts invite the same kind of questions or even analysis. Sometimes other strategies work better with different kinds of texts. If we decide to work with questions, we must value and respect children's own agendas and not control the talk and the children's thinking with our own adult questions (*even* if we have worked hard to come up with very good questions and believe our questions are better than theirs!). Our expectations can limit what we hear and prevent us from recognising what children *are* talking about by causing us to worry too much about what we would *prefer* they were talking about.

Building upon our experience and reflections and on what she has read of other teachers' insights (Gilles, Dickinson, McBride, & Van Dover, 1994), Willson is allowing time in discussions for children to think and build their own meanings, and is not rushing to fill up pauses with a new topic, a new question, or

her own ideas. She accepts that in any conversation about text, there will be a variety of questions, interests, and understandings. Not all questions or responses have to be *critical*—perhaps only a few are. Our own experience as readers reminds us that we all swing between the various reader roles: sometimes code breakers, sometimes text users, sometimes text participants, and occasionally text analysts.

Children's own interests are the best starting points for engaging them in learning, and as they gain confidence and skill we can gradually nudge them along to consider other textual features and cultural issues. We must listen and respond to their interests and concerns first, then support, encourage, and develop analytical readings as opportunities arise. In trying to teach children to become text analysts or critical readers, we must help *them* to ask the questions and accept that many of these questions will not appear on the surface to lead to the kinds of critical understandings we are seeking. But the bottom line is that if the children don't care about the answers, we may as well not bother with the questions.

Author's Note

Thanks to Allan Neilsen for the suggestion about models and frames.

References

Ash, B. H. (1992). Student-made questions: One way into a literary text. *English Journal, 81,* 61–64.

Christian-Smith, L. (1993). *Texts of desire.* London: Falmer.

Comber, B., & Simpson, A. (1995). Reading cereal boxes: Analysing everyday texts. *Broadsheet, 1.* South Australia: DECS.

Commeyras, M. (1994). Were Janell and Neesie in the same classroom? Children's questions as the first order of reality in storybook discussion. *Language Arts, 71,* 517–523.

Corcoran, B. (1992). The making and remaking of readers and writers: A retrospect and prospect. In J. Thomson (Ed.), *Reconstructing literature teaching* (pp. 71–82). Norwood, South Australia: Australian Association for the Teaching of English.

Freebody, P., & Luke, A. (1990). Literacies programs: Debates and demands in cultural context. *Prospect: Journal of Adult Migrant Education Programs, 5,* 7–16.

Gilbert, P. (1994). *Divided by a common language: Gender and the English curriculum.* Carlton, Victoria: Curriculum Corporation.

Gilles, C., Dickinson, J., McBride, C., & Van Dover, M. (1994). Discussing our questions and questioning our discussions: Growing into literature study. *Language Arts, 71,* 400–508.

Jongsma, K. (1991). Critical literacy: Questions and answers. *The Reading Teacher, 44,* 518–519.

Lankshear, C. (1994). *Critical literacy* (Occasional paper No. 3). Canberra: Australian Curriculum Studies Association.

Luke, A. (1988). The non-neutrality of literacy: A critical introduction. *Australian Journal of Reading, 11,* 79–83.

Mellor, B., O'Neill, M., & Patterson, A. (1992). Re-reading literature teaching. In J. Thomson (Ed.), *Reconstructing literature teaching* (pp. 40–55). Norwood, South Australia: Australian Association for the Teaching of English.

Morgan, W. (1992). *A post-structuralist English class: The example of Ned Kelly.* Carlton, Victoria: Victorian Association for the Teaching of English.

O'Brien, J. (1994). Show mum you love her: Taking a new look at junk mail. *Reading, 28,* 43–46.

Roller, C., & Beed, P. (1994). Sometimes the conversations were grand, and sometimes. . . . *Language Arts, 71,* 509–515.

Wallace, C. (1992). Critical language awareness in the EFL classroom. In N. Fairclough (Ed.), *Critical language awareness* (pp. 53–92). London: Longman.

Willson, P., & Simpson, A. (1994). Literature circles: Children reading, writing and talking about literature. *The Literature Base, 5,* 9–12.

Wilson, S. (1995). *And the Phantom wore purple.* Unpublished master's thesis, University of South Australia, Adelaide, Australia.

Children's books cited

Armstrong, W.H. (1989). *Sounder.* New York: HarperCollins.

Baker, J. (1991). *Window.* London: Julia MacRae.

Barbalet, M. (1991). *The wolf.* Ringwood, Victoria: Viking.

Base, G. (1988). *The eleventh hour: A curious mystery.* Ringwood, Victoria: Viking.

Browne, A. (1983). *Gorilla.* London: Julia MacRae.

Browne, A. (1984). *Willy the wimp.* London: Julia MacRae.

Browne, A. (1987). *Piggybook.* London: Methuen.

Macaulay, D. (1990). *Black & white.* Boston: Houghton Mifflin.

 Article Review Form at end of book.

WiseGuide Wrap-Up

- Mediated learning experience is built on the belief that the early learning of concepts cannot happen without the help, or mediation, of such people as parents, caretakers, and siblings.

- A successful program of comprehension instruction should include large amounts of time for actual text reading, teacher-directed instruction in comprehension strategies, opportunities for peer and collaborative learning, and occasions for students to talk to a teacher and one another about their responses to reading.

- More and different kinds of language interactions between teacher and students and among students as they talk about the text they read can promote students' literacy learning and lifelong valuing of language and literacy.

- Teachers can provide opportunities for students to learn to ask critical questions, which can lead to deeper awareness, appreciation, and critical insight into texts; however, teachers must accept the fact that many of these questions will not appear to lead to the kinds of critical understandings they are seeking.

R.E.A.L. Sites

This list provides a print preview of typical **Coursewise** R.E.A.L. sites. There are over 100 such sites at the **Courselinks**™ site. The danger in printing URLs is that web sites can change overnight. As we went to press, these sites were functional using the URLs provided. If you come across one that isn't, please let us know via email to: webmaster@coursewise.com. Use your Passport to access the most current list of R.E.A.L. sites at the **Courselinks**™ site.

Site name: ERIC Clearinghouse on Reading, English, and Communication

URL: http://www.indiana.edu/~eric_rec/

Why is it R.E.A.L.? This site offers a variety of teaching resources relating to the role of prior knowledge and schema in literacy development. The homepage provides access to READRO—a listserv discussion forum for reading educators, bibliographies, parent brochures, and book reviews exploring critical thinking, reading, and writing across the curriculum.

Key topics: critical thinking, reading, writing, reading/writing across the curriculum, prior knowledge, schema

Try this:

1. Locate the review of a book entitled *Reading Across the Curriculum,* edited by Mary M. Dupuis and Linda H. Merchant, and learn about ways of incorporating reading and writing instruction into the forgotten curriculum areas of physical education, business education, home economics, vocational education, and health education.

2. Navigate to the review of *Critical Thinking, Reading and Writing,* by Mary Morgan and Michael Shermis, and examine a free exemplary lesson plan from this book of valuable strategies.

Site name: Resources for The Center for Critical Thinking

URL: http://www.sonoma.edu/cthink/K12/k12class/trc.nclk

Why is it R.E.A.L.? This site provides links to a variety of teaching resources related to critical thinking. The resource list also includes instructional guides and lesson plans to help educators implement critical thinking strategies in classrooms.

Key topics: critical thinking, active learning

Try this: Before visiting the site, consider your prior knowledge and conceptions of critical thinking. Compare with the concept of critical thinking detailed at this site.

section

4

- Define *authenticity* as it applies to reading, writing, and thematic instruction.

- Describe the importance of a school district and the broader community within which it exists in engaging in a collaborative effort to develop curriculum standards.

- Discuss ways in which teachers' decisions and beliefs may unintentionally contribute to inequality among students in the classroom.

- Explain the value and relevance of IRA/NCTE *Standards for the English Language Arts*.

- Discuss the purpose of integrated instruction. Identify the benefits and advantages of integrated instruction over traditional instruction.

The State of the Field: Standards and Integrated Literacy Instruction

Few would disagree that, to be productive in the coming decades, citizens will need strong literacy and technological capabilities. We have already experienced a change in the form and context of the information we read, write, and view, due to the advent of electronic mail and the Internet. Changing expectations for spoken, written, and visual competencies will continue as technological advances arise. Parents, businesses, community members, teachers, and administrators are all concerned that the children of today be prepared to meet the challenges of the workplace of tomorrow.

One way to ensure that students are prepared for the literacy demands of the future is through the development of a list of standards that defines what students should know and be able to do in the English language arts. In 1996, the International Reading Association (IRA) and the National Council of Teachers of English (NTCE) published *Standards for the English Language Arts.* These content standards were developed by IRA and NCTE officers, committee members, parents, legislative leaders, administrators, researchers, and policy analysts, as well as thousands of K–12 classroom teachers across the country. The standards are based on current research and theory about how students learn language.

The standards represent a shared vision of what stakeholders across the nation expect students to learn and the high expectations they hold for achieving them. These standards can guide states and local school districts in developing their language arts curriculum standards. The development of standards by individual states and school districts will vary according to their philosophical beliefs about how children learn language and their students' needs; therefore, the nature of standards varies widely from state to state. Once the standards have been developed, specific outcomes and assessments must be created to match the standards.

Curriculum standards serve as guidelines for classroom instruction. Integrated instruction is one popular curricular organizational approach to teaching the language arts. Integrated instruction is based on the belief that reading, writing, listening, and speaking are interconnected and, therefore, should not be taught separately. With integrated instruction, rather than scheduling four separate blocks of instruction, one block of time is devoted to the language arts. During this time, students and teachers are involved in reading, discussing, writing, responding to, and dramatizing stories. Mini-lessons on reading strategies, the writing process or mechanics, and comprehension strategies can be provided. In this way, the language arts curriculum remains whole.

The articles in Section 4 discuss issues related to the development and purpose of English language arts standards and integrated and thematic teaching. These articles provide opportunities for further reflection and conversation about the goals of language arts education, students' needs, and teachers' instructional approaches. "Seeking Authenticity: What Is

'Real' About Thematic Literacy Instruction?" provides a definitional framework that can be used to determine the potential authenticity of teaching practices. "Developing Integrated Language Arts Standards, K–12" describes a process for developing integrated language arts standards in one urban setting. "Innocent and Not-So-Innocent Contributions to Inequity: Choice, Power and Insensitivity in a First-Grade Writing Workshop" explains teachers' need to reflect on the daily decisions they make that maintain or change inequity. "Challenging Expectations: Why We Ought to Stand by the IRA/NCTE Standards for the English Language Arts" argues the value and relevance of the standards document and the need to embrace rather than abandon the standards. "Reading-Writing Relationships, Thematic Units, Inquiry Learning . . . in Pursuit of Effective Integrated Literacy Instruction" raises some important questions about instruction that integrates reading and writing or that focuses on thematic units.

? ? Questions ? ?

Reading 15. Describe a literacy event that provides for purposeful communication, supports student choice, offers a real audience, uses a resource other than the basal, and presents literacy skills within meaningful instruction.

Reading 16. Compare the process of developing integrated language arts standards, as described in the article, with what you have learned in the past about curriculum development. What are some of the strengths and weaknesses of the Academic Area Outcomes: Prekindergarten–Grade 12 listed in the article?

Reading 17. The author of this article states that she saw how students segregated themselves and how they were segregated, based on participation opportunities created by her scheduling decisions. Describe one example she notes as

evidence for this statement. The author summarizes two major conclusions that can be drawn from her study: (a) there are times when what seems to be a minor decision can be a decision that contributes greatly to inequality, and (b) there are times when giving students choice increases the power and knowledge of an already "privileged" group of students while decreasing the opportunities for knowledge and power of an already oppressed group of students. What evidence was included in this article to support these conclusions?

Reading 18. How might the IRA/NCTE standards aid educators in moving from rote learning toward more active problem-solving instructional methods?

Reading 19. What was Shanahan surprised to discover about integrated instruction?

Describe a literacy event that provides for purposeful communication, supports student choice, offers a real audience, uses a resource other than the basal, and presents literacy skills within meaningful instruction.

Seeking Authenticity

What is "real" about thematic literacy instruction?

A framework that can be used to determine the potential authenticity of teaching practices is presented and explained.

Bette S. Bergeron
Elizabeth A. Rudenga

Bergeron directs the Elementary Education program and teaches at Purdue University Calumet in Indiana. Rudenga is Head of the Department of Education at Trinity Christian College in Palos Heights, Illinois, USA. Bergeron may be contacted at Department of Education, X-152, Purdue University Calumet, Hammond, IN 46323, USA.

As literacy educators and former classroom teachers we are intrigued by the current interest in "authenticity." References are made to authentic literature, writing samples, inquiry, and theme cycles. Although we are excited about the potential that genuine purposes offer in supporting more effective literacy instruction, we are perplexed by the inconsistent—and sometimes contradictory—uses of this term. Bottom line, we find ourselves asking how authenticity re-

ally affects classroom literacy instruction and children's literate lives.

To seek our own understanding of authenticity, particularly as it relates to teachers' use of themes within literacy instruction, we have begun to explore the authenticity of our present and past practices. Our past experiences, which include classroom teaching at the primary level (Bette) and special education instruction with middle and secondary students (Elizabeth), have informed our current work with pre- and inservice teachers and have shaped our interest in authentic literacy learning.

Instruction in letter writing, incorporated into our former classroom literacy lessons, provides a clear illustration of our own growth towards authenticity. Because people write letters beyond the context of the classroom, instruction in this area has the potential for authenticity. Our first instructional experiences with letter writing, however, were far removed from real-world purposes.

Workbook pages, completely decontextualized from the actual practice of written communication, formed the basis for our first lessons in letters. Students defined the parts of a letter that were already produced or, if they were to be more fully challenged, copied a class composition from the board. Realizing that students had no opportunities to produce letters of their own, we developed lessons where they responded to fictionalized prompts. For example, students contrived letters written by one fairy tale character to another. We discovered, however, that these letters served no communicative purpose.

As our understanding deepened regarding the communicative nature of real letters, we began to ask students to write in their own voices. As a class, we would brainstorm questions to pose to a favorite author or special class guest. While the audience became real, the purpose was still within the realm of the teacher's

Bergeron, Bette S., and Rudenga, Elizabeth A. (1996, April). Seeking authenticity: What is "real" about thematic literacy instruction? *The Reading Teacher*, 49(7), 544–551. Reprinted with permission of Bette S. Bergeron and the International Reading Association. All rights reserved.

authority. A final step towards authenticity occurred when we considered why letters are written outside of the classroom. The answer is, of course, obvious: We write to communicate with another who shares with us some part of our literate lives.

This exploration of letter writing instruction provided us with a way of thinking about degrees of authenticity and has led us to the development of a framework that can be used to ascertain the potential authenticity of teaching practices. Before describing this framework, however, we will share how authenticity has been previously conceptualized. With this knowledge base and the framework it has generated, we will then describe the potential for authenticity offered by thematic literacy instruction.

Authenticity within Literacy Instruction

The power of authenticity is in the potential of offering school experiences that closely resemble and are connected with students' real lives (Cronin, 1993; Newmann & Wehlage, 1993). When students are involved in real-life tasks, they strive to construct meaning from their experiences (Snowball, 1992). These tasks provide the potential for learning both the content and process of the curriculum. Communication plays an integral role in the development of authentic experiences. Rhodes and Shanklin (1993) purport that reading and writing events should reflect the same communicative purposes that are used outside of the classroom. They also offer three ways to increase instructional authenticity: (a) provide students with literacy materials and the opportunity to use language within natural social contexts, (b) offer students choices in negotiating the curriculum, and (c) follow the students' lead.

The level of authenticity in both reading and writing instruction depends to some extent on the resources and materials used. Authentic reading instruction, for example, is primarily defined through the use of trade books in lieu of basal texts. In a comparison of a variety of writing events, Edelsky and Smith (1984) argue that unauthentic tasks

A Framework for Authentic Literacy Learning

Purpose

Evaluation/practice . . . . Communication

- What is the goal of the literacy event?
- What is the level of student engagement?
- How does the literacy event support lifelong learning?

Choice

Teacher . . . . Student

- To what degree do teachers and students negotiate the curriculum?
- What is the level of student choice?
- What roles do students and teachers adopt?

Audience

Assigned . . . . Self-selected

- Who controls the audience selection?
- With whom will the literacy event be shared?
- To what extent does the intended audience exist outside the classroom?

Resources

Contrived . . . . Genuine

- How varied are available resources (e.g., genre, media, range of levels)?
- How accessible are instructional resources to the students?
- How are resources used beyond the classroom?

Relevance

Superficial . . . . Pertinent

- To what degree are activities reflective of curricular requirements?
- To what extent are skills presented in context?
- How does the literacy event support lifelong learning?

often frustrate students, promote passive participation, may contain false information, and are used for evaluation. When offered opportunities for authentic writing, however, students reflect on topics that they care about, consult various resources, and produce texts that are personally meaningful.

Our interest in thematic instruction has led us to consider the potential for authenticity within this approach. Thematically based learning supports students and teachers as they work together to negotiate a curriculum that engages all participants in more genuine inquiry (Weaver, Chaston, & Peterson, 1993). Themes can provide a basis for using language for real purposes across the curriculum and for real audiences (Pike, Compain, & Mumper, 1994). The teachers with whom we have worked often provide this real-life

connection as a rationale for using themes (Bergeron & Rudenga, 1994). As students begin to see connections within the school curriculum, they also discover relationships between the classroom and their lives at home. Learning, therefore, becomes more personal and relevant, which may lead to the internalization of life-long literacy skills.

A Framework for Authenticity

Our inquiry into authenticity has led us to develop a definitional framework that can be used as a guide when developing instruction (see the Figure). We anticipate that this framework will continue to evolve as our understanding and experiences develop. Our present conception of authenticity consists of five elements: Purpose, Choice, Audience, Resources, and Relevance.

The authentic *purpose* of an instructional activity appears to exist on a continuum from evaluation and practice to communication. When assignments are perceived as inauthentic, such as completing a worksheet on the parts of a letter, students do not become fully engaged as learners (Rhodes & Shanklin, 1993). Wortman (1993) suggests that even dialogue journals can become akin to worksheets when students become preoccupied with writing a text to meet the expectations of the assignment and an adult evaluator. To be purposeful, the literacy event needs to be embedded within a meaningful experience that has communication and shared meaning as its focus.

The degree of student *choice* within an activity also contributes to its authenticity. Choice implies that students are empowered within classroom interactions and decisions (Wortman, 1993). Students should have choice within the planning, exploration, and sharing of ideas (Snowball, 1992). In addition, activities become more authentic to students when they have a degree of control over the materials, amount of time devoted to an event, and the purposes of their learning (Rhodes & Shanklin, 1993). Within authentic instruction, the teacher's role should be to facilitate, model, demonstrate, and provide resources (Snowball, 1992; Wortman, 1993).

Choice is directly related to the intended *audience* of a literacy event. Within inauthentic events, the audience is controlled or assigned by the teacher. However, authentic experiences are defined through "the individual's choice to create and share meaningful and purposeful text for a self-selected audience" (Wortman, 1993, p. 1). This audience can also include the learner him/herself. When writing letters, for example, students should control both the communicative goal and receiver of the text.

A fourth element of authenticity is the *resources* of instruction. Authentic literacy resources include texts normally found within a child's environment, such as trade books, bus schedules, maps, and diaries. People are also valued resources, as they can offer firsthand accounts and personal knowledge to the process of inquiry. When students have access to multiple resources, activities can become more authentic, writers can more clearly communicate their message, and students can be more fully engaged in authentic literacy events (Wortman, 1993).

A final element of authenticity, *relevance,* is derived directly from our experiences with classroom teachers. Although students need choice within literacy events, teachers are also responsible for fulfilling requirements mandated by the curriculum. Activities that do not genuinely meet curricular needs become superficial. Within a wildlife unit, for example, students may be asked to cut out a paper chain of bears. This activity is irrelevant to the topic and the development of meaningful literacy learning. Relevant activities, however, reflect student and curricular needs, are pertinent to the curriculum, present skills within the context of a genuine literacy event, and engage children in purposeful, lifelong learning. For example, students involved with the wildlife unit can reference multiple resources to research an animal of their choice while meeting a curricular requirement of using details within descriptive paragraphs. The resulting descriptive paragraph can be integrated into a document prepared to increase the community's awareness of regional wildlife.

Authenticity within Thematic Literacy Instruction

For the past 2 years we have been working with classroom teachers to explore thematic literacy instruction. We are interested in this approach to instruction because of its potential to provide meaningful learning experiences for children. By working directly with teachers, we gain a better appreciation for the challenges and rewards of this approach.

We have found that both the conceptualization and authenticity of thematic instruction vary widely among teachers and even within a single classroom. Most teachers, however, have purposeful and participatory learning as a goal for their students. Below are examples of literacy events, incorporated within thematic inquiry, that have the potential for authenticity in regard to purpose, choice, audience, resources, and relevance. These activities have emerged from actual classrooms and therefore reflect the very real variation in authenticity as well.

The following literacy events were implemented in two elementary classrooms that both used *Number the Stars* (Lowry, 1989) as a basis for exploring World War II. The teachers include Lisa and her student teacher, Marvin (Grade 4), and Jane (Grade 5). These teachers believed that Lowry's text would provide students with a more personalized understanding of the World War II era. In addition, the use of this theme fulfilled curricular requirements in the areas of social studies and language arts within both classrooms. The activities used in these classrooms illustrate the potential for authenticity and providing students with purposeful literacy events. The classrooms are not intended as contrasts but instead illustrate how literacy learning, with various degrees of authenticity, can be enacted through themes.

Initiation. The topic of World War II was teacher-selected in both classrooms, partially in response to curricular requirements. Student choice was developed as this theme was initiated through the brainstorming of current knowledge and future questions to pursue. When Lisa's class developed an introductory web based on World War II, she noted that students presented some inaccuracies and misconceptions regarding this era. There were conflicting opinions, for example, regarding both the war's timeline and victors. These discrepancies and subsequent questions posed by the students became the basis for future inquiry. Similarly, Jane divided her bulletin board into the sections of place, people, timeline, and terms. As students delved into their research on World War II,

> As students begin to see connections within the school curriculum, they also begin to discover relationships between the classroom and their lives as home.

related information was posted under the appropriate headings. Students in both classrooms, therefore, provided direction for the inquiry, while the lessons themselves were relevant to the mandates of the curriculum.

Shared reading. The book *Number the Stars,* combined with classroom libraries complete with a variety of related texts and other resources, provided the framework for students'

> **Students in both classrooms provided direction for the inquiry, while the lessons themselves were relevant to the mandates of the curriculum.**

learning experiences within both classrooms. Students listened to their teachers read orally, volunteered to read aloud, read with partners, and explored the book independently. Story events were reviewed each day of the unit, and students developed predictions that were supported by previous text passages. Students led discussions as portions of the book were completed and shared personal interpretations of the events presented in the text. Teachers controlled the format of these sessions, but the focus on communication (purpose) and student interpretation (choice) provided for increased authenticity.

Jane used the book to explore characterization, a required literacy element. As a class, students brainstormed traits of a character they had selected. Next, they used a Venn diagram to compare this character with a member of their class. Students then chose a character from the story and independently compared their own personality traits with those of the character. Jane also developed an ingenious way too promote students' summarization skills. Students selected scenes and phrases from the book that hinted at its contents without revealing the story's ending. These selections were written or drawn by individual students and then "buried" in Jane's classroom. Next year's Grade 5 students would uncover this story "time capsule."

Although the goal of these activities was to provide exposure to required skills, students gained ownership over the process of selection and were motivated by the genuine audience the activities offered. These literacy events, therefore, provided for purposeful communication, sup-

ported student choice, offered a real audience, used a genuine trade book as a resource, and provided for relevance by presenting required literacy skills within meaningful instruction.

Vocabulary. The use of a literature-focused theme promoted vocabulary development within the context of an authentic text. In both classrooms, students selected terms from the book that they wanted to learn. Teachers modeled how to use contextual cues to define unfamiliar terms and posted students' selected vocabulary within the classroom. As Jane's students read independently, they were asked to record unfamiliar words and the corresponding page number on index cards that fit into the book library pocket. When the passage was completed, students transferred the words into personal logs where they recorded both the sentence in which the word was found and a personal definition. Although students had control over the selected vocabulary and the activity itself met requirements in developing word knowledge, students perceived it as less authentic because its purpose was more evaluative than communicative. The audience was clearly seen as being the teacher.

Writing. Students in both classrooms engaged in a variety of writing experiences related to the story. Lisa and Marvin's fourth-grade students selected a topic from their original brainstorming web to create a newspaper article. This activity addressed the curricular requirements of finding details within a paragraph, summarizing information, and writing a report. Students began their inquiry by writing down everything they currently knew about their selected topic and suggesting avenues for future inquiry. A variety of resources, including locally published newspapers, were used as they pursued their research. The students' completed articles, developed into a class newspaper, had the real-world audience of their school peers.

Students also engaged in a journalistic activity within Jane's classroom, where they worked in collaborative groups to develop news-

casts based upon events from World War II. They sought information from a variety of resources, and current newscasts were used as models for their presentations. Had there been time for students to present their newscast to the school body or community at large, however, a more authentic audience and purpose might have been established. Teachers often find that the reality of time constraints can inhibit the implementation of desired literacy events (Bergeron & Rudenga, 1994).

Response logs were used in both classrooms as a way to reflect individually on the story and to relate events with students' lives. The logs also supported class discussion of the text and provided a place to consider new directions for inquiry as the text's meaning was actively constructed. Neither teacher assigned letter grades to the logs, but they did find valuable assessment information about individual students. The communicative purpose, focus on student choice, and reflective audience supported the authentic nature of this activity.

Mapping. The story provided an avenue for developing mapping skills, required in both class curricula. Students in Lisa and Marvin's classroom were invited to complete maps of Denmark, the setting of *Number the Stars,* from sources that included their social studies textbook. As students shared their individual discoveries, a class map was created. The story also provided an excellent framework for discussing current events, supported by newspaper clippings, and comparing maps of Europe during World War II with today's changing political boundaries. Jane's students developed maps of story settings. Students were able to base the maps on their personal interpretations of the story; they also incorporated the required skills of developing a compass rose and map key.

Each of these mapping exercises provided a personalized means for meeting curricular requirements. A more authentic mapping lesson, however, would involve students in reading or creating maps to be actually used. Within this unit, for example, students could study local road maps to prepare for a visit to a nursing home, where they could interview residents for firsthand accounts of the World War II era.

Creative arts. Students in both classrooms engaged in creative arts activities. The Grade 4 students, for example, jointly decided upon story events to be used in the creation of a collaborative class mural. The book was used as a reference to check on specific details, surrounding events, and character descriptions. Their audience—the school body—appreciated the detailed final creation. Jane's students also chose important story events to create a "photo album" of the book. Student groups selected their interpretations of noteworthy incidents, which were collaboratively drawn and captioned. The completed entries were bound as a book for their classroom library. As they expressed themselves through these art forms, students reached out to the real-world audience of their peers.

Home connections. Perhaps the greatest potential of authentic thematic instruction is in the links that are naturally forged between the classroom and students' home lives. Jane's students began a classroom museum, where they shared and exhibited items from home that related to the World War II era. Grade 4 students wrote letters to self-selected audiences, including parents, grandparents, and neighbors, to invite them into the classroom to share related experiences. Students also interviewed community members to gain a more personalized understanding of World War II from those who lived through this important historical event. As students shared their discoveries, based on responses to the letters and interviews, they deepened their understanding of curricular content and their own appreciation for others within their community.

Conclusion

These brief examples do not necessarily meet each element of authenticity. What they do provide, however, is an understanding that ideal learning and classroom realities can be accommodated as teachers and their students collaboratively develop genuine purposes for learning. Thematic learning can provide one possibility for supporting this growth towards authenticity.

More questions arise as we continue to seek ways to enhance the authenticity of classroom literacy events. For example, future inquiry can explore how teachers achieve authenticity when restricted by mandated literacy programs and how students can be empowered while covering required curricular elements. Also to be considered is how connections between literacy instruction and children's lives beyond the classroom can most effectively be forged. In addition, a basic question we have considered focuses on whether authenticity in a "pure" form is realistically obtainable. In effect, is there room for compromise within authentic literacy events?

Cronin (1993) suggests that the concept of authenticity exists on a continuum and that making lessons more authentic does not require a complete reversal of present practices. Instead, teachers attempt to move more closely towards authenticity as their professional knowledge grows and student choice continues to be fostered. The examples that we have provided show that teachers and students can effectively expand classroom literacy enactments toward greater authenticity. The framework presented in this article can play a role in supporting teachers as they consider changes toward more authentic literacy instruction.

References

Bergeron, B. S., & Rudenga, E. A. (1994, December). *Teacher beliefs and thematic instruction: Implications for teacher education and inservice.* Paper presented at the meeting of the National Reading Conference, San Diego, CA.

Cronin, J. F. (1993). Four misconceptions about authentic learning. *Educational Leadership, 50*(7), 78–80.

Edelsky, C., & Smith, K. (1984). Is that writing—Or are those marks just a figment of your curriculum? *Language Arts, 61,* 24–32.

Lowry, L. (1989). *Number the stars.* Boston: Houghton Mifflin.

Newmann, F. M., & Wehlage, G. G. (1993). Five standards for authentic instruction. *Educational Leadership, 50*(7), 8–12.

Pike, K., Compain, R., & Mumper, J. (1994). *New connections: An integrated approach to literacy.* New York: HarperCollins.

Rhodes, L. K., & Shanklin, N. (1993). *Windows into literacy: Assessing learners K-8.* Portsmouth, NH: Heinemann.

Snowball, P. (1992). Whole language: The authentic classroom. *Teaching K–8, 22*(8), 54–56.

Weaver, C., Chaston, J., & Peterson, S. (1993). *Theme exploration: A voyage of discovery.* Portsmouth, NH: Heinemann.

Wortman, B. (1993). Authenticity: How writing becomes real. *Teachers Networking, 12*(4), 1, 3–5.

 Article Review Form at end of book.

Compare the process of developing integrated language arts standards, as described in the article, with what you have learned in the past about curriculum development. What are some of the strengths and weaknesses of the Academic Area Outcomes: Prekindergarten–Grade 12 listed in the article?

Developing Integrated Language Arts Standards, K–12

Regina G. Chatel

St. Joseph College, West Hartford, Connecticut

In September 1995, the Hartford Public Schools published *Academic Area Outcomes: Prekindergarten–Grade 12*. The outcomes are considered as a starting point in the improvement of teaching, learning, and curriculum revision based on continuous assessment and accountability. The document delineates student outcomes and assessment by grade level in literacy, English language arts, mathematics, science, social studies, the arts, foreign language, health, physical education, TESOL, and career readiness. The creation of this document was no small feat in light of the educational, social, political, and economic situation in Hartford.

The Hartford Public School District is the largest school district in Connecticut, enrolling 26,400 students in 32 schools. Enrollment is 93 percent minority, comprised of 50.2 percent Hispanic and 42.8 percent African American. Most of Hartford's students reside in AFDC-dependent households (Assistance to Families with Dependent Children).

During the 1994–95 school year, the Hartford public school system faced a unique educational period. It was experiencing educational innovations on many different levels, among them, changing demographics in Hartford; personnel changes at the building and central office, including a turnover of 20 out of 32 principals within the previous two years; the restructuring of central office staff; and the arrival of Educational Alternatives, Inc., a private for-profit educational management company. Hartford was the only school district in the country to be taken over by a private management firm.

Within these management changes, there was a refocusing on teaching and learning. This was achieved through the curriculum renewal process, which was the outgrowth of the district's strategic plan, *We Believe in Tomorrow: A Framework for the Strategic Direction of the Hartford Public School*. The plan included ten strategic goals that could be summarized in three broad categories: curriculum and student outcomes, parent and community involvement, and school organization and management.

District Teacher and Administrator Input

District teacher and administrator input was gathered through a survey instrument. It should be noted that information was gathered before and during the effort to create a committee which would write the outcomes. Each teacher was asked to write down the unwritten curriculum. Teachers and administrators responded to the following questions:

- What should students know at the end of a grade level in reading, writing, speaking, listening, and viewing?

- What should students be able to do at the end of a grade level in reading, writing, speaking, listening, and viewing?

- What are some possible ways to assess students in reading, writing, speaking, listening, and viewing?

The committee facilitator analyzed and synthesized the school-generated curricula, which revealed the following:

- A rich and varied curriculum existed in a few of the grade levels

Regina G. Chatel, "Developing Integrated Language Arts Standards, K–12," *English Leadership Quarterly*, May 1997, by the National Council of Teachers of English. Reprinted with permission.

and schools, but this was not consistently evident across the entire district.

- Speaking, listening, and viewing were not consistently addressed in the feedback given by teachers and administrator; those columns were left blank.

- There were two differing philosophies of reading-language arts instruction, one being a skills-based model and the other a meaning-based integrated language arts model.

- Existing curricula did not appear to be responsive to the needs of the Connecticut Mastery Test, which is given statewide in grades 4, 6, and 8, and the Connecticut Academic Performance Test, which is given in grade 10.

To address the issue of educational equity for all children, the committee felt it critical to create a unifying curriculum framework and to build upon those elements in the existing curriculum and assessment practices which reflected current research in English language arts.

Creating a Cohesive Document

In order to create a cohesive document, a set of unifying definitions developed by the director of curriculum, instruction, assessment, and staff development guided the development and format of the outcomes:

- Academic Area Outcome = a description of what students should know at the end of each grade level by academic area.

- Assessment of Outcomes = the answer to the question, How do we know they know?

Much discussion focused on the difference between standards and outcomes, the difference between a framework and a guide, and exactly what was meant by assessment. Was the call for assessment to be interpreted as identification of possible assessment tools and measures or a statement of student behavior? The question of performance standards— or "How good is good enough?"— was not addressed by the committees

and the final document. That question is being considered in the curriculum-writing process, which is currently in effect.

The Document

The committee grappled with the dilemma of realistic expectations for the given population. Some committee members felt that the outcomes being considered were not achievable by Hartford's students, whereas other members felt that there was nothing that Hartford's students could not achieve if given appropriate instruction and resources. In the end, it was decided that the outcomes had to reflect the highest standards possible and not compromise on achievement. Even though some students would be unable to reach all of the outcomes, the expectation of teachers, students, and parents was that Hartford's goals were high for all children.

Even though some students would be unable to reach all of the outcomes, the expectation of teachers, students, and parents was that Hartford's goals were high for all children.

Reflecting on the Framework

Although the *Academic Area Outcomes: Prekindergarten—Grade 12* document was created before the IRA–NCTE standards were released, it is important to review it in light of the most current guidance from the profession. Using the IRA–NCTE standards as the measure, this work examines the philosophy and a sample set of outcomes and assessment to determine the extent to which they reflect these standards.

Literacy Philosophy

The introduction to the outcomes states that Hartford Public Schools' literacy philosophy for prekindergarten through grade 6 is

to promote learning throughout the educational continuum, utilizing interactive instruction to emphasize the integration of the communication arts throughout the curricula and beyond the school day. Each staff member and pupil must be committed to the rewards of

lifelong learning and recognize the diversity of our population as a resource for teaching and learning. Parents and the larger community must also realize the importance of the communication arts in our highly technological society, and become more involved in promoting literacy beyond the school day.

The Hartford literacy philosophy includes a focus on (1) learning as a lifelong process, (2) interactive teaching, (3) integration of the communication arts, (4) recognition of diversity, (5) the parent, school, and community partnership, and (6) the highly technological nature of our society. In addition, the English language arts philosophy, which is a separate philosophical statement for grades 7–12, states that

The English Language Arts Department seeks to improve students' awareness of the role the English language and its literature play in their personal, cultural and career development. The English program emphasizes the development of comprehension, critical thinking, coherence, cogency and fluency as they are reflected in students' reading, writing, speaking, listening and viewing. It also provides experiences and activities to help students become more appreciative of the arts. We select literary works for excellence in content and style, relevance to student interests, and cultural heritage. Our philosophy is to promote humanistic attitudes, aesthetic, and critical skills to provide a foundation for a lifetime of literary enrichment.

An examination of this statement shows the desire to (1) improve students' awareness of the role that English and its literature play in their personal, cultural, and career development; (2) develop comprehension, critical thinking, coherence, cogency, and fluency as they are reflected in the use of the language arts; (3) develop appreciation of the arts; (4) provide experience with literature which is of literary merit and relevant to students' lives and cultural heritage; (5) promote humanistic attitudes, aesthetic appreciation, and critical skills.

However, two different philosophies, one for literacy development for grades prekindergarten–6 and one for English language arts grades 7–12, are simply unnecessary. The document should have one philosophy for English language arts which encompasses all grade levels. An examination of all grade level outcomes and assessment supports their philosophical continuity and congruence. The existing distinction somehow implies that one develops literacy only through grade 6 and then switches focus to the development of the English language arts upon entering grade 7. In fact, the development of the language arts is all about development of literacy at all grade levels. Therefore, one philosophical statement would serve to unify the language arts across all grades (Chatel, 1996).

A review of the Hartford document in light of the new IRA–NCTE standards shows that it does address each of the dimensions of language learning presented in the standards. Content, purpose, and development are addressed by the outcomes document in that it delineates the what, why, and how of the English language arts at each grade level. The document states that all students will read a broad range of texts and genres, select and apply meaning-making processes and strategies, and study and use standard structures of the English language. The purpose is clearly defined in terms of the language arts being for obtaining and using information, for aesthetic appreciation and expression, for learning from and reflecting on the literary experience, and for problem solving and broader applications to life. Finally, philosophically, the language arts are said to be integrated in purpose, use, and development. This framework is user friendly in that it is clearly divided by content area, has a manageable but comprehensive number of outcomes, states the philosophy of each content area in the introduction, and briefly explains the development of the document, giving it broad community appeal.

Further Considerations

Although *Academic Area Outcomes: Prekindergarten–Grade 12* appears to be flawless and a wonderful example of the English language arts standards put into operation, the literacy and the English language arts sections of the document are problematic in three ways: (1) the format which treats each of the language arts separately, (2) the statement of reading at least at grade level for each grade, and (3) the lack of visual representation as a language art.

The problem of format is being grappled with by all educators undertaking curriculum restructuring. How does one write outcomes which encompass all of the language arts? The very nature of dividing the language arts into reading, writing, speaking, listening, and viewing implies their separateness and contradicts the integrated language arts philosophy espoused in the introduction to the outcomes. The IRA–NCTE standards document attempts to be integrative in nature, but it is this very approach which has led to much criticism.

Second, the statement of reading "at least at grade level" for each grade appears to be a case of the document trying to be all things to all people. The outcomes document is intended to facilitate change in philosophy, teaching, learning, and assessment. Its clarity, organization, comprehensiveness, and research base make it a powerful tool. Yet the use of the phrase "reading at least at grade level" implies that there is such an entity which is achievable, measurable, and desirable. IRA and NCTE have indicated that there can be no expectation that all students in a given grade achieve at the "grade level" for that "grade level" designation on a normed achievement test because it is an indication of the *average* or *range* of scores. This appears to be a politically, and not an educationally, motivated outcome which is es-

The IRA–NCTE standards document attempts to be integrative in nature, but it is this very approach which has led to much criticism.

sential to the acceptance of the document within the broader Hartford social context.

Finally, the lack of visual representation as a language art is understandable in light of the lack of standards from IRA and NCTE when the document was being developed. Even today, visual representation is not a concept which is fully developed or understood. It should be included in the next revision of *Academic Area Outcomes: Prekindergarten–Grade 12.*

Summary

Academic Area Outcomes: Prekindergarten–Grade 12 is the result of a collaborative effort between the educational community and the broader community within which it exists. Parents, legislators, administrators, and regular and special educators want to know not only about the existing school programs, but about the future directions their schools are going to take. The collaborative writing process attempts to "satisfy a community's reasonable expectation that [schools] provide meaningful information on how they are performing [and future performance expectations]" (Schmoker, 1996, p. 47). In addition, Schmoker states that "people accomplish more together than in isolation; regular, collective dialogue about agreed-upon focus sustains commitment and feeds purpose; [and] effort thrives on concrete evidence of progress" (p. 48). From this perspective, the collaborative effort builds in accountability and ownership for implementation of the new outcomes document. The accountability and ownership place a responsibility on the schools to actually implement the outcomes and on the community to support them. The groundwork for implementation of the outcomes has been prepared by the collaborative nature of its creation.

Finally, *Academic Area Outcomes: Prekindergarten–Grade 12* is intended to facilitate change in the teaching, learning, and assessing of the English language arts and other content areas

in Hartford. It is a unifying frame
work for the development of curriculum guides in that it provides a vision of the high educational goals to
which Hartford aspires for all of its
children.

Works Cited

Chatel, R. G. 1996. Struggle for Standards:
The Hartford Experience with Literacy
Across the Curriculum. *Cascade*, 1:4–6.

Connecticut State Board of Education. 1987.
Connecticut's Common Core of Learning.
State of Connecticut.

Crabbe, A. B. 1994. *Toward Active Learning:
Integrating the SCANS SKILLS into the
Curriculum.* Washington, DC: Tech Prep
Executive Leadership Program.

Hartford Public Schools. 1995. *Academic Area
Outcomes, Prekindergarten–Grade 12.*
Hartford, CT: Hartford Public Schools.

IRA/NCTE Joint Task Force on Assessment.
1994. *Standards for the Assessment of
Reading and Writing.* Urbana, IL: NCTE.

Mitchell, R. 1996. *Front-end Alignment: Using
Standards to Seek Educational Change.* The
Education Trust. Washington, DC:
American Association for Higher
Education.

Schmoker, M. 1996. *RESULTS: The Key to
Continuous School Improvement.*
Alexandria, VA: ASCD.

**Article Review
Form at end of
book.**

The author of this article states that she saw how students segregated themselves and how they were segregated, based on participation opportunities created by her scheduling decisions. Describe one example she notes as evidence for this statement. The author summarizes two major conclusions that can be drawn from her study: (a) there are times when what seems to be a minor decision can be a decision that contributes greatly to inequality, and (b) there are times when giving students choice increases the power and knowledge of an already "privileged" group of students while decreasing the opportunities for knowledge and power of an already oppressed group of students. What evidence was included in this article to support these conclusions?

Innocent and Not-So-Innocent Contributions to Inequality

Choice, power, and insensitivity in a first-grade writing workshop

Even the most well-intentioned decisions can lead to inequality of opportunity in the classroom.

Jo Anne Pryor Deshon

Jo Anne Pryor Deshon teaches third grade at John R. Downs Elementary School in Newark, Delaware.

Me, insensitive? When I get down on my knees, I am the perfect height to give hugs and handshakes to each child entering the room. I spend more time on my shins that on my feet as I look up and listen to students during writing conferences. I sit on the floor with groups of them and raise my hand to be called on to ask a question or make a comment after a student author has shared his or her writing. I eat lunch with a different group of children each week. I smile and wave as I say good-bye to each child as he or she leaves the curb and heads for the bus. I call periodically to tell a parent what a wonderful child he or she has. Someone who shows she cares in such ways could not be insensitive!

Indeed, in my classroom, I thought I made every effort to be fair and to provide all my students equal opportunity and equal attention, which is the way I thought it should be. During writing time, I tried to provide students with the chance to express themselves and share their writing, for, as Dyson (1993) notes, children can use writing for social ends, as a way to negotiate status. I believed that the opportunity for children to write and share their writing was one way of promoting equality in the classroom.

Since 6 of my students participated in our school's Chapter I reading program, in early October, I rearranged their writing time to accommodate the pull-out program. I made sure that these 6 students always had the same amount of time to write as the other students.

But after reading Stanovich's (1986) ideas about "Matthew effects"

Jo Anne Pryor Deshon, "Innocent and Not-So-Innocent Contributions to Inequality: Choice, Power, and Insensitivity in a First-Grade Writing Workshop," *Language Arts*, January 1997, by the National Council of Teachers of English. Reprinted with permission.

in reading acquisition—situations that result in rich-get-richer and poor-get-poorer patterns of achievement—I was haunted by my classroom experiences that matched his descriptions. My first-grade writing workshop appeared to benefit the "privileged" children (those who come to school already reading and writing or on the brink of doing so) more than children who did not have literacy-rich preschool experiences. Thus, I feared that children like those receiving Chapter I instruction might not be getting all they needed from my attempts at writing workshop. Moreover, these concerns interacted with the fact that in my school, the children needing a great deal of extra help in reading and writing are disproportionately represented by African American children and/or children from low-income homes.

As I read the work of Anyon (1980), which practically accused public schools of offering different types of educational experiences and curriculum knowledge to children of different social classes, and the writings of others, questions came to mind. Did the non-random distributions of environmental quality, to which Stanovich (1986) referred, support Anyon's accusation? Could the "perverse plot against black success," to which Delpit (1986) referred, actually exist? Are teachers consciously and intentionally contributing to inequality? Can educators end inequality in classrooms and school systems? Because of my concerns about issues like these, I decided to do a study that would allow me to focus on two questions: (1) How are knowledge and power interrelated in a first-grade writing workshop?; and (2) How do status and power differences surface and subsequently influence students in writing workshop?

In this article, I first present the writing workshop structures I used in my classroom, including the effort I made to accommodate the 6 Chapter I students. Then, I evaluate the effect these different structures had on each group of students' opportunities to interact and share their

writing with me and with their peers. Finally, I address the issue of whether equal instruction is necessary or even fair to all students.

Who would have thought it would take reading, writing, videotaping, analyzing, and reflecting to discover that a seemingly minor decision regarding writing workshop scheduling contributed significantly to inequality in my first-grade classroom? If I had taught without reflection, I never would have understood what a poor and insensitive choice I made, and I never would have taken steps to solve the problem it created. This work helped me realize how easy it is to make culturally insensitive decisions as a European American teacher of linguistically and culturally diverse children.

Data Collection in the Classroom

I collected data in my integrated and heterogeneously grouped first-grade classroom. Twenty-five students (14 boys and 11 girls) had participated in a process approach to writing for 32 weeks before the research study began. Ten of those students (40%) represented cultural minorities (9 African Americans and 1 Hispanic American). Over 50% of the students came from low-socioeconomic backgrounds, as evidenced by the fact that 12 received free lunch and 2 received lunch at a reduced cost. In my class, writing workshop, as described by Graves (1983) and Calkins (1994), occurred 3 times a week for 45–60 minutes (a 5- to 10-minute mini-lesson, 24–35 minutes of writing time plus peer and teacher/student content conferences, and 10–15 minutes of sharing time).

The data collection period lasted for 10 writing workshop sessions from May 8, 1995, through May 31, 1995. Data included (1) videotapes of "official" peer content conferences (students signed up for a conference to be held in a designated area of the room), (2) videotapes of sharing sessions, (3) copies of student

Who would have thought it would take reading, writing, videotaping, analyzing, and reflecting to discover that a seemingly minor decision regarding writing workshop scheduling contributed significantly to inequality in my first-grade classroom?

work, (4) teacher journal and field notes, and (5) site documents (lesson plans, report cards, and portfolios). All the children's names throughout this article are pseudonyms.

I adopted a naturalistic inquiry approach (Lincoln & Guba, 1985) in this study. Because I was the full-time teacher responsible for conferencing and classroom management, most of my persistent observing occurred after the children had gone home when I viewed the videotapes of peer conferences and sharing sessions. My inductive data analysis began with a coding of "interaction events." When an author chose to share a piece for a peer conference or sharing session, the "interaction event" consisted of three parts: the author reading his or her piece, the audience responding to the piece, and the author responding to the audience's response. I categorized these interaction events by participant demographics (gender, race, and socioeconomic background), audience response characteristics (question or comment and criticism or compliment), and author-response characteristics (pleased, displeased, ambivalent). If the interaction event occurred during a sharing session, I was also interested in who was called on to (1) ask questions/offer comments and (2) be the next author to share.

The Impact of Teacher Decisions

The Chapter I Reading teacher tested children in September and began her small-group, pull-out program in October. By then, the daily schedule that I initiated the second week of September was a familiar routine for the students. If I had kept the schedule as it was, 6 of my students would have missed the beginning of writing workshop when they left at 10:00 a.m. for Chapter I reading. Switching the schedule would have been difficult, however, since I allow one hour for writing workshop. Because of bus, cafeteria, playground, and enrichment class schedules, I did not have one hour before or after the 30-minute Chapter I program. I decided it did not really matter if the "Chapter" kids were to miss the beginning of writing workshop. Although it would take a little of my conferencing time, I could give those children the mini-lesson when they returned. The lesson would be abbreviated and rushed, but it would basically be the same mini-lesson the other students had while the Chapter I children were out of the room. When the "Chapter" students returned to class and the rest of the children stopped writing to participate in a sharing session, I could give the "Chapter" kids a choice: They could continue writing or join us for sharing. I believe kids learn to write by writing

I saw how students segregated themselves and how they were segregated, based on participation opportunities created by my scheduling decisions.

and, thus, thought it necessary to insure that all students had the same amount of time to write, even if it meant not having the chance to participate in other parts of writing workshop. So I wanted to give each child equal writing time. I did not think that the "Chapter" kids' missing sharing time would matter.

Student Behavior

Analysis of the data yielded interesting patterns that I would not have noticed or reflected on during the course of the school day. I saw patterns in the writing workshop participation of the 4 Chapter I students who were ethnic minorities and across the entire class that broke down along ethnic and gender lines. I saw how students segregated themselves and how they were segregated, based on participation opportunities created by my scheduling decisions.

After returning from the pull-out program, "Chapter" kids chose to stay in their seats to write or draw. They joined the rest of us for sharing after most of the other children had already shared and discussed their writing. They missed the models of sharing prevalent during this time—the pieces that were shared, the questions that were asked, the answers that were given, and the comments that were offered. Three of the 6 "Chapter" kids never participated in a peer conference or shared a piece of writing at a sharing session. Over the 10 sessions of data collection, there were 2 days when some of the

"Chapter" kids did not come to sharing time.

"Chapter" kids were consistently called on last by their peers to share their texts. I believe that this pattern was a result of their coming late to sharing sessions rather than intentional exclusion. Nevertheless, children who were called on last by their peers to share writing had fewer and shorter opportunities for sharing and receiving feedback. Some days I told the students who had not had a chance to share that they could share after lunch (if there was time). Some days I tried to let them share quickly before lunch (but we were always in a hurry, and often the class was restless as sharing time grew longer). Consider the following sharing session comments I made at various times during the data collection:

We don't have time for another author, but it looks like James, Lisa, and Jordan all wanted to share. If we have time, we will do it later. (They did not share later that day.)

Kaleigh might be our last author. We'll see how quickly she can share and get questions.

You know what, let's stop right there and just raise your hand right now if you did not get a chance to share. Amy, Juliana, uh, James, Jordan, and Lisa. Now fortunately, uh, Amy you conferenced with someone this morning. Jordan and Lisa got a conference this morning. . . . I will try to give Amy, Juliana, James, Jordan, and Lisa a chance to share, but especially Juliana and James 'cause they did not have a chance to peer conference yet today. Right now, would you put away your papers and get ready for lunch?

James, can you be pretty quick and pretty loud? Because I would like to do a drug unit lesson as soon as sharing circle is done. . . . Go ahead, James, quickly!

I noticed that the ethnic minority students preferred to share their texts with large groups. For example, 54% of the students who read a piece during more than one sharing session were minority students, but 44% of the students who never peer conferenced were minority students. I realized that I was a teacher who encouraged peer conferences: I developed mini-lessons related to conferencing and occasionally extended writing time and decreased sharing time in order to increase opportunities for conferences. Thus, I ended up disadvantaging students in my class who preferred sharing with larger audiences. Although I did mini-lessons related to sharing sessions (procedures for sharing sessions, characteristics of a good audience, the difference between questions and comments, asking questions that will help the author revise), I did not encourage large groups to share during writing time.

Although students chose to conference with peers of varying academic ability (based on report card grades), they rarely crossed gender lines. Only 21% of the peer conferences crossed gender lines. Generally, students who did peer conference shared their pieces more than once (at other peer conferences or during sharing sessions) and eventually published those pieces. Students who conferenced with peers typically received higher language arts grades on report cards. Students with higher grades usually had more opportunities to increase their knowledge as they read their pieces of writing aloud and received feedback from their peers.

After I chose one person to begin the sharing session, the students chose who would share next. Three of the students with the highest grades in language arts were consistently the second, third, or fourth person to share during sharing sessions. One might conclude that higher grades are not only an indication of knowledge but also of power and status.

Conclusions from the Study

I thought I was being sensitive and fair when I decided to adjust the writing workshop schedule to accommodate the Chapter I reading program. I did not think about the fact that during sharing sessions, "Chapter" kids who chose to remain at their seats to write worked in isolation because their desks were scattered throughout the room. At first, I rationalized that this was not a problem because all of my students know that they can change their seats during writing time to work near a friend. Although, I encouraged "Chapter" kids to sit near one another if they wanted to conference with a friend, they still began from positions of isolation while other students never had to deal with this problem.

I also did not think about the fact that during sharing sessions, "Chapter" kids who chose to remain at their seats would have to talk with a peer at their ability level rather than with more capable peers who could act as scaffolds to them as they progress (Vygotsky, 1978). The other children were always heterogeneously grouped, thus allowing for mixed-ability conferencing. "Chapter" kids ended up being ability-grouped during the Chapter I program and during parts of writing workshop. I never asked myself if it would have been more valuable for "Chapter" kids to participate in a sharing session.

Although I had anticipated that the mini-lessons I repeated for "Chapter" kids would be rushed and abbreviated, I did not fully realize how often they would also be interrupted by children asking me questions or misbehaving. It wasn't fair that certain students consistently had lessons that were rushed, abbreviated, and interrupted.

I also did not realize how my favoring of peer conferences over larger group sharing time affected the opportunities of some students to interact with others about their writing. The structure I used for writing workshop ended up privileging those students who had opportunities to participate in all aspects of the workshop and who could choose whichever form of sharing writing they preferred—peer conferencing or sharing time—without the added pressure of time constraint or the problem of student power structures that insured that more advanced students would have greater chances to share their work.

Teachers need to reflect on the daily decisions they make, reevaluate the role and value of choice in the classroom, and recognize the realities and impact of power differences. This study shows (1) there are times when what seems to be a minor decision can be a decision that contributes greatly to inequality; and (2) there are times when giving students choice increases the power and knowledge of an already "privileged" group of students while decreasing the opportunities for knowledge and power of an already oppressed group of students.

Collaboration for Understanding: A Move Towards Equality

Having all students present for the entire workshop will not solve the problem of classroom inequality. There will continue to be students with more knowledge, power, and status. Delpit (1986) encourages educators to combine process-oriented and skills-oriented approaches so that skills may be learned in meaningful contexts. She believes that " 'skills' within the context of critical and creative thinking" are necessary "if minority people are to effect the change which will allow them to truly progress" (p. 384). In addition, she suggests it is the responsibility of the dominant group members to develop a vocabulary that will invite minority colleagues to participate in a dialogue that will address the concerns of poor and minority communities. Willis (1995) believes literacy programs "clearly put some children at a disadvantage, while giving an advantage to others" because school literacy is narrowly defined by white middle-class European American culture (p. 44). Teachers must consider the role of language and culture as they seek equality for all students in their classrooms.

Like researchers, classroom teachers need to study and reevaluate writing workshop from all perspectives. We must consider research that deals with literacy instruction in a pluralistic society and encourages readers to analyze the multiple causes of failure in school among subordinated groups of students (cf., Delpit, 1986, 1988; Heath, 1983; Lensmire, 1994; Taylor & Dorsey-Gaines, 1988; and Willis, 1995). We need to (1) ask ourselves and our colleagues "difficult" and "painful" questions about inequality, diversity, and appropriate instructional methods and materials, (2) become a part of the dialogue, and (3) contribute to this critical analysis.

The data from my classroom, along with research by Stanovich (1986) and Anyon (1980), motivated me to ask questions, dialogue with colleagues, and seek answers. Just as Delpit described, some of my students make little progress. These students are often members of groups subordinated by society (African American and/or low-socioeconomic status). If writing workshop is the most effective method to teach writing, why do some children benefit more than others? Would some of my students benefit from a different form of instruction or even a different structure of writing workshop?

This study provides evidence of one teacher's innocent and not-so-innocent contributions to inequality, of how decisions and beliefs may unintentionally give an already privileged group of students more knowledge and power. Although students with less knowledge of the code in power need to be taught the skills that will give them access to the code, society must recognize the cost of accepting one dominant view and the benefits of honoring diversity. Educators need to realize that everyone is affected by inequality (some benefit and others suffer) and that the daily decisions teachers make contribute to maintaining or changing inequality.

This study provides evidence of one teacher's innocent and not-so-innocent contributions to inequality, of how decisions and beliefs may unintentionally give an already privileged group of students more knowledge and power.

References

Anyon, J. (1980). Social class and the hidden curriculum of work. *Journal of Education, 26,* 67–92.

Callkins, L. M. (1994). *The art of teaching writing* (2nd ed.). Portsmouth, NH: Heinemann.

Delpit, L. (1986). Skills and other dilemmas of a progressive Black educator. *Harvard Educational Review, 56,* 379–385.

Delpit, L. (1988). The silenced dialogue: Power and pedagogy in educating other people's children. *Harvard Educational Review, 58,* 280–298.

Dyson, A. H. (1993). *Social worlds of children learning to write in an urban primary school.* New York: Teachers College Press.

Graves, D. H. (1983). *Writing: Teachers & children at work.* Portsmouth, NH: Heinemann.

Heath, S. (1983). *Ways with words: Language, life and work in communities and classrooms.* Cambridge: Cambridge University Press.

Lensmire, T. J. (1994). *When children write: Critical revisions of the writing workshop.* New York: Teachers College Press.

Lincoln, Y. S., & Guba, E. G. (1985). *Naturalistic inquiry.* Newbury Park, CA: Sage.

Stanovich, K. E. (1986). Matthew effects in reading: Some consequences of individual differences in the acquisition of literacy. *Reading Research Quarterly, 21,* 360–406.

Taylor, D., & Dorsey-Gaines, C. (1988). *Growing up literate: Learning from inner-city families.* Portsmouth, NH: Heinemann.

Vygotsky, L. (1978). *Mind in society: The development of higher psychological processes.* Cambridge, MA: Harvard University Press.

Willis, A. I. (1995). Reading the world of school literacy: Contextualizing the experiences of a young African American male. *Harvard Educational Review, 65,* 30–49.

Article Review Form at end of book.

How might the IRA/NCTE standards aid educators in moving from rote learning toward more active problem-solving instructional methods?

Challenging Expectations

Why we ought to stand by the IRA/NCTE *Standards for the English Language Arts*

The authors believe that critically examining issues like portfolio use in conjunction with the English Language Arts Standards can help teachers define expectations and build supportive learning environments.

Mark A. Faust
Ronald D. Kieffer

Faust teaches at the University of Georgia (Language Education Department, 125 Aderhold Hall, Athens, GA 30602, USA). Kieffer teaches at the same university.

Four years of hard work involving literally thousands of participants culminated in 1996 with the presentation of 12 standards for the English language arts, K–12. The Standards document itself, published jointly by the International Reading Association (IRA) and the National Council of Teachers of English (NCTE), was immediately and we believe unjustly denounced by many educators and journalists across the U.S. (see for example Boxer, 1996; Hufstader, 1996; Rochester, 1996;

Taukatch 1996). Certainly a project of this magnitude deserved a more considered reaction than it received from many outspoken critics.

We agree with Brewbaker (1997) that the surge of negativity following the release of the English Language Arts (ELA) Standards reveals more about "the low esteem Americans feel toward their teachers" and about the existence of widespread disagreement over the ultimate goals and purposes for creating standards than it does about the actual language of the document. Unfortunately, we know many teachers who have interpreted the well-publicized controversy as a signal that the standards project can be safely ignored. In opposition to this reaction as well as to charges that the standards are written in a "voiceless committee-speak" (Maloney, 1997),

we argue that *Standards for the English Language Arts* (1996) is a document well crafted to play a pivotal role in discussions about school reform and the professional development of teachers.

Now that supplemental materials are becoming available (e.g., the Standards in Practice Series published by NCTE), the time is right for a second (or a first) look not just at the original list of standards but at the whole document, which was wisely and carefully prepared to be "a guide for discussion" rather than a blueprint for reform. Educational leaders at all levels need to participate in deciding what impact, if any, these standards ought to have on policy decisions. Our increasingly diverse and fast-paced society poses numerous challenges to language arts professionals. One of them

Faust, Mark A., and Kieffer, Ronald D. (1998, April). Challenging expectations: Why we ought to stand by the IRA/NCTE *Standards for the English Language Arts. Journal of Adolescent & Adult Literacy,* 41(7), 540–547. Reprinted with permission of Mark A. Faust and the International Reading Association. All rights reserved.

surely is to develop evaluation instruments that reflect what children (and teachers) really need to know about language and be able to do with language.

We believe the ELA Standards document is a powerful tool for guiding discussion about the connection between evaluation and learning that is applicable across a wide spectrum, including policy making, curriculum development, and classroom practice. To elaborate on this claim, we (a) situate the NCTE/IRA standards project as a professional rather than a government-sponsored effort, (b) describe how the ELA Standards aim at national consensus by avoiding a narrowly prescriptive definition of content in favor of one that provides a framework for curriculum development and evaluation, and (c) discuss some of our own research findings that suggest possible connections between the ELA Standards and portfolio practices that support the creation of challenging expectations for all students.

The Drive for National Standards

To some extent the standards projects that have been completed or are currently under way in several academic disciplines reflect societal forces common to them all. None has escaped the public perception—some would say misperception (Berliner & Biddle, 1995)—that the quality of schooling is in decline. Alleged evidence of this decline is routinely trumpeted by local and national media thirsty for sensational stories about ignorant children and incompetent teachers. State legislatures nationwide are stepping in to stem what many still perceive to be the "rising tide of mediocrity" alluded to in the now-famous *A Nation at Risk* document published in 1983. National standards are viewed from this perspective as a sensible and powerful top-down tool for demanding excellence in education.

In contrast, the Standards Project for the English Language Arts (SPELA) represents a concerted effort to resist widespread calls for a national core curriculum requiring definitive, grade-level performance standards, the dangers of which are

well documented (Eisner, 1993; Pearson, 1993). Despite severe criticism from the press, the withdrawal of U.S. government funding, and the challenge of acknowledging a diverse constituency, the ELA Standards project achieved consensus about shared national values "based on current research and theory about how students learn—in particular, how they learn language" (*Standards for the English Language Arts,* p. vii). Furthermore, the leadership of IRA and NCTE deserve high praise for guiding the production of a document that clearly situates the debate about standards in relation to the uncertain future of educational reform.

"Back to basics" remains a familiar theme. Nonetheless, when asked, most people acknowledge that children today require a different education than that which served the needs of their grandparents. While disagreement about educational priorities persists, evidence mounts suggesting that many U.S. schools are struggling to keep pace with large-scale demographic and societal transitions (Cohen, Milbrey, & Talbert, 1993; Sizer, 1992). Change is inevitable, but what exactly the curriculum of the future will look like remains unclear. What we need now is a sense of direction. As noted by Linda Darling-Hammond (1994), passive, rote learning is still the norm in far too many classrooms across the U.S., where children are deprived of the "active engagement in problem solving, invention, and management of information resources, and ideas" that they need to be prepared for life in the next century (p. 479).

We believe the ELA Standards offer a clear vision for curriculum development and evaluation, one that has been evolving at least since the 1970s. From a historical perspective, the ELA Standards project appears not as an isolated event prompted by politicians and bureaucrats, but as an important phase in a long tradition of reform efforts (Applebee, 1974; Myers, 1994). In fact, a similar, though less ambitious, project had already taken place in 1987 when a dozen groups of teachers, calling themselves the English Coalition, convened to consider "what should be the curriculum content of K–12 English language arts" (Myers, 1994, p. 68). The work of the English

Coalition (see Lloyd-Jones & Lunsford, 1989), like the current standards project, was focused on building a national consensus regarding what children should know about language and be able to do with language. This tradition—not political pressure—provides one reason why the ELA Standards deserve renewed consideration. Another reason can be found in the purposes and goals for creating standards adopted by the authors of *Standards for the English Language Arts.*

What the ELA Standards Are Supposed to Do

A focus on defining curriculum content, K–12, distinguishes the ELA Standards from other types of standards representing different goals and purposes. The expression of legitimate concerns about the best way to define content standards (e.g., Zorn, 1997) needs to be differentiated from concerns that imply completely different goals and purposes. Critics, like Albert Shanker (1996), disregard the fact that there are at least three different types of standards (O'Neil, 1993). *Content standards* seek to identify what students should know and be able to do. *Performance standards* (which Shanker and others appear to favor) would make possible comparative judgments about levels of achievement. By definition, they require standardized assessment instruments to ensure fairness in judging who's up to par and who's not. Furthermore, though proponents of performance standards rarely acknowledge this, fairness also demands appropriate *delivery standards* to ensure that all students have an equal opportunity to learn. Each way of defining standards poses a different set of challenges and raises different concerns.

The decision by the authors of the ELA Standards document to focus on developing content standards that capture "the essential goals of English language arts instruction" (p. viii) makes sense given the impossibility of defining specific content objectives that would be appropriate for all students. However, demographic diversity is not the only issue here. Even in nations where the population is less diverse and where the educational systems are more centralized than in the U.S. (e.g., France, Germany, and Japan), proposals for a national curriculum have been rejected (Darling-Hammond, 1994).

Current disagreements among language arts professionals worldwide take place within an even larger context of debate as nations move beyond the industrial revolution into an uncertain future. Shifting demographics, changes in workforce requirements, new communication technologies, as well as new knowledge about language and language learning present enormous challenges as we seek to define what schoolchildren should know about language and be able to do with language.

Standards for the English Language Arts does not presume to be the ultimate answer to these challenges. Although the authors do claim to "reflect some of the best ideas already at work around the country," they do not adopt a "prescriptive framework." Instead, the Standards offer "starting points for an ongoing discussion about classroom activities and curricula" (p. 24).

If the standards work, then teachers will recognize their students, themselves, their goals, and their daily endeavors in this document; so, too, will they be inspired, motivated, and provoked to reevaluate some of what they do in class. (p. 24)

Is this a reasonable notion of what content standards can and should do? Is this approach to standard setting viable given a large and diverse body of language arts professionals? Do the ELA Standards succeed in reconciling a yearning for national values with local concerns about losing control over curriculum development? A close look at the ELA Standards themselves suggests that the answer to these questions is yes.

Achieving a Delicate Balance

Standards for the English Language Arts is a document carefully worded to be inclusive. It is designed to be discussed, not merely followed, by practitioners (K–12) representing different viewpoints on language and language learning. We have noticed that the document works in several ways to define common ground without attempting to dictate specific practices at the local level. First, an "expanded definition of literacy" based on "six language arts: reading, writing, speaking, listening, viewing, and visually representing" (p. 6) offers teachers a broad canvas as they seek to envision learning experiences keyed to one or more purposes of language use: "obtaining and communicating information," "literary response and expression," "learning and reflection," and "problem solving and application" (pp. 17–18). An emphasis on using language for purposes that extend beyond classroom walls is a hallmark of these Standards.

Second, the ELA Standards propose an array of challenging expectations about what students ought to be doing in classrooms. Unlike standards that merely delineate an inert body of grade-level content knowledge (that can be easily tested), the ELA Standards "present a number of dimensions along which students' development may be seen and evaluated" (p. 19). The task of measuring levels of achievement involves criteria that the authors assert" are best defined locally, in the contexts of specific schools and students' needs" (p. 19).

Respect for teachers as professionals is another hallmark of these Standards, which are specific enough to guide decision making but not so specific that they become impositional. *Standards for the English Language Arts* promotes consensus while respecting diversity in yet another way that can best be illustrated by a close look at the wording of the Standards themselves. Take for example Standard No. 3:

Students apply a wide range of strategies to comprehend, interpret, evaluate, and appreciate texts. They draw on their prior experience, their interactions with other readers and writers, their knowledge of word meaning and of other texts, their word identification strategies, and their understanding of textual features (e.g., sound-letter correspondence, sentence structure, context, graphics). (p. 25)

By itself, this statement briefly summarizes what we know about reading and what successful readers are able to do. To supplement this, the Standards document provides three pages of explanation that clarify what is at issue when the standard is discussed. In addition, key words such as *strategy, comprehension,* and *interpretation* appear in a glossary that is useful and in some instances provocative (see for example how the authors handle definitions of *text* and *communication*).

Standard No. 3 does not embody a particular view of reading. What it offers is a glimpse into what any view of reading should entail. In other words, we should agree that reading involves an "appreciation" of texts, but what exactly does the word *appreciation* mean in a given context? And, for that matter, what do we believe we are talking about when we use the word *text*? Here are questions worth discussing. The implication across all 12 Standards is that questioning ought to be an integral aspect of standards-based curriculum development and evaluation. In fact, we believe the ELA Standards function more as a guide to asking the right questions than as a set of explicit directives for curriculum development.

Taken as a whole, *Standards for the English Language Arts* raises questions ranging from the "essential goals of English language instruction" (p. viii) to very specific issues related to our understanding of language and language learning. Questions about students as language users with diverse aspirations, talents, and needs, as well as questions about research and technology, spring to mind as one peruses the ELA Standards. Other questions are raised by the supposition that a single set of expectations might apply across all grades. How will we know that a particular standard is being satisfied? Perhaps most important, the Standards can be used to prompt reflection and discussion about the assumptions underlying classroom practice. Although the ELA Standards surely allow for a variety of responses to these and other challenging questions, the questions themselves evoke a powerful sense of our mission as language arts professionals.

Challenges posed by the need for curricular reform and the responsibility of setting high expectations for all students require a teaching force that is open to change (Darling-

Hammond, 1994; Salinger, 1996). The ELA Standards document clearly positions teachers as learners. In the next section, we describe a research project we conducted with two teachers in which we created our own portfolios and reflected on our use of student portfolios to connect evaluation with learning.

Teachers Using Portfolios Talk About Standards

During the 1993–1994 academic school year, we participated in a study with two classroom teachers: Cheryl Hilderbrand, a high school English teacher from Butts County, Georgia, USA, and Linda Morrison, a second-grade teacher from Jackson County, Georgia, USA. We focused on portfolio implementation by making portfolios a dominant feature in our classrooms and by developing our own portfolios along with our students.

Each of us created very different portfolios. Linda developed a portfolio that represented her changing teaching practices. Ron's electronic portfolio put into perspective the various aspects of his life—the teacher, the researcher, the parent. Cheryl created a portfolio that explored the connection between her life as a learner in a global sense and her ongoing effort to model portfolio process for her students. Mark's portfolio was an attempt to revisit 5 crucial years in his life as a high school English teacher where he made some dramatic changes in his philosophy of teaching. What we created were "learning portfolios," aptly described by Wolf and Siu-Runyan (1996).

Our portfolios provided each of us with ways to reflect on diverse and sometimes conflicting purposes for evaluation—tools to judge progress, vehicles for response, and narrative accounts of students as readers, writers, and thinkers. As we documented our individual portfolio processes through interviews, direct observation, dialogue journals, and monthly interactive sessions, we shared and reflected upon ways our portfolios represented our growth as educators.

After analyzing the data, we realized that standards and expectations were at the heart of our discussions. Although we did not directly discuss the Standards project, our conversations and questions were typical of the kinds of interactions that we feel the NCTE/IRA Standards might and ought to generate. In particular, our conversations during the year focused on ways that teachers might use portfolios selectively for multiple purposes aimed at enhancing their ability to create conditions that support a range of literate behaviors in their classrooms. We focused on five areas (process, purpose, community building, learning, teacher practices) with underlining themes of the teacher as learner, connections between evaluation and learning, and equity and excellence for all.

The Teacher as Learner

Many of our discussions focused on questions about ourselves as learners. How does doing a portfolio change one as a teacher or a learner? What happens in our classrooms when we create our own portfolios and share them with our students? Our classroom student portfolios and the portfolios that we created as teachers helped us realize how and why our teaching practices evolved in certain directions, and they enhanced our ability as teachers to make life-affirming decisions in our relations with our students.

For example, Mark had been questioning the metaphor of "translating" theory into practice. His own portfolio furthered this questioning by helping him to better understand how and why his teaching practice evolved in a certain direction. In this way, portfolios were used to foster self-knowledge about past and current teacher and learner practices.

Linda's hope in her second-grade classroom was to connect evaluation and learning in ways that were real and purposeful. One way that Linda addressed this issue was by letting her second graders see her as a continual learner.

When you think about what your goals are for your children, your goal is helping them to become lifelong learners, and I think that's what most good teachers want. When you delve into this yourself

and start showing them that you're still learning, that is so incredibly powerful even for second graders. When they find out that sometimes I struggle for things, that she doesn't know everything. It is so powerful for them to find out that you struggle, that you're still learning, that you're changing. You know what they're going through to a certain extent.

Linda's teacher portfolio offered a way to model the learning process so her students could learn how to see themselves as learners engaged in a similar process. Important aspects of anyone's learning process are "knowing what to do when you don't know what to do," having a knack for identifying problems as well as solving problems, and making a habit of reflecting on what you are doing and why you are doing it. Portfolios can be used to focus attention on learning how to learn, which is "at the heart of all of the standards and is reflected in various ways in each of them" (see *Standards for the English Language Arts*, p. 9).

Portfolios not only help students learn about their own learning, but also help teachers learn about their teaching.

I think that creating a portfolio definitely pulls the learning together and helps students see connections between activities. And it affirms some things in my teaching, affirms some things that I believe in, but it affirmed for me the idea that what goes on in the classroom can be important to the students. It's hard to see that on a test or an essay or even in an evaluation of the course of the unit. But, in the portfolio there is a sense that they really believe that some of these things were important. And the things that were important to them were that there was a pattern to them. (Cheryl)

Because portfolios naturally support teachers and students in designing learning experiences, we advocate using portfolios for the purpose of enhancing the capacity of teachers and learners to make curricular decisions for themselves. Portfolios, used in conjunction with the Standards, offer teachers and students a way to address the question of what's important now. They help teachers make crucial decisions about instruction and learning that can be passed on to future teachers and help students build a sense of continuity across the curriculum.

Connections Between Evaluation and Learning

What happens when teachers talk to one another about evaluation and learning? The ELA Standards are written so that students and teachers can generate their own questions about experiences they have had, values that they place on their learning and teaching, and relevancy of experiences to their lives. Portfolios offer one way of supporting the kind of conversation envisioned by the authors of *Standards for the English Language Arts.* When serving as containers for students and teachers to gather meaningful reflections, responses, questions, and comments from peers, teachers, parents, and themselves, portfolios by definition address what children should know and what children are able to do. The benefits of these activities are stated directly in the Standards document:

All students have the ability to learn, but teachers can make that ability accessible by helping students reflect upon, and monitor their own learning. When students see themselves as able learners, capable of monitoring and controlling their learning, they are more willing to tackle challenging tasks and take the risks that move their learning forward. (p. 9)

The strength of the Standards, as we see them, are that they are written as dynamic, process-oriented entities that can be useful as tools for self-evaluation and learning. Portfolios enabled teachers and students to focus on change in ways that support learning. During our interactions, we came to realize that portfolios are best viewed as dynamic learning events rather than as static entities. Portfolios can serve as catalysts for change that can transform the way teachers and students see their classrooms as learning environments.

One of our coresearchers, Cheryl, kept returning to the idea of portfolios as focal points for building retrospective awareness:

In order to grow and be ready for these profound experiences and be open to them, you have to have established the process of self-evaluation and looking at yourself—where am I and what am I doing. Maybe that's the most important part of the portfolio. You say to yourself, "Here is where I am and here is where I want to go." Sadly, some people go

through their lives totally unaware that they can make any changes in themselves.

We agree that one of the most powerful aspects of portfolio creation is the potential for learners to document and reflect upon change. Furthermore, we agree that the process is not clear-cut; it can't be standardized. From the teacher's perspective, approaching portfolio use as a process can help to distinguish among competing evaluation purposes so that standards may be upheld without at the same time perpetuating the illusion that learning can be standardized.

How can we provide opportunities for evaluation that are meaningful to students and at the same time include grades? The challenge is to dissociate evaluation from grading without denying the social necessity of grades, and yet have an evaluation that is serious enough to represent the learning that is going on at a particular time and place. The evaluation should be asking what did I learn rather than how well did I perform according to some arbitrary and specific standard that somebody else has set. When teachers develop their own portfolios along with their students or colleagues, the conversations about standards create a vision for further exploration into understanding how evaluation and learning work together.

Equity and Excellence for All

Perhaps the most important connection between the new standards and portfolios resides in the discussions that teachers have about expectations, equity, and excellence for all. On the basis of our discussions, we are convinced that portfolios provide a means to support excellence for all of our students in ways that are equitable and self-assuring to learners. We strongly agree with the language of the Standards document:

It is, in fact, teachers' responsibility to recognize and value all children's rich and varied potentials for learning and to provide appropriate educational opportunities to nurture them. If we learn to recognize and value a variety of students' abilities in the language arts and then build on those strengths, we make it

possible for all students to attain high standards. Some will do so quickly and others more slowly, but to bridge the wide disparities in literacy attainment and to prepare all students to become informed and literate citizens, we must hold these high expectations for every student and every school. (p. 8)

Building excellence for all students means addressing unequal opportunities and expectations. Portfolios create opportunities for teachers and students to listen to each other in productive ways. For Ron, the portfolio was an integral aspect of the community building process. Sharing of portfolio items in conjunction with discussions about expectations made for professional growth and a building of a collaborative environment. Mark added to this idea by saying that portfolios were meant to be shared. They can be a powerful force for building classroom communities. One of the keys to Linda's success was the way she encouraged students to get in tune with one another, to develop a sense of community through trust and support. Cheryl helped her students share their reactions to situations. Then, using a variety of means, she helped them shape their reactions into responses. The four of us are dedicated to working toward creating environmental conditions that support a range of literate behaviors for all of our students.

Standards Can Generate Conversations

Through our conversations with other teachers, we have realized that teacher and student portfolios can serve distinct purposes with respect to the IRA/NCTE Standards:

1. Portfolios can support teachers' examinations of their own learning.

2. Portfolios can be used to facilitate connections between evaluation and learning.

3. Portfolios can support a definition of excellence that is appropriate for all students.

We believe that critically examining the role of portfolios in classrooms can further the discussion of the Standards document and raise questions that will help teachers in their quest for more supportive classroom learning environments. Questions such as these from Cheryl and Linda reveal the sense of direction that emerges out of this kind of conversation:

What are things we want the kids to do? How would you help them do better? How can we create a better situation so that they'll be more successful? What level of achievement are we aiming for beyond where we are now? Where are we now and how will you measure that? How will we measure what it is we want them to do? (Cheryl)
One of the things I kept coming back to was this connection between the portfolio and learning. I feel like I have really struggled with this idea the last couple of years. How do I show student growth in a meaningful way? (Linda)

We think that the ELA Standards discussions can support questions like these and generate conversations around issues that are respectful of teachers' struggles with evaluation.

Now that President Clinton has added his voice to the chorus of demands for national testing based on grade-level performance standards, it is imperative that those who believe as we do that this is a misguided notion speak out in favor of alternative routes to achieving national consensus with regard to educational standards. *Standards for the English Language Arts* offers a clear sense of direction to language arts profession- als seeking to define challenging expectations for their students. This document also challenges us to reconsider our expectations concerning the connection between standards and language learning. Finally, *Standards for the English Language Arts* offers a platform from which to challenge the expectations of politicians and bureaucrats that we will cooperate with public policies that are inconsistent with our goals and purposes as teachers.

References

Applebee, A. (1974). *Tradition and reform in the teaching of English.* Urbana, IL: National Council of Teachers of English.

Berliner, D., & Biddle, B. J. (1995). *The manufactured crisis: Myths, fraud, and the attack on America's public schools.* Reading, MA: Addison-Wesley.

Boxer, S. (1996, March 24). Teachers, teach thyselves. *The New York Times,* p. E2.

Brewbaker, J. (1997). On Tuesday morning: The case for *Standards for the English Language Arts. English Journal,* 86, 76–82.

Cohen, D. K., Milbrey, W. M., & Talbert, J. E. (Eds.). (1993). *Teaching for understanding: Challenges for policy and practice.* San Francisco: Jossey-Bass.

Darling-Hammond, L. (1994). National standards and assessments: Will they improve education? *American Journal of Education,* 102, 478–510.

Eisner, E. (1993). Why standards may not improve schools. *Educational Leadership,* 50, 22–23.

Hufstader, P. (1996, May 1). Strunk and White would nix English standards' vagueness. *Education Week,* p. 39.

Lloyd-Jones, R., & Lunsford, A. (1989). *The English coalition conference: Democracy through language.* Urbana, IL: National Council of Teachers of English.

Maloney, H. B. (1997). The little standards that couldn't. *English Journal,* 86, 86–90.

Myers, M. (1994). NCTE's role in standards projects. *English Education,* 26, 67–76.

National Commission on Excellence in Education. (1983). *A nation at risk.* Washington, DC: U.S. Government Printing Office.

O'Neil, J. (1993). Can national standards make a difference? *Educational Leadership,* 50, 4–8.

Pearson, P. D. (1993). Standards for the English language arts: A policy perspective. *Journal of Reading Behavior,* 25, 457–475.

Rochester, J. M. (1996, May 15). The decline of literacy. *Education Week,* p. 34.

Salinger, T. (1996). IRA, standards, and educational reform. *The Reading Teacher,* 49, 290–298.

Shanker, A. (1996, April 7). Where we stand. *The New York Times,* p. E7.

Sizer, T. (1992). *Horace's school: Redesigning the American high school.* Boston: Houghton Mifflin.

Standards for the English language arts. (1996). Urbana, IL: National Council of Teachers of English/International Reading Association.

Taukatch, A. (1996, March 18). Communication-speak. *The New York Times,* p. A14.

Wolf, K., & Siu-Runyan, Y. (1996). Portfolio purposes and possibilities. *Journal of Adolescent & Adult Literacy,* 40, 30–37.

Zorn, J. (1997). The NCTE/IRA standards: A surrender. *English Journal,* 86, 83–85.

 Article Review Form at end of book.

What was Shanahan surprised to discover about integrated instruction?

Reading-Writing Relationships, Thematic Units, Inquiry Learning . . .

In pursuit of effective integrated literacy instruction

Shanahan reviews research and raises questions about instruction that integrates reading and writing or that focuses on thematic units. He concludes with guidelines for integrated instruction.

Timothy Shanahan

Shanahan is Professor of Urban Education and Director of the Center for Literacy at the University of Illinois at Chicago. He is a Senior Research Associate with the Laboratory for Student Success (Mid-Atlantic Regional Laboratory). His research focuses on reading-writing relationships, family literacy, and early intervention. He was a winner of IRA's Albert Harris Award for 1997. He can be contacted at 1040 W. Harrison (M/C 147), Chicago, IL 60680, USA and at shanahan@uic.edu.

I bought it hook, line, and sinker. It just sounded right from the first time I heard it. I wasn't skeptical in the least. That was the way it worked . . . that was the way it must work. Integrated instruction would make the difference. It had to. It seemed so

obvious. No question about it. And, yet. . . .

I first came across curriculum integration while still an undergraduate. It was 1970, the U.S. was embroiled in an unpopular war, the high point of the civil rights movement was a fresh memory, assassination had become a cruel and frightening part of our politics, and many were in open rebellion against authority and tradition. I was 18 years old. I had been tutoring children in an inner city school. Like many young volunteers, I thought I could change the world, or I did until confronted with the reality of an African American fourth grader named Andre, who struggled with the simple preprimers that I had been given. I didn't have a clue. So, I took a class in reading—not to become a teacher, just to figure out how to deal with Andre.

The idea of integrated instruction was one of the many things I found out about in Dorsey Hammond's 9:00 a.m. section of Elementary Reading Instruction. And it clicked. It was so obvious to me that the schools had been going about these things all wrong. Just another example of how the system didn't work, I figured. Soon after I enrolled in the elementary education program and, eventually, became a primary grade teacher. From day one, I tried to integrate reading and writing instruction in my own classroom, as that had been one of the types of integration I had learned about in Professor Hammond's course (the other ways of pulling the curriculum together didn't grab me as quickly). So, at a time when elementary writing instruction was far

Shanahan, Timothy. (1997, September). Reading-writing relationships, thematic units, inquiry learning . . . in pursuit of effective integrated literacy instruction. *The Reading Teacher,* 51(1), 12–19. Reprinted with permission of Timothy Shanahan and the International Reading Association.
All rights reserved.

too rare, I was trying to teach writing as a part of my reading program. At a time when basals were dominant and didn't include writing, my students were reading self-selected tradebooks and writing to improve their reading ability. I was integrating instruction as I had been taught. It was the right thing to do. I just knew it.

Before long I had enrolled in a Ph.D. program and was in search of a dissertation topic. I flirted with lots of interesting ideas: prevention of reading problems through early intervention, classroom reading assessment, comprehension strategy instruction. All were and are fascinating and important, and each seemed to be attracting a lot of attention in the education community. None, however, seemed quite as "lonely" as reading-writing relationships. It seemed an orphan, despite being central to my belief system as a teacher. So, I set out to map the specifics of the relationship between reading and writing, believing that if the connections were better understood teachers and curriculum makers would be more likely to combine them.

Of course, my personal "discovery" of integrated teaching has been repeated again and again during our century, each ah-ha moment an echo of past discoveries by other fresh-faced teachers. Oh, the emphasis hasn't always been on the connections between reading and writing. Sometimes it has been on thematic units, whole language, inquiry-based learning, project methods, content area reading, writing across the curriculum, or literature in the reading class. Even the ideas of language arts or social studies as school subjects have been the result of efforts to integrate. Breaking down disciplinary boundaries has been an attractive hope. Progressive yearnings for coherence and authenticity reverberate across 20th-century education, reassuring hopeful teachers and researchers that experience doesn't need to be fractionated, that we are not alone, that we can do better.

And though integration is popularly championed, it remains elusive, still more a notion than an idea. Few innovations have been as widely accepted, or as poorly understood. I embraced reading-writing relationships in the same way that my own students now embrace thematic units—with a certainty of belief, rather than a power of understanding.

Teaching Reading with Writing

Reading-writing relationships are a good place to start. Reading and writing, as much as any pair of subjects, overlap; that is, they clearly depend on many of the same cognitive elements. You need to know the meanings of many words in order to read *or* write, for example. You need to know something about how sounds and symbols relate. You need to have some ideas about how text relates to the world. Given this, it might be possible to teach reading through writing, or vice versa. I set out to identify specifics of this overlap so that I would have a clearer idea of how reading and writing should be combined in the classroom.

Boy, was I surprised. Research doesn't always work as you think it will, and that certainly was the case this time (Shanahan, 1984). Yes, reading and writing were related, but not to the degree that I had expected. They were as separate as they were the same. It took a lot of reflection on my results, and several other studies, before I grasped the importance of my findings. If reading and writing were as similar as various metaphors had claimed (Tierney & Pearson, 1983, for example), then their instructional combination would not be as valuable. The similarities of reading and writing allow cross-learning opportunities. However, if they were as closely related as I had expected, then there would be no need for instruction in both (Shanahan, 1988; Shanahan & Tierney, 1990; Tierney & Shanahan, 1991). Educators had assumed such a close relationship that they could expect reading instruction to be sufficient to accomplish the goals of both reading and writing.

Reading and writing could be thought of as two separate, but overlapping, ways of thinking about the world (McGinley & Tierney, 1989). That they offered separate perspec-

Though integration is popularly championed, it remains elusive.

tives meant that by processing information both ways (through reading *and* writing) we could increase our chances of understanding. For example, awareness of an author's choices is central to effective critical reading, but this information is well hidden in text (Olson, 1994; Shanahan, 1992), and children become aware of it rather late in their development. Writing, however, because it affords one an insider's view of this aspect of text, provides a powerful, complementary way of thinking about reading that would not be available if reading and writing were identical. Similarly, reading a text and writing about it can provide alternative perspectives that deepen one's understanding that many study skills approaches try to combine reading and writing activities in various ways (McGee & Richgels, 1990).

However, the cognitive separation of reading and writing also means that the integration of instruction in this area will not automatically lead to learning. Thus, adding writing to the reading curriculum does not necessarily mean that students will improve in reading (Shanahan, 1988). Improved learning is only likely to be the result if reading and writing are combined in appropriate ways.

My research also demonstrated that the nature of how reading and writing were connected changes with development (Shanahan, 1984, 1987; Shanahan & Lomax, 1986, 1988). Studies have long shown that what is learned in reading changes as students come to terms with the process (Chall, 1996). Beginners are much more word bound or word oriented than are more proficient readers and writers. As they develop a comfortable grasp of basic word recognition and spelling, their attention begins to shift to other issues of interpretation and communication. Apparently, the developmental lines of reading and writing are sufficiently similar that they can be combined successfully, though in different ways, throughout literacy education. Young children's invented spelling, for example, can have a powerful impact on their word recognition ability (Clarke, 1988), though the cross-disciplinary benefits of this activity are likely to dissipate as children become more proficient in word recognition (for most this occurs by about the second or third grade). This doesn't mean that older children no longer benefit from the connections between reading and writing, just that the benefits change. Older writers' experimentation with text organization or structure can have a positive impact on reading comprehension, for instance (Nauman, 1990; Shanahan, 1984).

Another lesson we learned from the work on reading-writing relationships has been that integration is not necessarily just an alternative way of teaching the same things. "Another interesting approach to reading-writing relationships considers how using reading and writing in combination leads to different learning and thinking outcomes than would their separate uses" (Tierney & Shanahan, 1991, p. 265). Research in this arena has focused heavily on how students learn to synthesize information from a variety of sources (for example, Spivey & King, 1989). The types of judgments, evaluations, and comparisons described in such studies reveal important aspects of reading and writing that, traditionally, have not been taught. Traditional language arts curricula had not previously extended much interest in how students could best make sense of the alternative, and sometimes contradictory, information presented in multiple texts. Many of the best instructional attempts to combine reading and writing have as their aim the fostering of those reading and writing abilities that have been neglected by separate curricula.

Thematic Units and Other Approaches to Integration

Of course, reading and writing are a special case of integration. They involve two closely allied disciplinary partners. But what about other kinds of curricular integration? Currently, the most popular and ambitious attempts to break down disciplinary boundaries are those that involve thematic instruction. Thematic units hold the promise of unifying the entire curriculum by bringing together social studies, science, mathematics, art, music, and language arts into a coherent program of study. Typically, students are expected to engage in

some type of inquiry into a basic thematic idea established by the teacher, though there are a plethora of approaches, including those in which the students determine the purposes of the inquiry.

Although such teaching is appealing, my experience with reading-writing relationships urges caution. Combined reading and writing does not necessarily lead to improved learning, and there is reason to believe that other more ambitious forms of integration will not necessarily maintain even traditional levels of learning in the various subject areas (Brophy & Alleman, 1991; Kain, 1993; Shanahan, Robinson, & Schneider, 1995). I am not suggesting that integration should not be used, only that successful integration is not automatic.

The real test, of course, is to consider whether integrated instruction actually accomplishes the purposes for which it is adopted. Unfortunately, far too many teachers and teacher educators think about integration in the way that I did when I first became a teacher; they often see it as an end in itself—a bulwark against traditional approaches—rather than as a way to effect particular educational outcomes.

Proponents of thematic units usually emphasize one or more of four major categories of claims. Some, for example, claim that integration will lead to greater amounts of learning, with the focus on traditional disciplinary outcomes (Beane, 1995; Lehman, 1994). The idea here is that as a result of taking part in thematic activities, students will read better, understand science more thoroughly, or have higher math scores. Another set of claims emphasizes that students will have a deeper grasp of the ideas that are studied (Lipson, Valencia, Wixson, & Peters, 1993; Nissani, 1995). These proponents would gladly sacrifice the breadth and superficiality of the traditional curriculum for a more thorough and well-organized understanding of fewer concepts. "For most young people, including the privileged, the separate subject approach offers little

more than a disconnected and incoherent assortment of facts and skills. There is no unity, no real sense to it all" (Beane, 1995, p. 618).

A third set of claims focuses less on the amount of learning, and more on its applicability. That is, teachers believe that the combination of subjects within units, activities, and projects will increase the possibility that students will be able to apply what they know to real problems (Schmidt et al., 1985). Finally, there is the claim of greater motivation (Lehman, 1994). According to this idea, students are likely to find integrated instruction to be more meaningful, and thus, they will enjoy it more and be more curious and committed to learning.

Surprisingly, given the long history and nearly universal acceptance of the idea of integration at all levels of education, there have been few empirical investigations of its effects. A few studies have suggested that integrated teaching leads to either similar or slightly better levels of achievement than the traditional curriculum, but others have found less learning—especially with lower achieving students—as a result of such approaches (Kain, 1993). I have been able to identify no study, in any field with any age level, that has clearly demonstrated more coherent or deeper understandings, or better applicability of learning as a result of integration. Improved motivation is the one positive outcome for which there is convincing evidence. Integrated instruction does lead to better attitudes towards learning (Friend, 1985; Mansfield, 1989; Olarewaju, 1988; Schell & Wicklein, 1993; Wasserstein, 1995).

> Surprisingly, given the long history and nearly universal acceptance of the idea on integration at all levels of education, there have been few investigations of its effects.

Some Guidelines for Integrated Instruction

It would be easy to conclude from this that thematic units and other integrated instruction aren't worth the trouble. I believe that would be a mistake, however, as the claims of depth, coherence, and applicability are reasonable—if not proven—and it is apparent that children like this type of instruction; teachers, too, find it rewarding (Berlin & Hillen, 1994). My hunch is, as my findings with reading-writing relationships suggest, that thematic units can be beneficial if particular issues are attended to sufficiently during planning and implementation. In the remainder of this article, I will suggest a few guidelines for successful integration.

First, it is essential to know what integration is supposed to accomplish. Without a clear conception of the desired learning outcomes, it is impossible to plan, teach, or assess in powerful ways. I work with several urban schools that operate under a policy that encourages thematic instruction. Unfortunately, the policy does not specify any purposes for the requirement, and it is, consequently, difficult for teachers to implement it well, even when they are especially supportive of the policy. Of course, there can be no standard of quality with regard to integration if no one is certain why they are doing it. Integration is so widely accepted that it is especially necessary that we attend to specific rationales for our instructional choices. Research leads me to believe that unit instruction will not automatically lead to learning, so it is essential that we be candid and specific about our intentions.

Not long ago some colleagues and I published a critique of those instructional units that focused on topics rather than themes (Shanahan et al., 1995). We began from the premise that thematic units should add intellectual depth to the curriculum. Themes, we argued, would do more to reduce the fragmentation and overemphasis on minor facts and figures common in traditional curricula. We got a lot of mail from teachers and teacher educators illustrating the great depth of study possible in topic-oriented instruction, though these excellent examples of units on World War II, gardening, personification, and so on rarely seemed to be especially integrated; like traditional instruction, they seemed more the province of particular subject areas. Many other responses from teachers correctly suggested that we had misinterpreted the purposes of their forays into bears and penguins. We had claimed these to be topical, when actually bears and penguins were mo-

tifs, more of a unifying decoration than something to be learned. To illustrate my point: Have you ever gone to a party or restaurant with a sports motif? How much did you learn about sports?

Such units are designed more to make school fun than to necessarily create any great depth of knowledge. There is nothing wrong with making learning fun, and such instruction apparently helps to accomplish that—though my preference as parent, teacher, and teacher educator would be for enjoyment to come more from the meaning of the inquiry and the success of the learning.

Focus on integration as an end in itself or for the fun alone can, I fear, have some unfortunate consequences. For example, careful analysis of integrated instruction in the social studies has shown that far too often the activities do not lead to any kind of academic learning (Brophy & Alleman, 1991). To me, the major benefits of thematic units have to do with the opportunity to teach what is now neglected, to create a richer set of understandings, or to help students learn to apply skills and knowledge across curricular bounds. I wonder about the value of units that just try to repackage the traditional curriculum or that don't have any apparent learning goals.

Second, successful integration requires a great deal of attention to the separate disciplines. My research on reading and writing showed that maximum cross-curricular benefits would result only if *both* reading and writing received instructional attention; if you are not learning to write, you are unlikely to apply many insights across reading and writing. Brophy and Alleman's (1991) analysis of some of the cross-curricular activities recommended for social studies instruction found that the activities often seemed more relevant to art or reading than appropriate for helping students to develop much understanding of history, geography, or culture.

Similarly, studies have shown that integration can lead to *reductions* in the amount of language arts instruction.

The amount of time teachers spent in language arts and reading activities where language was the major focus decreased

as the amount of integration increased. The two teachers who spent the least time in integrated activities allocated approximately 20% more time on the average . . . for language and reading instruction than did the two teachers who integrated the most. (Schmidt et al., 1985, p. 313)

Incidental uses of reading within a larger inquiry will not lead to maximum progress in reading.

Also, not all disciplines will be useful for pursuing a particular inquiry (Shanahan et al., 1995), and it can be helpful during the planning to consider the specific disciplinary concepts that will be appropriate to a particular thematic exploration. If a subject is not really appropriate for a particular unit (that is, the unit will not lead to valuable learning in that subject), then it would be best to keep that part of the curriculum separate. In my experience, reading is easy to include in all inquiries, though this can lead to practice without instruction. This shows students the value of reading, which is useful, but it does not necessarily help them to read better. Conversely, math is often difficult to include in sufficiently demanding ways that would be expected to lead to greater understanding of mathematics, and thematic approaches alone would probably lead to less math learning.

Third, curricular boundaries are social and cultural, not just cognitive. Disciplines are more than collections of information; they provide ways of thinking and stances from which to approach the world. For literacy educators, one useful way to think about integration is as a fundamental social act of moving across cultures (Shanahan, Robinson, & Schneider, 1993). It is worth knowing how to read and write science text, and various instructional approaches help students to handle the special vocabulary demands and organizational style of science (Vacca & Vacca, 1993). But, more essentially, readers and writers need to develop an understanding of how scientists think about text, and how their thinking differs from that of historians, reporters, or novelists. I have little patience with those who claim they can successfully teach science or social studies with novels alone, though novels certainly can have their place in both subjects.

Different fields have their own cultural ideas on the purposes, processes, and uses of text, and it is these cultural practices that can best be exposed through integrated teaching. Scientists think, speak, and write like scientists; and historians, artists, and mathematicians have their own socially agreed upon ways of approaching the world, too. Much of what we have learned about multiculturalism with ethnic, racial, and linguistic groups is relevant here. These cultural differences are becoming clearer to me as I work on a project with a team assembled by the International Reading Association and the Council of Chief State School Officers that is examining the literacy demands inherent in the various U.S. national educational standards in math, science, history, social studies, civics, and the arts. Integrated instruction will serve literacy learning best if it focuses on genres as cultural ways of communicating, and on being able to translate information from one form to another. These connections should be made explicitly, and process talks in which disciplinary similarities and differences are explored should be a regular part of integrated instruction.

Different fields have their own cultural ideas on the purposes, processes, and uses of text.

In an earlier work, I have shown how a literacy focus within history can be a useful base for exploring certain kinds of interpretation (Shanahan et al., 1993), and Dyson (1989) has shown how writing helps younger children to struggle with the truth value of fiction. But science, too, can be a source for this type of cultural exploration. For example, one assignment that I have long used with children is to have them write descriptions of objects such as seashells, potatoes, and shoes. We then examine these descriptions and try to translate them into alternative genre; students quickly discover that specific measurements and color gradations are essential for the purposes of scientific description, but metaphor is usually more appropriate for fiction. As students develop this kind of awareness, I can, as a teacher, encourage considerations of the underlying purposes for these differences. I am sympathetic to those approaches to integra-

tion that put children in touch with people from various disciplinary backgrounds—directly through classroom visits and field trips, or less directly through correspondence, conference calls, or electronic communication—so that issues of underlying intentions can be explored most directly.

Finally, integration does not do away with the need for direct explanation or drill and practice. There is more to learning than just doing, or we could profitably abolish schools and put children to work. Students can gain valuable learning while pursuing a well-planned thematic unit or conducting their own personal inquiries; such endeavors are motivational and they can help students to recognize the utility of what is being studied. However, for most children, such work does not provide sufficient practice to make them fluent readers, good multipliers, or effective sellers. Even within integrated instruction there is a need for minilessons and guided practice. Part of the problem with traditional curricula is that they have so thoroughly abstracted what is being studied, and then focused on the mastery of these bits of information, that students often doubt the relevance or value of what is being learned. Conversely, a common problem in integrated instruction can be that the focus is so much on relevance that students never practice anything enough to get good at it.

Integrated instruction, in all of its many forms, is a hopeful notion that promises greater unity and attachment. However, it is likely to remain a missed opportunity—like the loneliness of beauty or the right word left unsaid—unless we are sufficiently hardheaded about how it works. Integrated instruction works best when there are clearly specified outcomes that take advantage of the best and most rigorous thinking of the disciplinary fields, but that go beyond this base to outcomes that would only be possible from integration. Integrated instruction works best when it makes children conscious of the connections being made, and when it focuses their attention on the cultural differences

that exist across disciplines and how to translate across these boundaries. Integrated instruction works best when, within the context of meaning, students are still given opportunities for enough instruction, guidance, and practice to allow them to become accomplished.

References

Beane, J.A. (1995). Curriculum integration and the disciplines of knowledge. *Phi Delta Kappan, 76*, 616–622.

Berlin, D.F., & Hillen, J.A. (1994). Making connections in math and science: Identifying student outcomes. *School Science and Mathematics, 94*, 283–290.

Brophy, J., & Alleman, J. (1991). A caveat: Curriculum integration isn't always a good idea. *Educational Leadership, 49*, 66.

Chall, J. S. (1996). *Stages of reading development* (2nd ed.). Fort Worth, TX: Harcourt Brace.

Clarke, L.K. (1988). Invented versus traditional spelling in first graders' writings: Effects on learning to spell and read. *Research in the Teaching of English, 22*, 281–309.

Dyson, A.H. (1989). *Multiple worlds of child writers*. New York: Teachers College Press.

Friend, H. (1985). The effect of science and mathematics integration on selected seventh grade students' attitudes toward and achievement in science. *School Science and Mathematics, 85*, 453–461.

Kain, D.L. (1993). Cabbages—and kings: Research directions in integrated/interdisciplinary curriculum. *Journal of Educational Thought, 27*, 312–331.

Lehman, J.R. (1994). Integrating science and mathematics: Perceptions of preservice and practicing elementary teachers. *School Science and Mathematics, 94*, 58–64.

Lipson, M., Valencia, S., Wixson, K., & Peters, C. (1993). Integration and thematic teaching: Integration to improve teaching and learning. *Language Arts, 70*, 252–263.

Mansfield, B. (1989). Students' perceptions of an integrated unit: A case study. *Social Studies, 80*, 135–140.

McGee, L.M., & Richgels, D.J. (1990). Learning from text using reading and writing. In T. Shanahan (Ed.), *Reading and writing together* (pp. 145–169). Norwood, MA: Christopher-Gordon.

McGinely, W., & Tierney, R.J. (1989). Traversing the topical landscape: Reading and writing as ways of knowing. *Written Communication, 6*, 243–169.

Nauman, A. (1990). Structure and perspective in reading and writing. In T. Shanahan (Ed.), *Reading and writing together* (pp. 57–76). Norwood, MA: Christopher-Gordon.

Nissani, M. (1995). Fruits, salads, and smoothies: A working definition of interdisciplinarity. *Journal of Educational Thought, 29*, 121–128.

Olarewaju, A.O. (1988). Instructional objectives: What effects do they have on students' attitudes towards integrated science. *Journal of Research in Science Teaching, 25,* 283–291.

Olson, D.R. (1994). *The world on paper.* New York: Cambridge University Press.

Schell, J.W., & Wicklein, R.C. (1993). Integration of mathematics, science, and technology education: A basis for thinking and problem solving. *Journal of Vocational Education Research, 18,* 49–76.

Schmidt, W.H., Roehler, L., Caul, J.L., Buchman, M., Diamond, B., Solomon, D., & Cianciolo, P. (1985). The uses of curriculum integration in language arts instruction: A study of six classrooms. *Journal of Curriculum Studies, 17,* 3035–320.

Shanahan, T. (1984). The reading-writing relation: An exploratory multivariate analysis. *Journal of Educational Psychology, 76,* 466–477.

Shanahan, T. (1987). Shared knowledge of reading and writing. *Reading Psychology, 8,* 93–102.

Shanahan, T. (1988). Reading-writing relationships: Seven instructional principles. *The Reading Teacher, 41,* 880–886.

Shanahan, T. (1992). Reading comprehension as a dialogic process. In M. Pressley, K.R., Harris, & J.T. Guthrie (Eds.), *Promoting academic competence and literacy: Cognitive research and instructional innovation* (pp. 129–148). New York: Academic Press.

Shanahan, T., & Lomax, R. (1986). An analysis and comparison of theoretical models of the reading-writing relationship. *Journal of Educational Psychology, 78,* 116–123.

Shanahan, T., m& Lomax, R. (1988). A developmental comparison of three theoretical models of the reading-writing relationship. *Research in the Teaching of English, 22,* 196–212.

Shanahan, T., Robinson, B., & Schneider, M. (1993). Integration of curriculum or interaction of people? *The Reading Teacher, 47,* 158–160.

Shanahan, T., Robinson, B., & Schneider, M. (1995). Avoiding some of the pitfalls of thematic units. *The Reading Teacher, 48,* 718–719.

Shanahan, T., & Tierney, R.J. (1990). Reading-writing connections: The relations among three research traditions. In J. Zutell & S. McCormick (Eds.), *Literacy theory and research: Analyses from multiple paradigms* (pp. 13–34). Chicago: National Reading Conference.

Spivey, N.N., & King, J.R. (1989). Readers as writers composing from sources. *Reading Research Quarterly, 24,* 7–26.

Tierney, R.J., & Pearson, P.D. (1983). Toward a composing model of reading. *Language Arts, 60,* 568–580.

Tierney, R.J., & Shanahan, T. (1991). Reading-writing relationships: Processes, transactions, outcomes. In P.D. Pearson, R. Barr, M. Kamil, & P. Mosenthal (Eds.), *Handbook of reading research* (Vol. 2, pp. 246–280). New York: Longman.

Vacca, R.T., & Vacca, J.L. (1993). *Content area reading* (4th ed.). New York: HarperCollins.

Wasserstein, P. (1995). What middle schoolers say about their schoolwork. *Educational Leadership, 53*(1), 41–43.

 **Article Review Form at end of book.**

WiseGuide Wrap-Up

- Themes can provide a basis for real-life connections between the school curriculum and students' home life, which may lead to more personal and relevant learning.

- When a school district and the broader community within which it exists collaborate to develop curriculum standards, the outcome may result in accountability and ownership for implementation of the new standards.

- The daily decisions teachers make contribute to maintaining or changing inequality among students in the classroom.

- IRA/NCTE *Standards for the English Language Arts,* used in conjunction with such assessments as portfolios, can help teachers define expectations and build supportive learning environments.

- Teaching reading and writing in combination leads to different learning and thinking outcomes than would their separate uses.

- Integrated instruction leads to better attitudes toward learning.

R.E.A.L. Sites

This list provides a print preview of typical **Coursewise** R.E.A.L. sites. There are over 100 such sites at the **Courselinks**™ site. The danger in printing URLs is that web sites can change overnight. As we went to press, these sites were functional using the URLs provided. If you come across one that isn't, please let us know via email to: webmaster@coursewise.com. Use your Passport to access the most current list of R.E.A.L. sites at the **Courselinks**™ site.

Site name: Student Achievements: Sample Lesson Plans

URL: http://users.neca.com/rchatel/Students.html#Lesson Plans

Why is it R.E.A.L.? This site provides exciting language arts lesson plans, which focus on reading comprehension and decoding skills development. Each lesson plan is linked to other exciting web sites, including The Lesson Plans Page and AskEric Lesson Plans. These links expand the visitors' instructional repertoire in the English Language Arts.

Key topics: reading comprehension, decoding skills, language arts skills

Try this: Visit this site to discover how children's literature might be used to teach reading comprehension.

Site name: Developing Educational Standards: Overview

URL: http://putwest.boces.org/standards.html

Why is it R.E.A.L.? This site provides an annotated list of K–12 Internet sites that deal with curriculum frameworks and standards development in all content areas at the national, state, and local levels. The exciting part of the web page is the alphabetical listing of all states and content areas. This is a case of finding everything you might ever want to know about standards in one place.

Key topics: standards, curriculum frameworks

Try this: Visit your state to find out the current level of standards development.

Site name: Standards at McREL

URL: http://www.mcrel.org/standards/

Why is it R.E.A.L.? The Mid-continent Regional Educational Laboratory has received national and international recognition for its work in standards-based education and has provided assistance to more than thirty school districts and several state departments of education as they develop their own academic standards and implement assessments. This web site consists of Internet resources—lesson plans, activities, curriculum resources—linked with corresponding subject-area content standards and articles and publications on standards.

Key topics: standards, curriculum resources

Try this: Navigate to the Connections+ site and explore some of the language arts lesson plans, activities, and teachers' guides.

section 5

Evaluating Readers and Writers: Comprehensive Assessment

Learning Objectives

- Identify strategies for understanding and supporting children's reading.

- Define fair grading practices that will allow included students to demonstrate their progress.

- Identify key principles for effective assessment.

- Discuss the relationship of assessment to teaching and learning.

- Discuss ways that teachers' beliefs about students as writers mediate their acceptance of new methods of assessment.

You probably remember taking standardized achievement tests at some point in your education. Your parents wanted you to "do good," and teachers reminded you that it was a "very important test." Standardized testing takes place in most schools across the nation each year. The results of this testing are used to measure student progress. This information is used to identify achievement trends for each school district and to make comparisons with state and national achievement levels. Standardized testing is very time consuming, and many question its value. Assessment should be about improving instruction; although standardized test results may be helpful in monitoring a school's overall effectiveness in educating children, they offer teachers little insight into meaningful program change. However, others feel that standardized testing is necessary to guarantee the continuous evaluation of students' performance.

Since standardized test results are not very beneficial to informing classroom instruction, alternative forms of assessment have emerged, including portfolio assessment, performance assessment, and outcome-based assessment. Alternative assessments are usually informal, analyze reading using real books, provide natural experiences with text, and are concerned with carefully analyzing overall student growth in the reading process. These assessments are more "authentic," in that they are as similar as possible to real-world, meaningful literacy tasks.

Standardized testing provides a limited view of readers, whereas authentic assessment can provide a more comprehensive view. Although many school districts are moving toward the use of authentic assessments, it is more than likely that standardized testing will continue to be required. Teachers must be informed of the benefits and limitations of both. Choosing appropriate assessment instruments that match the instructional goals and objectives of a reading program is critical to children's literacy development and to effective teaching.

The articles included in Section 5 discuss issues related to standardized and alternative assessment. These articles can provide teachers with a clearer understanding of comprehensive assessment. "Motivating Readers: Better Ways to See and Support Student Reading Progress" provides specific strategies that allow teachers to observe, understand, and assist students as they read. "Can Grades Be Helpful and Fair?" discusses the implications of developing a school policy that allows for included students to demonstrate their progress, while remaining fair to general education students. "Literacy Assessment Reform: Shifting Beliefs, Principled Possibilities, and Emerging Practices" offers thirteen key principles for effective literacy assessment based on personal ideas, classroom practice, theory, and research.

Questions

Reading 20. Summarize the five strategies that Calkins promotes. Calkins suggests that teachers "promote talk" in the classroom. What types of classroom setting and teacher attitudes encourage students to talk?

Reading 21. What mixed messages about grading adaptations are teachers currently sending? How can a teacher implement a fair policy for grading adaptations?

Reading 22. Discuss the philosophical beliefs on which the author bases his principles of effective assessment. What do all thirteen principles have in common?

Reading 23. How can writing assessments be aligned with standards? What beliefs do teachers hold about their students as writers?

Summarize the five strategies that Calkins promotes. Calkins suggests that teachers "promote talk" in the classroom. What types of classroom setting and teacher attitudes encourage students to talk?

Motivating Readers

Better ways to see and support student reading progress

Lucy Calkins

Lucy McCormick Calkins is founding director of the renowned Teachers College Writing Project, a national coalition of teachers, teacher-educators, professors, and writers. She also codirects the Teachers College Reading Project. Lucy is the author of The Art of Teaching Writing *(Heinemann, 1995), is currently working on a book for parents, and plans to soon begin writing* The Art of Teaching Reading.

Two children sit, shoulders touching, each reading a copy of the same book, pausing occasionally to laugh or marvel or puzzle over a line. Another pair sits together with one book held between them, moving their hands one atop the other along a line of print as they read in quiet unison. Around the room, in nooks and corners, other children read on their bellies, read on their backs with arms stretched overhead.

This is it, we think. This is the closest we come to seeing our students' reading lives unfold before us.

But then we think of all we can't see. Did Josh "get" the ending of his book? Can Jessie make a movie in her mind out of such a difficult text? What's really going on?

How Can We Track What We Can't See?

We yearn to get our hands on children's reading, to see it, to measure it. It's partly this desire that leads us to ask them to write summaries, log entries, and book reviews in response to their reading. I want to challenge that practice, and offer strategies for understanding and supporting children's reading lives.

Strategy I: Rethink Those Reading Logs

My nine-year-old son, Miles, loves nothing more than to curl up with a beloved book. He reads before he goes to sleep—and as he eats his breakfast, rides in the car, catches his breath after a soccer game. Yet if Miles were told that every night he needed to write about his reading, he'd probably tackle reading—and writing about it—with the same "I hope this is adequate" attitude he has toward math dittos. Many of the students we teach don't yet love books the way Miles does. How much more daunting must it be for them to not only read but also to write about their reading! Writing should have a

purpose for the writer. Something is wrong if our children are writing about their reading just to prove to us that they did it. There are other ways to check that our students are reading.

Strategy 2: Watch Closely

We can do a fast check on our students' reading progress simply by watching them during independent reading. We can make notes for ourselves on the books the children have chosen to read or the page they are on today compared to yesterday. But we also should be watching for signs of comprehension. If kids are engrossed in their books, they are probably comprehending them. If a child continues reading even as she walks to the carpet for the whole-class meeting, she probably comprehends the book. If a child laughs aloud at his book, or wipes away a tear, he is probably comprehending.

Strategy 3: Children Clarify the Text

If we want to check a child's comprehension more closely, we can sit with

"Motivating Readers: Better Ways to See and Support Student Reading Progress" by Lucy Calkins, published in *Instructor,* September 1996. Copyright © 1996 by Scholastic Inc. Reprinted by permission.

that child and volunteer to read the upcoming bit aloud to him. As we read, we'll stumble onto text that we won't understand. If it says, "Mandy slammed the door loudly," we'll ask, "Is she mad? Why?" We may also ask, "Who is Mandy, anyway?" Our young companion won't feel that he is being grilled, and yet we'll learn whether he grasps what's going on in the book.

Strategy 4: Promote Talk

As adults, we rarely write about our reading. Instead, we *talk* about it. We talk to friends and colleagues. In our minds, we carry on conversations with the author, with characters, with other readers. If we want our students to be wide-awake, thoughtful readers, we must give them opportunities to talk about their reading. If children know that first thing during reading time, they'll have a chance to talk about what they read last night, to chat about the author's craft, the characters, the clues they've picked up—then readers will read differently, rehearsing as they read.

Strategy 5: Make Good Use of Sticky Notes

We may want to ask our students to put sticky notes in their books as a way of place-holding for the conversations they'll later have. The advan-

Five Things Kids Can Do with Sticky Notes in Reading

In Kathleen Tolan's sixth-grade class as P.S. 125 in New York City, children have invented a host of ways to use sticky notes as reading tools. Here are a few of them.

1 Check them to get to know yourself as a reader.

Sometimes Kathleen's students reread their sticky notes to "spy on themselves" as readers. After rereading her stickies, DeVoia announced, "I thought I was the type of reader who noticed beautiful language, but mostly I just argue with the author!"

2 Categorize them.

Students put their stickies into categories, then choose one category to talk about. They've even compiled a list of "Ways to Talk a Very Long Time Off a Single Sticky," which includes tips such as: ask each other for specific examples; think of exceptions; and make comparisons to other books.

3 Leave them for the next person.

Kids select one or two stickies to leave behind in a book so that other readers will encounter them.

4 Pick one to write from.

Kathleen's students sometimes select one note for their writer's notebooks and then fill an entire page with further thoughts.

5 Collaborate on them.

Reading partners decide together on an angle for their sticky-noting. They may decide to note sections where the character seems to be changing, for example, or where the book reminds them of their own lives.

tage of the notes is that they promote a great many TPWs (thoughts per word). It's not unusual for, say, a third grader to write an entire page that contains one thought. "I like the part when . . ." he may write, and then proceed into a retelling of the selected section. How much more efficient for this child to simply leave a sticky note in the section saying, "I like it." A few pages later, another

note might ask: "Why?" as the child questions the character's motives. Another might say, "The author is slowing down" as the child remarks on the pace of the book. Later, in the classroom, children can talk at some length about what they've noticed.

 **Article Review Form at end of book.**

What mixed messages about grading adaptations are teachers currently sending? How can a teacher implement a fair policy for grading adaptations?

Can Grades Be Helpful *and* Fair?

While the practice of making exceptions or substitutions for grading criteria is relatively common, many teachers and students believe it can be unfair. How can we recognize learning differences and make grading adaptations more equitable?

Dennis D. Munk and William D. Bursuck

Dennis D. Bunk is Assistant Professor of Education at Carthage College, Kenosha, WI 53140-1994 (e-mail: munk@cns.carthage.edu). William D. Bursuck is Professor of Special Education at Northern Illinois University, DeKalb, IL 60115 (e-mail: bursuck@niu.edu).

Joshua is a 6th grader with a learning disability in reading. At the beginning of the last grading period, Joshua was transferred into several general content classes, including geography and science. His special and general education teachers worked cooperatively to adapt his lessons so that Joshua could finish on time and understand the material. Inclusion was proving to be a positive experience for him. He was excited about receiving his first report card since the change, but as he scanned the column of C minuses and D pluses, his spirits fell. Why did his teachers tell him he was doing well when he obviously wasn't?

Could, or should, Joshua's teachers have done something to prevent his disappointment?

Research suggests that situations like Joshua's are common: 60 to 70 percent of included students with disabilities receive below-average grades in their general education classes (Donohue and Zigmond 1990). In fact, more than half of all students with disabilities have grade-point averages below 2.24, with 35 percent below 1.75 (Valdes et al. 1990).

Unfortunately for included students, standard letter grades are still the most popular way of indicating student performance. This situation probably reflects a lack of familiarity with alternative grading systems. For example, researchers who conducted a nationwide study of 225 schools found that 68 percent had a grading policy, while just 39 percent of the school districts had policies that stipulated grading adaptations (Polloway et al. 1994).

Figure 1 provides an overview of the common grading adaptations. Although researchers have yet to look at their relative merits, educators might want to experiment with the options presented here (see Munk and Bursuck in press).

Teacher Practices and Perceptions

The practice of adapting individualized grading criteria is not unusual. As many as 50 percent of general education teachers use grading adaptations for students who do not have disabilities (Bursuck et al. 1996). The most common of these include basing grades on improvement, giving multiple grades (for example, grades for tests and grades for effort), and weighing grades for specific assignments. The most helpful adaptations, according to the teachers, include grading on improvement, basing a grade on meeting the objectives of an individualized education plan (IEP), and assigning separate grades for process and for product (Bursuck et al. 1996).

Consider the case of Joshua, for whom adaptations could have resulted in grades that better reflected how his inclusive placement was working. Joshua's teachers cold have varied the weight of individual assignments to reward Joshua's effort and minimize the effects of his reading disability. In Joshua's case, his performance on study guides and group projects could have been weighted greater than the pencil-and-paper tests on which he performed poorly, even when allotted more time. Or, Joshua could have received two grades: one for his effort and one for the quality of his work products. Either of these adaptations could have resulted in a report card grade more representative of Joshua's experience in general education classes.

Teachers are unlikely to use these alternatives, however, if they do not deem them acceptable. For example, when we surveyed 338 general education teachers, 73 percent of them said they believed limiting

Munk, Dennis D., and Bursuck, William D. (1997). "Can Grades Be Helpful *and* Fair?" *Educational Leadership* 55, 4: 44–47. Reprinted with permission of the Association for Supervision and Curriculum Development. Copyright © 1997 by ASCD. All rights reserved.

grading adaptations to students with disabilities was unfair (Bursuck et al. 1996). They felt that such limitations discriminated against students who didn't meet qualifications for special education. Further, they said, such limitations did not address the fact that extenuating circumstances such as relocation can affect any student's grade, and they ignored individual differences among all students.

Teachers who perceive grading adaptations for students with disabilities as unfair are not only less likely to use them, but they are also probably less likely to present a positive rationale for adaptations to their students. In the words of one teacher, "All students learn differently and deserve to be treated as individuals."

On the other hand, teachers who support grading adaptations for students with disabilities cite their desire to not punish students for their disabilities, to promote student learning, and to recognize effort. Even teachers who support the use of adaptations, however, believe that passing a student regardless of his or her performance is unfair.

> Unfortunately for included students, letter grades are the most popular way of indicating student performance.

What Do Students Think?

Teachers should anticipate that some students will think grading adaptations give the students to whom they are applied an undeserved or unfair break. Indeed, in a survey of 275 secondary students, we found that most believed the grading system should be the same for everyone (Bursuck et al. 1997). The students said that giving passing grades no matter what, grading some students on a different scale, and giving pass-fail grades were most unfair. They said that giving separate grades for achievement and for effort was most fair, but 64 percent of the students still disapproved of this adaptation. One student responded, "Why should good students keep trying if they won't get higher grades?"

General education students from four achievement levels (low through above-average) were in agreement, except that low-achieving students approved of pass-fail grades. As would be expected, students with disabilities held different views. They said grading based on improvement, varying the weight of certain products, and use of a different scale were most fair.

A different pattern of responses emerged regarding methods for calculating GPAs. Average and low-achieving general education students and special education students were more likely to say that all classes should count the same toward the GPA, while high-achieving students thought it more fair to have difficult classes count more. The most common reasons for viewing adaptations as unfair were that they created a disincentive for taking harder classes and they provided the students who received them with an unfair advantage. Like their teachers, students who favored adaptations cited a need to reward effort and to recognize learning differences. Also like their teachers, students said that no one should ever be passed "no matter what."

Figure I	Common Grading Adaptations
Adaptation	**Example**
Changing Grading Criteria	
Vary grading weights of certain activities or products.	Increase credit for participation in classroom group activities and decrease credit for essay exams.
Modify or individualize curricular expectations.	Indicate on the IEP that the student will work on addition while the other students work on fractions.
Use contracts and modified course requirements for quality, quantity, and timelines.	State in the contract that student will receive an A- for completing all assignments at 80 percent accuracy, attending all classes, and completing one extra credit report.
Grade on improvement by assigning extra points.	Change a C to a B if the student's total points have increased significantly from the previous marking period.
Changes to Letter and Number Grades	
Add written comments to clarify details about criteria used.	Write on the report card that the student's grade reflects performance on IEP objectives and not on regular classroom curriculum.
Add information from student activity log over a period of time.	Note that while the student's grade was the same this quarter, daily records indicate the student completed math assignments with less teacher assistance.
Add information about effort, progress, and achievement from portfolios or performance-based assessment.	State that the student's written language showed an increase in word variety, sentence length, and quality of ideas.
Use of Alternatives to Letter and Number Grades	
Use pass-fail grades.	Student receives a pass for completing 80 percent of daily work with at least 65 percent accuracy, and attending at least 90 percent of classes.
Use competency checklists and show percentage of objectives met.	Attach a checklist to the report card indicating that during the last quarter, the student mastered addition facts, two-digit addition with regrouping, and counting change to one dollar.

Mixed Messages

We do not yet have a well-defined, systematic approach to grading adaptations. At this point, therefore, we must consider the following, sometimes conflicting, information:

- Included students with disabilities may not experience success when teachers use traditional grading systems, and these students perceive the use of adaptations for some, but not all, students to be fair.

- As many as 50 percent of general education teachers already use informal grading adaptations, but only a quarter of these teachers perceive the use of adaptations for some, but not all, students to be fair.

- Only about a third of all school districts have a policy to guide the use of grading adaptations.

- General education students from all achievement levels perceive the use of adaptations for some, but not all, students to be unfair.

- Teachers and students consider some adaptations (for example, assigning separate grades for effort and product) to be helpful.

Recommendations

Our current knowledge suggests the following recommendations for developing, communicating, and implementing grading adaptation policies.

Developing a School or District Policy

- Consider input from teachers, students in both general and special education classes, and parents. When people help formulate a policy, they are more likely to perceive it as fair.

- Include selection guidelines (for example, a menu of acceptable adaptations), and a specific process for documenting the use of adaptations (for example, the adaptation should be described in a student's IEP) in the policy. Discourage informal or inconsistent uses of adaptations.

- Delineate any adaptations that should never be used (for example, passing a student no matter what).

Communicating a Grading Adaptation Policy

- In the school handbook, clearly describe the policy for using adaptations, the menu of acceptable adaptations, and the process for selecting and documenting adaptations.

- Explain the policy to teachers formally (inservice training sessions) and informally (individual meetings). Explain the policy to students when you discuss schoolwide grading procedures.

Implementing Grading Adaptations

- Document the use of grading adaptations in a student's IEP.

- Monitor student grades to determine whether the chosen adaptation is effective.

- Keep information about specific students who receive adaptations confidential.

- Expect that other students will notice when you use adaptations. Be prepared to explain your rationale to them.

> **Research suggests that 60 to 70 percent of included students with disabilities receive below-average grades in their general education classes.**

Although we continue to learn about grading adaptations as a way to meet the needs of special and general education students in inclusive classrooms, questions do remain. For example, selecting the most appropriate adaptations would be easier if we knew that certain ones were clearly superior. And, if teachers and students perceive them to be fair, adaptations would be even more attractive.

References

Bursuck, W. D., D. Munk, and M. Olson. (1997). "The Fairness of Report Card Grading Adaptations: What Do students With and Without Disabilities Think?" Manuscript submitted for publication.

Bursuck, W. D., E. A. Polloway, L. Plante, M. H. Epstein, M. Jayanthi, and J. McConeghy. (1996). "Report Card Grading Adaptations: A National Survey of Classroom Practices." *Exceptional Children* 62, 4: 301–318.

Donohue, K. and N. Zigmond. (1990). "Academic Grades of Ninth-Grade Urban Learning Disabled Students and Low Achieving Peers." *Exceptionality* 1: 17–27.

Munk, D., and W. D. Bursuck. (in press). "Report Card Grading Adaptations for Students with Disabilities: Types and Acceptability." *Intervention in School and Clinic.*

Polloway, E., M. H. Epstein, W. D. Bursuck, T. W. Roderique, J. L. McConeghy, and M. Jayanthi. (1994). "Classroom Grading: A National Survey of Policies." *Remedial and Special Education* 15, 3: 162–170.

Valdes, K. A., C. I. Williamson, and M. M. Wagner. (1990). *The National Transition Study of Special Education Students* (Vol. 1). (ERIC Document Reproduction Service No. ED324 893.) Menlo Park, California: SRI International.

 Article Review Form at end of book.

Discuss the philosophical beliefs on which the author bases his principles of effective assessment. What do all thirteen principles have in common?

Literacy Assessment Reform

Shifting beliefs, principled possibilities, and emerging practices

Distinguished Educator Rob Tierney articulates thirteen key principles for literacy assessment.

Robert J. Tierney

Tierney has done considerable work with teachers and students on assessment issues from portfolios to report cards to studies of teacher and student change. He is currently Professor and Director, School of Teaching and Learning, The Ohio State University, 1945 N. High Street, Columbus, OH 43210, USA.

Developing better assessment practices requires more than simply choosing a new test or adopting a packaged informal assessment procedure. Indeed, it is difficult to imagine "plastic wrapped" versions of what these new assessment systems intend. Unfortunately, some assessment practices may be repackaged versions of old tests rather than new ways of doing assessment. And some assessment practices, regardless of

the label (authentic assessment, alternative assessment, student-centered assessment, responsive evaluation, classroom-based assessment, or constructive assessment), may be compromised as they are made to fit tenets or principles out of character or inconsistent with the aspirations of these possibilities. . . . Not surprising, professionals may differ in whether or not new forms of assessment live up to their promise. . . .

I have tried to make the ramifications of my definition of assessment more explicit with the articulation of a number of principles, which I describe in this article. . . .

My goal is aligned with constructivists' ways of knowing and the notion of responsive evaluation that Guba and Lincoln (1989) as well as others (e.g., Lather, 1986; Stake, 1983) have espoused. . . .

I also find my views aligning with critical theorists (e.g., Baker & Luke, 1991; Freire & Macedo, 1987; Gee, 1990; hooks, 1989, 1994) who suggest that the point of literacy is to reflect upon, and be empowered by, text rather than to be subjugated by it—that literacy contributes to social transformation as we connect with what we read and write, not in acquiescence, but in reaction, reflection, and response.

I contend that to be both accountable and empowered, readers and writers need to be both reflective and pragmatic. Readers and writers need to be inquirers—researching their own selves, considering the consequences of their efforts, and evaluating the implications, worth, and ongoing usefulness of what they are doing or have done. Teachers can facilitate such reflection by encouraging students to keep traces of what

Adapted from Tierney, Robert J. (1998, February). Literacy assessment reform: Shifting beliefs, principled possibilities, and emerging practices. *The Reading Teacher*, 51(5), 374–390. Adapted with permission of Robert J. Tierney and the International Reading Association. All rights reserved.

they do, by suggesting they pursue ways to depict their journey (e.g., webs or a narrative or listing of steps) and by setting aside time to contemplate their progress and efforts. These reflections can serve as conversation starters—conversations about what they are doing and planning to do and what they did and have learned. I suggest moving toward conversations and notes rather than checklists, rubrics, and more formal evaluations, which seem to distance the student from what she/he is doing, has done, or might do.

These principles . . . reflect a need for a major paradigm shift as regards how we assess, why we assess, and the ways these assessments are manifest in the classroom. . . . Currently, there are several efforts occurring that are simultaneously studying and supporting such shifts (see, for instance, Tierney, Clark, Fenner, Wiser, Herter, & Simpson, in press). I am optimistic enough to think we have the makings of a movement that is beginning to establish its own identity—one that is aligned with contemporary views of learning, and more consistent with pluralistic and constructivist ethics (see especially Moss, 1996).

The Principles

Principle 1: Assessments should emerge from the classroom rather than be imposed upon it. . . . Learnings may be fleeting, emerging, reinforced, and challenged. Oftentimes teachers expect certain learnings; at other times, teachers are surprised at what is learned.

The learnings that occur in classrooms are difficult to predict. . . . While most teachers may begin the year with a sense of what they want to cover, generally they do not consider their plans to be cast in stone. . . . They are more apt to begin with a menu of possibilities and an open-ended agenda, which allows for learning that is opportunistic and individualized.

With the movement to more child-centered approaches, teaching and learning have become less prescriptive and predetermined and have given way to notions of emergent literacy and negotiated curriculums. Most teachers espouse following the lead of the child.

Unfortunately, testing practices tend to abide by a different orientation. Many forms of traditional tests do not measure what is valued and what is occurring in classrooms. Changes in testing have not kept pace with shifts in our understanding of learning and literacy development. . . . Indeed, I often argue that one of the reasons for emergent assessment is to ensure that assessment practices keep up with teaching and learning rather than stagnate them by perpetuating the status quo or outdated views of literacy learning. . . .

Principle 2: Effective testing requires teacher professionalism with teachers as learners. Many of the assessment practices in schools (especially standardized tests) have a dysfunctional relationship with teachers and learners. . . . Actual testing practices in schools seem more estranged than reciprocal, more detached than intimate. . . . Testing divisions in school districts generally have detached themselves from teachers and students or have forced teachers and students to work on their terms. . . .

Quite often teachers will make reference to the tests that they are required to use, principals will allude to the district and state policy, and the district and state lay the responsibility on the public. Some systems seem to be either resistant to change or entrenched in their commitments.

But, teachers relinquishing control of assessment leads to a loss of self-determinacy and professionalism, which is problematic. . . . It removes responsibility for instructional decisions from the hands of those who need to be making them. . . . It depersonalizes the experience and serves as an excuse for relinquishing responsibility. Essentially, the external control of testing and standardization of testing procedures tend to perpetuate teacher and student disenfranchisement.

Teachers are in a better position to know and learn about an individual's development than outsiders. They are with the student over time across a variety of learning situations. As a result they become aware of the subtle changes and nuances of learning within and across individuals. They are sensitive to student engagement, student interests, student personalities, and the idiosyncrasies

of students across learning activities. They are less likely to overstate or ascribe too much significance to results on a single test that may have an alienating impact upon a student. They are in a better position to track and assess learning in the context of teaching and child watching, and therefore to help students assess themselves. Effective teachers are effective learners themselves; they are members of a community of learners in a classroom.

Teachers, in partnership with their students, need to devise their own classroom assessment systems. These systems should have goals for assessment tied to teaching and learning. These goals should be tied to the types of learning and experiences deemed desirable and, therefore, should be established by those most directly invested in the student's education—the teachers and the students themselves. These standards/features should be open ended and flexible enough to adjust to the nuances of classroom life. Tied to these goals might be an array of assessment activities from formalized procedures to very informal, from student self-assessment activities to teacher observations to periodical assessments via portfolios or other ways of checking progress.

Teachers and students need to be willing to change and recognize that there exists no quick fix or prepackaged way to do assessment. . . .

More direct forms of assessment might involve ongoing monitoring of students by sampling reading and writing behaviors, maintaining portfolios and journals, holding periodic conferences, and keeping anecdotal records. . . .

Principle 3: Assessment practices should be client centered and reciprocal. The notion that assessment should empower students and caregivers suggests an approach consistent with a more client-centered approach to learning. . . . In attempts at being client centered, teachers are apt to consider what students take away from tests or teacher-student conferences. A shift to client-centered approaches addresses how assessment practices are helping students assess themselves— i.e., the extent to which students might know how they can check their own progress. . . . It suggests that we should shift the whole orientation of assessment from developing better methods of assessing students toward better methods of helping students assess themselves.

So how might client-centered assessment look? It would look like child-centered learning. Teachers would strive to help students assess themselves. Their orientation would shift from subjecting students to assessment practices to respecting students for their self-assessment initiatives. This entails a shift from something you *do to* students to something you *do with* them or help them *do for themselves*—a form of leading from behind. . . .

Various forms of self-analysis can complement portfolios and be wonderful springboards for such conversations. For example, sometimes I will have students represent their progress and goals with bar graphs or other visual representations (e.g., Venn diagrams, landscapes) in a fashion akin to "then," "now," and "future" and use these graphs as conversation starters. In turn, the visuals serve as the basis for having students delve into their portfolios and examine evidence about what they have achieved and what they might focus upon or set their sights on.

Principle 4: Assessment should be done judiciously, with teachers as advocates for students and ensuring their due process. A useful metaphor, if not rule, for rethinking assessment can be derived from aligning assessment with judicial processes. . . .

Consider how students are put on trial in our school systems. They may or may not have an advocate, they may or may not be given adequate representation, and the evidence that is presented may or may not best represent their cases. They may not see the reports that are developed. Indirect indicators such as standardized tests, of questionable (if not circumstantial) quality, serve as the basis for decisions that restrict opportunities. In a host of ways assessment activities appear less judicious than they should be. Indeed, students are rarely given the right to appeal or to provide their own evidence—it is as if the students' right to due process is violated. . . .

Principle 5: Assessment extends beyond improving our tests to the purposes of assessment and how results from assessment are used, reported, contextualized, and perceived. Any consideration of assessment needs to be broadly defined to encompass an exploration of the relationship between assessment and teaching, as well as facets such as report cards, parent-teacher-student conferences, and the student's ongoing record. These facets should not be viewed as exempt from scrutiny in terms of the principles described herein. They should be subjected to the same guidelines. . . .

Report cards, records, and other elements must be examined in terms of whether they adequately serve the ends for which they are intended. Do report cards serve the needs of the student, teacher, and parent? Do they represent a vehicle for ongoing communication and goal setting? Are they done judiciously? If not, how might the method of reporting be changed to afford such possibilities? Or, take, if you will, the student's records. For what purposes are the records used? Are the records adequate for these purposes?

Changes in assessment should be viewed systemically. When teachers contemplate a shift in classroom assessment, it is rarely a matter of simply making selected adjustments or additions. What a teacher does with one facet should and will affect another. . . . We need to keep an eye on achieving students' engagement in their own learning as we negotiate future goals and possibilities against the type of judgments that are made and reported by whom and how.

We should not underestimate the importance of parent or caregiver involvement in such efforts. Rather than keep the parent or caregiver at arm's length in the negotiations over reform, we need to embrace the concerns that parents have and the contributions that they can make. In those situations where teachers pursue alternatives to report cards, parent contributions may be crucial. Parents need to be informed of the goals and engaged in contributing to the efforts. Because not all parents might see the advantages, they may need choices. And, there are ways to avoid holding all parents hostage to

what one parent or a small number express as concerns. . . .

Principle 6: Diversity should be embraced, not slighted. Oftentimes those assessing students want to remove any cultural biases rather than recognize diversity and support individual empowerment. They often pursue culture-free items and analysis procedures as a way of neatening and comparing. In pursuit of straightforward comparisons they assume that to be fair more items are needed, and therefore, the use of authentic assessment procedures will create problems, especially since the "time-consuming nature of the problems limits the number" (Linn, Baker, & Dunbar, 1991, p. 18). In addition, they seem to support as a given the use of the same analysis systems for the responses of all students. They expect a respondent to interpret a task in a certain way and respond in a set manner and may not tolerate variation in response, even if such variation might be justified. Whereas they might allude to the context-specific nature of any assessment, they tend to retreat from considering individuals on their own merits or in their own ways.

The term *culture-free tests* seems an oxymoron. I suspect that it is well nigh impossible, and certainly questionable, to extract cultural influences from any test or measure of someone's literacy. Literacy, your own and my own, is inextricably connected to cultural background and life experiences. Culture-free assessments afford, at best, a partial and perhaps distorted understanding of the student. In other words, assessments that do not build upon the nature and nuances of each individual's experiences should be viewed as limited and perhaps flawed. Just as teachers attempt to engage students by building from their background of experiences, so assessment should pursue a goal of culture sensitivity. Classroom teaching does not occur by ignoring or removing diversities. Nor should such a view of assessment be dismissed because of its ideological or sociopolitical considerations: Recognition or validation of one's own experience would seem a basic human right.

We need to aspire to culturally based assessment practices. . . .

For years standardized test developers and the National Assessment of Educational Progress have retreated from dealing with issues of nonuniformity and diversity as they have pursued the development of scales for straightforward comparisons across individuals. In conjunction with doing this, they have often revised their assessment instruments to ensure that results fit their models or views of literacy. . . .

Principle 7: Assessment procedures may need to be nonstandardized to be fair to the individual. As teachers try to avail students of every opportunity within their control, they are constantly making adjustments as they "read" the students—their dispositions, verbal abilities, familiarities, needs, and so on. We look for ways to maximize the learning for different students, and we know that different students may need different amounts of encouragement and very different kinds of support. If we standardized our teaching, we know what would apt to be the end result —some students with wonderful potential would reveal only certain sides of themselves and might not achieve their potential or even reveal who they are and what they might contribute and learn.

Allowing for individual or even group differences creates havoc with the desire to standardize assessment. Standardization approaches each individual and group in the same way—that is, students perform the same tasks at the same time, and then their responses are assessed using the same criteria. But if different students' learning repertoires are different and different students enlist different strategies and have different values, etc., and different approaches to testing, then what may be standard for one student may be unique for another.

Different students respond in different ways to different forms of assessment depending upon their histories—cultural, classroom, or personal. As my previous principle suggested, how students respond should be looked at as different across situations and against a "comparative canvas, one that takes into account the nature of the community that students inhabit, both the community of the classroom and the community of society with all of its past and pre-

sent conditions and hopes for the future" (Purves, 1982, p. 345). Green and Dixon (1994) have emphasized that students construct "situated repertoires associated with particular models for being a student . . . not generic ones" (p. 237). . . .

Principle 8: Simple-minded summaries, scores, and comparisons should be displaced with approaches that acknowledge the complex and idiosyncratic nature of literacy development. Straightforward comparisons across individuals are usually arbitrary, biased, and narrow. Assuming an approach to assessment with a new openness to complexity, respect for diversity, and interest in acquiring a rich picture of each student, then how might decisions be made about students? Those decisions that require reflection upon the individual's progress and prospects will likely be bountiful. Teachers who pursue an open-ended and diverse view of students will find little difficulty negotiating new areas of pursuit with and for individual students. Decisions that demand comparisons from one individual to the next will be problematic, but these difficulties are not insurmountable. They require a willingness to deal with uncertainties, to entertain possibilities, and to negotiate decisions, including the possibility that there will be lack of agreement. The problems with comparisons are confounded when people assume that straightforward continuums or single scores can adequately describe students.

Comparisons based upon scores are so problematic for a host of reasons: (a) Each student's development is unique; (b) the literacies of one student will be different from another, and even the same literacies will involve differing arrays of facets; and (c) some of these facets will be unique to a certain situation. Literacy development is sufficiently different from one student to the next that the types of comparisons that might be made are quite complex and multifaceted. The term *literacy abilities* rather than *literacy ability* seems in order. If you were trying to portray the character of these developments, you might find yourself gravitating to describing individuals on their own terms. Unfortunately, the terms of comparison in place with stan-

dardized tests and NAEP assessments and implicit in many of the attempts to score portfolios and other classroom-based data are often insensitive to such complexity. Looking at different individuals in terms of a single score masks variability and individuality. Again, test makers err on the side of a level of simplification not unlike a massive "conspiracy of convenience" (Spiro, Vispoel, Schmitz, Samarapungavan, & Boerger, 1987, p. 180).

The drive for uniformity is quite pervasive. Our assessment and instructional programs oftentimes include long lists of skills as outcomes to be assessed, taught, and mastered. It is assumed that skills are neatly packaged and discrete and that each makes a uniform contribution to literacy development. It is assumed that students acquire these skills to mastery and that their ability to use them is uniform across literacy situations. In authentic reading and writing situations within which genuine purposes are being pursued, this is unlikely. Across literacy situations certain attributes may be more likely to be enlisted than others, and they are apt to be enlisted as clusters rather than one by one or discretely.

Too often literacy educators have ignored the complexities of the issues and have fallen back on convenience rather than exploring possibilities. Take, if you will, the attempts to wed some of the data emerging from performance assessment (e.g., portfolios) with rubrics. The data generated from a portfolio might involve a rich array of samples or observations of the students' work across situations and time. These samples are apt to represent the students' pursuit of different goals, utilizing different resources, including content, under varying conditions. In some ways student classroom samples may vary as much as the works of art from an artist's portfolio. Each sample may represent very different achievements and processes. When you hold them, examine them, and discuss their significance you are in touch with the actual artifact and not some distant derivative.

It is at this point, some would argue, that we can use a rubric to affix a score or scores or a sum total score to the student's work. But we need to examine a question that is the reverse of what is often asked. Instead of asking how we rate the portfolio, we should be asking whether the rubric measures up to the portfolio or to the assessment of complex performance. Moreover, in classrooms do we need a measure that is a distant derivative when we have the primary sources—the actual samples—to examine and reexamine using an array of lenses or perspectives? Whereas I argue for the context-specific nature of any assessment, advocates of rubrics seem to want to dismiss idiosyncrasies and variation—that is, they would retreat from being willing to consider individuals on their own merits or in their own ways. Unless rubrics are used to prompt a consideration of possible ways to analyze work or as conversation starters in conjunction with revisiting the students' work samples, I see few advantages to their use in classrooms.

Sometimes assessment of reading and writing becomes more far-fetched by adding together a set of subscores. A key assumption often undergirdlng the use of such scores—especially the suggestion that they can be added and used as the basis of comparative decision making—is that the full and detailed portrait of an individual's literacies has been afforded. Unfortunately, these dimensions are not exhaustive, these determinations of degree are not accurate, and they should not be added. To be able to do so, we would have to do the following:

1. include all of the attributes or be assured that the partial listing that was developed is representative;

2. determine how these attributes are configured across situations;

3. assume that ample evidence will be provided for assessing these attributes;

4. develop scales for assessing attributes; and

5. generate an algorithm that works across individuals by which we might combine the elements and their dimensions.

I would posit that we do not have such samples, sampling procedures, ways of procuring evidence, adequate scales, or algorithm. And it is problematic to assume that an al-gorithm that simply represents sums would ever be adequate. The complexity of literacy is such that we cannot assume a basis for generating or combining scores.

Literacy assessments cannot and should not be so rigid. Perhaps there are some benchmarks that are appropriate across all students. Perhaps there are benchmarks appropriate to some readers and not others. But such benchmarks are likely to represent a partial view of any student's literacies. The use of scores and continua as ways of affording simplification and comparability has a tendency to camouflage the subjectivity of assessment and give test developers the allusion of objectivity. The use of scores and continua is not more objective; it is arbitrary. Guba and Lincoln (1989) have suggested the shift toward accepting the inevitability of relativism and the complexities across different settings may require the ongoing, ecumenical, and recursive pursuit of shared possibilities rather than a single set of absolute truths.

Principle 9: Some things that can be assessed reliably across raters are not worth assessing; some things that are worth assessing may be difficult to assess reliably except by the same rater. Oftentimes, test makers and researchers will perseverate on whether or not they can consistently measure certain abilities. They tout reliability as the major criteria for whether or not a test is valid. The end result is that some things that are worth measuring are discarded and some things that are not worth measuring or valuing achieve an elevated level of importance. . . .

Unfortunately, reliability is translated to mean that two different scorers or raters will be able to assess the same thing in the same way. Unless a high degree of agreement across raters is achieved, test makers will deem a measure unreliable and therefore question its worth. In so doing, they may be making the mistake of assuming that reliability equates to agreement when verifiability may be a better approach. . . .

One should not be seduced into thinking that variables that are easy to define should be looked at to the exclusion of those that are difficult to assess. It may be foolish to exclude some facets because they are difficult to assess or because they look different either across students or situations or by the raters. Likewise, one should not be seduced into thinking that every reading and writing act is the same and involves the same variables. If the only literacy facets scored are those common across students and those that can be scored with high reliability across different students' responses, then certain facets will be given more weight than they deserve, and some important facets may be excluded.

Principle 10: Assessment should be more developmental and sustained than piecemeal and short-sighted. . . . If assessment goals are tied to development, then we need to look at patterns and long-term goals. What we see or look for in a single selection or case may not be helpful in looking for patterns across cases, selections, or circumstances. For example, as a reader or writer reads and writes a single selection, we might look for engagement and active involvement. Across situations we might want to consider the extent to which the interest and engagement are maintained across a range of material for different purposes. We also might be interested in the extent to which the student has developed a value for reading and writing that is reflected in how he or she uses reading and writing inside and outside the class. This may be apparent in her or his self-selection of books or self-initiated writing to serve different purposes. . . .

A shift toward assessment that examines students over time aligns assessment with classroom practices that pursue sustained engagement and aim to help students derive an understanding of patterns. It shifts our teaching and learning to long-term possibilities rather than the specific and short-term objectives of a lesson.

Principle 11: Most interpretations of results are not straightforward. Assessment should be viewed as ongoing and suggestive, rather than fixed or definitive. In many ways teaching involves constant redevelopment or continuous experimentation and adjustments to plans, directions, and future goals. To appreciate the complexities and sophistication of teaching, consider the image one conjures up for a sportsperson. In certain sports (e.g., baseball, tennis) involving eye-hand coordination with racquets or bats, players will begin their swing and constantly be making subtle adjustments as balls with different velocities, rotations, and angles are thrown at them. But sporting events pale in comparison with the dynamics of teacher-student interactions—the adjustments, just in time decision making, and ebb and flow of activities that occur. Teachers deal with students whom they may be trying to respond to, motivate, mobilize, develop, and coach while understanding their needs, beliefs, strategies, and possible ways of responding as they are interacting with one another and dealing with the rest of their lives. Not surprising, teachers have to be a mix of ecologist, developer, advocate, coach, player, actor-director, stage manager, mayor, and sometimes counselor. Teachers are always planning and recognizing the need to make constant adjustments to what they are doing and what they might do next.

For these purposes, the typical assessment data (e.g., scouting reports of students provided by school records, premeasures of abilities, standardized or even informal assessments) may provide limited guidance to teachers in terms of the moment-by-moment decision making and even planning for the next day or week or even month. Too often typical student records seem as limited as a mug shot taken of the learner; you may be able to identify the learner (depending upon your ability to see likenesses) but may not. Certainly, the mug shot will not afford you an appreciation of the character of the student, nor will it help you understand the range of things that the student can do, nor will it support your ability to negotiate either long-term or short-term learning goals.

Most classroom-based assessments offer more promise but are still limited. Classroom-based assessment procedures may give teachers a better sense of how students will proceed in like circumstances and may also afford a fuller picture of the student across time. Portfolios, for example, are equivalent to scrapbooks involving multiple snapshots of the learner in a variety of contexts. Such assessments might afford a fuller and richer depiction of the learner and his

or her pattern of development, but judgments—especially prescriptions—are never as straightforward as they might appear. The possibility of obtaining a complete vision of a learner is complicated by our inability to constantly monitor a learner, delve into and interpret his or her innermost thoughts, and achieve more than one perspective on the learner. It is also tied to the ever-changing nature of learning. Apart from the fact that our snapshots of classroom learning tend to be still shots of the learner, these images are tied to a place and time that has become more historical than current. Such limitations might be viewed as a problem if we were to perseverate on wanting to pin down what to do next with a student and be sure to stick to a set course. Instead, they should be anticipated and viewed as tentative bases for where and when one might begin. While we can develop short- and long-term goals and plans, we should not approach our teaching as if our prescriptions should not be altered, assessment fixed, nor directions more than suggestive.

Likewise, we should not approach assessment as if our results need be final or base our subsequent actions as if we have derived a decision that is any better than a hunch. We should avoid assuming that our assessments do anything more than afford us information that we might consider. No assessment should be used as restrictively or rigidly as decisions made in courts of law, yet I fear that many are. Instead we should reinforce what needs to occur in classrooms—constant adjustments, shifts, and ongoing decision making by teachers who are constantly watching, learning, coaching, and responding to students, peers, and others.

Principle 12: Learning possibilities should be negotiated with the students and stakeholders rather than imposed via standards and assessment that are preset, prescribed, or mandated. . . . Historically, standard setting (and the proficiency testing that it spurs) has tended to restrict access and experimentation at the same time as it has tended to support agendas tied to gatekeeping and exclusion.

The standard-setting enterprise and the proficiency-testing industry

have the potential to perpetuate the view that we can set targets that we can easily reach. Unfortunately, it is problematic to assume that development is simply setting a course for the student from A to B—especially when A is not taken into account and B is tied to views of outcomes looking for expertise rather than individual assessment of development. Without ample consideration being given for where students are and how and why they develop and their aspirations, we are apt to have our targets misplaced and our learning routes poorly aligned. I was in attendance at one of the many sessions on standards sponsored by the International Reading Association and the National Council for Teachers of English, when a speaker talked abut standards using the analogy of a basketball player of the caliber of Michael Jordan as the "standard." As the speaker discussed the worth of setting standards based upon what we view as aspirations, I mulled over my height and my skill and what I might do to improve. Then I reminded myself of my reasons for playing basketball and where I am insofar as my background in basketball. I play basketball for fun, to be with my sons, and for exercise. We need to realize that we should be asking who is deciding? Whose standards are being represented? In some ways the quest for educational improvement via standards and in turn proficiency testing places a premium on uniformity rather than diversity and favors prepackaged learning over emerging possibilities.

In a similar vein, advocates of standards emphasize the importance of the role of making judgments by comparisons to Olympic skating and other activities where success is measured by the trophies one achieves or the graded measures that are applied. I think we need to challenge this metaphor and question the emphasis on judgment rather than support. I prefer to think of a teacher as a coach rather than a judge—a supporter and counselor versus a judge and award- or grade-giver. I would like to see teachers view their role as providing guidance, handholding, and comments rather than As, Bs, and Cs or some score. In my view of a more ideal world, I see teachers, students, and caregivers operating in a kind of public sphere where they are part of the team negotiating for a better self. In this regard, I find myself fascinated with several classroom projects: with the kind of self-reflection and analysis occurring amidst the community-based preschool efforts of Reggio Emilia (Forman, 1993, 1994) where teachers, students, and community work together developing and implementing curriculum plans, ponder the right questions to ask to spur students' reflections, develop insights, and learn; with the work of Short, Harste, and Burke (1996) on developing inquiry in Indianapolis schools (as they engage students and teachers in considering the anomalies, patterns, and ways of looking at themselves); with the work of the Santa Barbara Classroom Discourse Group (1992a, 1992b), a community of teachers, researchers, and students interested in understanding how life in classrooms is constructed and how expectations and practices influence opportunities to access, accomplish, and learn in school; and with the work of Fenner (1995) who uses a general form of Toulmin's (1958) analysis of argumentation to examine classroom conversations and student self-assessments with portfolios and looks for ways to help students look at themselves in terms of evidence, assumptions, claims, and goals. Fenner's approach to self-assessment moves us away from the typical checklist that asks students to detail in rather vague and unsubstantiated fashion their strengths and goals in a kind of "hit and miss" fashion. . . .

I fear that standards will perpetuate the effects uncovered when Ellwein, Glass, and Smith (1988) surveyed the history of the effects of various statewide proficiency testing—gatekeeping and the removal rather than enhancement of opportunities. Indeed, in Ohio and I would suspect other states, Ellwein et al.'s (1998) findings are being replicated. With the introduction of proficiency testing more students are dropping out. Ironically, the tests were intended to improve instruction, but fewer students are taking them, which in turn suggests that more students are passing them. So by keeping these dropouts invisible, advocates of proficiency testing and legislators claim the reform is having

positive effects—that is, as more students leave or drop out, abhorring or deterred by the situation, legislators and advocates (including the media) erroneously suggest or advertise falsely that more students are passing.

Closing Remarks

My principles for assessment emanate from a mix of child-centered views of teaching, developmental views of children, constructivist views of knowing, critical theoretical views of empowerment, and pluralistic views of society. I view them as suggesting directions and guidelines for thinking about the why, how, where and when, who, and what of assessment.

Why?
  To develop culturally sensitive versus culturally free assessments
  To connect assessment to teaching and learning
  To connect assessment to students' ongoing goal setting, decision making, and development
  To become better informed and make better decisions
  To develop assessment that keeps up with teaching and learning

How?
  Collaborative, participatory, client centered
  Coach-like, supportive and ongoing rather than judgmental, hardnosed, and final
  Supplemental and complementary versus grade-like and summative
  Individually, diversely, not prepackaged
  Judiciously
  Developmentally
  Reasoned

Where and when?
  Amidst students' lives
  Across everyday events and programs
  In and out of school
  Opportunistically, periodically, continuously

Who?
  Students, teachers, and stakeholders

What?
  Ongoing learning: development, resources, and needs
  Complexities
  Individuals and groups
  Evidence of progress and decision making
  Programs, groups, and individuals

In describing the essence of my proposition, I would like to return to where I began. I believe an overriding principle, which is perhaps my 13th or more of a penumbra, is *assessment should be assessed in terms of its relationship with teaching and learning including the opportunities learners are offered and the rights and respect they are accorded.*

Shifts in my own thinking about assessment began occurring when I asked myself this question: If I were to assess assessment, what criteria might I use? My answer to this question was that assessment practices should empower teachers, students, and their caregivers. In other words, assessment practices should enrich teaching and learning. As I explored how tests might be used as tools of empowerment for teachers and learners, I became interested in whether this type of assessment actually helped teachers and students (as well as the student's caregiver, resource teachers, principal, and others) achieve a more expanded view of the student's learning. I also wanted to know whether testing contributed to developing goals and formulating plans of action, which would suggest that assessment practices were empowering. . . .

The use of standardized tests, tests accompanying the published reading programs, and even teacher-made tests do not expand teachers' views of their students' learning over time, nor suggest ways the teacher might help them. Nor are such tests integrated into classroom life. They tend to displace teaching and learning activities rather than enhance them.

Likewise, students rarely seem to be engaged in learning how to assess themselves. When my colleagues and I interviewed teachers with whom we began working in assessment 10 years ago, most teachers did not conceptualize the goal of testing to be helping students reflect or obtain feedback on their progress, nor did they envision tests as helping students establish, refine, or achieve learning goals. When we interviewed students, we found that students in these classes tended to have a limited and rather negative view of themselves, and they had set few learning goals. Attempts to examine the impact of more learner-based assessments yielded quite contrasting results. In classrooms in which portfolios were becoming an integral part of classroom life, teachers and students had developed a fuller sense of their own abilities (Carter, 1992; Carter & Tierney, 1988; Fenner, 1995; Stowell & Tierney, 1995; Tierney, Carter, & Desai, 1991).

A study by Shavelson, Baxter, and Pine (1992) provides other confirmation of the worth of aligning assessment to the teaching and learning in classrooms. In their attempts to examine variations in instructional programs, they concluded that direct observations and more emergent procedures captured the shifts in learning while traditional methods (multiple choice, short answer) did not. Such findings should come as no surprise to those of us who have been involved in research on the effects of teaching upon learning; that is, very few literacy researchers would rely upon a standardized test to measure the effectiveness of particular teaching strategies with different students. Instead, we are apt to pursue a range of measures, and some of us would not develop our measures a priori. In fact, several efforts have demonstrated the power of new assessment approaches to evaluate and guide program development and teacher change effectively (see Tierney et al., 1993).

Designing these new assessment approaches has to do with a way of teaching, testing, and knowing that is aligned with a set of values different than what has been and still is espoused by most educational reformers. Unfortunately, the power of some of the psychometricians and their entrenched values related to testing make the emergence of alternative assessment procedures difficult. Indeed, I see the shift as involving a cultural transformation—a shift away from what I view as a somewhat totalitarian practice tied to "old science" and metaphors that equate student learning to quality control.

Mike Rose (1995) suggests in *Possible Lives* that classrooms are created spaces, and the successful ones create spaces where students feel safe and secure; they are the classrooms in which students are willing to stretch, take risks, and pursue their interpretive authority for themselves and with others. In a similar vein, Kris Gutierrez and her colleagues (Gutierrez, Rymes, & Larson, 1995), in discussing teacher-student discourse, assert the need for spaces where students and teachers can connect or transact with each other, rather than pass by one another. The key is finding ways to effect involvement and transaction rather than detachment and monolithic responses.

Assessment must address making futures possible and pursuable rather than impossible or improbable. We must create spaces where students, teachers, and others can achieve futures and spaces wherein the dynamics and practices are such that they challenge but do not undermine the ecology of who students are and might become.

References

Baker, A., & Luke, A. (1991). *Toward a critical sociology of reading pedagogy*. Philadelphia: John Benjamin's.

Basso, K. (1970). "To give up on words": Silence in Western Apache culture. *Southwest Journal of Anthropology, 26,* 213–230.

Bober, S. (1995, July). *Portfolio conferences.* Presentation at Lesley College Literacy Institute, Cambridge, MA.

Bruner, J. (1990). *Acts of meaning.* Cambridge, MA: Harvard University Press.

Carter, M. (1992). *Self-assessment using writing portfolios.* Unpublished doctoral dissertation, The Ohio State University, Columbus.

Carter, M., & Tierney, R. J. (1988, December). *Writing growth: Using portfolios in assessment.* Paper presented at the National Reading Conference, Tucson, AZ.

Ellwein, M. C., Glass, G. V., & Smith, M. L. (1988) Standards of competence: Prepositions on the nature of testing reforms. *Educational Researcher, 17*(8), 4–9.

Fenner, L. (1995). *Student portfolios: A view from inside the classroom.* Unpublished doctoral dissertation, The Ohio State University, Columbus.

Forman, G. (1993). Multiple symbolizations in the long jump project. In C. Edward, L. Gandini, & G. Forman (Eds.), *The hundred languages of children* (pp. 171–188). Norwood, NJ: Ablex.

Forman, G. (1994). Different media, different languages. In L. Katz & B. Cesarone (Eds.), *Reflections on the Reggio Emilia approach* (pp. 41–51). Urbana, IL: ERIC/EECE.

Freire, P., & Macedo, D. (1987). *Literacy: Reading the word and the world.* South Hadley, MA: Bergin & Garvey.

Gee, J. (1990). *Social linguistics and literacies: Ideologies in discourse.* New York: Falmer Press.

Green, J., & Dixon, C. (1994). Talking knowledge into being: Discursive and social practices in classrooms. *Linguistics and Education, 5,* 231–239.

Guba, E. G., & Lincoln, Y. S. (1989). *Fourth generation evaluation.* Newbury Park, CA: Sage.

Gutierrez, K., Rymes, B., & Larson, J. (1995). Script, counterscript, and underlife in the classroom: James Brown versus Brown v. Board of Education. *Harvard Educational Review, 65,*445–471.

Haney, W. (1993). Testing and minorities. In L. Weis & M. Fine (Eds.), *Beyond silenced voices* (pp. 45–74). Albany, NY: State University of New York Press.

hooks, b. (1989). *Talking back.* Boston: South End Press.

hooks, b. (1994). *Teaching to transgress: Education as the practice of freedom.* New York: Routledge.

Lather, P. (1986). Research as praxis. *Harvard Educational Review, 56,* 257–277.

Linn, R. L., Baker, E. L., & Dunbar, S. B. (1991). Complex performance assessment: Expectations and validation criteria. *Educational Researcher, 20*(8), 15–21.

Moss, P. (1996). Enlarging the dialogue in educational measurement: Voices from interpretive research traditions. *Educational Researcher, 25*(1), 20–28.

Ogbu, J. (1988). Literacy and schooling in subordinate cultures: The case of Black Americans. In E. Kintgen, B. Kroll, & M. Rose (Eds.), *Perspectives on literacy* (pp. 227–242). Carbondale, IL: Southern Illinois University Press.

Ogbu, J. (1991). Cultural perspective and school experience. In C. Walsh (Ed.), *Literacy as praxis: Culture, language and pedagogy* (pp. 25–50). Norwood, NJ: Ablex.

Phillips, S. (1983). *The invisible culture: Communication and community on the Warm Springs Indian reservation.* New York: Longman.

Purves, A. (1982). Conclusion to an international perspective to the evaluation of written composition. In B. H. Choppin & T. N. Postlethwaite (Eds.), *Evaluation in education: An international review series* (Vol. 5, pp. 343–345.). Oxford, England: Pergamon Press.

Rose, M. (1995). *Possible lives.* Boston: Houghton Mifflin.

Santa Barbara Classroom Discourse Group. (1992a). Constructing literacy in classrooms; literate action as social accomplishment. In H. Marshall (Ed.), *Redefining student learning: Roots of educational change* (pp. 119–150). Norwood, NJ: Ablex.

Santa Barbara Classroom Discourse Group. (1992b). The referential and intertextual nature of classroom life. *Journal of Classroom Interaction, 27*(2), 29–36.

Shavelson, R., Baxter, G. P., & Pine, J. (1992). Performance assessment: Political rhetoric and measurement reality. *Educational Researcher, 21*(4), 22–27.

Short, K. G., Harste, J. C., & Burke, C. (1996). *Creating classrooms for authors and inquirers.* Portsmouth, NH: Heinemann.

Spiro, R. J., Vispoel, W. L., Schmitz, J., Samaraungavan, A., & Boerger, A. (1987).

Knowledge acquisition for application: Cognitive flexibility and transfer in complex content domains. In B. C. Britton & S. Glynn (Eds.), *Executive control processes* (pp. 177–200). Hillsdale, NJ: Erlbaum.

Stake, R. (1983). The case study method in social inquiry. In G. Madaus, M. Scriven, & D. Stufflebeam (Eds.), *Evaluation models* (pp. 279–286). Boston: Kluwer-Nijhoff.

Tierney, R. J., Carter, M., & Desai, L. (1991). *Portfolio assessment in the reading-writing classroom.* Norwood, MA: Christopher Gordon.

Tierney, R. J., Clark, C., Fenner,, L., Wiser, B., Herter, R. J., & Simpson, C. (in press). A portfolio discussion: Assumptions, tensions and possibilities. *Reading Research Quarterly.*

Tierney, R. J., Wile, J., Moss, A. G., Reed, E. W., Ribar, J. P., & Zilversmit, A. (1993). *Portfolio evaluation as history: Evaluation of the history academy for Ohio teachers* (occasional paper). National Council of History Education, Inc.

Toulmin, S. (1958). *The uses of argument.* Cambridge, England: Cambridge University Press.

Wile, J., & Tierney, R. J. (1996). Tensions in assessment: The battle over portfolios, curriculum and control. In R. Calfee & P. Perfumo (Eds.), *Writing portfolios in the classrooms: Policy and practice, process and peril* (pp. 203–218). Hillsdale, NJ: Erlbaum.

 **Article Review Form at end of book.**

How can writing assessments be aligned with standards? What beliefs
do teachers hold about their students as writers?

New Writing Assessments

The challenge of changing teachers' beliefs about students as writers

Shelby A. Wolf
Maryl Gearhart

*Shelby A. Wolf is assistant professor of
education at the University of Colorado,
Boulder; Maryl Gearhart is adjunct
associate professor of education at the
University of California, Berkeley.*

New writing assessments are built on
the belief that young children learning to write are engaged in making
meaning. As Dyson (in press) has
taught us, children create a written
world surrounded by talk, drama,
and drawing—a world that combines
their "symbolic resources and social
intentions," a world that often fore-
grounds the micropolitics of their
classroom situations including gender, race, or class. Thus, as evaluations of the writing of children, new
assessments capture the ways young
writers express themselves to multiple audiences through a variety of
genres for multiple purposes, manipulate language to achieve particular
effects, and respect the abundant variety in language use and dialect
across diverse groups.

In this article, we suggest that
these new assessments will be utilized effectively by teachers and children only if teachers understand
their contents and purposes and
agree to endorse and embrace them.
When teachers assess students'
growth as writers, they ask themselves, "Where has this child been?"
"Where is she now?" and "Where can
I advise her to go next?" Answers to
these questions require a teacher's
commitment to assessments that
honor young authors' efforts to make
their own meaning. To accomplish
this, teachers must validate language
variety and stretch children to new
genres and styles as well as clarity
and creativity of expression. This requires a discerning eye and a willingness to engage with children in
constructive criticism about their
writing. In this view, a teacher's "assessments" become a reader's "analytic response to text" (D. P. Wolf,
1993; D. P. Wolff, Bixby, Glenn, &
Gardner, 1991; S. A. Wolf & Gearhart,
1993a, 1993b).

In the sections that follow, we
examine ways that elementary teachers' beliefs about their students as

writers mediate their acceptance and
investment in new methods of assessing students' narrative writing.
Our findings emerged from a 2-year
collaboration with the teachers of one
elementary school. While our venture
resulted in considerable growth
among teachers, we encountered
some resistance as well, resistance
engendered by our hesitancy to address deep issues about the philo-
sophic foundations that undergird
teachers'—and our own—current
practices.

We begin with a description of
the writing assessments we created
in collaboration with the teachers of
one elementary school, through a
program entitled Writing What You
Read (WWYR). Next, we explore
where the teachers were prior to the
onset of WWYR and then describe
the overall impact of WWYR on
classroom practice.[1] We then turn to
two teachers who represent case examples of resistance and explore the
quite varying reasons for their rejec-
tion. We conclude with remarks
about what we have learned about
new assessments in conflict with differing philosophies.

Reprinted with permission from *Theory Into Practice*, Autumn 1997, 36(4) (theme issue on "New Directions in Student Assessment").
Copyright 1997 College of Education, The Ohio State University.

The WWYR Program

Young authors are often encouraged to write about life experiences and the life of their individual imaginations and then to analyze the effectiveness of their written expressions. "Write what you know" is the advice often given to novice writers, encouraging them to take what they know about life and put it on paper. Yet professional writers, including numerous children's authors, seem to suggest alternative advice—"Write what you read"—implying that writers are often inspired by what they know about literature.

Learning about literature was one key feature in the first year of the Writing What You Read professional development program. Following the participating teachers' request to focus on narrative, we began by asking teachers to analyze literature in terms of the following narrative components: genre, theme, character, setting, plot, point of view, style, and tone. Teachers read sections of Atwell's (1987) *In the Middle* and Lukens' (1990) *A Critical Handbook of Children's Literature,* and we drew on additional articles and books in the areas of children's literature and literary criticism (e.g., Huck, Hepler, & Hickman, 1987; Lurie, 1990; Sloan, 1991; S. A. Wolf & Heath, 1992). We also examined curricular materials crafted to highlight the critical features of narrative and the connections among literary texts, topics, and themes.

Learning about children as writers was a second key component of our first-year program. We provided numerous examples of young children writing their own stories as well as analyzing narratives. We discussed children's oral insights and written work in the same way that we examined professional texts, stressing children's developing understandings of character revelation, the symbolic use of setting, the often sequential nature of plot, and the explicit and implicit revelation of theme. We analyzed children's beginning and more accomplished uses of language to set a tone and to create their own voice or style. We evaluated children's awareness of audience, delineating what attempts children made to make their writing clear to others.

We also stressed that indices of children's development could not be readily equated to "grade-level expectations"—that very young writers were quite capable of more accomplished pieces than older students, depending on their purpose and experience. We emphasized that children are interested in criticism that would help them become better writers—encouraging the teachers to think of a developmental model that would scaffold children toward stronger writing through specific commendations and recommendations.

Teachers' understandings of the components of narrative and their students as writers then became the motivation for integrating curricular possibilities, instructional techniques, and assessment tools. Our goal was to help teachers assess children's narrative writing in the same way that they critically respond to literature. Our hope was that teachers could offer their students explicit guidance, equipped now with the "tools of the literary trade"-an understanding of genre influences, the technical vocabulary, and the orchestration of the narrative components of a text—within a framework designed to strengthen young children's writing.

Together we developed two tools to support teachers in narrative assessment—a narrative feedback form to assist teacher-student conferences (Figure 1)* and a narrative rubric to help teachers evaluate students' present understandings and future possibilities (Figure 2). Year 2 focused heavily on practice and implementation of these methods.

Teachers' Beliefs Prior to WWYR

When we began our workshops, we found that the majority of teachers assumed their students lacked knowledge necessary to competent writing. Writing in the classroom was viewed in one of two ways—as an opportunity to express and develop creative imagination (a belief that limited the teacher's role for fear of restricting the child's expression)or as an opportunity to practice and master composition skills (a belief

*Figure 1 is not included in this publication.

that motivated a sequential, stepping-stone curriculum). Patterns of belief were associated with grade level.

The primary teachers had a tendency to work from a readiness model and a skills view of writing (cf. Goldenberg & Gallimore, 1991; Sulzby, 1991). Because the kindergarten teachers believed their students were not ready for writing skills, the only writings assigned were stories children dictated to their parents at home—stories that received no critical evaluation from the teachers. The first-grade teachers did not give their students opportunities for "real writing" until after January, when they thought the children were "ready to write." There was initially no mention of young children needing to write for meaning; most first grade writing projects were handled as exercises with prescribed story starters and fill-in-the-blank pattern books.

In this context, assessment could not possibly have the function of enhancing children's efforts with meaning making. Indeed, there was a common assumption—linked to the skills view—that children could not write and would not want to write without the teacher's warm, uncritical acceptance to ensure a child's interest and imagination. Thus, viewing their role as one of praise and motivation, the primary teachers did not evaluate their children's writing, and their comments reflect this point of view: "Any attempts with the written word receive praise and encouragement." "I want the child to truly like to write."

At higher grade levels, we found a juxtaposition between the teachers' concerns with creative voice and with skill. Teachers might assign narratives on specific topics (usually associated with heroes and holidays) guided by explicit criteria, or they might provide time for opportunities to "just write": "I want children to express themselves in a way that does justice to what they imagine and think, to find the words." "I want children to see relationships between their thoughts and words."

Still, the teachers did not understand ways of helping children enhance these relationships. They were not particularly explicit in their analyses of narrative and, not want-

Figure 2 Narrative Rubric

Theme	Character	Setting
explicit ◄———► implicit didactic ◄———► revealing	flat ◄———► round static ◄———► dynamic	backdrop ◄———► essential simple ◄———► multi-functional
• Not present or not developed through other narrative elements	• One or two flat, static characters with little relationship between characters; either objective (action speaks for itself) or first person (author as "I") point of view	• Backdrop setting with little or no indication of time and place ("There was a little girl. She liked candy.")
• Meaning centered in a series of list-like statements ("I like my mom. And I like my dad. And I like my. . . .") or in the coherence of the action itself ("He blew up the plane. Pow!")	• Some rounding, usually in physical description; relationship between characters is action-driven; objective point of view is common	• Skeletal indication of time and place often held in past time ("Once there was . . ."); little relationship to other narrative elements
• Beginning statement of theme— often explicit and didactic ("The mean witch chased the children and she shouldn't have done that."); occasionally the theme, though well stated, does not fit the story	• Continued rounding in physical description, particularly stereotypical features ("wart on the end of her nose"); beginning rounding in feeling, often through straightforward vocabulary ("She was sad, glad, mad.")	• Beginning relationship between setting and other narrative elements (futuristic setting to accommodate aliens and spaceships); beginning symbolic functions of setting (often stereotypical images—forest as scary place)
• Beginning revelation of theme on both explicit and implicit levels through the more subtle things characters say and do ("He put his arm around the dog and held him close. 'You're my best pal,' he whispered.")	• Beginning insights into the motivation and intention that drives the feeling and the action of main characters often through limited omniscient point of view; beginning dynamic features (of change and growth)	• Setting becomes more essential to the development of the story in explicit ways: characters may remark on the setting or the time and place may be integral to the plot
• Beginning use of secondary themes, often tied to overarching theme, but sometimes tangential; main theme increasingly revealed through discovery rather than delivery, though explicit thematic statements still predominate	• Further rounding (in feeling and motivation); dynamic features appear in the central characters and in the relationships between characters; move to omniscient point of view (getting into the minds of characters)	• Setting may serve more than one function and the relationship between functions is more implicit and symbolic—for example, setting may be linked symbolically to character mood ("She hid in the grass, clutching the sharp, dry spikes, waiting.")
• Overarching theme multilayered and complex; secondary themes integrally related to primary theme or themes; both explicit and implicit revelations of theme work in harmony (" 'You can't do that to my sister!', Lou cried, moving to shield Tasha with her body.")	• Round, dynamic major characters through rich description of affect, intention, and motivation; growth occurs as a result of complex interactions between characters; most characters contribute to the development of the narrative; purposeful choice of point of view	• Setting fully integrated with the characters, action, and theme of the story; role of setting is multifunctional—setting mood, revealing character and conflict, serving as metaphor

Figure 2 Narrative Rubric *(Continued)*

Plot	**Communication**
simple ◄———————► complex static ◄———————► conflict	context-bound ◄—► reader-considerate literal ◄———————► symbolic
• One or two events with little or no conflict ("Once there was a cat. The cat liked milk.")	• Writing bound to context (you have to be there) and often dependent on drawing and talk to clarify the meaning; minimal style and tone
• Beginning sequence of events, but occasional out-of-sync occurrences; events without problem, problem without resolution, or little emotional response	• Beginning awareness of reader considerations; straightforward style and tone focused on getting the information out; first attempts at dialogue begin
• Single, linear episode with clear beginning, middle, and end; the episode contains four critical elements of problem, emotional response, action, and outcome	• Writer begins to make use of explanations and transitions ("because" and "so"); literal style centers on description ("sunny day"); tone explicit
• Plot increases in complexity with more than one episode; each episode contains problem, emotional response, action, outcome; beginning relationship between episodes	• Increased information and explanation for the reader (linking ideas as well as episodes); words more carefully selected to suit the narrative's purpose (particularly through increased use of detail in imagery)
• Stronger relationship between episodes (with the resolution in one leading to a problem in the next); beginning manipulation of the sequence through foreshadowing, and subplots	• Some experimentation with symbolism (particularly figurative language) which show reader considerations on both explicit and implicit levels; style shows increasing variety (alliteration, word play, rhythm, etc.) and tone is more implicit
• Overarching problem and resolution supported by multiple, episodes; rich variety of techniques (building suspense, foreshadowing, flashbacks, denouement) to manipulate sequence	• Careful crafting of choices in story structure as well as vocabulary demonstrate considerate orchestration of all the available resources; judicious experimentation with variety of stylistic forms which are often symbolic in nature and illuminate the other narrative elements

Wolf & Gearhart

ing to stifle creativity, they tended to avoid giving advice on content, focusing their assessment feedback mostly on convention or genre-general characteristics such as the importance of a clear "beginning, middle, and end."

Upper-grade teachers represented a departure from a focus on the child's expressive imagination toward detailed assignment-specific expectations. A good story had a "beginning, middle, and end/conclusion; stays to the point; lots of detail; at least two paragraphs; complete sentences; [no] run-on sentences; [no] rambling; proper punctuation; neat; completed all parts of the assignment." With assessment criteria such as these, upper-grade teachers conveyed a traditional view of students not as makers of meaning but as compliant learners.

The Impact of WWYR

Year 1 represented the more intensive focus on children as writers, and its impact was evident by the end of the year. We were heartened that many teachers reported a shift in focus away from skill mastery toward the making of meaning through narrative ("I don't [just] correct the convention. I have begun to ask questions to get them to think of ways to improve writing."). Kindergarten teachers expressed interest in facilitating more opportunities for "letting them tell stories."

Teachers at all grade levels reported really reading and listening to their children's stories ("I've enjoyed children's writing.") and building instruction on children's spontaneous interests and understandings of literature ("I'm now beginning to have the students look for and share their favorite phrases from the literature we read and tell us why it appeals to them."). Many teachers were beginning to recognize students as authors, a change that had potential to support assessment as a reader's response.

However, that potential was limited by complaints that WWYR may be "too sophisticated," and the apparent source of those complaints was the belief that students could not analyze narrative in the ways we were recommending: "We still have a problem with [theme] in class; they tend to think every theme is friendship." "Trying to explain plot to my kids is often difficult." "Some miss the point completely." Kindergarten and some primary teachers were particularly likely to distance themselves from the relevance of our program, and they wished for a focus just on their grade levels.

During year 2, we focused our workshops intensively on methods of assessment. Perhaps because we had far less time to share, celebrate, and criticize students' writing, the patterns of impact on teachers' beliefs were little different from the first year. Again, we found some teachers delighted with their students' writing ("I was just so impressed with what they had come with [portfolios from the prior year] and how much better their writing had gotten.") and surprised by their students' positive attitudes toward writing ("We talked about what was our favorite part of the year, and . . . a great many students said *writing* was! . . . It wasn't as much of a chore for them as I thought it was!").

In this context, more teachers expressed awareness that children can handle explicit feedback ("and then children want to fix it right away, and they go away happy and wanting to change, they're very eager to go back and write."). Indeed, at this point, some teachers were actively confronting ways that their prior assessment practices had emphasized incompetence, rather than competence: "I need to be able to see a lot more positive things from the students and not always think about the best student and evaluate from top down."

But the pattern of mixed impact persisted, as some teachers continued to raise concerns about their students' capacities as writers: "Weaving a good story is beyond them." "They don't have a clue on what revision is all about." "There isn't that much that [third graders] accomplish in a year's time that you could measure." Their deep beliefs in either a "skills" view or a "creative writing" view were the two predominant counters to the WWYR approach to assessment.

On the one hand, the teachers invested in skills either rejected WWYR for its irrelevance or suggested revisions of WWYR assessments that fit a "scope and sequence" analysis of writing growth. Thus the first quote illustrates a primary teacher's worries about time lost to teaching writing skills.

Spending so much time and attention to the rubric and the feedback form . . . I actually did less writing than I normally would have done. . . . [Now] they don't even know how to write a sentence. (2nd-grade teacher, 6/11/93)

In her view, the purpose of a "writing" program is to provide students opportunities to practice composing grammatical sentences, and therefore WWYR is limited in its relevance. The second quote illustrates a revisionist position grounded in a deep commitment to a skills view of writing development:

I think that [WWYR should have] some type of structure so that . . . in first grade . . . you would lay out what the narrative should contain—a simple plot, a simple scene, no more than two characters, and then, the next year, you would take one of those and develop it further, maybe the third year you'd put dialogue in, so you're following the sequence down the line. (1st-grade teacher, 7/2/93)

On the other hand, the teachers invested in "creative writing" felt that WWYR's analytic emphasis violated their understandings of whole language, writing process approaches. Our substantive focus on narrative content was viewed as inconsistent with a child-centered classroom. When some teachers planned a narrative assignment or had specific criticisms of children's writing, they felt guilty about restraining the freedom of the child.

When I read Graves [1983] and Atwell [1987] . . . they say . . . when we assign a topic to the children, we're still making them dependent upon us as writers. [On the other hand], you cannot draw from an empty well. If you don't give the child something to draw from, then all they do is pull from their own limited experience. And yet, there has to be time when what's important to them is what they're writing about rather than the assigned topic. . . . So do we have two *different* writing [methods]? . . . It is overwhelming. (5th-grade teacher, 6/30/93)

This teacher is ambivalent, worried that constructive assessment may silence children's voices.

Case Examples

We have selected two cases that represent patterns of resistance to WWYR founded on beliefs about students as writers. Neither case is typical of our 16 teachers. Indeed, as we report elsewhere (Gearhart, Wolf, Burkey, & Whittaker, 1994), there were teachers whose knowledge, beliefs, and practice were deeply and positively impacted by their involvement with WWYR. The cases below, however, serve to highlight two persistent philosophical orientations that would not be moved in the face of new assessments. Although both teachers, Bert and Peter (the names are pseudonyms), gave a polite nod to our program, their firmly-held beliefs were not swayed by the methods we used.

Bert

An experienced teacher new to the primary level, Bert tended to follow the lead of his grade-level colleague in planning narrative units and utilizing methods of narrative assessment. Less knowledgeable about narrative than his partner, Bert was able to make minor use of some of the WWYR materials we distributed, such as "the [guide]book . . . that's helpful," but, for the most part, the materials seemed overwhelming to him: "There seems to be so much coming at you, you really have limited time to touch base with resource materials."

Bert's comments about writing assessment in early workshops led us to believe that he did not see children as capable authors ("I used to ask older kids things. But with the primary grade I don't."). In year 2, we noted changes in his understandings of the developmental nature of children's writing. He learned that children were capable of handling theme, particularly if it was explicitly discussed in class. Thus, with regard to the *Frog and Toad* unit he and his colleague designed (Lobel, 1971, 1979), Bert said, "The kids understood the theme of friendship. It was something that they could easily write down and identify with."

Nevertheless, Bert's emphasis on "simpler" and "basic" curriculum for primary children did not change, as he conveys in his reflections on the relevance of the WWYR rubric.

As we practice grading other papers, you know, I scratch my head and say, "I'm kinda glad I'm in the [primary] grade 'cause it's pretty basic and it's pretty simple . . ." So I keep it kinda simple and don't feel like I need to, you know, refer to the rubric so much. (Bert, 1st-grade teacher, 6/14/93)

With this rationale, he departed from his colleague by providing his students with a simpler version of the WWYR assessment materials. When his students planned their stories, they used a form that included four components (theme, plot, character, setting) but omitted the communication circle in the center of the form.

When I'm talking with first graders, and they're beginning to write for the first time in January or February . . . it just seemed to be a simpler approach, for what I was trying to do with kids who were writing for the first time. (6/14/93)

Comparing the remaining four components to the children's familiar game of four-square, Bert felt that the communication circle in the form was too complex for his students. By removing the communication circle—which encompassed the necessary writing tools of style, tone, and audience awareness—he virtually eliminated attention to language. He felt strongly that while first graders could write a brief plot, with two characters in a limited setting with a minimal theme, they could not manipulate language for particular effects.

Overall Bert's attitude represents his determination to simplify materials for younger children. He had little faith in his students' abilities to become accomplished writers.

Peter

Peter was an upper grade teacher who joined the faculty and the WWYR project in the second year. Peter's resistance to WWYR derived from multiple sources—his limited understandings of narrative, his com-

mitment to "creative" writing, and his beliefs that his students' capacities were limited.

Uncomfortable with the analytical WWYR workshop conversations, he commented that the workshops were the most "intellectual" experiences he had ever had concerning text. His own difficulties with the material were linked to his beliefs that his students had comparable difficulties. Peter felt, for example, that the subtle devices of motivation and intention were unavailable to his children.

These stories that I'm reading [to the students] are not just telling of events, but there is a plot to it, and there is a theme to it, and I think kids don't really do that, at least not the ones that I have worked with. (Peter, 6th-grade teacher, 6/5/93)

His students, he felt, saw writing as an assignment to finish rather than a meaning to be communicated: "They didn't quite grasp theme. . . . They just wanted to write it and finish it and turn it in and get it graded and be done." We heard much from Peter about what his students could not do.

Perhaps because he viewed the "technical" aspects of writing to be beyond his students' capacities, Peter was resistant to the critical stance we asked teachers to take in their assessments of students' writing, believing that a teacher should not tamper with a child's personal writing process. He believed many children cannot handle specific feedback.

Last year, I had this one girl. She just—the blood would just drain out of her face. It was really painful for me, 'cause she was one of the most rambling writers I ever encountered and she needed a lot of help. But she couldn't handle . . . the criticism. So, for me, it was more of an issue of helping her with that issue alone, rather than even with the writing. (6/5/93)

Prior to being introduced to WWYR, Peter's teaching reflected a particularly open-ended view of process writing, which emphasized that children's writing was sacrosanct and not to be criticized by the teacher. Thus, in his teaching, Peter was most concerned with enhancing his students' creativity. He labeled himself a "writing process" teacher, and felt that a major part of the process was "allowing [children] to

write whatever they feel like writing, and then guiding each individual child along, in terms of where they are with their writing."

But Peter's guidance was limited both by his lack of knowledge about narrative and his strong aversion to giving any assessment feedback at all. Because Peter focused on the negative aspects of criticism, he could not see the role of constructive criticism in helping to build a student's confidence.

Peter's differentiation of creativity from criticism represents a novice approach to central ideas in process writing. The purpose of any kind of conferencing, whether with the teacher or with peers, is to hold a conversation about the effectiveness of the writing—to compliment and question different choices, to encourage an expansion of the writer's vision. By avoiding attention to criticism, Peter set up an atmosphere for "anything goes"—an atmosphere that may serve to make children feel more comfortable for a while, but one that will not support a writer's growth in developing new styles, genres, and audiences in the future.

Unexamined Beliefs

In the past 2 decades, teachers in the writing classroom have shifted from a concern for convention to an emphasis on communication and making meaning (Atwell, 1987; Dyson & Freedman, 1991). Through the workshops they attend and the reading they do, teachers are becoming more and more knowledgeable about a new view of writing as a process to be supported rather than a final product to be achieved. Still, the gap between awareness of new writing reforms and the ability to implement the reforms is large, and there is many a slip between the cup of knowledge and the lip of belief. In this article, we have examined the slips between the knowledge about narrative writing that we offered and the beliefs of teachers about their students' capacities by demonstrating how elementary teachers' beliefs about their students as writers mediate their acceptance and investment in new methods of assessing students' narrative writing.

While teachers in our study grew demonstrably in their competencies with narrative assessment, their growth was most typically marked by only partial alignment with a fundamental tenet of WWYR that children are eager to "make meaning" through narrative and will make use of the insights of a thoughtful reader. Not every teacher was ready and able to embrace a developmental approach that veered from a sequential step-by-step vision. Teachers might be charmed by their students' writing, excited by their students' growth, and eager for more involvement and opportunities for response to children's work, but otherwise daunted by our requests for substantive critique. Even as they commented on growth and shared with pride examples of their students' stories, they complained about what their students could not understand and accomplish. We regard this attitude of complaint and negativity as a failing of our inservice methods. Teachers held beliefs that we did not attempt to unsettle directly.

One unexamined belief was that writing is a set of skills that can be charted hierarchically and should be taught and assessed sequentially. Skills are seen as discrete and dichotomous in nature—a child has either mastered them (e.g., writing a complete sentence) or not, and, if not, it is the teacher's job to ensure mastery. This belief provided a basis for rejecting WWYR's views of narrative (as beyond most students' level of maturity) and of pedagogy (as presuming a voice that the child does not yet possess).

A second unexamined belief was that teachers tended to perceive criticism as a way of silencing children. In our work, we had advocated for constructive criticism as an opportunity for children to develop a creative voice, and we did not recognize that teachers might perceive criticism as negative. Even though *we* were convinced, we had not persuaded some teachers that criticism is a way of expanding children's voices and helping them to find new genres and styles in which to express themselves. To be sure, creativity is vital in writing, but there is little creativity without dialogue, communication, and collaboration. Assessment is critical.

As Bakhtin's work demonstrates, "Meaning is always a function of at least two consciousnesses. thus, texts are always shared" (Clark & Holquist, 1984, p. 151). To share a text does not mean to look at it and put a smiley face or a quick compliment at the top of the page ("Good work!"). To share a text means to value the work with substantive attention, to ask questions, to push the metaphors, and to guide the writing.

In hindsight, we recognize that we were much like some of the teachers in our study, equally guilty in our failure to offer sound criticism. We were so eager to have the teachers feel comfortable with new assessments that we failed to question their long-held beliefs about what children could not do and what children could not tolerate. When we shared examples of children's writing with the intention of countering the teachers' focus on children's limited competence, we left unchallenged the teachers' belief that the writing we displayed was from exceptionally gifted children. Nor did we question specific practices—such as designating the home as the context for kindergartners' dictated stories and reserving the classroom for the teaching of skills—and as a result, teachers felt validated in continuing such practices.

To counter teachers' beliefs that students lack both skill and voice, as well as to improve our own inservice practices with new assessments, we would make three changes. First, we would create a primary focus to allow us to share what is known about the development of very young writers and to address squarely the tendencies of primary teachers to see WWYR as irrelevant to their students.

Second, for teachers of all grade levels, we would ask teachers to develop cases of their students as writers. Teachers could share their students' writing and tell stories about their students as young authors. Videotapes of children's engagement with their work, peers, parents, and teachers could provide memorable images of children's eagerness to compose, share their work with others, and respond to critique.

Third, we would model effective conferencing, either directly with children in their classrooms or through videotapes of teachers holding productive assessment conferences. These models would serve to demonstrate the validating and growth-nurturing powers of criticism, as opposed to a more negative view.

Conclusion

The art of excellent teaching often lies in the balance between comfort and challenge—how to help our students feel comfortable with new ideas and simultaneously challenge them to reflect on and extend their accomplishments. This is particularly true in writing, for as students are invited in to the substantive work of making meaning, they need an atmosphere that will endorse their risks as well as encourage them to expand their meanings. The same is true in helping teachers come to new methods of teaching writing.

In our own work to increase teachers' knowledge of current ideas in the curriculum, instruction, and assessment of writing, we did not sufficiently address teachers' beliefs—their convictions about what children and their teachers can and cannot do. In the balance between comfort and challenge, we tipped the scales too often in favor of comfort.

Thus, in our criticisms of our work—often the product of extended discussions between ourselves as well as insights from our teachers in final interviews and follow-up conversations—we have come to discover that there are no crystal ball secrets for the future success of new assessments. In Lloyd Alexander's (1992) humorous tale, *The Fortune Tellers,* a young man asks if he will have a long life. The old seer gazes into his crystal and replies, "The longest. . . . Only one thing might cut it short; an early demise."

Will it be the case that new assessments are destined to be short lived? Certainly, such a prediction is not unnecessarily dire considering the early death of the California Learning Assessment System (McDonnell, 1996). However, we are hopeful that the lessons learned here and elsewhere will serve to help those who are attempting to "build assessments toward which [we] want educators to teach" (Resnick &

Resnick, 1992, p. 59). Life, as the fortune-teller intimates, is what you make it—"You shall wed your true love if you find her and she agrees." To secure such agreement in our work to develop and implement new assessments, we must make our conversations with teachers open to criticism as well as collaboration.

Notes

The work reported herein was supported in part by the Apple Classrooms of Tomorrow℠ Project, Advanced Development Group, Apple Computer, Inc.; the California Assessment Collaborative; and the Educational Research and Development Center Program cooperative agreement R117G10027 and CFDA catalog number 84.117G as administered by the Office of Educational Research and Improvement, U.S. Department of Education.

The findings and opinions expressed in this report do not reflect the position or policies of Apple Computer, the California Assessment Collaborative, the Office of Educational Research and Improvement, or the U.S. Department of Education.

1. In prior reports, we have described our program in detail, reported on its impact on teachers' understandings of narrative genre, and analyzed the role of this knowledge in teachers' capacities to interpret and score children's writing in meaningful ways (Baker, Gearhart, Herman, Tierney, & Whittaker, 1991; Gearhart, Herman, Novak, & Wolf, 1995; Gearhart & Wolf, 1994; Gearhart, Wolf, Burkey, & Whittaker, 1994; Herman, Gearhart, & Baker, 1993; S. A. Wolf & Gearhart, 1993a, 1993b, 1994).

References

Alexander, L. (1992). *The fortune-tellers,* New York: Dutton Children's Books.

Atwell, N. (1987). *In the middle: Writing, reading, and learning with adolescents.* Portsmouth, NH: Boynton/Cook-Heinemann.

Baker, E. L., Gearhart, M., Herman, J. L., Tierney, R., & Whittaker, A. K. (1991). Stevens Creek portfolio project: Writing assessment in the technology classroom. *Portfolio News, 2*(3), 7–9.

Clark, K., & Holquist, M. (1984). *Mikhail Bakhtin.* Cambridge, MA: Harvard University Press.

Dyson, A. H. (in press). Children out of bounds: The power of case studies in expanding visions of literacy development. In J. Flood, S. B. Heath, & D. Lapp (Eds.), *A handbook for literacy educators: Research on teaching the communicative and visual arts.* New York: Macmillan.

Dyson, A. A., & Freedman, S. W. (1991). Writing. In J. Flood, J. M. Jensen, D. Lapp, & J. R. Squire (Eds.), *Handbook of research on teaching the English language arts* (pp. 754–774). New York: Macmillan.

Gearhart, M., Herman, J. L., Novak, J. R., & Wolf, S. A. (1995). Toward the instructional utility of large-scale writing assessments: Validation of a new narrative rubric. *Assessing Writing, 2,* 207–242.

Gearhart, M., & Wolf, S. A. (1994). Engaging teachers in assessment of their students' writing: The role of subject matter knowledge. *Assessing Writing, 1,* 67–90.

Gearhart, M., Wolf, S. A., Burkey, B., & Whittaker, A. K. (1994). *Engaging teachers in assessment of their students' narrative writing: Impact on teachers' knowledge and practice* (CSE Technical Report No. 377). Los Angeles: University of California, Center for Research on Evaluation, Standards, and Student Testing.

Goldenberg, C., & Gallimore, R. (1991). Local knowledge, research knowledge, and educational change: A case study of early Spanish reading improvement. *Educational Researcher, 20*(8), 2–14.

Graves, D. (1983). *Writing: Teachers and children at work.* Portsmouth, NH: Heinemann.

Herman, J. L., Gearhart, M., & Baker, E. L. (1993). Assessing writing portfolios: Issues in the validity and meaning of scores. *Educational Assessment, 1,* 201–224.

Huck, C., Hepler, S., & Hickman, J. (1987). *Children's literature in the elementary school.* New York: Holt, Rinehart, & Winston.

Lobel, A. (19971). *Frog and toad together.* New York: Scholastic.

Lobel, A. (1979). *Days with frog and toad.* New York: Harper & Row.

Lukens, R. (1990). *A critical handbook of children's literature.* New York: HarperCollins.

Lurie, A. (1990). *Don't tell the grown-ups: Subversive children's literature.* Boston: Little, Brown.

McDonnell, L. M. (1996). *The politics of state testing: Implementing new student assessments* (Deliverable to CRESST/OERI). Los Angeles: University of California, Center for Research on Evaluation, Standards, and Student Testing.

Resnick, L. B., & Resnick, D. P. (1992). Assessing the thinking curriculum: New tools for educational reform. In B. R. Gifford & M. C. O'Connor (Eds.), *Changing assessments: Alternative view of aptitude, achievement and instruction* (pp. 37–75). Boston: Kluwer.

Sloan, G. D. (1991). *The child as critic: Teaching literature in elementary and middle schools.* New York: Teachers College Press.

Sulzby, E. (1991). The development of the young child and the emergence of literacy. In J. Flood, J. M. Jensen, D. Lapp, & J. R. Squire (Eds.), *Handbook of research on teaching the English language arts* (pp. 272–285). New York: Macmillan.

Wolf, D. P. (1993). Assessment as an episode of learning. In R. Bennett & W. Ward (Eds.), *Construction vs. choice in cognitive measurement* (pp. 213–240). Hillsdale, NJ: Erlbaum.

Wolf, D. P., Bixby, J., Glenn, J., & Gardner, H. (1991). To use their minds well: Investigating new forms of student assessment. *Review of Research in Education, 17,* 31–74.

Wolf, S. A., & Gearhart, M. (1993a). *Writing What You Read: Assessment as a learning event* (CSE Technical Report No. 358). Los Angeles: University of California, Center for the Study of Evaluation.

Wolf, S. A., & Gearhart, M. (1993b). *Writing What You Read: A guidebook for the assessment of children's narratives* (CSE Resource Paper No. 10). Los Angeles: University of California, Center for the Study of Evaluation.

Wolf, S. A., & Gearhart, M. (1994). Writing What You Read: A framework for narrative assessment. *Language Arts, 71*(6), 425–445.

Wolf, S. A., & Heath, S. B. (1992). *The braid of literature: Children's worlds of reading.* Cambridge, MA: Harvard University Press.

 Article Review Form at end of book.

WiseGuide Wrap-Up

- Effective strategies can be used to allow teachers to observe, understand, and assist students as they read.

- Policies can be developed that allow for included students to demonstrate their progress and that are fair to the general education students.

- Effective principles for literacy assessment are sensitive to complexity and diversity and begin from inside rather than outside the classroom.

- Assessment should be measured in terms of its relationship to teaching and learning.

- Teachers' beliefs about their students as writers can mediate their acceptance of and investment in new methods of assessing students' narrative writing.

R.E.A.L. Sites

This list provides a print preview of typical **Coursewise** R.E.A.L. sites. There are over 100 such sites at the **Courselinks**™ site. The danger in printing URLs is that web sites can change overnight. As we went to press, these sites were functional using the URLs provided. If you come across one that isn't, please let us know via email to: webmaster@coursewise.com. Use your Passport to access the most current list of R.E.A.L. sites at the **Courselinks**™ site.

Site name: National Assessment of Educational Progress

URL: http://nces.ed.gov/nationsreportcard/

Why is it R.E.A.L.? The National Assessment of Educational Progress (NAEP) is mandated by Congress to provide objective data about the levels of knowledge, skills, and student performance at national, regional, and, on a trial basis, state levels. This site provides access to information and data about government-mandated, nationwide assessments at the national, regional, and state levels.

Key topics: nationwide assessment

Try this: Navigate to the State-by-State Results site and find your state's 1994 NAEP Reading Report. Discuss the implications of the information on students and teachers in your state.

Site name: The National Center for Fair and Open Testing

URL: http://www.fairtest.org

Why is it R.E.A.L.? The National Center for Fair and Open Testing (FairTest) is an advocacy organization working to end the abuses, misuses, and flaws of standardized testing and to ensure that the evaluation of students and workers is fair, open, and educationally sound. The site provides survey information on state-by-state assessment practices for K–12, university, and employment tests. The site also provides links to publications, articles, and fact sheets on standardized and alternative assessment.

Key topics: standardized educational testing and alternative assessment

Try this: Navigate to the State-by-State Survey of State Assessment Practices and find your state's report. Discuss the results of the survey for your state in light of what you know about how assessment must be integrated with curriculum and instruction to support learning.

When Children Struggle with the Reading Process: Literacy and Diversity and the At-Risk Learner

Learning Objectives

- Discuss why providing delayed readers with exemplary reading instruction may not be enough to assure their academic success and what other high-quality programs need to be considered.

- Identify administrative policies and instructional procedures that may contribute to the failure of remedial reading.

- Identify critical features of successful reading programs for at-risk first-grade students.

- Discuss why teachers should take language differences into account in the teaching-learning process.

- Describe teaching strategies that can be used to help diverse groups of learners read and comprehend material that would appear to be considerably beyond their reading levels.

- Identify the characteristics of effective individualized instruction for special education students in a resource classroom.

Every day, a wide range of children come together in classrooms across the nation. These children come from homes that are culturally, linguistically, racially, and ethnically diverse and some are economically disadvantaged. Some children have learning disabilities or special needs, such as speech and hearing impairments, visual disorders, emotional disturbances, autism, mental retardation, and giftedness. The diversity within a classroom creates a unique learning community. For some children, reading acquisition is easy; for others, it is difficult. It is important to understand the literacy needs of all types of children.

How do teachers design instruction to meet the needs of all students? First, and most important, teachers must believe that all children can learn to read. Beliefs, attitudes, and expectations about children influence instruction. Believing that all children can become readers is the first step in creating an effective literacy program and developing a sense of community that respects the unique qualities of each child.

The role of the classroom teacher is a critical factor in ensuring that all children are successful readers. Teachers must be knowledgeable about the reading process, which takes into account every child's prior knowledge, experiences, and home language. They must create learning environments that support cognitive, language, and social development through authentic learning activities relevant to the children's lives. Teachers must communicate high expectations to all children that will enhance their potential for success.

Regardless of optimal classroom instruction and environments, some children experience great difficulty acquiring literacy. These children may require additional support from professionals outside the classroom. Some children may be identified with a learning disability that qualifies them for special education services. These children may be pulled out of the classroom for supplemental instruction in a resource room, or a special education teacher may provide support in the regular classroom. Many schools have reading specialists to assist children who are at-risk but do not qualify for special education services. The reading specialist is usually trained in one of several intervention programs, such as Reading Recovery, Success for All, and Early Intervention in Reading. It is important that supplementary instruction is consistent with regular classroom instruction and is in addition to, rather than a replacement for, regular classroom instruction.

Teachers must be knowledgeable about effective instructional practices that meet the diverse needs of all students. It is also important for teachers to understand the program components and teaching practices of special education and intervention programs. The articles in Section 6 discuss issues related to effective literacy instruction and programs for at-risk and special needs learners. "There's More to Teaching At-Risk and Delayed Readers Than Good Reading Instruction" describes one school's experiences with designing high-quality programs across the curriculum that go beyond providing excellent reading instruction for children with severe reading difficulties. "The 11 Deadly Sins of Remedial Reading Programs" examines the factors of remedial reading programs that are inconsistent with research and presents some ideas about constructing effective early intervention programs. "Preventing Reading Failure: A Review of Five Effective Programs" presents the common features identified in successful early intervention programs that appear to be related to preventing reading problems. " 'Dat Teacher Be Hollin at Us'—What Is Ebonics?" provides a reason for teachers to take language differences into account in the teaching-learning process. "Boosting Reading Success" describes several teaching strategies that can be used to help diverse groups of learners read and comprehend material that would appear to be considerably beyond their reading levels. "Broken Promises: Reading Instruction in the Resource Room" identifies the characteristics of effective individualized instruction for special education students in a resource classroom.

? Questions ?

Reading 24. Why can the experiences of teachers during the past three years at Benchmark School provide timely and important information today about reading instruction for struggling readers? What are the key components of a reading program for children who read below grade level?

Reading 25. What recommendations does the author offer concerning phonics and word recognition? Why shouldn't teachers treat reversals as a symptom of a reading problem?

Reading 26. At the beginning of the article, Pikulski calls attention to the mythical town first referred to in Slavin, Madden, Karweit, Dolan and Wasik (1991). In this town, 30 percent of the children were falling ill from contaminated drinking water. The town council rejected a proposal by the town engineer to build a water treatment plant. The town council felt it was too expensive of a project, because then funds would not be available to treat current victims and because 70 percent of the children never fell ill. What is the relevance of this mythical town and its reluctance to build the water treatment plant to the current state of education? Pikulski concludes the article with the statement, "It's time we built the water treatment plant!" What arguments does he include in his article to support this statement?

Reading 27. What is the evidence that Ebonics is a language? Why should a student's primary or home language be a consideration in the teaching-learning process?

Reading 28. Which models and strategies are particularly effective for teaching diverse and struggling readers? What kinds and levels of material are best for students with special needs?

Reading 29. Why does the title of this article declare that reading instruction in the resource room is a broken promise? What kind of reading instruction should students with learning disabilities receive, according to the authors?

Why can the experiences of teachers during the past three years at Benchmark School provide timely and important information today about reading instruction for struggling readers? What are the key components of a reading program for children who read below grade level?

There's More to Teaching At-Risk and Delayed Readers Than Good Reading Instruction

Irene W. Gaskins

Gaskins, founder and Director of Benchmark School, has taught at the elementary, middle school, high school, and university levels. She works with children daily as she collaborates with staff to develop programs and foster professional development. She may be contacted at Benchmark School, 2107 N. Providence Road, Media, PA 19063, USA.

Benchmark is a school for children who read below grade level, have average or better potential, and whose reading delay cannot be attributed to primary emotional or neurological problems. Most enter the school as non-readers. During the early years of the school some children attended the school for a half-day reading program, returning in the afternoon to their regular schools, and others attended full day for a total elementary program. Both options included a daily, 2½-hour reading block that featured a great deal of reading and responding to what was read (Gaskins, 1980). The half-day program was phased out during the early years of the school because it separated the teaching of reading from the rest of the curriculum. Now all children who attend the school receive a full elementary or middle school curriculum. At present the student body consists of 125 lower school students and 50 middle school students.

During Benchmark's first 25 years, the staff taught over 3,000 delayed readers who were enrolled in either the regular school year or summer school programs. The responses of these students to instruction at Benchmark, and at the schools they attended after Benchmark, as well as study of the professional literature, have led us to make some tentative hypotheses about what works in teaching delayed readers. We hope that our hypotheses about programming for at-risk and delayed readers will lead to fruitful discussions with other professionals as we continue to refine our understanding of how best to meet students' needs.

Foundation Upon Which Successful Programs Are Built

Research suggests that the foundation of a school initiative to provide at-risk and delayed readers with the skills and strategies they need to meet with and maintain success in regular classrooms is composed of at least four critical elements.

Staff Development

The cornerstone of instructional programs that produce significant results in student progress is staff

Gaskins, Irene W. (1998, April). There's more to teaching at-risk and delayed readers than good reading instruction. *The Reading Teacher*, 51(7), 534–547. Reprinted with permission of Irene W. Gaskins and the International Reading Association. All rights reserved.

development (Darling-Hammond, 1996). Staff development needs to be ongoing, collaborative, and in-depth as it engages teachers and support staff in exploring and understanding research-based principles and theories about instruction, curriculum, and cognition. The goal is that staff development will lead to the staff creating, and taking ownership of, quality programs that meet the needs of at-risk and delayed readers. Understanding instructional principles and theories allows teachers to make informed decisions about long-term program planning and on-the-spot instruction. Another important aspect of staff development is principals and supervisors spending time in classrooms to support, coach, and collaborate with teachers as they meet the daily challenges of providing at-risk and delayed readers with quality instruction. . . .

Quality Instruction and Support Services to Address Roadblocks

A second critical ingredient is quality instruction and support services tailored to address the academic and nonacademic roadblocks that stand in the way of success in regular classrooms (Dryfoos, 1996). For example, delayed readers, unlike their more successful classmates, often do not figure out on their own how to learn a word or make an inference. For them, learning these skills may be contingent upon instruction from the very best teachers—instruction that includes explicit explanations, modeling, and scaffolded practice that is engaging and meaningful. And, more than likely, they will need this kind of high-quality instruction not merely during reading instruction, but across the curriculum. Our experience at Benchmark suggests that teaching delayed readers how to read is only a first step in dealing with their roadblocks to academic success. In addition to high-quality instruction across the curriculum, students often need additional support services to address social and emotional needs and maladaptive cognitive styles. . . .

Congruence

The third critical ingredient is congruence between the remedial program and regular classroom programs. Although there is movement in the United States toward an inclusion model that brings specialists into regular classrooms to collaborate with the classroom teacher in teaching at-risk and delayed readers, many programs continue to pull students out of their regular classrooms for remedial instruction that is poorly coordinated with the curriculum and instruction of the regular classroom (Johnston, Allington, & Afflerbach, 1985). No matter how good, pull-out instruction is not usually sufficient to create successful students. At-risk and delayed readers have the best chance for success if classroom instruction and remedial instruction are not only of high quality but also congruent. Research has consistently shown that even when academic progress of at-risk and delayed readers is accelerated as a result of remedial programs, these learning gains are difficult to maintain unless there is congruence between remedial and regular classroom instruction (Shanahan & Barr, 1995). Remedial teachers must prepare delayed readers with the skills and strategies they need for success in regular classrooms.

Time

Missing in most initiatives to teach at-risk and delayed readers is sufficient time to accomplish the goal of preparing students to be successful in the mainstream. Most initiatives envision support in terms of a year or two. The Benchmark staff's experience suggests that (a) preparation for success in the mainstream requires that delayed readers spend more time receiving quality instruction than their peers in regular classes, and (b) delayed readers continue to need support over many years. Thus, ideally, programs for every at-risk and delayed reader should begin as early as possible and continue across the curriculum throughout the elementary and middle school years. . . .

The Development of Programs for Delayed Readers

Reading Lots of Books

During the 1970s, Benchmark students were taught reading in small groups of 2 to 4 students who had similar needs; groups progressed through basal reader levels at rates 1½ to 2 times that of students in regular schools, for example, moving from the 1-2 level to the 3-1 level in one year. While regular school students typically read one basal per level and spent hours completing workbook pages and skillsheets, our students read 5 to 10 basal readers at each level, as well as many trade books. Workbooks and publishers' skillsheets were seldom used. In the early years of the school, we used out-of-date basals discarded by other schools and trade books donated by schools, staff, and parents. Parents supported their children's reading by making sure that their children read each evening for 30 minutes at their independent level, and by reading to their children for an additional 20 minutes from children's literature supplied by the school. In class each day teachers held individual book conferences with students about their home reading. These home and school reading activities continue today. . . .

During the mid-1970s we decided that the age of entry to the Benchmark program might be a factor in the difficulties some of our former students experienced when they returned to the mainstream. As a result, we began giving first preference in admissions to the youngest students. These younger children exhibited less emotional overlay and fewer behavior problems than the older students, confirming our suspicions that entering Benchmark after years of failure made remediation more difficult. As with the older students, we were successful in teaching these younger children to read.

In following the progress of these students as they returned to regular schools, we learned that they were often found happily engaged in reading trade books (even when they should have been attending to other aspects of the curriculum) and that they made insightful contributions to discussions about what they had read. Our follow-up also revealed that these former students had difficulty demonstrating in writing their understanding of trade books, basal reader stories, and content area subject matter. Difficulty expressing themselves in writing, difficulty handling content area assignments, and difficulty exhibiting style and dispositional characteristics of successful students (e.g., attentiveness, organization, conscientiousness) were the problems most often cited when discussing the poor academic performance of former Benchmark students. As a result, we became convinced that merely accelerating the reading ability of delayed readers was not sufficient for school success. Many, if not most, of our students seemed to need reading instruction, plus something more. Consequently, our search for an appropriate program for delayed readers widened beyond teaching students how to read trade books and basals.

Expressing Ideas in Writing

One problem that concerned us was our students' poor written expression. We searched professional journals for insights into how to teach our delayed readers to express themselves adequately in writing. We discovered, and our experience confirmed, that children with reading problems usually demonstrate an even greater and more enduring lag in writing skills than they do in reading (Critchley & Critchley, 1978; Frauenheim, 1978; Kass, 1977). We invited Graves (1977) to present several inservice programs at Benchmark. With these inservice meetings as a catalyst, the staff collaborated to develop a process approach to writing that not only succeeded in teaching our reluctant writers to write, but also seemed to enhance their reading ability (Gaskins, 1982). In the years since we implemented a process approach, we have continued to refine our writing program and, through explicit explanations, teach students how to write both expository and narrative text.

Once the process writing program was in place, we added hand-me-down computers to our classrooms, so that students could learn word processing skills. Students found revising and editing much more palatable when revised copies of their pieces could be produced by computer rather than by recopying drafts. Word processing also improved the legibility, spelling, and organization of students' writing.

Reading in the Content Areas

Another newly discovered problem we addressed about the same time as we initiated a process approach to writing was the difficulty our students experienced reading and learning from content area textbooks. Once again, a review of the research was conducted. . . . Based on our study and the needs of our students, the staff developed methods to address intent to learn; schema development; active involvement in searching for meaning; and the synthesis, reorganization, and application of what was learned (Gaskins, 1981). A key feature of these lessons was providing students with advance organizers, discussions about what was to be accomplished, what they presently knew, and an overview of the new content. Lessons also featured the scaffolding necessary for success, including daily reviews, homework checks, guided practice, and corrective feedback. We later learned that explicit strategy instruction that would put students in charge of their own learning was missing from these lessons. We had developed excellent lessons in how to read a text, but these lessons were too teacher driven to create students who understood how to be self-regulated learners, thinkers, and problem solvers.

Learning Words and Decoding

In the early 1980s we became convinced that instruction in neither synthetic phonics nor context clues was meeting all of our students' needs in decoding. . . .

With Patricia Cunningham and Richard Anderson as consultants, we developed a Grades 1–8 program for teaching students to identify un-

known words using analogous known words (Gaskins et al., 1988). In this program students are taught key words for the 120 most common phonograms (spelling patterns) in our language, as well as how to use these key words to decode unknown words (Gaskins, Downer, & Gaskins, 1986). For example, knowing the key word *king* helps a student decode *sing*, and knowing the key words *can* and *her* helps a student decode *banter*. As a result of being taught to use known words to decode unknown words, our students improved significantly in their decoding ability (Gaskins, Gaskins, Anderson, & Schommer, 1995). . . .

Between 1970 and 1994 the staff continued to evaluate our reading program, study the professional literature, and make changes to address our delayed readers' needs; yet as we began our 25th year, two literacy issues still puzzled us. These were how to help all students achieve automaticity in reading words and how to improve students' spelling ability. Although by the early 1990s the vast majority of our students read with automaticity and good comprehension upon graduation from Benchmark, about 15% were exceedingly slow readers, and these same students tended to be poor spellers. We suspected that we had designed a word identification program that eventually worked for most of our students, but not all. . . .

Although the analogy approach to word identification that we designed in the early 1980s produced better results than our previous attempts to teach delayed readers to decode, we had a hunch we could make it even better. We had observed that nearly all of our students arrived at Benchmark stranded in the early phases of word learning. Even after a year of instruction, many still had not learned the key words with high-frequency phonograms in a fully analyzed way. Thus they were unable to call them to mind to use in decoding unknown words. In 1994 we added a sight-word-learning strategy to our word identification program. We now teach students how to learn sight words by analyzing the sounds they hear in each word and matching those sounds to the letters they see.

Our initial data suggest that current students who have been taught to fully analyze words in this way are making significantly better progress in word learning than a comparison group who received only the analogy program but were not instructed in word learning (Gaskins, Ehri, Cress, O'Hara, & Donnelly, 1996).

Understanding How to Learn

Despite the changes we made in our curriculum during the late 1970s and early 1980s, we still did not produce students who could enter regular schools and be successful across the curriculum. Some students who were reading on a level commensurate with their regular school peers when they graduated from Benchmark were not as successful as we would have expected. Teachers in the regular schools often described our former students as employing unproductive strategies for learning, remembering, and completing assignments. Thus, during the 1980s, teaching students how to learn became the focus for inservice meetings, research seminars, and teacher-supervisor classroom collaboration.

We discovered that students who are delayed in reading also usually do not figure out on their own the strategies that are characteristic of successful students (Chan & Cole, 1986; Wong, 1985). They have few intuitions about how the mind works nor have they discovered, as most successful students have, how to take control of the learning process. We began to explore the literature about the cognitive and metacognitive strategies that are characteristic of successful students and, as a result of this study, set about developing a comprehensive strategies instructional program (Gaskins, 1988; Gaskins & Elliot, 1991). . . .

Applying Strategies Across the Curriculum

We began teaching a course called Psych 101 to middle school students and LAT (Learning and Thinking) to lower school students. We organized these courses around a formula for intelligent behavior (IB): IB = knowledge + control + motivation

(Gaskins & Elliot, 1991). With respect to the first element of intelligent behavior, we guided students to the awareness that acquiring knowledge includes knowledge about more than the content of school subject matter. They also need knowledge about skills and strategies, as well as about the traits and dispositions that undergird successful school performance. Each of these was discussed with students as it related to how they learn. . . . Acquisition of different kinds of knowledge, however, is only one part of what it takes to be intelligent. *How* and *if* knowledge is used were issues central to our students' success or failure.

The "how" and "if" involve control, the second element of intelligent behavior. We taught students that being in charge of how their brains work—the control element of intelligent behavior—requires active involvement and the ability to reflect on and manage one's thinking. Students were taught that they needed to take charge of tasks, situations, and their own personal learner characteristics and were shown how to do it. The *how* was to be accomplished by learning strategies for acquiring, understanding, remembering, and completing tasks, as well as by learning how to select, apply, and monitor these strategies.

The third element of intelligent behavior is motivation—the affective component of intelligent behavior. We shared with students that motivation is the result of one's beliefs, attitudes, values, and interests. Examples were given of how approaching learning opportunities believing that you are not intelligent, or that you have an enduring ability deficit, can be self-fulfilling. The examples illustrated that such beliefs are not conducive to taking charge of learning. In fact, these beliefs tend to result in such learning characteristics as lowered expectations for success, nonpersistence, and passivity (Johnston, 1985; Torgesen, 1977).

We also taught that motivation to use strategies was specific to students' beliefs about the relationship of effort to success for a particular task. Because of this, teachers guided students to connect their successes with what they did to achieve suc-

cess. Teachers emphasized that the critical factor in a successful performance is not how much time a student spent working *hard,* but rather what the student did to work *smart.*

Teachers attended Psych 101 and LAT with their students and, as a result, began to incorporate what they had heard into their own teaching. Two of the most valuable outcomes of Psych 101 and LAT lessons are that they provide students and staff with both a rationale and a common language for strategies instruction.

Some of the first comprehension strategies we taught in small reading groups were surveying, predicting, and setting purposes; identifying key elements in fiction—the characters, setting, central story problem, and resolution; and summarizing using the key elements. Other strategies followed: accessing background knowledge, making inferences, monitoring for understanding and taking remedial action when necessary, noticing patterns in text, identifying main ideas in nonfiction, organizing information, summarizing nonfiction in one's own words, and analyzing and taking charge of tasks. . . .

Teacher reports and follow-up data, however, from the early years of Benchmark's strategies instruction made us aware that our students did not automatically transfer the strategies they were learning in reading and social studies classes to the areas of the curriculum in which the strategies had not been taught. This was not unlike what other researchers have found with respect to transfer (e.g., Olsen, Wong, & Marx, 1983). Therefore, the next 3 years were devoted to applying to the teaching of mathematics and science what we had learned about teaching comprehension strategies in reading and social studies. . . .

The results of our strategies programs were and continue to be exciting, but we have not found a way to develop strategic students quickly. Becoming strategic across the curriculum takes many years of instruction and scaffolded practice in all subject areas, as well as instruction tailored to students' developmental levels.

Identifying Roadblocks to School Success

The schoolwide focus during the past several years has been to revisit an earlier concern about students' maladaptive styles that interfere with academic success. . . . Beginning in 1978, we gathered data regarding 32 possible academic and nonacademic roadblocks to school success that our teachers had observed in our students. Academic roadblocks, for example, include poor comprehension, poor written expression, and poor handwriting; nonacademic roadblocks include poor attention, inflexibility, impulsivity, lack of persistence, poor home support, frequent absences, and disorganization. . . .

Our review of the literature confirmed, just as Monroe (1932) had found over 50 years earlier, that in teaching delayed readers we are dealing with students who usually have more than one roadblock to school success and who have more differences than similarities (Gaskins, 1984). In light of these findings, it appeared that our program for at-risk and delayed readers had to be more comprehensive than we had initially envisioned.

We concluded that poor reading might result from, or even cause, a number of the roadblocks, and that these might persist even if the reading problem itself were solved. In view of the variety of characteristics exhibited by our delayed readers, we began to suspect that at least some of our students might need an educational program that included remedial reading, writing, and strategy instruction plus something extra to address cognitive styles, dispositions, and feelings.

Taking Charge of Personal Style and Motivation

Based on a review of the research, we developed a training program in the early 1980s to teach students how to cope with maladaptive cognitive styles (Gaskins & Baron, 1985). For our initial research project we chose to address three of our students' problematic thinking styles: impulsivity, inflexibility, and nonpersistance. . . .

In teaching students how to take charge of unproductive thinking styles, we also created the prototype for a staff-student mentor program.

In the early 1990s the middle school staff attempted to build on these programs and find better ways to coach students to take charge of their personal styles and their learning and to apply the strategies they had been taught. The goals of the middle school staff were for students to learn to be self-regulated learners and advocates for themselves. . . .

During the 1995–96 school year Joanne Murphy (1996) completed a follow-up study of 118 graduates of Benchmark who were in the age range 18 to 25. She found that reading level at the time of graduation from Benchmark was not as good a predictor of success in future academics as was the number of roadblocks indicated by students' teachers at the time of graduation from Benchmark. The fewer roadblocks, the more likely the student would be to do well in his or her schools after Benchmark, regardless of reading level. Based on this study and our earlier work, we were convinced that, in addition to teaching students strategies across the curriculum for reading, writing, understanding, and remembering, we also needed to do a better job of making students aware of their unproductive styles and of providing them with the rationale and strategies that would enable control of them. Styles that we targeted for emphasis were attentiveness, active involvement, persistence, reflectivity, and adaptability. Knowledge of and control over sounds, letters, words, and text were necessary, but learning how to control one's cognitive style would assure that students could put to good use what they knew about words and text. We were convinced that if we did not address maladaptive styles we would invite continued school difficulties.

In the fall of 1994 the middle school staff responded to these motivational and style issues by beginning to revamp the mentor program to better meet our 50 middle school students' needs for choice, collaboration, competence, and productive cognitive styles. . . .

Middle school mentors have become students' contact people with staff and parents. They keep track of students' progress in all courses and are in regular contact with parents. . . .

Conclusions Based on Benchmark Experiences

Our work at Benchmark School suggests that, contrary to what we had hoped, providing delayed readers with 2 or 3 years of remedial instruction is usually not sufficient to prepare them for success in regular classes. Most delayed readers need much more. Throughout elementary and middle school they need an integrated, full-day program taught by well-trained and caring teachers who collaborate with parents; orchestrate conditions that are motivating; and teach students the strategies they will need in regular classrooms for reading, writing, understanding, remembering, completing tasks, and taking control of maladaptive styles. The program must be undergirded by ongoing and reflective professional development, including follow-up of former students. Further, it must be distinguished by its quality. Teaching at-risk and delayed readers the skills and strategies that are congruent with success in the mainstream must begin early and continue for many years. There are no shortcuts. But, given instruction by the best teachers that is congruent with instruction in regular classrooms and that is provided over ample time, at-risk and delayed readers can be successful in the mainstream. . . .

References

Chan, L. K. S., & Cole, P. G. (1986). The effects of comprehension monitoring training on the reading competence of learning disabled and regular class students. *Remedial and Special Education, 7,* 33–40.

Critchley, M., & Critchley, E. A. (1978). *Dyslexia defined.* London: William Heinemann Medical Books.

Darling-Hammond, L. (1996). The quiet revolution: Rethinking teacher development. *Educational Leadership, 53,* 4–10.

Dryfoos, J. G. (1996). Full-service schools. *Educational Leadership, 53,* 18–23.

Frauenheim, J. G. (1978). Academic achievement characteristics of adult males who were diagnosed as dyslexic in childhood. *Journal of Learning Disabilities, 11,* 476–483.

Gaskins, I. W. (1980). *The Benchmark story.* Media, PA: Benchmark Press.

Gaskins, I. W. (1981). Reading for learning—Going beyond basals in the elementary grades. *The Reading Teacher, 35,* 323–328.

Gaskins, I. W. (1982). A writing program for poor readers and the rest of the class, too. *Language Arts, 59,* 854–861.

Gaskins, I. W. (1984). There's more to a reading problem than poor reading. *Journal of Learning Disabilities, 17,* 467–471.

Gaskins, I. W. (1988). Teachers as thinking coaches: Creating strategic learners and problem solvers. *Journal of Reading, Writing, and Learning Disabilities, 4,* 35–48.

Gaskins, I. W., & Baron, J. (1985). Teaching poor readers to cope with maladaptive cognitive styles: A training program. *Journal of Learning Disabilities, 18,* 390–394.

Gaskins, I. W., Downer, M. A., Anderson, R. C., Cunningham, P. M., Gaskins, R. W., Schommer, M., & the teachers of Benchmark School. (1988). A metacognitive approach to phonics: Using what you know to decode what you don't know. *Remedial and Special Education, 9,* 36–41, 66.

Gaskins, I. W., Downer, M. A., & Gaskins, R. W. (1986). *Introduction to the Benchmark School word identification/vocabulary development program.* Media, PA: Benchmark Press.

Gaskins, I. W., Ehri, L. C., Cress, C., O'Hara, C., & Donnelly, K. (1996). Procedures for word learning: Making discoveries about words. *The Reading Teacher, 50,* 2–18.

Gaskins, I. W., & Elliot, T. T. (1991). *Implementing cognitive strategy instruction across the school: The Benchmark manual for teachers.* Cambridge, MA: Brookline.

Gaskins, R. W., Gaskins, I. W., Anderson, R. C., & Schommer, M. (1995). The reciprocal relationship between research and development: An example involving a decoding strand for poor readers. *Journal of Reading Behavior, 27,* 337–377.

Graves, D. H. (1977). Research update—Language arts textbooks: A writing process evaluation. *Language Arts, 54,* 817–823.

Johnston, P. (1985). Understanding reading disability: A case study approach. *Harvard Educational Review, 55,* 153–177.

Johnston, P. H., Allington, R. L., & Afflerbach, P. (1985). Congruence of classroom and remedial reading instruction. *The Elementary School Journal, 85,* 465–478.

Kass, C. E. (1977). Identification of learning disability (dyssymbolia). *Journal of Learning Disabilities, 10,* 425–432.

Monroe, M. (1932). *Children who cannot read.* Chicago: University of Chicago Press.

Murphy, J. (1996). *A follow-up study of delayed readers and an investigation of factors related to their success in young adulthood.* Unpublished doctoral dissertation, University of Pennsylvania, Philadelphia.

Olsen, J. L., Wong, B. Y. L., & Marx, R. W. (1983). Linguistic and metacognitive aspects of normally achieving and learning-disabled children's communication process. *Learning Disabilities Quarterly, 6,* 289–304.

Shanahan, T., & Barr, R. (1995). Reading Recovery: An independent evaluation of the effects of an early instructional intervention for at-risk learners. *Reading Research Quarterly, 30,* 958–996.

Torgesen, J. K. (1977). The role of nonspecific factors in the task performance of learning-disabled children: A theoretical assessment. *Journal of Learning Disabilities, 10,* 27–34.

Wong, B. Y. L. (1985). Self-questioning instructional research: A review. *Review of Educational Research, 55,* 227–268.

 Article Review Form at end of book.

What recommendations does the author offer concerning phonics and word recognition? Why shouldn't teachers treat reversals as a symptom of a reading problem?

The 11 Deadly Sins of Remedial Reading Programs

Some sure-fire ways to make programs for treating reading difficulties fail.

Jerry Milligan

Jerry Milligan is Professor of Literacy Education, Washington State University, Pullman, WA.

Some Chapter One programs, resource rooms, remedial reading programs and adult literacy programs are exceedingly successful. Many of these same programs, however, are ineffective and may even be counterproductive. This is evidenced by the number of students who still aren't effective readers, even after receiving years of remedial help.

It can be useful to consider policies and procedures that may be inconsistent with recent research and current thinking. Although I make no claims of originality for this idea, I believe that programs for treating reading difficulties can become more successful by avoiding the pitfalls that often cause programs to fail.

Each of the following 11 administrative policies and instructional procedures, I believe, contributes to the failure of reading difficulty programs.

1. *Delay the start of the program.* The later in a student's life the program begins, the more likely it is to fail. Programs not initiated until the student is discovered to be reading at least a year below grade level seldom have positive results.

In recent years, I've observed programs in Canada, the United States and New Zealand. Those that commence as soon as the beginning reader appears to need assistance are quite successful and inexpensive because the child often needs help for less than a year. In contrast, programs that are delayed often fail and are expensive because the student usually remains in the program for many years.

> **"The more anxious a student is, the more likely the program is to fail."**

2. *Analyze word identification skills.* Most programs commence with a diagnostic instrument, such as a word list, an analysis of a student's oral reading errors and comprehension questions about the oral reading. This instrument assesses the student's ability to reproduce text without error, recognize words in isolation and decode unfamiliar words.

Identifying individual words and decoding unfamiliar ones are the skills that poor readers use. But diagnoses that focus on these skills invariably lead to the third method for making a program fail.

3. *Teach phonic skills systematically.* This leads to a program's failure in two ways. First, it requires the reader to focus on the "meaningless" aspects of language, such as individual words and parts of words. Second, learning phonic skills is boring for the student and counterproductive because it takes time away from productive activities.

Attending to meaningless aspects of language is the strategy of poor readers. In contrast, good readers see through the surface structure of print to its meaning.

4. *Avoid having students read.* Research suggests that the most efficacious way to learn and improve reading skills is by reading. There is no other way. The more time that's spent filling in blanks, marking vowel values and responding to graphemes in insolation, whether it's part of computer instructional software or on worksheets, the more likely the program is to fail.

5. *Use controlled-vocabulary reading materials.* The purpose for controlling the vocabulary of text is to make the reading material easier. Although this was the method for many years, it doesn't work. Controlled vocabularies usually make reading materials *more* difficult because the materials lack the qualities of predictable text.

These materials that have been matched to the reading level of very poor readers are not only boring,

Reprinted with permission of the publisher, *Teaching K–8*, Norwalk, CT. From the August/September 1993 issue of *Teaching K–8*.

they're also difficult to read—even for good readers.

6. *Disregard the importance of background knowledge.* Learning to read becomes difficult when materials about which the reader has very little background knowledge are chosen. It has been well established that prior knowledge affects the reader's interest and the ease with which materials can be read. It still amazes me to see how well exceedingly disabled readers who happen to be interested in motorcycles can read and discuss motorcycle company promotional brochures.

Teachers can make reading easy for even the poorest readers by having them read the lyrics of familiar songs, poems and stories that have been read to them often (or tape recorded for repeated listening). Allow students to read about topics they like.

7. *Encourage readers to sound out unfamiliar words.* When readers come upon an unfamiliar word, it isn't uncommon for teachers to suggest that they "sound it out." Occasionally, the readers pronounce the word correctly. Far more often, however, they pronounce the first grapheme, and then they make several unsuccessful attempts at the entire word.

Sounding it out requires readers to look more closely at print, and this slows their reading. Examining print makes such extraordinary demands on the reader's memory that fluent reading becomes nearly impossible.

Good readers skip the word and try to decipher the print without knowing all the words.

8. *Insist upon accuracy in oral reading and discourage guessing.* Making word-perfect oral reading an objective also combats improvement. Insisting upon perfect oral reading leads the reader to examine each word carefully. Focusing on words is characteristic of many poor readers. Reading too carefully isn't efficient, nor is reading without guessing (and it's nearly impossible to do correctly). Predicting, or informed guessing, is what good readers do.

9. *Treat reversals.* Letter reversals and letter-sequence reversals are symptoms of a reading difficulty, not causes of one. Reversals are not uncommon among students who can't make sense out of print. This problem disappears, however, as soon as students begin to understand print and begin to monitor their own reading.

Since a reversal usually changes a sentence so that it no longer makes sense, the only effective way to treat it is to wait until the reader has finished the sentence, and then ask that student if it makes sense. Next, have the student reread to find the miscue.

10. *Be certain that poor readers understand the seriousness of the problem and the repercussions of failure.* Since high anxiety and learning to read are nearly incompatible, the more anxious a student is, the more likely the program is to fail. Sometimes, teachers and parents believe, incorrectly, that poor readers

aren't trying hard enough. Quite often, the harder one tries, the more difficult learning to read becomes.

However, there are teachers who are masters at creating opportunities for readers to be successful and who focus on success while minimizing difficulties.

11. *Maintain a complex system of testing and record keeping.* Many teachers are compelled to do such a massive amount of testing and record keeping that they have to devote as much as 25 percent of their time to this task. The teacher could be using this time to facilitate reading improvement. Measuring and recording growth doesn't make children grow faster and taller, and it doesn't make readers read better.

Although few programs fall victim to all of these pitfalls, many employ enough of them to render the programs ineffective or counterproductive. Many programs, though, are quite effective. In these, reading isn't treated as a *series* of skills, but as *one* skill that can be learned and refined with practice.

In the most successful programs, assistance is provided very early, the teachers make learning to read easy by providing sufficient prior knowledge, and the teachers encourage students to read about topics the *students* are interested in. In this type of program, students discover that reading can be easy and pleasurable.

 Article Review Form at end of book.

At the beginning of the article, Pikulski calls attention to the mythical town first referred to in Slavin, Madden, Karweit, Dolan and Wasik (1991). In this town, 30 percent of the children were falling ill from contaminated drinking water. The town council rejected a proposal by the town engineer to build a water treatment plant. The town council felt it was too expensive of a project, because then funds would not be available to treat current victims and because 70 percent of the children never fell ill. What is the relevance of this mythical town and its reluctance to build the water treatment plant to the current state of education? Pikulski concludes the article with the statement, "It's time we built the water treatment plant!" What arguments does he include in his article to support this statement?

Preventing Reading Failure

A review of five effective programs

Pikulski reviews and identifies critical features of five successful reading programs for at-risk first-grade students.

John J. Pikulski

Pikulski teaches courses in literacy education at the University of Delaware. He is a past member of the International Reading Association Board of Directors. Pikulski can be contacted at the College of Education, University of Delaware, Newark DE 19716, USA.

Slavin, Madden, Karweit, Dolan, and Wasik (1991) write of a mythical town where 30% of the children were falling ill from contaminated drinking water. Many became permanently disabled; many died. The town spent millions for the medical care of these victims. At one point, a town engineer proposed building a water treatment plant that could virtually eliminate the illnesses. The town council rejected the proposal as being too expensive, because funds would not then be sufficiently available to treat current victims and because some 70% of the children never fell ill.

Slavin et al. (1991) compare the situation in the mythical town to our efforts to remediate reading problems. Enormous amounts are spent annually in efforts to remediate reading problems, or so-called "learning disabilities," while a fraction of that funding is expended on *preventing* those problems. This focus on correc-tion rather than prevention continues in spite of an impressive and growing body of authoritative opinion and research evidence which suggests that reading failure is preventable for all but a very small percentage of children (e.g., Clay, 1985; Hall, Prevatte, & Cunningham, 1993; Hiebert, Colt, Catto, & Gury, 1992; Hiebert & Taylor, 1994; Ohio State University, 1990; Pinnell, 1989; Reynolds, 1991; Slavin, Madden, Karweit, Livermon, & Dolan, 1990; Slavin, Madden, Karweit, Dolan, & Wasik, 1992; Taylor, Frye, Short, & Shearer, 1992; Taylor, Strait, & Medo, 1994). These positive findings are particularly important since I could

Pikulski, John J. (1994, Sept.). Preventing reading failure: A review of five effective programs. *The Reading Teacher,* 48(1), 30–39. Reprinted with permission of John J. Pikulski and the International Reading Association. All rights reserved.

locate very little evidence that suggested that programs designed to correct reading problems beyond second grade were successful. Indeed, one study (Kennedy, Birman, & Demaline, 1986) suggested that efforts to correct reading problems beyond third grade are largely unsuccessful.

On the surface, successful programs for the prevention of reading problems may seem expensive, but they are actually very cost effective when compared against the costs involved in remedial efforts; in retaining students for 1 or more years of schooling; and in placement in expensive, yet minimally effective, special education programs (Dyer, 1992; Slavin, 1989; Slavin et al., 1992; Smith & Strain, 1988). In addition, there is no way to calculate the savings in human suffering, humiliation, and frustration that would occur if children did not experience the painful school failure that all too often follows them through school and life.

The term *early intervention*, used in a variety of ways in the professional literature, often refers to programs designed for preschool children. Research reviews suggest strongly that these programs will play a critical role in efforts to eradicate reading and school failure (Slavin, Karweit, & Wasik, in press). This article, however, focuses upon five school-based early intervention programs designed for implementation early in a child's school career, primarily in first grade: Success for All (Madden, Slavin, Karweit, Dolan, & Wasik, 1991); the Winston-Salem Project (Hall et al., 1993); the Boulder Project (Hiebert et al., 1992); the Early Intervention in Reading (EIR) Project (Taylor et al., 1992), and Reading Recovery (Pinnell, 1989; Pinnell, Fried, & Estice, 1990). These programs were chosen for review on the basis of three criteria: (a) they were described in reasonable detail in a nationally distributed U.S. education journal that subjected its articles to review by an editorial board; (b) their primary focus was working with first-grade, at-risk students, those identified as likely to make limited progress in learning to read; and (c) data were presented which suggested that they were "effective," that is, student participation in the programs led to substantially better reading achievement than that of similar students who had not participated in the programs.

The primary purpose of this article is to compare these five programs on a number of dimensions and to identify common features that seem related to preventing reading problems. The identification of features that are common to successful early intervention programs may be useful for those working with students who require early intervention or for those planning such programs. No attempt will be made to "prove" the effectiveness of these five programs. The articles cited earlier should be consulted for evidence of their effectiveness. The position taken here reflects Archambault's (1989) suggestion that there comes a time when we should stop focusing on justifying program effects and focus instead on recommendations for program improvement. Likewise, no attempt will be made to determine which of the five programs is best. While all of them have proven effectiveness, some might be better than others depending on the circumstances of individual schools or school districts. For example, schools that have a high percentage of at-risk students might consider total school intervention programs like Success for All or the Winston-Salem Project. EIR and the Boulder Chapter 1 program are designed for use with small groups of students and so can serve a larger number of students than Reading Recovery, which requires one-to-one tutoring. However, some children may require the intense one-to-one support of Reading Recovery. It also might be more effective to provide some children with one form of early intervention and other children with a different form even within the same school.

Five Programs of Early Intervention for the Prevention of Reading Problems

Success for All

This project has been implemented primarily in schools in Baltimore, Maryland and Philadelphia, Pennsylvania (USA) that serve students from very low socioeconomic, innercity communities. Success for All is a total school program for kindergarten through third grades that focuses both on regular classroom instruction and supplementary support. Students in Grades 1 through 3 are heterogeneously grouped in classrooms of about 25 students, except for a 90-minute daily reading period in which they are regrouped by reading level across all three grades, in groups of 15 to 20 students. This allows whole group, direct instruction and eliminates seatwork using Dittos and workbooks.

Individual tutoring sessions of 20 minutes supplement group instruction for those students who are falling behind. Tutoring sessions emphasize the same strategies and skills as classroom reading activities. Where possible, the classroom teacher is also the child's tutor. Most children attend a half-day preschool and a full-day kindergarten.

The Winston-Salem Project

This project has operated in the first-grade classrooms of two schools in Winston-Salem, North Carolina (USA). One school serves students from middle class backgrounds; the other serves students from low socioeconomic backgrounds. In both schools classroom instruction is reorganized into four 30-minute blocks in which students are instructed in heterogeneous groups.

The Basal block consists primarily of selective use of instructional suggestions from a recently published basal reading program that includes an anthology of children's literature and accompanying paperback books. The Writing block consists of 5–10-minute minilessons and student independent writing activities. The Working with Words block consists of "word wall" activities in which students learn to read and spell words that are posted by the teacher each week, and a "making words" activity in which students manipulate groups of letters to form as many words as possible. During the Self-Selected Reading block, students read self-selected books, including informational books related to science and social studies topics.

First-grade teachers who first implemented the program were encouraged with the reading progress of their students, but believed many of the students needed continued support. Therefore, they continued to teach the same class of students, using the same intervention procedures, through the second grade.

Students spend a sizable amount of time in reading-related activities—a total of 3 hours and 15 minutes. At the school with a high proportion of at-risk students an additional 45 minutes of small group instruction is added to the schedule. Small group size is achieved by having Chapter 1 (federally funded) and special education teachers teach reading during these 45 minutes.

Early Intervention in Reading (EIR)

This first-grade intervention program has been implemented in several schools in the state of Minnesota, USA, representing both middle and lower socioeconomic levels. It is conducted almost completely by the regular classroom teacher. In addition to their regular reading instruction, these teachers work daily with the 5–7 lowest achieving students in each of their classes for an additional 20 minutes of reading instruction.

The small group instruction focuses on the repeated reading of picture books or summaries of these books and on developing students' phonemic segmentation, blending abilities, and other word recognition skills. Students also work individually or in pairs for 5 minutes with an aide, a parent volunteer, or the teacher rereading materials from their small group instruction sessions.

The Boulder Project

This program involves Chapter 1 teachers and students from two schools. The project involves reorganizing and modifying the Chapter 1 instruction that is federally funded for children at risk who come from disadvantaged homes.

In order to create small groups, a Chapter 1 teacher works with three children for 30 minutes each day while a teacher's aide instructs another group of three at the same time. After a half year the teacher and the aide exchange groups. It appears that the teacher plans and coordinates

students' instructional programs. The program focuses on the repeated reading of predictable tradebooks, teaching word identification skills through the use of analogy or word patterns, writing words from the word pattern instruction, and writing about topics of choice in notebooks.

Reading Recovery

Reading Recovery is an individual tutoring program in which a tutor meets with a child for 30 minutes each day outside the child's regular classroom. Although the tutor determines instructional strategies, Reading Recovery lessons operate within a clearly defined framework. Each day teachers and students are involved in 5 major activities.

The first activity is the reading of familiar stories. Students read at least two stories from books they have read previously. Second, the teacher takes a running record of a book that was introduced to the student the previous day. A running record is a set of notations that records the child's oral reading. Next is working with letters, though letter activities can occur at several points in the lesson. Fourth, the child dictates a sentence or short story that the teacher records and then rereads to the child, guiding her or him to write it accurately. The teacher then rewrites the message on a strip of paper, cuts it into individual words, and asks the child to reconstruct the message. This material is taken home daily for further practice. The final activity is the reading of a new book. Before reading, the teacher and child thoroughly explore the book and the teacher introduces concepts, language of the story, or specific vocabulary items as needed.

Comparing the Five Programs

Relationship of Early Intervention to Regular Classroom Instruction

The five programs vary greatly in their coordination with or connection to the reading instruction in the students' regular classrooms. Reading Recovery and the Boulder Project ap-

pear to be exclusively supplementary programs that assume no responsibility for the students' regular classroom reading instruction; both are conducted outside the classrooms. This is not to suggest that either program fails to recognize the importance of the ongoing classroom instruction that children receive. Clay 1985), who developed Reading Recovery procedures, for example, states:

The first essential of a satisfactory early intervention program is to have a good reading instruction program in the schools. . . . Against the background of a sound general program it is possible to develop a strategy for reducing the number of children with reading difficulties. (p. 48)

However, the descriptions of the Reading Recovery and Boulder Project don't address the complex issue of how to improve poor classroom reading instruction.

Although EIR instruction is implemented primarily by the students' regular classroom teacher and takes place within the classroom, no mention is made of attempts to alter the classroom reading instruction or to coordinate classroom activities with the EIR instruction. The EIR activities are simply added to the classroom schedule.

Success for All and the Winston-Salem Project, on the other hand, involve classroom instructional changes at several grade levels. Success for All provides preschool and full day kindergarten experiences for all students and implements a clearly defined approach to teaching reading. Chapter 1 teachers, school-wide special education teachers, and Success for All tutors provide classroom reading instruction in order to reduce reading group size. Students in Grades 1 to 3 are grouped across all classes according to their reading achievement.

The Winston-Salem Project also seems focused on schoolwide change. Classroom reading instruction is organized into 4 instructional blocks for all students, whether at risk or not. An additional 45 minutes of instruction is provided for all students at the school serving a high percentage of at-risk students.

Quality instruction for at-risk students in the regular classroom is desirable. Allington and McGill-Franzen (1989) document the need for improving classroom instruction for at-risk students and for coordinating regular and compensatory instruction. Although the positive effects of all five programs are well documented, the impact of some might be even greater if classroom instruction were improved. School districts or schools that are adding early intervention programs should also carefully review their regular instruction. Efforts should be made to ensure that students receive quality classroom reading instruction that is carefully coordinated with the compensatory instruction.

Organization for Early Intervention

Success for All and EIR use some individual tutoring, and Reading Recovery employs it exclusively. Most EIR instruction takes place in small groups, and Success for All provides moderate-sized group instruction with individual tutoring for students needing extra help. Small group instruction is used by the Boulder (three students) and Winston-Salem (five to six students) projects.

Wasik and Slavin (1993) reviewed evidence that one-to-one tutoring is the most powerful form of instruction. The positive results of the EIR and the Boulder Project, however, suggest that at least some at-risk students can make progress with very small group instruction. In a comprehensive program of early intervention it might be efficient to begin with small group instruction, but to move to one-to-one tutoring for students who are not making sufficient progress.

Amount of Instructional Time

In all five programs students spend more time in reading and writing activities than do students not at risk. None of the early intervention programs was a substitute for regular classroom instruction. In the three add-on programs, students receive about 30 extra minutes of individual

or small group reading instruction. Of the two classroom intervention programs, the Winston-Salem Project seems more ambitious in terms of time allotment—over 2 hours of instruction in the 4 blocks, with an additional 45 minutes of small group instruction in some schools. Success for All involves 90 minutes of reduced-sized group classroom instruction and 20 minutes of tutoring.

Devoting extra time to reading instruction appears a necessary but not sufficient factor for at-risk student success. For example, Hiebert et al. (1992) compared the progress of the students in their Boulder Project against a comparison group of students who received an equal amount of special help in a traditional program. The comparison group made essentially no demonstrable progress in reading during first grade in spite of extra instructional time. Lyons, Place, and Rinehart (1990) report similar results in a study comparing Reading Recovery and Chapter 1 programs. Indeed, there is little evidence to suggest that added time for reading instruction in many compensatory or special education programs yields positive effects (Rowan & Guthrie, 1989). Indeed, one study (Glass & Smith, 1977) suggests that the more time at-risk students spent in some pullout, compensatory programs' the poorer their progress. Although additional time for reading seems essential, what is done instructionally during that time is what makes the difference.

Devoting extra time for reading instruction appears a necessary but not sufficient factor for at-risk student success.

Length of Intervention

Reading Recovery has a clearly specified time frame. It is exclusively a first-grade program, and intervention lasts until a student is achieving at an average level for his or her class, or for up to a maximum of 100 sessions. EIR is also exclusively a first-grade program that lasts most of the school year. The Boulder Project is a first-grade program, but Hiebert et al. (1992) note that some children need, and should receive, help beyond first grade. The Winston-Salem Project echoes this sentiment and has ex-

tended the project into second grade. The philosophy of Success for All seems to have been laid down from its inception—the amount and intensity of intervention must vary with students' needs; some will require preschool intervention, home support, and help during and beyond primary grades.

At-risk students' needs will be met most fully and efficiently only if intervention programs of various durations are available. A growing case can be made that treatment is most effective if it comes early in a child's school career—in first grade or perhaps even before; however, some students will need additional, intense support beyond first grade.

Types of Texts and Materials Used

A great variety of texts is used in these programs. Predictable, easy-to-read texts and authentic tradebooks are extremely popular for first-grade classroom use at this time. Such texts also figure prominently in these programs and seem, with the possible exception of Success for All, to be the major type of texts used. Each project uses texts that students can read successfully; initial texts are easy, and those introduced thereafter present increasing levels of challenge.

There is a very clear absence of traditional workbook and isolated skill practice materials in all of the programs. The Winston-Salem Project mentions the use of workbooks, but these are part of a recently published reading program, which emphasizes open-ended responses rather than isolated skill-drill or multiple choice items.

Success for All and the Winston-Salem Project include the use of basal materials. In addition, Success for All uses kindergarten and first-grade texts specifically written to include vocabulary that exercises phonic skills. The Boulder Project includes the use of "little books" that appear to be written with vocabulary that focuses upon word patterns that students are taught.

All these successful projects rely on texts that use natural, non-controlled vocabulary, but only Reading Recovery uses them exclusively. The others use some specially written texts in order to reduce reading demands or exercise word recognition skills. In order to ease reading demands, for example, EIR uses written summaries of trade books in the beginning phases of intervention. Later, complete trade books are used.

Some combination of this variety of text types seems ideal. For example, predictable texts are particularly advantageous at the beginning stages of intervention, since students can use extratextual clues such as recurring phrases or strong picture clues, but students sometimes become overly focused on such clues and pay insufficient attention to word-level information. The Boulder Project's use of pictureless versions of some books is a reasonable approach to this potential problem.

There is great value in using interesting, motivating, quality literature, but it also seems possible to develop texts, as in the Success for All and Boulder Projects, that specifically attempt to exercise word identification skills. These books can also be interesting and motivating. Dr. Seuss creations such as *The Cat in the Hat* were written with vocabulary restrictions but have become favorites of children.

Text Level Strategies

The instructional strategies of all five programs show that classifying beginning reading programs as either code emphasis or meaning emphasis is a myth that has far too long been argued by extremists. Each program is clearly oriented toward ensuring that students conceptualize reading as a meaning constructing process, but each also emphasizes teaching word identification strategies to help students become independent readers. There is a firm research base for the position that a balance between the reading of meaningful, connected texts and systematic word identification instruction results in superior achievement (Adams, 1990).

In all five programs repeated reading is the most common instructional activity with books and other texts. The impact of repeated reading

on young readers' developing fluency is well documented (e.g., Dowhower, 1987; Herman, 1985; Samuels, 1979). The procedures used vary. In Reading Recovery, the teacher familiarizes the student with the content and vocabulary of a new book, the student does a first reading and then reads the same book the next day. Finally, the book becomes part of a library from which the student can choose books for later rereadings. Other programs have students do repeated readings in pairs or small groups. The number of times the texts are reread varies from program to program, and the number of times a particular book is read varies even within a program. Although instruction in comprehension strategies is provided, most of the instructional time is spent with text level activities designed to develop word recognition fluency, since poor word identification skills are a major stumbling block for these students.

Word Level Strategies

All of the programs include instruction that focuses students' attention on letters and words. EIR, Reading Recovery, and Success for All include very deliberate instruction in phonemic awareness—ensuring that children develop a conscious understanding that spoken words are composed of identifiable sounds. Success for All and EIR also provide instruction in blending sounds into words. Both the Winston-Salem and Boulder Projects focus on working with word patterns (e.g., *in, pin, tin*), based on the work of Cunningham (1991). The specific approaches to word recognition vary among the programs, but systematic instruction in word recognition is a major focus for all programs.

Writing Component

All five programs prominently include writing activities, most of which seem geared to reinforcing word recognition. As Clay (1985) puts it, "A case can be made for the theory that learning to write letters, words and sentences actually helps the child to make the visual discriminations of detailed print that he will use in his reading" (p. 54). Clarke (1988) also suggests a positive effect

of writing on reading progress, particularly for at-risk students. In some of the programs (Reading Recovery, EIR, and the Boulder Project) the writing activities are brief: Students write a few words, a sentence, or a few sentences related to the vocabulary in stories they are reading or word patterns that have been taught. More extended writing is included in the Winston-Salem and Success for All programs, both of which operate as classroom instruction models as well as supplementary programs.

Assessment Procedures

All five projects include regular, ongoing assessment. In Reading Recovery running records are taken daily as a check of reading fluency. In EIR, running records are taken every 3 days. The Boulder Project checks oral reading weekly and includes more extensive assessments quarterly. Oral reading is monitored in all three supplementary programs. This seems appropriate, since word recognition is a prominent difficulty for their students. In Success for All students are formally evaluated every 8 weeks. Writing portfolios are kept for students in the Winston-Salem Project, and teacher observations are also considered important. Successful early intervention programs include systematic, regular assessment in order to monitor progress and provide a basis for instructional planning.

Home Connections

Only the Winston-Salem Project fails to mention efforts to extend instructional time by having students take materials home for reading to parents or others. However, this may be an oversight, since the project description notes dramatically greater parent participation in school activities since the initiation of the project. Success for All has the most substantial parent component, including establishing a parent support team at every school. Students in Success for All schools are expected to read books from classroom libraries at home for 20 minutes every day. Boulder Project students are expected to take books home nightly and are rewarded with gift books for regular at-home reading. In EIR, students are expected to read a story summary at home every third day. In Reading Recovery students take a sentence or two home for reading each day and are also encouraged to take home and read books. Although the amount of home reading expected of students varies, at-home reading appears as a consistent element in all projects.

Teacher Training

All five programs use experienced, certified teachers, and two use teacher aides. In the EIR program, an aide may briefly meet with one or two children to listen to them read a story; however, the instruction is conducted by the regular classroom teacher who has been trained in EIR procedures. In the Boulder Project a teacher aide conducts the same activities as a certified teacher, who seems responsible for planning and decision making.

All five programs have built-in consultation available at least throughout the first year of implementation. Teachers who are using the intervention for the first year can meet with others who are familiar with the program. This seems a very important point for anyone who is planning to initiate an early intervention program.

Reading Recovery provides the most defined and intense consultation. First-year teachers meet weekly with teacher leaders. These meetings include observations of the first-year teachers working with students and follow-up discussions of instructional strategies. The Boulder and EIR projects seem to include more flexibly scheduled, less intense consultation.

The length of initial teacher training varies. Again, Reading Recovery is most specific. Teachers attend a 30-hour workshop before the beginning of the school year and also meet 2½ hours weekly thereafter for the first year. Teachers in the Winston-Salem Project meet for a week before the school year and spend an unspecified amount of time in consultation with the curriculum coordinator through the year. The Success for All program and the EIR program provide only 1 or 2 days of training before the beginning of the school year. The written information about the Boulder Project does not describe training prior to the beginning of the school year.

General Conclusions

Those planning early intervention programs in reading should consider the multiple dimensions of these five programs. It seems reasonable to conclude that attention to the following issues will increase the probability of program success.

- Students' total program of reading instruction should be considered when planning for early intervention. Tutoring and extra time pull-out programs certainly can be effective; however, for maximum impact, early intervention programs should try to ensure that students are receiving excellent and coordinated instruction both in their classrooms and in the special intervention programs.

- Children who are experiencing difficulty with reading should spend more time receiving reading instruction than children who are not experiencing difficulty. Quality instruction must be provided during this extra time.

- For at-risk children to be successful readers, individual or very small group (no more than 4 or 5 students) instruction is essential. Some children will definitely require one-to-one tutoring.

- Special reading instruction for at-risk students is most profitably focused on first grade. Where school resources are limited, they should be spent on first-grade intervention that leads to the prevention of reading difficulties. Some students will need support beyond first grade.

- Texts for early intervention programs should be very simple so that students will be successful in reading them. Predictable texts have merit, particularly at the beginning stages of the program. Interesting literature that uses natural language patterns seems important although texts constructed to encourage application of word identification skills may also be beneficial.

- Reading the same text several times seems a very effective approach to helping at-risk children develop reading fluency. Instructional procedures should ensure that students see reading as an act of constructing meaning.

- In early intervention programs, at-risk children need instruction that focuses their attention on words and letters. Phonemic awareness and phonics instruction should be included. Focusing on word patterns also appears to have merit.

- Writing is important in early intervention programs. When children write words they attend to the details of those words, which supports development of word identification skills. Students should write daily; the writing activities should be relatively brief; and the instruction should ensure that students focus attention on features and details of letters and words.

- Ongoing assessment that monitors student progress is necessary. The assessment of oral reading fluency is an informative, effective assessment procedure.

- Effective early intervention programs encourage communication between home and school. Students should be provided with materials for daily reading at home.

- Professionally prepared, accomplished teachers are the mainstay of successful early intervention programs. Initial training should be provided so that teachers learn to deliver consistently effective instruction. Continuous professional support should also be available, at least through a teacher's first year of implementation.

The devastating effects of reading failure are widely acknowledged. Stanovich (1986) offers cogent arguments and good evidence that children who encounter problems in the beginning stages of learning to read fall further and further behind their peers—the poor do get poorer. A substantial portion of the enormous number of dollars spent annually on marginally, if at all, effective compensatory and special education programs needs to be redirected toward preventing initial reading failure. It's time we built the water treatment plant!

References

Adams, M. J. (1990). *Beginning to read: Thinking and learning about print.* Cambridge, MA: MIT Press.

Allington, R., & McGill-Franzen, A. (1989). School response to reading failure: Instruction for Chapter 1 and special education students in grades two, four, and eight. *The Elementary School Journal, 89,* 529–542.

Archambault, F. X. (1989). Instructional setting and other design features of compensatory education programs. In R. E. Slavin, N. L. Karweit, & N. A. Madden (Eds.), *Effective programs for students at risk* (pp. 220–261). Boston: Allyn & Bacon.

Clarke, L. K. (1988). Invented versus traditional spelling in first graders' writings: Effects on learning to spell and read. *Research in the Teaching of English, 22,* 281–309.

Clay, M. M. (1985). *The early detection of reading difficulties.* Portsmouth, NH: Heinemann.

Cunningham, P. M. (1991). *Phonics they use: Words for reading and writing.* New York: HarperCollins.

Dowhower, S. L. (1987). Effects of repeated reading on second-grade transitional readers' fluency and comprehension. *Reading Research Quarterly, 22,* 389–406.

Dyer, P. (1992). Reading recovery: A cost-effectiveness and educational-outcomes analysis. *ERS Spectrum, 10,* 10–19.

Glass, G. V., & Smith, M. L. (1977). *Pull-out in compensatory education.* Washington, DC: Department of Health, Education, and Welfare.

Hall, D. P., Prevatte, C., & Cunningham, P. M. (1993). *Elementary ability grouping and failure in the primary grades.* Unpublished manuscript.

Herman, P. A. (1985). The effects of repeated readings on reading rate, speech, pauses, and word recognition accuracy. *Reading Research Quarterly, 29,* 553–564.

Hiebert, E. H., Colt, J. M., Catto, S. L., & Gury, E. C. (1992). Reading and writing of first-grade students in a restructured Chapter 1 program. *American Educational Research Journal, 29,* 545–572.

Hiebert, E., & Taylor, B. (Eds.). (1994). *Getting reading right from the start: Effective early literacy interventions.* Needham Heights, MA: Allyn & Bacon.

Kennedy, M. M., Birman, B. F., Demaline, R. E. (1986). *The effectiveness of Chapter 1 services.* Washington, DC: Office of Educational Research and Improvement, U.S. Department of Education.

Lyons, C. A., Place, W., & Rinehart, J. (1990). *Factors related to teaching success in the literacy education of young at-risk children* (Tech. Rep. No. 10). Columbus, OH: The Ohio State University.

Madden, N. A., Slavin, R. E., Karweit, N. L., Dolan, L. J., & Wasik, B. A. (1991). Success for All: Ending reading failure from the beginning. *Language Arts, 68,* 47–52.

Ohio State University. (1990). *Reading Recovery 1984–1990.* Columbus, OH: Author.

Pinnell, G. S. (1989). Reading Recovery: Helping at-risk children learn to read. *The Elementary School Journal, 90,* 161–183.

Pinnell, G. S., Fried, M. D., & Estice, R. M. (1990). Reading Recovery: Learning how to make a difference. *The Reading Teacher, 43,* 282–295.

Reynolds, A. J. (1991). Early schooling of children at risk. *American Educational Research Journal, 28,* 392–422.

Rowan, B., & Guthrie, L. F. (1989). The quality of Chapter 1 instruction: Results from a study of twenty four schools. In R. E. Slavin, N. L. Karweit, & N. A. Madden (Eds.), *Effective programs for students at risk* (pp. 195–219). Boston: Allyn & Bacon.

Samuels, S. J. (1979). The method of repeated readings. *The Reading Teacher, 32,* 403–408.

Slavin, R. E. (1989). Students at-risk of school failure: The problem and its dimensions. In R. E. Slavin, N. L. Karweit, & N. A. Madden (Eds.), *Effective programs for students at risk* (pp. 3–23). Boston: Allyn & Bacon.

Slavin, R. E., Madden, N. A., Karweit, N. L., Livermon, B. J., & Dolan, L. (1990). Success for All: First year outcomes of a comprehensive plan for reforming urban education. *American Educational Research Journal, 27,* 255–278.

Slavin, R., Madden, N., Karweit, N., Dolan, L., & Wasik, B. (1991). Research directions; Success for All: Ending reading failure from the beginning. *Language Arts, 68,* 404–409.

Slavin, R. E., Madden, N. L., Karweit, N. L., Dolan, L., & Wasik, B. A. (1992). *Success for All: A relentless approach to prevention and early intervention in elementary schools.* Arlington, VA: Educational Research Service.

Slavin, R. E., Karweit, N. L., & Wasik, B. A. (Eds.) (in press). *Preventing early school failure: Research on effective strategies.* Boston: Allyn & Bacon.

Smith, B. J., & Strain, P. S. (1988). *Does early intervention help?* Reston, VA: Council for Exceptional Children.

Stanovich, K. E. (1986). Matthew effects in reading: Some consequences of individual differences in the acquisition of literacy. *Reading Research Quarterly, 21,* 360–407.

Taylor, B. M., Frye, B. J., Short, R., & Shearer, B. (1992). Classroom teachers prevent reading failure among low-achieving first-grade students. *The Reading Teacher, 45,* 592–597.

Taylor, B. M., Strait, J., & Medo, M. A. (1994). Early intervention in reading: Supplementary instruction for groups of low achieving students provided by first grade teachers. In E. H. Hiebert & B. M. Taylor (Eds.), *Getting reading right from the start: Effective early literacy interventions* (pp. 107–121). Needham Heights, MA: Allyn & Bacon.

Wasik, B. A., & Slavin, R. E. (1993). Preventing early reading failure with one-to-one tutoring: A review of five programs. *Reading Research Quarterly, 28,* 178–200.

Article Review Form at end of book.

What is the evidence that Ebonics is a language? Why should a student's primary or home language be a consideration in the teaching-learning process?

"Dat teacher be hollin at us"— What Is Ebonics?

Geneva Napoleon Smitherman

Michigan State University

Edited by Bonny Norton Peirce

University of British Columbia

I had my first taste of linguistic pedagogy for the Great Unwashed when my European American elementary school teachers attacked my Ebonics (though it was not called that in those days) and demoted me half a year. Effectively silenced, I learned to negotiate success in the educational system by keeping my mouth shut—relatively easy for a ghetto child in those days. However, this strategy failed me when, as a university student, I had to take a speech test. Because I had not yet developed oral code-switching skills, I flunked the speech test and was forced into speech therapy along with several of my peers (many Black, a few Brown). The speech therapist (a young woman studying for her PhD in the field) did not know what to do with any of us because nobody was dyslexic, nor were any of us aphasic —in fact, there was not even a stutterer amongst us! Frustrated by this absence of the language deficiencies she was being trained to cure, the speech therapist ended up teaching us to memorize the standard middle-class, U.S. midwestern pronunciation of the words on the speech test. Thus, the second time around, we all passed the test.

This experience not only rescued me from the ghetto streets (where at the time I was enjoying a high degree of success—more in my memoirs), it also aroused the fighting spirit in me and took me from literature into critical linguistics, after which I entered the lists of the language wars. It should be noted, though, that for every Ebonics speaker like me, who escaped the malaise of the streets and who survived to call the educational system into account, as I sought to do in *Martin Luther King Jr. Elementary School Children v. Ann Arbor Board of Education* (the *King* case)—for every Ebonics-speaking Geneva Napoleon Smitherman—there are many thousands gone.

Which brings us to December 18, 1996, when the Oakland, California, School Board passed its resolution recognizing Ebonics as the primary language of its African American students and committing the district to use this medium to teach literacy skills in the U.S. language of wider communication, that is, Standard American English (SAE). Like those in most other urban school districts in this country, Oakland's African American students, particularly those from under- and working-class homes (like mine), whose primary language is typically Ebonics, are experiencing a severe educational crisis. For example, 71% of Oakland's Black students are tracked in special education or learning disabilities-type programs, as were many of my

homiez[1] back in the day. There is no inherent intellectual deficiency in these students. Further, most approach schooling enthusiastically and highly motivated to learn (because they know what time it is in this most advanced technological country). Notwithstanding that many urban schools suffer from inadequate funding, poor facilities, and limited resources, language is the major factor in the failure of Ebonics-speaking students.

Much of the public debate and media (mis)coverage of the Oakland resolution completely missed the beat—and the volumes of linguistic research on Ebonics that date back to 1884, when Harrison published a 47-page treatise on what he termed *Negro English* in the journal *Anglia*. People of African descent have been speaking Ebonics for centuries, although the proper terminology for this language was not coined until 1973, when a group of African American scholars, principal among them psychologist Dr. Robert Williams, caucused at the national conference Cognitive and Language Development of the Black Child, held in St. Louis, Missouri (see Williams, 1975). Ebonics is not nonstandard English, nor is it synonymous with Rap (although Rappers use Ebonics in their musical lyrics). Ebonics is a superordinate term that refers to all the West African–European language mixtures (i.e., pidgins and creoles) developed in various language con-

[1] Friends from one's neighborhood.

Reprinted from "'Dat teacher be hollin at us'—What Is Ebonics?" by Geneva Napoleon Smitherman, *TESOL Quarterly*, Spring 1998. Copyright Teachers of English to Speakers of Other Languages, Inc.

tact situations, principally in the so-called New World, as a result of the African slave trade. Africans created a language, with its own morphology, syntax, phonology, and rhetorical and semantic styles and strategies of discourse. This new code, which enabled them to communicate with each other and with the European slavers, was based on the common structural features of their West African languages (e.g., Yoruba, Wolof, Mandinka) and the lexicon of the European languages (e.g., English, French, Dutch). The Ebonics that has created the current controversy in the U.S. is only one variety of this language; it can be referred to as *United States Ebonics* (USEB).

Space will not permit a full delineation of the grammatical integrity and communicative practices of USEB. A few examples should suffice to exemplify the distinctive nature of this language. Consider the USEB sentence *The coffee be cold*. As in the case of Efik and other Niger-Congo languages, Ebonics has an aspectual verb system, in this example conveyed by the use of the English verb *be* to denote iterativity. Thus, *The coffee is generally cold*, if translated into SAE.

The condition of iterativity (whether habitual or intermittent) is obligatory for the use of *be*. Thus *The coffee be cold today* is ungrammatical. SAE's *The coffee is cold today* would be *The coffee cold* in USEB. This latter pattern has been labeled *zero copula* or *copula deletion*. However, like such West African languages as Twi and Yoruba, the use of a copulative verb is not obligatory in most contexts; in the underlying structure, there was never a copula to be deleted. Thus, USEB generates sentences like *They gone home*, or *Dat boy, he too slow for me*.

Unlike English, which inflects verbs to indicate tense and person, USEB follows the uninflected pattern of West African languages, relying on stress or the encoding of contextual information to convey time. In *I look for him everywhere last week*, past tense is conveyed by *last week* without the redundancy of the morpheme *-ed* on *look*. In response to the question *Is he married?* the USEB speaker may reply *He BEEN married* (i.e., stress on the verb *been*), meaning that the man in question married in the remote past and is still married. However, if the

speaker responds, *He been married* (no stress on *been*), the man in question is divorced. This use of stress to convey a difference in meaning parallels the operation of tone in some West African languages.

Ebonics is also a system of communicative practices, in which may be found some of the richest and most expressive forms of African survivals in the African American speech community. In the ritualized insult tradition known as *Signification/Playin the Dozens/Snappin*, speakers deploy irony, exaggeration, indirection, and humor aimed at a person for play and corrective criticism. Consider the following brief excerpt from a longer conversation among several "Sistas" at a bridal shower:

Linda: Girl, what up with that head? [referring to her friend's hairstyle]

Betty: Ask yo momma. [causes laughter from the other Sistas]

Linda: Oh, so you goin there, huh? Well, I DID ask my momma. And she said, "Caint you see that Betty look like her momma spit her out?" [laughter from all, including Betty]

The usual expectation in a conversation is that a speaker's question will be answered honestly and sincerely; Betty's unexpected indirection produces laughter from the listeners. The surface meaning of *yo momma* for those outside the USEB speech community is simply *your mother/mom*, with the direct meaning of "You should go and ask your mother about this situation." However, within the discourse rules governing USEB practices, the utterance is a signal that an insult has been hurled but that it is one within the established African American verbal tradition. The speaker is indirectly saying, "Let the game of the Dozens begin." Linda clearly recognizes the entry into the game context by her response, "Oh, so you goin there, huh?" and proceeds to cap[2] this exchange with a more clever retort. Whereas Betty's intragroup expression, "Ask yo momma," is humorous and sets up a challenge, it is formulaic and stylized. It cannot and does not beat "Well, I DID ask my momma. And she said, 'Caint you see that Betty look like her momma

[2]Win.

spit her out?'" (Troutman & Smitherman, 1997, p. 152).

It has been 20 years since I served as advocate and chief expert witness for a group of Ebonics-speaking children whose parents successfully sued the Ann Arbor, Michigan, School District for failing to teach the children to read (see Smitherman, 1981a, 1981b). In this federal court case, the failure was demonstrated to be the result of traditional pedagogy, derived from an inadequate knowledge base, that did not take the children's language into account in the teaching-learning process. Because of the highly charged, supersensitive nature of race and racial issues in the U.S., the lesson of *King* was capitalized on in a sporadic and limited fashion around the country (e.g., in Taylor's 1980s experiment in a college composition class outside Chicago; see Taylor, 1989). Now, two decades later, the literacy crisis among Africans in America—among those most in need of literacy, the working and underclasses—has reached an all-time high. Oakland, California, is only the tip of the iceberg. Teachers of English, literacy instructors, and educational policy makers, wherever they are around the globe, need to take language differences into account, regardless of whether the differences are perceived to constitute a different language or a variety of the language of wider communication. The research evidence is clear: When students' primary/home language is factored into language planning policy and the teaching-learning process, it is a win-win situation for all.

The Author

Geneva Smitherman (also known as *Dr. G*) is University Distinguished Professor and Director, African American Language and Literacy Program, Michigan State University. An educational activist as well as a linguist, she has been at the forefront of the struggle for Black language rights for over 20 years. She is author of over 100 articles and papers and is author or coauthor of eight books on the language, culture, and education of African Americans, most notably the classic work *Talkin and Testifyin: The Language of Black America* (Houghton Mifflin, 1977; Wayne State University Press, 1986). Dr. G is the daughter of rural sharecroppers and has roots in the Traditional Black Church.

References
and Suggestions
for Further Reading

Asante, M. (1990). African elements in African-American English. In J. E. Holloway (Ed.), *Africanisms in American culture* (pp. 19–34). Bloomington: Indiana University Press.

Baugh, J. (1983). *Black street speech.* Austin: University of Texas Press.

Dillard, J. L. (1972). *Black English: Its history and usage in the United States.* New York: Random House.

Ebonics [Special issue]. (1997). *Black Scholar, 27*(1).

Ebonics [Special issue]. (1997). *Journal of Black Psychology, 23*(3).

Harrison, J. A. (1884). Negro English. *Anglia, 7,* 232–239.

Holloway, J. E., & Bass, W. K. (1993). *The African heritage of American English.* Bloomington: Indiana University Press.

Kochman, T. (1981). *Black and White styles in conflict.* Chicago: University of Chicago Press.

Labov, W. (1972). *Language in the inner city.* Philadelphia: University of Pennsylvania Press.

Mufwene, S. S., Rickford, J., Baugh, J., & Bailey, G. (Eds.). (in press). *African American English.* London: Routledge.

Perry, T., & Delpit, L. (Eds.). (1997). The real Ebonics debate: Power, language, and the education of African-American children [Special issue]. *Rethinking Schools, 12*(1). (Also Perry, T., & Delpit, L. (Eds.). (in press). *The real Ebonics debate: Power, language, and the education of African-American children.* Boston: Beacon Press.)

Smitherman, G. (1977). *Talkin and testifyin: The language of Black America.* Boston: Houghton Mifflin. Paperback, Detroit, MI: Wayne State University Press, 1986.

Smitherman, G. (Ed.). (1981a). *Black English and the education of Black children and youth.* Detroit, MI: Wayne State University, Center for Black Studies.

Smitherman, G. (1981b). "What go round come round": *King* in perspective. *Harvard Educational Review, 62,* 40–56.

Smitherman, G. (1992). Black English, diverging or converging?: The view from the National Assessment of Educational Progress. *Language and Education, 6*(1), 47–61.

Smitherman, G. (1994). *Black talk: Words and phrases from the hood to the amen corner.* Boston: Houghton Mifflin.

Smitherman, G. (1997). Black language and the education of Black children: One mo once. *Black Scholar, 27*(1), 28–35.

Taylor, H. U. (1989). *Standard English, Black English, and bidialectalism: A controversy.* New York: Peter Lang.

Troutman, D., & Smitherman, G. (1997). Black women's discourse. In T. A. van Dijk (Ed.), *Discourse as social interaction* (Vol. 2, pp. 148–156). London: Sage.

Turner, L. D. (1949). *Africanisms in the Gullah dialect.* Chicago: University of Chicago Press.

Vass, W. K. (1979). *The Bantu speaking heritage of the United States* (Monograph Series, Vol. 2). Los Angeles: University of California, Center for Afro-American Studies.

Williams, R. L. (Ed.). (1975). *Ebonics: The true language of Black folks.* St. Louis, MO: Institute of Black Studies.

 Article Review Form at end of book.

Which models and strategies are particularly effective for teaching diverse and struggling readers? What kinds and levels of material are best for students with special needs?

Boosting Reading Success

Language, literacy, and content area instruction for deaf and hard-of-hearing students—and bilingual students, and students learning English as a second language, and everyone else who needs a little help.

Barbara R. Schirmer

Barbara R. Schirmer (CEC Chapter #214), Associate Professor of Special Education, Lewis & Clark College, Graduate School of Professional Studies, Portland, Oregon. For an extensive bibliography of reading resources, contact the author at Lewis & Clark College, Graduate School of Professional Studies, 0615 S.W. Palatine Hill Road, Portland, OR 97219-7899 (e-mail: schirmer@lclark.edu).

Here is the story of Linda and Ben. Linda is a fourth-grade teacher, and Ben is one of 28 children in her class. Linda has taken advantage of abundant research on strategies for teaching reading comprehension; Ben, who is profoundly deaf, has particularly benefited—as have all the diverse learners in Linda's class.

The fact is that *we know how to help children achieve success in reading.* Research from the 1960s to the present has provided teacher-tested, proven strategies that can be tailored to any child, any class. The names of some of these strategies may sound daunting, such as Concept-Text-Application, Semantic Maps, and Directed Reading Thinking Activity. Many of them, such as K-W-L (What I **K**now, What I **W**ant to Learn, and What I **L**earned) (Ogle, 1986) are a result of an explosion of reading re-

search in the 1980s and are old friends to many teachers and students. (See Samuels & Farstrup, 1992; Schirmer, 1994; Zakaluk & Samuels, 1988 for other reading resources.)

No teaching strategy can enable children to understand *all* text material, regardless of the level of the material (see box, "Factors Contributing to Text Readability"),* but teachers may use various strategies to provide children support in comprehending material that would appear to be considerably beyond their reading levels. These strategies can be used just as effectively by general education teachers with classrooms of diverse learners as by special education teachers with small, self-contained classrooms of deaf and hard-of-hearing children.

Teaching Strategies That Enhance Comprehension

For the purposes of discussion, let's consider two models of instructional strategies. Both models offer substantial support for reading content-area text material. One model requires that the teacher devote class time to reading the material, and the other model requires that the students read the material independently. Linda used both in her fourth-grade class.

*Not included in this publication.

In-Class Text Reading

Linda used a variety of strategies for in-class reading. She found that when she developed a theme, such as "government," many of the strategies made sense as she guided her students through the steps indicated here. As mentioned previously, Ben, a profoundly deaf child, was one of her students. Ben is also assisted throughout the day by a sign language interpreter and bimonthly by a consultant teacher of deaf and hard-of-hearing students.

Some of the strategies Linda used were the Guided Reading Procedure, Concept-Text-Application, K-W-L, Directed Reading Activity, and Directed Reading Thinking Activity. The latter two strategies are usually used with narrative text but have been found to work effectively with expository text (Alvermann & Swafford, 1989).

Step 1. Activating and Building Background Knowledge

Because Linda was *theming* her instruction, she did not have to incorporate extensive background-building activities—she was presenting and reinforcing a common set of concepts within each of the subject areas. The

From "Boosting Reading Success: Language, Literacy, and Content Reading Instruction for Deaf and Hard-of-Hearing Students," by Barbara R. Schirmer, *Teaching Exceptional Children,* September/October 1997, pgs. 52–55. Copyright 1997 by The Council for Exceptional Children. Reprinted with permission.

For the teacher of deaf and hard-of-hearing students, language is the curricular foundation on which the school day is built. The child's acquisition of language in face-to-face communication, reading, and writing is the focal point of instruction. The opportunity that content area instruction provides deaf and hard-of-hearing students to use language expressively and receptively is at least as important, and often considerably more important, than the specific concepts taught within individual subject areas.

It is often said that the teacher of deaf and hard-of-hearing children is a teacher of *language first*. But language is meaningful only when it is used within communicative contexts. In classrooms with deaf and hard-of-hearing students, language and content instruction need not be mutually exclusive, nor does one need to be emphasized at the expense of the other, because subject areas can provide students meaning-centered milieu for language and literacy development.

Meeting this triple agenda of language acquisition, literacy development, and content area learning is a challenge not only to special education teachers but also to general education teachers with deaf and hard-of-hearing students in their classrooms. In reality, it is a challenge for teachers of all children with disabilities who also have language-learning difficulties, as well as children learning English as a second language.

Teachers of deaf and hard-of-hearing children must consistently and consciously offer opportunities for the following:

- Interpersonal communication in spoken English or American Sign Language among students and between the students and teacher (with the assistance of a sign language interpreter if the teacher or other children in the class do not know American Sign Language).

- Intrapersonal language to reflect on new concepts and skills.

- Writing that incorporates the variety of patterns of expository writing and the purposes uniquely available in each subject area.

- Reading the bodies of information in content area subjects, information that is as likely to be in the form of newspaper and magazine articles as in the form of textbooks, biographies, self-help books, and reference materials.

Reading has traditionally presented the greatest challenge to teachers of deaf and hard-of-hearing students, as it has for teachers of bilingual children and children with language disabilities. Regardless of how effectively the child can comprehend complex concepts when presented teacher-to-student, reading about these concepts requires that the child be able to manipulate English sentence structure, and this is a daunting task for the child who is not proficient in English.

An example of a difficult English sentence structure for deaf children is one that includes words expressing time relationships such as "before" and "after." When events are not written in sequence but are signaled through one of these words, the deaf child may misunderstand the meaning. (For example, a child who is deaf might comprehend the sentence, "Before Todd was allowed to go to the movies, he had to clean up his room," to mean that first Todd went to the movies and then he cleaned his room.)

This challenge has led many teachers of deaf and hard-of-hearing children to rewrite subject-matter material into simpler English syntactic structures or to ignore written material altogether. Neither approach enables children to become autonomous readers of expository material, which they ultimately must be for success in college and the workplace, as well as to be informed citizens throughout their lives.

---

consultant teacher had explained to Linda that deaf children like Ben typically miss much incidental information and, therefore, often have fragments of knowledge about any given topic (see box, "Language Learning"). In building background knowledge, Linda tried to expand on the knowledge that Ben—and other children—already had and to draw the connections between bodies of knowledge.

When Linda began the 4-week theme on government, she engaged the children in a discussion about rules at school and at home and asked them to figure out the criteria of workable rules (e.g., clear, easy to understand, realistic, can be obeyed without breaking another rule, can be enforced). Knowing that deaf and hard-of-hearing children benefit from visual representation of concepts, Linda used this discussion and the subsequent presentation about laws to begin a *semantic map* representing important concepts that would be incorporated throughout the theme on government. Each day, she and the students added new information to the map. Ben was able to see how new information connected to previously learned information, and the map served as an *advance organizer* for reading text material. Figure 1 shows the semantic map as it had evolved by the third week of the government theme.

Step 2. Teaching New Vocabulary

Linda read each text passage ahead of time to determine whether it included any terminology that was either so new or complex that she would want to design a vocabulary-building activity. She also noted whether terms seemed to be defined in context.

For example, at one point during the month-long theme, the term *debate* was important in an upcoming text passage. Linda decided to use a *Concept Attainment* model instead of a dictionary activity because she knew that the children, and particularly Ben, would benefit from

Figure 1 Semantic Map on Government Theme

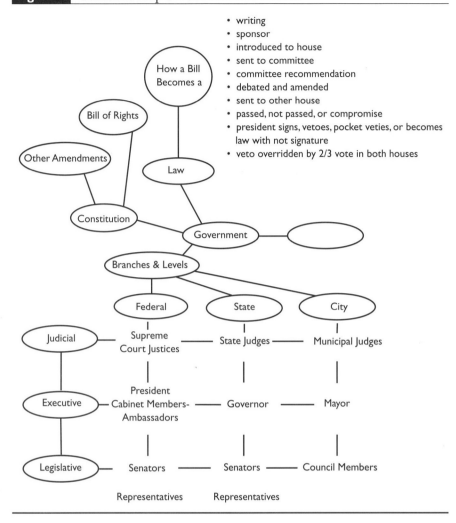

- writing
- sponsor
- introduced to house
- sent to committee
- committee recommendation
- debated and amended
- sent to other house
- passed, not passed, or compromise
- president signs, vetoes, pocket veties, or becomes law with not signature
- veto overridden by 2/3 vote in both houses

developing a conceptual framework, rather than a static definition of this term. Linda began by presenting examples and nonexamples of "debate." (An *example* of "debate" is disagreeing and trying to show someone else why your idea is right. A *nonexample* of "debate" is compromising or having no opinion.) She then encouraged the children to identify important attributes of the term, separate relevant from irrelevant attributes, and identify subordinate, superordinate, and coordinate terms.

Step 3. Setting a Purpose for Reading the Text Material

On some days, Linda herself would set the purpose for reading a text—but she often used the *K-W-L* ap-proach because she liked the idea of encouraging the children to deter-mine what they wanted to learn by creating their own questions. The K-W-L approach involves three steps:

K The children brainstorm what they know about a topic the teacher has identified, and they develop categories for their ideas.

W Children create questions or state-ments regarding what they want to learn about the topic.

L In groups or in the whole class, children discuss what they learned after reading the text material.

Linda had found it difficult to ensure Ben's participation in full-class discussions because lively dis-cussions tended to outpace his interpreter. By the time he could in-sert an idea or answer a question, the discussion was often well ahead of his point. One modification that Linda sometimes made to the K-W-L approach was to start by asking the children to write their ideas. At other times, she asked the children to form small, heterogeneous groups in which at least one child took on the role of facilitator—to make sure that all group members participated.

Step 4. Reading Silently

Linda encouraged silent reading as much as possible, particularly for Ben. Silent reading has benefits over oral round-robin reading for most children; but for deaf and hard-of-hearing children, silent reading is es-pecially crucial:

- Deaf and hard-of-hearing children like Ben cannot simultaneously watch the public reader and read the material themselves. They are forced to make a choice during oral reading situations that hearing children do not have to make. They must either watch the child reading aloud or in sign (or watch the interpreter), in which case they are doing no reading themselves, or they can read the passage themselves, in which case the child whose turn it is to read publicly is losing at least one member of the audience.

- For deaf or hard-of-hearing children, comprehension suffers during oral reading because the child must concentrate on saying or signing the words correctly, and a child like Ben has no opportunity to reread or engage in other strategies when he does not understand the material (Samuels & Farstrup, 1992; Schirmer, 1994).

Step 5. Discussing the Material and Recording Key Concepts on Semantic Maps, Graphic Organizers, or Outlines

Linda found that discussion—plus the use of visual aids—after reading provides children with opportunity to clarify information, point out relationships between concepts, and add information on the topic.

Linda built on the semantic map that she and the students created throughout the entire 4 weeks of the "government" unit, adding new information every day. The students used the map to review information presented previously, discuss relationships between concepts, predict information in upcoming text passages, and summarize what they had learned. For Ben, a visual reminder of what he had learned was always available.

Independent Text Reading

While Linda typically used her semantic map throughout the theme, both when she devoted class time to reading the text and when she expected the students to read some portions of the text independently, several times she developed a *thematic organizer* for the children prior to having them read a text passage at home. She found that when she developed a thematic organizer for a passage that included a lot of new information, many of the children still demonstrated poor comprehension and were very frustrated with the assignment. This was noticeably true for Ben. Figure 2 shows a thematic organizer used for the government unit.

She observed that it was more effective to teach the new concepts first, then have the children read the thematic organizer, and finally assign the text for independent reading at home. In essence, combining the presentation of the material with a thematic organizer served as a *scaffold*, or support, that enabled the children to read the text material independently. The more the children were able to read independently, the more class time she had for presenting subject area material, exploring other teaching models and techniques, and working with individual children. She kept in mind, however, that independent reading strategies do not offer students as much support for comprehending the text as strategies used for in-class reading.

Organizers and overviews can be helpful to learners—particularly deaf and hard-of-hearing students and other students with language difficulties.

- *Organizers* are written in a narrative form at the child's

---

Figure 2   Thematic Organizer for Text Passage on Elections and Voting

- Have you ever wondered how someone gets to be the President, Governor, Mayor, Senator, or Member of congress? Would you like to be a lawmaker some day?

- Lawmakers are elected by citizens who have registered to vote. The person who wants to be a lawmaker is called a candidate. The candidate "runs for office." This means that the candidate gives speeches and talks to the voters.

- Most candidates belong to a political party. The two biggest political parties in the United States are the Democratic and Republican.

- You will read about how people get elected to public office. When you finish this chapter, you will know:

  who can vote,
  what a political campaign is,
  and how elections are held.

---

reading ability level. The information contained in an organizer includes (a) topics and subtopics to be covered in the text, (b) explanation of how the new concepts relate to the prior knowledge or previous experiences of the reader, (c) examples of the concepts, (d) new or relevant vocabulary, and (e) expected learning outcomes (Lenz, Alley, & Schumaker, 1987).

- *Overviews* are graphic representations of the hierarchical and parallel relationships between key text concepts. Originally developed in the late 1960s, overviews can take many forms —maps, flowcharts, bubble charts—to attach new information to prior knowledge.

Scaffolding—for Teachers

Just as many students need supports in their climb toward higher reading comprehensions, so do most teachers welcome suggestions for the difficult job of teaching reading—particularly for children who are deaf or hard of hearing or have other special language needs. Try the "scaffolds"—or steps—that Linda and Ben used. These same strategies are just as valuable to teachers in inclusive settings with children demonstrating other kinds of disabilities and children who are bilingual.

The opportunity to read expository material in subject areas should be as integral to every child's educational experience as the opportunity to read narrative material. Language acquisition, literacy development, and content area instruction are important for all children. And effective teaching strategies are crucial tools for all teachers.

References

Alvermann, D. E., & Swafford, J. (1989). Do content area strategies have a research base? *Journal of Reading, 32,* 388–394.

Lenz, B. K., Alley, G. R., & Schumaker, J. B. (1987). Activating the inactive learner: Advance organizers in the secondary content classroom. *Learning Disability Quarterly, 10,* 53–67.

Ogle, D. M. (1986). K-W-L: A teaching model that develops active reading of expository text. *The Reading Teacher, 39,* 564–570.

Samuels, S. J., & Farstrup, A. E. (Eds.). (1992). *What research has to say about reading instruction* (2nd ed.). Newark, DE: International Reading Association.

Schirmer, B. R. (1994). *Language and literacy development in children who are deaf.* Needham Heights, MA: Allyn & Bacon. (ERIC Document Reproduction Service No. ED 340 011)

Zakaluk, B. L., & Samuels, S. J. (1988). Toward a new approach to predicting text comprehensibility. In B. L. Zakaluk & S. J. Samuels, (Eds.), *Readability: Its past, present, and future* (pp. 121–144). Newark, DE: International Reading Association. (ERIC Document Reproduction Service No. ED 292 058)

Article Review Form at end of book.

Why does the title of this article declare that reading instruction in the resource room is a broken promise? What kind of reading instruction should students with learning disabilities receive, according to the authors?

Broken Promises

Reading instruction in the resource room

Sharon Vaughn

University of Texas at Austin

Sally Watson Moody

Jeanne Shay Schumm

University of Miami

In this study, we were interested in the potential influence of reforms on grouping and instruction that students with learning disabilities receive during reading in special education resource room settings. The questions that guided our investigation were:

- What grouping structures do teachers use for reading instruction in the resource room?

- In what ways do teachers provide differentiated instruction, materials, and curriculum for students?

- What word knowledge and comprehension practices do teachers implement during reading instruction? . . .

Method

Participants

Teachers and students from a large southeastern school district were included in this study. . . .

Fourteen special education, elementary school teachers who were teaching in resource room settings participated in this study. . . .

Sixty-one males and 21 females participated in the study. Seventy-seven of the 82 students in the study were identified by the school district as LD, while the remaining 5 students were identified as educable mentally disabled (n = 2), and orthopedically impaired (n = 3). . . .

Procedures and Measures

Teacher Interviews

The teachers were interviewed at the beginning and end of the school year. Both the pre- and the postinterview protocols consisted of open-ended questions designed to elicit information about teachers' backgrounds and perceptions about grouping during reading instruction, factors that contributed to their decision to use particular reading practices, and their perceptions about effective materials and practices for students with reading problems. . . .

The 14 participants were formally interviewed, individually, in sessions that lasted from 30 to 60 min. Teachers were interviewed informally during the three classroom observations. . . .

Observations

Observations were conducted using an adapted version of the Classroom Climate Scale (McIntosh et al., 1993), an observation measure originally designed to provide information about teacher and student interaction in settings that include mainstreamed students with learning disabilities. The scale was adapted for use in a resource room setting. An additional form was added to the scale to obtain information on group size, composition, and instructional materials used. . . .

Each of the 14 classrooms was observed three times (beginning, middle, and end of the year) during the same reading/language arts instructional period. Each observation lasted for a complete reading/language arts lesson (60 to 90 min).

Teacher Self-Report

To further investigate the instructional groups and materials used by the teacher, we developed a teacher self-report measure. The measure was an adaptation of a previously developed list of flexible grouping components (e.g., size, composition; Flood, Lapp, Flood, & Nagel, 1992). On the days of the classroom observations, teachers were asked to complete the checklist as it pertained to their lesson that day. There were four questions asked, each with a list of possible answers. Teachers were instructed to check as many responses as applied to their grouping for that day's lesson. Questions included:

- What was the composition of your groups?

From "Broken Promises: Reading Instruction in the Resource Room," by Sharon Vaughn, Sally Watson Moody, and Jeanne Shay Schumm, *Exceptional Children,* Winter 1998, pgs. 211–225. Copyright 1998 by The Council for Exceptional Children. Reprinted with permission.

- What type of leadership was used in your groups?
- Who selected the materials that were used in the different groups?
- What types of materials did you use for the different groups?

Background Information Form

There were 14 items related to demographic information, professional preparation for teaching reading, and instructional grouping. An additional three items were designed to obtain information regarding current reading and grouping practices. Teachers were asked to complete the background form at the time of the initial interview.

Results

Classroom Climate Scale: Quantitative Report

The grouping formats investigated in this study through the use of the Classroom Climate Scale included

- Whole group instruction (all students are involved in the same activity, assignment, discussion, and question and answer session).
- Group activities (students are working in two or more groups with three or more students in a group).
- Pairs (one student is working with another).
- Independent activities (students are engaged individually on an activity/assignment that is the same as the rest of the students in the class).
- Individualized activities (students are not involved in pairing or group activities and are working individually on a differentiated assignment). . . .

Grouping Practices

The range of reading ability of students during the observed reading classes were 3 to 4 grade levels much like what a teacher would expect in the general education classroom. Eleven of the 14 teachers used primarily whole group instruction (all students in the room during that period participated in the same reading lesson) followed by seat work that was largely completed independently while the teacher moved from student-to-student to provide assistance. Of the three teachers who used different grouping procedures rather than primarily whole group instruction, one used small group instruction with 4 to 5 students in a same-ability group with follow-up work completed individually and occasionally in pairs. The other two teachers taught reading by dividing the students into two same-ability groups with approximately four students in each group.

Teachers provided a range of explanations for using primarily whole group instruction. Some teachers indicated that they thought it was "right" to have students on the same level with the same materials and that it keeps students from being stigmatized. . . .

Some teachers indicated that they preferred whole group instruction because they thought the students learned more.

Three teachers commented about their large class sizes and how that allowed for little individualization.

The two teachers who provided small groups, pairing, and more individualized work provided these explanations. "I think it is necessary for them to be grouped according to their instructional level and using materials that they are actually able to read, not a book too hard that they aren't able to read." The second teacher spent considerable time having students read individually to her every day. "I think that is the secret of reading. That you listen to each student every day of the year."

Individualized Instruction

Only a few of the teachers provided differential work for the students to complete independently or one-on-one with the teacher. Nine of the teachers provided no individualization of work. In these nine classrooms, all students, regardless of ability, were asked to read the same book and complete the same activities. These teachers stated that they did provide differential expectations for each student in terms of the amount or quality of the work they completed. . . .

The teachers who provided highly individualized instruction frequently provided one-to-one instruction along with materials and assignments tailored to meet the individual needs of students. . . .

Overall Approach to Reading Instruction

Ten of the 14 teachers identified whole language as the primary approach they used to teach reading. Most of these teachers indicated that their reading program also included direct instruction or attention to individual learning styles. The other four teachers mentioned whole language as part of their instruction, but indicated that they implemented other instructional practices. The teachers who identified whole language as their primary instructional approach provided numerous explanations including: (a) students are more motivated, (b) skills are taught in context, (c) stigma is reduced since all kids do the same thing, and (d) the types of reading materials are broader (e.g., books and literature). . . .

None of the teachers was confident that whole language was adequate to teach reading to students with disabilities, and many indicated they used it because it "was what their school did" or to "conform to what they did in the classroom. . . ." Some teachers felt that the school wanted them to use whole language. Some of the concerns expressed about whole language were that students might not be really reading but memorizing the story and that students do not learn to decode words. . . .

More than half of the teachers provided some comment about the importance of attending to the learning styles of students. . . .

Teaching Word Recognition and Decoding

Three of the teachers provided ongoing word recognition or decoding instruction. Two of these teachers used phonics worksheets to supplement instruction, and all three taught word families. . . .

Some of the other teachers commented on the importance of phonics instruction for some of their students, but were never observed teaching it and did not indicate that they taught it. . . . Several teachers indicated that they thought there was a controversy between whole language and phonics instruction. . . .

Several teachers indicated that they did not teach decoding. . . . Another teacher felt that it was useless to teach letter or sound recognition. . . .

Teaching Comprehension

Most of the teachers (11) taught reading comprehension by either reading the story aloud to the students and asking questions, or having the group take turns reading the story followed by the teacher asking questions. Observations revealed that the questions asked were largely factual and literal. In one teacher observation, the students worked in pairs and asked each other questions about the story. Of the 41 observations there is only one record of a comprehension strategy being taught to the students.

What's Special About Special Education?

We asked the teachers who participated in this study what they thought was special about special education. Caring, patience, reteaching, extra help, small group instruction, and individualization were the most prevalent responses.

Students' Reading Achievement

Stanford Achievement Test (SAT) scores for total reading were available for 76% of the students who participated in this study. The SAT is a group-administered test given at the end of each school year—scores at the end of the previous school year prior to the start of the study, and then scores at the end of the school year the study was conducted were obtained. Total Reading Percentile scores prior to the start of this study were $M = 15.56$ ($SD = 11.78$), and for the same students at the end of the study year were $M = 14.19$ ($SD = 10.87$). These results reveal that, at least relative to their peers, the students in this study made little or no growth in reading.

Discussion

In light of the many reforms in general and special education, the purpose of this study was to better understand how grouping and instruction for reading were implemented in special education resource rooms. Our expectation was that special education resource room teachers would provide differential reading instruction and that a range of grouping practices would be implemented including individual one-on-one instruction, small group instruction, paired learning, and, less frequently, whole group instruction. Furthermore, we expected that students would be provided reading materials that corresponded with their instructional reading levels and were designed to meet their specific reading problems. In other words, we expected that the reading instruction would be significantly different from that provided in the general education classroom, particularly since these students were placed in the special education resources room because they were identified as having a specific reading disability.

The interviews and observations from the special education resource room teachers who participated in this study were surprisingly similar to the general education teachers who participated in a separate year-long study the previous year (Schumm et al., 1996). Both the general education teachers in that study and the special education teachers in this study implemented primarily whole group instruction for reading, used the same reading materials for all students, and provided little differentiated instruction. In brief, most of the students with learning disabilities who participated in the resource room reading program did not receive an individualized reading program nor were they provided reading material that corresponded with their instructional reading level.

After each observation, teachers in this study were asked to identify the types of materials they used during the observed reading period. The majority of responses by the special education teachers (31 of 42 responses) corresponded with our observations—teachers used the same materials for all of the students. One special education teacher in this study provided this representative statement: "We were told that you were supposed to use one book. If the third grade is using a third-grade level basal, then everyone in the room uses the third-grade basal." When asked what she would do if one student was having trouble with learning a skill and whether she would then teach the student individually, the teacher responded, "No, I would probably do a group lesson on the skill so he doesn't feel singled out. Chances are there are others who need it, too. . . ."

There are a number of explanations for these general findings. First, the number of students for whom the teacher was responsible during our targeted periods ranged considerably in size, from 5 to 19. It could be that the large numbers of students that the special education teachers were asked to instruct at any one time prevented them from providing differential instruction and encouraged the provision of whole group reading instruction. To further address this issue, we examined the classroom observations of the seven teachers who had eight or fewer students in their class at one time to see if their grouping practices and differentiated instruction varied from that of the teachers as a whole. Results indicated that with these seven teachers, one provided a highly individualized program, a second teacher provided an individualized program to a lesser extent, and the other five teachers provided instructional programs that closely resembled those of the teachers who had much larger groups of students at one time.

Another possible explanation is that special and general education teachers are provided the same reading courses and many of the same inservice experiences, and so their beliefs about grouping, reading, and appropriate instructional practices, as well as their skills for teaching reading, are similar. Considering the emphasis in the past 10 years on whole language instruction (Altwerger, Edelsky, & Flores, 1987; Goodman, 1986), mixed-ability grouping (Eldredge & Butterfield, 1986), the fear of providing extensive skills instruction to low-performing readers

(Allington, 1983; Hiebert, 1983), and the perceived stigma associated with providing students with different level reading materials (Schumm et al., 1995), it may be that special education teachers, like many of their general education colleagues (Moody et al., in press; Vaughn et al., 1996), perceive that many aspects of differentiated instruction are not effective or are no more effective than whole group instruction. Comments from their interviews suggest that many of these teachers perceived that differentiated instruction and grouping by ability may have negative outcomes (e.g., be harmful to the self-concept of students), or ultimately result in students spending more time on individual seat work activities (Haynes & Jenkins, 1986).

Most of the teachers in this study indicated that whole language best described their approach to reading instruction. In line with the principles held by most whole language advocates (Goodman, 1986; Goodman, Crites, & Whitemore, 1991), what little phonics instruction was provided was taught within the context of reading and writing, largely incidentally, and with little documented monitoring or skills development. Some teachers were comfortable with this approach and indicated that they "just taught phonics as the child needed it." However, our observations revealed this rarely occurred. Other teachers expressed concern about the lack of phonics instruction and commented that "students would not learn to read if we don't teach them the letters and sounds." Other teachers indicated that they felt caught in the cross fire between phonics and whole language instruction (Mather, 1992). . . .

We think that the findings of this study reveal a series of broken promises. The most obvious is the broken promise to the student and the parent that an individualized reading program will be provided to each student to meet their specific needs. With few exceptions, teachers are struggling to provide individualized instruction to students when they are responsible for teaching eight or more students at one time. Other broken promises occur for special education teachers who expect that they will have the resources and

time to provide an appropriate education to students with reading disabilities. These broken promises deny the intention of IDEA which specifies "specially designed instruction, at no cost to the parents, to meet the unique needs of a child with a disability" (20 USC 1401 et seq.). . . .

Implications for Practice

While the solutions will be challenging to implement, we have identified several implications from our research. First, if special education is supposed to meet the pedagogical principles designed for successful reading experiences for students (Kameenui, 1993), it will not occur when teachers are asked to meet the needs of "small classes" of students at one time. Second, there is increasing evidence that reading procedures designed specifically for poor readers require intensive, specific interventions that differ considerably from what can be provided in large, whole group reading activities (Torgesen, Wagner, Rashotte, Alexander, & Conway, 1997). Furthermore, there is considerable evidence that these specific interventions must include instruction characteristic of code-based programs (i.e., phonics; Adams, 1990; Blachman, 1989, 1994; Felton, 1993; Foorman, (in press), Spear-Swerling & Sternberg, 1996). Third, students with reading problems need to have many opportunities to practice reading material that is on their level and not too difficult in terms of word recognition (Anderson, Hiebert, Scott, & Wilkinson, 1985; Chinn, Waggoner, Anderson, Schommer, & Wilkinson, 1993; Spear-Swerling & Sternberg, 1996). Fourth, teachers are "starving" for professional development experiences that provide them with research-based reading practices that yield effective outcomes for students with severe reading difficulties.

We are concerned that many of the teachers perceive themselves as "victims" of the waves of reform that occur within their school district. One teacher said to us, "I feel that I am at the bottom of a cement mixer where they whirl around ideas and down load them on my desk." Regardless of what aspects of reform schools choose to implement, we think it is essential that they evaluate

the effects of whatever changes they implement on teachers (e.g., morale and perceptions of effectiveness), as well as on student outcomes. . . .

References

Adams, M. J. (1990). *Beginning to read: Thinking and learning about print.* Cambridge, MA: MIT Press. *

Allington, R.L. (1983). The reading instruction provided readers of differing ability. *Elementary School Journal, 83,* 255–265.

Altwerger, B., Edelsky, C., & Flores, B. (1987). Whole language: What's new? *The Reading Teacher, 41,* 144–154.

Anderson, R., Hiebert, E., Scott, J., & Wilkinson, I. (1985). *Becoming a nation of readers: The report of the Commission on Reading.* Champaign, IL: Center for the Study of Reading. (ERIC Document Reproduction Service No. ED 253 865)

Blachman, B.A. (1989). Phonological awareness and word recognition: Assessment and intervention. In A. Kamhi & H. Catts (Eds.), *Reading disabilities: A developmental language perspective* (pp. 133–158). Boston, MA: College-Hill. *

Chinn, C.A., Waggoner, M.A., Anderson, R.C., Schommer, M., & Wilkinson, I.A.G. (1993). Situated actions during reading lessons: A microanalysis of oral reading error episodes. *American Educational Research Journal, 30,* 361–392.

Eldredge, J.L., & Butterfield, D. (1986). Alternatives to traditional reading instruction. *The Reading Teacher, 40,* 32–37.

Felton, R.H. (1993). Effects of instruction on the decoding skills of children with phonological-processing problems. *Journal of Learning Disabilities, 26,* 583–589.

Flood, J., Lapp, D., Flood, S., & Nagel, G. (1992). Am I allowed to group? Using flexible patterns for effective instruction. *The Reading Teacher, 45(8),* 608–616.

Foorman, B.R. (in press). *The case for early reading intervention: Foundations of reading acquisition.* Mawah, NJ: Lawrence Erlbaum. *

Goodman, K.S. (1986). *What's whole in whole language.* Portsmouth, NH: Heineman. *

Goodman, Y.S., Crites, A., & Whitemore, K. F. (1991). Teaching skills in whole language classrooms. In K. S. Goodman, L.B. Bird, & Y.M. Goodman (Eds.), *The whole language catalogue* (p. 308). Santa Rosa, CA: American School Publishers. *

Haynes, M.C., & Jenkins, J.R. (1986). Reading instruction in the special education resource room. *American Educational Research Journal, 23(2),* 161–190.

Hiebert, E.H. (1983). An examination of ability grouping for reading instruction. *Reading Research Quarterly, 18,* 231–255.

Kameenui, E.J. (1993). Diverse learners and the tyranny of time: Don't fix blame; fix the leaky roof. *The Reading Teacher, 46(5),* 376–383.

Mather, N. (1992). Whole language reading instruction for students with learning disabilities: Caught in the cross fire. *Learning Disabilities Research and Practice, 7*(2), 87–95.

McIntosh, R., Vaughn, S., Schumm, J.S., Haager, D., & Lee, O. (1993). Observations of students with learning disabilities in general education classrooms. *Exceptional Children, 60,* 249–261.

Moody, S.W., Vaughn, S., & Schumm, J.S. (1997). Instructional grouping for reading: Teachers' views. *Remedial and Special Education.*

Schumm, J.S., Moody, S.W., & Vaughn, S. (1996). *Grouping for reading instruction: General education teachers' perceptions and practices.* Manuscript in preparation.

Schumm, J.S., Vaughn, S., & Elbaum, B.E. (1996). Teachers' perceptions of grouping practices for reading instruction. *NRC Yearbook,* 543–551.

Schumm, J.S., Vaughn, S., Haager, D., McDowell, J., Rothlein, L., & Saumell, L. (1995). General education teacher planning: What can students with learning disabilities expect? *Exceptional Children, 61,* 335–352.

Spear-Swerling, L., & Sternberg, R.J. (1996). *Off track: When poor readers become "learning disabled."* Boulder, CO: Westview Press. *

Torgesen, J. K., Wagner, R. K., Rashotte, C. A., Alexander, A. W., & Conway, T. (1997). Preventive and remedial interventions for children with severe reading disabilities. *Learning Disabilities: A Multidisciplinary Journal, 8*(1), 51–61.

Vaughn, S., Schumm, J. S., Jallad, B., Slusher, J., & Saumell, L. (1996). Teachers' views of inclusion. *Learning Disabilities Research & Practice 11*(2), 96–106.

 Article Review Form at end of book.

WiseGuide Wrap-Up

- Providing an exemplary reading program adapted to the needs of individual students is not sufficient to assure the academic success of delayed readers.

- Policies and procedures that are inconsistent with recent research and current thinking can contribute to the failure of remedial reading programs.

- Successful early intervention programs have common features that appear to be related to the prevention of reading problems.

- Traditional pedagogy does not take into account the language of students that is different from the standard, middle-class U.S. community.

- Several strategies can be used to help diverse groups of learners read and comprehend material that would appear to be considerably beyond their reading levels.

- Effective instruction for special education students in a resource classroom must be provided in order to meet their special needs.

R.E.A.L. Sites

This list provides a print preview of typical **Coursewise** R.E.A.L. sites. There are over 100 such sites at the **Courselinks**™ site. The danger in printing URLs is that web sites can change overnight. As we went to press, these sites were functional using the URLs provided. If you come across one that isn't, please let us know via email to: webmaster@coursewise.com. Use your Passport to access the most current list of R.E.A.L. sites at the **Courselinks**™ site.

Site name: LD Online
URL: http://www.ldonline.org/index.html
Why is it R.E.A.L.? This site is a guide to learning disabilities for parents, teachers, and children. Included are highlights of new information in the field of learning disabilities, the basics about learning disabilities, material from leading organizations and professionals, a comprehensive list of resources and events, and personal essays, artwork, and stories by adults and children with learning disabilities.
Key topic: learning disabilities
Try this: What are the most recent findings about the implications of learning disabilities for learning to read?

Site name: The Council for Exceptional Children
URL: http://www.cec.sped.org/
Why is it R.E.A.L.? This is the site for the largest international organization dedicated only to special education. It includes information about the organization, its special interest groups, and its publications. It also includes information about professional standards and accreditation, training and events, public policy, and legislative information.
Key topic: learning disabilities
Try this: Visit the web site and find out what is being discussed about teaching literacy to exceptional learners.

Site name: Center for Applied and Special Technology
URL: http://www.cast.org/
Why is it R.E.A.L.? CAST is a not-for-profit organization whose mission is to expand opportunities for individuals with disabilities through the development of and innovative uses of technology. This site has publications, sample software programs, and teaching strategies that are interactive and that demonstrate the universal curriculum concept for students of all learning abilities.
Key topics: innovative technology, learning disabilities
Try this: Navigate to the Teaching Strategies section and connect to the Customizing with Software link. Preview some of the available software programs designed to customize learning. Choose one of the programs to review. Present why you think this software program facilitates individualization of learning materials and experiences.

section 7

Learning Objectives

- Define the transactional approach toward technology.

- Discuss ways that technology can provide links between reading and writing, assisting students with special needs, and extend the reading process.

- Discuss how the influence of technology has changed how we become literate and what it means to be literate.

- Identify the benefits of educators' creating and using an interactive World Wide Web site with students.

- Analyze ways in which electronic reading and writing are transforming literacy.

Technology as an Integral Part of Literacy Instruction

WiseGuide Intro

Students of today literally have the world at their fingertips. Computers and the Internet provide students with access to resources from around the world and have the potential to transform the teaching and learning of literacy. It is an exciting time for teachers and students, yet with this excitement comes the challenge of meeting new and changing literacy demands as the form, context, and space for reading and writing change. Educators must be knowledgeable about these new forms of literacy, as well as about the most effective method of incorporating technology into the curriculum in order to prepare children for the future.

As with any educational material, computers and other technology should be thought of as tools to achieve the goals and objectives of the reading program. A teacher's decisions about what and how to teach with technology will closely align with his or her beliefs about teaching and learning. For example, some computer software programs, such as simulations, word processing programs, and Internet applications (such as electronic mail and the World Wide Web), can be used to promote critical thinking, cooperative learning, experimentation, inquiry, and authorship. Other software programs, such as drill-and-practice, tutorials, and games, provide practice in skills that have already been taught. CD-ROM encyclopedias and videodiscs can be used for research purposes. Different applications serve different purposes and meet different objectives, and they should be chosen based on the teacher's instructional goals.

There are thousands of software programs, CD-ROMs, and World Wide Web sites available to teachers. It is important to evaluate these programs and sites carefully to determine if they are appropriate for your students' needs and match your instructional goals. Software programs must also be compatible with the computer hardware available. Reviews of software programs and web sites are published in educational journals and computer magazines, as well as electronic magazines and other web sites. Catalogs and demonstration copies of software can also be of help in selecting the right program.

The Internet can also serve as a powerful tool for professional development. Mailing lists, discussion forums, and bulletin boards can provide an avenue for collaboration with other teachers and educators from around the world with similar interests. Liszt Select (http://www.liszt.com) and TileNet (http://tile.net/lists/) are two web sites that contain extensive sets of mailing lists. Another professional use of the Internet is for the development of lessons in the classroom. Hundreds of web sites are dedicated to providing educators with resources for promoting the effective teaching of literacy. Information about many of these web sites has been provided for you in the WiseGuide Wrap-Ups for the sections in this volume and also at the **Courselinks** web site.

As we enter the next millennium, teachers must be cognizant of their role in preparing students for the future as technology continues to redefine what it means to be literate. The articles in Section 7 discuss issues that will assist teachers in making thoughtful decisions about the best and most appropriate use of technology for teaching and learning literacy. "Literacy Technologies: What Stance Should We Take?" explores several different stances taken by literacy educators toward technology in regard to their perception of the relationship between technology and literacy. "Can Technology Help Teach Reading Right?" proposes ways in which technology can help children become literate. "Caity's Question: Literacy as Deixis on the Internet" discusses the Internet's implications for what it means to be literate and how we become literate. "Using the World Wide Web to Build Learning Communities: Writing for Genuine Purposes" explains the benefits of teachers' and students' creating an interactive web site. "Reading and Writing with Computers: Literacy Research in a Post-typographic World" discusses the importance of future research that analyzes the extent to which electronic reading and writing are transforming literacy.

Questions

Reading 30. Bruce describes a variety of stances toward technology, including neutrality, opposition, utilitarian, skeptical, transformational, and aesthetic. However, he argues that these stances are incomplete, due to their perception of the relationship between technology and literacy. Discuss what you believe Bruce means by this statement. Discuss how the transactional stance toward technology enhances and broadens the relationship between technology and literacy. Do you feel this stance has merit?

Reading 31. Name and briefly discuss several software packages mentioned in the article.

Summarize the two opposing views on how young children best learn to read. How does technology play a role in each?

Reading 32. What is a deictic term? Why does Leu say that literacy is a deictic term? What are the four important changes in what it means to be literate?

Reading 33. How does the World Wide Web (WWW) serve as an "animator and tool for creating and sharing ideas, for improving literacy, and for welcoming others into your classroom community of learners"?

Reading 34. What does a "post-typographic world" mean? Are reading and writing different with technology?

Bruce describes a variety of stances toward technology, including neutrality, opposition, utilitarian, skeptical, transformational, and aesthetic. However, he argues that these stances are incomplete, due to their perception of the relationship between technology and literacy. Discuss what you believe Bruce means by this statement. Discuss how the transactional stance toward technology enhances and broadens the relationship between technology and literacy. Do you feel this stance has merit?

Literacy Technologies

What stance should we take?

Bertram C. Bruce

University of Illinois at Urbana-Champaign

Technology. The word seems unavoidable now in discussions of literacy theory and practice. Parents ask the teacher or school principal what the school is doing about computer literacy and networking. Librarians are alternately invigorated or distressed thinking about what new information technologies mean for their work. Teachers wonder about whether these technologies will improve children's literacy skills or take them forever away from traditional reading and writing. Theorists debate whether the book is dead. Nearly everyone struggles just to stay minimally aware of new technological developments and their social implications. The question of what form literacies will take in a century likely to be defined by a new technological environment (Bruce, 1995; Burbules & Bruce, 1995; Reinking, 1995; Reinking, McKenna, & Kieffer, in press) has become a present issue for nearly everyone involved with literacy today.

Underlying both the excitement and the unease about technology[1] are deeper issues about literacy and its relation to the physical world, the nature of knowledge, social change, linguistics, aesthetics, and morality. At the core are questions about what it means to be human. If we open up the current debates to these underlying issues, we may find not only that we arrive at different conclusions, but that our understanding of literacy itself has changed.

Adopting a Stance Toward Technology

The issues regarding technology that concern parents, teachers, administrators, researchers, and others challenge us to ask some basic questions. For a start: What should be the stance of literacy educators and researchers toward technology? Where does technology fit with respect to other concerns about reading and writing processes, learning, multiculturalism,

[1]By "technology," I mean here information and communication technologies, though not necessarily limited to the modern digital forms of these technologies.

texts, assessment, and sociocultural contexts? Will new technologies fundamentally alter the nature of literacy or are they a passing fad? Several possibilities emerge immediately:

Neutrality. Some say no stance toward technology is needed, thus arguing for neutrality. They stress that literacy is about feelings and ideas; technology is about things. Texts and objects are separate realms. This stance accepts technologies as potentially valuable, and technology as a valid area of study, but it does not connect either specific technologies or technology studies to its primary concerns about the life of texts.

Opposition. Others go beyond the neutral position to stand in opposition or resistance to technology. For them, the inevitable uses of technologies for surveillance, regimentation, and social stratification far outweigh the alleged benefits. Slouka (1995) worried about a retreat from reality into the virtual worlds of new technologies. He argued that "the real significance of our retreat from the world may be not so much in the technology that makes it possible as in the revolution in attitude that makes it appealing"(p. 68).

Reprinted with permission from the National Reading Conference.

Following Ellul (1980), many fear that technicizing society will progressively destroy the last bit of our humanity. Some argue further that, in this materialistic, technologically driven world, a major function of literacy, and especially literature, is to support human values against the technical.[2] Like Dilthey and other early hermeneuticists (Palmer, 1969), who saw the imperative for counterposing human to natural sciences, they feel compelled to hold human conceptions against the technological. Only through the human realm of interpretation and adherence to human values can we then avoid reduction to the level of the machine.

Utilitarian. In contrast, others argue for a utilitarian stance, saying "technology provides marvelous new tools for teaching and learning that can improve literacy education." Surely, they must be employed with care, but one can find many ways to make use of these new tools. Many recent studies (Bruce & Rubin, 1993; Bruce & Sharples, 1995; Garner & Gillingham, 1996; Handa, 1990; Shutte, 1996) on electronic communication in classrooms might then be cited as evidence that the use of new technologies can have beneficial effects on learning and teaching. The utilitarian could be characterized as having a stance toward technology analogous to what Rosenblatt (1978) called the efferent stance toward literature, one that sees a text as a repository of information. Technologies are then repositories of capabilities for teaching and learning.

Skeptical. Representing the pessimistic side of utilitarianism, but closely allied to it philosophically, is one of practical skepticism. Proponents of this stance might say, "I've seen many so-called 'marvels'; show me that technology really makes a difference and I'll begin to listen more." Unlike one who adopts the oppositional stance, the practical skeptic does not see great dangers in technology, just overblown rhetoric about it. The great willingness of technology to break down when it is needed most is the skeptic's first line of argument, but the educational system's inertial resistance to change is

their best answer to the optimistic utilitarian (Neilsen, in press; Peyton, 1990).

Transformational. Going beyond utilitarianism, and sitting at the far extreme from the oppositional position, are those who argue that new technologies are transformational: They will replace or radically transform the basic definition of literacy (Reinking, McKenna, Labbo, & Kieffer, in press; Soloway, 1993; Spender, 1995). This position sees the end result of this transformation as essentially positive, though the process itself is not without difficulties along the way. The transformationalist argues that our task then is to understand and guide this transformation.

Aesthetic. Following Rosenblatt again, there are numerous examples of an aesthetic stance toward technology. Many artists, for example, see new information technologies as affording rich opportunities for creativity in electronic media. They talk of a paradigm shift as artists move from using the computer to create or reproduce art to accepting electronic representations per se as finished art (ad319, 1994).

The aesthetic response reminds us that if technology does lead to changes that the course is not easy to predict. Do we really know what the fundamental skills for 21st-century literacy will be? It is unlikely that they are simply keyboarding skills or knowing how to use a CD-ROM. Nathan Shedroff (*internet.au*, 1997), a professional web-page designer, suggests one possibility when he says:

Few people are ever taught to create successful, satisfying experiences for others. Mostly, those folks are in the performing arts: dancers, comedians, storytellers, singer, actors, etc. I now wish I had more training in theater and performing arts to rely on . . . especially improvisational theater. That's like the highest form of interactivity. (pp. 40–41)

The aesthetic stance can thus be added to the neutral, oppositional, utilitarian, skeptical, and transformational stances to form an incomplete list of possible positions one might assume with respect to new technologies. The differences among these stances are sharp, signifying much more than nuanced differences in interpretations of empirical data. They speak to different views of literacy

and technology, but also to different conceptions of language, of education, and of basic human values. Moreover, the stance one adopts entails distinctly different choices regarding uses of technologies and overall curricular goals. And beyond a host of immediate practical decisions, that stance shapes what counts as literacy studies and how we conceive of literacy practices. In fact, it defines to a large extent the very purpose of literacy.

The Reflexivity Problem

But oddly, despite the differences between these positions, they all share at least one important assumption. They each construct "technology" and "literacy" as distinct realms, with literacy over here and technology over there. In fact, technology is not just over there, but out there, at most in a distant suburb of literacy, if not on another planet. The point of contact among the stances, and thus their point of difference, is over how the realms of literacy and technology ought to relate, whether we should be building a wall to keep technology out or a highway to bring it in. In either case, the shared starting assumption is that we are discussing two autonomous realms, as shown in Figure 1.*

This view of technology as autonomous from literacy derives from what Latour (1991) called the "technology/society divide" (p. 103), a divide deeply ensconced in our discourse about technology. It manifests itself clearly in the extreme positions, that one can stand opposed to a technology outside of us, or that we will be transformed by that technology, but also in the belief that one could be neutral about technology, or see it as only a tool. . . .

A Transactional View

The assumption that technology and literacy are separate, autonomous realms serves to distance us from the concrete reality of literacy, both as it is practiced today and as it changes in new sociotechnical contexts. The assumption has been challenged from many quarters, though not always in mainstream literacy dis-

[2]This stance is one that might derive from Heidegger (1977), though Heidegger himself would be unlikely to share its inherent optimism.

*Not included in this publication.

course. Haas (1995), for one, has argued for re-attending to the materiality of literacy, how it is practiced in terms of specific bodily, temporal, spatial, and technological relations. Similarly, Bromley (1997) addressed it in his discussion of the "social chicken or the technological egg." Researchers in the new field of social informatics*[9] essentially take the negation of that myth as their starting point.

What alternative is there to the autonomy myth? How might we think about technology in relation to literacy practices in a way that does justice to the dynamic and situated sociotechnical processes of literacy?

Soros's word "reflexive," discussed above, suggests one clue, remind us as it does of Dewey's early work (1884) on the stimulus arc in psychology. For Dewey, the reflexive nature of perception was crucial to his theories of knowing and learning. Rejecting both naïve realism, which posits events "out there" independent of the perceiver, and subjectivism, which has no way of accounting for common knowledge, Dewey was led to a constructivist theory of meaning. In his view, knowing was a process in which the individual learned through reflection on ordinary experience and through communication with others.

Within this theory, the actual process of interpreting experiences is *transactional* (Dewey & Bentley, 1949; Rosenblatt, 1978). This means, in short, that each encounter with phenomena is a unique event, neither wholly determined by external processes nor independent of them. In the case of literacy technologies, a transactional account tells us that technologies do not transform or determine literacies, nor could they ever be irrelevant to literacy practices. Instead, they are part of the continual reconstruction of literacies. As such, they too are constructed out of the evolving literacy practices. A

*Footnotes 3–8 are not included in this publication.

[9]See the Center for Social Informatics (http://www-slis.lib.indiana.edu/CSI); the Network for Socio-Cultural Analysis of New Educational Technologies (http://owl.qut.edu.au/scanet); and the Science, Technology, Information, and Medicine group (http://gaia.lis.uiuc.edu/leep3/stim).

transactional account is not an alternative stance, but rather, a conception of a mutually constitutive relation between technologies and social practices.

There are at least two major ways in which a transactional account figures in sociotechnical analysis of literacy. One is that our reading of technology is itself transactional; we bring to that reading all our unique sociocultural history, just as we do to a reading of Toni Morrison, Judy Blume, or Maurice Sendak. This holds not only for the disinterested researcher, but also for the participants within any literacy situation who use that technology. The second is that a technology within a literacy setting participates in a transaction with the other technologies, texts, artifacts, physical spaces, and procedures present there. For Dewey, these transactions are more richly textured and more organic than might be inferred from terms like "interaction" or "reflexivity." All the actors in a literacy environment—observers, participants, texts, technologies, discourses, and so on—become integral parts of the sociotechnical practice defining literacy in that environment. Thus, the transactional view leads not to another stance *toward* autonomous technology, but to a conception of literacy as a sociotechnical practice.

That view of literacy is consistent with a large body of work on the social construction of technological systems (Bijker, Hughes, & Pinch, 1987; Bijker & Law, 1992), sociotechnical processes (Bromley, 1997; Latour, 1991, 1993; Law, 1991; Winner, 1986); the use of information systems (Kling, 1980; Star, 1989; Taylor, Kramarae, & Ebben, 1993), the technologies of writing (Haas, 1995; Senner, 1989), and processes of situated learning (Lave & Wenger, 1991). These studies of technologies in use show clearly that any technology is deeply intertwined with social relations, in terms of its construction, distribution, use and interpretation (Bruce & Hogan, in press).

As a transactional analysis implies, technologies and social relations are not merely intertwined. The construction of power and agency in social situations derives from a subtle interplay of material and social processes. This interplay leads us to

question many taken-for-granted boundaries. Thus, Winner (1986) can ask whether artifacts have politics, and Latour (1991) whether technology is society made durable. Questions such as these have major implications for literacy research and practice.

Implications for Literacy Research and Practice

An immediate consequence is that the technologies of literacy are not optional add-ons, but are part of the definition of every form of literacy. Thus, a theory of literacy in a particular setting or community needs to incorporate an analysis of the relevant technologies, much as we more often include analyses of textual content, pedagogical procedures, personal backgrounds, or institutional agendas. That we often do not incorporate such an analysis may be due in part to implicitly assuming that those technologies are known and fixed. But when we look at literacy cross-culturally, or historically, that assumption becomes untenable. . . .

The lesson here is that analysis of literacy technologies and the relations of technologies to texts; discourses; ideologies; and race, class, and gender formations are inseparable from studies of literacy. And as Luke (1996) wrote, "literacy training is not a matter of who has the 'right' or 'truthful' theory of mind, language, morality, or pedagogy. It is a matter of how various theories and practices shape what people do with the technology of writing" (p. 309). That we often conceive of writing without mentioning its technologies is less a statement about their centrality to literacy practices and more a statement about how deeply these technologies are embedded in our daily practices. . . .

Conclusion

To ask, as I do in the title of this article, what stance we should take toward technology, presupposes a view of technology that is fundamentally limited. In essence, the flaw is an assumption of autonomy—conceiving of technology and literacy as neatly separable realms, such that one could say, "I'm studying literacy now and plan to start on technology in literacy study next year." The cases above shed doubt on that separation and point us toward a view of literacy as sociotechnical practice and remind us that research in literacy is the study of social practices associated with a particular array of technologies.[*11] Thus, technologies do not oppose, replace, enhance, or otherwise stand apart from literacy, but rather, they are part and parcel of it. Technology is within us, imbued with our beliefs and values, and we are within it.

*Footnote 10 is not included in this publication.

[11]The converse point is equally valid. Technology studies are at the core of studies about the writing and reading of artifacts, devices, texts, and social relations (cf. Akrich, 1992; Latour & Woolgar, 1986). A literacy perspective is essential to understanding these processes.

References

ad319. (1994). *New perspectives: Art & design in the digital age* [www document]. Retrieved June 19, 1997 from URL http://gertrude.art.uiuc.edu/ad319/paper2.html

Akrich, M. (1992). The de-scription of technical objects. In W.E. Bijker & J. Law (Eds.), *Shaping technology/Building society: Studies in sociotechnical change* (pp. 205–224). Cambridge, MA: MIT Press.

Bangert-Drowns, R. (1993). The word processor as an instructional tool: A meta-analysis of word processing in writing instruction. *Review of Educational Research, 63* (1), 69–93.

Beach, R. (1993). *A teacher's introduction to reader-response theories*. Urbana, IL: National Council of Teachers of English.

Bijker, W. E., Hughes, T. P., & Pinch, T. (1987). *The social construction of technological systems*. Cambridge, MA: MIT Press.

Bijker, W.E., & Law, J. (Eds.). (1992). *Shaping technology/Building society: Studies in sociotechnical change*. Cambridge, MA: MIT Press.

Bromley, H. (1997). The social chicken and the technological egg. *Educational Theory, 47* (1), 51–65.

Bromley, H. (in press). Introduction: Data-driven democracy? Social assessment of educational computing. In H. Bromley & M. W. Apple (Eds.), *Education/technology/power: Educational computing as a social practice*. Albany, NY: SUNY Press.

Bruce, B.C. (1993). Innovation and social change. In B. C. Bruce, J.K. Peyton, &

T.W. Batson (Eds.), *Network-based classrooms: Promises and realities* (pp. 9–323). New York: Cambridge University Press.

Bruce, B.C. (1995). *Twenty-first century literacy* (Technical Report No. 624). Urbana, IL: University of Illinois, Center for the Study of Reading.

Bruce, B.C. (1996). Technology as social practice. *Educational Foundations, 10* (4), 51–58.

Bruce, B.C., & Hogan, M.P. (in press). The disappearance of technology: Toward an ecological model of literacy. In D. Reinking, M. McKenna, L. Labbo, & R. Kieffer (Eds.), *Literacy for the 21st century: Technological transformations in a post-typographic world*. Hillsdale, NJ: Erlbaum.

Bruce, B.C., Peyton, J.K., & Batson, T.W. (Eds.). (1993). *Network-based classrooms: Promises and realities*. New York: Cambridge University Press.

Bruce, B.C., & Rubin, A. (1993). *Electronic quills: A situated evaluation of using computers for writing in the classroom*. Hillsdale, NJ: Erlbaum.

Bruce, B.C., & Sharples, M. (Eds.). (1995). *Computer Supported Cooperative Writing* [Special issue of *Computer Supported Cooperative Work*], 3 (3–4), 225–409.

Burbules, N.C., & Bruce, B.C. (1995). This is not a paper. *Educational Researcher, 24* (8), 12–18.

Cleverley, J. (1991). *The schooling of China: Tradition and modernity in Chinese education* (2nd ed.). North Sydney, Australia: Allen & Unwin.

Dewey, J. (1884). The new psychology. *Andover Review II*, pp. 281–285.

Dewey, J. (1966). *Democracy and education*. New York: Macmillan. (Original work published 1916)

Dewey, J., & Bentley, A.F. (1949). *Knowing and the known*. Boston: Beacon.

Eisenstein, E.L. (1983). *The printing revolution in early modern Europe*. Cambridge, UK: Cambridge University Press.

Ellul, J. (1980). *The technological system* (J. Neugroschel, Trans.). New York: Continuum.

Epstein, I. (Ed.). (1991). *Chinese education: Problems, policies, and prospects*. New York: Garland.

Foucault, M. (1972). The discourse on language (A.M. Sheridan Smith, Trans.). In M. Foucault, *The archaeology of knowledge and the discourse on language* (pp. 215–237). New York: Pantheon.

Garner, R., & Gillingham, M.G. (1996). *Internet communication in six classrooms: Communication across time, space, and culture*. Mahwah, NJ: Erlbaum.

Green, K. (1996). *1996 campus computing survey*. Encino, CA: Campus Computing.

Haas, C. (1995). *Writing technology: Studies on the materiality of literacy*. Hillsdale, NJ: Erlbaum.

Handa, C. (Ed.). (1990). *Computers and community: Teaching composition in the twenty-first century*. Portsmouth, NH: Boynton/Cook, Heinemann.

Heidegger, M. (1977). *The question concerning technology and other essays* (W. Lovitt, Trans.). New York: Harper & Row. (Original work published 1954)

internet.au. (1997, February). Interview: vivid: strikingly bright. *internet.au*, no. 16, pp. 40–41.

Jenner, W.J.F. (1992). *The tyranny of history: The roots of China's crisis*. London: Penguin.

Kling, R. (1980). Social analyses of computing: Theoretical perspectives in recent empirical research. *Computing Surveys, 12*, 61–110.

Latour, B. (1991). Technology is society made durable. In J. Law (Ed.), *A sociology of monsters: Essays on power, technology, and domination* (pp. 103–131). New York: Routledge.

Latour, B. (1993). *We have never been modern* (C. Porter, Trans.). Cambridge, MA: Harvard University Press.

Latour, B., & Woolgar, S. (1986). *Laboratory life: The construction of scientific facts* (Rev. ed.). Princeton, NJ: Princeton University Press.

Lave, J., & Wenger, E. (1991). *Situated learning: Legitimate peripheral participation*. Cambridge, UK: Cambridge University Press.

Law, J. (Ed.). (1991). *A sociology of monsters: Essays on power, technology, and domination*. New York: Routledge.

Luke, A. (1994). On reading and the sexual division of literacy. *Journal of Curriculum Studies, 26*, 361–381.

Luke, A. (1996). Genres of power? Literacy education and the production of capital. In R. Hasan & G. Williams (Eds.), *Literacy in society* (pp. 308–338). New York: Longman.

Malone, T.W., & Rockart, J.F. (1991). Computers, networks, and the corporation. *Scientific America, 265* (3), 128–136.

McLuhan, M., & Fiore, Q. (1967). *The medium is the massage: An inventory of effects*. New York: Bantam.

Neilson, L. (in press). Coding the light: Generation and authority in a rural high school telecommunications project. In D. Reinking, M. McKenna, L. Labbo, & R. Kieffer (Eds.), *Literacy for the 21st Century: Technological transformations in a post-typographic world*. Hillsdale, NJ: Erlbaum.

Palmer, R.E. (1969). *Hermeneutics: Interpretation theory in Schleirmacher, Dilthey, Heidegger, and Gadamer*. Evanston, IL: Northwestern University Press.

Peyton, J.K. (1990). Technological innovation meets institution: Birth of creativity of murder of a great idea? *Computers & Composition, 7*, 15–32.

Reinking, D. (1995). Reading and writing with computers: Literacy research in a post-typographic world. In K.A. Hinchman, D.J. Leu, & C.K. Kinzer (Eds.), *Perspectives on literacy research and practice*. Forty-fourth yearbook of the National Reading Conference (pp. 17–33). Chicago: National Reading Conference.

Reinking, D., McKenna, M., Labbo, L., & Kieffer, R. (Eds.). (in press). *Literacy for the 21st century: Technological transformations in a post-typographic world.* Hillsdale, NJ: Erlbaum.

Rosenblatt, L.M. (1978). *The reader, the text, the poem: The transactional theory of the literary work.* Carbondale, IL: Southern Illinois University Press.

Schutte, J. (1996). *Virtual teaching in higher education: A new intellectual superhighway or just another traffic jam?* [www document]. Retrieved on June 19, 1997 from URL http://www.csun.edu/sociology/virexp.htm

Selfe, C.L., & Selfe, R.J., Jr. (1994). The politics of the interface: Power and its exercise in electronic contact zones. *College Composition and Communication, 45,* 480–504.

Senner, W.M. (1989). *The origins of writing.* Lincoln, NE: University of Nebraska Press.

Slouka, M. (1995). *War of the worlds: Cyberspace and the assault on reality.* New York: Basic Books.

Soloway, E. (1993). Reading and writing in the 21st century. *Communications of the ACM, 36,* 23–27.

Soros, G. (1997, February). The capitalist threat. *The Atlantic Monthly, 279* (2), 45–58.

Spender, D. (1995). *Nattering on the nets.* North Melbourne, Australia: Spinifex.

Star, L.S. (1989). Institutional ecology, "translations," and boundary objects: Amateurs and professionals in Berkeley's Museum of Vertebrate Zoology, 1907–39. *Social Studies of Science, 19,* 387–420.

Taylor, H.J., Kramarae, C., & Ebben, M. (1993). *Women, information technology, scholarship.* Urbana, IL: University of Illinois, Center for Advanced Study.

Triolo, P.S., & Lovelock, P. (1996, November–December). Up, up, and away—with strings attached. *The China Business Review,* pp. 18–29.

Winner, L. (1986). *The whale and the reactor: A search for limits in the age of high technology.* Chicago: University of Chicago Press.

Yutang, L. (1936). *My country and my people.* London: Heinemann.

 Article Review Form at end of book.

Name and briefly discuss several software packages mentioned in the article. Summarize the two opposing views on how young children best learn to read. How does technology play a role in each?

Can Technology Help Teach Reading Right?

Caught in the phonics-versus-whole language crossfire, reading teachers are using technology tools to forge an effective middle path.

Donna Harrington-Lueker

Donna Harrington-Lueker is a freelance education writer based in Newport, RI.

At the 58th Street Elementary School in Los Angeles, Jody Doram's kindergartners will get their fair share of phonics instruction this year. They'll push letters into the slots of an electronic phonics desk and hear words sounded out for them, and they'll take turns at the classroom Macintosh, clicking on letters, then listening as the computer reads a selection from Aesop's fables. They'll recite their ABCs, practice saying words like "popcorn" with an initial puff of air, and learn to spell and sound out their names.

"Phonics just never left our classrooms," says Doram, who also uses big books, story time, computer games, and a variety of other strategies to get her inner-city children ready to read.

A Fierce Debate Over How to Teach

As a primary teacher in Los Angeles, Doram has had a front-row seat at the great debate over phonics versus whole language, a debate that

reached its fiercest level last year when the California legislature demanded that schools return to explicit instruction in phonics after nearly a decade of using a whole language approach to reading (see *California vs Bellwether**). The catalyst: the state's next-to-last-place finish on the 1994 National Assessment of Educational Progress (NAEP) reading exams. Only students in Louisiana scored lower.

But like many of her colleagues in California and other states where reading instruction has come under fire, Doram has staked out a middle ground, adopting strategies from both phonics and whole language.

"I tell beginning teachers: Adopt whole language exclusively, and you'll have holes in your program," says Doram. "Teachers have to take the best of whatever's out there."

Tim Lauer, a K–2 teacher at Buckman Elementary School in Portland, Ore., agrees. "People want you to choose a camp. They want you to say whether you're whole language or phonics," he says. But K–3 teachers have to use a number of different strategies because their children's needs are so diverse. Some children arrive at school knowing their ABCs and reciting *Green Eggs*

*Does not appear in this publication.

and Ham. Other often disadvantaged students or language-minority children lack this background. Faced with 30 or more students, all at different levels of readiness, experienced teachers adapt.

Eclectic Use of Technology

Ask about their use of technology, and these teachers' answers are similarly eclectic. Though hampered by outdated equipment and limited access, many teachers use CD-ROM books, word processing, the Internet, and skill software to supplement print materials. These teachers also say they're keeping close tabs on children's progress, identifying specific reading skills children might be having trouble with. To do so, they're making increasing use of spreadsheet programs and electronic portfolios.

"I'm doing what I've always done," says one first-grade teacher. "I'm teaching children, not philosophies."

Code Cracking or Comprehension?

The controversy Doram, Lauer, and others have opted out of is a bitter

"Can Technology Help Teach Reading Right?" by Donna Harrington-Lueker, published in *Electronic Learning,* December 1996. © 1996 by Scholastic Inc. Reprinted by permission.

one (see *A Century of Controversy**). Behind the public controversy are two opposing views of how young children best learn to read. Proponents of whole language argue that children learn to read the same way they learn to speak: by absorbing the language around them. Phonics advocates, on the other hand, argue that beginning readers need explicit instruction in letter-and-sound combinations, the building blocks of language. "It's critical that children learn to stick with a word and sound it out," says Bill Honig, former state superintendent of instruction in California. (Honig, who has become a standard-bearer for phonics, ironically was superintendent of instruction when California adopted whole language in 1987.)

Toward a Blended Approach

While academics and policy makers squabble, classroom teachers experiment. Pam Williams, a first-grade teacher at W. T. Cooke Elementary School in Virginia Beach, Va., uses The Little Planet literacy series, a multimedia program with video and laser disc, to help her first graders with the sequencing. At Cardiff Elementary School in Cardiff, Calif., parent volunteers work with small groups of students on specific skills using the Learning Company's *Reader Rabbit's Interactive Reading Journey* among other tools. "It's heavily into phonics," says second-grade teacher Jane Ditmars. Tim Lauer in Portland uses Holt, Rinehart and Winston's *Impressions* series, one of the first textbooks to use real children's literature, and supplements it with the phonics-intensive *Story Box Books* from Rigby.

As for technology, Lauer emphasizes the link between reading and writing and encourages even his youngest students to publish stories using the computer. (A 3-inch type font is ideal for the big books the class uses to read together, says Lauer.) With a fast T1 connection and a Macintosh he uses as a Web server, Lauer has begun to showcase his students' work on the classroom's home

page of the World Wide Web (*http://buckman.pps.k12.or.us*). Recent projects include a timeline his students developed after reading My Dream of Martin Luther King, Jr. by Faith Ringgold. "It creates a sense of audience," says Lauer of the Web site, which parents routinely visit.

For Challenged Readers: Skills

Clearview Elementary School in Chula Vista, Calif., takes another tack. Clearview has a student body that speaks 23 different languages, a challenge for any early literacy program, experts say. To meet that challenge, says language arts specialist Lee Woldt, Clearview uses technology to teach phonics explicitly, especially at the K–2 level.

"That's where you want to put the effort and systematically attack," says Woldt of the school's decision to use the approach in the early grades. Students in kindergarten and first grade use IBM's *Writing to Read,* a phonics-based software program that combines computer drills with books on tape and story writing.

But whole language also has a prominent place in the school's literacy efforts. "Research shows kids like being bathed in language," says Woldt. "Why would you not want to do that? . . . People can no longer say, 'Because I learned this way [phonics], all else is idiocy.' "

High-Tech Whole-Language

Lee Sattelmeyer, a third-grade whole language teacher at Lomond Elementary School in Shaker Heights, Ohio, has adapted technology to his students needs' as well. "At first," the third-grade teacher says, "I tended to use technology to remediate. Now, I look at it as a way to enlarge."

Sattelmeyer's extensive in-class library includes books in print and on CD-ROM. Kids use three Apple IIs and a single Macintosh for publishing their own stories and reports. Sattelmeyer has students use *HyperStudio* to create multimedia group projects integrating Internet research.

Sattelmeyer, who has taught for 23 years, also uses simulation software such as MECC's *Oh, Deer,* in which students are asked to weigh the factors affecting the deer population as part of his reading program. Shaker Heights itself has a problem of too many deer, Sattelmeyer says, which leads to "lots of discussion and debate."

Sattelmeyer is no whole language purist. At the beginning of the year, nearly a quarter of his students "weren't reading as well as they should have," Sattelmeyer says. "I was picking up real problems with vowel sounds." His solution: having the students use a drill-and-practice phonics program called WordMunchers from MECC. "I'll use anything I can that will enhance kids' learning," he says.

Using Technology to Keep Track

Like other K–3 teachers, Sattelmeyer keeps running records—ongoing observation notes on children's reading. Last year he experimented with Sunburst's *Learner Profile,* which let him use a bar-code scanner to enter data on each child. He's also exploring *Grady Profile* from Auerbach and Associates to create electronic portfolios.

Lauer uses his Apple PowerBook to record his observations on each child's reading and to list the books the child has read; he hopes to someday put the files on the school's building-wide network. "I've seen too many kids fall through the cracks because the paper trail was too slow," says Lauer.

Four times a year, teachers at Clearview Elementary enter data on a child's progress along with standardized test scores into an Excel spreadsheet, says principal Ginger Hovenic. Clearview administrators use the information to keep tabs on overall achievement levels, while classroom teachers use it to identify children who might be falling behind.

The school's tracking effort and its commitment to early intervention have paid off. "We have the data to show that all our kids are leaving first grade as readers," says Hovenic.

*Does not appear in this publication.

Careful Use of Electronic Books

Interactive books may be the most visible connection between reading and technology. But teachers say the jury is still out on the role of e-books in early reading.

According to K–3 teachers like Karen Beard, a Title I reading teacher at Spring Creek Elementary School in East Ridge, Tenn., the gee-whiz graphics and hyperlinks of e-books capture children's interest, an important feature for beginning readers. The books also build in extensive "scaffolding": for example, a child can click on a word he or she doesn't recognize and the computer will pronounce it. The animation, illustrations, and background information in the books provide beginning readers a rich context for understanding the story.

But e-books are costly: $25 or more for a single title, teachers point out. And while some are sophisticated pedagogically, many do little more than let kids turn the pages electronically.

The hyperlinks can sometimes be a big distraction as well. "I think kids get enamored of the bells and whistles, and reading is secondary," says Sattelmeyer.

Barbara Fox, a reading expert at North Carolina State University, wor-ries that the scaffolding may actually get in the way of learning. To become fluent readers, Fox says, children may need to practice "without the computer telling them every single word."

Moving Toward Consensus?

While some see this diverse mix of approaches as a boon, others argue that the best way to enhance children's reading skills is for the educational community to reach a consensus about best practices in reading and where technology fits in. Jean Osborn of the Center for the Study of Reading at the University of Illinois puts the challenge succinctly: "Other fields have agreed-on knowledge. They don't keep arguing over basic questions like, Are there electrons? . . . It's just terribly important to have a consensus."

That worry applies to the use of technology as well. Reading software too often amounts to nothing more than electronic worksheets. And even in cases where software is built on solid research, teachers often aren't aware of the underlying pedagogy or don't have access to a powerful enough computer to take advantage of it.

Without consensus, reading teachers, especially inexperienced ones, may fall into what Stanford University professor Bob Calfee calls the "Cuisinart approach" to reading: a little bit of this and that all mixed together without any overriding sense of what good reading instruction should be.

So how far away is anything resembling consensus? It depends on whom you ask. At the moment, phonics proponents say the momentum is theirs. California is moving toward explicit instruction in phonics, while Ohio, Alabama, New York, Tennessee, Wisconsin, Virginia, Nebraska, North Carolina, and other states have taken their own steps toward incorporating phonics into classrooms or teacher prep programs.

But resistance is high to an all-or-nothing approach. "Phonics isn't the panacea," says Regie Routman, a language arts resource teacher in Shaker Heights, Ohio, and author of *Literacy at the Crossroads: Crucial Talk about Reading, Writing, and Other Teaching Dilemmas* (Heinemann, 1996). "I worry that we'll go overboard the other way." Adds Stanford University professor Calfee, "A lot of people just aren't going to be willing to put the [whole language] genie back in the bottle."

 Article Review Form at end of book.

What is a deictic term? Why does Leu say that literacy is a deictic term? What are the four important changes in what it means to be literate?

Caity's Question

Literacy as deixis on the Internet

Donald J. Leu, Jr.

Syracuse University, Syracuse,
New York, USA

Several years ago, more than I wish to admit, our 4-year-old daughter, Caity, turned to me and asked a simple, but profound question. "Dad," she said, "is today tomorrow?" Intuitively, I knew there was something important behind this question, but, like many busy parents, I didn't take time to think about the special nature of her query before I answered.

"No," I said, trying my parental best to be helpful and clear up any confusion. "Today is today and tomorrow is tomorrow."

Thinking about this a bit later, my response troubled me. I was quite certain there was something more complicated behind Caity's question. Why did she ask it? What did it mean?

Thinking about Caity's question eventually led me to an understanding of *deixis,* a linguistic term used to capture the special qualities of words like *today, tomorrow,* and *here* whose meanings are dependent upon the time or space in which they are uttered (Fillmore, 1966, 1972, 1975). Tomorrow is a Sunday when I write this word, but when you read this article *tomorrow* could mean any day of the week. Time references like *now, today, tomorrow, yesterday,* or *last week* are deictic in nature; their meaning is entirely dependent upon the temporal context in which they appear. Fillmore points out that many

locational and personal terms are also deictic. *Here* is next to me, but my *here* is likely to be your *there; I* means *me* when I say it, but my *I* is your *you,* or a third person's *him.*

Discovering the changing meanings for deictic terms is an important linguistic challenge for young children who have come to believe that words have fixed meanings (Murphy, 1986). To many young children, "A word is a word is a word," to rephrase a famous quote by Gertrude Stein, since most words have meanings that do not change substantially in time or space. Young children do not understand that the meaning of a deictic word like *tomorrow* may change drastically depending upon when it was said. Tomorrow is not always tomorrow; sometimes it is also today.

When Caity asked, "Is today tomorrow?" she was sorting through the slippery, conditional meanings for deictic terms we use to express time. Caity was really asking, "Is today the tomorrow you told me about yesterday?" It was a wonderful question for a young child to ask as she attempted to figure out the changing meanings for these deictic terms. Clearly, it was a question I did not fully appreciate when she asked it.

"Is Today Tomorrow?"

I recalled this story last spring with a smile as I sat in the stands watching Caity's high school graduation ceremonies. My mind wandered across

many stories about Caity, stories that taught me important lessons about life, literacy, and learning. I kept coming back to this one, though, thinking about its meaning to our lives today.

As I sat watching the ceremonies, it seemed to me that Caity's question might also help us to understand the cusp on which we currently find ourselves. Here we stand between traditional forms of literacy and new forms of literacy that are continually appearing. In our rapidly changing world, new information and communication technologies regularly redefine what it means to be literate. Literacy, it seems, is not literacy is not literacy. Instead, literacy has become a deictic term; its meaning is continually changing, dependent upon the technological context in which it occurs. What it means to be literate has become a moving target, one we can never completely define because information and communication technologies continually change. As the meaning of literacy changes, our role as literacy educators is also being fundamentally altered.

One of the most visible technologies changing the nature of literacy is the Internet, an extensive set of computers around the world connected to one another and capable of quickly exchanging vast amounts of information. One text on the Internet ultimately leads to millions and millions of other texts, many of which contain additional media resources such as video, audio, animation, and

Leu, Donald J., Jr. (1997, September). Caity's question: Literacy as deixis on the Internet. *The Reading Teacher,* 51(1), 62–67. Reprinted with permission of Donald J. Leu and the International Reading Association. All rights reserved.

e-mail. Moreover, new forms of communication are continually being developed on the Internet that regularly require new forms of literacy learning in order to effectively exploit their potential. Internet relay chat sessions, MOOs (MUD, object-oriented), MUDs (multiuser dungeon), videoconferencing, push technologies, and other communication forms not yet imagined are on their way to your classroom. The Internet is providing new technologies to classrooms and, as a result, redefining literacy, learning, and teaching for each of us.

If you have any doubt about the Internet entering your classroom and changing the nature of literacy, learning, and teaching, consider these observations:

- Each year, Linda Hubbard, a fifth-grade teacher at Carminati Elementary School in Tempe, Arizona, USA, engages her students in Internet activities during a science unit on exploring space. They "log in" as visitors to the current space shuttle in orbit, discover information about crew members, monitor the progress of science experiments, ask the astronauts questions, and study the tracking maps of the shuttle's orbits (http://shuttle.nasa.gov/index.html). They also travel through space to each of the nine planets in our solar system by taking **The Nine Planets Tour** (http://seds.lpl.arizona.edu/billa/tnp/), an exciting and informative multimedia experience for students.

- Over 200,000 children have traveled to a computer in Australia to explore a wonderful series of adventures about Max, the Koala, and his friends (http://www.gil.com.au/max). These stories have been written and illustrated by Alex, a 5-year-old boy, and his father, Scott. They are accompanied by delightful music and interactive animations. Alex, it appears, is quickly becoming the most widely read 5-year-old author in the world.

- Following California's lead, most states in the U.S. have set aside "Net days" where parents and teachers get together, with support from business and state

governments, to wire their school classrooms. Information about inexpensively wiring your school is available on the home page for **Net Day** (http://www.net-day96.com/).

- The percentage of school classrooms (K–12) connected to the Internet in the U.S. has been tripling each year (U.S. Congress, 1995). If this rate continues, every classroom will have at least one Internet connection by the spring of 1999, a widely publicized goal of the Clinton administration.

- Brian Maguire, a third-grade teacher in upstate New York, and a parent in New Jersey have developed a wonderful site for young children to exchange writing and pictures about monsters at **Minds Eye Monster Exchange** (http://www.csnet.net/minds-eye/). The location includes a chat room, lesson plans, and many other features to support communication and literacy learning between young children at schools around the world. Over 200 classrooms and 6,000 young children have participated in these exchanges.

- Doug Crosby, a first-grade teacher at Cherry Valley School, in Polson, Montana, USA, has had students in his classroom communicating with other students around the glove via e-mail for several years. They have a map above their computer with pieces of yarn from their location to all of the places from which they have received e-mail. Doug's class members share many experiences on their home page (http://www.digisys.net/cherry/Mr.Crosby_fg.htm).

- Tim Lauer and Beth Rohloff, K–2 teachers in Portland, Oregon, USA, and their students have written an amazing set of curriculum resources for primary-grade children and made these available to others on their classroom home page (http://buckman.pps.k12.or.us/room100/room100.html). Students from around the world visit their computer in Oregon to read about Martin Luther King, Jr., bus safety rules, a space alphabet book, and more. (See Figure.)*

*Does not appear in this publication.

Hundreds of thousands of similar stories take place on the Internet each day as teachers and students explore the potential of this resource to fundamentally redefine what it means to become literate.

Changes in Why We Need to Be Literate

Why are these changes taking place? Manguel (1996), in an outstanding new history of reading, notes that the function of literacy has never been static; it continually changes in different historical, cultural, and technological contexts. In earliest societies, literacy was a way to record sheep, crops, and taxes. Among many religions, it was a way to enforce a common dogma. In a post-Reformation world, literacy was viewed as the means to individual salvation by Luther and his Protestant followers. In a Jeffersonian democracy, literacy was seen as essential to the survival of the civic enterprise as informed citizens made reasoned decisions at the ballot box. In an industrial world, literacy was seen as a means to accurately transmit production information from top to bottom in a hierarchically organized company.

In the information age in which we live, literacy is essential to enable individuals, groups, and societies access to the best information in the shortest time so as to identify and solve the most important problems and communicate this information to others. Information access, problem solving, and communication are essential to success in the information age in which we live.

It is no accident the Internet has appeared at this time. The Internet is currently the most efficient way to store, access, and communicate large amounts of information to vast numbers of people interested in identifying and solving important problems. To prepare our students for the challenges of their tomorrows, the Internet and future technologies will be central to our mission. Doug Crosby, Linda Hubbard, Alex and Scott Balson, Brian Maguire, Tim Lauer, Beth Rohloff, and many others are pioneering new forms of literacy within the Internet. The rest of us will quickly follow and homestead these new forms in the years to come.

Increasingly, new abilities will be required for literacy in a digital, information age.

Changes in What It Means to Be Literate

Clearly, the Internet is changing what it means to be literate. Traditional reading and writing are but the initial layers of the richer and more complex forms of literacy required in this electronic context. While the exact nature of these changes will continue to evolve, at least four important changes are already apparent.

First, being literate will require our students to acquire new and increasingly sophisticated navigational strategies. On the Internet, where so many new forms of information and communication are available, each of us will be required to learn how to efficiently exploit these forms to accomplish the tasks we determine to be important. The new navigation strategies required in CD-ROM hypermedia have been noted earlier (Bernstein, 1991; Leu & Reinking, 1996). The Internet multiplies this problem many millions of times over, at least once for every Web site that exists. Our students must learn strategies not only to navigate the browsers used to explore the Web but also to effectively navigate each Web site they encounter. Each site on the Internet contains information organized as a unique manner. Unitary forms of narrative and expository discourse knowledge, useful in a world of traditional text with static, well-established norms for text organization, will be insufficient in a world of variably designed Web pages.

Second, being literate is quickly changing from an end state to an endless developmental process. Increasingly, "becoming literate" is a more precise term than "being literate," reflecting the continual need to update our abilities to communicate within new technologies that regularly appear. Changes in the strategic knowledge required to navigate traditional text environments have been glacial; changes in the strategic knowledge required to navigate Internet environments are meteoric. New versions of Web browsers ap-

pear every 6 months, and the designs of most Web sites are updated more frequently than this. Somehow, we must seek ways to support our students in continually acquiring new forms of strategic knowledge as Internet technologies change. Just as Caity discovered that tomorrow has many different meanings, literacy will not be literacy, will not be literacy. Individuals unable to keep up with the new information strategies generated by new information technologies will quickly be left behind.

Third, literacy on the Internet will require new forms of critical thinking and reasoning about the information that appears in this venue. Anyone may publish anything on the Internet. Traditional forces, guaranteeing some degree of control over the accuracy of information in published books, do not exist. As a result, students may sometimes encounter Web pages created by people who have political, religious, or philosophical stances that profoundly distort the nature of the information they present to others. Or, sometimes a person simply gets the facts wrong on a Web page. This requires us to help our students become "healthy skeptics" about the accuracy of information they encounter. Such skills have not always been central in classrooms where textbooks and other traditional information resources are often assumed to be correct.

A fourth change is also apparent in the new forms of literacy required on the Internet: We need to support children in becoming more aware of the variety of meanings inherent in the multiple media forms in which messages appear (Flood & Lapp, 1995). We have gradually come to recognize that traditional texts contain multiple meanings. When additional media (video, audio, animations) are added to a literacy context, we provide opportunities for an even wider range of meanings to be generated and combined in subtle but important ways. To authors interested in either limiting or expanding interpretations of their texts, the effective use of these media is an important new challenge. As teachers, we need to help students develop the new composing, comprehension, and response abilities that result from new combinations of media sources possible on the Internet (McKillop, 1996).

Changes in How We Become Literate

Internet technologies will also change how we become literate. Previously I have argued that electronic contexts for literacy, because they are powerful, complex, and continually changing, will be even more dependent upon social learning strategies than traditional literacy contexts (Leu, 1996). No one person knows everything there is to know about the Internet; each of us has useful information that can help others. I may know something about how to search for information, but you may know a really good location for students who want to publish their work. By sharing our information, we can help one another learn about these rich information resources. Literacy learning on the Internet is best accomplished through social interactions with others, perhaps even more naturally and frequently than in traditional print environments.

As we think about how to use the Internet in our classrooms, we need to look first to instructional practices that take advantage of social learning opportunities. Workshop experiences and cooperative learning activities may be especially useful with the Internet since they allow groups of students to share experiences and learn from one another (Leu & Leu, 1997). In addition, the Internet is also developing its own forms of socially mediated learning, many of which appear to be very promising for classroom instruction. These include listservs, chat sessions, collaborative Internet projects, and teleconferences with CUSeeMe and other technologies. We need to seek ways to use these new technologies to support our students' learning experiences.

New Opportunities for Each of Us on the Internet

If we are to prepare our students for their tomorrows, we need to embrace the opportunities the Internet provides for new forms of literacy. No matter how technologically challenged any one of us feels, each of us must enter this new world and make every attempt to keep up with the changes taking place in what literacy means. Continually becoming literate is as important for us as it is for our students. consider, for example, these opportunities available on the Internet for our classrooms:

- Seek answers to important questions from experts. Students engaged in inquiry projects may e-mail their questions to subject area experts around the world including astronauts, architects, paleontologists, earth scientists, and many others. Useful lists of e-mail addresses for subject area experts may be found at **Ask an Expert** (http://www.askanexpert. com/askanexpert/index.html) or **Ask a Mad Scientist** (http://128.252.223.239/-ysp/MSN/).

- Participate in a collaborative Internet project at **Monarch Watch** (http://www.keil.ukans.edu/~monarch/). This location, sponsored by the Department of Entomology at the University of Kansas, Manhattan, contains an extremely comprehensive set of resources for studying Monarch butterflies and sharing observations, especially of their migration. Find out about migration patterns, join one of several science projects, learn how to raise and release Monarchs in your classroom, learn how to start a butterfly garden near your classroom, and communicate with scientists who study these beautiful creatures.

- Publish students' writing as you seek more authentic writing experiences for your students. A number of locations exist on the Internet where students may publish their writing. Incorporate them into your classroom writing projects and encourage students to revise and edit their works before submitting them for publication. Locations include **The Book Nook** (http://i-site.on.ca/booknook. html), which publishes reviews of books students have read; **Cyberkids** (http://www. cyberkids.com/), which invites

Subscribing and Unsubscribing to RTEACHER, a Listserv on Literacy and Technology. (Note: There is no charge for subscribing to this listserv.)

RTEACHER, a listserv, assists a diverse population of educators interested in issues of literacy and technology. Over 200 educators participate in discussions of this column and other issues of literacy and technology. To subscribe to the *RTEACHER* listserv you must possess an e-mail account. When you are in your e-mail account, do the following:

1. Address your message to listserv@listserv.syr.edu
2. Leave the first line of your message blank
3. In the second line, type
     SUB RTEACHER fullname
       e.g., if your name is Jane Doe, type: SUB RTEACHER Jane Doe
4. Be certain your message does not contain any other information. Disable your "signature" option, if you have one, so this is not included at the end of your message.
5. Send your message.
6. Shortly, you will receive a confirmation message. Read this message and follow the directions within 48 hours to confirm your subscription.

To unsubscribe from the RTEACHER listserv do the following:

1. Address your message to listserv@listserv.syr.edu
2. Leave the first line of your message blank
3. In the second line, type: UNSUB RTEACHER
4. Be certain your message does not contain any other information. Disable your "signature" option, if you have one, so this is not included at the end of your message.
5. Send your message.
     If you experience problems, please send a message to: djleu@mailbox.syr.edu

submissions from students ages 7–11; **KidPub** (http://www.kidpub.org/kidpub/), which publishes all submitted work; and **Children's Voice** (http://schoolnet2.Carelton.Ca/engish/arts/lit/c-voice/welcome.html), which sponsors a listserv for publishing student work as well as a zine (an electronic magazine) containing student work.

- Enrich your study of another country by developing "key pal" relationships with a classroom in the country you are studying. Visit **Intercultural E-mail Classroom Connections** (http://www.stolaf.edu/network/iecc/), **Global Heinemann Keypals** (http://www.reedbooks.com.au/heinemann/global/global1.html), or **Pitsco's Launch to Keypals** (http://www.keypals.com/p/keypals.html) to find lists of teachers and classrooms from different parts of the world who

are interested in forming collaborative keypal relationships. Or visit **Web66** (http://web66.coled.umn.edu/schools.html) and explore the lists of classrooms around the world connected to the Internet. Send a message to several schools, inviting them to exchange e-mail messages with your class.

- Participate in a collaborative Internet project with other classrooms around the world. Pay a visit to **NickNack's Telecollaborative Learning** (http://www1.minn.net:80/~schubert/NickNacks.html#anchor100100) to learn how to develop these projects. Then visit one of several locations where teachers list their projects in an effort to get others to join their classrooms in a variety of learning activities: **Classroom Connect's Teacher Contact Database** (http://www.classroom.net/contact/); **The Global Schoolhouse Projects Registry** (http://www.gsh.org/gsh/class/projsrch.html); or **Kidproject** (http://www.kidlink.org:80/KIDPROJ/).

Tomorrow Will Quickly Become Today for Each of Us

As we met Caity after her graduation ceremonies, it was clear how quickly all of the tomorrows from yesterdays past had suddenly become today.

"Dad. Is today tomorrow"

Caity's question from long ago had acquired a new and even more important meaning as we confronted how quickly the time had passed since she had first entered school. The same will be true for each of the students in our classrooms. Their tomorrows will quickly become their todays. We need to begin, now, to engage our students in the electronic literacies of their future. Each of the experiences listed above, and more to appear in future columns, will help your students become literate within the new technologies appearing on the Internet. The rewards for our students are as important as the futures we wish to provide them.

References

Bernstein, M. (1991). The navigation problem reconsidered. In E. Berk & J. Devlin (Eds.), *Hypertext/hypermedia handbook* (pp. 285–298). New York: McGraw-Hill.

Fillmore, C.J. (1996). Deictic categories in the semantics of "come." *Foundations of Language, 2,* 219–227.

Fillmore, C.J. (1972). How to know whether you're coming or going. In K. Huldgaard-Jensen (Ed.), *Linguistik 1971* (pp. 369–379). Amsterdam: Athemaiim.

Fillmore, C.J. (1975). *Santa Cruz lectures on deixis.* Lecture presented to Indiana Linguistics Club, Indiana University, Bloomington, IN.

Flood, J., & Lapp, D. (1995). Broadening the lens: Toward an expanded conceptualization of literacy. In K.A. Hinchman, D.J. Leu, & C.K. Kinzer (Eds.), *Perspectives on literacy research and practice* (pp. 1–16). Chicago: National Reading Conference.

Leu, D.J., Jr. (1996). Sarah's secret: Social aspects of literacy and learning in a digital, information age. *The Reading Teacher, 50,* 162–165.

Leu, D.J., Jr., & Leu, D.D. (1997). *Teaching with the Internet: Lessons from the classroom.* Norwood, MA: Christopher-Gordon.

Leu, D.J., Jr., & Reinking, D. (1996). Bringing insights from reading research to research on electronic learning environments. In H. van Oostendorp & S. de Mul (Eds.), *Cognitive aspects of electronic text processing* (pp. 43–76). Norwood, NJ: Ablex.

Manguel, A. (1996). *A history of reading.* New York: Viking.

McKillop, A.M. (1996, December). *Visual and media literacy: A new look at some old definitions.* Paper presented at the meeting of the National Reading Conference, Charleston, SC.

Murphy, S.M. (1986). Children's comprehension of deictic categories in oral and written language. *Reading Research Quarterly, 21,* 118–131.

U.S. Congress, Office of Congressional Assessment. (1995). *Teachers and technology: Making the connection.* Washington, DC: U.S. Government Printing Office.

 Article Review Form at end of book.

How does the World Wide Web (WWW) serve as an "animator and tool for creating and sharing ideas, for improving literacy, and for welcoming others into your classroom community of learners"?

Using the World Wide Web to Build Learning Communities

Writing for genuine purposes

This article explains how professors of literacy development, classroom teachers, and inservice facilitators can help students and teachers create interactive World Wide Web sites. A summary of recent literature on technology, a theoretical foundation, and explanations and examples are included.

Gerald H. Maring

Beau J. Wiseman

Kurt S. Myers

Maring teaches at Washington State University (Department of Teaching and Learning, Pullman, WA 99164–2132, USA). Wiseman is a graduate student at the same university. Myers is a senior engineer/scientist at Lockheed Martin–Idaho Technologies in Idaho Falls, Idaho, USA.

What is the World Wide Web? According to Ned Desmond, editor of Infoseek [http://www.infoseek.com], one of the major search engine services on the World Wide Web, the Web, often abbreviated WWW, consists of an incredibly large number of documents that are hyperlinked in such a manner that one can click on one word within a document and be immediately taken to another document. The WWW is part of a larger network of information called the Internet. The WWW first contained text, but soon graphics, audio, and even three-dimensional animation were added. By early 1997, there were about 40 to 50 million pages out there in cyberspace on the Web.

Further questions arise: (a) Is use of the WWW for the technologically elite or (b) is it a tool that ordinary teachers and students in public and private schools and in higher education can use to promote content learning in general and literacy development in particular?

Our answers are "no" to (a) and "yes" to (b). At the start, we want to emphasize that our "yes" stems from experiences using the WWW interactively to enhance learning communities, social learning, and literacy development, and not from projects that are primarily about launching more information or student work into cyberspace.

First, we review some of the current professional articles related to classroom use of the WWW. Second, we briefly explain some of the benefits (in terms of literacy development theories and community of learners/literate environment perspectives) of helping students place

Maring, Gerald H., Wiseman, Beau J., and Myers, Kurt S. (1997, November). Using the World Wide Web to build learning communities: Writing for genuine purposes. *Journal of Adolescent & Adult Literacy*, 41(3), 196–207.
Reprinted with permission of Gerald H. Maring and the International Reading Association. All rights reserved.

their writing on the WWW so that they can write for genuine purposes and to real audiences (Tompkins & Hoskisson, 1995). Third, we describe our efforts helping preservice teachers to create interactive Web sites and to place six different types of coauthored or individually written literacy-related lessons or projects on the WWW. (Note: Interactive web sites are those designed to invite user feedback and to initiate dialog.) Finally, we offer, on the basis of our experience, practical, time-saving advice so that other teachers and college or university faculty can help their students create interactive Web sites.

Using Internet/WWW Technology in Classrooms

In the past few years, an increasing number of related articles have appeared in the professional literature. December's (1994) article in *Educational Technology* was one of the first professional publications for teachers that explored publishing on the Internet. December described uses of such technologies as e-mail and the World Wide Web and presented four case studies illustrating how people can use the Internet to make information widely available to readers.

Chobrak (1995) offered advice about building a WWW homepage for individual school buildings. Included in her article were ideas for installing a WWW Browser and a sample lesson plan with objectives, procedures, and evaluation.

Dyrli and Kinnaman (1995) explained what they felt teachers should know about local area networking (i.e., among classrooms or building within a school district) and global communications. They presented various reasons why teachers should connect their classrooms to the Internet or commercial online systems and how WWW and browsing software may revolutionize teaching and learning.

In October 1995, Anderson-Inman began a Technology Tidbits department in the *Journal of Adolescent & Adult Literacy* "to open a window . . . onto ideas for using technology in ways that support your goals as a teacher . . . so that

[teachers will] be better informed about the potential that technology brings to the teaching and learning process . . . [and] will want to try more" (p. 154). Shotsberger (1996) noted that more and more teaching-related WWW sites are being developed and offered ideas related to good design (e.g., many shorter Web pages with few links rather than a few long pages with many links). He concluded by stating that "student work, the centerpiece of any course, should be prominently displayed in instructional sites" (p. 50).

In terms of instructional materials for teachers, commercial products are being rapidly developed. *Classroom Connect: The Internet Made Easy in the Classroom* is a monthly 20-page newsletter for K–12 educators containing helpful short articles and advertisements. Further information about it can be obtained by e-mail: connect@classroom.net or by URL at http://www.classroom.net.

On the classroom level, teachers and their students have joined networks and globally shared their visual art combined with storytelling and writing. Teacher Kristi Rennebohm Franz (1996) and her primary-grade students in Pullman, Washington, USA, began collaborating on the International Education and Resource Network (I*EARN) with schools around the world as early as January 1993. Their global communication involved science water habitat projects and social studies, geography, and social action projects. Their subsequent Global Art Projects/GAP, shared with 10 schools of the I*EARN network, focused on the themes A Sense of Family and Habitats: A Sense of Place. These GAPs involved "parallels" between pupils' drawings and their storytellings and explanations put in writing. In addition, the projects united children, teachers, families, and communities around the world by means of shared art and writing.

Finally, it is worth noting that a number of recently published textbooks and trade books contain important how-to's of Web site and homepage development. *The Net, the Web, and You* (Kurland, 1996) is helpful for the reader with limited knowledge. It defines terms, offers pictures of screen displays, and describes how features and parts of the Web work

and interact. *Publish It on the Web* (Pfaffenberger, 1996) is a straightforward how-to text. Its inside cover contains a CD. The book includes sections on Web browsers and editors.

Theoretical Grounding: Benefits to Teachers and Students

The benefits of students collaborating to place their work on the WWW and to receive feedback and critique from outside audiences are myriad. Major elements of the endeavor necessarily involve students in writing for genuine purposes and for real audiences (Tompkins & Hoskisson, 1995). By responding to feedback from WWW users (teachers and students in our case, but different audiences in other cases, such as scientists or newspaper editorial writers), students have the opportunity to revise and improve the quality of their ideas and writing and to continue to dialog with classmates, teachers, and others at a distance about the common subjects simultaneously at hand, on the screen, and in cyberspace.

Above all, having students coauthor some of their assignments and participate in other team writing projects gives them a powerful exposure to functioning within a literate environment that becomes a community of learners (McCaleb, 1994; National Education Association, 1995; Palmer, 1993; Peterson, 1992; Short Burke, 1991). Students who are members of a learning community collaborate in the various phases of the writing process (brainstorming, topic selection, connecting concepts, writing rough drafts, peer editing, revision, writing final drafts, and publishing). Tierney and O'Flahaven (1989) described a community of learners as a literate environment, where "members facilitate their own and each others' learning by sharing, offering support, suggesting possibilities, and evaluating ideas in a social context" (p. 301). Rousculp and Maring (1992) observed that a community of learners who focus on literacy processes becomes "a dynamic classroom community that is rich in social relationships, in partnerships, and in collaborations involving talking, reading, thinking, and writing" (p. 384). Maring (1993) further noted:

A community of learners does not exist at the beginning of a class. Rather, it forms in the middle and in the end of the course . . . it is a Spirit . . . it is a group where friendships begin and deepen and endure. . . . it is an opportunity for partnerships and for dialog . . . it is inclusive of diversity . . . it grows in a place where there are celebrations that pertain to the personal matters of students as well as to academic successes and cultural events. (p. 1)

The challenge of putting coauthored writing projects (that are clearly useful to others and are the result of meaningful inquiries into the available literature) on the WWW enables individual students to become bonded into an enthusiastic community of learners. The research and classroom practice described by Salaman (1993) and by Resnick, Levine, and Teasley (1991) related to team writing as "socially distributed cognition" have clear connections to much of what goes on in any classroom that is truly trying to use a community of learners approach or framework. However, a learning community will not be achieved if the colearners feel the effort involves "busy work," work that is simplistic or in a "transmission model" (Harste, 1990), or entries and writing on the WWW that are of little real value to themselves or anyone else.

A key point we want to make here is that we observed the emergence of learning community indicators in our courses as the three semesters of our project progressed. Each semester, a few students have difficulty adjusting to a learning community approach because many of our lower division and even some upper division university courses are dominated by lectures. In these courses, students mostly study on their own and compete for grades that are curved and derived from multiple choice tests and individually written assignments. Building trust and helping students to act responsibly and respectfully with one another are not easily accomplished learning community realities. Most students are accustomed to functioning and being successful in university classes where these processes and outcomes (trust building, finding time to meet with colearners, working effectively as team members) are not used or expected by professors.

In addition, "stand and deliver" is a teaching method many of our students were used to from their high school years. Nevertheless, within a few weeks, we, as well as visitors to our classroom, readily observed during each workshop segment of the weekly class schedule an intense level of engagement among the students as they huddled around their small group's computer. They critiqued one another's verbal ideas and writing and listened intently to suggestions. Clearly, they were beginning to function as team writers. They wanted to show their best ideas and work after multiple revisions so that it would showcase their own abilities and thinking and also be attractive to teachers in the field who would browse and read it on the Web.

As they brainstormed their ideas and began to get them into writing and onto their homepages, we often observed students (a) accommodating and then incorporating one another's viewpoints, (b) making subsequent revisions based on peer editing suggestions, and (c) responding more critically to the written assignment guidelines and directions they were given and to the journal articles and professional texts they consulted in order to select and craft their units and assignments. Soon after one coauthoring team learned to use a scanner to place their author photos onto their homepage, they offered to help the next small group of students who asked to learn this skill.

About midpoint in the courses, students were encouraged to e-mail comments to one another about their work. These comments ranged from general encouragement to specific questions like "How did you get that three-dimensional figure on your title page?" However, just as often, students would get up from their work stations to simply check out what was on their classmates' screens. Then spontaneous talk-to-learn exchanges would occur. In short, we observed that our classroom environments were "language rich" because they were "tech rich."

To encourage even more sharing among students and coauthoring teams, we required from midpoint on in the courses that students engage in whole-class sharing times in which

they would verbally summarize literacy strategies that were especially adaptable to one or more specific content areas and grade levels. This sharing helped students realize that as individuals and members of coauthoring teams they had found and constructed many teaching ideas, held diverse viewpoints, and could recommend resources for teaching literacy to many other students in the class.

At the end of each semester, one of the more common comments heard was "Looking back, I can't believe how much reading I did in this course, how much I drafted and revised, and that I got so much writing that I am proud of on the WWW. . . ."

A final indication of the emergence of a learning community and quality and usefulness of student work was that "outsiders" browsed our students' work on the WWW and wanted to become "insiders"; that is, members from afar. Here are a few examples, in the form of e-mail from teachers received during the spring 1997 semester.

Example 1. Two teachers from the west side of the state were interested in partnering with preservice learning community members in our campus classroom on Washington's eastern border. In this example, one teacher (a building technology/media specialist) invited a second teacher to join in.

Dear Jerry. . . . Dave is one of a team of teachers. This high school has three teams of teachers who teach in integrated blocks of 170 minutes. They have a project centered curriculum that Dave will share with you that will be a great place to start. Their students will be working in teams of three. Each team is assigned a country and they are to develop a presentation that will attract foreign investors to their country. The presentation can be multimedia, informational brochures, a Web page. . . . They will bring their classes over to the tech rich classroom for those blocks. I will be responsible for setting up accounts, shared directories, . . . e-mail, Internet, [and] software and providing training and other related support. They are the curriculum experts. They are very excited about the idea of this WWW partnership. Dave should contact you soon and I will leave details up to you two to work out and provide whatever support is needed. This will be VERY cool.

Professor Maring . . . we are integrated teams of ninth-grade teachers. Each of us has about 90 students in three curricular areas. All include social studies which is either world geography or Washington history. The other areas are science, word processing, English, and family and consumer education. We will be using our district's "Classroom of the Future" in the next few weeks. This includes six online computers with software. . . . My team's project will almost certainly be to have the students prepare an invitation from the country they are studying to potential investors.

Example 2. A teacher in a self-contained sixth-grade classroom wanted to collaborate via the WWW.

I want to create an integrated social studies/science/language arts student centered project for a Middle Ages unit for this spring. I have *The Midwife's Apprentice, Door in the Wall,* and *Catherine, Called Birdy* in class sets . . . but no study guides—I need vocab and chapter review questions (literal and inferential). The student projects will be multiple intelligence based and integrated. Please have your students look at my current Web site to see the student centered project template and philosophy we use. . . . Hope to hear from a student soon.

Offering Ideas and Inviting Feedback

Our purpose in this section is to show what we accomplished so other teachers can adapt our procedures and guidelines to their own contexts.

The use of computers and of the WWW by preservice teachers in Washington State University's College of Education was pioneered in the area of literacy methods by over 150 students in six sections of two specific courses during two semesters in 1996: Content Literacy in Middle and Secondary Schools and Survey of Elementary Language Arts and Reading. The students and the teacher of these classes worked together as learning community members, developing literacy strategies and other classroom teaching ideas for themselves and to share with other educators. During the spring 1997 term, we continued to use the WWW in two sections of the middle and secondary school literacy methods course and began its use in a graduate-level content literacy course.

We decided to put on the WWW six categories of assignments: (a) traditional units, (b) integrated units (each with embedded content literacy strategies and service learning dimensions), (c) collaborative research projects, (d) service learning reflective essays, (e) literature focus units (Thompson & Hoskisson, 1995), and (f) theme cycles (Altwerger & Flores, 1994; Gamberg, Kwak, Hutchings, Altheim, & Edwards, 1988; Goodman, 1986). Traditional units were developed by writing teams of students who were exploring in the same subject area, while integrated units were developed by groups of students from differing subject areas. Collaborative research projects were of a smaller scale and contained literacy strategies. The elementary reading course completed similar units in keeping with written guidelines for the creation of theme cycle or literature focus units.

We spent over half of our class time working in one of our college's two computer labs. To complete their assignments, our students relied upon written guidelines and step-by-step directions that had been developed and revised over many years. (See Maring, Myers, and Wiseman, 1996, for a more detailed explanation as well as step-by-step directions, though by now somewhat dated, for putting documents on the Web, linking Web pages, saving documents, attaching mail tags, and placing photos.) Because these guidelines had helped students produce desktop-published work in spiral-bound course handbooks from 1992 through 1995, we felt it would be an easy matter of using these same directions for the Web. Hence, we began our WWW adventure in January of 1996 with the view that we simply needed to try out, revise, and write down step-by-step directions.

To make the literacy strategies developed within the three classes accessible to other teachers for their adaptation and use and to receive feedback, it was decided that the Internet would be an effective means of communication with teachers statewide and beyond. For our general systems design, we relied on the expertise of Marc Fleisher, one of our college's two technology consultants. (Note: If your school has a homepage that one of your staff created, you

have a tech expert who can help you adapt and implement an interactive WWW system for your classes.) In addition, within the classes, three students came forward and identified themselves as having considerable background and interest in computer technology. They indicated during a first class session that they would sincerely enjoy taking the leadership and service learning opportunity to build a system and help their classmates get their written work up on the WWW.

One of these students, Dawn Hanson, devised a title for the three, and henceforth, we referred to them as our tech experts, or "techies" for short. Other students had various levels of working knowledge, but most knew only how to do word processing and felt themselves "pretty much computer illiterate." One student, who became extremely enthusiastic by the end of the course ("this is the greatest thing to do"), began class by wanting to know if she could use her typewriter to do her assignments. She stated that she did "not even know how to use a Macintosh or any other computer, for that matter."

Relying on our technology consultant, our three tech experts, and other more experienced students within the classes, we created a development structure for putting documents on the WWW. Class title/homepages were developed by the instructor and tech experts for both the elementary and secondary literacy methods classes, and the various assignment categories developed by small groups of students were linked to the class title page in table-of-contents formats for viewing on the WWW (see Figure 1).

For each group's unit, a folder was created within our class folder on our WWW server (a computer that stores and connects information to the Internet and/or other computers). Within their individual folders, groups created an index/title page, which would function as the main link to the rest of their unit, to be accessed through a link from our class title/homepage. Each group set up WWW links within its unit, linking all the sections to its main index/title page. These links enabled access to each part of the unit, with return links back to the index page (see Figure 2).

Figure 1 Part of One of Our First Homepages

```
This is the Teaching and Learning 450 (Content Literacy in Middle
   and Secondary Schools) Home Page. It contains links to Content
Literacy Strategies and Units developed by students within the class.
  The work completed by these students falls under the following
 categories (with headings described in greater detail in the links
  below): traditional units, integrated units, cooperative research
                projects, and service learning essays.
```

Click here for the major headings of Traditional Units.

Click here for the major headings of Integrated Units.

Click here for the major headings of Cooperative Research Projects.

Click here for the major headings of Reflection Essays.

Click here for the major headings of Content Literacy Strategies.

```
To access the table of contents for Fall     To access the table of contents for
1996 traditional units, integrated units,    Spring 1996 traditional units, integrated
cooperative research projects, and            units, cooperative research projects, and
service learning essays, click here.          service learning essays, click here.
```

Figure 2 Links within Units

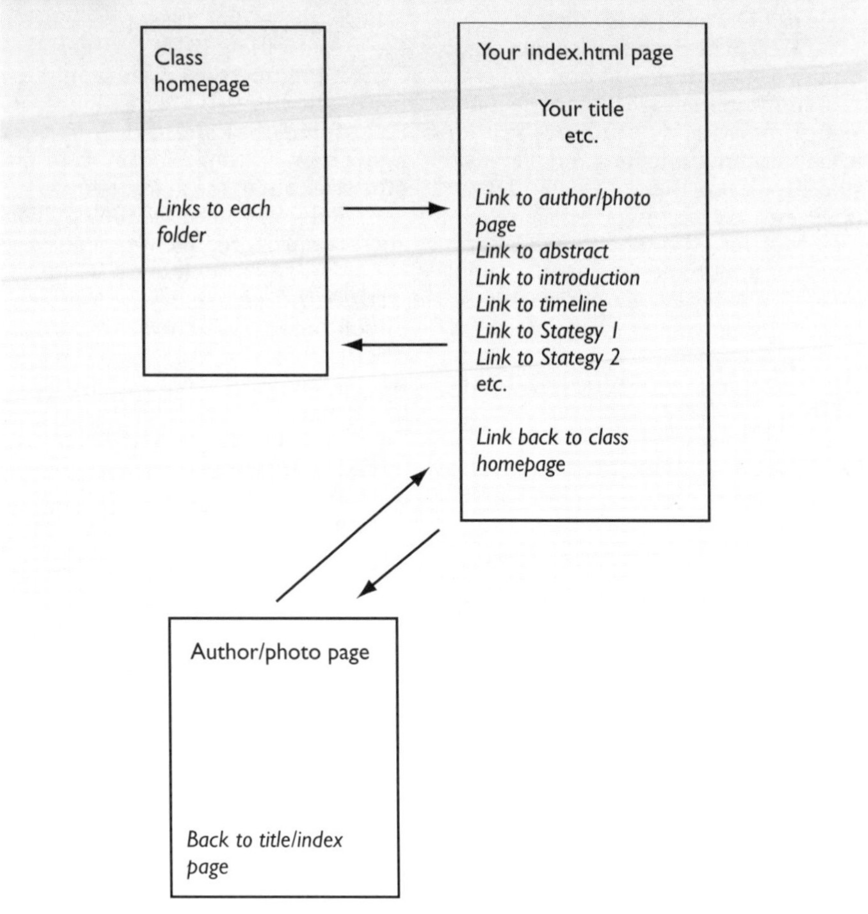

Each unit was required to have author photographs scanned and inserted onto a page within the unit and also to have mail tags. The mail tags were designed so that educators or students browsing our units on the WWW could e-mail comments and suggestions via our class mailing list. In short, the use of mail tags is essential for teachers and students who want to create Web sites that are interactive.

The majority of our students used PageMill for Web page development during 1996. In 1997, we began to use Claris Home Page, Graphic Converter, Ofoto, and ScreenPlay were used for scanning pictures or taking video photos and converting them to GIF files inserted and seen as pictures on our author/photo pages within our unit (see Figure 3).*

Figure 4* shows a project homepage within the class's homepage. Notice how it contains a link at the bottom inviting browser feedback.

As is evident from the preceding overview, the task our students took upon themselves was substantial and led to much engagement. With the infrastructure previously built into our Education Department's computer lab and with the dedicated assistance of our tech experts, the coauthors and team writers in our class learning communities were able to publish their writing on the WWW as well as to communicate with larger educational communities.

We received feedback from nearby (e.g., professors, librarians, a provost, students who would be taking the course in a subsequent semester, teachers in our own college town) and from afar (e.g., a Form 12 student in Australia, learning community members vacationing in Connecticut and another in Beijing, the office of our state department of education, professors at universities in other states and in Canada). From teachers, we received comments including the following.

This is an excellent example of the usefulness of the WWW. . . . I found your ideas interesting and helpful.

I am a social studies teacher . . . and would like to be a part of your curriculum partnership. [We are] involved in major curriculum work in preparation for a four period day next fall. There are many faculty who are interested in your work. . . . We all have access to the WWW. Thanks for sharing your work and offering your help.

I would love to use some of these ideas and provide feedback. I will share your Web site with all the faculty. . . . I think it would be super to have preservice students build units that will be used and evaluated in the "real world." Doing assignments like that [was] always much

*Figures 3 and 4 are not included in this publication.

more interesting for me when I was a student. Plus . . . it will allow students to network with teachers and enhance their portfolios for interviews.

This summer I want to align our state-required Essential Academic Learning Requirements for Reading and Writing with our content in Northwest History, World History, and Current World Problems [the subjects I teach]. . . . I want to write an electronic (html) portfolio assessment this summer . . . after reading a few of your projects. I want to integrate service learning into all this. So your homepage will help.

We received a very large number of e-mail return tag comments from former learning community members.

Thank you SO VERY MUCH for having current students respond to the units and literacy strategies we wrote last semester. Their feedback and encouragement really inspired me to study hard as I prepare to become a teacher.

The collaborative research project on censorship and propaganda . . . is very important to the field of literacy. The suggested activity is quite good. . . . However, I think pupils should check further into the historical aspect of the issue and research how and why certain works came to be taboo.

As the semester progressed, our tech experts developed several pages of written directions to help their classmates with such tasks as making links, attaching e-mail tags, making photo pages, and dealing with unique or mysterious problems and glitches.

Evaluation Questions

Here are answers to a few questions readers may be asking about our WWW project:

1. *What criteria for evaluation do we give students and use?* As we mentioned earlier, we provided our students with written guidelines related to the content of what they place on the WWW. In a nutshell, students are evaluated on the basis of how well their work complies with these directions and the suggestions they are given by the professor, other students, and teachers. To facilitate this process at grading time and to focus students' attention before the end of the term, we developed and used a two-page, end-of-term course checklist. This document

listed each component of the various WWW, hard copy, coauthored, and individually authored assignments. It was designed in such a way that ratings could be assigned both for team writing and individual writing.

2. *Is everything the students do put on the WWW?* No, the students complete a series of "Building Your Knowledge Base" assignments before they begin to place some of the work in our course homepage. Other assignments like "Mid-Term Sharing of Favorite Content Literacy Strategies" and end-of-course "I search" portfolio coversheets (Rousculp & Maring, 1992) are submitted in hard copy.

3. *Is all of the work students share via WWW exemplary?* No. Preservice teachers perform during any given time frame according to their level of motivation and in keeping with their abilities. In addition, the work of individual coauthors who contribute to a team writing effort may be outstanding while the contributions of other members of the project may be only "good" in light of the topic selected for development.

4. *Who critiques the student work and suggests improvements?* In addition to feedback from the course professor, the students seek out suggestions from their peers, classroom teachers, and instructors of other courses. Some of this occurs face to face over hard copy. However, the best feedback our students get is in the form of truly substantive remarks via e-mail from teachers in the field. Here is such an e-mail example.

Hi! I teach in San Jose, CA and wanted to give you some feedback on a few of your units. I looked at FAMILIES first and was a bit surprised at the constant forcing of appreciation and awareness. The ideas are not really off base, but they seem sort of superficial (especially activity 2 and 6). Activity 1, 4, and 5 are pointed in the right direction. 6 is very cliché. Sound teaching provides all learners with an avenue for personal expression . . . my experience with a very diverse inner city and suburban group of students has helped me see that they first want to be seen as

individuals with their own unique gifts and talents. Culture is not a trivial thing and the children themselves can provide us with so much that doesn't come from strategies . . . just let them talk or if you don't have access to children from different backgrounds, let them be bathed in the literature of various cultures . . . maybe have penpals in a different country or state. They see through any surface attempts at being sensitive to culture. . . . The personal experiences of the teacher are paramount . . . read and study, study . . . study . . . then the children will benefit from the richness of the world cultures. . . . I hope you keep up your interest and appreciation.

5. *What happens if a teacher visiting the WWW site finds something offensive or objectionable?* When students forget to periodically spell check their work in progress, they receive valid criticism. But, up to this point, we have not encountered substantive objections. We should emphasize that instead of viewing such "objections" as a problem, this is one of the outcomes we are looking for. Objections create opportunities for dialog, clarification, and growth. In general, the teacher in the learning community would want to protect and help her or his students and would try to safeguard students' ownership of their ideas.

In the example offered in the preceding question, the coauthors involved and the class as a whole agreed with the substance and the spirit of the feedback. We have not received feedback that has found our work objectionable or offensive.

6. *What is the instructor's role?* Even though in the case of our Web site the instructor is a professor, we believe a learning community is more productive and creates qualitatively better work when the "instructor of record" serves as a teacher in the sense of being a helper, a guide, a facilitator; one who shares advice and information not so that it will be regurgitated, but because it might well help students who are constructing meaning.

We have observed that students are very engaged in their work when constructing Web sites and that they actually consult one another more than they do the professor. This situation occurs when written guidelines are clear and call for many critical and creative responses. With such a high level of student engagement and ownership, it might happen that the professor would feel uneasy about not being at the center of attention. Such occurrences, however, indicate that having the course centered around students is essential for a community of learners.

7. *Are grades given?* Yes, at the end, after multiple revisions and chances to improve, and in light of other assignments students complete that are not placed on the Web. Grades must be assigned because they are an administrative requirement. Most students seemed to want to do their best because their work would be seen and used by others rather than because it might be assigned low grades.

Adapting Our Procedures to Other Classrooms

By adapting our procedures to your course or classroom, you and your students can build a community of learners that offers its unique ideas to others worldwide. As we have, you should focus on what your course is about and on using technology. After all, technology in most class situations is a tool for learning and for building a community of learners more than it is the major objective of the course.

Step 1: Select an experienced technology consultant and recruit student tech experts. Again, if your school has a WWW homepage constructed by a staff member, you have a tech expert right there, and you and your students have access to technology. Larger universities usually have at least one tech expert per college, whereas most smaller institutions of higher education have one who serves the entire campus.

(a) Provide your consultant and a number of student tech experts with an overview and examples of the assignments you want your students to place on the WWW. (b) Suggest that they read this article as a resource. If you teach in an elementary or middle school, you should probably seek out tech experts from a nearby high school or college. Perhaps they can earn credit for a service learning project that involves helping you and your students. (c) Ask your technology consultant and your tech experts to create folders on a server for your class and to design passwords so that your students can place drafts of their writing onto the server. These experts can also advise you about further technical matters and choices related to your class Web site and the procedures and programs you will need. (d) Describe to your tech experts your plans and expectations so that they can give you directions and advice about what will and will not work on your system server and about parameters for your students.

Step 2: Provide your students with models of written work from previous semesters and examples of WWW applications that involve dialog and interaction. It is essential that students have the hope that the work they will put on the WWW is interesting and significant to them and to others who read and respond to it. Our students were truly excited about "putting our work on the WWW and getting feedback from teachers." We felt we were pioneers, in a sense. Soon, though, the novelty of the WWW will wear off. At that point, placing work on the WWW that is perceived by the students and their audiences as relevant, interesting, and significant will become the larger part of the motivation for "doing all this extra work."

As soon as your first semester's efforts are on the WWW, these will serve as effective motivators and examples to students who hope to follow in the footsteps of the last class. Hard-copy assignments written by previous students can also show your current students some possible formats and styles. In this way, students have the benefits of following a style guide and will be able to see that they, too, can be part of a learning community that offers its critical and creative ideas to interested WWW users.

Instruct your writing teams to follow guidelines designed to help them produce consistent formats. Explain that coauthors should be reader-friendly writers who save their readers the frustrations of feeling they have just traversed so many idiosyncratic and stylistic labyrinths. Explain that members of the class will also feel a better sense of community with one another if their work, though unique in content, follows common formatting and writing guidelines.

Step 3: Personalize your class's WWW effort, explaining that their ideas are of great value and worth sharing. We found that students' inclusion of author photos and biographical information helped motivate them to realize that their ideas actually stemmed from their history as readers and writers as well as such factors as their life and career goals; intellectual interests; personalities; spiritualities; physical, recreational, and social avocations; human/cultural views and experiences; and sociopolitical stances, concerns, and questions. We feel that students will soon be putting "just more stuff" up on the WWW if their assignments do not encourage them to express what Belenky, Clinchy, Goldberger, and Tarule (1986) call their self(s), voices, and minds as these have emerged in the literate environment of their learning community.

Step 4: Design your reading and writing assignments so that your students can engage in coauthoring. Collaboration in researching, reading, and writing has a trifold benefit: (a) students investigate more content and in greater detail than they can as individual researchers, (b) writing team members who are more computer literate help others take advantage of this "zone of proximal development" (Vygotsky, 1978), and (c) the community of learners in the class is enhanced because individuals learn from others and from the give and take of group work. However, be sure you schedule adequate research and reading/writing workshop time so that students can engage in all stages of the reading and writing process.

Step 5: Use an "editor" like the PageMill or Claris Home Page programs. PageMill is a Macintosh program for creating Web pages. Allow time for your students to walk through the PageMill tutorial (or through some other program you select for helping them translate their writing onto WWW) in small groups of two or three. They will demonstrate basic competency when they can create two pages of text with hypertext links between them. PageMill or Claris Home Page are effective tools for students since they do not require learning a complicated HTML/hypertext markup language.

Step 6: Edit your Web pages and link them into a single, central document that serves as your homepage. This step, which involves securing links among the subdocuments the students have created, their title pages, and a central entry point (the class homepage) is one of the most technically sophisticated steps of the project. In our classes, to accommodate the volume of writing and to ensure consistent formatting, we chose to use tables to display our project title links on the class homepage.

Step 7: Create a class e-mail list. It is a prerequisite for this step that students in your classes have and use e-mail. You and they can use e-mail addresses to communicate with any individual in the class. In this step, you need to have your systems administrator create a class e-mail list, which is like an electronic class newsletter that sends messages to you, your tech experts, and your technology consultant as owners of the list and to your students as subscribers.

Step 8: Add e-mail return tags to your class's homepage or, even better, to each project's title page. This step is absolutely essential if

you want to have your students write for genuine purposes and to real audiences and if you want to have interactive involvements with other WWW users who are interested in your work and writing. Former students can make suggestions, and students not yet enrolled in your class can build their anticipation by browsing what your students have created.

Ask your students to help find interested persons, groups, or classes who will browse your class Web site and who will dialog with you via your e-mail return links. Once they e-mail back to you, they will be a part of your community of learners.

Step 9: Share and archive feedback you receive over the WWW. Keep your productions online for a year or more. You can expect to receive feedback after your class has ended. If it is kept in an archive, former and future students can enjoy and profit from comments and suggestions. With each new semester, you will have new products and writing on the WWW. The quality of work and writing produced will improve with each passing semester, because you and your students will be able to stand on the shoulders of learning community members from previous years.

Welcoming Others into Your Classroom

Although our purpose in this article is to encourage other educators to create interactive Web sites that promote student literacy development, readers should also feel free to visit our learning community by browsing our Web sites at http://www.educ. wsu.edu/tl/450/. We have stored completed units and strategies for teaching and learning as well as current student work under construction. Increasing numbers of these sites contain feedback from teachers in the field or have been constructed in partnership by coauthoring teams of students taking undergraduate or graduate courses in literacy development on campus interacting with teachers or student teachers in the field.

Before we decided to embark on the adventure of getting our work and writing on the WWW, our classes were designed to be embodiments of the learning community approach (Rousculp & Maring, 1992). However, the actual adventure clearly animated us even more to function as a truly literate environment, which, in turn, transformed us into a more sophisticated community of learners.

Elementary and middle school teachers whose pupils write reports from theme cycles and literature focus units, secondary teachers whose pupils create reports within traditional and integrated content area units, and college-level instructors who invite preservice and inservice teachers to write literacy strategies for teaching and learning within units of instruction can model and adapt our procedures. After the projects are on the WWW, both students and teachers can look forward to receiving and responding to comments and suggestions from near and far. In short, the WWW, used this way, is not primarily a vehicle for the "transmission model" of education (Harste, 1977). Rather, it serves as an animator and tool for creating and sharing ideas, for improving literacy, and for welcoming many others into your classroom community of learners.

References

Attwerger, B., & Flores, B. (1994). Theme cycles: Creating communities of learners. *Primary Voices K–6, 2,* 2–6.

Anderson-Inman, L. (1995). Technology Tidbits: An introduction. *Journal of Adolescent & Adult Literacy, 39,* 154–155.

Belenky, M., Clinchy, B., Goldberger, N., & Tarule, J. (1986). *Women's ways of knowing.* New York: Basic Books.

Chobrak, K. (1995). Build a WWW homepage for your school. *Library Media Activities Monthly, 11*(9), 39,42.

December, J. (1994). Electronic publishing on the Internet: New traditions, new choices. *Educational Technology, 34*(7), 32–36.

Dyrli, O.E., & Kinnaman, D.E. (1995). Connecting classrooms: School is more than a place—What every teacher needs to know about technology. *Technology and Learning, 10*(8), 82–88.

Franz, K.R. (1996). Real teaching in the social context of the virtual school. In B. Robin, J.D. Price, J. Willis, & D.E. Wills (Eds.), *Technology and Teacher Education Annual, 1996.* Charlottesville, VA: Association for the Advancement of Technology in Education.

Gamberg, R., Kwak, W., Hutchings, M., Altheim, J., & Edwards, G. (1988). *Learning and loving it: Theme studies in the classroom.* Portsmouth, NH: Heinemann.

Goodman, K. (1986). *What's whole in whole language.* Portsmouth, NH: Heinemann.

Harste, J. (1977). Foreword. In M. W. Olson (Ed.), *Opening the door to classroom research* (pp. v–viii). Newark, DE: International Reading Association.

Kurland, D.J. (1996). *The Net, the Web, and You.* Belmont, CA: Wadsworth.

Maring, G.H. (1993). *Tying service learning to content literacy for preservice and "early years" teachers.* Paper presented at the Wallace-DeWitt/Council of Chief State School Officers Conference for Integrating Service Learning into Teacher Preparation and Advancing Institutional Change, Cullowhee, NC.

Maring, G.H., Nyers, K., & Wiseman, B.J. (1996). *Using the World Wide Web to promote literacy development and learning communities: Guidelines and directions for teachers.* Bloomington, IN: ERIC Clearinghouse on Reading, English, and Communication. (ERIC Document Reproduction Service No. ED 396 298)

McCaleb, S.P. (1994). *Building communities of learners: A collaboration among teachers, families, and community.* New York: St. Martins.

National Education Association. (1995). *Creating a community of learners—A teacher TV videotape* (videotape). West Haven, CT: NEA Professional Library.

Palmer, P. (1993). *To know as we are known: A spirituality of education.* San Francisco: Harper.

Peterson, R. (1992). *Life in a crowded place: Making a learning community.* Portsmouth, NH: Heinemann.

Pfaffenberger, B. (1996). *Publish it on the Web.* Boston: AP Professional.

Resnick, L.B., Leving, J.M., & Teasley, S.D. (Eds.). (1991). *Perspectives on socially shared cognition.* Washington, D C: American Psychological Association.

Rousculp, E.E., & Maring, G.H. (1992). Portfolios for a community of learners. *Journal of Reading, 35,* 378–3835.

Salaman, G. (Ed.). (1993). *Distributed cognitions: Psychological and educational considerations.* New York: Cambridge University Press.

Short, K.G., & Burke, C. (1991). *Creating curriculum: Teachers and students as a community of learners.* Portsmouth, NH: Heinemann.

Shotsberger, P.G. (1996, March/April). Instructional uses of the World Wide Web: Exemplars and precautions. *Educational Technology,* 47–50.

Tompkins, G.E., & Hoskisson, K. (1995). *Language arts: Content and teaching strategies.* Columbus, OH: Merrill.

Tierney, R., & O'Flahavan, J. (1989). Literacy, learning, and students' decision-making: Establishing classrooms in which reading and writing work together. In D. Lapp, J. Flood, & N. Farnan (Eds.), *Content area reading and learning* (pp. 297–303). Englewood Cliffs, NJ: Prentice Hall.

Vygotsky, L. (1978). *Mind in society.* Cambridge MA: Harvard University Press.

Article Review Form at end of book.

What does a "post-typographic world" mean? Are reading and writing different with technology?

Reading and Writing with Computers

Literacy research in a post-typographic world

David Reinking

University of Georgia and the National Reading Research Center

[Edited by Doug Fisher]

Richard Lanham (1989), in an article about how electronic texts are changing reading and writing, points out how technological change often requires businesses and professions to address the question "What business or profession are we really in?" For example, as technological advances led to alternative forms of transportation early in this century, railroads had to decide if they were in the railroad business or the transportation business. The decline in railroads as they moved to the margins of the transportation industry testifies to the outcome of those that stayed in the railroad business. More recently, those who produce newspapers have faced decisions about whether they are in the newspaper business or the information business. Some major newspapers are hedging their bets, such as the *Atlanta Journal-Constitution*, which has added an on-

line news service available to readers who subscribe electronically. And the Steinway Company, a leading manufacturer of pianos, is threatened by competition from companies such as Yamaha that manufacture electronic keyboards. Steinway must decide if it is in the piano business or the music business. I am sure that for many who make and play Steinway pianos, such a decision is an agonizing and emotional one. To them, a piano is more than a device that produces music; the physical and sensory characteristics of a well-crafted piano evoke a strong aesthetic response that electronic keyboards do not. The risk of losing that aesthetic is more salient to them than any of the keyboard's potential advantages. . . .

Evolving forms of electronic reading and writing point to fundamental changes in the way we communicate and disseminate information, the way we approach the task of reading and writing, and the way we think about people becoming literate.

I believe that our conceptions of literacy, and by extension our research agenda, must respond to these changes, or, as Marshall McLuhan has cautioned, we risk driving into the future looking in the rearview mirror. . . .

I hope to convince you that virtually every area of interest among literacy researchers must now be reconsidered because we are poised to enter the post-typographic era that McLuhan (1962) and others predicted 30 years ago. However, it is not television and the other video media, at least in analog form, that will usher in the post-typographic culture as McLuhan argued; it is the digital forces of the computer in all of its shape-shifting forms and uses. . . .

To support my position and to comment on the research that has been done or needs to be done, I will address the following key questions:

1. To what extent are reading and writing changing? That is, what evidence is there that we are moving into a post-typographic era?

2. Could books be moving to the margins of the literacy; and, if so, how much should we care?

3. Is reading and writing with a computer really that different? And, if so, how?

4. How might incorporating electronic reading and writing into our conceptions of literacy reconfigure our research agenda?

Plenary Research Address presented at the National Reading Conference, San Diego, California, December 3, 1994.

Reprinted with permission from the National Reading Conference.

5. How much does the research involving computers speak to these issues? What do we most need to know if we are headed toward a post-typographic world?

Are We Moving Toward a Post-Typographic Era?

To address this question, it is necessary to consider the term *post-typographic*. Obviously, it is meant to demarcate a shift to a time when typography or print no longer dominates. However, its significance is rooted in the understanding that, throughout history, literacy has been a dynamic concept, intimately related to the tools and materials (i.e., the technology) used to read and to write (Kaufer & Carley, 1993). It also is meant to acknowledge that technology fundamentally shapes the entire spectrum of literate activity and its consequences. For example, as Jay Bolter (1991) has pointed out, the conceptual units of writing, such as paragraphs, chapters, and books, are linked to typography, as are our notions abut diverse topics such as copyrights, plagiarism, authorship, and the literary canon. . . .

When the technology of reading and writing remains relatively stable as it has until recently in our lifetimes, the role of technology in shaping literacy is of little more than historical interest. As Jay Samuels used to say when I was a graduate student, "If scientists were fish, water is the last thing they would investigate." Using the term *post-typographic* highlights that electronic texts are increasingly becoming a destabilizing influence, requiring us to examine assumptions so basic that they have been transparent. Considering that we may be entering a post-typographic world means facing the discomforting reality that our assumptions about literacy are not immutable laws of nature, but only the natural consequence of one way to read and write.

The pace at which we are moving away from print has of late accelerated to a point that is difficult to ignore. New examples appear almost daily. *Newsweek* just joined the other news magazines by announcing an interactive version available through a commercial on-line service. An article in *Scientific American* (Stix, 1994) reported that the exchange of information among leading scientists is increasingly bypassing conventional journal publication. As noted in that article, the 1994 edition of the *Directory of Electronic Journal, Newsletters and Academic Discussion Lists*, published by the Association of Research Libraries, lists 440 electronic academic journals, a fourfold increase from 1991 (see also the *Los Alamos E-Print Archives*, available on the World Wide Web as http://xxx.lanl.gov/). Currently, about 100 have some type of peer review. The article also documents that the number of journals and books purchased by libraries has decreased steadily since 1985.

The move toward electronic reading and writing is not limited to scholars and scientists. We sign for deliveries with a stylus on an electromagnetic tablet. Nurses use a similar technology to chart patients, medications and vital signs, which are sent wirelessly to computers in a physician's office. The clerk in an auto parts store conducts an electronic search for a needed part, which is then displayed graphically on a CRT screen. Hotels include special phone links for guests who wish to use modems. Britannica and other companies are increasingly marketing electronic versions of encyclopedias in place of their printed counterparts. Students at major universities such as Stanford, UCLA, and MIT, where many dormitories have direct Internet connections, are using computers to register for courses, to research topics in libraries around the world, to submit their work to instructors, and to find out who in their dormitory wants to chip in on a pizza. Traffic on the Internet has been doubling every 8–10 months. Publishing companies are tentatively experimenting with electronic texts. Rental cars are being equipped with electronic street maps. Anyone who thinks these are isolated examples that will eventually disappear is living in a time warp that is increasingly difficult to sustain.

If we in our field have been slow to acknowledge these developments, the general public, corporate America, and the government have not. Both *Newsweek* and *Time* recently published cover stories about the Internet, and *Newsweek* has an ongoing feature entitled "Cyberscope" that deals with aspects of the Internet and computer-based communication. Vice President Al Gore's superhighway metaphor has become part of the national vocabulary. We read of high-stakes corporate jockeying that is occurring in response to ambiguity about the future of conventional forms of communication and entertainment. . . .

Hopefully, we in our field will begin to provide thoughtful and measured responses to such developments. It would be unfortunate indeed if we found ourselves on the trailing edge of a shift toward a post-typographic world with nothing of substance to add to the discussion. We risk more than looking foolishly provincial, for by continuing to invest only in the print business we will miss the opportunity to shape the new world of digital literacy.

Are Books Moving to the Margins of Literacy, and Should We Care?

. . . Rarely before the present have we had any reason to question the centrality of books in our conception of literacy. Only occasionally are we confronted with their abiding and pervasive effect on us. . . .

However, books, and indeed writing itself, were not always viewed with such veneration and respect, and such an awareness lends perspective to our indignation about the thought of losing the ideal of the book. For example, Socrates considered writing inhuman, a manufactured product outside of the mind, and ultimately a destroyer of memory. This position persisted into the Middle Ages, when St. Thomas Aquinas wrote that "it is fitting that Christ did not commit his teaching to writing, on account of his own dignity and . . . whereby his doctrine would be imprinted on the hearts of his hearers." And, when relatively inexpensive printed books were beginning to replace handwritten illuminated manuscripts, a 16th-century administrator lamented,

Could a portable, private instrument like the new book take the place of a book made by hand and memorized as one made it? Could a book which could be read quickly and even silently take the place of a book read slowly aloud? Could students trained by such printed books measure up to the skilled orators and disputants produced by manuscript means?

Will future citizens of a post-typographic world smirk at our own resistance to a changing literacy landscape, as a feeble attempt to preserve a literacy that is not necessarily better but only more familiar? Given the increasing flexibility and power of electronic texts, the arguments for elevating books over electronic texts are already beginning to sound shallow and desperate. The fact that some prefer to take a book rather than a computer to read in bed or at the beach hardly seems to be a firm foundation upon which to argue for the preservation of books at all costs. It may, in fact, seem foolish, when considering the computer's capability to provide a whole library at one's disposal in a single, portable, highly interactive, and increasingly readable device. The strong aesthetic response that we associate with books, especially certain genres of fiction, is real, but learned. It does not negate the possibility that an equally powerful aesthetic response could reside within creative forms of electronic reading and writing, a possibility entertained by a *New York Times Book Review* article (Coover, 1993) on the emerging genre of hypertextual fiction. Opposing such electronic forms of creativity on preference alone is no more justifiable than rejecting all forms of textual creativity except those that are consistent with Western literature. . . .

Is Reading and Writing Different with a Computer?

Implicit in the viewpoint that we are entering a post-typographic era is that the differences between printed and electronic texts are substantial enough to alter current conceptions of literacy. I believe the differences are that important, although they are not obvious to the print-based mind. I will briefly highlight five differ-

ences here that I have written about more extensively elsewhere (Reinking, 1992, 1994a; Reinking & Chamlin (1994b), because they are an important starting point for setting a post-typographic research agenda and for thinking about how we can prepare future generations of readers and writers.

Interactivity and Malleability

The first difference is that electronic texts are truly interactive, and they are interactive because they are so malleable. The interaction that is referred to between readers and printed texts and that fills the literature about reading processes has a metaphorical, not a literal, meaning. Until now, describing reading as an interactive or transactional process has emphasized the active role of a reader in making meaning, not a text's capability to be modified by or respond to individual readers. Printed texts are fixed, inert entities that stand aloof from the influence and needs of a particular reader. Electronic texts, on the other hand, can alternately respond to individual readers while inviting them to manipulate the text to meet their personal needs. George Landow (1992) has pointed out that the flashing cursor on the screen is the visual representation of a reader's intimate presence within a text and lack of restrictions in modifying it. Likewise, electronic texts can be programmed to monitor what a reader is doing or not doing while reading a particular text, and to adjust the textual presentation accordingly. . . .

Interactivity and malleability also undermine the authority we ascribe to printed texts. As Bruce Edwards (1991) has observed,

The authority of the text is its finality as an unerasable hardcopy product. In contrast, . . . the digitized word facilitates discovery, retrieval, recombination, and revisions of ideas and form. . . . Its authority or meaning is located in the interaction between the author and the electronic community of readers in and for which the text was created. (p. 74)

. . . One does not have to look too hard to substantiate the position that interactivity (often associated with a multimedia approach) is becoming the touchstone of contemporary culture. Everything from the

remote control to the hands-on museum could be cited. We can say that is too bad, that interactive media are inferior to books, but if we wish to take that stand, we had better marshal some convincing reasons soon, because just saying it won't preserve the status quo.

The Ascendancy of Nonverbal Elements

The ascendancy of nonverbal elements is also a characteristic of electronic texts. Nonverbal elements include pictures, icons, movies, animations, and sound. Not only are such elements available in electronic texts, but they can easily and cheaply be integrated with written prose.

Multimedia is a term that has only recently been associated with reading and writing. This development, as Jay Lemke (1994) pointed out, means that we must reorient our thinking about the relationship between alphabetic, iconographic, and nonverbal modes of communication. In electronic texts, images and sound compete equally with alphabetic symbols, forcing us to consider their respective contribution and value toward expressing meaning. We can no longer blithely accept the notion that graphical information is subservient to the primacy of the alphabetic code. Electronic texts force us to acknowledge our biases for words over other modes of communication and to think about whether such biases are justifiable. Does saying we are in the literacy business mean automatically that we are also in the alphabetic code business? . . .

One consequence is that electronic texts require a renewed self-consciousness about the meaning contained in the visual forms of a text. We look at, not through, electronic texts to find their meaning. . . . It's one thing when Ted Turner wants to colorize some classic old movies; it may be another when students can easily alter or extend everything from a Whitman poem to the principal's latest memo.

As readers and writers of electronic texts, we will be pushed toward a more complex definition of what a text is and what successful readers and writers must know about to create one. . . . A glimpse of the future is found in the Apple

Classrooms of Tomorrow project carried out by Rob Tierney and his colleagues (Tierney et al., 1992). When high school students were given access to various state-of-the-art hardware and software for use in school and at home over several years, their views of text began to change. As one student stated about his writing after two years in the project,

Now I incorporate graphics with my text a lot more. I relate it or I try to link it together so that it looks like one unit. . . . I try to make it look more aesthetic and I try to have it more pertinent to what the text is. . . . The things we created weren't really something that could be done on a page. . . . It was something you had to become involved with. . . . It makes it more non-linear sometimes. (p. 4)

Researchers too may find a multimedia approach useful in reporting their investigations. For example, a research report in electronic form could include a video of an interview with a subject rather than a transcript.

New Textual Structures

The characteristic of electronic texts that has received the most attention is the degree to which they invite nonlinear reading and writing, often manifested in what have been referred to as hypertexts. Various definitions of hypertext have been proposed, but they always include nonlinear access to separate but interconnected nodes of text. Although hypertext has existed as a concept since the 1940s, and as a term since the 1960s, its surging popularity is due not only to technological advances but also, I think, to the view that it is a harbinger of the post-typographic world.

Much more could be said about hypertexts, but I will highlight two points that are pertinent to my theme. First, hypertexts remind us that acquiring the discipline to organize one's thoughts into a linear, hierarchical argument is a large part of what we call being literate only because the technology of print does not invite other ways to structure an argument, not because that is the natural way we think. Hypertexts provide a means to express ourselves in ways that reflect more directly the complexity of our thinking and the interrelatedness of ideas. As Bolter

(1991) has argued, "When technology provided us with printed books and photographs, our minds were repositories of fixed texts and still images. When the contemporary technology is electronic, our minds become pulsing networks of ideas" (p. 207).

Second, hypertexts further the educational, social, and political ends of literacy that we have always valued. For example, as Henrietta Shirk (1991) commented about hypertexts in composition instruction, "Writers will no longer create in solitary environments; they will become contributing members of hypertext development teams" (p. 198). In other words, hypertexts turn the notion of a community of writers and readers into an objective reality. . . .

Given the now feasible alternative of nonlinear reading and writing, insisting that students be taught to read and write only printed texts is like insisting that they use only straight lines when they draw.

Expanding the Boundaries of Freedom and Control

As illustrated by hypertexts and recent developments such as the Internet, another characteristic of electronic texts is that they expand exponentially readers' freedom to access textual information and writers' freedom to disseminate their ideas without the barriers of conventional publishing. At the same time, computers provide unprecedented opportunities to control readers' access to text and to monitor their strategic actions while reading a particular text. These countervailing forces raise some familiar issues that are taking on new shapes and forms.

The control made possible by electronic texts is derived from the fact that only a limited amount of textual information can be presented on a computer screen at one time. Text displayed on a computer is as if we are viewing the textual world through a window (see Wilkinson, 1983), and what is hidden is just as important as what is visible. The two-dimensional placement of text on a printed page requires an additional dimension when displayed on a computer screen, and that additional dimension is time (see Daniel & Reinking, 1987). That is, creating

an electronic text requires deciding not just *where*, but *when* the text will be displayed. . . .

The issue of control in electronic texts also reminds us that free access to textual information in even a democratic print-based society is often an illusion (see Kaufer & Carley, 1994). As someone has said, "The only people who have freedom of the press are those who own one." Control of readers' access to text in a post-typographic world is less subtle and is therefore more difficult to disguise with excuses—such as having limited funds to buy only "good" books.

The Pragmatics and Conventions of Literate Activity

Electronic reading and writing also change the pragmatics and conventions of written communication. . . . The social and interpersonal conventions of literacy in a typographic world may be transformed in a post-typographic one. The handwritten letter on a particular stationary, for example, continues to communicate something beyond its prose. Those of us who regularly use E-mail (clearly the prominent example of this characteristic) are struggling to discover the pragmatics of this new form of communication. What meanings are being sent and received between the lines? What is appropriate "netiquette" in a discussion group? When is it ethical to forward a message without permission from its author? The social dynamics of accidentally sending a private message to an entire discussion group is not only a hazard of E-mail communication; it is also a literacy event worthy of study for the way it affects written communication in a post-typographic world. . . .

Columnist Dave Barry has described E-mail as the CB radio of the 90s, only with a lot more writing. There is a serious side to Barry's tongue-in-cheek comparison, as Howard Rhinegold (1993) has highlighted in his book *The Virtual Community: Homesteading on the Electronic Frontier*. He acknowledged that his original attraction to E-mail discussion groups was his enjoyment of writing as a performing art, itself an interesting new mode of writing. However, he has come to see the real value of E-mail discussion groups as "virtual communities" or "electronic agora"—functioning much like the marketplace in ancient Athens, "where citizens met to talk, gossip, argue, size each other up, [and] find the weak spots in political ideas by debating about them" (p. 14). As Rhinegold has pointed out, E-mail is a blend of opposing values both altruistic and self-serving, compassionate and unfeeling, time saving and time consuming. As such, it encompasses a wider range of communicative modes and purposes than any single type of printed document.

A typographic world is finding that it is increasingly difficult to absorb the pragmatics and conventions of electronic texts. For example, in academia the new American Psychological Association manual struggles to create citations of electronic sources that conform to print-based citations, and promotion committees are ambivalent about how electronic publications should count as professional products.

Some Things That We Know and That We Need to Know

Given the scope and depth of the changes that are likely to occur as we move into a post-typographic world, our current research base is extremely thin. Further, much of the research has been conceptualized from the standpoint of print and is of marginal usefulness. Yet we have learned some things that are useful, and some current research seems to be moving in the right direction. I wish to highlight a few promising areas of research now, in addition to those I have already alluded to.

Existing research clearly indicates that, under some conditions, the unique characteristics of electronic texts can effect increases in learning during independent reading (e.g., Reinking, 1988; Reinking & Rickman, 1990). For example, consider how a reader encountering an unfamiliar word can instantaneously obtain a definition of the word, perhaps as a dictionary entry surrounded by conceptually as opposed to alphabetically related words; a

pronunciation of the word; a video or animation pertaining to the word's meaning; a concordance of similar uses of the word in different contexts, and so forth. Consider as well the capability of the computer to sense that a reader is having difficulty and on that basis prescribe remedial action or even alter the text to accommodate the reader. It could sense difficulties from sources as mundane as performance on inserted questions, or as exotic as eye movements or galvanic skin response. In conducting such research we must consider the distinction between short-term and long-term effects—what Gabriel Salomon and his colleagues (Salomon, Perkins, & Globerson, 1991) have called the effects *with* and *of* technology.

We need to understand more about the strategies that readers and writers use when reading and writing electronic texts. . . . We also need to investigate navigational aids to deal with the lost-in-hyperspace problem inherent in exploring large, interconnected textual networks, which is made possible by browser applications such as Mosaic or Netscape on the Internet. One intriguing solution has been explored by Jay Bolter (personal communication), who has developed virtual reality texts. Readers virtually enter a textual world that they see through special goggles. In this textual world, topics appear on objects that resemble large buildings, connected by skyways representing links. To read the textual nodes related to a particular topic, one moves a special glove to enter a building where the texts can be displayed on the walls of rooms. This application may seem bizarre until we think of it as an electronic version of what we do when we enter a large library, which can be conceptualized as a huge text organized around topics linked by the Dewey decimal system.

There is consistent evidence that introducing innovative computer applications aimed at moving instruction in different directions does not alone change instruction and learning. The most thoroughly documented and extensively researched example is the work of Chip Bruce (Bruce & Rubin, 1993) and his colleagues investigating QUILL, a comprehensive process-writing ap-

plication implemented over several years and schools. They found that teachers molded the QUILL activities to fit their existing ideas about writing, which were sometimes contrary to the underlying purposes of the program. We need more research that investigates how technology affects the intricate social fabric of classrooms. . . .

We also know that computers can help students learn more mundane aspects of reading and writing, such as the alphabetic principles underlying conventional writing, and that this aspect of instruction can be accomplished in engaging ways that frees teachers to concentrate on less transient aspects of literacy (see McKenna, 1994; Roth & Beck, 1981).

We can also learn from past mistakes. We need look no further than the research on the IBM *Writing to Read* program for a good example of research run amok (see Krendl & Williams, 1990). The enthusiasm for using computers must be tempered with sound research and thoughtful theories. As researchers we must heed Thoreau's caution against inventions that are an "improved means to an unimproved end."

Some Proposals and Concluding Remarks

Most of all, we in the field need to promote solid scholarship that analyzes the extent to which electronic reading and writing are transforming literacy. . . . I do not underestimate the difficulties in making technology more central to the field. As Robert Samuelson (1993) stated in a *Newsweek* column earlier in 1995, "new technologies gush uncertainties." The emerging technologies of electronic communication change rapidly, and as Samuelson points out, they require major investments in infrastructure and training to be used effectively. Acknowledging that we are moving towards a posttypographic world also threatens the security of our print-based academic accomplishments. It will also be difficult to encourage discussion of technology and literacy in an atmosphere where people are labeled either as technophiles or as Luddites. My interest in technology does not mean that I enjoy reading technical magazines about computers, or that I have no reservations abut the computer's influence on literacy.

Despite these difficulties, I believe we can confront the challenges we will face in moving toward a post-typographic world. It would not be the first time that we have redefined the nature of our business. Fifteen years ago, we saw ourselves predominantly as being in the reading comprehension business, and around 5 years ago we began to see ourselves as being in the literacy, not just the reading, business. . . .

Being in the literacy business means seeing our business as intimately related to textuality, and that in turn means that our business has always been related to technology. That is the perspective we need for literacy research in a post-typographic world, and the one that I hope I have stimulated you to think more about.

References

Barthes, R. (1974). *S/Z* (R. Miller, Trans.). New York: Hill & Wang. (Original work published 1970).

Baumann, J.F., Dillon, D.R., Shockley, B.B., Alvermann, D E., & Reinking, D. (in press). Perspectives in literacy research. In L. Baker, P. Afflerbach, & D. Reinking (Eds.), *Developing engaged readers in school and home communities*. Hillsdale, NJ: Erlbaum.

Bolter, J. D. (1991). *Writing space: The computer, hypertext, and the history of writing*. Hillsdale, NJ: Erlbaum. (Also available as hypertext computer program.)

Bolter, J.D., Joyce, M., Smith, J.B., & Bernstein, M. (1993). *Storyspace* [Computer program]. Cambridge, MA: Eastgate Systems.

Brandt, D. (1990). *Literacy as involvement: The acts of writers, readers, and texts*. Carbondale, IL: Southern Illinois Press.

Bruce, B.C., & Rubin, A. (1993). *Electronic quills: A situated evolution of using computers for writing in classrooms*. Hillsdale, NJ: Erlbaum.

Cherryholmes, C. H. (1993). Reading research. *Journal of Curriculum Studies, 25*, 1–32.

The Cognition and Technology Group at Vanderbilt University (1994). Multimedia environments for developing literacy in at-risk students. In B. Means (Ed.), *Technology and education reform: The reality behind the promise* (pp. 23–56). San Francisco: Jossey-Bass.

Cooper, M.M., & Selfe, C.L. (1990). Computer conferences and learning: Authority, resistance, and internally persuasive discourse. *College English, 52*, 847–869.

Coover, R. (1993, August 29). Hyperfiction: Novels for the computer. *The New York Times Book Review*.

Daniel, D.B., & Reinking, D. (1987). The construct of legibility in electronic reading environments. In D. Reinking (Ed.), *Reading and computers: Issues for theory and practice* (pp. 24–39). New York: Teachers College Press.

DeGroff, L. (1990). Is there a place for computers in whole language classrooms? *The Reading Teacher, 43*, 568–572.

DeYoung, M.J., & CBIEL at the Pennsylvania State University. (1993). *Martin Luther King's letter from a Birmingham jail* [Computer software]. Santa Barbara, CA: Intellimation.

Edwards, B.L. (1991). How computers change things: Literacy and the digitized word. *Writing Instructor, 10*(2), 68–76.

Fey, M.H. (1994). Finding voice through computer communication: A new venue for collaboration. *Journal of Advanced Composition, 14*(1), 221–238.

Gallego, M.A. (1992, December). *Telecommunications: Beyond the dialogue journal*. Paper presented at the meeting of the National Reading Conference, San Antonio, TX.

Goodenough, A. (1991). *Amanda stories* [Computer software]. Santa Monica, CA: Voyager.

Grudin, R. (1992). *Book: A novel*. New York: Penguin.

Horney, M. (1994, December). *Project literacy: Hypermedia for hearing-impaired readers*. Paper presented at the meeting of the National Reading Conference, San Diego, CA.

Kaufer, D.S., & Carley, K.M. (1993). *Communication at a distance: The influence of print on sociocultural organization and change*. Hillsdale, NJ: Erlbaum.

Kinzer, C., Risko, V., Meltzer, L., Carson, J., Bigenho, F., Peter, J., & Henley, A. (1994, December). *Multimedia tools to enhance preservice, reading teacher preparation*. Paper presented at the meeting of the National Reading Conference, San Diego, CA.

Koskinen, P.S., Wilson, R.M., Gambrell, L.B., & Neuman, S.B. (1993). Captioned video and vocabulary learning: An innovative practice in literacy instruction. *The Reading Teacher, 47*(1), 36–43.

Krendl, K.A., & Williams, R.B. (1990). The importance of being rigorous: Research on writing to read. *Journal of Computer-Based Instruction, 17*, 81–86.

Labbo, L. (1994, December). *Examining the influence of computers on young children's opportunities for literacy development*. Paper presented at the meeting of the National Reading Conference, San Diego, CA.

Landow, G. (1992). *Hypertext: The convergence of contemporary critical theory and technology*. Baltimore: The Johns Hopkins University Press.

Lanham, R.A. (1989). The electronic word: Literary study and the digital revolution. *New Literary History, 20*(2), 265–290.

Lanham, R.A. (1993). *The electronic word: Democracy, technology, and the arts*. Chicago: University of Chicago Press.

Larson, D. (1993). *Marble Springs* [Computer software]. Cambridge, MA: Eastgate Systems.

Leu, D., & Hillinger, M. (1994, December). *Reading comprehension in hypermedia: Supporting changes to children's conceptions of a scientific principle*. Paper presented at the meeting of the National Reading Conference, San Diego, CA.

Lemke, J.L. (1994, April). *Multiplying meaning: Composing multimedia text*. Paper presented at the meeting of the American Educational Research Association, New Orleans, LA.

McIntyre, S.R. (1992, December). *Computer-mediated discourse: Electonic journaling and effective practice*. Paper presented at the meeting of the National Reading Conference, San Antonio, TX.

McKenna, M. (1994, December). *Effects of a program of computer-mediated books on the progress of beginning readers*. Paper presented at the meeting of the National Reading Conference, San Diego, CA.

McLuhan, M. (1962). *The Gutenberg galaxy: The making of typographic man*. Toronto, Canada: University of Toronto Press.

Means, B. (Ed.). (1994). *Technology and education reform: The reality behind the promise*. San Francisco: Jossey-Bass.

Means, B., et al. (1993). *Using technology to support educational reform*. Washington, DC: Office of Educational Research, U.S. Office of Education.

Miller, L., & Olson, J. (1994). Putting the computer in its place: A study of teaching with technology. *Journal of Curriculum Studies, 26*(2), 121–141.

Moulthrop, S. (1991). Reading from the map: Metonymy and metaphor in the fiction of forking paths. In P. Delany & G.P. Landow (Eds.), *Hypermedia and literacy studies* (pp. 119–132). Cambridge, MA:MIT Press.

Mouthrop, S., & Kaplan, N. (1994). They became what they beheld: The futility of resistance in the space of electronic writing. In C.L. Selfe & S. Hilligoss (Eds.), *Literacy and computers: The complications of teaching and learning with technology* (pp. 220–237). New York: Modern Language Association.

Murphy, J.W. (1988). Computerization, postmodern epistemology, and reading in the post-modern era. *Educational Theory, 38*(2), 175–182.

Myers, J. (1993). Constructing community and intertextuality in electronic mail. In D.J. Leu & C.K. Kinzer (Eds.), *Examining central issues in literacy research, theory, and practice. Forty-second Yearbook of the National Reading Conference* (pp. 251–262). Chicago: National Reading Conference.

Neilsen, L. (1995). *Coding the light*. Manuscript in preparation.

Neuman, S.B. (1991). *Literacy in the television age: The myth of the TV effect*. Norwood, NJ: Ablex.

Newman, D. (1990). Opportunities for research on the organizational impact of school computers. *Educational Researcher,* *19,* 8–13.

Ong, W. (1982). *Orality and literacy: The technologizing of the word.* New York: Methuen.

Persig. R. (1992). *Zen and the art of motorcycle maintenance* [Computer software]. Santa Monica, CA: Voyager.

Poetry in motion [Computer software]. (no date). Santa Monica, CA: Voyager.

Reinking, D. (1988). Computer-mediated text and comprehension differences: The role of reading time, reader preference, and estimation of learning. *Reading Research Quarterly, 23,* 484–498.

Reinking, D. (1991). [Review of the book *Writing space: The computer, hypertext, and the history of writing*]. *Journal of Reading Behavior, 23,* 511–514.

Reinking, D. (1992). Differences between electronic and printed texts: An agenda for research. *Journal of Educational Multimedia and Hypermedia, 1*(1), 11–24.

Reinking, D. (1994a). *Electronic literacy.* (Perspective in Reading Research No. 4). University of Georgia, University of Maryland: National Reading Research Center.

Reinking, D., & Chamlin, L. (1994b). Graphic aids in electronic texts. *Reading Research and Instruction, 33,* 207–232.

Reinking, D., & Pickle, J. M. (1993). Using a formative experiment to study how computers affect reading and writing in classrooms. In D.J. Leu & C.K. Kinzer (Eds.), *Examining central issues in literacy research, theory, and practice. Forty-second Yearbook of the National Reading Conference* (pp. 263–270). Chicago: National Reading Conference.

Reinking, D., & Rickman, S.S. (1990). The effects of computer-mediated texts on the vocabulary learning and comprehension

of intermediate-grade readers. *Journal of Reading Behavior, 22,* 395–411.

Reinking, D., & Watkins, J. (in press). *A formative experiment investigating the use of multimedia book reviews to increase elementary students' independent reading* (Research Report). University of Georgia, University of Maryland: National Reading Research Center.

Reitsma, P. (1988). Reading practice for beginners: Effects of guided reading, reading-while-listening, and independent reading with computer-based speech feedback. *Reading Research Quarterly, 23,* 219–235.

Rheingold, H. (1993). *The virtual community: Homesteading on the electronic frontier.* Reading, MA: Addison-Wesley.

Roth, S.F., & Beck, I.L. (1987). Theoretical and instructional implications of assessment of two microcomputer word recognition programs. *Reading Research Quarterly, 22,* 197–218.

Salomon, G., Perkins, D.N., & Globerson, T. (1991). Partners in cognition: Extending human intelligence with intelligent technologies. *Educational Researcher, 20*(3), 2–9.

Samuelson, R.J. (1993, December 20). Lost on the information highway. *Newsweek,* p. 11.

Shirk, H.N. (1991). Hypertext and composition studies. In G.E. Hawisher & C.L. Selfe (Eds.), *Evolving perspectives on computers and composition studies* (pp. 177–202). Urbana, IL: National Council of Teachers of English.

Spiro, R.J., Coulson, R.L., Feltovich, P.J., & Anderson, D.K. (1988). *Cognitive flexibility theory: Advanced knowledge acquisition in ill-structured domains* (Tech. Rep. No. 441). Urbana-Champaign, IL: University of Illinois, Center for the Study of Reading.

Stix, G. (1994). The speed of write. *Scientific American, 271*(6), 106–111.

Sulzby, E. (1994, December). *Emergent writing on and off the computer: A final report on project CIEL (computers in early literacy).* Paper presented at the meeting of the National Reading Conference, San Diego, CA.

Tierney, R.J., Kieffer, R.D., Stowell, L., Desai, L. E., Whalin, K., & Moss, A. G. (1992). *Computer acquisition: A longitudinal study of the influence of high computer access on students' thinking, learning, and interaction.* (Apple Classrooms of Tomorrow Report No. 16). Cupertino, CA: Apple Computer.

Tobias, S. (1987). Mandatory text review and interaction with student characteristics. *Journal of Educational Psychology, 79,* 154–161.

Tobias, S. (1988). Teaching strategic text review by computer and interaction with student characteristics. *Computers in Human Behavior, 4,* 299–310.

Tuman, M.C. (1992a). *Word perfect: Literacy in the computer age.* London: Falmer Press.

Tuman, M.E. (Ed.) (1992b). *Literacy online: The promise (and peril) of reading and writing with computers.* Pittsburgh, PA: University of Pittsburgh Press.

Weir, S. (1989). The computer in schools: Machine as humanizer. *Harvard Educational Review, 59,* 61–73.

Wilkinson, A.C. (1983). Learning to read in real time. In A.C. Wilkinson (Ed.), *Classroom computers and cognitive science* (pp. 183–199). New York: Academic Press.

 Article Review Form at end of book.

WiseGuide Wrap-Up

- Technology is an integral part of literacy.

- Technology can provide a link between reading and writing, assisting students with special needs, and extend the reading process.

- Technology has changed how we become literate and what it means to be literate.

- The creation of and participation in interactive web sites can promote student literacy development.

- Electronic reading and writing are fundamentally changing the way people communicate, read, and write and, thus, the way educators think about helping people become literate.

R.E.A.L. Sites

This list provides a print preview of typical **Coursewise** R.E.A.L. sites. There are over 100 such sites at the **Courselinks**™ site. The danger in printing URLs is that web sites can change overnight. As we went to press, these sites were functional using the URLs provided. If you come across one that isn't, please let us know via email to: webmaster@coursewise.com. Use your Passport to access the most current list of R.E.A.L. sites at the **Courselinks**™ site.

Site name: Classroom Connect

URL: http://www.classroom.net/

Why is it R.E.A.L.? This site has lots of information about the use of technology in the classroom. The site includes lesson plans that include technology, chat areas for students, education web sites for students, and links to other resources.

Key topic: technology in the classroom

Try this: From the opening page, click on Resource Station; then click on Lesson Plans. Find a lesson plan of interest to you and discuss how you would implement the plan in the classroom.

Site name: Global Schoolhouse

URL: http://www.gsn.org/

Why is it R.E.A.L.? This exciting web site has great collaborative learning projects for teachers, parents, kids, and teens. The site motto is "We provide the training wheels needed to get you started!"

Key topic: technology in the classroom

Try this: Explore the learning projects for teachers. Discuss how these projects would enhance instruction in your classroom.

Site name: Technology Integration

URL: http://www.mcrel.org/resources/technology/index.asp

Why is it R.E.A.L.? This site has a host of publications on a variety of aspects of technology, including Internet safety, the impact of technology, technology and teacher education, and funding for technology.

Key topic: technology

Try this: Click on the Internet Safety icon and then Parents' Guide to the Internet. Read the recommendations for parents and make suggestions about ways teachers could use this guide to inform parents.

Index

Note: Names and page numbers in **bold** type indicate authors and their articles; page numbers in *italics* indicate illustrations.

decoding
    disabled students' difficulty with, 167
    importance of, 62
    in special education, 188–89
    See also phonics
deictic terms, 203
delayed readers, 165–69. *See also* remedial
    reading
delivery standards, 126
demonstrations
    of comprehension strategies, 88
    and learning, 23, *25*
    by teachers, 5–6
Deshon, Jo Anne Pryor, 120
Detective Donut and the Wild Goose Chase, 73
Developing Educational Standards:
    Overview web site, 137
developmental delays, screening for, 31–32
difficulty, optimal, 87
direct instruction, in phonics, 64
disabled students
    grading for, 142–44
    identifying and teaching, 28–33
    web sites about, 192
    See also at-risk children; remedial
        reading
discussion
    as assessment, 141
    and comprehension, 87, 88–89, 94,
        97–98, 99–100
    critical questions for, 102–7
    role in learning, 26
disrupting text, 102
Distar, 64
diversity
    and assessment, 147–48
    as challenge to instruction, *19*
Dougherty Stahl, Katherine Anne, 61
Down by the River, 72
Duffy-Hester, Ann M., 10, 61
dyscalculia, 29, 31
dysgraphia, 29–30
dyslexia, 29, 31
dysnomia, 29
dyspraxia, 29

E

early intervention, successful programs for,
    173–79
Early Intervention in Reading, 175
Ebonics, 180–81
e-books, 202, 219–21
eclectic approach, 10–11, 13–15, 17–18
Educational Alternatives, Inc., 116
education reform, and standards, 126
efferent reading, 89
e-mail
    and conventions of literacy, 220–21
    exchange programs for, 206
    use in collaborative learning, 212, 215
embedded phonics approaches, 64
emergent literacy perspective, 16
employment, role in learning, 24, *25*
engagement, 23, 24, *25*

English as a second language (ESL)
    programs, 43–45
English Coalition, 126
ERIC Clearinghouse on Reading, English,
    and Communication web site, 108
Ettenberger, Shari, 53
evaluation
    role in learning, 26, 129
    of web projects, 213–14
    See also assessment
excellence, encouraging, 129
expectations, role in learning, 23, *25*
experts, reaching via Internet, 206
explicit instruction, 87–88

F

fairness, in assessment, 148
family literacy, 42–48
fast mapping, 40
Faust, Mark A., 125
feedback, role in learning, 24, *25*
Feuerstein's Instrumental Enrichment, 82
Fielding, Linda G., 86
First Grade Studies, 11
The First R, 12
five-finger test, 60
Freppon, Penny A., 49
functional magnetic resonance imaging
    (fMRI), 30
funding, as challenge to instruction, *19*
fund-raising, for family literacy programs,
    47–48

G

Gaskins, Irene W., 165
Gavelek, James R., 92
Gearhart, Maryl, 154
gentle inquisition, 89
Girls Speak Out: Finding Your True Self, 74
Global Heinemann Keypals, 206
Global Schoolhouse Network web site, 224
The Global Schoolhouse Projects Registry,
    206–7
goals, 5, 83. *See also* standards
Gorilla, 104
grading
    for disabled students, 142–44
    and meaningful evaluation, 129
grade-level standards, 118, 130
grammar, infants' understanding of, 37,
    39–40
grammatical morphemes, 40
grand conversations, 89
grouping practices, 188
guessing, 172
guided practice, 88

H

habits, role in learning, 22
Harrington-Lueker, Donna, 200
Hartford Public Schools curriculum
    guidelines, 116–19

Harvey, Jenny, 32–33
From Head to Toe, 71–72
hearing-impaired children, reading
    instruction for, 183–86
Hoffman, James V., 10
holistic instruction. *See* balanced instruction
homepages, creating, 211–12
Honig, Bill, 49–50
hypertext, 220

I

IEA Reading Literacy Study, 12
immersion strategies, 16–17, 23, *25*
impatience, of teachers, 83
inclusion, 142–44, 166, 183–86
independent learning, and mediation, 82
individual cognitive activity, 95–98
individual differences, 58–59, 60
individualized instruction, 188, 190
inequality in classrooms, 120–23
infants, language acquisition in, 37–41
inferences, 72–73
instruction
    authenticity in, 111–15
    balanced (*see* balanced instruction)
    for comprehension, 78, 86–90, 189
    in critical literacy, 102–6
    demonstrations in, 5–6, 88
    equality in, 120–23
    in how to learn, 168
    integrated, 109, 131–35
    introducing holistic approach, 3–8
        (*see also* whole language approach)
    involving parents in, 7, 35, 177–78
    major challenges in, 18, *19*
    most commonly used techniques, 16–17
    phonics in (*see* phonics)
    politics and, 55
    poor strategies for, 171–72
    remedial (*see* remedial reading
        programs)
    setting goals for, 5, 83
    technology in (*see* technology)
    traditional approaches to, 63–64, 89, 93
instructional conversations, 89
instructional materials, 15
integrated instruction
    assessment of, 131–33
    described, 109
    guidelines for, 134–35
intelligent behavior, elements of, 168
intentionality, in mediated learning, 82–83
interactive books, 202, 219
Intercultural E-mail Classroom
    Connections, 206
interest, in reading, 4, 72
International Reading Association
    language arts standards of, 109, 118,
        125–30
    position on phonics, 11
Internet
    classroom applications for, 208–11
    impact on literacy, 203–7
    web site creation, 211–13
    See also technology

invention vs. convention, 98–99
IRE format, 88

J

Job Training Partnership Act, 45
juxtaposing texts, 102

K

Kantrowitz, Barbara, 28
Kenan Family Literacy Model, 44
Kidproject, 207
KidPub, 206
Kieffer, Ronald D., 125
knowledge. *See* construction of knowledge;
  prior knowledge
K-W-L approach, 185

L

Lab School of Washington, 31, 32
language, and knowledge construction,
  93–94
language acquisition
  complexity of, 22
  for hearing-impaired children, 184
  in infants, 37–41
  keys to success in, 23–24
language acquisition device, 39
language arts standards. *See* standards
LAT, 168
LD Online web site, 192
learning
  cultural factors in, 81
  evaluation and, 26, 129 (*see also*
    assessment)
  importance of mediation in, 80–85
  roadblocks to, 169
  setting goals for, 5
learning disabilities, 28–33, 192
Learning Disabilities Association, 30
learning portfolios, 128–30
learning theory, 21–26, 27
legislation, requiring phonics, 11–12
lesson plans, 137
letter recognition, 62–63
letter writing, 111–12
Leu, Donald J. Jr., 203
libraries, in classrooms, 58–59
linguistic method of phonics instruction, 64
literacy
  critical, 101–7
  current abilities of U.S. students, 12
  differential development in, 148–49
  family programs, 42–48
  goals of, 204
  impact of Internet on, 203–7
  impact of poverty on, 42
  major challenges to, 18, *19*
  making meaningful, 6
  philosophies of, 3–4, 117–18
  power of, 4
  relation to technology, 195–98, 217–22
  standards for (*see* standards)

texts about, 51
  See also reading
literacy education
  for at-risk children, 50, 165–69
  authenticity in, 111–15
  equality in, 120–23
  major challenges to, 18, *19*
  philosophies of, 3–4, 117–18
  poor strategies for, 171–72
  relevant theory for, 21–26, *27*
  technology in (*see* technology)
  See also instruction
literacy portfolios, 3–4
literature
  authentic vs. decodable texts, 70–75, 88
  controlled language, 58, 171
  discussing, 92–100, 102–7, 141
  electronic future of, 217–22
  selection guidelines, 72–73
  values in, 101–2
  writing about, 154–61
  See also books
Look to the North: A Wolf Pup Diary, 74
low-income students, 4–5, 42

M

magnetic resonance imaging (MRI), 30,
  37–38
mail tags, 212, 215
Making Words, 64
malleability, of e-books, 219
Maple Tree Even Start program, 43–45
mapping, from authentic literature, 114–15
Maring, Gerald H., 208
*Martin Luther King Elementary School
  Children v. Ann Arbor Board of Education*,
  180, 181
mathematics, learning disabilities for, 29, 31
McIntyre, Ellen, 51–52
meaning
  at heart of instruction, 52
  mediated learning of, 84–85
mediated learning experiences, 80–85,
  94–95
Meta-Phonics, 64
Michigan Family Literacy Research, 43
Mid-Continent Regional Educational
  Laboratory web site, 137
Milligan, Jerry, 171
Minds Eye Monster Exchange, 204
minority students
  classroom inequalities for, 120–23,
    180–81
  learning disabled, 32
miscues, 62
Monarch Watch, 206
Moody, Sally Watson, 187
Moon, Jennifer, 10
mothers, influence on language
  development, 41
motivation
  and integrated instruction, 133
  strategies for, 140–41
  teaching about, 168
A Mouse Told His Mother, 73

Mr. Putter and Tabby Fly the Plane, 73
Mr. Putter and Tabby Row the Boat, 73
multimedia, 219–20
multiple readings, 87
multiple strategies, 15–16
Munk, Dennis D., 142
My Best Sandwich, 72
Myers, Kurt S., 208

N

narrative rubric, *156–57*
National Assessment of Educational
  Progress web site, 162
National Center for Fair and Open Testing
  web site, 162
National Center for Family Literacy, 44, 77
National Council of Teachers of English
  language arts standards, 109, 118,
  125–30
National Institute on Early Childhood
  Development and Education
  web site, 77
neocerebellum, 39
Net days, 204
networking, 7–8
neural networks, 39–40
NickNack's Telecollaborative Learning, 206
Nine Planets Tour, 204
nonverbal elements, in e-books, 219–20
Number the Stars, 114

O

oppositional stance, 195–96
optimal difficulty, 87
oral reading, 58, 59
organization, learning, 83
organizers, 186
Orton-Gillingham approach, 64
overviews, 186

P

Parecki-DeBruin, Andrea, 42
parents
  and alternative assessment, 147
  challenge of engaging, *19*
  influence on language development,
    41, 58
  keeping informed, 7
  mediation of learning by, 83
  role in reading education, 35, 177–78
  training for, 44
Paris, Scott G., 42
parody, 102
Pearson, P. David, 53–54, 86
peer conferencing, 122
peer learning, 88, 94
Peirce, Bonny Norton, 180
performance standards, 126
philosophies
  of literacy, 3–4, 117–18
  of reading instruction, 13–14
phonemes, 38

Putting it in *Perspectives*
-Review Form-

Your name:_____   Date: _____

Reading title: _____

Summarize: Provide a one-sentence summary of this reading: _____

_____

_____

_____

Follow the Thinking: How does the author back the main premise of the reading? Are the facts/opinions appropriately supported by research or available data? Is the author's thinking logical?

_____

_____

_____

_____

_____

Develop a Context (answer one or both questions): How does this reading contrast or compliment your professor's lecture treatment of the subject matter? How does this reading compare to your textbook's coverage?

_____

_____

_____

_____

_____

_____

Question Authority: Explain why you agree/disagree with the author's main premise.

_____

_____

_____

_____

_____

_____

_____

COPY ME! Copy this form as needed. This form is also available at http://www.coursewise.com
Click on: *Perspectives*.